IN SEARCH
OF GOD THE
MOTHER

BLACK

Sino

ISTANBUL

Nikomedia

Kyzikos

Lampsakos
Daskyleion

BOLU

Troy

Sangarios River

ANKARA

Boğa

Assos

ESKIŞEHIR
(Dorylaion)

Findik

Porsuk River

Gordion

Pergamon

KÜTAHYA

Pessinous

Kyme

Aizanoi

Midas City

Phokaia

MANISA

Arslankaya

Dokimeion

Smyrna

Sardis

AFYON

Erythrai

Klazomenai

Çepni

Kolophon

Klaros

DINAR

KONYA

NIĞD

Ephesos

Magnesia

Aphrodisias

BURDUR

Çatalhöyük

Priene

Miletos

Hacilar

Didyma

Iasos

Halikarnassos

Bayandir

Tarsos

Knidos

ELMALI

Kastabala

MEDITERRANEAN   SEA

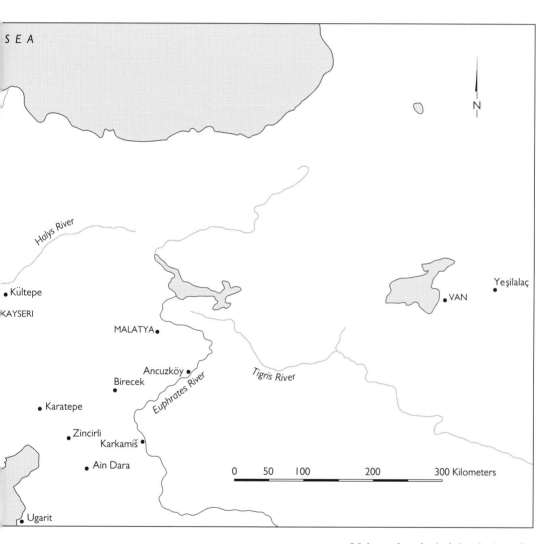

S E A

Halys River

• Kültepe

KAYSERI

MALATYA •

Ancuzköy •

Birecek
•

Euphrates River

• Karatepe

Zincirli
•

Karkamiš •

• Ain Dara

• Ugarit

Tigris River

• VAN

Yeşilalaç
•

0   50   100   200   300 Kilometers

M A P   I.   Major archaeological sites in Anatolia
connected with the Phrygian Mother Goddess (modern
cities in majuscule, ancient sites in minuscule).

Rhone River

Marseilles

Tiber
River

Rome
Ostia
Naples
Pompeii
Velia

Locri

Syracuse

Panticapaeum

BLACK SEA

Thasos

Delphi

Thebes
Athens
Chios

Pergamon
Sardis
Smyrna
Ephesos

Olympia

Corinth

Samos

Sparta

Amorgos

MEDITERRANEAN SEA

Alexandria

Nile River

N

0   500 Kilometers

MAP 2.   Major archaeological sites
in the Mediterranean region connected
with the Phrygian Mother Goddess.

LYNN E. ROLLER

IN SEARCH
OF GOD THE
MOTHER

The Cult of Anatolian Cybele

UNIVERSITY OF CALIFORNIA PRESS

Berkeley *Los Angeles* *London*

University of California Press
Berkeley and Los Angeles, California

University of California Press, Ltd.
London, England

© 1999 by
The Regents of the University of California

Library of Congress Cataloging-in-Publication Data

Roller, Lynn E.
    In search of god the mother: the cult of Anatolian Cybele / Lynn E. Roller.
        p.   cm.
    Includes bibliographical references and index.
    ISBN 0-520-21024-7 (alk. paper)
    1. Cybele (Goddess)—Cult. 2. Goddesses—Mediterranean Region.
3. Mediterranean Region—Antiquities.   I. Title.
    BL820.C8R65 1999
    291.2′114′093—dc21   98-20627
                                        CIP

Printed in the United States of America
9 8 7 6 5 4 3 2 1

To Sarah Fredrica and Charles Raymond

CONTENTS

List of Illustrations   *xi*

Preface   *xv*

Abbreviations   *xix*

Introduction   *1*

1. Prolegomenon to a Study of the Phrygian Mother Goddess   9

PART 1. THE MOTHER GODDESS IN ANATOLIA

2. The Evidence from Prehistory   27

3. The Bronze and Early Iron Ages   41

4. The Cult of the Mother Goddess in Phrygia   63

PART 2. THE MOTHER GODDESS IN GREECE

5. The Early Cult   119

6. The Classical Period   143

7. The Hellenistic Period   187

PART 3. FROM CULT TO MYTH

8.   The Myth of Cybele and Attis   237

PART 4. THE ROMAN MAGNA MATER

9.   The Arrival of the Magna Mater in Rome   263

10. The Republic and Early Empire   287

11. The Roman Goddess in Asia Minor   327

Epilogue   345

Bibliography   347

Index   367

ILLUSTRATIONS

MAPS

1.   Archaeological sites in Anatolia   ii

2.   Archaeological sites in the Mediterranean region   iv

FIGURES

1.   Seated female figurine, Çatalhöyük   32

2.   Seated female figurine, Hacilar   33

3.   Relief of Kubaba, Karkamiš   50

4.   Relief of Kubaba, Karkamiš   51

5.   Urartian cult relief, Yeşilaliç   55

6.   Cult niche, Yeşilaliç   55

7.   Relief of Phrygian Mother, Gordion   56

8.   Relief of Phrygian Mother, Ankara/Bahçelievler   57

9.   Relief of Phrygian Mother, Ankara/Etlik   58

10.   Relief of Phrygian Mother, Boğazköy   59

11.   Head of Phrygian Mother, Salmanköy   60

12.   Relief of Phrygian Mother, Gordion   76

13.   Miniature relief, Gordion   76

14.   Relief of attendant figure, Gordion   77

15.   Aniconic idol, Gordion   78

16.   Phrygian altar, Dömrek   80

17.   Phrygian shrine, Kalehisar, distant view   81

18.   Phrygian altar, Kalehisar   82

19.   Arslankaya, general view   87

20.   Arslankaya, relief in niche   88

21.   Arslankaya, relief on side   88

22.   Büyük Kapikaya   89

23.   Kumca Boğaz Kapikaya   90

24.   Midas Monument, Midas City   91

25.   Unfinished Monument, Midas City   92

26.   Hyacinth Monument, Midas City   93

27.   Areyastis Monument   94

28.   Maltaş Monument, main relief   95

29.   Maltaş Monument, shaft behind relief   95

30.   Bakşeyiş Monument, main relief   97

31.   Bakşeyiş Monument, shaft behind relief   97

32.   Stepped altar with idol, Midas City   98

33.   Cult relief and shaft, Findik   99

34.   Arslantaş, lion relief over grave   103

35.   Ivory figurine of goddess, Bayandir   106

36.   Silver figurine of priest, Bayandir   107

37.   Meter naiskos, Miletos   129

38.   Temple model, Sardis   130

39.   Meter naiskos, Kyme   133

40.   Meter naiskos, Athenian Agora   146

41.   Meter naiskos, Athenian Agora   147

42.   Meter and two attendants, Piraeus   150

43.   Attic red-figure krater, Ferrara, Side A   152

44.   Attic red-figure krater, Ferrara, Side B   153

45.   Relief with votaries and statue of goddess, Thasos   158

46.   Relief with Kouretes and Nymphs, Piraeus   159

47.   Meter naiskos, Piraeus   160

48.   Relief of Angdistis and Attis, Piraeus   179

49.   Meter statuette, Gordion   190

50.   Meter on a lion's back, Gordion   191

51.   Meter enthroned, Gordion   191

52.   Relief of Artemis and Meter, Sardis   197

53.   Meter with older and younger god, Ephesos   201

54.   Meter with worshippers, Kyzikos   205

55.   Marble statue of Meter, Pergamon   208

56.   Terracotta statuette of Meter, Pergamon   209

57.   Marble statue of Attis, Pergamon   213

58.   Bronze matrix, provenience unknown, Side A   214

59.   Bronze matrix, provenience unknown, Side B   215

60.   Relief of Meter and Attis, provenience unknown   225

61.   Votive relief, Lebadeia   226

62.   Plan of west side of Palatine hill, Rome   272

63.   Restored elevation of Magna Mater temple, Rome   273

64.   Head of Magna Mater, Palatine, Rome   275

65.   Attis figurine, Palatine, Rome   275

66.   Terracotta glans penis, Palatine, Rome   276

67.   Terracotta evergreen cone, Palatine, Rome   277

68.   Republican denarius illustrating the Magna Mater   290

69.   Republican denarius illustrating the Magna Mater   290

70.   Statue of Gallus, Rome   294

71.   Bronze group of Magna Mater in lion-drawn chariot   295

72. Relief illustrating Augustan temple of Magna Mater, Ara Pietatis   310

73. Relief on pediment of Augustan temple of Magna Mater, Ara Pietatis   311

74. Relief of Claudia Quinta, Rome   312

75. Marble statue of Magna Mater, Palatine, Rome   313

76. Meter relief, Kyzikos   333

77. Temple of Zeus and Meter, Aizanoi   338

78. Underground shrine to Meter, Temple of Zeus and Meter, Aizanoi   339

PREFACE

In the summer of 1979, I spent my first field season in Turkey working with the Gordion Project, sponsored by the University of Pennsylvania's University Museum. I was two years out of graduate school, recently embarked on my first regular academic appointment at the University of California at Davis, and looking for new research horizons. A fortuitous invitation from my dissertation supervisor, Professor Keith DeVries of the University of Pennsylvania, to take part in the Gordion Project offered an opportunity that seemed irresistible then and set me on path that proved to have a decisive influence on my professional life. A field trip I took with other members of the Gordion team to Midas City, just five days after I arrived in Turkey, is still a vivid memory. We came around the bend of a winding, unpaved road, and suddenly the Midas Monument stood before our eyes, its impressive form towering over the village at its feet and standing out brightly in the full morning sun. Even then I remember thinking, "Some day I must come back and explore this further."

I have never forgotten the impact the rock monuments of the highlands of Phrygia made on me (as they have done on so many travelers), and I have tried to convey that overpowering sense of awe and inspiration as the underlying force of this book. It is no surprise to me that people of Mediterranean antiquity found a special kind of religious experience in the dramatic natural landscape, particularly in the mountains where they lived, nor is it surprising that one divinity they associated with this experience, the Phrygian Mother, made a profound and lasting impact on her followers.

This positive impression remained with me even as I began to read more widely in ancient literature and in modern scholarship about the Phrygian Mother Goddess, better known as Cybele. Particularly in modern works, the initial impression one receives of this divinity is almost unremittingly negative. In large part, this results from the very unflattering, often sinister portrait of her created by such pivotal Latin authors as Virgil, Martial, Juvenal, and especially Catullus, whose masterful portrait of the destructive Mother Cybele in his poem 63 has had a decisive impact on virtually everyone, scholar or layperson, who has addressed this topic. Chapter 1 seeks to show why the negative picture of the Phrygian Mother has resonated so powerfully in the nineteenth and twentieth centuries, but the troubling image of the Mother Goddess found in so many of the Greek and Latin sources remains. The inconsistent status of a deity that projected such power in her homeland yet met with a very mixed reception outside of Phrygia demanded fuller consideration than was offered by any modern work of scholarship I have seen.

Another incentive for me to work on this subject is the Phrygian Mother's basic identification as a mother goddess. The years during which I was working on this project coincided with a growth in public interest, spurred on in large part by the women's movement, in female divinities, particularly in mother goddesses, and Cybele was clearly a powerful female deity and a mother goddess with a definite impact on human society in antiquity. Yet the role of the Phrygian Mother in defining feminine elements in religious consciousness has been largely ignored, and what literature there is on the topic of mother goddesses in the ancient world is often unsatisfying and vague, offering little aid to my efforts to ground a definition of a mother goddess in a specific space and time.

I began the research for this study in 1986 during an extensive summer research trip in Turkey, followed by a fall sabbatical at the American Academy in Rome, and began to write the manuscript in 1990. As I finish the work in 1998, the initial impetus that led me to this topic, namely, my fascination with Phrygia and its rich artistic, cultural, and religious traditions and my desire to explore what led people in Mediterranean antiquity to worship a mother goddess, still remains. This book is the result.

A work with such a long period of gestation and covering such a wide territory has benefited from the contributions of many people and institutions, and it is a pleasure to record my debts to them. In some cases, it is too late to do so personally, although I still wish to acknowledge the contributions of the pioneers of Anatolian studies, particularly William Ramsay, Gustav and Alfred Körte, Emilie Haspels, and Rodney Young, all of whom played critical roles in rescuing the accomplishments of the ancient cultures of Anatolia from oblivion. My own study has received extensive financial support from many sources. My home institution, the University of California at Davis, most generously provided a Faculty Development Award and a term in residence at the Davis Humanities Institute in 1990, as well as annual Faculty Research Grants. A grant-in-aid from the American Council of Learned Societies in 1992 supported a research trip to Turkey, which enabled me to make an extensive visit to the Phrygian highlands and many of the archaeological monuments in Turkey connected with this project. A fellowship from the National Endowment for the Humanities in 1992–93 offered a necessary relief from academic duties that made it possible for me to complete the greater part of the manuscript. I spent part of that year as a fellow at the National Humanities Center in North Carolina, an institution that provided a wonderful support staff and the company of a stimulating group of scholars; I would like to offer particular thanks to Eleanor Winsor Leach, Richard Seaford, Michael Maas, and the center's director, W. Robert Connor, all of whom took an interest in my work and discussed many of the ideas in it. During the spring of 1993, I was a visiting scholar at Wolfson College, Oxford, an opportunity that provided a cordial atmosphere and the superb research facilities of the Ashmolean Library; my special thanks go to John Boardman, John Lloyd, and Donna Kurtz, all of whom facilitated my presence there. Brian Rose generously shared information from the post–Bronze Age excavations at Troy, Mary Jane Rein provided much valuable material on the Sardis temple model, and Naomi Hamilton gave much-needed assistance with the Çatalhöyük figurines. Machteld Mellink, Michael Jameson, and Oscar Muscarella, who have long encouraged my interest in the Phrygian Mother Goddess, also deserve special thanks. Erich S. Gruen, Richard Seaford, and Thomas H. Carpenter read portions of the manuscript in draft and made many helpful comments on it. I would also like to thank others who helped improve several chapters of the manuscript: Charlayne Allan, Susan Burdett, Crawford H. Greenewalt, Jr., Eugene Lane, Stephen Miller, and the anonymous readers for the University of California Press. The members of my Feminist Study Group at Davis, Alison Berry, Cynthia Brantley, Carole Joffe, Suad Joseph, Anna Kuhn, Kari Lokke, Francesca Miller, and Stephanie Shields, provided much-appreciated intellectual and moral support. My student assistants Katherine Dhuey, Julie Hines, and Heather-Lark Curtin were an invaluable help in the final stages of the preparation of the manuscript. Very special thanks go to my husband, John Wagoner, who accompanied me on my research trip to Turkey in 1992, took many of the photographs in this work, and offered support and encouragement at every stage of the project.

Many of the photographs were generously provided by museums and excavation collections. I would like to thank the Museum of Anatolian Civilizations, Ankara; the British Museum; the Archaeological Museum of Antalya; the German Archaeological Institute, Istanbul; the Archaeological Exploration of Sardis; the Istanbul Archaeological Museum; the Archaeological Museum of Ferrara; the J. Paul Getty Museum, Malibu; the Agora Excavations, American School of Classical Studies; the State Museum in Berlin; the Greek National Archaeological Museum in Athens; the Gordion Excavation Project; the National Museum in Copenhagen; the Metropolitan Museum, New York; the Archaeological Museum in Venice; the Soprintendenza Archeologica in Rome; the German Archaeological Institute, Rome; the American Academy in Rome; the Capitoline Museum, Rome; and the Musée du Louvre, Paris.

Finally, I would like to record two special debts. The first is to my Turkish colleagues, the Turkish Archaeological Service, its representatives who aided our work at Gordion, and the many local Turkish archaeological museums that preserve the information necessary for a study of the Phrygian Mother. My special thanks go to the Museum of Anatolian Civilizations in Ankara, its director Ilhan Temizsoy, and its staff, who have afforded every courtesy to members of the Gordion Project and have assembled the most valuable collection of Phrygian art and artifacts in the world. My second debt is to the Gordion Project for ongoing support: I would like to thank G. Kenneth Sams, the director of the Gordion Project; Mary Voigt, the Gordion field director; Ellen Kohler, keeper of the Gordion records; Elizabeth Simpson, director of the Gordion Furniture Project; and the many individual staff members of the project for their encouragement of my work and of my general interests in Phrygian history and culture. All of the above contributed much to the merits of this study, while its deficiencies are always mine.

This book is dedicated to my twin daughter and son. Their birth in the summer of 1995 slowed down the production of the book, but contributed enormously to my understanding of a mother goddess.

It seems impossible to avoid inconsistency in transliterating ancient names into modern English. In transliterating Phrygian words I have followed the principles set forth by Claude Brixhe and Michel Lejeune in their *Corpus des inscriptions paléo-phrygiennes* (Brixhe and Lejeune 1984). In transliterating Greek and Latin words, I have tried to stay as close to the original language as possible; this has resulted in the goddess being called Kybele in discussions of the Greek world and Cybele in discussions of the Roman world. Similarly, the title of the Mother Goddess's eunuch priests is given as Gallos in discussions of Greek cult and as Gallus in connection with Roman cult. In recording dates, I use B.C. for dates before Christ and C.E. for dates after Christ.

All translations of Greek and Latin texts are my own.

ABBREVIATIONS

For guidelines to abbreviations of ancient authors and works not given here, see Lidell and Scott, *A Greek-English Lexicon*, and the *Oxford Latin Dictionary*.

ABV	J. D. Beazley, *Attic Black-Figure Vase-Painters* (Oxford, 1956)
*ARV*²	J. D. Beazley, *Attic Red-Figure Vase-Painters,* 2d ed. (Oxford, 1963)
CARC	*Cybele, Attis and Related Cults: Essays in Memory of M. J. Vermaseren,* edited by Eugene Lane (Leiden, 1996)
Carchemish I–III	D. G. Hogarth, C. L. Wooley, T. E. Lawrence, and R. D. Barnett, *Carchemish: Report on the Excavations at Djerabis on Behalf of the British Museum*, vols. 1–3 (Oxford, 1914–52)
CCCA	M. J. Vermaseren, *Corpus Cultae Cybelae Attidisque,* 7 vols. (Leiden, 1977–89)
CIG	*Corpus Inscriptionum Graecarum*
CIL	*Corpus Inscriptionum Latinarum*
Délos	*Exploration archéologique de Délos*, 25 vols. (Paris, 1909–61)
Délos XXIII	A. Laumonier, *Les figurines terre-cuites. Délos XXIII* (Paris, 1956)
Et. mag.	*Etymologicum magnum*
FGrHist	F. Jacoby, *Fragmente der griechischen Historiker* (1926–58)
IG	*Inscriptiones Graecae*
IGRRP	R. Cagnat, *Inscriptiones Graecae ad Res Romanas Pertinentes,* vol. 4, ed. G. Lafaye (Paris, 1927)
MAMA	*Monumenta Asiae Minoris Antiquae*

OGIS	W. Dittenberger, *Orientis Graeci Inscriptiones Selectae* I–III (Leipzig, 1903–5, reprinted Hildesheim, 1960)
Olynthus IV	D. M. Robinson, *Terracotta Figurines: Excavations at Olynthus* IV (Baltimore, 1931)
Olynthus XIV	D. M. Robinson, *Terracotta Figurines from 1934 and 1938: Excavations at Olynthus* XIV (Baltimore, 1952)
RE	A. Pauly et al., *Realencyclopädie der classischen Altertumswissenschaft* (1893–)
SEG	*Supplementum Epigraphicum Graecum*
SIG[3]	W. Dittenberger, *Syllose Inscriptionum Graecarum,* 3d ed. (Leipzig, 1915–24)

INTRODUCTION

Dea magna, dea Cybebe, dea domina Dindymi
procul a mea tuus sit furor omnis, era, domo:
alios age incitatos, alios age rabidos.

Great goddess, goddess Cybele, goddess and mistress of Dindymus, may all your
insanity, Lady, be far from my home. Drive others to frenzy, drive others mad.

(Catullus 63.91–93)

With these words the Roman poet Catullus prayed to the Mother Goddess Cybele
and created a striking portrait which was to influence the popular image of her for
generations to come. She was the great goddess, the mistress to whom men owed
absolute obedience, a vengeful lady who could, and did, destroy those in her power.
Other views of the Great Mother in ancient Greece and Rome echo these sentiments
of power and ferocity: "She delights in the clangor of castanets and drums, the roar
of flutes, the clamoring of wolves and bright-eyed lions," reported the anonymous
author of the sixth-century B.C. Greek "Hymn to the Mother of the Gods." The notion of a maternal deity who was a nurturing, comforting, kindly figure seems remote from the Mother Goddess of ancient Mediterranean society.

The divinity known as Cybele (Kybele in Greek), as the Great Mother, or simply
as Mother, is one of the most intriguing figures in the religious life of the ancient
Mediterranean world. Evidence for human devotion to this goddess extends from
the early first millennium B.C., the earliest era to produce material clearly indicating
worship of a mother deity, to the final days of paganism in the Roman Empire in the
fifth century C.E. We encounter the Mother Goddess most vividly in the poetry,
hymns, and religious monuments of ancient Greece and Rome, but her original
home was Anatolia (modern Turkey). Her most characteristic and enduring features

were formed in Phrygia, in central Anatolia. From there, her worship was widely diffused, attracting an enormous number of followers and covering the full geographical span of the Mediterranean cultural sphere, in Europe, western Asia, and North Africa. The long life of her cult and the literally thousands of offerings to the Mother demonstrate clearly that her worship was deeply felt.

The identity and nature of the Mother Goddess in ancient Mediterranean society is the major theme of this work. These issues are explored by chronologically reviewing the primary evidence, archaeological, literary, and epigraphical, for the Great Mother Cybele. The study also includes an analysis of several of the key myths, rituals, and subordinate figures associated with Cybele and examines the varied reactions of people to her in antiquity, ranging from praise and thanksgiving to unalloyed disgust. As we shall see, an examination of the Great Mother in the ancient Mediterranean world tells as much about the people who worshipped her as it does about the goddess herself.

First, a word of explanation is in order about the identity of Cybele and how we know she was a mother goddess. Her name first appears in Phrygian inscriptions of the seventh century B.C., where she is addressed as Matar, or "Mother" in the Phrygian language. While this word usually appears alone, in two cases there is a qualifying adjective, *kubileya,* a word that appears to have meant "of the mountain" in the Phrygian language.[1] Therefore in the earliest written texts addressed to the goddess, she was simply "the Mother" or "the Mother of the mountain." Dedications in Phrygian texts of the second century C.E., written in Greek, address her as Μήτηρ Θεά (*Meter Thea*), the Mother Goddess.[2] In Greece, she was Μήτηρ (*Meter*), or Mother, but she acquired a further identity, that of Μήτηρ θεῶν, the Mother of the gods, an identity that placed her firmly in the Greek pantheon. In the Roman world, the goddess was the Magna Mater, the Great Mother, and she was frequently addressed as the Mater Deum Magna Idaea, the Great Idaean Mother of the gods, a title that gave her a central place both in the Roman pantheon and in the legendary tradition of Rome's founding by the Trojan Aeneas, from Mount Ida.

In addition to these cult titles, in Greece and Rome the Mother Goddess was frequently called Kybele or Cybele, a name derived from her Phrygian epithet *kubileya.*[3] In Greek and Latin texts, Kybele or Cybele is a proper noun, not an adjective. As a personal name for the goddess, it gained wide currency in literature, particularly poetry, but it is never used in religious texts such as hymns and votive dedications. In the context of her worship, she was always simply "the Mother." Because her oldest

---

1. Brixhe and Lejeune 1984: nos. B-01 and W-04, *kubileya;* the only other recorded Phrygian epithet of Matar is *areyastin* (ibid.: no. W-01a). *Kubileya* may either mean "mountain" in general or be the name of a specific mountain. For a discussion of the goddess's name, see Brixhe 1979: 40–45 and ch. 4 below.

2. Haspels 1971: 199–200.

3. Brixhe 1979: 43.

and most widely used name in various languages was Mother, in this study she is regularly called the Mother Goddess.

The concept of a mother goddess is one with many emotional associations, both ancient and modern. In particular, Mother Cybele has attracted a great deal of attention in both popular and scholarly literature, and has been the subject of several synthetic studies.[4] Yet these earlier studies are often framed by unwarranted preconceptions about the nature of the Phrygian Mother Goddess and Cybele's Asiatic background, ranging from uncritical celebration of her supposedly primeval origins to horror at her allegedly barbaric Eastern nature. Therefore, this study commences with a review of earlier literature on the subject and an analysis of the theoretical problems, including those relating to matriarchy, class conflict, and Orientalism, that have colored so many earlier discussions of the Mother.

The major goal of this study is to follow the development of the Mother's worship in the areas of the ancient Mediterranean world where her impact was the strongest. Since the Phrygians were the first to address the goddess directly as "Mother," an important task is to define the Phrygian Mother. I start by examining the antecedents of the Phrygian deity, in central Anatolia and elsewhere, which entails a review of the Phrygians' forerunners in Anatolia. Material from the Anatolian Neolithic, particularly from the site of Çatalhöyük, has often been trumpeted as evidence for the existence of the Anatolian Mother Goddess as early as 6000 B.C., and it is important to examine whether this claim can be substantiated. The contributions of the complex cultures of the Bronze and Early Iron Ages that preceded the Phrygians in Anatolia—those of the Hittites, Neo-Hittites, and Urartians—can also usefully be considered to see what effect their religious practices and images had on the Phrygians.

The evidence for the Mother Goddess in Phrygia itself is clearly at the center of the study. Who was the Phrygian Mother? How was she was represented? What were her areas of concern? To answer these questions, one must turn primarily to the archaeological material, the cult monuments, votive offerings, and sacred spaces of the Mother in Phrygia, for our limited familiarity with the Phrygian language severely restricts our ability to understand what the Phrygians thought about their Mother Goddess. Yet the archaeological evidence is very enlightening; an analysis of Phrygian monuments dedicated to the Mother provides much information about the symbols and rituals of the Phrygian people, and offers significant insights into the motives of the Phrygians and their attitudes toward their principal divinity.

From Phrygia, knowledge of the Mother Goddess passed to the Greeks, and so I turn next to an examination of the Greek Meter. The body of data pertinent to the Mother Goddess in the Greek world is so extensive that this section is divided into three parts in chronological order, presenting the cult of Meter in the Archaic, Clas-

---

4. The most comprehensive of these are Showerman 1901, Graillot 1912, Cumont 1929, and Vermaseren 1977.

sical, and Hellenistic periods. The Mother's transition from Phrygia to Greece apparently occurred in a rather informal way during the late seventh and sixth centuries B.C. The Greek goddess Meter became an accepted part of Greek religious life, a potent figure of poetic inspiration and private worship. Her presence in Greek religious life is attested through frequent references in Greek literature and through hundreds of votive offerings. Yet, while Meter's impact on Greek religious imagery and practice is clear, her role in public life was somewhat ambivalent. The appeal of Meter lay in her capacity to induce ecstatic religious expression on an individual basis, and so her worship often lay outside the socially binding forces of Greek political religion, with its emphasis on the cults of the family and city and the Panhellenism of the Greek people. This circumstance made the goddess suspect in the eyes of many Greeks, a trend that became even more apparent during the fifth and fourth centuries, when Meter's Phrygian roots made her a symbol of the Greeks' eastern enemy, Persia. By the Hellenistic period, however, the decline of the independent city-state made the civic cults of Greek religion less powerful, and so the individual expression that characterized the Meter cult became even more prominent, both on the Greek mainland and in the Greek cities of western Anatolia.

It is from Rome that we receive the most vivid portrait of the Mother Goddess. In contrast to the Greek situation, the Romans formally solicited the Magna Mater in the late third century B.C. and brought her to Rome to be a deity of the Roman state. She was transported directly to Rome from Anatolia, although in a very Hellenized form, and installed in a place of honor on the Palatine amid the distinguished cults of the Roman Republic. I give special attention to the circumstances of the goddess's arrival in Rome, and then offer a broad overview of her place in Roman social and religious practice. The Magna Mater received the support of many illustrious political figures, from the Scipiones to Augustus, and her cult figures prominently in the works of almost every major author of the late Republic and early Empire. Yet the Mother was an uneasy resident in the Roman pantheon too; she was lauded as the savior of the state, yet held at arm's length, largely because of general disgust at the eunuch priests who attended her. The dichotomy in the Roman reaction to the Magna Mater becomes particularly pronounced in the clash between pagan and Christian in late antiquity, in which the Mother Goddess played a significant role. This is such a complex topic that I have decided not to treat it here, however, and so conclude my discussion of the Mother in the Roman world with a review of the goddess in her Anatolian homeland during the first two centuries of the Roman Empire.[5]

5. I mention the role of Cybele, the Magna Mater, in late Roman texts and documents because several of the early Christian authors provide our best sources for the myth of Cybele and Attis, the most complex and best-attested mythical cycle connected with the Mother Goddess; this is discussed extensively in chapter 8. I hope to return to the topic of the Mother Goddess in the later Roman Empire in a subsequent study.

One other aspect of the Mother's cult receives special attention: the myths and legends describing her birth and her love affair with the young shepherd Attis. Because this affair supposedly ended in the castration and death of Attis, the tale of Cybele and Attis is one of the best-known aspects of the Mother Goddess, and one that has received the widest attention. Although often claimed as a traditional Phrygian story, the narrative was apparently created during the Hellenistic period to explain the existence of the god Attis, and it was repeated by many Greek and Latin authors as a rationale for some of the more bizarre features of the Mother's worship, particularly the practice of ritual castration. There are some Phrygian elements at the core of the myth, but the story as we know it was very much a product of Greek and Roman society. For this reason I discuss it between parts 2 and 4, dealing with Greece and Rome respectively.

Thus the major sections of this book present the evidence for the Mother Goddess in a chronological framework. This approach delineates many of the changes in the Mother's worship as it spread from Anatolia to Greece and from Greece to Rome, looking at three threads, Phrygian, Greek, and Roman, whose blending is often confused and uneven. In following these threads, the principal emphasis throughout this study is on the primary evidence for religious practice. This includes the physical evidence of shrines and sacred places, representations of the deity, offerings made to her, symbols used to address her, and also the written evidence of cult dedications and regulations. In a world of complex, often confusing polytheism with no sacred text or dogma, the evidence for what people did in religious practice is often the most telling way to determine what a particular divinity or cult meant to its followers. The evidence of literary texts is certainly valuable and receives extensive attention. Indeed, no one would want to ignore them, for the Mother Goddess appears in the works of a great many ancient authors, ranging from Pindar and Euripides to Catullus and Virgil. Literary texts are often less representative than cult practice of what people thought about a divinity, however, for they often reflect the perspectives of the educated elites of Greece and Rome. This is a particularly important consideration in reviewing the narrative accounts of the mythic cycle of Mother Cybele and her young lover Attis. Here we receive the opinions only of a literary viewpoint, not of cult worship, and only of the Greeks and Romans, not of the Phrygians. Such a limited perspective can be a misleading guide to the thoughts and experiences of many of the Mother's adherents.

Another goal of this study is to examine the meaning of the concept "mother goddess." A closer look at the Mother Goddess of ancient Mediterranean society reveals a number of paradoxes, which challenge many of the modern assumptions of what a mother goddess is, or ought to be. The goddess was always addressed as "Mother" and yet rarely appears with a child. She was a potent female deity in societies in which women had few rights and almost no public presence. Originally an Oriental deity, the goddess enjoyed her greatest authority and prestige in the western Mediterranean, in Rome under the Roman Empire. Although frequently scorned by the literati of Greek and Roman society, the goddess nonetheless attracted an enormous following among potentates and common people. Although she was widely regarded as a symbol of power and fertility, the goddess's closest divine associate was the young male god Attis, who castrated himself. Clearly, we cannot assume that the Mother Goddess simply replicated the status of a human mother on the divine level. An examination of these paradoxes leads the reader onto the slippery slope of human psychology, as this study attempts to analyze what made people turn to a mother goddess and what they hoped to gain from a deity who seems far from modern-day images of maternal behavior.

Finally, I want to touch on one crucial question about this goddess—namely, of what was she the mother? This is fully explored in subsequent chapters, but the question admits of so many misunderstandings that some preliminary remarks are appropriate here. As noted above, this Mother does not fit into the conventional female roles of reproduction and nurturing. She is rarely associated with childbirth or with attributes referent to agricultural or animal fertility. In Phrygian texts and monuments, the most prominent aspect of the Mother Goddess is her association with mountains, hollows, and wild spaces. The awesome character of the mountainous Anatolian landscape and the sense of sacred space in the natural environment clearly were key factors in defining her divinity. We seem to see a goddess whose position of power over the natural environment, rather than any specifically maternal function, was the chief factor that gave her the status of a Mother. This power in turn afforded protection to the Phrygian state and the Phrygian people, apparently making her the mother of the state.

The visual image of the goddess in Greece, derived from Phrygian representations, also lacks obviously maternal qualities, but Greek texts provide a fuller definition of the Hellenic concept of her identity as a Mother. One of the earliest testimonia to her presence in Greece, the sixth-century B.C. Homeric Hymn 14, addresses her as the Mother of all gods and humans, and the title "Mother of the gods" became her principal designation in Greek literary texts and in cult dedications. The Greek tradition also recalled the figure of Ge, or Earth, who was the original mother of the Titans, and the goddess Rhea, a Titan herself, who was the progenitor of the six major Olympian gods. Ge and Rhea each could also be characterized as a *kourotrophos,* or nurturer of children, and thus the Mother of humanity as well.[6] As Ge and Rhea were assimilated with the Anatolian Mother Kybele, all of these elements became part of the character of the Greek Meter.

In her Roman form, too, the goddess was the Great Mother of the gods, the Mater Magna Deum. She shared in the character of both the Phrygian and the Greek Mother goddesses. Yet she also took on the role of protector of the Roman

6. E. Simon 1966: 75–76; 1987: 164–66.

state, a situation analogous to her position in Phrygia. In Virgil's *Aeneid,* she is the protector of the founding hero Aeneas, to whom she is *alma mater,* the foster mother; she also became a symbol of the magnificence of the Roman state, which Aeneas would found.[7] Toward the end of the Roman Empire, all of these elements were present. The goddess was addressed both as the Mother and protectress of all[8] and as Mother Earth.[9] She had become the Mother of the gods, the Mother of the state, and the Mother of life.

7. *Aeneid* 6.784–88.
8. Julian, *Oration* 5.159.
9. Augustine, *Civ. Dei* 4.10, 7.16, 7.24.

1 · PROLEGOMENON TO A STUDY OF THE PHRYGIAN MOTHER GODDESS

Efforts to understand the cult of the Mother Goddess Cybele are not new. A deity with such a long life, wide diffusion, and all-encompassing character has, not surprisingly, already attracted a great deal of attention. Although rarely openly articulated, however, the modern cultural values framing many of the earlier scholarly discussions of this goddess and her cult have substantially influenced the interpretation of the ancient material. This is to an extent the case with any discussion of Mediterranean antiquity, but it seems to be particularly pronounced in the case of the Anatolian Mother Goddess. The vivid picture created by Euripides, Catullus, and Virgil of the powerful Mother, often in the company of desexed males, has evoked forcefully expressed reactions ranging from horror at the goddess's so-called repulsive nature to uncritical celebration of the goddess's supposed ancestral prominence. Moreover, modern perceptions of the nature of maternal deities have greatly influenced the picture of the Mother Goddess in the ancient Mediterranean world, since such perceptions are almost always based on the Judaeo-Christian image of the loving, nurturing mother subservient to her husband and closely bonded to her children. Thus many discussions of the Mother Goddess rely on modern projections of what a mother goddess ought to be, rather than on ancient evidence defining what she was.

Such preconceived attitudes are particularly noticeable in two broad areas. The first is gender, specifically the effect of the goddess's female gender on the evaluation of her cult. The second can be termed racial consciousness—namely, the Asiatic origins of the goddess's cult and the perceived tension between her eastern background and the status of her cult in Greece and Rome, a point that impinges on questions of social class as well. Modern cultural attitudes toward issues of gender and race have often become so deeply embedded in the scholarly literature that they impede efforts to evaluate the primary evidence for the ancient deity and place it in the specific context of ancient Mediterranean society. Therefore it seems useful—indeed, imperative—to review previous approaches to this topic and scrutinize the underlying assumptions that have informed them.

I start by considering how discussions of the goddess's cult have been affected by the goddess's female gender and her identity as a mother goddess. This is especially evident in modern efforts to use the cult of the Anatolian Mother Goddess to examine questions related to the history of consciousness. These efforts have been largely dominated by two premises: first, that a mother goddess is one of the earliest manifestations of the human concept of divinity, and second, that belief in a mother goddess is an inevitable part in the maturing stage of human social development. The ideas generated by discussions of these premises were later to rebound back into discussions focused more specifically on the Anatolian Mother Goddess.

Although the thesis that the original deity of all human beings was Mother Earth can be traced back to the Greek poet Hesiod in the eighth century B.C. (if not earlier), the close association between the worship of a mother goddess and a primitive stage in the development of human society appears to owe its initial formulation to Johann Jakob Bachofen in his influential work *Das Mutterrecht,* originally published in 1861. Bachofen frequently equates a belief in Mother Earth with a lower order of human consciousness: "a lower, more primordial view of the full, unrestricted naturalness of pure tellurism . . . the unbidden wild growth of mother earth."[1] Bachofen then states that "all great nature goddesses, in whom the generative power of matter has assumed a name and a personal form, combine the two levels of maternity, the lower, purely natural stage, and the higher, conjugally regulated stage."[2] Bachofen used this supposedly natural development to support his idea that human social organization underwent a similar progression, from hetaerism, defined as unrestricted sexual relations, to matriarchy, or dominance of women regulated by legal marriage. For Bachofen, worship of a mother goddess was proof of the existence of a matriarchal phase of human society. Arguing that a further development beyond the belief in a mother goddess was "an ascent to a higher culture," Bachofen posits that this lower, supposedly more primordial, stage of mother goddess worship was, in the natural course of events, superseded by a belief in male deities: "[Man] breaks through the bonds of tellurism and lifts his eyes to the higher reaches of the cosmos. Triumphant paternity partakes of the heavenly light, while childbearing motherhood is bound up with the earth that bears all things; . . . the defense of mother right is the first duty of the chthonian mother goddesses."[3] In this passage, Bachofen is articulating the specific thesis of his work—namely, that progress from the wor-

1. Bachofen 1967: 97. All quotations from Bachofen here are from this source.
2. Ibid.: 97, 98.
3. Ibid.: 109–10.

ship of chthonian, or earthbound, mother goddesses to the worship of uranian, or heavenly, sky gods, is not only inevitable and natural, but part of the rise of human consciousness. According to Bachofen, while motherhood is common to all earthly life, consciousness of fatherhood is limited to man (*sic*) alone; thus the replacement of the mother goddess by the father god is seen as a good thing, because it puts human beings on a higher plane than animal life. Here, too, Bachofen viewed religious practice as parallel to the development of human society. Indeed, for him it was a proof of that development. He concluded that just as a father god superseded a mother goddess, patriarchy, or dominance by men, evolved as a system superior to matriarchy.

In the late twentieth century, it is easy to dismiss Bachofen's work as naive and patronizing, but that would ignore its tremendous influence on subsequent approaches to the topic of the Anatolian Mother Goddess. Like most educated men of his generation, Bachofen had read widely in Classical Greek and Latin literature, and he drew most of his material in support of his thesis from the literature of Mediterranean antiquity.[4] In particular, his principal piece of evidence for his concept of mother goddesses and matriarchy was directly related to one of the indigenous peoples of Anatolia—namely, a statement by the Greek historian Herodotos concerning the Lycians. Bachofen quotes the following passage:

> In their customs they [the Lycians] resemble the Cretans in some ways, the Carians in others, but in one of their customs, they are like no other race of men. They call themselves after their mothers and not after their fathers. If one asks a Lycian who he is, he will tell you his own name and his mother's, then his grandmother's and great-grandmother's, etc. And if a citizen woman co-habits with a slave, the children are considered legitimate, but if a male citizen, even the first citizen among them, co-habits with a foreign woman or concubine, the children have no citizen rights at all.

> (Herodotos 1.173)

Bachofen used this as a starting point for his thesis that the whole of the ancient world (not just the Lycians) was a matriarchal society.[5]

Bachofen's interpretation of this passage has frequently, and justifiably, been criticized on a number of grounds. The principal one is that what Herodotos is describing is not a matriarchal, but a matrilineal society—that is, one in which descent is traced through the maternal line.[6] The two terms, *matriarchy* and *matriliny,* are by no means equivalent, for the presence of a matrilineal kinship system does not automatically imply that women hold power in such a society. Moreover, there is another important criticism to be made—namely, that this passage cannot support

---

4. For a critique of Bachofen's use of ancient Greek and Latin sources, see Pembroke 1967.
5. Bachofen 1967: 121–56.
6. Pembroke 1967: 1.

even the weaker hypothesis of matriliny in Anatolia, for Lycian society was in fact not matrilineal. This can be determined from a study of Lycian grave inscriptions, which show that the Lycians identified themselves by patronymics and thus presumably did trace descent through the paternal line.[7]

Bachofen's specific connection between Anatolia and matriarchy has, however, proved to be remarkably tenacious. Bachofen's ideas were accepted by the late-nineteenth-century explorer and archaeologist William Ramsay, whose own work in Anatolia was instrumental in drawing the attention of Classical scholars to the history and monuments of pre-Greek Anatolia, especially Phrygia. In particular, Ramsay was the first traveler and researcher to demonstrate clearly that the principal deity of Phrygia was indeed a mother goddess, through his publication of a Phrygian inscription that records the goddess's name of Mother, or "Mater kubile," as he read it.[8] Ramsay's writings indicate that he was significantly influenced by Bachofen's basic thesis that human social development proceeded from hetaerism to matriarchy and then to patriarchy: "I shall show that the early Anatolian social system knew no true marriage and traced descent only through the mother."[9] In a later work, Ramsay described the early people of Anatolia as the product of "a matriarchal system, a people whose social system was not founded on marriage, and among whom the mother was head of the family and relationship was counted only through her."[10]

Although Ramsay does not cite Bachofen as his source, his key ideas parallel those of the Swiss scholar closely, as is evident in Ramsay's confusion between matriarchy and matriliny (descent through the mother), in his statement that descent through the mother was the older system, and in the belief that no "true" marriage existed in early Anatolia, paralleling Bachofen's presumption of the social stage called hetaerism. For Ramsay, too, the prominence of the Mother Goddess in Anatolian religious practice provided the clearest proof of the existence of this supposedly matriarchal social system among the pre-Phrygian inhabitants of Anatolia. Such a social system predisposed them to a religion that was "a glorification of the female element in human life." This in turn produced a national character that was "receptive and passive, not self-assertive and active,"[11] in other words, stereotypically feminine. These pre-Phrygians were conquered by a "higher caste"—namely, the masculine, warlike Phrygians who introduced the supremacy of the father in the family and in the social system.[12] Thus the older social system was superseded by "a higher type of society," in which descent was traced through the father.[13] In Ramsay's view also, this

---

7. Pembroke 1965.
8. Ramsay 1888: 380. The correct reading of the text is "Matar Kubileya"; see Brixhe and Lejeune 1984: 46, no. W-04.
9. Ramsay 1888: 367.
10. Ramsay 1895: 94.
11. Ramsay 1899: 40.
12. Ramsay 1888: 367–68.
13. Ramsay 1895: 94.

sequence of events was clearly seen as an advance, even though the worship of the Anatolian Mother Goddess was retained by the immigrating Phrygians.[14]

This supposed connection between matriarchy, Anatolia, and the worship of the Mother Goddess rapidly became part of the conventional wisdom in subsequent studies of the goddess. It was repeated by Grant Showerman in his 1901 study,[15] and was especially emphasized by Henri Graillot, whose book *Le culte de Cybèle, mère des dieux,* first published in 1912, is still one of the most frequently cited studies on the Mother in Rome. Graillot stated explicitly that the "predominance of the feminine aspect of divinity" was a survival of the matriarchy characteristic of earlier peoples. As proof of this, he cited the existence of matriarchy in Lycia, again quoting the same passage from Herodotos, 1.173.[16] In an influential essay, originally published in 1906 but frequently reprinted, the Belgian scholar Franz Cumont accepted without question Bachofen's basic thesis that the prominence of a mother goddess in Anatolia was indicative of the early stage of matriarchy there, and applied this directly to his analysis of the Roman Cybele.[17] In a more recent study of Anatolian religion, published in 1971, Roberto Gusmani also uncritically accepted the concepts of matriarchy and the mother goddess as particularly applicable to Anatolian religion.[18]

In most of these works after Ramsay, the existence of matriarchy in Anatolia is stated as an apparent fact, with no documentation brought forward in support. Yet a closer reading of these statements shows that the association of matriarchy with the worship of the Anatolian Mother Goddess rests on a circular argument. The question being posed was: why did the Anatolians worship a mother goddess? The answer given was: clearly because this was a matriarchal society—that is, a society in which women were more powerful than men. Yet how do we know that Anatolian society was matriarchal? Clearly, because they worshipped a mother goddess. Moreover, since both a mother goddess and a matriarchal society were seen as early phases in human development, there was always the implicit assumption in all of these works that the Anatolian peoples themselves were somehow more "primitive" because they had not developed past the mother goddess stage.

Ultimately, this argument rests on the assumed existence in prehistoric society of a mother goddess whose chief function was to oversee and promote human fertility. The idea, widely repeated in both popular and scholarly literature, has been around for several decades; for example, Robert Graves, writing in 1948, advocated a return to a pre-Christian "White Goddess," asserting that Christianity is "an ancient law suit. . . . between the adherents of the Mother-goddess who was once supreme in the West and those of the usurping Father-god."[19] More recently, advocates of fem-

14. Ramsay 1895: 94.
15. Showerman 1901: 230–32.
16. Graillot 1912: 5, 365.
17. Cumont 1929: 45.
18. Gusmani 1971: 308. Note also the comments of Laroche 1960: 126.
19. Graves 1948: 529 and passim.

inist spiritualism have come to see the Mother Goddess as some sort of idealized feminist leader, representative of a period of prehistory in which women were dominant over men.[20] Ironically, while this approach seeks to exalt the status of a mother goddess rather than downgrade it, as Bachofen did, it too relies on the concept of matriarchy as a historical reality and thus is open to many of the same criticisms as have been applied to Bachofen's work.

One circumstance that has encouraged such tenacity of belief in prehistoric matriarchy and a primeval mother goddess is the existence of a large body of figurines depicting nude females. These figurines, a prominent feature of the archaeological assemblages of many Paleolithic and Neolithic settlements, have routinely been interpreted as images of a mother goddess and brought forward as proof of this early stage of human religious activity. They have been widely regarded as depictions of females who are pregnant, and who incorporate the symbolism of female sexuality and fecundity into one image.[21] Two often-repeated assumptions are particularly ubiquitous and need to be examined. The first is that such prehistoric figurines offer evidence of religious activities; the second, that they are the specific product of a mother goddess cult. Figurines from several geographical areas and time periods have been interpreted in this way, and the conclusions drawn have then been applied to discussions related only to Mediterranean Neolithic figurines and the prehistory of the Mother Goddess cult in this region.

In reality, figurine groups from prehistoric Mediterranean sites offer little support for the hypothesis of a mother goddess cult. The assumption that these figurines must be fertility idols is based in large part on the assumption that they depict pregnant women. This is incorrect, for the figurines depict a wide variety of female types, from youth to old age and from slimness to corpulence.[22] The total assemblage of prehistoric female figurines represents a normal range of female appearances, such as would be found in any cross-section of human society. Nor should it be assumed that female figurines are invariably religious artifacts; the great variation in their appearance and in the contexts in which they were found indicates that they served a variety of functions, not all religious.[23]

20. See esp. Stone 1976, and Gimbutas 1982, 1989, a strong champion of this ideology.

21. For examples of such argumentation, see Renaud 1929; James 1959; Vermeule 1964: 21–22; Patai 1967: 15; Hawkes 1968; Gimbutas 1982: esp. 236–38; Lerner 1986: 39–40; and Gimbutas 1989. One common point in these discussions is their methodologically flawed approach. Prehistoric figurines are often grouped together indiscriminately without reference to their dates, archaeological contexts, functions, or even appearance. Furthermore, figurines from Paleolithic, or hunter-gatherer sites have often been treated together with those from Neolithic, or agricultural sites, without regard for the differences in social and economic structures of these two types of communities. Material from prehistoric Mediterranean sites is often grouped together with figurines from central Europe and North America and analyzed according to the same principles, disregarding the differing cultural contexts. Good critiques of the vagueness involved in these ideas are given by Ucko 1962: 38–40, Ucko 1968: 409–19, Ehrenberg 1989: 66–76, and Talalay 1994: 167–73.

22. Ucko 1962; Rice 1981: 402–12. See also the discussion of this problem in Anatolian material in chapter 2 and the sources cited there, esp. Hamilton 1996: 225–26.

23. Talalay 1994.

Studies that have examined figurines from Neolithic sites in the eastern Mediterranean with particular reference to the mother goddess interpretation reveal significant regional differences in the form and uses of the figurines.[24] Despite claims that most anthropomorphic Neolithic figurines represent females, a substantial minority clearly depict males, while many others have no indication of sex at all. In the majority of the figurines that clearly represent females, gender is normally indicated, not by emphasizing female sex organs, but by a large hip-waist ratio or by depicting large abdomens and buttocks, signs of obesity that often develop normally in older women. Moreover, the contexts of these objects rarely support an identification with a divine figure, for most were found in household deposits, in rubbish dumps, or in graves. Interpretations as servant figures (in Egypt), teaching devices, toys, or objects of sympathetic magic appear much more plausible. Nor can we automatically assume that the figurines that do depict women with children represent a mother goddess; they may instead simply express a personal wish for more children.

It is also worth emphasizing that modern assumptions of the universality of a female goddess embodying fertility cannot be maintained for much of the ancient Mediterranean world. In Egypt, for example, the earth, far from being the Mother of all life, was normally personified as male.[25] In Greece and Crete, the goddess Meter (Mother) had little to do with human reproduction, and was in any case an uneasy visitor to the Hellenic pantheon, outside the circle of Olympian deities. The fact that a maternal deity was marginal to the Hellenic religious experience in historical periods makes it uncertain whether her cult existed in prehistoric times. Moreover, it is unclear why an emphasis on a fertility divinity should be particularly characteristic of Neolithic societies. There seems to be a tacit assumption that female fecundity would have been more highly valued then because human life was more at risk, given the high rates of maternal and infant mortality. Yet this is not a condition exclusive to the Neolithic period; high rates of death in childbirth and infant mortality have been a regular condition of the human race until well into our own century. While such circumstances may have helped shape the religious consciousness of Neolithic peoples, in themselves they are not sufficient to enable us to postulate the existence of a mother goddess.

In ancient Anatolia, the picture is somewhat different, because there is indeed evidence from historical times demonstrating the existence of a divinity acknowledged as a mother goddess there, and this divinity may well have had a prehistoric predecessor. The evidence for such a predecessor, to be discussed in chapter 2, does not rely on vague generalizations about female fertility idols, but rather relates to particular objects from ritual contexts. Such a cult, however, was not an inevitable

---

24. Ucko 1962 and 1968, esp. 409–19; Voigt 1983: 186–93; Talalay 1987, 1991, and 1994.
25. Frankfort 1958: 173–74. The concept of the divine Mother embodied in the goddess Isis was a relatively late phenomenon, strongly influenced by Roman cult practices.

feature of religious experience, but rather was located only in certain areas and connected with identifiable social conditions. Indeed, the specific nature of the Anatolian material argues against the existence of a universal mother goddess.

Nevertheless, this idea dies hard. The sense of inevitability of a mother goddess being part of early human religious consciousness has informed almost every study of the Anatolian Mother Goddess, and Paleolithic and Neolithic figurines invariably form a prominent part of the discussion. This idea forms the basic thesis of the study of E. O. James,[26] and is also a major theme in the work of Marija Gimbutas.[27] Both of these authors state that this Neolithic fertility goddess was the direct ancestress of the Graeco-Roman Cybele. In the most recent general study of the goddess Cybele and Attis,[28] Maarten Vermaseren begins his discussion of the Anatolian goddess's cult by positioning it squarely in this supposedly primordial concept: "Throughout antiquity the earth was regarded as a goddess and worshipped as such," and he says later: "As far back as the Paleolithic Age one finds in the countries around the Mediterranean a goddess who is universally worshipped as the Mighty Mother."[29]

In addition to belief in the historical reality of matriarchy and universal mother goddess worship, another, very different line of approach was taken by the Swiss psychologist Carl Jung and his disciple Erich Neumann. Jung proposed that matriarchy and mother goddess worship comprise an archetype of the individual human consciousness, which he called the "Mother complex."[30] The Anatolian Mother Goddess contributed heavily to the negative aspects of this archetype as the symbolic cause of homosexuality, adultery, and impotence in sons: "The effects of a mother-complex on the son may be seen in the ideology of the Cybele and Attis type: self-castration, madness, and early death."[31] Neumann developed the concept of the Mother archetype even more extensively in his work *The Great Mother*.[32] He described a variety of archetypes of female activities and behavior, both good and bad, and ascribed them to different aspects of the primordial Great Mother Goddess. To Neumann, the concept of matriarchy was very real, but it was a psychological, not a historical, reality, still alive in the psychic depths of modern-day man. In developing this argument, Neumann's work, even more than Jung's, relied heavily on material connected with the Anatolian Mother Goddess, particularly the practice of ritual

26. James 1959, especially pp. 13–46.
27. Gimbutas 1982: 152, 195–200. Gimbutas 1989: 316–17 and passim.
28. Vermaseren 1977.
29. Ibid.: 9, 13. Others pursuing this line of argument include Hawkes 1968: 25. It is certainly true that concept of the so-called Neolithic fertility goddess has been extensively criticized, e.g., by Ucko 1962 and 1968, Burkert 1985: 11–12; Talalay 1991, 1994.
30. Jung 1954.
31. Ibid.: 19.
32. E. Neumann 1963.

castration (a central feature of the cult of the Roman Cybele), which he saw as symbolic of the devouring mother and of a society governed by "savage instincts."[33]

This type of psychological probing of human consciousness as a means of examining human prehistory has little to contribute to an understanding of the Mother Goddess in the Mediterranean world. It does not offer anything meaningful to our understanding of early religious imagery, but rather uses these supposedly divine sanctions to justify socially constructed modes of behavior. Neumann's arguments are particularly weak, since they rely on vague generalizations about Woman as Vessel, or Woman as Primordial Nature, without defining what these mean or whose perceptions create these archetypes, men's, women's, or both. Both Jung and Neumann also rely on an (unstated) concept of arrested development—namely, that the religious images of the so-called primitive peoples represent an immature stage of human development, while civilized societies have matured beyond that stage, and so have rejected the Great Goddess as a viable religious symbol.

The link between mother goddesses and primitive man apparently lies behind attempts to find the origin of the mother goddess in the structure of hunter-gatherer societies.[34] In Mediterranean studies, one of the main proponents of this point of view has been Walter Burkert, whose hypothesis places the origin of the mother goddess in the hunter's need to support his family, specifically his wife and mother, and in the hunter's projection of the mother onto a great goddess. In the death of the hunter's prey, Burkert thus sees the death of the goddess's companion, father Attis, "whom the goddess loves, emasculates, and kills."[35] Thus the act of ritual castration is seen as critical to a mother goddess's cult, a survival of the Stone Age.[36] Burkert's argument, however, is also susceptible to a number of objections. His picture of Paleolithic man the hunter as the principal provider for a dependent wife and mother is a projection of modern Western middle-class values into prehistory. Comparative studies of hunter-gather societies indicate that such a model is incorrect, for it is unlikely that males were the sole or even the principal food providers in such societies.[37] Thus Burkert's model becomes another example of using the past to rationalize a culturally constructed mode of behavior, although Burkert sites the inevitability of such behavior, not in the primitive psyche of Jung's archetypal human personality, but in the primitive past of human reality. Moreover, Burkert's assumption that the practice of ritual castration in the worship of a mother goddess is a sur-

33. Ibid.: 43–44, 276–77. A similar argument in Patai 1967: 16–17. A valuable critique of these arguments is offered by Wehr 1985.

34. Although not, strictly speaking, a structuralist viewpoint, the *locus classicus* for this approach remains Frazer 1906.

35. Burkert 1983a: 80–82.

36. Burkert 1979a: 104–5.

37. Ehrenberg 1989: 65.

vival of Stone Age times is quite dubious; most of the evidence for the practice from the Mediterranean world is connected with the Magna Mater cult in Rome, and there is little to support the notion that this was a prominent feature of the Mother Goddess cult in its Anatolian homeland.[38]

These efforts to locate the cult of the mother goddess in early human psychological or social development have another feature in common—namely, the claim that belief in a mother goddess was universal. Bachofen maintained strongly that the original primacy of the female in matters of religion was a universal phenomenon,[39] and other scholars cited material from Europe, the Near East, Iran, India, and North America.[40] Jung argued that his image of the Mother archetype was a static, eternal entity, and Neumann stated clearly that the primordial archetype of the Great Mother does not refer to a concrete image existing in space and time, but was represented in the myths and artistic creations of all mankind.[41] Burkert uses his thesis of ritual killing to explain the social development of all humanity: "Man [should] recognize that he still is what he once was long ago."[42] Vermaseren also claims universality for the worship of the mother goddess: "As long as mankind has existed, [she] has been present . . . the Goddess is an integral part of humanity, forever."[43] Yet it is clear that most of these scholars were using as their principal model the Mother Goddess of ancient Mediterranean society, the Greek and Roman Cybele. They took one culturally specific example of a mother goddess and applied it indiscriminately to the human condition.

Thus we can see that the Mother Goddess's female gender has affected scholarly approaches toward the study of her cult in several explicit ways. The assumption that belief in a mother goddess is characteristic of a matriarchal society led to the assertion that ancient Anatolia was a matriarchy. The assumption that belief in a mother goddess is characteristic of all early human societies created the myth of an era of universal mother goddess worship. This in turn has affected the evaluation of the historically attested Anatolian Mother Goddess by skewing efforts to determine the origins of her cult. At the same time, there is a less attractive implicit assumption. Scholars who used the theories of the Bachofen and Jungian school (often unaware that they were doing so) to discuss the cult of Anatolian Cybele tended to infer that the presence of a mother goddess was typical of early social structure. Indeed, both Ramsay and Burkert state this quite forthrightly. Therefore the worship of this goddess identified its followers, in the eyes of many scholars, as a group that was less developed socially. The upshot of such thinking was the assumption that the native

38. On the origin of the eunuch deity Attis, see Roller 1994. The myth of Cybele and Attis and the meaning of ritual castration will be fully explored in chapter 8.
39. Bachofen 1967: 91.
40. Renaud 1929: 507–12. E. Neumann 1963: 179–208.
41. E. Neumann 1963: 3.
42. Burkert 1983a: 82.
43. Vermaseren 1977: 11.

peoples of Anatolia were still in a primitive state, one that other groups such as the Classical Greeks and Romans passed beyond.

This implicit sense of the inferiority of people who worshipped a mother goddess carried over from discussions based on gender to those based on ethnicity, specifically concerning the goddess's eastern origins. As in the case of gender, discussions of the Oriental nature of the mother goddess cult have often been framed by certain preconceived notions about the nature of Oriental cult, notions that have substantially colored the modern picture of the goddess's cult rituals and practices. This has been particularly true in discussions focused on the transfer of the cult from Anatolia to Greece and Rome, and on perceived tensions between the two areas.

One critical circumstance affecting an analysis of differing cultural influences is the fact that we are very unevenly informed about the cult as it was practiced in both the eastern and western Mediterranean areas. It is fairly certain that the cult of the Anatolian Mother Goddess was well established in Phrygia by the Iron Age (ca. 800 B.C.), and in this Phrygian form spread to the west coast of Anatolia. Here the Phrygian Mother Goddess was adopted by the Greeks, who gradually assimilated her to their own female deities, especially Rhea and Demeter. Yet this process is traceable only through the archaeological record. Virtually no written records survive from the Anatolian Iron Age, and Greek written sources are highly fragmentary, offering little explanation as to why the Greeks should have wished to adopt the Mother Goddess cult. The cult of the Great Mother was imported into Rome directly from Anatolia in 204 B.C. under a specific set of political and cultural circumstances that, in contrast to the situation mentioned above, are richly described in our literary sources. From this point on there is a much fuller record of how the goddess was worshipped and by whom, why she was worshipped, and what exactly her rituals entailed.

This dearth of information about the earlier, eastern aspect of the cult, contrasting sharply with the richer documentation from the Roman era, has been a source of unease for many scholars writing on the topic. For most, the problem has been solved by simply ascribing every aspect of the cult as it was practiced in Rome, particularly the unattractive aspects, to an eastern origin. Why did devotees of the Magna Mater have processions accompanied by loud music, clashing cymbals, and pulsing drums? Why did they hold orgiastic rites punctuated by loud cries of ritual possession? And, most puzzling, why did the priests of the goddess castrate themselves? Because that was how things were done in Phrygia! The fact that there is virtually no evidence from Phrygia to support any of these claims has not deterred wide acceptance of this line of reasoning.

This scholarly *horror vacui* took on a hidden political agenda from its earliest appearance. Bachofen again is the most obvious, if crudest, example of this. To Bachofen, the Romans clearly elevated the cult to a higher plane by taking it away from its older, Oriental roots and bringing it to the more civilized West:

To the Occident, with its purer, chaster nature, history entrusted the task of bringing about the lasting victory of the higher principle, so liberating mankind from the fetters of the lowest tellurism in which the magic of the Orientals held it fast . . . but in times of stress the oracle announced that Rome was in need of the mother whom only Asia could provide. [This refers to the arrival of the cult in Rome in 204 B.C. at the command of the Sibylline oracle.] Without the support of its imperial idea this city destined to provide the connecting link between the old and new worlds could never have triumphed over the Asiatic nature-bound conceptions of material motherhood.[44]

The concept that everything disagreeable about the cult could be ascribed to its eastern origins received a special twist in the analysis of Cumont, to whom the excesses of the cult derived in part from primitive Anatolian religious customs, which, according to him, survived into Christianity and Islam.[45] Such primitive customs included worship of the sacred pine tree, identification of the goddess as Earth, and her association with a weak consort Attis, a practice derived directly from matriarchal rule. The cult's especially savage aspects, however, could be squarely attributed to the violent nature of Phrygia itself. The extremities of the harsh climate in central Anatolia made the Phrygians particularly susceptible to the worship of a vegetation god. Moreover, the savage nature of the people who lived there induced a tradition of religious extremism: "Violent ecstasism was always an endemic sickness in Phrygia."[46] Like many scholars, Cumont was particularly obsessed with the practice of ritual castration and made a great deal of the "emasculated Orientals" who followed the goddess. In doing so, he perpetuated the image of the Oriental as effeminate, inferior both because of his race and because of his supposedly feminine qualities.

Graillot too stressed the outrageous aspects of the Mother Goddess cult, calling it "a cult characterized by orgiasm, ecstasism, and sexual aberration." Graillot considered this typical of the Anatolian character. In reviewing the evidence for the cult of the Mother in Greece, Graillot stressed that the Greek cities rejected these excesses and, in his opinion, would never have lowered themselves to such practices, which were "repugnant to the Hellenic spirit."[47]

Today such language seems almost embarrassing, and, viewed in the historical context of scholarship (remembering that both Cumont's essay and Graillot's book were written in the first decades of this century), is best interpreted as a form of Orientalism, the consistent downgrading of west Asiatic culture and history that has characterized much European writing about the Near East in the nineteenth and twentieth centuries.[48] Such attitudes were not original to Cumont and Graillot, but their focus on matriarchy and on the supposed sexual aberrations in the Mother

44. Bachofen 1967: 99–100.
45. Cumont 1929: 45.
46. Ibid.: 47.
47. Graillot 1912: 21.
48. Said 1979: 167–97, 309–21. Kabbani 1986.

Goddess cult reinforced these stereotypes, implying that the Oriental followers of the Anatolian Mother were weak and depraved.

A mitigating point that may offset such embarrassing language is that scholarly works from the generation of Cumont and Graillot were disadvantaged by their limited information about Anatolia. Comparatively few of the monuments and inscriptions providing evidence about the Mother Goddess's Phrygian cult that are available now had been excavated in their time, and so their lack of knowledge about Anatolian religious practices is understandable. With a larger body of evidence to work with, it can be shown that few aspects of the Mother Goddess cult attributed by these scholars to Phrygia are in fact attested there. The climate of central Anatolia is no more extreme than that in most parts of the United States and Canada, nor is there any evidence in Phrygia for some of the most characteristic features of the Greek and Roman Mother Goddess cult, such as the worship of the god Attis and the symbolism of the sacred pine tree. Yet more recent surveys on the Mother Goddess, particularly those of the cult of the Magna Mater in Rome, continue to cite Cumont and follow the same Orientalist clichés.[49]

Several studies of the identity and nature of the god Attis have carried these racist attitudes to a more extreme point, presumably because the castration of the Mother Goddess's priests, which was said to have been done in imitation of Attis, evokes a more personally threatening image. This threatening quality has been averted from Classical studies by the assumption that although the Greeks must have known about the cult of Attis, they rejected it because of their supposedly more enlightened attitudes. In particular, it has enabled scholars of ancient Greek religion, as opposed to Roman religion, to adopt a high moral ground. "We can console ourselves with the feeling that the Greeks rejected the unnatural situation of the Attis cult," wrote Otto Kern in 1935. This attitude was reiterated in 1990 by the Dutch scholar H. S. Versnel: "The male attendant of the Great Goddess and his repulsive myth and ritual were obviously kept at bay."[50] Indeed, the assumption that extreme violence culminating in ritual castration was a hallmark of the Mother Goddess cult in Anatolia has become almost a truism, rarely questioned in the scholarly literature. Moreover, the assumption has been inverted to the point where virtually every reference to castration is taken as proof of the worship of Attis, even when neither Meter nor Attis is mentioned.[51]

---

49. Note, e.g., the comments of Bömer 1963: 866–901, and Bömer 1964. Other examples are cited below.

50. Kern 1935: II, 232. Versnel 1990: 107–8. Note a similar comment by Ferguson 1944: 110.

51. An excellent example of this is the scholarly treatment of an incident of self-castration mentioned by Plutarch in the context of the mutilation of the Herms in Athens on the eve of the Sicilian expedition in 415 B.C. (Plutarch, *Nikias* 13, 2). A number of scholars, e.g., Foucart 1873: 64–65; Graillot 1912: 22–23; Burkert 1979a: 104; Garland 1987: 130–31; Versnel 1990: 107–8; and Shear 1995: 175, have asserted that this proves that ritual castration was practiced in Athens during the late fifth century B.C., despite the fact that Plutarch's narrative contains no allusion to any religious ritual and merely describes the act of a single, mentally disturbed individual.

Scholars of Roman religion too have framed their discussions of Cybele and Attis within a similarly biased vision. One still reads that the Romans imported the savage rituals of the Magna Mater wholesale from the East because they did not know what they were getting.[52] This is so despite the fact that there is ample documentation in Roman historical and literary sources that many Romans, including several emperors, not only knew exactly what the cult entailed, but fully supported it. Likewise, the assumption that the unattractive features of the cult attested in Roman practice must have originated in Phrygia, because no Roman would have done such things, is also widely repeated.

One must certainly take into account the fact that several ancient authors themselves express similar sentiments; for example, Dionysios of Halikarnasos, writing in the late first century B.C., is quite forthright in his efforts to separate the Roman positive features of the Magna Mater cult from the Phrygian negative features, and the same point of view appears in the work of other ancient authors.[53] Yet with few exceptions, the disparaging opinions of the Phrygian Mother Goddess expressed by Dionysios of Halikarnassos and other ancient writers have been accepted uncritically, largely because they reinforce the similar prejudicial attitudes of more modern scholars toward the Orient, while the positive image of the Magna Mater cult in Roman literature, for example, that in Virgil's *Aeneid*, has been regarded as an anomaly requiring special explanation. It is a sad commentary on modern Classical scholarship that myths of rape and incest, the myths of violence to women that populate the Greek and Roman landscape so abundantly, are considered a natural part of the Greek and Roman experience, while a myth of castration, of violence to men, must be explained away as a foreign import, the mark of an inferior Oriental people.

An essay by Garth Thomas is particularly emphatic on this point.[54] In discussing the circumstances surrounding the introduction of the cult into Rome, Thomas (like many others) is puzzled by the contradiction between the ancient sources that describe the event as one that was highly desired, attracting the patronage of many of the most important Roman Republican families, including the Scipiones and the Claudii, and the later picture of the cult as a thing steeped in barbarism and sexual aberration: "I would need to know how an oriental deity whose cult contained so many traits that were completely alien and even repugnant to Roman religious sensibilities, could ever have been glossed over so as to make the cult innocuous enough for Roman aristocrats," he remarks; and later, discussing the role of Scipio Nasica: "[I]t is beyond credibility that a Roman nobleman would have identified himself with the non-Roman aspect of the cult, or that such identification would have been acceptable within the social attitudes of the time. . . . But how else do we imagine

52. See, e.g., the statements of Thomas 1984 and Gruen 1990: 5.
53. Dionysios of Halikarnassos 2.19. For a discussion of this dichotomy, specifically with relation to Virgil's *Aeneid,* see Wiseman 1984. This topic is pursued more fully in part 4.
54. Thomas 1984.

that a barbarian deity, whose worship consisted of mystery and orgy, whose character was that of an eastern fertility goddess, suddenly became a civilized, Roman deity . . . whose cult became that of a national and protective goddess?"[55]

This is one of the most explicit modern statements of bias against the cultural traditions of the East. It relies on vague and undefined clichés (e.g., "eastern fertility goddess"), and on the unstated and unexamined notion that an Oriental cult was by definition degenerate, one that the Romans had to rise above. As Thomas himself notes,[56] such a position creates significant difficulties in reconciling this modern picture of the East as backward and barbaric with the ancient testimonia. The recent date of this essay, 1984, and its publication in the frequently cited series *Aufstieg und Niedergang der römischen Welt* indicates that such prejudicial views of the Orient are still an active part of the scholarly literature.

The assumption of taint attached to the eastern origins of the Mother Goddess underlies a number of comments in modern scholarly discussions about the social background of the goddess's devotees. While little is known about the origins and social class of the Mother's followers in any area of the Mediterranean, several modern discussions have filled in the gaps with unsupported notions about whom the cult ought to have appealed to. To explain the popularity of the Anatolian Mother Goddess in Rome, many scholars have simply assumed that most of the goddess's followers were persons of no account. Thus, for Cumont, the Phrygian cult of the Mother in Rome was supported primarily by slaves, non-citizens, Asiatic merchants, and Levantine types.[57] In discussing the visit of the priest Battakes to Rome in 108 B.C.,[58] Graillot states quite emphatically, and in direct contradiction to the ancient testimonia describing the event, that the crowd that followed the priest of the Magna Mater doubtless included "Orientals, slaves, disenfranchised individuals, Levantine merchants, and women, who were profoundly attracted to the cults of the Orient; among the citizens, the plebeian element would have been dominant."[59] In other words, everyone in Rome was there but the male aristocrats. And Graillot then chides these aristocrats for failing to suppress "the contagion of metroac fanaticism" (fanaticism of the Mother Goddess cult) either through indifference and lack of will or through complicity.[60]

Other studies have pursued the question of the social origins of the Mother's adherents in much the same vein. In his discussion of the organization of the cult of

55. Ibid.: 1504, 1506–7.
56. Ibid.: 1504.
57. Cumont 1929: 50.
58. The incident is described by Diodoros 36.13.1–3 and Plutarch, *Marius* 17–18.
59. Graillot 1912: 97–98. Graillot maintains this despite Plutarch's statement that the strongest opposition to Battakes' presence came from the tribune of the plebs, A. Pompeius. I strongly suspect that in mentioning "Levantine merchants" as among the low-life types prominent among the Mother's followers, both Cumont and Graillot were reflecting the strong anti-Semitism of their time.
60. Graillot 1912: 98. A more moderate voice in this debate is that of Toutain 1911: 111–19, who stresses the personal satisfaction and salvation that the cult's devotees found.

Meter in the Piraeus, W. S. Ferguson is at pains to insist that the Athenian citizens who took part in it omitted the "more repulsive" features of the Phrygian cult. According to Ferguson, a separate organization existed for Athenian citizens who worshipped Meter; this was to avoid the "social let-down" that might have come from joint participation in the cult with metics (free non-citizens).[61] I have already noted the difficulties faced by Thomas as a result of his insistence that the cult of the Magna Mater in Rome was barbaric, unfit for proper Romans, notwithstanding the undoubted fact that many of the most prominent Republican aristocratic families took part in the cult. These examples suggest that in discussing the identity and social origins of those attracted to the Mother's cult, previous treatments of the ancient evidence have been strongly affected by biased presuppositions, in this case the presupposition that the cult of the Mother Goddess would not have appealed to respectable people.

This disparity between the picture of the cult created in the primary sources and its treatment in secondary sources should induce caution in any subsequent study of this material. In trying to avoid the prejudices that have colored much scholarship in the past, a particularly rigorous analysis of the principal evidence is needed. The reader will have to decide if I have been any more successful than my predecessors in avoiding these pitfalls. But there is an important function to be served in drawing attention to these earlier presumptions, if only to stress that the primary evidence from Mediterranean antiquity, literary, epigraphical, and archaeological, must form the principal basis of this study. The gaps and inconsistencies in the ancient evidence (and there are many) should be pointed out and then let stand. Perhaps then we can avoid reading values from our own culture into the ancient evidence and allow the Mother Goddess to speak for herself.

61. Ferguson 1944: 110.

1 · THE MOTHER GODDESS IN ANATOLIA

2 · THE EVIDENCE
FROM PREHISTORY

Astudy of a mother goddess in the ancient Mediterranean world must address the question of her origins. Although the existence of this divinity in historic periods is securely attested by literary texts and inscriptions that address her as "Mother" in a variety of local languages, the evidence for her existence in prehistoric periods is much shakier. Certainly, the peoples of the ancient Mediterranean took great pride in the antiquity of their Mother Goddess; the Romans, for example, regarded the cult of the goddess known as the Magna Mater, or Cybele, as one with roots extending back into the dim past.[1] The basis for the belief of these peoples concerning their own religious traditions needs to be examined, and since textual evidence that might provide a clear answer is unavailable for the prehistoric era, we must consider what other classes of material may provide testimonia for the existence of such a divinity. The goal of this chapter is therefore twofold: to determine whether there is evidence from Mediterranean prehistory of the existence of a female divinity (or divinities) who was identified as a mother goddess, and, if so, whether this divinity was the ancestor of the Mother Goddess Cybele, so well attested in historic eras.

Identification of a mother goddess in prehistoric religious practice, however, is a tricky task. While many extravagant claims have been made about the inevitability and ubiquity of a mother goddess in Mediterranean prehistory, as we saw in chapter 1, such claims are frequently unfounded; this is particularly true of the casual equation of any prehistoric female figurine with a mother goddess. There are, however, two Neolithic sites in central Anatolia, Çatalhöyük and Hacilar, which have attracted considerable attention because they have produced material strongly remi-

1. Ovid, *Fasti* 4.249–52; Apuleius 11.4.

niscent of the Phrygian Mother Goddess cult. Evidence from both sites suggests that powerful female figures played a role in the religious consciousness of the community. These figures were represented with symbol systems similar to those of the historically attested Phrygian Mother. And both sites are located in regions that contained cult centers of the Phrygian Mother in historical periods.

The earlier of the two (although the later one excavated) is the well-known site of Çatalhöyük, situated about 40 kilometers south of Konya, in south central Turkey.[2] Çatalhöyük is a large Neolithic mound that was continuously occupied between 6200 and 5400 B.C., when it was abandoned for unknown reasons.[3] The earliest levels of the site have not been reached, so the initial date of the settlement is not known; moreover, only a small portion of the mound has been investigated and many aspects of the settlement are still imperfectly understood.

The form of the settlement has been extensively described in excavation reports and in several subsequent studies; hence it need only be summarized briefly here. The lowest levels of the settlement consisted of a series of contiguous houses with party walls. Higher levels, in contrast, appear to have included discrete units of one or more rooms, often arranged around courtyards. Some rooms had parallel walls with narrow spaces in between. While doorways have been found, in some cases these were deliberately taken out of use and plastered over. In most instances access to a house was by ladder through an opening in the roof, and communication between parts of the settlements was presumably across the rooftops, which were flat. There is no evidence of large-scale public buildings or elaborate houses that might signify social stratification by rank. When the houses of one level were destroyed, either by fire or simply by abandonment, a new house was built directly on top of the previous one.[4] This pattern was continued for at least eight centuries. Because occupation at the site in subsequent millennia was limited, the material from the Neolithic levels was remarkably well preserved, making it possible to examine a number of features in Neolithic society about which we are frequently poorly informed.

Among these features are the symbol systems reflecting the spiritual and social life of the community. Çatalhöyük is remarkable for the frequent occurrence, at all

2. Çatalhöyük, first excavated between 1961 and 1965, is currently being investigated anew, and so all suggestions made here concerning interpretations of its material should be regarded as tentative. Results of the first three seasons of new excavations are presented in Hodder 1996. For reports of the original excavation, see Mellaart 1962, 1963a, 1964, 1966, and 1967. A report on the nearby mound of Çatalhöyük West, a settlement of Chalcolithic date, was published by Mellaart 1965. Todd 1976, gives a useful summary of the original excavation and its finds, and discusses several problems of interpretation. A more recent book on the Çatalhöyük cult material, Mellaart, Hirsch, and Balpinar 1989, contains beautiful illustrations of the Çatalhöyük paintings, although the text relies on many of the same clichés about the Great Mother Goddess as a perpetual fertility deity discussed in chapter 1; for a review of the conflicting opinions on this book, see Mallett 1992–93.

3. The population may not have completely abandoned the site, but shifted to another area of the mound; see Hodder 1996: 360–61.

4. Abandonment often appears to have been preceded by intentional burning; see ibid.: 365.

twelve excavated levels of habitation, of individual rooms with wall paintings, plaster reliefs on walls and benches, and a variety of objects, including several unusual figurine types, all suggesting that the rooms had been used for a ritual purpose. This functional interpretation is based entirely on the rooms' decoration or on their contents, for the rooms themselves were identical in form and size to other rooms in the settlement that were used for habitation or storage. It is misleading to call such rooms "shrines," since it seems unlikely that they were designated for ritual usage at the time of their construction; recent investigations suggest that the "shrines" may originally have been intended for habitation and were only later used for ritual activities.[5] They occur randomly throughout the settlement. Almost every level had at least one such room, and some have several: levels 2, 3, 6, and 8 were especially rich in them.

The paintings and plaster reliefs found in a number of the rooms have received special attention, since they are among the most striking finds of the Anatolian Neolithic. I shall consider the paintings first. These were found throughout levels 3–12, painted directly onto the plaster of the walls. In some rooms, the same wall was painted, then covered with a thick coat of white plaster, then repainted and replastered several times, suggesting that the paintings reflect the room's use for certain special activities and were later intentionally removed.

The subject matter of the paintings covers a rich variety of material. Some are nonfigurative elements, such as abstract designs (rooms E.VI.2, A.III.8), motifs of human hands on the walls (A.VI.4, E.VI.15), and a landscape (E.VII.14).[6] Figurative subjects include several scenes of men hunting wild animals, such as deer and wild cattle, and others in which the cattle form a backdrop for men in leopard skins or deer skins performing some type of dance (A.III.1, F.V.1). There are two scenes that appear to depict vultures denuding human corpses of their flesh (E.VII.8, E.VII.21).

Another frequent form of decoration was plaster reliefs molded directly onto the walls. These occur primarily on level 6 and below. Several plaster reliefs depict wild animals, including a bull and a stag, sometimes raised and sometimes cut into the walls. Other raised reliefs include the forms of two antithetically placed leopards (E.VII.44), which had been painted and replastered at least four times. There are also seven examples of a human being, two sets of pairs and three individual figures, all shown with an enlarged abdomen and legs and arms stretched wide apart; these may represent a woman giving birth. Other furnishings in the rooms included clay benches, often with bull horns placed in a row on them. Other sets of bull horns were found mounted in a row on the walls (E.VI.8, 10, 14, 31). Also found on the

5. Ibid.: 363.
6. The letter/number designations refer to the method of numbering rooms in the excavation. In each case, the first notation, a letter, refers to the excavation sector, the second, a Roman number, to the excavation level, and the third, an Arabic number, to the individual room. See Todd 1976: 23.

walls in rooms of levels 7 and 6 were molded objects resembling human breasts; sometimes these were molded around vulture, fox, or weasel skulls or around boar's jaws, with the boar's teeth projecting from them (E.VI.8).

The site also yielded a number of figurines from different contexts, including human, animal, and schematic figurines.[7] Most are of clay, although all the schematic figurines and most of the human figurines up to level 6 are of stone. The human figurines have received the most attention. Several of these depict females, often with exaggerated breasts, hips, buttocks, and abdomens, of a type found widely throughout the Mediterranean Neolithic. While clearly representing women, they do not draw particular attention to women's reproductive roles. Some were shown standing, while a few were seated or crouching.[8] The number of female figurines increases in level 6, and there are more large-breasted females in the higher levels. There were several male figures, one shown riding a leopard and another with a leopard-skin cap. Other figurines have no indication of gender. Among the more unusual figurine types uncovered were pairs of figures made out of one piece of stone or clay; some show two figures side by side, other pairs appear to embrace, and one may be a group of a mother and child. Probably the most widely illustrated figure is that of a female seated on a throne supported by two felines (from room A.II.1); she appears to be shown in the act of giving birth, with the child's head appearing between her legs (fig. 1).

Çatalhöyük has thus produced abundant material that can directly be connected with belief in a mother goddess. Figurines and wall paintings and reliefs do illustrate women in the process of giving birth or holding young children. Many of these were found in rooms whose contents or decoration suggest ritual use. And such material was not isolated in one or two limited areas, but was found throughout the levels of the site's occupation. The original excavator, James Mellaart, was quite forthright in interpreting the female figurines and reliefs as representations of the Anatolian Mother Goddess, the prehistoric forerunner of the Greek and Roman Cybele, and in this he has been followed by many people in both popular and scholarly literature.[9]

On the other hand, while much has been made of the scenes referent to female fertility and childbirth, a more imposing motif informing this material is that of animal imagery. Many of the figurative scenes on the walls have direct or indirect allusions to the hunt. Men are shown in the act of hunting wild animals, while other scenes depict the same animals that form the quarry in the hunting scenes, but standing alone. In some paintings, the men shown with wild animals seem not to be hunting

7. For valuable observations on the range and context of the Çatalhöyük figurines, see Hamilton 1996. I am grateful to Naomi Hamilton for sharing her ideas on the figurines with me.
8. Illustrated in Mellaart 1963b and Mellaart 1964: 73–81.
9. See esp. Mellaart 1963b. Supporters of the Mother Goddess hypothesis include, among others, Vermaseren 1977, Burkert 1979a: 120, Robertson 1996: 303.

them so much as teasing them, pulling at the tongue or tail of the animal. Other scenes present men wearing leopard skins or deer skins engaged in dancing or some other ritual activity. Some of the figurines depict individuals wearing leopard skins, suggesting that these are not divine figures, but representations of the inhabitants of the site. Animal imagery dominates even in scenes connected with death, those of vultures denuding a corpse of flesh.

Such animal images carry over into the material associated with female fertility. Two female figures with legs spread apart, as if in the act of giving birth, are placed antithetically, as if mirroring the pairs of leopards. The use of boars' jaws and vulture skulls on which to mold female breasts further entwines the metaphor of human fertility with animals, as does the figurine of the corpulent woman giving birth while seated on a throne supported by two felines. One particularly striking plaster relief depicts a woman with abdomen enlarged and legs spread apart, presumably in the act of giving birth; on the wall below her legs is a row of bull horns (E.VI.8). The implication appears to be that the woman will give birth to a bull, although the damaged state of the relief makes this interpretation uncertain.[10]

Rather than interpreting these reliefs and figurines as purely religious symbols, it may be more fruitful to see them as symbols of the community's economic and social structure. There is abundant evidence demonstrating the importance of domesticated animals, especially cattle, to the economy of the site. The use of bull horns mounted on benches or on walls may recognize this importance and express a wish for the continued fertility of cattle. Similarly the birth-giving female above cattle horns may recognize the dependence of humans on cattle.[11] The find spots of some of the female figurines are also instructive. Several were uncovered on the floor of domestic areas near hearths or in grain bins. The large enthroned figurine of the birth-giving female from level 2 (fig. 1) was found in a grain-storage room adjacent to a living room. Here, too, the symbolism of human reproduction may express human dependency on cereals and other domesticated plants. Also worth noting is that several deposits of grain, evidently intentional offerings, were placed in the room (E.VI.44) with the two antithetically placed plaster leopards.

Other examples of the entwining of human and animal imagery may allude to social grouping within the community. The painted figures wearing differing types of animal skins may represent groups or clans that used the animal as a totem.[12] In this case, the pairs of antithetically placed leopards depicted in plaster reliefs on walls might allude to the space allotted to this group. Some bones of wild animals were found, indicating that hunting was practiced, but the primary reason for this may not have been dietary needs;[13] instead, animal symbols such as leopard skins, boars'

10. Todd 1976: 53–56.
11. Hamilton 1996: 226.
12. Ibid.: 227.
13. Todd 1976: 120.

FIGURE I.
Seated female figurine
from Çatalhöyük. Sixth
millennium B.C. Courtesy,
Museum of Anatolian
Civilizations, Ankara.

jaws, and vulture skulls may have signified different groups in which both males and females were prominent.

Another point worth noting is the increased incidence of female figurines in the later levels of the site. This could indicate an increase in prominence of certain women or groups of women in the community.[14] Figurines referent to human fertility and reproduction are not common; the frequent repetition of the enthroned birth-giving female in modern literature has distorted this point, but this figure and one other showing a woman and child are the only two depictions of children. Several female figurines depicting full-breasted women more likely represent older women whose maturity gave them a greater degree of status.

The material from Çatalhöyük certainly suggests that symbolic imagery played an important role in the community, for the paintings, plastered features, and figurines

14. Hamilton 1996: 226.

FIGURE 2.   Seated female
figurine from Hacilar. Sixth
millennium B.C. Courtesy, Museum
of Anatolian Civilizations, Ankara.

rarely depict the type of mundane activities that undoubtedly made up the day-to-day occupation of this site. Instead, we see allusions to a number of economic and social concerns: the economic prosperity of the site and the desire to ensure that prosperity; the division of the community into social groups and the ways in which each group maintained its position; and the activities of women and the status of women, particularly older women in the community. These are all tentative suggestions, which should be regarded as working hypotheses, but they do indicate that the symbol systems at Çatalhöyük need not signify the cult of a mother goddess, particularly since it is not certain at this point whether any of the paintings or figurines represents a divinity. It also seems unlikely that this imagery was very widespread. Mellaart suggested that the settlement owed its size and prosperity to the fact that it was the spiritual center of the Konya plain,[15] but at present it seems safest to assume that the symbol systems demonstrated at Çatalhöyük are representative only of this site, and not of the Konya plain in general.

Let us turn now to the material from another important Anatolian Neolithic site, Hacilar, which lies about 26 kilometers southwest of the modern Turkish city of Burdur. It was excavated from 1957 to 1960, also by James Mellaart.[16] Occupation at the site included a small aceramic Neolithic settlement, dated ca. 7000 B.C., and, discontinuous from this, a settlement of the later Neolithic and early Chalcolithic periods in nine identifiable habitation levels, ranging in date from ca. 5700 to 5000 B.C. The arrangement of the settlement was somewhat different from that of Çatalhöyük, for at Hacilar the dwellings consisted of separate houses built around courtyards. These houses often consisted of more than one occupation room, plus separate storage areas. Considerable evidence for household activity was found in each room, including hearths, grinding stones, and other evidence of food and textile preparation. No examples of figured wall paintings were uncovered, and there seems to be little to indicate that such paintings ever existed.[17] The furnishings of each house were in general quite similar. There is no evidence of either any large community structure or elite residence or separate cult or shrine rooms.

The evidence for the symbolic or spiritual life of the community is drawn entirely from a rich sequence of figurines found at the site.[18] Most of the figurines are made of clay, although there are a few stone pieces. All were found in domestic contexts. The fullest series comes from level 6, an occupation level that was destroyed by fire in about 5600 B.C., and thus is contemporary with the later levels at Çatalhöyük.

15. Mellaart 1975: 106.

16. Mellaart published preliminary excavation reports of his work at Hacilar in *Anatolian Studies,* 1958–61. The final report is Mellaart 1970.

17. There was evidence of painted plaster at Hacilar, but not of figurative designs. Mellaart 1970: 20, postulated, quite reasonably, that textile hangings may have been used as wall coverings, and the rich series of geometric ornaments found on the Hacilar pottery suggests the type of ornamental patterns that may have been used in textiles.

18. These are discussed as a group in ibid.: 166–85.

Approximately forty-five figurines were found in the houses from this level, representing a cross-section of female types. They depict a range of ages, from young to older women. (Age designation is assumed from the slenderness of the figure, the hip-to-waist ratio, the size of the breasts, and the size of the abdomen.) Several figurines appear to be pregnant, while others seem to be older women with sagging breasts and abdomens. The figurines appear in a variety of poses, standing, seated, reclining. Some are shown with smaller human figures, presumably children, although in at least one case the woman may be copulating with a young male.[19] One is shown squatting, with her legs drawn apart, perhaps in the act of giving birth.[20] Several figures cup their hands under their breasts to lift them up and call attention to them,[21] while others place their hands on the upper edge of the breasts and push down, as if to express milk.[22] Many are totally naked, and the female anatomical features of breasts, buttocks, and abdomen are clearly delineated; in contrast, the non–gender specific parts of the anatomy, such as the face, arms, and legs, are shown in a very schematic fashion. A few of the slender figures assumed to be young girls are shown wearing a garment like a bikini brief, while other, apparently older women have a pattern of nets or dots painted on the skin, perhaps representing tattoo marks or the textile patterns of clothing.

Most of the figurines illustrate a range of ages, poses, and allusions to the life passages of youth, childbearing, and old age, in other words, a cross-section of female types that one would likely have encountered in any human settlement. There are, however, several figurines depicting subjects beyond the boundaries of normal human activities. Women are shown seated on thrones supported by two felines (fig. 2).[23] Other women cradle felines to their breasts,[24] in a pose similar to that of women cradling human babies.

The prominence of the figurines in level 6 is remarkable, given that only scattered examples of figurines were found in the lower levels, most of them of much cruder workmanship. It seems unlikely, however, that the figurines' period of use was limited to level 6, but rather that the circumstances of this level's destruction by fire preserved these figurines. This suggests that the figurines were limited to specific purposes or functions and may have been deliberately destroyed after such functions had been served. The find spots of the figurines are also informative; all were found on household floors, most clustered near the hearths. Several were found embedded in piles of grain. Most are in excellent condition; they were not broken or damaged intentionally. This too suggests that, because of the fire that destroyed the settle-

19. Women with children, ibid.: nos. 519, 575, 573, figs. 218–20. Woman copulating, ibid.: no. 528, pl. VI and fig. 227.
20. Ibid.: no. 525, fig. 201.
21. Ibid.: nos. 486, 507, 513, 514, 515, 522, 534, 569, 576.
22. Ibid.: nos. 529, 531, 570, and pl. v.23.
23. Ibid.: nos. 518, 523, figs. 228–29.
24. Ibid.: nos. 539, 577, 518, figs. 196–97, 228.

ment, we have been fortunate in finding the figurines in the circumstances under which they were actually used.

These are important points to keep in mind when trying to determine the function and meaning of the Hacilar figurines. The excavator definitely considered all of them to represent goddesses, and considered the figurines shown with children to be representations of the mother goddess.[25] Few, however, have anything unusual in their appearance or pose to suggest divinity, and most seem to represent human females in the normal poses, activities, and life stages of women in a typical human community. They may be representations of specific individual women, or they could represent archetypes of female personalities and activities; they may symbolize ancestors, or they could be objects used as teaching devices to initiate young women into the community.[26] The lack of individual male figures, coupled with the emphasis on female anatomy in the figurines, implies strongly that womanhood was being represented, but whether we can move from this tentative conclusion to an assumption that they represent a goddess or goddesses as mothers is much less certain.

Two factors make this group of figurines unusual and present close parallels to the representations of females at Çatalhöyük. One is the association of females with predators: the motif of the woman seated on the leopard throne is found at both sites, and the Hacilar figures shown cradling leopard cubs to their bosoms indicate a close connection between human fertility and predators. The other is the association with grain and agriculture: at both sites, the representations of females in the mother role were deliberately placed into grain bins. These included the examples in which feline predators are present.

While the excavator did not hesitate to interpret the material from both sites as clear evidence for the presence of the cult of a Mother Goddess in the Anatolian Neolithic and for the continuity of this cult into the historic period, there are a number of other factors that make this interpretation less certain. In the first place, it is not at all certain that any of the artifacts proposed as evidence of mother goddess worship are even religious objects, in the conventional sense of objects intended primarily or exclusively for a religious function, such as cult statues of deities and votive objects and shrines dedicated to deities. We cannot even be certain that the inhabitants of Neolithic communities in central Anatolia conceptualized their spiritual world as one populated by discrete anthropomorphic entities called gods, and it is therefore even less certain that they would have envisioned the need for a mother goddess, in the sense of a single female deity who monitored human reproduction.

We can state with some confidence that the inhabitants of these two sites felt the need to express their concerns about the economic and social health of the commu-

---

25. Ibid.: 171–74.
26. Note the range of activities and functions postulated for figurine groups in the Peloponnesos in Greece (Talalay 1993: 37–44).

nity through complex symbol systems. One common motif is that of human-animal relationships, which bear on both life and death. This could represent a need to propitiate a spiritual world in which various abstract powers were thought to be represented by different animals. It could also, following up on a suggestion made above, represent a social system in which the community was divided into groups represented by separate animal totems, each competing for prestige within a larger group. In this context, the images of human women and birth seem to be a part of a much larger concept. Pregnant women are depicted in poses and with decorations similar to leopards, spread out in plaster reliefs and sometimes antithetically placed. The large statuette of the woman giving birth while supporting herself on a throne flanked by two felines closely connects human birth and wild animals. This image is present at Hacilar also, in figurines depicting a woman seated on a throne supported by felines or women cradling felines to their breasts. These could represent the women of the group whose symbol was a leopard, or more generally, identify the most important women in the community whose status was manifest through the symbolism of a powerful animal. The figurines and paintings could also communicate the motives of the whole community: the desire for mastery over the natural environment symbolized by taming these fierce animals, and the desire that the prosperity resulting from such control be extended to agricultural prosperity and fertility, either for the whole group, or for one part of the group. This suggestion is supported by the find spots of some figurines, buried in grain bins, where they may well have been intended to express the wish to extend the power represented by animals such as wild felines to agricultural prosperity and fecundity.

Using the figurine groups as evidence for the worship of a mother deity is equally problematic. At both sites there were a large number of figurines depicting women, the majority of them shown in normal life stages, such as would be encountered in a typical village settlement. Interpreting these female figures as symbols of quasi-divine status—namely, "the goddess in her younger aspect," "the mistress of animals," "the goddess with her young consort"[27]—has the effect of objectifying aspects of women's lives. Such interpretations also serve to limit their meaning to women's reproductive capacities and imply that women had no part in creating these images. We have no idea of the identity of the makers of these objects, nor of the process by which meaning was attached to them, but parallels with other cultures suggest that women did create and use such figurines for a variety of reasons, including as vehicles of sympathetic magic, teaching devices, or toys.[28] Many of the more conventional scenes of females with children may well represent a wish for more children or a prayer for the safety of children or mothers. The scarcity of representations of males also argues against the interpretation of these figurines as symbols of deities,

---

27. Mellaart 1963b, 1970: 171.
28. Ucko 1962; Voigt 1983: 187–93; Talalay 1991, 1993.

for then we would have to explain the lack of representations of male divinities, or postulate the existence of a monotheistic religion, which seems very unlikely. The group of predominantly female figurines may point to a society in which gender roles were defined so that men and women lived quite separate lives, and the figurines could have been used in activities in which men had little part, such as teaching and nourishing the young, but these activities need not have been limited to religious actions.

Thus what we see here is not the worship of a mother goddess, but rather the existence of conceptual framework of religious activities in which control of human fertility and animal totems would bring prosperity to the people. It is surely significant that the Çatalhöyük object that shows the closest affinity to later cult statues, including first-millennium B.C. representations of the Phrygian Mother, was found in the upper level of habitation, shortly before the site's abandonment. We may see the concepts of divinity, status, and power symbolized by animals such as the leopard, the vulture, or the boar, which ensured the prosperity of the group, or enhanced the status of some members of the group. What we seem to see here is not a universal belief but rather a belief system in the process of construction, and one that was subject to change over the occupation period of a site.

As yet, these two sites are the only ones in Anatolia that have produced material that can be brought to bear on the question of a mother goddess in prehistory. At the time when Hacilar and Çatalhöyük were excavated, relatively little was known about the Anatolian Neolithic, but since then a large number of other Neolithic sites in Turkey have been investigated; several have yielded quite striking evidence bearing on ritual activity, although little to suggest the existence of the cult of a mother goddess.[29] This further suggests that belief in a mother goddess was not natural or inevitable, but was in fact the product of specific social and cultural circumstances.

Certain other points should be noted concerning the prehistoric material. The interpretation of Neolithic figurines as mother goddesses, as in these two Anatolian sites, rests on the modern assumption that such a goddess would be depicted with an iconographic image denoting human female reproductive capacity. Yet in the historical era, the goddess called Meter or Magna Mater was almost never portrayed with any overtly maternal characteristics; she is never shown giving birth, and only rarely holds a child. Instead, her most constant historical iconography consists of images of power, such as the wild animals that accompany her, her placement on a throne or in a votive niche, and her crown.

Finally, we should note that the iconography and personality of the goddess Meter / Magna Mater changed significantly during the centuries when her worship is historically attested. The Meter in the cult of fifth-century B.C. Athens was very

29. Hodder 1996: 3–4, commenting on the place of Çatalhöyük within the Neolithic of central Anatolia.

different from the goddess worshipped by the emperor Julian in the fourth century C.E. We should not expect to find the historical images of Meter transferred literally back into prehistory, without allowing for equivalent or greater changes that may have taken place over a much longer period of time. If we are to seek the ancestor of the Phrygian Mother in prehistory, then we must look for some indication in Neolithic cult material of images that were especially enduring, such as the strength and awe symbolized by predators, especially felines and raptors. As we shall see, images of hunting and of the power and strength found in the lion and in birds of prey were key symbols in the Phrygian cult of the Mother Goddess and remained prominent in her Greek and Roman cults. The Neolithic sites in south central Turkey give us some indication of how such symbols may have been formed.

3 · THE BRONZE
AND EARLY IRON AGES

The figurines and paintings depicting female figures with felines from Çatalhöyük and Hacilar furnish a concentration of religious artifacts and symbols
that appear to anticipate the Phrygian Mother Goddess. Yet after this rich
body of material from the Neolithic period, there is very little evidence from Anatolia pointing to the existence of a mother goddess until the first millennium B.C.,
when the Phrygian Mother Goddess becomes a prominent figure in the religious life
of the region. Such a long gap, from the sixth to the first millennium B.C., seems surprising, even more so in light of the Phrygian Mother's remarkable presence in the
ancient Mediterranean world for the next millennium and more. Given her continuing impact on ancient society from the Iron Age through the late Roman period,
one would expect the Phrygian Mother Goddess to have an extensive background in
the earlier Anatolian cult as well.

The goal of this chapter is therefore to trace whether any aspects of the Phrygian
Mother Goddess, such as her nomenclature, iconographic form, or attributes, can
be found in the Bronze Age and Early Iron Age cultures that preceded the Phrygians
in Anatolia. As we shall see, there was no single deity addressed as "Mother" in Anatolia during the Bronze and Early Iron Ages. Yet the earlier cultures of Anatolia did
indeed influence the identity and portrayal of the Phrygian goddess. Many of the
symbols and cultic rituals associated with the Phrygian Mother were not limited to
this divinity, but are also found among the Phrygians' predecessors in Anatolia. Analyzing what such symbols are and how they contributed to the cult of the Phrygian
Mother will be a valuable aid in defining the origins and meaning of the goddess.

The chief focus of this section is on the complex cultures that preceded the Phrygians in central and eastern Anatolia. These include the Hittites, the dominant
people in central Anatolia during the Middle and Late Bronze Ages, and the Neo-

Hittites in the southeast and the Urartians in eastern Anatolia, both civilizations of the Early Iron Age contemporary with the Phrygians. Certain symbols found in Phrygian expressions of divinity were also prominent among these peoples: they include the sacred mountain, the sources of water that spring from the ground, and the links between the symbolism of animal predators and civic ritual. Because the same concepts continued to recur in different time periods and different cultural groups, it seems likely that they carried a meaning of sacredness that was not specific to one ethnic group but survived in the basic consciousness of the people who lived in this area.

THE HITTITE BACKGROUND

The immediate predecessors of the Phrygians in central Anatolia were the Hittites, and one might expect several features of Phrygian cult practice to be found in Hittite religion as well. Indeed, several prominent Phrygian sites, including Gordion, Ankara, and Boğazköy, were built directly over earlier Hittite settlements, and at least one site, Gordion, was continuously inhabited throughout the Late Bronze and Early Iron Ages, although one or more significant shifts of population do seem to have occurred.[1] The Hittites did occasionally represent a prominent female deity, the Sun Goddess of Arinna, holding a child, and it is possible that this deity may have been conceived of as a mother goddess (although she is not addressed as Mother).[2] The differences in religious practices between the two cultures, however, are more notable. The large Hittite pantheon with its multitude of deities, both male and female, is far removed from the Phrygian world, in which the Mother Goddess is the only deity attested iconographically or in written texts. The large temples dominating the economy and urban planning of Hittite cities find no counterpart in Phrygian settlements. Nonetheless, certain aspects of Hittite religious symbolism recur in Phrygian symbolism.

Chief among these is the sacred mountain. To the Hittites, the mountains supported their gods and offered the opportunity to contact them. This is most vividly demonstrated at the Hittite capital city of Hattusa (modern Boğazköy), where the major settlement was located, not in the valley, but on the mountainside above. The mountainous upper city was almost totally devoted to religious purposes, and over thirty temples have been uncovered there.[3] A mountain formed a frequent iconographic symbol as well. Mountains themselves could be personified as deities, nor-

1. The relationship between the Phrygian immigrants and the earlier Hittite settlements is a complex one, and more work will be needed to clarify it, but in Gordion there seems to have been no period of abandonment after the collapse of the Hittite Empire; see Sams and Voigt 1990; Voigt 1994: 276–78.

2. Muscarella 1974: no. 125, the Sun Goddess of Arinna. We should note that the Phrygian Mother never sits and holds a child on her lap, so this image is unlikely to be a predecessor of the Phrygian goddess.

3. Mellink 1991: 130.

mally male deities, and as such were represented alone or standing as supports for more important deities. In depictions from both the Middle and Late Bronze Age the Hittite weather god, the principal male deity, often appears standing on a mountain; a notable example is the pair of mountain gods that support the weather deity at Yazilikaya, the impressive set of rock relief sculptures decorating the funerary complex of Tudhaliyas near Boğazköy.[4] This acknowledgment of the sacred aura of mountains may have been an important element in defining the Phrygian Mother as a mountain deity.

Another important feature of Hittite religious iconography that may be ancestral to Phrygian usage is the presence of the raptor, the bird of prey, as a divine attribute. The bird itself is a hunter, and it is also a frequent companion of a hunting deity, present in the Middle Bronze Age,[5] the Hittite Empire period,[6] and in the Early Iron Age.[7] The deity is usually male, but at least one example, a stamp seal impression from Boğazköy, illustrates a seated goddess holding a bird of prey and a bowl, the same attributes as the Phrygian Mother Goddess.[8] While none of these objects reproduces the precise iconography of the Phrygian goddess, they do establish the suitability of these symbols as divine attributes. They also suggest that interest in the hunt and in a deity that could master the wildness of the open countryside through hunting was an important feature of Anatolian religious consciousness, one that survived into the Early Iron Age.

A third aspect of Hittite religious practice that reappears in Phrygian cult is the attention paid to underground water sources, especially springs. Ground water was always a major water source for the peoples of Anatolia, a circumstance reflected in religious art and iconography throughout the Bronze Age.[9] We can see specific examples in sanctuaries located near springs, such as the spring shrines at Eflatun Pinar and at Boğazköy, a shrine located beside an underground spring near Temple I.[10] A similar phenomenon can be noted in Phrygia, for images of the Phrygian Mother have been found near water sources at Gordion and Ankara.[11] In addition, there are

4. N. Özgüç 1965: 63 (the weather god standing on a mountain on seals of the Assyrian Colony period). Bittel 1976a: fig. 248 (mountain god alone); fig. 239 (mountain god supporting the weather god).

5. Seals from the Assyrian Colony period, N. Özgüç 1965: nos. 65, 66, 69; an Old Hittite rhyton, bird of prey held by both a seated figure and a figure standing on the back of a stag, Bittel 1976b: pls. 3–5, Muscarella 1974: no. 123. Bittel identifies the deity as male, Muscarella as female, but I find Bittel's interpretation of the deity's conical cap as a masculine attribute more persuasive.

6. A relief from Yeniköy, Bittel 1976a: fig. 247, Akurgal 1961: 47b; stamp seals from Boğazköy, Güterbock 1940: no. 64, Beran 1967: no. 161; a stamp seal in Oxford, Akurgal 1961: pl. 52.

7. T. Özgüç 1971: 9–11, fig. 7, pls. 11–12. For a discussion of the Hittite hunting deity and its relation to Phrygian cult, see Mellink 1983: 351–52.

8. Güterbock 1942: 77, no. 220; Beran 1967: 30, no. 135.

9. See Deighton 1982: 1–39 and passim.

10. Bittel 1976a: fig. 257 (Eflatun Pinar); Neve 1970: 157–59, figs. 15–17, and Macqueen 1986: 121, figs. 106–7 (spring shrine at Boğazköy).

11. The largest relief of Phrygian Matar from Gordion (described in chapter 4 below; see Mellink 1983: pl. 70) was found near the Sangarios River; Phrygian idols were carved into the rock at Faharad Çeşme, a spring near Ankara.

several Hittite sanctuaries, including Boğazköy, that contain sunken holes or pits, probably intended to receive votive offerings.[12] This too is a feature that recurs in Phrygian religious monuments, particularly in the Phrygian highlands, where shafts for depositing votive offerings were cut behind several of the rock façades.[13]

One should not overstate the ties between Hittite and Phrygian cult practice. No single Hittite religious monument, temple, or statue can be said to provide a close forerunner to Phrygian shrines and iconographic images. Yet we can sense that the two cultures had a similar awareness of the divine properties in the natural features of the landscape. Whether the Phrygians were the direct heirs of Hittite cult tradition or whether both cultures were reacting independently to the same natural phenomena is difficult to determine; our inability to read Phrygian texts means that we are poorly informed as to what the Phrygians thought about the sacred quality of mountains and springs. But it seems clear that for both peoples, the need to address and control the natural environment in which they lived was a powerful force in defining their relationship with their deities.

THE NEO-HITTITE BACKGROUND

The Anatolian people whose religious iconography and cult monuments share the most direct connections with the Phrygians are the Neo-Hittites, the successor states to the Hittite kingdom in southeastern Anatolia during the early first millennium B.C. The chief period of political and artistic prominence of Neo-Hittite culture, ca. 900–700 B.C., is roughly contemporary with early Phrygian material, although the Neo-Hittite states reached a higher degree of complexity at an earlier stage. The political interests of the Neo-Hittites and the Phrygians were frequently intertwined, suggesting that they had a fair amount of contact with each other,[14] and the artistic influence of the Neo-Hittites on the Phrygians is readily observable in sculptural works at several Phrygian sites.[15]

Within the Neo-Hittite pantheon, particular interest has focused on one important female deity, Kubaba. Although she was only a minor deity in Bronze Age Anatolia, Kubaba became a more conspicuous presence in Neo-Hittite society during the early first millennium B.C. and was worshipped at a number of Neo-Hittite cities. It has long been recognized that she is the deity whose Hellenized name is

12. Ussishkin 1975; Deighton 1982: 23–25.
13. Examples include shafts behind the Phrygian carved façades at Maltaş, Deliklitaş and Fındık, discussed in chapter 4 below.
14. On the relations of the Neo-Hittites and Phrygians, see Mellink 1979; Hawkins 1982; and Mellink 1983: 358–59.
15. Note sculpted orthostate blocks from Ankara (Akurgal 1962: pl. 137) and Gordion (Sams 1989), both of which show clear Neo-Hittite influence; the bronze cauldrons from the great tumulus at Gordion were probably Neo-Hittite imports (DeVries, in Young et al. 1981: 109–10).

Κυβήβη, Kybebe.[16] Since Kybebe and Kybele, the Greek name for the Phrygian Mother Goddess, were often equated in later Greek and Roman literature, many have assumed that the Neo-Hittite Kubaba must be the direct forerunner of the Phrygian Mother.[17]

The picture, however, is more complex than that of a simple equation between the two. The Phrygians did indeed use some of the visual iconography of Kubaba to depict their Mother Goddess, but this need not mean that the Phrygians identified their own Mother Goddess with a deity from the pantheon of another people. To understand the relationship between Kubaba and the Phrygian Mother, we need to review the evidence on the Neo-Hittite goddess in greater detail.

The cult of Kubaba was already well established in Anatolian religion by the mid second millennium B.C., when the goddess's name appears in several Bronze Age texts and on cylinder seals from a number of sites in central and eastern Anatolia and northern Syria. In these Late Bronze Age sources, Kubaba appears to have been a fairly minor deity, at home in southeastern Anatolia, particularly in Karkamiš. No iconographic representation of her from the second millennium B.C. is known.[18] In Neo-Hittite society during the early first millennium B.C., Kubaba became a more conspicuous presence, largely because of her position as the principal deity of the city of Karkamiš.[19] As Karkamiš gained greater political power in the region, Kubaba, known as the "Queen of Karkamiš," became a prominent figure in Neo-Hittite cult.[20] During the ninth and eighth centuries B.C., the influence of Karkamiš within the Neo-Hittite political sphere (southeastern Anatolia and northwestern Syria) expanded substantially, and so the number of sites where the cult of Kubaba is attested, both iconographically and by inscription, increases to include virtually all of this region.[21]

Moreover, the cult of Kubaba was not limited to Neo-Hittite centers. The name Kubaba appears in an Aramaic text of the fifth or fourth century B.C. from Kastabala, in Cilicia.[22] In western Anatolia, Kubaba was worshipped in Sardis, according to the

16. Brixhe 1979 has a good discussion of this problem, with earlier bibliography.

17. The idea was first proposed by Albright 1929, and was expounded in detail in a seminal essay by Emmanuel Laroche (Laroche 1960). Laroche's conclusion, that Kubaba was the direct predecessor of the Phrygian goddess, has been widely accepted by most scholars who have addressed this topic, including Bittel 1963: 17; Dupont-Sommer and Robert 1964: 7–8; F. Naumann 1983: 18; Hanfmann 1983: 224–25; Mellink 1983: 358–59; and Burkert 1985: 177. Reservations about the equation of the two divinities have been expressed by Akurgal 1949: 111; Brixhe 1979: 40; Graf 1984; and myself, Roller 1994b.

18. On Kubaba in the Bronze Age, see Güterbock 1954: 110; Laroche 1960: 115–19 and fig. 1. Bronze Age sites where Kubaba is attested include Kültepe, Boğazköy, Karkamiš, Ugarit, and Comanna.

19. For the Karkamiš excavations, see *Carchemish* I–III. The evidence on Kubaba at Karkamiš has been gathered by Hawkins 1981a; the inscriptions from Karkamiš that mention Kubaba have been re-published by Hawkins 1981b.

20. On Kubaba as queen of Karkamiš, see Hawkins 1972: 98–105; 1981b: 147.

21. Laroche 1960: 120–22 and fig. 2, traces the spread of the Kubaba cult; see Hawkins 1981a for a full list of sites and texts.

22. Dupont-Sommer and Robert 1964: 7–15.

testimony of Herodotos. He calls her simply Kybebe, the local deity, but the identification with Kubaba is assured through the occurrence of this name in a graffito in Lydian script on a fragment of local pottery found in Sardis.[23] The spread of this cult to the west may imply that the worship of Kubaba was common to several Anatolian peoples, and was not limited to the sphere of influence around Karkamiš.

The precise connection of the Neo-Hittite goddess Kubaba with the Phrygian Mother is problematical. There are many parallels between visual images of the Phrygian goddess and those of Kubaba, and since the Phrygian images are of somewhat later date, we may assume that the Phrygian representations were influenced to some extent by their Neo-Hittite counterparts. There are, however, significant differences between the two divinities in other areas, in their attributes and in the forum in which they were displayed. Moreover, the role of each goddess in the religious life of her community may have been less closely related to that of the other than the similarity of sculptural images suggests. As our knowledge of the monuments depicting these goddesses and of the dedicatory texts attached to them grows, the assumption of a close relationship between them seems less convincing.[24]

One point that has been thought to furnish close contact between the two Anatolian divinities is their nomenclature.[25] In the case of the Hittite and Neo-Hittite deity, the word "Kubaba" is simply her name; if the name carries a specific meaning, it is not known. The name is consistently written in the Neo-Hittite script with the hieroglyph "deus," then the syllable "Ku" followed by the hieroglyph for "bird" and the syllabic symbols "ba-ba." The name of the Phrygian deity, in contrast, is completely different: she is Matar, or "Mother," as is attested in ten texts in the Paleo-Phrygian language.[26] "Kubileya" is an epithet attached to Matar. It occurs only twice in the extant corpus of Paleo-Phrygian texts and probably refers to a topographical feature;[27] Byzantine lexicographers define it as the Phrygian word for "mountain."[28] The Greek name for the goddess, Kybele, surely comes from this Phrygian epithet,

---

23. Herodotos 5.102. For the graffito, see Gusmani 1975: 28 no. A II 5. The cult of Kybebe in Sardis is discussed by Hanfmann 1983: 223–25, and Rein 1993.

24. One must remember that Laroche wrote his essay on the Kubaba/Kybele relationship in 1958, prior to the discovery and publication of many of the major monuments depicting the Phrygian Mother, including the reliefs from Ankara/Bahçelievler (published by Temizer 1959), Gordion (discovered in 1957–58; see Mellink 1983: 349), Boğazköy (discovered in 1958, published by Bittel 1963), and Ankara/Etlik (first published by F. Naumann in 1983), and before the publication of Emilie Haspels's essential study on the Phrygian highland monuments in 1971.

25. Laroche 1960: 113, thought that the two words were dialectical variations of the same name in Asia Minor.

26. Brixhe and Lejeune 1984: nos. M-01c, M-01d I, M-01d II, M-01e, W-01a, W-01b, W-03, W-04, W-06, and B-01.

27. On Matar Kubileya/Kubeleya, see Brixhe and Lejeune 1984: nos. W-04, B-01.

28. *Suda* and *Et. mag.*, s.v. *kubelon*. Brixhe 1979: 43–45, has proposed that this was the name of a specific mountain in the region of modern Dinar, although it should be noted that neither of the two Paleo-Phrygian texts in which the epithet occurs are at all close to the Dinar region. The nomenclature of the Phrygian Mother is explored in greater detail in chapter 4.

but the Phrygian texts make it clear that the word "Kybele" was not her name in Phrygia. Thus the name of the Phrygian goddess has no connection with that of the Neo-Hittite Kubaba. The similar sound of the Herodotean Kybebe and the Kybele of the Greek poets may be nothing more than a coincidental similarity of the names as they were transliterated into Greek, rather than an actual relationship in the languages spoken in Iron Age Anatolia.[29] That Kubaba was not the Mother Goddess is further demonstrated by the Kastabala inscription. In the Aramaic text, the goddess's name is Kubaba. Yet in the Hellenistic and Roman periods, the goddess of Kastabala was equated with Artemis and Hekate, not with Kybele or Meter.[30]

The iconographic images of Kubaba and the Phrygian Mother also seem to demonstrate several points of contact. Kubaba's form and costume are well known from a number of sculpted reliefs from first-millennium Neo-Hittite centers, primarily Karkamiš, Malatya, and Zincirli, ranging in date from ca. 950 to 700 B.C.[31] The goddess was depicted in a seated pose on orthostate reliefs from Malatya and Ancuzköy and on two reliefs from Karkamiš.[32] In other reliefs, she stands, represented either full-front, as in another relief from Karkamiš, now in the British Museum (fig. 3), and one from Mahrada,[33] or in profile, at Karkamiš, Zincirli, and Birecik.[34] Her typical costume is a long gown, frequently belted, and a high, elaborate headdress, often, as at Karkamiš, with a veil extending from the headdress down the back and sides of her gown. This was not a special outfit limited to the deity, for human women depicted in sculpted reliefs at Karkamiš wear an identical costume.[35]

In several respects, the appearance of the Phrygian goddess resembles that of Kubaba.[36] In a typical Phrygian image, the Phrygian goddess, normally depicted standing in a frontal pose, also wears a long gown, belted at the waist, and a high elaborate headdress, from which a veil extends down her side and back. In addition to the general similarity of costume, several specific details in the Phrygian sculptural works suggest that the Phrygian depictions were derived from Neo-Hittite sculpted reliefs. For example, the veil along the side of Kubaba's skirt in the London relief

29. Graf 1984: 119.

30. Dupont-Sommer and Robert 1964: 88–89.

31. Representations of Kubaba have been discussed as a group by Akurgal 1949: 107–11; Bittel 1981: 261–64; and F. Naumann 1983: 17–38, 291–93, who lists ten representations of Kubaba in Neo-Hittite art. The Karkamiš reliefs from the Long Wall of Sculpture are known to date to the reigns of the earliest kings of Karkamiš, ca. 900 B.C. (Mallowan 1972: 82; Hawkins 1982: 439–41).

32. Malatya, Orthmann 1971: pl. 42f; F. Naumann 1983: pl. 1, 2. Ancuzköy, Orthmann 1971: pl. 5g. Karkamiš reliefs, Orthmann 1971: pls. 29f and 34f; F. Naumann 1983: pls. 1, 3, and 292, no. 4.

33. Relief from Karkamiš, Orthmann 1971: pl. 34e; F. Naumann 1983: pl. 3, 3. Relief from Mahrada, Orthmann 1971: pl. 38g.

34. Reliefs from Karkamiš, Orthmann 1971: pl. 23e, F. Naumann 1983: pl. 2, 1 and 2, 2; and Orthmann 1971: pl. 23b, F. Naumann 1983: pl. 2, 3. Relief from Zincirli, Orthmann 1971: pl. 58e, F. Naumann 1983: pl. 3, 1. Relief from Birecik, Orthmann 1971: pl. 5c, F. Naumann 1983: pl. 3, 2.

35. Note the women depicted approaching Kubaba on the Long Wall of Sculpture, *Carchemish* II (1921): pls. 19–22. Hawkins 1972: fig. 4.

36. See Mellink 1983: 354, and F. Işik 1989, a general comparison of Neo-Hittite and Phrygian sculptural styles. This discussion of the Phrygian monuments of necessity anticipates the more detailed descriptions and analyses of the Phrygian representations of Matar in chapter 4.

(fig. 3) is shown as a flat ridge extending out from the skirt, a detail that is depicted in almost identical fashion on reliefs of the Phrygian goddess from Gordion and from Ankara (figs. 7, 8, and 9).[37] The headdresses worn by Kubaba and the Phrygian Mother offer another close parallel. On a relief of the Karkamiš goddess (fig. 4), her headdress is a complicated affair with superimposed rows of beads, tongues, and rosettes.[38] We can compare this to a Phrygian head from Salmankӧy,[39] where the Phrygian goddess's crown has a remarkably similar series of ornaments (fig. 11).

Yet in contrast to the similarities in physical appearance and costume, the attributes held by the two goddesses are quite different and point to an individual character for each. The Neo-Hittite goddess regularly holds a mirror, her symbol of femininity and beauty.[40] This emphasis on the feminine aspect of her personality is especially noticeable when she is paired with her male consort, the weather god, as on the relief from Malatya. Her other frequent attribute is the pomegranate or, in one case, a stalk of wheat. The pomegranate is a less individual symbol, for it appears with other divinities as well, and its religious implications remain unknown.[41]

The Phrygian goddess, in contrast, has a different set of attributes, of which the principal one is the predatory bird.[42] Not only is she regularly shown holding and restraining the hunting bird,[43] but the Phrygian bird also appears as an independent hunter.[44] The Phrygian bird does point to Kubaba, since the Neo-Hittite hieroglyph "bird" appears between the phonetic syllables "Ku" and "ba-ba."[45] Yet the Neo-Hittite goddess is never a hunting deity, and a bird of prey never forms one of her attributes. On the other hand, the element of the hunt was clearly an important part of the character of the Phrygian Mother, and allusions to hunting appear in several objects associated with her.[46]

37. The relief from Gordion, Mellink 1983: pl. 70; F. Naumann 1983: pl. 5, 3. Relief from Ankara-Bahçelievler, Mellink 1983: pl. 71, 1; F. Naumann 1983: pl. 5, 2. Relief from Ankara-Etlik, F. Naumann 1983: pl. 5, 4. In the Phrygian reliefs, this veil ridge appears only on the figure's right side, since the Phrygian Mother is almost always shown with her veil tucked into her belt on the left.
38. Orthmann 1971: pl. 23b; F. Naumann 1983: no. 6, pl. 2, 3. A similar headdress appears on the relief from Zincirli, Orthmann 1971: pl. 58e; F. Naumann 1983: pl. 3, 1.
39. F. Naumann 1983: no. 24, pl. 7. 2. Note also the comments of F. Işik 1989: 67.
40. Akurgal 1949: 107–8; Laroche 1960a: 123; F. Naumann 1983: 27–36.
41. Akurgal 1949: 109; Laroche 1960a: 123.
42. One attribute that the two goddesses have in common may be the pomegranate; in the Boğazköy relief (Bittel 1963: 9), the goddess holds a round object in her left hand, and a miniature relief from Gordion also depicts the Phrygian goddess holding a round object (Güterbock 1974, Roller 1988a: 45, fig. 3). In both cases, however, the identification of the round object as a pomegranate is not certain. For a discussion of the Phrygian Mother's attributes, see Mellink 1983: 351–53.
43. Note the reliefs from Gordion, F. Naumann 1983: pl. 5, 3, Mellink 1983: pl. 70; and Ankara, F. Naumann 1983: pl. 3, 2; and the sculpture from Ayaş, Bittel 1963: pls. 11 c, d; Prayon 1987: pls. 2 a, b.
44. A fragmentary red stone statuette of the Phrygian Mother from Gordion with hunting birds on her skirt, Mellink 1983: 352–53 and pl. 73, 1. Note also a bone ornament from Gordion that illustrates a hawk hunting a hare, Young 1964: pl. 84, fig. 14; and the bird of prey as a Phrygian votive, Mellink 1963–64; Mellink 1983: 352–53; Roller 1988a: 47. On the hawk as a hunting motif suitable to the Phrygian goddess, see Mellink 1963–64; 1983: 352–53; Roller 1988a: 47; and chapter 4 below.
45. Laroche 1960b: 76–78, no. 128; Hawkins 1981a: 258.
46. A good example is a schematic idol from Boğazköy, a work set into a framework decorated with relief sculpture depicting various hunting scenes, including wild animals hunting their prey and humans

The lion, another symbol of the hunt, is a characteristic attribute of the Greek Kybele, and is therefore often mentioned as a point of contact between the Phrygian and Neo-Hittite goddesses. On reliefs from Karkamiš and from Malatya, Kubaba or her consort appears with a lion.[47] Yet the lion is a comparatively rare symbol in Phrygian religious iconography, appearing primarily in monuments in western Anatolia. The vivid impression created by one of these monuments, Arslankaya,[48] and the adoption of this western Phrygian symbol in Lydian and Greek representations of the goddess[49] should not obscure the fact that in central and eastern Phrygia, the lion only occasionally forms a part of the Phrygian Mother's iconography.[50] And it is precisely this region of Phrygia that had the most extensive contact with Neo-Hittite art and culture. The mirror, a reference to beauty and femininity, is also absent from the iconography of the Phrygian goddess. Thus, in contrast to the similarities in costume, there is little or no correspondence between the attributes of the Phrygian goddess and those of the Neo-Hittite Kubaba.

One point of contact between Neo-Hittite and Phrygian attributes is furnished by a relief of the Phrygian Mother from Etlik in Ankara, in which the Phrygian goddess is accompanied by a composite lion/human creature (fig. 9). Since such composite animal/human figures are rare in Phrygian sculpture, it is likely that this creature was modeled on a Neo-Hittite example.[51] The winged sun that surmounts this composite creature is also a Neo-Hittite feature, one that can appear together with Kubaba; in a relief from Karatepe, another such composite creature, this one a bird-human, supports a winged sun.[52] Yet even this parallel is not exact. The winged sun of the Ankara/Etlik relief is placed over her attendant, not over the goddess herself, as it would be in Neo-Hittite reliefs. This suggests that while the Phrygians may have borrowed the symbol of the winged sun from Neo-Hittite iconography, they attached a different meaning to it.

A major point of dissimilarity between the two goddesses is the setting in which the sculpted reliefs of each divinity were displayed. The reliefs of Kubaba come almost entirely from the context of court sculpture, advertising the goddess's chief

---

hunting from horseback with bow and arrow (Neve 1970: figs. 9 a–d; Boehmer 1972: 206, 210, no. 2144A; also illustrated by F. Naumann 1983: pl. 9e, and Prayon 1987: pl. 35).

47. Orthmann 1971: pl. 29f (Karkamiš); pl. 42f (Malatya).

48. Haspels 1971: 87–89, figs. 186–91.

49. On Lydian representations of the goddess with a lion, see Hanfmann and Waldbaum 1969, and Hanfmann 1983: figs. 1–3 and pl. 43. On Greek representations, see F. Naumann 1983: 130–35.

50. One of the few examples is the fragmentary relief on Kalehisar, near Alaca Hüyük; the relief is badly worn, but there seems to be a lion's tail near the Phrygian stepped altar. On Kalehisar, Brixhe and Lejeune 1984: 242–43, pl. 124.

51. The closest parallel may be found on a Neo-Hittite relief from Ain Dara, illustrated by Orthmann 1971: 312, pl. 3c. There is no exact parallel for the Phrygian creature in Neo-Hittite art (F. Naumann 1983: 66).

52. For the Karatepe relief, see Orthmann 1971: pl. 15d; F. Işik 1989: 82–83; Kubaba does not appear in this relief. Kubaba appears with a winged sun in the reliefs from Birecik, Orthmann 1971: pl. 5c, and from Malatya, Orthmann 1971: pl. 42f.

function as a protector of cities. Three of the Kubaba reliefs from Karkamiš were placed on the Great Staircase and Long Wall of Sculpture, a series of orthostate reliefs forming a processional entrance to the main center of the city.[53] Karkamiš texts also refer to reliefs of Kubaba placed in temples and statues dedicated to her.[54] While the original setting of the other Neo-Hittite reliefs is less certain, their form indicates that they too were orthostate blocks intended for display in an official public context.[55] In general, the Neo-Hittite reliefs seem to have been displayed in a setting reflecting court propaganda, designed to direct the viewer's attention to the power of the king and the goddess who protects him.[56]

Phrygian cult reliefs were displayed in a much wider variety of settings. The Phrygian reliefs all depict the goddess as if standing in a doorway, a key feature lacking in Neo-Hittite works. The Phrygian doorway not only frames the goddess but often reproduces in stone the form of an actual Phrygian building.[57] Yet the Phrygian reliefs were not set into central areas of Phrygian settlements, such as on temple or palace walls, but were frequently placed on the boundaries of the city near gates.[58] Moreover, most of the reliefs depicting the Mother Goddess in her architectural frame were individual works, not part of a larger sculptural program, as were the reliefs of Kubaba at Karkamiš. Phrygian cult reliefs were also displayed in non-urban settings. They are found in funerary contexts, in conjunction with major burial tumuli.[59] They also occur regularly in remote mountainous settings, both the striking reliefs of the highlands of southwestern Phrygia,[60] and the reliefs and altars in similar outdoor settings in central Anatolia.[61] No example of this type of placement is known with a Kubaba relief.

In general, the points of closest contact between Kubaba and the Phrygian Mother seem to rest on fairly superficial features. The names of the two divinities were unrelated in their Anatolian languages and only sound alike in Greek. The sculptural forms of the Phrygian reliefs were strongly influenced by Neo-Hittite sculptural style, but more individual details of attributes and placing of the reliefs suggest that the characters of the two divinities were quite different.

There are other differences between the two divinities. The Neo-Hittite goddess

---

53. Laroche 1960a: 120–22; Hawkins 1972; F. Naumann 1983: 30–31.
54. Laroche 1960a: 120–22.
55. F. Naumann 1983: 27–36.
56. Hawkins 1981a: 259; 1981b: 147–49.
57. Note the parallels with architectural finds from Gordion, Young 1963: 352, Mellink 1983: 356–59. The identity and function of the building depicted in the relief is not clear, and suggestions include a temple (Mellink 1983: 359) and a palace (Roller 1988a: 49). The form and meaning of the Phrygian architectural frame receive more detailed analysis in chapter 4.
58. Note the setting of reliefs from Boğazköy, Bittel 1963: 7–8, and Midas City, Haspels 1971: 36–40, 73–77.
59. Buluç 1988 discusses the series of Phrygian reliefs from Ankara (illustrated by Güterbock 1974: 97–99; Prayon 1987: pls. 6–8) and presents a convincing case for their placement on funerary monuments.
60. Haspels 1971: 73–111.
61. Mellink 1981; Roller 1988a: 45.

had a consort, with whom she was sometimes represented, and her personality and attributes seem to develop in part as a reaction to her male partner. The Phrygian deity, by contrast, always appears alone; she sometimes had male attendants,[62] but she is never shown with a male divinity of equal status. Indeed, depictions of the Phrygian Mother rarely stress her feminine aspects; she does not appear as a feminine counterweight to a male god, but, through her association with the hunting bird, is a symbol of power in her own right, combining both male and female stereotypes. Kubaba, moreover, was one in a pantheon of several divinities, who can also appear with her on Neo-Hittite reliefs, but the Phrygian Mother Kybele is the only Phrygian deity represented in art, and the only Phrygian deity known to us.

Taken together, these factors suggest that the two goddesses were in fact two separate deities in the Early Iron Age. The similarities between the sculptural forms of the two can be ascribed to the fact that the Phrygian immigrants into central Anatolia did not have an indigenous sculptural tradition to draw on to represent their deity, and so imitated the sculpted reliefs of their neighbors to the southeast, the Neo-Hittite kingdoms. This would have been the most politically prestigious source of religious sculpture known to them. We can imagine that Phrygian kings who wished to consolidate their power would have wanted to develop an impressive court religious iconography to serve as a visible manifestation of the favor they claimed to enjoy from the Phrygian Mother Goddess, and the most prominent Neo-Hittite female deity, whose name included the symbol of the bird of prey, furnished a particularly handy model. The documented activities of the Phrygian king Midas in southeastern Anatolia and the political alliances he formed there furnish a clear example of how such contact would have been made.[63]

Thus the influence of the Neo-Hittites on Phrygian religious practice was apparently limited to fairly superficial factors. While the Phrygians adopted several iconographic forms from Neo-Hittite religious art, they applied new meaning and new attributes to the sculptural types. The Neo-Hittite religious tradition contributed greatly to the external appearance of the Phrygian Mother, but little to her character or symbolism.

THE URARTIAN COMPONENT

Another strong influence on Phrygian religious monuments and practices can be found in the monuments of the Urartians, an Iron Age people whose sphere of influence was centered on the region around Lake Van and included eastern Anatolia, northern Iraq, and northwestern Iran. From their chief city of Tušpa (modern Van, on the eastern shore of Lake Van), the Urartians dominated eastern Anatolia

62. As in Boğazköy, Bittel 1963: 10, and at Gordion, Mellink 1983: 352.
63. Mellink 1979; Hawkins 1982: 416–22; Roller 1983: 300–301; Mellink 1983: 358–59; Muscarella 1989: 336.

during the period ca. 850–700 B.C. The Urartians worshipped a large pantheon of both male and female deities, none of whom was a Mother Goddess. Yet several of the Urartian cultic monuments present striking similarities to those of the Phrygians, visible in the choice of iconography and the placement of monuments.[64]

One point of similarity lies in the common interest of both peoples in addressing the deities of the mountains. The Urartians also lived in a very mountainous region of Anatolia, and they apparently attached a religious aura to the mountains of their homeland. Several Urartian cult monuments consisting of a cult niche carved into the live rock of the mountainside reflect this attachment.

Two monuments from the Early Iron Age, Meher Kapisi, near Tušpa (Van), and Taş Kapisi, in Yeşilaliç (fig. 5), may serve as examples.[65] Both monuments, dated to the eighth century B.C., consist of an oblong niche framed by three receding moldings, carved as if to imitate the recessed moldings on a doorway. The niche at Yeşilaliç has a set of broad steps leading up to it (fig. 6). On both works an inscription in Urartian cuneiform above the doorway states that the function of the doorway is to allow the deity to make an epiphany from a mountain. This parallels almost exactly the Phrygian practice of carving an architectural niche resembling a door frame onto a natural outcrop of live rock.[66] In most of the Phrygian examples, the niche, like the Urartian niches, is empty, but in a few instances (the best known being Arslankaya and Büyük Kapikaya), the figure of the deity, here the Phrygian Matar, was carved from the rock together with the niche, suggesting that the Phrygians too conceived of their goddess as making an epiphany from the rock cliffs of the natural landscape. Other Phrygian examples parallel the Urartian models further by including a set of steps leading up to the niche and an inscription over the doorway.[67]

The form of the door in the Urartian niches is, not surprisingly, modeled on Urartian architectural forms and parallels the type of doorway carved into niches in the citadel of Van. Yet while the form of the Urartian niche is different from that on the Phrygian monuments, the general concept is the same in both cultures, namely, that an architectural structure from the human settlement is being used to frame and incorporate the mountain deity. The deity brings the power of the sacred landscape into the human sphere. This was evidently a key feature in the cult practices of eastern Anatolia. It survived past the demise of the Urartian kingdom until the second/first centuries B.C., as exemplified by a Hellenistic rock-cut niche at Alyar, on the upper Zap River.[68]

64. On Urartian history and art, see van Loon 1966. F. Işik 1987 discusses the connections between Urartian and Phrygian rock monuments.

65. F. Işik 1987: 173, pl. 33b; Salvini 1994 (Meher Kapisi). F. Işik 1987: pl. 34b (Taş Kapisi).

66. The numerous Phrygian examples, discussed in detail in chapter 4, have been collected and illustrated by Haspels 1971: 73–111.

67. The best examples are the Midas Monument and the nearby Areyastin Monument (Haspels 1971: 73–80).

68. F. Işik 1987: 172–73, pl. 32b.

FIGURE 5. Urartian cult relief at
Yeşilaliç, distant view. Eighth century B.C.
Photograph by author.

FIGURE 6. Urartian cult relief at
Yeşilaliç, close-up of cult niche. Eighth
century B.C. Photograph by author.

FIGURE 7. Relief of the Phrygian
Mother from Gordion. Seventh–sixth
century B.C. Courtesy, Museum of
Anatolian Civilizations, Ankara.
Photograph by Elizabeth Simpson.

FIGURE 8. Relief of the Phrygian
Mother from Ankara/Bahçelievler. Seventh
century B.C. Courtesy, Museum of Anatolian
Civilizations, Ankara. Photograph by
Elizabeth Simpson.

FIGURE 9.   Relief of the Phrygian Mother
from Ankara/Etlik. Seventh century B.C. Courtesy,
Museum of Anatolian Civilizations, Ankara.
Photograph by Elizabeth Simpson.

FIGURE 10. Relief of the Phrygian
Mother from Boğazköy. Early sixth century B.C.
Courtesy, Museum of Anatolian Civilizations,
Ankara. Photograph by Elizabeth Simpson.

KYBELE BAŞI
Eski Frig çağı (M.Ö. 8.Yüzyıl)
Boğazköy   124

FIGURE 11.   Head of the Phrygian Mother
from Salmanköy. Seventh–sixth century B.C.
Courtesy, Museum of Anatolian Civilizations,
Ankara. Photograph by Elizabeth Simpson.

Another parallel between Urartian and Phrygian monuments may be found in the Urartian tradition of placing freestanding stelai onto the rock-cut platforms often found in shrines. These can be stelai set upright in an open area, as at Altintepe,[69] or stelai placed in front of carved niches, either as separate objects or carved into the live rock. Examples of the latter include Yeşilaliç and the monuments on the Van citadel itself.[70] The importance of such stelai in Urartian cult is further demonstrated by their frequent appearance in cult scenes on Urartian cylinder seals, which depict these stelai as tall, narrow objects with rounded tops.[71] The Phrygians also used such portable stelai, as we see in a miniature pair of stelai from a Phrygian house in Boğazköy; here a schematic Phrygian idol was set up on a stone basis between the two stelai.[72] In addition, some of the major Phrygian rock reliefs, such as the Midas Monument, have cuttings in the rock platform in front of the cult relief; they are of a size and shape indicating that similar stelai were placed there also.

Urartian monuments also provide parallels for the Phrygian practice of using religious art in a funerary setting, for in Urartu there is a similar conjunction of religious and funerary monuments. The practice of carving chamber tombs into rock cliffs was common in eastern Anatolia, and many of the Urartian examples have an elaborate exterior façade, frequently reproducing architectural structures. Such architectural façades are found on Phrygian tombs also, particularly in the rock-cut tombs of the Phrygian highlands.[73] While the precise details of the Urartian and Phrygian tombs are not identical, in both cultures there seems to have been a desire to transfer the structures of the living into the structures of the divine and the dead.

Thus there are a number of formal similarities between Urartian and Phrygian cult monuments, in the choice and form of monuments used, and in their outdoor setting. Since the Urartian cult places for the most part are earlier than the Phrygian, the Phrygians may have drawn their ideas from Urartian material. Formal contact between Urartu and Phrygia in the Early Iron Age is attested through an alliance between Urartu and the Phrygian king Midas, offering the potential for Phrygian knowledge of Urartian cult practices.[74] But the Urartian impact on Phrygian monuments seems to extend beyond formal congruencies and imitation. We sense a similar concept of a deity at home in the mountains whom it was necessary to address and propitiate by bringing the architectural structures of the people to the deity's home.

69. T. Özgüç 1969: 28–33, figs. 29–33.
70. Yeşilaliç, F. Işik 1987: 175. At Van, the Analikiz Monument, F. Işik 1987: pl. 35c.
71. C. Işik 1986: figs. 1–2, 4–6.
72. Neve 1970: pl. 9; Boehmer 1972: 206, 210 no. 2144A. These are the stelai with hunting reliefs cited in n. 46 above.
73. F. Işik 1987: 168–72. Note, e.g., a Urartian rock tomb with architectural niche at Alyar (F. Işik 1987: pl. 28c) and similar rock-cut tombs in Phrygia, at Arslantaş (Haspels 1971: figs. 130–34) and Hamamkaya (Prayon 1987: pl. 14).
74. Luckenbill 1926–27: II, nos. 25 and 55; DeVries, in Young et al. 1981: 221.

CONCLUSION

Thus we can see that several Anatolian cultures, both those earlier than and those contemporary with the Phrygians, left a legacy of religious artifacts and symbols that clearly had an impact on the Phrygians. In some instances, the contact with other Anatolian peoples and beliefs may have come through a continuity of population, as in the survivals of Hittite iconography of the hunting deity. In other instances, the similarities can be ascribed to a conscious desire by the Phrygians to imitate a more prestigious form of monumental religious art. In every case, however, the most enduring symbols are the basic ones furnished by the Anatolian landscape, the mountains, the water, and the predators that roamed the mountains. The recurrence of these sacred symbols appears to arise not from one specific cultural group but from the relationship of the people to the land where they lived. Therefore it is important to turn now to the Phrygian monuments to see how the Phrygians used the symbols of the natural landscape to create their own definition of divinity.

4 · THE CULT OF THE MOTHER GODDESS IN PHRYGIA

The enduring portrait of a mother goddess in the ancient Mediterranean world begins with the Phrygian Mother. The goddess's name, physical appearance, and many features of her cult were distinctive traits of Phrygian culture, and in their Phrygian form were transmitted to other parts of Anatolia, to Greece, and eventually to Rome. Despite significant changes during succeeding centuries in several aspects of the Mother's cult, the divinity we meet in Greece, Rome, and throughout the Roman Empire ultimately derived from the goddess of the Phrygians.

Since many of the definitive and influential features of the Mother's cult evolved in Phrygia, it is important to try to approach the goddess from the perspective of the Phrygians. We need to determine what kind of deity the Phrygian Mother was on her home ground, so to speak, in the period before the wide dissemination of her cult throughout the Mediterranean world. This investigation of the Phrygian goddess therefore focuses primarily on evidence from Phrygia itself. In many modern scholarly discussions, the Phrygian goddess is presented from the perspectives of the Greeks and Romans. Yet the divinity we meet in Greek and Roman cultural spheres had acquired some characteristics that were distinctly different from those of the goddess of the Phrygians. Even their name for her, Kybele (Greek) or Cybele (Latin), was not her name in ancient Phrygia. Thus we cannot assume that the testimonia and cult practices of the Greeks and Romans reproduce the Mother Goddess of the Phrygians.

Much of this chapter is devoted to a full discussion of the Phrygian evidence.[1]

---

1. Several important discussions of the Phrygian material have contributed significantly to this chapter: on Phrygian sculpture, see F. Naumann 1983: 39–100 and Prayon 1987; on Phrygian epigraphical

This evidence is drawn from a wide geographical territory. It includes all of central Anatolia, extending from the districts around modern Afyon and Kütahya in the west (the territory of the Roman province of Phrygia) to the district around Elmali (ancient Lycia) in the south, the region around Bolu (ancient Bithynia) in the north, and northwest to the Sea of Marmara. Phrygian culture also influenced the region beyond the Halys River to Pteria in the east, and the region of ancient Tyana, near modern Niğde, in southeastern Anatolia.[2] The goddess surely enjoyed a much wider following in Anatolia than this: we meet a Lydian form of her in Sardis,[3] for example, and in Hellenized form, the Mother Goddess was worshipped in several Greek cities in western Anatolia.[4] Outside of Phrygia, however, she seems to have been only one divinity among many, and not necessarily the most important one. Within Phrygia proper, the goddess clearly was the most important deity and received the most important cult. When the Greeks called her the Phrygian goddess, they were reflecting her high status within her homeland as well as her place of origin.

I shall begin by reviewing the evidence for the Phrygian Mother's cult during the period before Phrygia came under extensive Greek influence. The upper chronological limit of this discussion is the early first millennium B.C., the time of the first evidence of Phrygian immigration into central Anatolia,[5] and the lower limit is in the latter half of the fourth century B.C., when central Anatolia came under the political control of the Greeks following the conquests of Alexander.[6] Within this time span, two types of material, epigraphical and archaeological, furnish information. The epigraphical texts, the inscriptions pertinent to the goddess's cult, comprise the only body of written material from Phrygia, for no works of literature in the Phrygian language survive.[7] The archaeological material, much more extensive, includes rep-

texts, see Brixhe 1979 and Brixhe and Lejeune 1984. Emilie Haspels's invaluable 1971 study is the only work to combine an analysis of both epigraphical and archaeological material, but this work discusses only the Phrygian highlands and does not cover the full geographical range of Phrygia. Mellink's 1983 study, although brief, offers many acute insights.

2. The name "Phrygia" does not imply a political unity, for there was no independent Phrygian state during much of the flourishing period of Phrygian culture. Central Anatolia was under the control of the Lydians from the early sixth century B.C. until 547 B.C., when Persian hegemony commenced. The territory is defined rather by the extent of inscriptions in the Phrygian script and by other typically Phrygian cultural forms, including the religious apparatus of the Mother Goddess. See Ruge 1941: esp. 785–86, and Brixhe and Lejeune 1984: x.

3. Hanfmann and Waldbaum 1969; Hanfmann 1983: 223–25; Rein 1993, 1996. The Lydian evidence is discussed in chapter 5.

4. Herodotos 4.76 (on Kyzikos); F. Naumann 1983: 113–17, 124–35; Rein 1996 (Kyme, Smyrna, and Miletos, and others). The material is extensively discussed in chapter 5.

5. For the evidence of Phrygian migration into Anatolia, see Herodotos 7.73; Crossland 1982: 842; Sams and Voigt 1990: 458–59; Voigt 1994: 276–77.

6. There had certainly been Greek cultural influence in central Anatolia before the fourth century B.C., and Hellenic models may lie behind several representations of the seated Phrygian goddess in the fifth and fourth centuries B.C., as discussed below. Such influence seems to have been fairly superficial, however, and was limited to some modifications in the representational images of the goddess; it apparently did not disturb the basic character of the inhabitants' religious beliefs. For a further discussion of this issue, see Roller 1991: 131–32.

7. There are, of course, several Greek and Latin authors who describe the cult of the goddess and the reactions of her worshippers, but their testimonia are likely to have been influenced by the position of the

resentations of the goddess, evidence for her sacred places, and votive offerings. At the end of this chapter, I attempt to provide a general overview of the nature of the Phrygian Mother Goddess and her place in Phrygian society.

THE EPIGRAPHICAL EVIDENCE

The information available from epigraphical texts, while helpful, is constrained by several factors. Despite the widespread use of an alphabetic script in Phrygia,[8] the amount of written material available for study is small. It is limited to inscriptions on the rock façades that are found throughout western Phrygia, a few scattered stone monuments in the central and eastern zones, and graffiti on pottery.[9] While several hundred texts in the Phrygian language survive, most of them are quite short, often consisting of only a few words or a personal name. The longest extant Phrygian text consists of nine lines.[10] Whole classes of material, such as literary texts, have not been found, and historical records are very few.[11] The extant texts can be transliterated easily enough, since the Phrygian script is a modified form of the Greek alphabet, but the small amount of material available for study means that the language has not yet been fully translated. It can, however, be determined from the surviving texts that the Phrygian language was part of the Indo-European language family, probably of the same branch as Greek. The language's grammatical and lexical similarities to Greek make it possible to gain information from the texts even when they cannot be deciphered fully, and these texts thus form a good starting point for an examination of the cult of the Mother Goddess.[12]

The majority of the inscriptions on stone seem to be concerned with subjects related to the goddess's cult. This can be determined from both their placement and their content. Many were incised onto cult façades, niches, altars, or other rock monuments connected with the goddess's worship.[13] Some texts mention the goddess specifically, while others use similar expressions of language but refer to other figures. Several of these texts have long been known and discussed, while others were dis-

---

cult in Greek and Roman society rather than in Anatolia, and so will for the most part be excluded from the current discussion.

8. On the origin and extent of the Phrygian alphabet, see Brixhe and Lejeune 1984: ix and 98–103. For the disappearance of this distinctively Phrygian script, Roller 1987b: 106–7.

9. All of the extant examples of Paleo-Phrygian inscriptions have been studied and published by Brixhe and Lejeune 1984. The corpus of Neo-Phrygian inscriptions, published by Friedrich 1932: 128–40, were written in the Greek alphabet and can be dated for the most part to the second and third centuries C.E. These have not been considered in the present discussion.

10. Brixhe and Lejeune 1984: 62–68, no. B-01.

11. For the subject matter attested in the extant Phrygian texts, see Roller 1989: 60.

12. On the relationship of the Phrygian language to Greek, see Friedrich 1941: 878–80, and Crossland 1982: 849. Phrygian grammar and vocabulary have been studied by M. Lejeune and Cl. Brixhe in a valuable series of papers: see Lejeune, 1969a, 1969b, 1970, 1979; Brixhe, 1979, 1982.

13. Of the forty-nine examples of inscriptions on stone published by Brixhe and Lejeune 1984, twenty-five were incised onto natural rock formations that appear to have been used as cult monuments. Several others are found on architectural blocks and may well have a religious significance, e.g., G-02, although the exact context in which the inscription was originally displayed can no longer be determined.

covered only recently. Virtually all lack objective criteria for dating. In most cases, the dates proposed by previous scholars for these inscriptions are derived, not from the text, but from the date of the monuments on which they were incised (in itself difficult to determine). For this reason the question of dating specific inscriptions is addressed in conjunction with a discussion of the archaeological monuments on which they are placed.

Probably the most important information to be gained from the Paleo-Phrygian inscriptions is the goddess's Phrygian name, Matar, which appears ten times in Paleo-Phrygian inscriptions. In every case, the word is found on cult façades or in cult niches, indicating that this was a religious term.[14] The Phrygian word was apparently *matar* in the nominative case and *mater-* in the oblique cases, for example, *materey* (dative), *materan* (accusative).[15] Lexical parallels with other Indo-European languages indicate that *matar* meant "mother." Thus the Phrygian epigraphical evidence demonstrates clearly that the Phrygian deity was a mother goddess.

In seven of these texts, the name Matar stands alone, without a corresponding adjective.[16] In three instances, however, it is followed by an epithet. One of these epithets, *areyastin,* is found in an inscription on a cult façade near Midas City.[17] The word is evidently an adjective in the feminine singular accusative, modifying *materan* in the text. Its meaning is unknown. The second epithet, which occurs twice, is more intriguing: it is *kubileya,*[18] or *kubeleya,*[19] in both instances in the nominative case modifying the word *matar.* This word seems to be the origin of the Greek name of the goddess, Kybele, but as these two inscriptions indicate, in Phrygia *kubileya* was not a proper noun but an adjective, presumably a divine epithet. It clearly was not an essential part of the goddess's name, for Matar could be used without an epithet or with another epithet. Since the goddess's customary Greek and Latin names derived from the word *kubileya,* however, it is worth considering in greater detail what it might have meant. Here the comments of Greek and Latin sources may provide some help.

The first ancient author we know of who speculated on the meaning of the name Kybele was the Roman geographer Strabo, who discusses this problem in two passages. In commenting on the city of Pessinous, the site of an important Hellenistic and Roman sanctuary of the Mother, Strabo notes that the goddess received her epithet "Dindymene" from the mountain Dindymon, just as the name "Kybele" came

---

14. The Old Phrygian inscriptions in which the word *matar/mater-* appears have been collected and studied by Brixhe 1979. They are also listed in the corpus of Brixhe and Lejeune 1984: nos. M-01c, M-01d I, M-01d II, e; W-01a, b; W-03; W-04; W-06; B-01.

15. Brixhe 1979: 41. This, of course, corresponds to the nomenclature of Greek and Latin literature, where the goddess was addressed as Meter, the Mother, or Magna Mater, the Great Mother.

16. Brixhe and Lejeune 1984: M-01c, M-01d I, M-01d II, M-01e, W-01b, W-03, W-06.

17. Ibid.: W-01a.

18. Ibid.: B-01.

19. Ibid.: W-04.

from Kybelon.[20] Here Strabo implies that Kybele referred to a specific mountain, but he is not consistent on this point, for in another passage he states that the people of Phrygia address the goddess with a variety of toponymic epithets, including Idaia, Dindymene, Sipylene, Pessinountis, Kybele, and Kybebe.[21] In fact, not all of these refer to geographical places. The first three are names of mountains: Idaia and Sipylene refer to sites in western Anatolia, Mount Ida in the Troad and Mount Sipylos near the city of Magnesia on the Meander, both situated outside of the earlier Phrygian heartland; there was also a mountain Dindymon, although this name was apparently used for several different mountain ranges.[22] Pessinous was a not a mountain, however, but a city located in a valley in central Phrygia. Kybebe was not a toponymic epithet at all, but rather was the Hellenized form of the name of the Neo-Hittite goddess Kubaba, whose cult became conflated with that of the Phrygian Mother.[23] Thus the implication of Strabo's comment is that the word Kybele may have been either a specific toponym, perhaps the name of a mountain or perhaps not, or simply an alternative name for the goddess.

A passage in Ovid's *Fasti,* however, indicates more pointedly that the word *kubileya* alludes to a topographical feature.[24] In his discussion of the rites of Cybele in Rome, the Roman poet mentions the Phrygian river Gallos, located "between green Cybele and lofty Celaenae." Here the word Kybele (Cybele) does appear to designate a place name, although it is uncertain whether the name refers to a city (thus paralleling Ovid's mention of Celaenae) or to a geographical feature such as a mountain. Moreover, Ovid's geography seems rather vague, for the Gallos, the river that flows through Pessinous,[25] lies a considerable distance from Celaenae (modern Dinar); thus describing the placement of "green Cybele" with reference to the river and the city Celaenae provides little help in determining the location of Ovid's Cybele. In fact, the rather imprecise allusions of both Strabo and Ovid imply that in the first century B.C., the specific location of the topos Kybelon/Cybele, if such had ever existed, was no longer known.

Byzantine lexicographers clearly were intrigued by the etymology of Kybele, for they too attempted to define it. Hesychios states that word *kybela* meant "the mountains of Phrygia, and caves and hollow places."[26] The word is also defined as the

20. Strabo 12.5.1–3.
21. Strabo 10.3.12.
22. No fewer than seven separate mountains in Anatolia were called Dindymon (see Jessen 1903). Of these, the two most widely attested were the mountain where the source of the Hermos River was located, on the border between Lydia and Phrygia (Herodotos 1.80; Strabo 13.4.5) and a mountain near Kyzikos, on the Sea of Marmara (Apollonios Rhodios 1.1093–1150; Strabo 1.2.4). The Dindymon mountain near Pessinous (Strabo 12.5.3) is yet another place.
23. Laroche 1960; Brixhe 1979: 40; Roller 1994b. The Kubaba/Kybele connection is explored in chapter 3.
24. Ovid, *Fasti,* 4.363–64. Cf. Brixhe 1979: 44.
25. Waelkens 1971. Devreker and Waelkens 1984: 13.
26. Hesychios, s.v. Κύβελα: ὄρη Φρυγίας. καὶ ἄντρα. καὶ θάλαμοι.

sacred mountain of the goddess in the *Suda* and the *Etymologicum magnum;* the latter quotes the first-century B.C. historian Alexander Polyhistor as a source.[27] In the work of Stephanus of Byzantium, Kybelon is called the sacred mountain of Phrygia.[28]

Thus citations in Classical literature make it appear likely that the epithet *kubileya* (or *kubeleya*) was derived from the name of a natural feature of the landscape, probably a mountain. The term may have been the regular Phrygian word for mountain or it may have been the name of one specific mountain. Phrygian inscriptions also support the association of the term with a mountain, for both occurrences of the word in Paleo-Phrygian texts are inscribed on mountainous rock façades. The two façades are, however, some two hundred kilometers apart, one in northern Anatolia, in Bolu province, and the other in central Phrygia, near modern Afyon. Moreover, if the passage in Ovid's *Fasti* has any validity, this would place the location of the mountain Cybele in an altogether different place, in the vicinity of Celaenae, roughly fifty kilometers to the south of Afyon. The presence of the term *kubileya* in three quite different locations implies that this term did not refer to one specific landscape feature. In sum, Greek and Roman sources indicate that the word meant simply "mountain" (thus Hesychios), or any sacred mountain dedicated to the Mother (thus Stephanos Byzantinus). "Matar Kubileya" would then be translated as "the Mother of the mountain."

Since *kubileya* was not the only Phrygian epithet used of the Mother Goddess, it is worth asking why this particular epithet became so prominent in Greek and Roman usage. The Greeks' choice of the name Kybele to address the Phrygian Mother Goddess may have resulted from several factors. The use of the epithet *kubileya* may have been more widespread in Phrygia than our limited knowledge of Phrygian texts suggests, leading the Greeks to adopt it when they adopted the cult of Meter. This suggestion is weakened, though, when one notes that during the Hellenistic and Roman eras, the Anatolian goddess continued to be addressed (in Greek) as Meter, or Mother, accompanied by various topographical epithets referring to the names of sacred mountains.[29] Moreover, the Greek proper adjective *Kybeleie,* Κυβελείη, could also refer to one specific place, a town near Smyrna on the Erythraian peninsula.[30] A votive text from Chios dedicated to Meter Kybeleie may refer to yet another Kybeleia, this one located on Chios, suggesting that at least some Greeks recognized that Ky-

27. *Suda,* s.v. Κυβέλη. ὀρεία γὰρ ἡ θεός. *Et. mag.,* s.v. Κύβελον = Alexander Polyhistor, *FGrHist* 273 F 12. Cf. also Σ Aristophanes, *Birds* 876.

28. Steph. Byz., s.v. Κυβελεία.

29. In the region around Midas City, she was Meter Angdisses (Haspels 1971: 297–99, nos. 6, 8, 13). In south central Phrygia, she was addressed as Meter Zizimmene (Mitchell 1982: no. 361). In the Greek cities of Asia Minor, the goddess was addressed with a large number of topographical epithets, discussed in chapters 7 and 11.

30. Hekataios, *FGrHist* 1 F 230; Strabo 14.1.33.

bele had originally been an epithet, not a separate name that referred to a specific place.[31]

The solution may lie in the regional variations of the Mother Goddess's cult in the Greek world. As a proper noun, rather than an adjective, "Kybele" first appeared in the Greek language in the mid sixth century B.C., and it became the common Greek name of the goddess during the fifth century B.C.[32] Within Greece, especially mainland Greece, the Mother Goddess was rarely associated with sacred mountains, and so the specifically topographical connotations of the name Kybele would have been less meaningful to the Greeks. It is possible too that the Greeks' choice of the name Kybele for the goddess may have reflected their familiarity with the Anatolian goddess Kybebe, as implied by Herodotos.[33] The similarity of the two words Kybebe/Kybele may have resulted in a syncretism of two names that were originally unrelated.

In addition to the Phrygian name Matar, three other names that occur in Paleo-Phrygian inscriptions, Midas, Baba, and Ates, may have significance for the goddess's cult. These names stand out because they too appear in Greek and Roman sources in the context of the cult of Kybele. The name Midas is perhaps the best known. It appears in a prominent inscription placed just above the large and intricately carved rock façade, commonly called the Midas Monument, at Midas City, a site in western Phrygia named for this text (fig. 24).[34] This façade was a cult monument dedicated to the Mother, with a space for her image in the niche, where the name Matar occurs in several graffiti, although not in the major inscriptions on the monument.[35] In the main Midas City text, Midas is in the dative case, followed by the titles *lavagtaei* and *vanaktei,* probably to be translated as "leader of the people" and "ruler."[36] These titles imply that the inscription was a dedication to a Phrygian king, not a divinity. The only individual king Midas known to us was ruler of Phrygia in the late eighth and early seventh centuries B.C., when Phrygia was at the height of its political power and geographical extent, and it seems likely that the Midas mentioned in this inscription is this historically attested Midas.[37] The text

31. Forrest 1963: no. 11 = Engelmann and Merkelbach 1973: 365–66, no. 211. Engelmann and Merkelbach assumed that this text referred to a place on the Erythraian peninsula, citing Strabo 14.1.33. Forrest, however, suggests (persuasively, I believe) that the Meter in the Chios text is the goddess worshipped in a Metroön in southeastern Chios; this would be the same deity mentioned in two other texts from Chios, Forrest 1963: nos. 9, 10.

32. This is discussed in greater detail in chapter 5; for the ancient sources, see chapter 5, nn. 17–20.

33. Herodotos 5.102. On the confusion between Kybebe and Kybele in Greek, see Brixhe 1979: 44, Graf 1984: 119; Roller 1994b and chapter 5 below.

34. Brixhe and Lejeune 1984: M-01a, with earlier bibliography. For illustrations and description of the monument, see Haspels 1971: 73–76 and 289, no. 1, and fig. 8.

35. For the graffiti within the cult niche, Brixhe and Lejeune 1984: M-01c, M-01d I, M-01 d II, M-01e.

36. Huxley 1959: 85–99.

37. It has often been assumed that Midas was a dynastic name used by several Phrygian kings, but all the testimonia on Midas, both Near Eastern and Greek, refer only to the one individual mentioned

also implies that a human ruler Midas was in some way connected with the cult of the Mother, a point reinforced by the appearance of the name Midas, together with Matar, in a graffito within the cult niche.[38]

Another well-known Phrygian name, Ates, occurs in several Paleo-Phrygian inscriptions. Ates, in the nominative case, is the name of the dedicator on the principal inscription of the Midas Monument. The same name, spelled Atas, also appears in two inscriptions carved onto natural rock façades near Çepni, southwest of Afyon. These façades have not been shaped into carved reliefs containing a cult niche, nor does the name Matar appear in the texts, but the recurrence of certain key formulae and the placement of the texts on rock façades suggests that they too have a religious connotation.[39] The name Ates/Atas appears twice, once in the nominative case, presumably the name of the dedicator,[40] and once in the dative, the recipient of the dedication.[41] In both inscriptions the obscurity of the texts makes it difficult to comment more closely on their precise meaning, but it is interesting to note that this name Ates/Atas, surely the eponym of the Greek and Roman god Attis, appears in religious contexts in Phrygia as well. This does not, however, necessarily imply that it was the name of a divinity in Phrygia. Ates, in various spellings, was a common proper name in Phrygia, in fact, the most frequently attested Phrygian personal name.[42] It may also have been a name found in the Phrygian royal family, just as it was a component of the names Alyattes and Sadyattes, both seventh-century B.C. kings of Lydia.[43]

There is another major inscription on the Midas Monument, placed vertically on the right side of the monument, in which the dedicator is Baba.[44] This name also has important implications in the cult of the Mother, for Baba, or its Greek form Papa, was an alternative name for Attis in Graeco-Roman cult.[45] A virtually identical inscription using the name Baba is found on an altar at the same site.[46] Apart from the name, neither text can be read, although the placing of both inscriptions implies that Baba too had some connection with the goddess. I shall offer some suggestions for

---

above. For the ancient sources on Midas and further discussion of the identity of the Phrygian king, see Mellink 1965; Roller 1983: 300–301; Muscarella 1989.

38. Brixhe and Lejuene 1984: M-01 d I.

39. Brixhe and Drew-Bear 1982: 73.

40. Brixhe and Lejeune 1984: W-08.

41. Ibid.: W-10.

42. Note the numerous citations of Zgusta 1964: nos. 119-1 through 119-21, a total of ninety-three citations of the name from central Anatolia. The Gordion excavations have yielded several more examples among the graffiti on Phrygian pottery; see Brixhe and Lejeune 1984: nos. G-107, G-118, G-119, G-120, G-123, G-124, G-128, G-148, G-221, G-224, G-234. Note also the comments of Robert 1963: 528–30. The high frequency of the occurrence of the personal name Ates in Phrygia is in marked contrast to the occurence of other personal names, most of which are attested by a single example.

43. This is implied by Herodotos 1.34. See also Roller 1988a: 48–49.

44. Brixhe and Lejeune 1984: M-01b.

45. In inscriptions of the Roman period, Baba, or Papa, was an epithet of the Phrygian Zeus (*MAMA* 5, 213 bis). Baba is also the name given by Greek sources (Diodoros 3.58,4; Arrian, *FGrHist* 156 F 22) as an alternative name for Attis, the youthful companion of the Mother in Graeco-Roman cult.

46. Brixhe and Lejeune 1984: 18–19, M-02.

the meaning of these three names in the context of the Mother's cult after an analysis of the archaeological evidence.

THE ARCHAEOLOGICAL EVIDENCE

The archaeological material related to the cult of the Phrygian Mother Goddess is substantial, extending throughout the whole range of the Phrygian cultural sphere. The depictions of the goddess and her companions, the votive offerings dedicated to her, and the cult façades, niches, and altars that constituted her places of worship are among the most dramatic and memorable monuments of central Anatolia. Some of these monuments have long been known, while others were discovered only recently. In this section, too, I shall focus on data from Phrygia, using material from other Anatolian sites and from Greece only when it may help clarify a point. As was true of the Paleo-Phrygian inscriptions, chronology presents a difficult problem here, for most of the Phrygian monuments lack objective evidence that might provide a firm date. Dates for specific works are given where they are available, and a general discussion of chronology follows at the end of this section.

Let us start with the pictorial monuments relevant to the cult. There are approximately twenty individual Phrygian sculptural representations depicting the goddess Matar.[47] There are also several aniconic figures that may be representations of her, as well as other pieces depicting smaller figures, who appear to be her attendants. These form the earliest body of Phrygian religious sculpture and will be discussed as a group.

The pictorial representations of the Mother Goddess display certain uniform features, suggesting that the Phrygians had a basic concept of how their goddess ought to look. She is always shown as a mature woman, standing upright, with her head, body, and legs perfectly frontal. Her arms are usually bent across her body and hold various objects. Her figure is heavily draped: she wears a gown that comes high up on her neck and has long sleeves and a long, full skirt, gathered at the waist by a belt. The sculpted costume represents a garment that was apparently made of ample and fairly thick material, allowing little indication of anatomy. The figure normally wears a tall, tiered headdress, the so-called *polos,* from which a long veil extends to the hem of her skirt. Often one or both sides of this veil are tucked into the figure's belt, where it appears as a series of horizontal catenary folds extending across the goddess's skirt. The iconographic schema of this costume was almost surely derived from the costumes worn by women, both human and divine, depicted in Neo-Hittite relief

47. The Phrygian representations of the goddess have been collected and studied by F. Naumann 1983: 39–100. To her catalogue on pp. 293–96 should be added the reliefs published by Mellink 1983: pl. 73, figs. 1 and 2, and the recently discovered ivory figurine from Elmali, *Antalya Museum Catalogue* 1988: no. 42. One of the pieces included in Naumann's catalogue, p. 295 no. 22, is probably not a representation of the goddess, but an attendant figure.

sculpture in southeastern Anatolia in the ninth and eighth centuries B.C., for both the details of the garment and its stylistic rendition are very close to Neo-Hittite female figures, especially those from Karkamiš and Malatya.[48] There is no trace of Hellenic influence in these representations of the standing Phrygian goddess.[49] The attributes of the Phrygian goddess and her placement on Phrygian monuments are, however, uniquely Phrygian features, which provide insight into her character. They also show marked regional differences.

The Archaeological Evidence: Central and Eastern Phrygia

I shall start with an analysis of representations of the goddess in central Phrygia, since several of these were found in informative archaeological contexts. The images of the goddess from central Phrygia, including the regions around Gordion, Ankara, and Boğazköy, are among the finest and best preserved. These include five large and impressive cult reliefs and statues, several smaller images of the goddess and her attendants, and a number of simple schematic idols. The five largest images, all of which were probably displayed in public shrines of the goddess, were found in Gordion (fig. 7),[50] in the Ankara districts of Bahçelievler (fig. 8)[51] and Etlik (fig. 9),[52] in Ayaş,[53] and in Boğazköy (fig. 10).[54] The size of the figures ranges from about one-third to two-thirds life-size, the figure from Boğazköy being the largest. All five of these works depict the goddess in the costume described above, the high headdress with veil, the garment with long sleeves, long skirt, and a broad belt. The piece from Ayaş (now apparently lost) was a freestanding work of sculpture, but the other four images of the Phrygian goddess are works of high relief. These four images include both the figure of the goddess and an architectural setting that frames her and presents her as if in the doorway of a building. In the works from Gordion and Ankara, the figure and architectural frame are carved from one piece, while in the Boğazköy piece, the goddess figure and the frame were made separately.[55]

---

48. See Mellink 1983: 354, and F. Işık 1989, who gives a careful analysis of the relationship between the Neo-Hittite and Phrygian costumes. Close parallels can be found in the procession of women to the goddess Kubaba on the Long Wall of Sculpture at Karkamiš (Wooley, in *Carchemish* II, 1922: pls. 19–22) and in a sculpture from Malatya (F. Naumann 1983: pl. I, 2). For an analysis of the similarities between the two sets of costumes, Neo-Hittite and Phrygian, see Roller 1994b and the discussion of this question in chapter 3.

49. Several scholars who have alleged Hellenic influence in the Phrygian representations of the goddess Matar have relied on an unrealistically low dating for these figures, e.g., F. Naumann 1983: 77; Prayon 1987: 201–4; Borgeaud 1988b: 87. Others have assumed that certain aspects of the goddess's appearance, such as the folds in her garment or the smile on the Boğazköy figure, must be of Greek origin, e.g., Temizer 1959: 179–87, Bittel 1963: 12–14. Both of these traits, however, are found on Neo-Hittite sculpture of the eighth and seventh centuries B.C. F. Işık 1989: esp. 67, 72, 100, gives a thorough and convincing analysis of the Neo-Hittite sources of the Phrygian Matar's dress, stance, and facial expression.

50. F. Naumann 1983: 295, no. 19, pl. 5, 3; Mellink 1983: pl. 70.

51. Temizer 1959; F. Naumann 1983: 294, no. 18, pl. 5, 2.

52. F. Naumann 1983: 295, no. 20, pl. 5, 4.

53. Bittel 1963: pl. II, c, d. F. Naumann 1983: 295, no. 21.

54. Bittel 1963: pl. 1–8. F. Naumann 1983: 295, no. 23, pl. 7, 1.

55. This can be seen clearly in the photograph in Bittel 1963: pl. 4.

The attributes held by the figures make this group of representations distinctive. In three of the five works, the reliefs from Gordion and Bahçelievler, and the Ayaş statue, the goddess is shown with similar attributes, a bird in her left hand and a drinking vessel in her right. The bird is grasped firmly in a restraining action suitable to a bird of prey, and the profile of each bird is that of a raptor such as a hawk or falcon.[56] The Gordion and Ayaş figures are shown holding a shallow open bowl, while on the Bahçelievler relief, the figure holds a small spouted jug; both are types of drinking vessels frequently found in Phrygian pottery.[57] The right hand of the figure on the Etlik relief also holds a drinking vessel of indistinct shape. In this work, there is no bird; instead, the figure's left arm is tucked under the fold of her veil next to her belt.

The Boğazköy relief is somewhat different. The upper torso and arms of the figure are not preserved, apart from a small fragment of the left hand, which appears to hold a round object, identified by the excavator as a pomegranate[58] This relief is also unique in that the goddess is not alone, but is accompanied by two small male figures, whose height is about even with the goddess's hips. Both figures wear loincloths but are otherwise nude. The figure on the goddess's right plays the double flute, while that on the left plays the lyre or cithara.

Another common feature of the central Phrygian reliefs is the architectural façade that frames the goddess, as if in a doorway. This is seen most clearly on the two reliefs from Ankara, which imitate a door placed in the short end of a building with a pitched roof, whose central point is supported by a vertical post. Above the point of the gable is an akroterion, resembling a set of horns curving inward. The depiction of the akroterion in the sculpted reliefs closely parallels actual stone akroteria found at Gordion.[59] In the Bahçelievler relief, the surface on either side of the doorway is decorated with an interlocking meander design reminiscent of the designs found on Phrygian pottery and furniture of the late eighth century B.C.[60] The whole schema of door, framing posts, roof, akroterion, and geometric pattern was evidently designed to represent the form and structure of an actual building. This schema was apparently followed in the relief of the goddess and her attendants found at Boğazköy, although because of its poor state of preservation only the outline of the archi-

56. Mellink 1983: 351–54. In his publication of the relief from Bahçelievler, Temizer 1959: 179–87, R. Temizer argued that the bird held by this figure was perhaps a pet such as a dove, on analogy with Greek korai, which are often shown holding birds (e.g., a kore from Miletos, inv. no. Berlin 1791, illustrated by Boardman 1978: fig. 89; a kore from Samos, Boardman 1978: fig. 97), but the profile of the bird held by Phrygian Matar seems clearly to indicate a raptor.

57. Mellink 1983: 351.

58. Bittel 1963: 9.

59. Several examples of such stone horn-shaped akroteria have been found at Gordion, all reused in later contexts. An example is illustrated by Young 1956: pl. 93, fig. 41. See also Sams 1994: 212–13, figs. 20.3.2, 20.3.4.

60. For similar meander patterns on Phrygian pottery, see Sams 1971: 584, fig. 2; for geometric patterns on Phrygian furniture, Young et al. 1981: 63, fig. 33, and 178, fig. 104; and Simpson 1988.

tectural frame is known.[61] The architectural frame of the Gordion relief is also very battered; only the side and horizontal upper frame of the doorway, along with the vertical support for the gable, are visible.

The Etlik relief preserves the left half (viewer's left) of the architectural façade, on which we see a composite human-animal figure on the building's left "wall." The figure, a creature with head and forelegs of a lion and the lower torso of a human being, wears a long skirt, which covers the right leg, while the nude left leg steps forward toward the Phrygian goddess in the door. Its arms are raised, as if to support the winged sun above it. The whole composition is reminiscent of Neo-Hittite art, where such composite creatures are frequent.[62] The winged sun is also a Neo-Hittite motif.[63] No one specific parallel between the Phrygian relief from Etlik and a Neo-Hittite relief, however, has been found.[64] The Etlik relief's gabled roof has another unique detail: to the left of the central akroterion (and presumably also on the missing right side) is an additional roof ornament, a horn that curves out and down along the slope of the roof.

The settings in which these reliefs were originally displayed provide interesting clues to their functions. The clearest context is provided by the Boğazköy work. This was set into a niche in the interior of the fortification wall around the Phrygian settlement on Büyükkale, near one of the city gates.[65] The Bahçelievler and the Etlik reliefs were found reused in later contexts, but both appear to have been part of a series of sculpted orthostate reliefs depicting real and fantastic animals: a horse, bull, lion, sphinx, and griffin.[66] All of these reliefs, goddess and animal, have cuttings for attachment clamps on the rear surface. They were found in several different parts of Ankara, but all were associated with Phrygian tumuli, suggesting that these two goddess reliefs were originally displayed in a funerary context.[67] The Gordion relief follows a different pattern still, for it was found outside the city in the bed of the Sangarios River, and may have been used in an extramural shrine.[68] The context of the work from Ayaş is unknown.

Another noteworthy piece, found in Salmanköy, near Boğazköy, is a nearly life-size head of a female figure wearing a large multitiered headdress similar to that on

61. Bittel 1963: 7, 14. Bittel proposed a reconstruction of the niche with geometric designs on the façade and a gabled roof (fig. 8), on analogy with other Phrygian cult reliefs of the goddess.

62. Orthmann 1971: 310–16.

63. See the reliefs illustrated by Orthmann 1971: pl. 15d (Karatepe); pl. 42f (Malatya); pl. 49a, 50c, 51c (Sakçagözü).

64. F. Naumann 1983: 66. Roller 1994b: 190.

65. Bittel 1963: 7.

66. Güterbock 1946: 74–80, and Güterbock 1974. Illustrations of some of animal figures are found in Güterbock 1946: figs. 22–29, and Akurgal 1949: pls. 48b, 49, and 50.

67. Buluç 1988: 19–21. Hans Güterbock had suggested that these reliefs were placed on the wall of a sanctuary of the goddess (Güterbock 1974: 98).

68. Mellink 1983: 356.

the Boğazköy goddess (fig. 11).[69] While its original setting is unknown, the piece provides further evidence of the tradition of representing the goddess in impressive sculptural works.

In addition to the major cult images discussed above, other smaller and less carefully crafted pieces can be connected with the cult of the goddess. Some of these appear to represent the deity herself, while others may depict attendant figures. Three further representations of the Mother Goddess are known from Gordion. One, a flat relief of red sandstone from a later context, lacks a head and lower torso (fig. 12).[70] The relief represents a standing figure with arms bent across the body. The right arm holds an open bowl, while the left grasps a large bird of prey by its legs. There is no clear detail of anatomy, although the long garment suggests a female figure. In addition to the raptor in the figure's hand, another bird stands upright at the left, while on the right side of the figure's skirt is a third raptor with a fish dangling from its mouth.

Two additional figures of the goddess in Gordion were found in the debris of houses located under later burial tumuli outside the walled areas of the city. Both may be indicative of the kinds of objects placed in household shrines. One, found under Tumulus E, is a fragment of a small alabaster piece, lacking a head and lower torso.[71] The two arms hold attributes that mirror those of the red sandstone relief: the bird, held firmly by the legs, is in the right hand, and an open bowl is in the left. A most interesting, although fragmentary relief, found under Tumulus C, shows the goddess in a different setting (fig. 13).[72] The work is a small limestone slab, divided into a horizontal row of panels by vertical strips. In one extant panel, a bull strides to the right, its head turned to face the viewer, while another, partially preserved panel shows a standing female, fully frontal, with her arms and hands extended out from her body. The female figure wears the same high polos, veil, and long full garment seen in the larger cult reliefs and is likely to be a miniature version of them. The relief's border frames this figure as if she were standing in a doorway, reinforcing the parallel with the major cult reliefs, although here the niche is a purely rectangular space without pediment or akroterion. Her right hand is incomplete, while her left hand holds a round object, perhaps a vessel of some kind. The depiction of the goddess flanked by striding animals recalls the orthostate relief panels from Ankara,[73] suggesting that the Tumulus C relief depicts in miniature the arrangement in which large-scale reliefs were displayed.

Two other figures from Gordion, one found in the nineteenth century (now in Is-

69. Boehmer 1972: no. 2162; F. Naumann 1983: 296, no. 24, pl. 7,2. This headdress, like the costume on the full-scale figures of the goddess, shows a strong affinity to Neo-Hittite sculpture; cf. the discussion in chapter 3.

70. Mellink 1983: pl. 73,1.

71. Ibid.: pl. 73,2.

72. Güterbock 1974: 98, pl. 13; Mellink 1983: pl. 73,4; Kohler 1995: 34, no. TumC 26.

73. Güterbock 1974: 98; Mellink 1983: 356; F. Naumann 1983: 63–64.

FIGURE 12. Relief of the Phrygian Mother from Gordion. Seventh–sixth century B.C. Courtesy, Gordion Excavation Project.

FIGURE 13. Miniature relief of the Phrygian Mother from Gordion, Tumulus C. Seventh–sixth century B.C. Courtesy, Gordion Excavation Project.

FIGURE 14. Relief of attendant figure from Gordion. Seventh–sixth century B.C. Courtesy, Gordion Excavation Project.

tanbul) and one uncovered more recently (fig. 14), may represent attendant figures.[74] In both cases, only the head and upper torso are preserved. Both works depict a figure with no headdress and bare upper torso. Both figures hold an open bowl in the right hand. Only the figure in Istanbul still preserves its left arm and hand, and that grasps a raptor by the legs. The lack of headdress, garment, and veil suggests that these are male figures, probably youths, since they are beardless.[75] They are reminiscent of the two small youths who accompany the Boğazköy goddess and are roughly of the same dimensions—that is, notably smaller than the figures of the goddess herself. The presence of such small male figures at both Boğazköy and Gordion may indicate that a young male attendant was part of the goddess's retinue.

In addition to iconic images of the goddess and her attendants, there is a series of aniconic idols that appears to be connected with the cult. Five are known from Boğazköy,[76] and approximately fifteen from Gordion (fig. 15).[77] The simplest of these

74. The earlier find is now in Istanbul; see Körte 1897: 25–27, and Mellink 1983: pl. 72, 1–3. The other figure, still in Gordion, is depicted by Mellink 1983: pl. 72, 4–5.

75. Mellink 1983: 352. Naumann included the piece in Istanbul in her catalogue of Kybele representations but interprets the other figure as male (F. Naumann 1983: 295, no. 22).

76. Examples are illustrated by Bittel 1963: fig. 2; Boehmer 1972: nos. 2144 A, 2147, 2148, 2160 (all stone pieces) and 1892 (bone); and F. Naumann 1983: pl. 9 a–e.

77. An example is illustrated in Young 1951: pl. VII, fig. 2; the rest are unpublished.

FIGURE 15. Aniconic idol
from Gordion. Seventh–sixth
century B.C. Photograph by author.

are merely roughly worked rectangular stones with a round knob on top, approximating a human head. On others, the round knob bears sketchy features of a human face. They do not have the costume or any of the attributes of the iconic images of the goddess, but their connection with her cult seems highly probable; similar schematic images are frequently found on the goddess's altars, including a set of double idols at Faharad Çeşme,[78] between Ankara and Gordion, and in the Phrygian highlands, to be discussed below. Most were found in residential contexts, although one in Boğazköy came from a Phrygian shrine near an earlier Hittite temple.[79] One particularly interesting example was recovered from a Phrygian house in Boğazköy. This is a schematic idol set up on a stone base flanked by two rounded stelai, on which there are hunting scenes in low relief; these depict wild animals hunting domestic animals and human beings hunting animals with bow and arrow.[80] In general, these idols appear to have been simpler images of the goddess, perhaps the focus of her worship in private contexts, such as domestic shrines, or were the offerings of less affluent individuals.

Objects used as votive offerings are also known. The goddess's most common

78. Mellink 1981: 97; F. Naumann 1983: 94, pl. 9f. See also Boehmer 1972: 206–7.
79. Boehmer 1972: 210, no. 2160; F. Naumann 1983: 93.
80. Boehmer 1972: 206, 210 no. 2144A; F. Naumann 1983: pl. 9e; Prayon 1987: no. 183, pl. 35.

attribute, a bird of prey, was a frequent choice. The Gordion excavations yielded several figurines of birds of prey, ranging from simple terracotta images to carefully crafted stone and metal objects.[81] One, an alabaster falcon, bore a dedicatory inscription.[82] Similarly, in Boğazköy, the small Iron Age shrine uncovered near an earlier Hittite temple had several votive figurines of birds.[83]

The substantial number of representational images, large and small, from several major Phrygian centers in central Anatolia certainly signifies the Mother Goddess's prominence, but evidence for rites connected with her worship is surprisingly limited. Exactly what kind of sacred space was allotted to Matar remains uncertain. There is no building that can be convincingly identified as her temple in any Phrygian settlement.[84] There do seem to have been intra-urban shrines of the goddess, such as the Phrygian open-air shrine in Boğazköy, but there is no evidence that a temple or sacred precinct formed a central nexus of city planning in Phrygia, as is the case in the Bronze Age levels at Boğazköy. In Gordion, the best-known Phrygian settlement in central Anatolia, cult objects both large and small were found throughout the city, within and without the walled citadel, suggesting that the cult was practiced in both public and domestic shrines.

There is also abundant evidence for extra-urban sanctuaries of the goddess. As noted above, the figured reliefs from Ankara and Gordion were found in extramural contexts, near funerary monuments and near the Sangarios River, respectively. Other sanctuaries lay in rural areas, quite remote from any urban association. One, on the cliffs above the Sangarios River near the modern village of Dömrek, about twenty kilometers north of Gordion, consists of several step altars and stelai carved out of the natural live rock (fig. 16).[85] Another is the sanctuary at Kalehisar, about 30 kilometers north of Boğazköy (fig. 17), consisting of a step altar with high back next to a long flat platform with a Paleo-Phrygian inscription, now much worn (fig. 18).[86] Traces of sculpted relief of a human figure, of which only the feet remain, suggest that a relief of the goddess might have stood here. A similar step altar with niches on each side was carved into the local granite near the Phrygian site of Pessinous, and a pair of basins, perhaps used for liquid offerings, was hollowed out from the rock

81. Four terracotta birds are known, Romano 1995: 58, nos. 149–52, as well as one of faience and one of glass; not all of these are necessarily raptors. Nineteen stone examples have been found, most of which are clearly raptors. One of these has been published, Young 1964: pl. 83, fig. 6; Mellink 1983: pl. 73, no. 3. For some general remarks on the use of stone birds in Phrygia, see Mellink 1963–64: 28–32.

82. Brixhe and Lejeune 1984: G-136.

83. Beran 1963; Boehmer 1972: 208–9.

84. Mellink 1983: 357–59, and 1993b: 297, has argued that Megaron 2 in Gordion (for the location of the building, see DeVries 1990: 376, fig. 7, labeled M 2) was a temple of the goddess, a temple that would have provided the model for the architectual frame in which the goddess stands. This building does not differ in form or in contents from the other megara in that section of the city, however, and its attribution as a temple seems quite unlikely. For another suggestion concerning the goddess's architectural frame, see Roller 1988a: 49. The meaning of the architectural frame is discussed in greater detail below.

85. Mellink 1981: 97. Keith DeVries, personal communication.

86. Brixhe and Lejeune 1984: 242–43, pl. 124; Prayon 1987: no. 9, pl. 5d.

FIGURE 16. Phrygian altar at Dömrek. Seventh–sixth century B.C. Photograph by author.

nearby.[87] The double idols at Faharad Çeşme, a spring between Ankara and Gordion, may also signify an extramural sanctuary.[88]

There is some evidence that the Mother Goddess's worship extended beyond central Phrygia. A small number of sculptural works of fairly schematic workmanship from the fringes of Phrygia that may represent the goddess are one indication of this. A stele from Daday, in north central Anatolia (ancient Paphlagonia), depicts a standing woman with a headdress and veil; she holds the right hand between the breasts, while the left is folded across her waist.[89] In a relief from Beydeğirmen, near Kayseri, the standing figure clasps both hands between her breasts and appears to hold a spindle in her right hand.[90] A stele from Mut (ancient Claudiopolis, in Cilicia) depicts the figure holding a spindle in the right hand, while the left is folded across the chest; a lion appears lying on the upper surface of the stele.[91] In each example, the figure is carved in high relief on a background framed by a raised edge, although this is not, strictly speaking, an architectural setting; moreover, the figures

87. Devreker and Vermeulen 1991: 111–12, figs. 9–10.
88. F. Naumann 1983: 94, pl. 9f; Prayon 1987: no. 47, pl. 15c.
89. F. Naumann 1983: 296, no. 25, pl. 8,1.
90. Ibid.: 296, no. 26, pl. 8,2.
91. Ibid.: 85 n. 242; cat. no. 25a.

FIGURE 17. Phrygian shrine at
Kalehisar, distant view. Seventh–sixth century B.C.
Photograph by John Wagoner.

have different attributes, making their identity uncertain. A cult that extended over such a large area could, however, have had significant local variations, apparent in variant types of sculptural images. The goddess's cult presence in Cilicia is further indicated by rock altars similar to those at Dömrek and Kalehisar.[92]

Before concluding this survey of the central Phrygian evidence, some comments on chronology are needed. A few monuments can be dated from their archaeological context. Two shrines at Boğazköy offer fixed points of chronology. The Phrygian shrine located on the site of an older Hittite temple was in use during the mid eighth century B.C.[93] The Boğazköy sculptural group of the goddess with her two youthful male attendants can be no later than the end of the sixth century B.C.; the excavator dated it to the middle of the sixth century.[94] Two Gordion objects found under burial tumuli, the small relief from under Tumulus C and the idol from under Tumulus E, have a fairly precise lower chronological limit, since they must have been made before the mid sixth century, the date of the construction of those tumuli.[95] Another chronological indicator may be the stone used in the cult reliefs from Gor-

92. Note the rock altars at Dibektaşi, north of Alanya, Zoroğlu 1994: 302–3 and pls. 27, 28.1.
93. Boehmer 1972: 208–9.
94. Bittel 1963: 7–8.
95. Kohler 1995: 34.

FIGURE 18. Phrygian altar at
Kalehisar, close-up. Seventh–sixth century B.C.
Photograph by John Wagoner.

dion, for this is a type of stone first used for sculpture in the Middle Phrygian Level;
thus the Gordion works are probably no earlier than the rebuilding of the city after
its destruction in approximately 700 B.C.[96] The monuments from the Ankara region
have no clear archaeological context, but certain comments can be made on stylistic
grounds: the Etlik relief shows close affinities with Neo-Hittite sculpture, and the
Bahçelievler relief was apparently one of a series of orthostate reliefs, several of
which show strong influence from the Assyrianizing phase of Neo-Hittite sculptural

96. For the date of the rebuilding of Gordion following its destruction, traditionally dated to 696
B.C., see Sams and Voigt 1990: 459–60. DeVries 1998 proposes the slightly earlier date of 709 B.C. for the
destruction.

style. They should probably be dated no later than the seventh century B.C., the latest period of Neo-Hittite influence in Phrygia, and may be earlier.[97] It seems likely that the Phrygian sculptural tradition of representing the goddess had been formed by the late eighth or early seventh century B.C. under Neo-Hittite influence. This tradition continued into the sixth century, and possibly later.

These suggested dates for the sculptural monuments of central Phrygia are surprisingly late, for Gordion was already an important Phrygian center in the ninth century B.C.[98] Ankara also was a major settlement during the eighth century, judging from the rich finds from the burial tumuli in Ankara, contemporary with the eighth-century Gordion tumuli. Yet no monumental representations of the goddess before the seventh century B.C. survive, although it should be noted that sculptural monuments of any kind are rare in Gordion in the levels immediately preceding the site's destruction. The presence of an eighth-century shrine at Boğazköy, in which the bird of prey formed an important symbol, suggests that the goddess was worshipped on the Anatolian plateau earlier; moreover, the lack of a specific cult center such as a temple may make it difficult to recognize the goddess's cult presence.

The evidence seems to point to a gradual development of formal cult symbols and materials. I noted in chapter 3 that the Phrygians used many symbols for their Mother Goddess that they had inherited from earlier Anatolian peoples, including the bird of prey and the presentation of the divinity standing in the sacred doorway, and developed these into specifically Phrygian forms of religious expression. The continuity with the past illustrated through the use of such older Anatolian symbols suggests strongly that the Mother Goddess became part of the Phrygians' religious tradition during their earliest presence as a distinct Anatolian people in the Early Iron Age, although the goddess may not have received a monumental expression in sculpture until the flourishing period of Phrygian civilization, the eighth and seventh centuries B.C. One may even wonder, following the bold hypothesis of Machteld Mellink, whether contact between the Phrygian king Midas and the Neo-Hittite rulers of the later eighth century B.C. exposed the Phrygians to the court iconography of the Neo-Hittite sculptural monuments and led them to develop an iconographic form for their own goddess.[99] The aniconic or partially iconic Phrygian monuments and the rock altars to Matar may be older forms of addressing the Phrygian Mother, which interest in making large iconographic monuments never fully obliterated.

Once the iconography of the goddess was formed, it seems to have been conservative. The changes observed in the representations of her are relatively minor, indicating little change in the cult for several centuries. While the evidence for central

97. Mellink 1983: 359; F. Işik 1989: 94–95, 103.
98. Sams 1989: 452; Sams 1994.
99. Mellink 1983: 358–59.

Anatolia is sparse, later developments in cult images of the Mother Goddess seem to come, not from internal developments within Phrygia, but from contact with the Greek world in the west, and are best considered after a review of the archaeological monuments in western Phrygia.

The Archaeological Evidence: Western Phrygia

While the cult material from western Phrygia has much in common with that from central Phrygia, there are some notable differences. One significant difference is the nature of the material available for study. In central Phrygia, the archaeological evidence consists primarily of representations of the goddess and other cult objects found during excavation in or near established Phrygian centers. In western Phrygia, apart from the important Phrygian center at Midas City, few sites have been carefully excavated.[100] On the other hand, the character of the terrain, with its prominent natural outcrops of limestone and tufa, permitted the carving of monumental cult reliefs onto the live rock. These reliefs could be associated with an urban settlement such as Midas City, but many were placed away from an urban area, and were often integrated into the landscape in quite dramatic settings. This in itself has created a major problem in examining the western Phrygian monuments, namely, that these monuments have always been exposed to the elements and are often in much poorer condition than their counterparts in central Phrygia. Information on chronology is sparse or nonexistent. Nonetheless, a distinctive image of the goddess emerges, one characteristic of this region.

The major concentration of monuments lies in the highlands of Phrygia, the mountainous country near the upper reaches of the Tembris and Sakarya rivers, within a roughly triangular area defined by the modern Turkish cities of Eskişehir, Kütahya, and Afyon. Twenty-three such monuments have been identified, in each case carved into the natural rock.[101] Each monument consists of a sculpted relief depicting an architectural façade, recognizable as a representation of the front of a building. These reliefs can range in detail from the simple schematic outline of a building to an elaborately rendered image with many architectural details. As a group, the façades have several features in common. Each one contains an oblong niche recessed into the stone, in some cases deep and in others shallow; often steps carved into the rock lead up to this niche. In several of the monuments, the niche is carved so as to imitate in stone the form of a wooden doorway with frame and crossbeams, as would be found in an actual wooden building.[102] The relief can include the pediment and gable of a pitched roof surmounted by an akroterion with two inward curved horns; these fea-

---

100. For the excavation of Midas City, see Gabriel 1952, 1965, and Haspels 1951.

101. The principal study of the monuments of the Phrygian highlands is Haspels 1971: 73–111. Since Haspels gives careful descriptions and analyses of these works, the discussion here can be much briefer. For their location and distribution, see also F. Naumann 1983: 42, fig. 3.

102. Note the comments of Haspels 1971: 73–74 and 100–101.

tures too parallel the known details of actual buildings in central Phrygia.[103] The doorway/niche is often surrounded by geometric patterns carved in the stone, some of which are quite intricate.[104] The fact that all the façades present the same basic appearance similar to that found in the reliefs of central Phrygia (note especially the architectural façade on the monument from Bahçelievler) suggests that the carved façade imitating the appearance of the front of a building was part of the basic iconography of these monuments.

Sixteen of these façades have an empty niche, but in the remaining seven, the figure of the goddess standing in the "doorway" can still be seen.[105] In three cases, the image is extremely worn, so that now one can determine only that at one time an image did exist.[106] On four others, however, the figure of the goddess is preserved well enough to determine that her general appearance was similar to that in the images found in the reliefs of central Phrygia: a standing female wearing a high headdress and long robe.

Some of the western Phrygian images of the goddess have traits that set them apart from the images of central Phrygia. The most distinctive is the monument known as Arslankaya, or "lion rock," carved onto a freestanding, pointed rock outcrop and forming a conspicuous feature at the entrance to a fertile valley (fig. 19).[107] The front of the rock bears an architectural relief that follows the standard pattern described above but is more richly decorated. The part of the relief's surface that imitates the front wall of a building is covered with geometric designs. In the center of this ornamental wall is a broad door frame, while above it is depicted the triangular end of a gabled roof surmounted by a horned akroterion. Two antithetically placed sphinxes, winged leonine creatures shown in profile with human heads turned to face the viewer, can be seen within the triangular space of the pediment. Within the niche, the "doorway," is the figure of the goddess, carved out of the background rock in high relief (fig. 20). She stands upright, and evidently wears a high headdress and long gown, which covers her arms and her whole body, although the figure is now so battered that the details of the garment are unclear.

The goddess's companions, her lions, make this relief particularly striking. Two huge lions are found on either side of her, their heads at the same height as the top of the goddess's headdress. They stand upright on their hind legs and each places a front paw on the top of the goddess's head. The goddess holds another lion, a cub,

103. Young 1956: pl. 93, fig. 41; Young 1963: 352.
104. Note the elaborate geometric patterns found in the Midas Monument, Haspels 1971: fig. 8; Arslankaya, fig. 189; Büyük Kapikaya, fig. 183; Maltaş, fig. 158; Değirmen, fig. 162.
105. F. Naumann 1983: 293–94, nos. 11–17.
106. This is true of the images found in Deliklitaş, Haspels 1971: figs. 210–12; Kümbet Asarkale, Haspels 1971: fig. 98; and Deliktaş, Haspels 1971: figs. 203–6. See also F. Naumann 1983: 294, nos. 15, 16, and 17.
107. Haspels 1971: figs. 186–91; F. Naumann 1983: 293, no. 11.

upside down by its hind legs so that its head swings down to her knees. In addition, on either side of the "building"—that is, on the two sides of the rock monument—are two huge lions, shown standing upright on their hindquarters, with the head of each lion reaching to the top of the carved pediment (fig. 21).

Another figured monument, Büyük Kapikaya, also reproduces an elaborate architectural façade (fig. 22). On this façade, there does not seem to have been a pointed gable and pediment; instead, the door is surmounted by a flat lintel, which extends the full width of the monument, effectively dividing the geometric designs of the façade into two panels, upper and lower. The lower panel of the "building" depicted in this relief is covered with intricate cross-and-square designs, while on the upper part is a round disk directly above the flat lintel of the door; this is flanked by geometric designs in the form of a checkerboard pattern.[108] The top surface is now missing, and it is difficult to tell how much higher the rock was in antiquity. The figure of the goddess stands within a recessed niche. Like the Arslankaya goddess, this goddess too had companions flanking her, as is indicated by the presence of two small bases on either side of the figure; the bases are now empty, apart from traces of bronze clamps, which presumably were used to attach accompanying figures.[109]

In two other monuments, Küçük Kapikaya[110] and Kumca Boğaz Kapikaya (fig. 23),[111] the outline of the architectural façade lacks the geometric ornament, but does have the pointed gable with central support. In these two works, the rock façade is approached by steps, as if it were on a step altar. Each of these two façades contains a niche with a relief statue, now much worn, depicting the goddess wearing her standard costume. In both cases, the figure of the goddess was alone, with no space for accompanying figures. In the Küçük Kapikaya monument, the goddess's right arm is clasped across her breast, but in neither work can it be determined whether she was holding attributes.

The remaining sixteen architectural façades with no central figure in the niche are similar enough to the sculpted façades that contain relief sculpture of the goddess to suggest strongly that these empty façades were also designed to hold a statue, presumably a portable image of the goddess.[112] In the case of the main façade at Midas City, the so-called Midas Monument, this assumption is reinforced by cuttings in the ceiling of the niche that could have supported such a statue,[113] as well as by the presence of graffiti within the niche recording the name Matar.[114] The type of image

---

108. Haspels 1971: figs. 182–84; F. Naumann 1983: 293, no. 12.
109. Haspels 1971: 87, suggests that the bases held two figures of bronze lions, but there is no surviving trace of any figure that would support her assumption. The two figures could just as easily have been two small human attendants, as in Boğazköy, or two other figures of a type not known to us.
110. Haspels 1971: fig. 185; F. Naumann 1983: 294, no. 13.
111. Haspels 1971: fig. 159; F. Naumann 1983: 294, no. 14.
112. Körte 1898: 82; Akurgal 1961: 110; Haspels 1971: 99; F. Naumann 1983: 41.
113. Haspels 1971: 75.
114. Brixhe and Lejeune 1984: M-01c, M-01d I, M-01d II, M-01e.

FIGURE 19. Arslankaya, general view.
Early sixth century B.C. Photograph by author.

FIGURE 20. Arslankaya,
relief in niche. Early sixth century B.C.
Photograph by author.

FIGURE 21. Arslankaya,
relief on side. Early sixth century B.C.
Photograph by John Wagoner.

FIGURE 22. Büyük
Kapikaya. Seventh–sixth century B.C.
Photograph by John Wagoner.

placed in these niches is unknown, but it seems reasonable to assume that they resembled the images of the goddess carved in one with the façades.

Although lacking a cult statue, the empty façades frequently surpass the façades with images in both size and degree of detail. The Midas Monument, the principal façade at Midas City, is particularly rich in geometric ornament (fig. 24). The main part of the façade, the front of the "building," is incised with an elaborate pattern developed around a motif of crosses and squares, with meander patterns woven around them. On the so-called "frame" of the building-relief, the horizontal cornice and side supports of the structure, is a running pattern of four lozenges around a square, while a row of lozenges is found above the horizontal cornice within the pediment, and on the raking cornice and sima. The elaborate patterns on the Midas Monument are echoed in similar patterns on the other carved façades at Midas City, the Unfinished Monument (fig. 25) and the Hyacinth Monument (fig. 26). They are also found in the nearby Areyastis Monument (fig. 27),[115] and in façades in other areas of the Phrygian highlands, including the partially buried Maltaş Monument (figs. 28

115. Haspels 1971: figs. 84–85.

FIGURE 23. Kumca Boğaz
Kapikaya. Seventh–sixth century B.C.
Photograph by John Wagoner.

and 29), and the smaller but even more ornate Bakşeyiş Monument (fig. 30).[116] These decorative patterns go beyond the simple meander present on the Bahçelievler relief in central Phrygia to very intricate and complex expressions of the geometric repertory. Clearly, the façades without a permanent cult statue were equally important in Phrygian cult.

The settings of the empty façades are quite varied. Some are located in rural settings, often in quite remote areas, while others, like Arslankaya, stand almost as guardian sentinels at the edge of a valley or plain. The Maltaş Monument, for example, stands at the entrance to the fertile Köhnüş Valley, while the Bakşeyiş Monument is perched on a rock overlooking a valley containing a major road. The site of Midas City has three prominent examples, the Midas Monument, the Unfinished Monument, and the Hyacinth Monument, and several smaller façades carved onto the outer sides of the rock outcrop forming the natural walls of the acropolis.[117]

116. The Maltaş Monument, Haspels 1971: figs. 157–58; the Bakşeyiş Monument, Haspels 1971: figs. 124–25.
117. Haspels 1971: the three elaborate monuments, 73–78, 80–81, figs. 8–9, 14–15, 34; the smaller monuments, Haspels 1971: figs. 16, 35.

90 THE MOTHER GODDESS IN ANATOLIA

FIGURE 24. Midas Monument, Midas City.
Seventh century B.C. Photograph by John Wagoner.

FIGURE 25.   Unfinished Monument, Midas City.
Seventh–sixth century B.C. Photograph by John Wagoner.

FIGURE 26. Hyacinth Monument, Midas City.
Seventh–sixth century B.C. Photograph by John Wagoner.

F I G U R E   2 7.   Areyastis Monument. Seventh–
sixth century B.C. Photograph by John Wagoner.

FIGURE 28. Maltaş Monument, main relief.
Seventh–sixth century B.C. Photograph by John Wagoner.

FIGURE 29. Maltaş Monument, shaft behind relief.
Seventh–sixth century B.C. Photograph by John Wagoner.

In addition to the reliefs of the goddess in cult niches, a few freestanding statues of a standing female are known that may represent the Mother Goddess.[118] Two examples from Midas City preserve only the lower half of the piece. This depicts the lower torso of a standing female clothed in a long gown, although there is no indication of a veil drawn across the body, as is found on the representations of the goddess in central Phrygia. One of these pieces had a tenon on the underside, as if to fasten it into another stone setting such as a niche.[119]

Other monuments of the Matar cult in western Phrygia include stone façades that lack sculpted representations of architecture but have been shaped with a flat surface displaying a Paleo-Phrygian text. The long Phrygian text from Bithynia naming Matar Kubileya and texts dedicated by and to Ates/Atas appear on such plain façades.[120] These were located in very remote areas, well away from Phrygian settlements. There are also a number of schematic stone sculptures, round heads set on rectangular forms, like the schematic idols in central Phrygia.[121] Some were found alone, but many were placed on stepped altars. Most are single figures, but there are several examples from Midas City of a pair of schematic figures, placed side by side, including one pair located on a stepped altar inscribed with a Paleo-Phrygian text.[122] No indication of sex is given, and so we have no way of knowing if these were double representations of the goddess, of the goddess and another figure, or of two attendants of the goddess.

Stepped altars are among the most frequent cult monuments.[123] They consist of steps leading up to a flat area cut into the natural rock. Many are surmounted by a rounded stele, while others are surmounted by schematic idols or, in two cases, by a carved façade imitating a building. Often clusters of them are found near the larger carved façades. Their function may not have been completely analogous to a Greek altar used for animal sacrifice,[124] but they do seem to have been platforms used to approach and address the deity. Several were found in Midas City, on the top of the plateau within the walled citadel (fig. 32). A great many such altars also exist in the area around the major monuments of the Köhnüş Valley north of Afyon. Most are set on high places, frequently apart from urban settlements (the altars within Midas City are an exception to this pattern).

Other sacred monuments include a series of perpendicular shafts sunk into the

118. Two examples from Midas City, Haspels 1971: figs. 53, 54; Mellink 1983: 354 n. 26; F. Naumann 1983: 88; Prayon 1987: nos. 1, 2. There is a third freestanding piece (unpublished) that may be from Midas City, very similar in style and iconography to these two; it is presently in the archaeological museum in Afyon.

119. Haspels 1971: 97; F. Işik 1989: 71.

120. Brixhe and Lejeune 1984: B-01, W-08, W-09, W-10.

121. Haspels 1971: 97–98. Examples are illustrated by F. Naumann 1983: pls. 10, 11.

122. Haspels 1971: figs. 28, 36; F. Naumann 1983: pl. 10a, e, f; pl. 11a. The text, Brixhe and Lejeune 1984: M-04.

123. Haspels 1971: 93–96: F. Naumann 1983: 46, 92–100.

124. Haspels 1971: 93, expresses doubt about the appropriateness of the term "altar."

F I G U R E 3 0. Bakşeyiş Monument, main relief.
Seventh–sixth century B.C. Photograph by John Wagoner.

F I G U R E 3 1. Bakşeyiş Monument, shaft behind relief.
Seventh–sixth century B.C. Photograph by John Wagoner.

FIGURE 32. Stepped altar with idol, Midas City. Seventh–sixth century B.C. Photograph by John Wagoner.

stone behind several of the carved façades.[125] These are found behind some of the larger elaborate façades, such as those at Deliklitaş, Maltaş (fig. 29), and Bakşeyiş (fig. 31), and also behind small plain façades at Findik (fig. 33).[126] It seems likely that these were used as depositories for offerings, perhaps intended to keep the offering closer to the goddess by placing it behind her "house"—that is, her sculpted façade —and within her sacred mountain.[127] Another area that may have been used for offerings is an open space to the left of the Midas Monument, where the natural rock floor was leveled and a row of four column bases was carved.[128] This is unique among the carved façades, so its exact function is uncertain.

The cult monuments in western Phrygia are rarely connected with a datable archae-

125. Haspels 1971: 100. F. Naumann 1983: 52–54.
126. Deliklitaş, Haspels 1971: figs. 210–14, Maltaş, Haspels 1971: fig. 157; Bakşeyiş, Haspels 1971: figs. 124–25; Findik, Haspels 1971: figs. 221–22.
127. The function of these shafts has been a subject of some speculation, and suggestions have included use in the taurobolium, an elaborate sacrifice of a whole bull, as had been suggested by Körte 1898: 97, or as a depository for the genitalia of the goddess's eunuch priests. The taurobolium was, however, a Roman, not a Phrygian cult practice, and the stabbing death of a bull became common only in the late Roman cult of the Graeco-Roman Kybele (see Rutter 1968). Moreover, we have no idea whether the notorious castration sacrifice of the Roman priests of Cybele, who were said to throw their genitals into a shaft, was practiced in Phrygia at this time. For a discussion of these shafts, see F. Naumann 1983: 53–54.
128. Haspels 1971: 75–76.

FIGURE 33.
Findik, relief and shaft
behind. Seventh–sixth
century B.C. Photograph
by John Wagoner.

ological context, and thus they present serious problems of chronology. The only excavated settlement is Midas City, where the main period of the settlement was the
seventh through fourth centuries B.C.[129] The rock façades at Midas City that lie outside the major inhabited area need not be connected with this settlement, and a date
as early as the eighth century B.C. has been proposed for the Midas Monument.[130]
Suggestions of dates for other monuments in the Phrygian highlands range from the
eighth century to the end of the sixth century B.C.[131] Often, however, the criteria for
assigning dates to these monuments appear to rest on purely subjective and unsupported grounds,[132] and so some additional comments are in order.

129. Ibid.: 140–43.
130. Ibid.: 108–9.
131. For various suggested dates, see Haspels 1971: 146 (eighth century); F. Naumann 1983: 293–94
(early sixth century); and Prayon 1987: 206–7 (late sixth century). See also F. Naumann 1983: 57, who
summarizes the opinions of earlier scholars.
132. For example, Haspels 1971: 143–46, assumed that the Midas Monument must date to the eighth
century B.C. because of its association with the great Phrygian king Midas, known to have lived in the late
eighth century. Other scholars, e.g., Akurgal 1955: 60; 1961: 86; and Prayon 1987: 71–79, have assigned a
sixth-century date to the façades on the assumption that they show Greek influence.

The Midas Monument is both the most impressive of the western Phrygian monuments and the only one associated with a datable context, and so it forms a good starting point for a discussion of chronology. The principal inscription on the Midas Monument appears to have been carved at the same time as the façade, and since the text is a dedication to Midas by another person, it seems likely that the text was written after the death of the Phrygian king Midas in the early seventh century B.C.[133] If the monuments and inscription were contemporary with Midas, this would imply that the Phrygians worshipped a living king, and we have no evidence to suggest that divine kingship was a feature of any Anatolian society. There is also a second inscription, running vertically along the right side of the monument. This contains the Phrygian λ, or *yod*, a letter not introduced into the Phrygian alphabet until the sixth century B.C.[134] The second text is in a different hand and appears to have been added after the façade was fully carved, since it is fitted in between the area of geometric designs and the finished right edge; an equivalent space on the left side of the monument is blank. The presence of the sixth-century letter form in this text indicates that the monument had been completed by the mid sixth century.[135] Thus the two inscriptions indicate a time frame for the monument between the early seventh and mid sixth centuries B.C.

Another factor that supports this chronological range is the use of abstract ornament on the carved façades of the Phrygian highlands. Intricate geometric patterns had long been part of the Phrygians' artistic repertory,[136] but the growing complexity of the abstract ornament on these architectural reliefs illustrates an increasingly sophisticated use of this medium. One type of geometric pattern is found on the Büyük Kapikaya and Midas Monuments, where the design on the façade is divided into two sections by the horizontal bar above the doorway. This is similar to the arrangement of the geometric patterns on the inlaid wooden "screens," or serving stands, found in Tumulus MM at Gordion, and may indicate that these monuments should be close in time to the date of the tumulus, the early seventh century B.C.[137]

A different type of geometric pattern use is found on some of the large façades with gables and akroteria, including the Midas Monument, the Areyastis Monument, and several others. Here the geometric patterns appear to be a translation of architectural terracottas into stone, for the designs are almost identical to the designs of actual Anatolian architectural terracottas.[138] These include the patterns of four

133. For the historical and chronological data related to the Phrygian king Midas, see Roller 1983: 300–301; Muscarella 1995.
134. Lejeune 1969a: 30–38; Lejeune 1970: 60–62.
135. DeVries 1988: 55–57.
136. Note the wide variety of geometric ornament on early Phrygian pottery (Sams 1971: 583–89) and Phrygian furniture (Young et al. 1981: 178, fig. 104, 184, fig. 110). In general, see Simpson 1988.
137. For the Tumulus MM serving stands, see Young et al. 1981: pl. 44. I owe this suggestion to Elizabeth Simpson.
138. This is another example of how the façades' sculpted form replicates in stone several of the architectural members of a building, for the function of these terracottas was to sheath wooden beams.

lozenges within a square, a checkerboard pattern and a row of tangential lozenges, all of which are found on terracottas from Gordion, Sardis, and other Anatolian sites.[139] This use of architectural terracottas had been introduced into central Anatolia by the early sixth century B.C.[140] The geometric ornament on the Midas Monument appears to represent an incipient stage of such terracotta design, and the Unfinished, Bakşeyiş, Areyastis, and Hyacinth Monuments have decorated motifs representing more elaborate patterns present in architectural terracottas.[141]

A third type of geometric design is that which covers the front of the façade on the Arslankaya Monument. This may also reproduce architectural terracottas, in this case placed directly on the front wall of a building; similar terracotta plaques were found in situ at the site of Akalan, near the Black Sea coast, and dated to the sixth century B.C.[142] Thus both the intricate decorative patterns and the imitations of architectural terracottas on the façades point to a chronological range for the construction of the highland façades extending through the seventh and sixth centuries B.C.

Foreign influences on the decorative motifs of the façades support this chronological range. One such feature is the type of rosette found on the Areyastis and Unfinished Monuments.[143] Each of these façades has two rosettes in the pediment and one in the akroterion, a feature that may reflect a continuation of Neo-Hittite influence, for the Phrygian rosettes resemble those found on Neo-Hittite reliefs.[144] This would suggest a date in the seventh century B.C. In contrast, the Arslankaya Monument may be somewhat later. The type of geometric pattern found in the front of this monument is a much simpler design than is found on many of the other façades, little more than a variation on the meander pattern. The type of the sphinxes in the pediment suggests a later date also, for the Arslankaya sphinxes have little in common with the Neo-Hittite representations of sphinxes,[145] but do recall sixth-century Greek sphinxes, which frequently have upturned wings and heads turned out to the viewer.[146]

Taken together, these factors suggest that the Büyük Kapikaya and Midas Monuments were among the earliest of the façades to be made; they appear to date from

139. For examples from Gordion, Young 1951: 6, pl. 3; Young 1953: 13–15, fig. 8, and 21–23, fig. 16; Åkerström 1966: pl. 72, 1, pls. 80–85; DeVries 1988: 54–55, figs. 4–6. For a thorough review of the Gordion architectural terra-cottas, see Glendinning 1996a. See also Åkerström 1966: pl. 51, 2 (Sardis); pl. 68 (Midas City); pls. 93, 95, 96 (Pazarli).

140. Glendinning 1996b: 102, correcting the chronology of Åkerström 1966: 156–57.

141. DeVries 1988: 54.

142. Åkerström 1966: 123, pl. 63, 2.

143. Areyastis Monument, Haspels 1971: figs. 84–85; Unfinished Monument at Midas City, Haspels 1971: figs. 14–15.

144. A very similar type of rosette was found on the headdress of Kubaba at Karkamiš (F. Naumann 1983: pl. 2, fig. 3, here fig. 4).

145. In the Neo-Hittite sphinx, the head is almost always shown in profile (one exception is the sphinx at Ain Dara, Orthmann 1971: 476, Ain Dara Ba/1, pl. 1), and the wings have a distinctly Neo-Assyrian look, cf. Orthmann 1971: 339–47.

146. Ridgway 1977: 156–60. Boardman 1978: 167.

the early to mid seventh century B.C. These monuments may have introduced the form of the façade decoration from the central Phrygian heartland into the Phrygian highlands. One may postulate that the basic outline of the façade was developed in the principal Phrygian centers such as Gordion and Ankara to imitate an actual Phrygian building, and the image of the goddess was taken from representations of her in central Phrygia also. The interest in setting such architectural façades into the mountainous terrain of the region caused this form of cult artifact to become especially popular and widespread. The construction of the monumental façades would have lasted until the second half of the sixth century, at which point the resources to construct such façades would have become more limited, as the Phrygians came under Lydian and then Achaemenian political control. The use of the façades as cult centers surely lasted much longer, perhaps as late as the third century C.E., for votive altars dedicated to the Mother Goddess continued to be placed at Midas City until that date.[147]

The cult monuments of western Phrygia parallel the central Phrygian monuments not only in their use of architectural imitation and geometric ornament but also in their settings in both urban (at Midas City) and extra-urban contexts. Many of the western Phrygian monuments were located in boundary zones: the Midas Monument was carved onto the natural rock fortifying the citadel at Midas City, recalling the placement of the Boğazköy monument near a city gate. The Arslankaya, Maltaş, and Bakşeyiş monuments are found at the entrance to valleys of Phrygian settlements. Other monuments were located in remote, extra-urban settings, similar to the central Anatolian monuments at Dömrek and Kalehisar. In the Phrygian highlands, there are many more monuments in remote settings, but this may result from the greater suitability of the terrain for such façades.[148]

Another similarity to the monuments of central Phrygia is the association with funerary contexts. The practice of carving tombs into rock cliffs was common in the western Phrygian highlands, and several of these Phrygian tombs reproduce architectural forms, some quite elaborately decorated with sculptural reliefs.[149] A notable example is the sculpted tomb called Arslantaş (fig. 34).[150] Here two lions are shown as if standing on their hind legs, placing their paws over the tomb chamber door in a manner very similar to the lions on the Arslankaya façade. The use of such rock

147. On the votive altars from Midas City, see Haspels 1971: 295–302. Because of the lack of precise chronological indicators, it is not even certain whether any of the Phrygian cult artifacts connected with the Mother Goddess can be dated to the period between the late sixth and the late fourth centuries B.C. At this point, the influence of Hellenism became much more pronounced in the aftermath of Alexander's campaigns in Anatolia. For a further discussion of this issue, see Roller 1991: 131–32.

148. We should note that the Phrygian settlements in this area are themselves frequently situated on natural rock outcrops, the "kales" of Emilie Haspels's study (Haspels 1971: 36–72), and so the monuments of the Mother Goddess in an urban setting, the carved façades and rock altars, often reproduce the natural character of those in a more remote, extra-urban setting.

149. Haspels 1971: 112–38.

150. For the monumental tomb at Arslantaş, see Haspels 1971: figs. 130–34.

FIGURE 34. Arslantaş, lion relief over grave.
Seventh–sixth century B.C. Photograph by John Wagoner.

façades as architectural chamber tombs implies that in this region of Phrygia, too, the cult of the Phrygian Mother could be attached to a funerary context.[151]

One notable difference between the monuments of central and western Phrygia is the choice of animal attributes. The bird of prey is absent from the Phrygian high-land monuments, whereas the lions of Arslankaya are rare on the central Phrygian monuments. Unfortunately, the Arslankaya Monument is the only one of the western Phrygian rock façades on which the attributes are well preserved, and so it remains uncertain how widespread the lion attribute was in western Phrygia. The lack of overlap in attributes may, however, signal regional differences in the Mother's cult.

The recent discovery of several Phrygian artifacts in south central Anatolia has provided important new information about the cult of the Mother. A group of tumuli at Bayandir, near modern Elmali, excavated in 1986, yielded a number of character-istically Phrygian metal artifacts, including cauldrons, omphalos bowls, and belts.[152] In one of these tombs an ivory statuette of a standing female figure was found, whose pose and costume are extremely similar to images of the Mother Goddess in the Gordion and Bahçelievler reliefs (fig. 35).[153] The Elmali statuette depicts a mature woman, who is shown wearing a polos, or high crown, and a long gown, belted at the waist, with long sleeves. A veil descends from the polos over the figure's back, with its two lower corners drawn up in front and tucked into the top of the belt. In her right hand, the figure grasps the left hand of a little girl standing beside her, who wears a similar costume. On her left shoulder is the figure of a little boy; he is nude, and sits as if straddling her shoulder with his legs while he grasps her polos for support.

The style of the piece bears close affinities to the ivory figurines from the Artemi-sion at Ephesos, especially the so-called Megabyzos figure,[154] suggesting a date in the late seventh or early sixth century B.C. The headdress, costume, and facial fea-tures of the Elmali statuette strongly resemble an ivory statuette of a female figure from Gordion,[155] indicating that this piece too is a Phrygian work. The other ob-jects from the same tomb, including fibulae, phiales, and elaborate metal belts, sup-port this conclusion, since they find extremely close parallels in the material from the early Gordion tumuli.[156]

151. Buluç 1988: 20.

152. Özgen 1988: nos. 29–62.

153. Ibid.: no. 42.

154. Akurgal 1961: figs. 158–59; Bammer 1984: fig. 92. The "Megabyzos" ivory figurine in fact depicts a woman (see Bammer 1985: 57).

155. Young 1966: pl. 74, fig. 5.

156. Note the close connections between several classes of objects in the early Gordion tumuli and the Elmali tomb groups: small bronze cauldrons, Özgen 1988: no. 33, cf. with Young et al. 1981: MM 1, pl. 50; bronze ladles, Özgen 1988: no. 35, cf. with Young et al. 1981: TumP 9, pl. 8; plain omphalos bowls, Özgen 1988: nos. 37, 39, cf. with Young et al. 1981: TumP 13–29, pls. 9–10, and MM 131–67, pls. 72–73; petaled omphalos bowls, Özgen 1988: nos. 36, 38, cf. with Young et al. 1981: MM 74–123, pls. 69–70; bowls with spool attachments, Özgen 1988: no. 40, cf. with Young et al. 1981: MM 55–69, pls. 66–67.

A major interest in this statuette is the presence of the two children, unique among representations of the Mother Goddess. It is possible that the group of a mother with two small children may depict a Phrygian version of the legend of Leto and her children Apollo and Artemis, for the cult of Leto was prominent in Lycia.[157] It seems more likely, however, that we have in this piece one of the few representations of the Mother Goddess as a mother—that is to say, a goddess with her children. Whether this alludes to a specific Phrygian legend that is no longer known or to a general concept of maternal qualities is uncertain. Certainly, the recent discovery of this piece is a good indication of how many aspects of the Phrygian Mother remain beyond our understanding.

The tumulus yielded another piece of great interest for the Phrygian cult of Matar, a silver statuette of a standing human figure, beardless, wearing a long gown belted at the waist and a high tiered headdress (fig. 36).[158] Shoulder-length ringlets fall in front of the ears, while the back of the head is shaved. The figure clasps both hands across the waist in a gesture of prayer. The costume of the figure is very similar to that worn by the goddess, but the anatomy of the figure indicates that it is male, not female, and the costume, unusual hairstyle, and gesture of the hands may signify that this statuette depicts a priest. The lack of a beard, a regular feature in representations of mature male figures in both Near Eastern and Greek art, further suggests that this individual is a eunuch.[159] If so, this is one of the few pieces of evidence within Anatolia for the eunuch priesthood that attended the Phrygian Mother, a distinctive feature of the goddess's cult in Greece and Rome. This statuette depicts a mature figure of dignity, implying that for the Phrygians, the priesthood carried considerable respect, an impression further supported by the costly material of the piece.

Transitional Cult Monuments

At the end of the series of Phrygian cult monuments representing Matar, probably in the second half of the sixth century B.C., are a number of seated statuettes depicting the Mother Goddess that seem to reflect direct Greek influence. The closest point of reference is the seated pose found in Meter statuettes in mid-sixth-century B.C. Ionia.[160] Examples include two pieces from sites near Konya (south central Anatolia) and statuettes from Zonguldak (Black Sea coast), Gordion, and Takmaköy (near Eskişehir).[161] In all of these works, the goddess is shown seated on a formal throne, and in the first three, she is framed in a niche. Greek influence seems especially evident in the statuette from Takmaköy, in which the goddess is shown wearing a cos-

157. Akurgal 1978: 260–61.
158. Özgen 1988: 38, no. 41.
159. Junge 1940: 19–20; Reade 1972: 91–92.
160. F. Naumann 1983: 120–21; La Genière 1985: 704. This point is discussed further in chapter 5.
161. Gordion piece, Roller 1991: fig. IIIb; other pieces, F. Naumann 1983: nos. 44–47.

FIGURE 35. Ivory figurine of goddess,
Bayandir. Late eighth–seventh century B.C. Courtesy,
Antalya Museum. (After E. and I. Özgen, *Antalya
Museum Catalogue* [Ankara, 1988], fig. 42.)

FIGURE 36.   Silver figurine of priest,
Bayandir. Late eighth–seventh century B.C. Courtesy,
Antalya Museum. (After E. and I. Özgen, *Antalya
Museum Catalogue* [Ankara, 1988], fig. 41.)

tume much like a Greek chiton.[162] In this work, a lion sits beside the throne and another on the goddess's lap, while the goddess holds a hare in her left hand against her chest. A Greek model is further suggested by the attribute of the lion on her lap, a feature that first appears after the introduction of the seated goddess into Greek iconography. The other pieces adopt the Greek seated pose but preserve the Phrygian costume. In two works from sites near Konya and the piece from Zonguldak, a female figure sits within a gabled niche with one hand under the breast and the other on the lap.[163] The figure from Gordion, also seated, has no surrounding niche, but this figure holds an object that, although damaged, appears to be a bird of prey.[164] All of these pieces appear to be contemporary with representations of the seated goddess outside of the Phrygian cultural sphere, in the Greek cities on the west coast of Anatolia. Knowledge of the Greek type of the seated goddess could have spread through Greek contacts with the Phrygians, particularly in northwestern Anatolia, where Greeks and Phrygians seem to have lived in close quarters.[165] The Greek influence is strongest in Phrygian sites closest to the Greeks (such as the statuette from Takmaköy) and less obvious in works from sites further east, such as the pieces from Gordion and Konya. Phrygian receptiveness to Greek iconography was part of a process that was to accelerate after Alexander's campaigns in Anatolia. By the third century B.C., most of the Phrygian cult objects were expressed in a purely Greek form, driving out the older Anatolian forms.[166]

THE CULT OF THE MOTHER GODDESS IN PHRYGIA: SUMMARY AND ANALYSIS

Taken together, the evidence gives a vivid picture of the Phrygian Mother. This is a divinity whose impressive costume, stance, and setting within an architectural frame establish her as an important cult figure, surely the most important cult figure in Phrygia, since she is the only divinity who is depicted iconographically. Her name was Matar, Mother. She could also be addressed with epithets, including the epithet *kubileya,* which evidently refers to her domain in the mountains. She first appeared in sculpted monuments in the early seventh century B.C., and cult symbols associated with her were in use during the eighth century B.C. She continued to be worshipped in her Phrygian form until the Hellenistic period, and in a more Hellenized

162. F. Naumann 1983: 122–24, pl. 15, fig. 2, 3.
163. Ibid.: 118–22, pl. 14, fig. 3, 4.
164. Roller 1991: 131–32 and pl. IIIb.
165. As discussed in chapter 5, extensive Greek-Phrygian contacts in northwestern Anatolia, in the region around the Sea of Marmara and the western Black Sea coast, offer the most likely forum for the cultural exchanges of religious ideas and forms; see Rein 1996. F. Naumann 1983: 137 discusses a Meter naiskos from Perinthos, a Milesian colony on the Sea of Marmara; this piece, which depicts the seated goddess holding a hare, furnishes a close parallel to the Takmaköy statuette.
166. This development is discussed in Roller 1991.

guise until late antiquity. The absolute prominence of the Mother Goddess in Phrygian cult is clear.

One definitive characteristic of the cult monuments from all regions of Phrygia is their uniqueness to Phrygia. The influence of earlier Anatolian cultures is certainly present: the visual form of the Phrygian Mother owes much to the Neo-Hittite tradition of sculptural representation, and several of the goddess's attributes, including the bird of prey and lion, were religious symbols in the Anatolian Bronze Age. Earlier Anatolian influence is present too in the practice of placing architectural façades on live rock in remote settings, for this recalls the Urartian doorway reliefs on mountainsides. Yet the specific combination of the goddess's name, form, and type of cult monument is recognizable as part of Phrygian culture. It represents a purely Phrygian response to the religious experience.

In lieu of being able to understand the Phrygians' statements about their Mother Goddess, her attributes provide the best clue to her character. The attribute of a drinking vessel, while common, is perhaps the least indicative, for this was an old convention in Anatolian cult scenes.[167] By symbolizing the liquid offerings that the goddess will receive from her worshippers, the drinking vessel establishes her divinity, but does not mark her in any distinctive way. In contrast, her animal attributes are both individual and memorable. She holds or is accompanied by various animals, birds of prey, lions, and fantastic creatures. Every one of these animals is a predator of one sort or another. The associations of the predator are not negative but reinforce the goddess's image of power. In central Phrygia, her most frequent animal attribute, the hawk or falcon, is a predator of practical value. The hawk hunts for itself, as we see in the representations of hawks hunting fish or hares,[168] but it can also be trained to hunt for man.[169] This attribute gives the goddess a helpful function in relation to humans. Such an image is reinforced by the small Boğazköy stele with a relief depicting men hunting; even human beings have become predators for a beneficial purpose. The Etlik relief shows the goddess with a fantastic creature, but one composed of elements of several predators. The position of this creature, next to the goddess and of equal stature with her, gives this predator too a beneficial quality, here as a guardian or protective figure.

The most complex animal images are those of the lion monuments. Although the lion is not the constant and ubiquitous companion of Matar in Phrygia, as it is in the images of the Greek Meter, nevertheless several noteworthy examples are known, both in central Phrygia, the rock altar at Kalehisar and the composite leonine figure

---

167. Mellink 1983: 351.

168. Note not only the hawk hunting fish on the relief of the goddess from Gordion described (fig. 12), but also the representation of a hawk seizing a hare, also from Gordion, Young 1964: pl. 84, fig. 14.

169. One of the incised drawings, or "doodle stones," on a block from Megaron 2 at Gordion may illustrate a hunting falcon held on a human hand, Young 1969: 271.

of the Etlik relief, and in the west, the Arslankaya Monument. The Arslankaya Monument, both the best preserved and the most complex, suggests that the lions served a dual function: they protect the goddess, thus emphasizing her strength, while at the same time she dominates them, symbolizing her mastery over the animal world. Like the raptors, the lions reinforce the goddess's image of power while making her appear beneficial to mankind.

Another attribute of the goddess, found only in the central Phrygian group, is a round object, held by the Boğazköy goddess and (perhaps) the figure from Gordion Tumulus C. This may be a pomegranate, a symbol of fertility, although both the infrequency and the uncertain identification of this object make this interpretation very tentative.[170]

The goddess could also be accompanied by male attendants. The two companions of the goddess in the Boğazköy group, the musicians, have attracted the most attention, but, as noted above, there are two male attendant figures from Gordion also. It is uncertain whether these represent human or semi-divine attendants, although their schematic bodies and beardless faces may be indicators of youth. The musical instruments that the Boğazköy youths hold are unique in the Phrygian material, but on analogy with the vessels held by the Gordion youths, it seems likely that these instrumentalists and their music also represent an offering to the deity.[171] Some scholars have tried to identify these youths with Greek companions of the goddess,[172] but it seems more likely that their association with her had an Anatolian precedent, for such instrumentalists are known elsewhere in Anatolia, at the Neo-Hittite site of Karatepe.[173] Like the predators, the musical instruments imply a positive character, for the lyre and flute were instruments of beautiful music, not the wild, unrestrained music associated with the cult of Kybele in Graeco-Roman sources.[174] The tympanum, the most common instrument of the Graeco-Roman Kybele, does not appear in Phrygian representations of the goddess.

The placement of the images of the goddess provides further clues to her identity. The location of these images suggests that the goddess's most frequent positions were on the edge of city settlements, particularly on the walls of these settlements, as in reliefs from Boğazköy and Midas City, or on the boundaries of settled territories, as in the Arslankaya and Maltaş monuments, both placed on the edge of fertile

170. As Bittel notes, the object in the goddess's hand in the Boğazköy relief is too poorly preserved for us to be certain of its identity (Bittel 1963: 9).

171. Bittel 1963: 20 and Fleischer 1973: 251 identify the two male figures in the Boğazköy group as divine but subordinate creatures attached to the goddess.

172. The suggestion of G. Neumann 1959, that the two youthful companions of the goddess from Boğazköy represent the two figures named by Apollonios Rhodios, *Argonautika* 1.1117–31, as the Daktyloi Titias and Kyllenes, is based on the unproven assumption that a Hellenistic Greek work would accurately reflect Phrygian religious practice in the Iron Age.

173. Orthmann 1971: 393–94. Karatepe A/27, Orthmann 1971: pl. 17f., furnishes a close parallel.

174. F. Naumann 1983: 79–80.

valleys. They were also placed near water sources (Gordion, Faharad Çeşme), on funerary monuments (the Bahçelievler and Etlik reliefs), or in extramural shrines in mountainous landscapes, such as the rock façades and altars in high places (Pessinous, Dömrek, Kalehisar, and many others). Smaller images were found in private houses. No monument was found attached to a building in the middle of an urban center.

The question of how the goddess was displayed is related to the problem of who worshiped her. The representation of the goddess on or near city walls indicates an official cult, for it is unlikely that such monuments would have been made without the consent of the governing authority of the city. Similarly, the construction of the large rock façades of Midas City and monuments of the Phrygian highlands such as Arslankaya must have demanded large financial resources, indicating the patronage of important figures in Phrygian society. A hint of who these figures may have been is provided by several inscriptions placed on cult monuments. The goddess's façade at Midas City is dedicated to Midas, the name of a Phrygian king, by Ates. The name Ates, also a royal name, is present in two inscriptions from Çepni, once in the nominative and once in the dative, and the name Baba also appears in the nominative in two inscriptions of Midas City. Although the Greeks associated these names with male gods in the cult of Kybele, it seems unlikely that these names in the Paleo-Phrygian texts are those of a divinity, especially when they appear in the nominative case in a dedicatory inscription. It seems quite probable, though, that they were names of Phrygian royalty. Following this hypothesis, the Phrygian kings not only made dedications, but could also be the recipients of cult dedications, since their names also appear in the dative. If so, we may wonder why a monument of the goddess was dedicated to a Phrygian king, to Midas or Ates. Did a Phrygian king receive divine honors after his death? This is quite possible in the case of Midas, and is implied by the appearance of his name in connection with the goddess in several Greek legends.[175] It seems likely that Phrygian kings would have played a critical role in the cult of the goddess and could have been honored jointly with her,[176] thus reinforcing the patronage implied by the size and placing of these monuments. One may even speculate that part of Matar's function as a mother goddess was to serve as the mother of the Phrygian state, perhaps reinforced by conjunction with the Phrygian king in the form of a sacred marriage. One piece of evidence supporting this suggestion is the use of the name Ates/Attis as the title of the principal priest of the Mother Goddess into the second century B.C. at the important Hellenistic Phrygian

175. Roller 1984: 267–68.
176. Roller 1988a: 48–49. Note also the comments of Buluç 1988: 20–21, who suggests that the Phrygian practice of placing objects into tumuli in pairs may represent pairs of gifts for the Mother Goddess and the royal personage in the tomb.

shrine of Pessinous.[177] The priestly function of a king would have been the only survival of royal authority after Phrygia ceased to be an independent state.

At the same time, we cannot say that the cult of the Mother was a cult limited to
the upper stratum of Phrygian society. The discovery of sculptural monuments such
as the small figures from private houses in Gordion suggests that the cult was important to the common people as well. The relief from Tumulus C, imitating a monumental relief in small scale, was uncovered in an ordinary house of unprepossessing
form, another indication of Matar's importance to people of limited means. The
same impression is given by the numerous schematic idols in humanoid form that
appear to represent the goddess, found in Gordion, Boğazköy, and Midas City.
These seem to be simpler versions of the larger and more elaborate depictions of the
goddess in sculpted relief. Since many of these images also came from ordinary private houses, this would seem to indicate that the cult enjoyed a strong following on
a popular level. Such an impression is reinforced by the find of several small votive
hawks, or raptors, at Gordion; the precise context of these objects is often unclear,
but the rather crude nature of these votives suggests that they were the offerings of
people of lower social status.

The meaning of the architectural façade is problematical and deserves further
comment. On several of the monuments, the details of doorway, lintel, pediment,
gable, and akroterion are so precisely represented that it seems certain that such
façades were intended to reproduce an actual Phrygian structure. But what building
did the façade represent? The most obvious answer would seem to be a temple of the
goddess, and several scholars have interpreted the façades as such.[178] This hypothesis is weakened by the fact that no temple has ever been found in a Phrygian settlement. The form and construction techniques suggested by the façades seem to have
been common to virtually all important Phrygian buildings, regardless of function.[179] Perhaps the goddess did not have her own house, so to speak. She may have
been closely identified as the protectress of the city, particularly of the royal family,
as suggested by the prominence of royal names in the Paleo-Phrygian texts. The frequent depiction of the goddess surrounded by an architectural façade may be an allusion, not to a temple, but to a royal residence where the goddess was venerated by
a king as part of the priestly function of his office.[180]

Yet the persistence of the goddess's architectural façade is puzzling, for it is not

177. Welles 1934: 55–61. Virgilio 1981: 24–34, letters 2, 4, 5, and 7. Cf. also Polybios 21.37.4–7; Livy
38.18.9–10. Note also the incident described by Diodoros 36.13.3, in which a Phrygian priest came from
Pessinous to Rome wearing a golden crown and other insignia regarded as signs of royalty.

178. F. Naumann 1983: 55. Mellink 1983: 356–59.

179. The form of the building suggested by the façade reliefs is found in virtually all the buildings of
the early-seventh-century B.C. Destruction Level at Gordion, despite their varying functions. See De-
Vries 1980: 33–35.

180. Roller 1988a: 49.

limited to official cult centers at Gordion and Midas City. It went with her into the wild, non-urban environment of the rock façades as well. Here the cult artifacts from earlier Anatolian civilizations may provide some help. The Urartian practice of representing a divinity framed in a doorway offers a parallel situation, for the Urartian texts make clear that the divinity is presumed to make an epiphany from the mountain.[181] This seems highly likely for the Phrygian Mother as well, particularly in view of the texts identifying her as Matar Kubeliya, the Mother of the mountains. Her presence in the mountains was part of her character, since this was where she was most at home. At the same time the doorway through which the deity appears replicates an urban structure, suggesting that the purpose of these door façades was to emphasize the deity's ability to connect the mountain with the human environment.

Thus in placing the Mother Goddess in an architectural façade and locating that façade in mountain contexts, the Phrygians were continuing an older Anatolian tradition, one that preceded the formation of Phrygia as a distinct cultural entity. Yet the Phrygians did not merely copy an older practice, but adapted it to their own needs. They used these façades only for their own special deity, the Mother Goddess. The distinctively Phrygian architectural details in the façades show that the Phrygians wished to place the Mother in their own settlements and transfer her persona as the mountain goddess to her urban cult in Phrygia. The Phrygian goddess was the divinity of the mountains, and her authority and her capacity to inspire awe appear to have resulted from her ability to transcend boundaries between the open natural terrain and the settled urban environment. She brought her predators to Phrygian settlements and she brought her "house," her symbol of civilization, to remote mountainous terrain. This same ability to communicate with both the wild and tame environment may underlie the use of architectural façades in funerary cult also, for here too the deity transcends boundaries, in this case the irrevocable boundary between the known environment of life and the unknown world of death.

One question that inevitably arises in an examination of the Phrygian Mother is the issue of her consort. As this review of the images of the goddess has shown, she is normally represented alone. The youthful figures from Boğazköy and Gordion are the only iconographic evidence we have of any male companions of the goddess in Phrygia, and their small size indicates that they are attendants, not equals. As is well known, in Greek and Roman cult, the goddess Meter or Magna Mater is frequently accompanied by a young male divinity, Attis, whose worship, involving the castration of his priests, was one of the most notorious features of the Mother's cult in

181. F. Işik 1987, pl. 34b (Yeşilaliç; see also figs. 5–6 in this volume); Salvini 1994 (Meher Kapisi). Cf. also Burney 1957: 42–44. Phrygian contact with Urartu during the reign of Midas would have made the Urartian model of the cult "doorway" available to the Phrygians (see chapter 3, n. 74).

later Greek and Roman society. The Graeco-Roman god Attis, however, had no counterpart in Phrygia. It seems clear that this eunuch divinity originated elsewhere, perhaps as a result of an erroneous combination of the Mother's small attendants with her principal human devotee, a priest regularly entitled Attis. The silver statuette from the Elmali tomb suggests that such priests were an important part of the Matar cult. The confusion resulting from a misrepresentation of these Phrygian cult features is more understandable if they were conflated by Greeks who had little knowledge of or interest in Phrygian cult ritual.

Finally, one may speculate on the identity of the divinity as Mother Goddess. She was addressed most often as Matar or "Mother." Since accompanying epithets appear only occasionally and inconsistently, it seems that her principal name was simply "the Mother." What concept of a mother goddess is suggested by her image in Phrygian cult? Apart from the ivory statuette from Elmali, she is never shown holding or nurturing a child; the youthful attendants depicted at Boğazköy and Gordion were surely her associates, not her offspring. There seems to be nothing in her image that suggests a fertility divinity: her appearance, while obviously female, does not emphasize eroticism or reproductive functions. Her only attribute that might possibly suggest fertility is the "pomegranate" that the Boğazköy figure holds, but the identification of this object as a pomegranate is not secure.

A much more consistent association is that of the predators who regularly accompany the goddess. They do not give the goddess a frightening image, but rather one of strength and control over the natural environment. The goddess becomes the Mother of the natural world, and her human worshippers approach her to gain her help in obtaining a measure of control over the natural environment for themselves, both by the choice of attributes and by placing her urban setting, her "house," on natural rock façades guarding the entrance to the cities and valleys of her people. Taken together, the material suggests that the Phrygian Mother Goddess was not limited by the conventional modern definitions of motherly qualities, of fertility and nurturing, but was focused on a figure of power and protection, able to touch on many aspects of life and mediate between the boundaries of the known and the unknown. Her power could be brought into the urban center to reinforce the status of Phrygia's rulers, but it transcended any purely political usage and spoke directly to the goddess's followers from all walks of life.

While this concept of divinity may well have a direct connection with the religious images of pre-Phrygian Anatolian societies, the cult of the Phrygian Mother was not an empty survival of a few forms, but a unique reshaping to reflect the religious practice of contemporary Phrygian society. In subsequent chapters, I shall return to several of these points, and the discussion of Phrygian cult during the period of Greek and Roman cultural influence will be aided by several comprehensible Phrygian religious texts in Greek. These furnish further clues concerning the reasons for such interest in a mother goddess, and also for the connection between the goddess and the power emanating from predators and from sacred mountains. But even without the aid of explanatory cult texts, first-millennium B.C. Phrygian monuments are dramatic and impressive in number, range, and quality. They communicate the enormous force exerted by the cult of the Phrygian Mother.

2 · THE MOTHER GODDESS IN GREECE

5 · THE EARLY CULT

The Phrygian Mother Goddess came to the Greek world from Anatolia and became a forceful presence there, making a lasting impact on Greek society. The goddess was conspicuous in several prominent situations: she received major cult shrines and numerous private votives in several Greek cities, and she was a figure of note in Greek literature, especially Athenian drama. From the beginning, however, the Mother Goddess was an ambivalent figure in Greek cult. As her prominence increased, she was Hellenized in name, appearance, and background, and became conflated with other, better-known Greek mother deities such as Rhea and Demeter. Yet she always retained her status as an outsider: she was the Asiatic Mother, the Phrygian Kybele, a foreigner whose position in Greek cult and Greek life was somewhat marginal. This tension between her popularity and her close integration into many facets of Greek myth and cult, on the one hand, and her status as an uneasy resident in the Greek world, on the other, help make the Mother Goddess a fascinating figure.

The earliest evidence for the Phrygian Mother Goddess in Greece, primarily archaeological and epigraphical, suggests that the cult of the goddess found a place in Greek life during the early sixth century B.C. The goddess first appears in the Greek world on the west coast of Anatolia: this is attested by small Greek votive reliefs depicting her, found in or near several East Greek cities, including Miletos, Smyrna, and Kyme. From there her worship spread to the Greek mainland and further west, to Greek cities in Sicily, Italy, and southern France. Her worship was formally recognized in Athens by the construction of a temple to her in the Athenian Agora, the Metroön, and this made her cult an important institution in Athenian life. Temples to Meter are also found at other Greek sites, such as Olympia and Kolophon. By the fourth century B.C., the cult of the Mother Goddess was known in virtually every

Greek city, a situation attested by inscriptions, frequent references in Greek literature, and literally hundreds of votive reliefs and statuettes depicting the seated goddess.

This general summary, available in many handbooks and surveys on the Greek goddess Meter (Mother) and on religion in Greece,[1] gives a false sense of smooth linear progression to a cult whose development and status in Greek society was by no means so simple. It masks many of the important questions about the Greek Mother Goddess. Why did the Greeks worship her so extensively, yet classify her as a barbarian goddess? To what extent was she Hellenized in myth and cult practice, and how did this change her Phrygian identity? How did the Greeks accommodate her to Rhea, the Greek mother of the gods? What was her relationship to the Potnia Theron, the female figure depicted with lions in earlier Greek art? And, perhaps most important, what did it mean to a Greek to worship a mother goddess? Of what was she the mother? These are all issues that take us beyond a simple review of the evidence for the cult of the Greek Meter into much more fundamental questions about the status of religion in Greek society, Greek attitudes toward foreign deities and toward foreigners in general, and the tension between the public image and private reality of cult practice. It will not be possible to treat all of these issues with equal confidence, but a discussion of them and their connection with the cult of Meter will offer a valuable look not only at the Greek Mother Goddess but also at many aspects of Greek life.

Chapters 5 and 6 survey the cult of Meter in Greece in the Archaic and Classical periods, the sixth through fourth centuries B.C. To some extent, these two periods form a unit, for it was during this time that the cult of the Phrygian Mother became established in the Greek world, undergoing significant alterations in the process. Yet the Persian Wars, the event that created the break between the Archaic and Classical periods, affected the Greek perception of Meter and led to observable changes in the status of her cult, and so it seems best to discuss these two periods separately. Chapter 7 deals with the cult in the Hellenistic Greek world. After the conquests of Alexander and the more frequent contacts between Greece and the Near East that ensued, the Phrygian Mother's Anatolian homeland came within the cultural sphere of the Greek world; as a result, the Hellenized face of the goddess became more complex, comprising the older Phrygian deity, the Greek Meter, and the composite goddess of the newly Hellenized East.

In the earlier periods, when she had only recently arrived from Anatolia, the Mother Goddess stands out more sharply than she does later. She was the first non-Greek divinity to establish a public presence and an important public cult in the

1. See among others, Graillot 1912: 18–24; Nilsson 1967: 725–27; Vermaseren 1977: 32–34; Burkert 1985: 177–79.

Greek world. Moreover, the cult of this foreign deity became prominent during the period when the Greek city-state, the polis, was still engaged in the process of self-definition and, on occasion, in self-defense, and Greek reactions to the Mother Goddess's Anatolian background changed accordingly. Questions about the Mother's origin, character, and position in Greek cult are therefore of value, not only for themselves, but also for the light they shed on early Greek society.

THE ARRIVAL OF THE MOTHER GODDESS IN THE GREEK WORLD

The circumstances of the goddess's first appearance in the Greek world and the establishment of her cult there will be the first issues to be considered. Meter, the Greek Mother Goddess, came to the Greek world from Anatolia—the Greeks themselves acknowledged this.[2] Her presence is first noticeable during the early sixth century B.C. through a combination of epigraphical testimony, votive reliefs and statuettes representing her, and scattered references in Greek literature.[3] Yet it is still very difficult to be certain how and why her cult became established in the Greek world. The lack of clear evidence about the early cult of Meter raises difficult issues apart from the problem of tracing the cult's foundation and spread. Greek sources of the fifth century B.C. and later, drawn primarily from Athens, the best-known cult center, describe a cult composed of distinctive characteristics that were apparently widely recognized by the early fifth century: these included worship through mystery cult and the use of orgiastic or ecstatic rites, which could be a conduit for a disturbed emotional state, a situation that, in the view of many Greek writers, carried a distinctly negative tone.[4] These unusual qualities were often ascribed by the Greeks to the goddess's Phrygian origins. Yet it is uncertain whether ecstatic rites were part of the Meter cult in early Greece; moreover, the assumption that these rites were a result of foreign influence may well be incorrect. Understanding the Mother Goddess in the Greek world thus depends on which aspects of the Meter cult were derived from Phrygia and which were primarily Greek. As we shall see, the Greek Meter is very much a composite figure, including both Anatolian and Hel-

2. Meter's Anatolian origins: Sophocles, *Philoktetes* 391–94 (Lydia); Euripides, *Bacchae* 78–79, 126–29 (Lydia, Phrygia); Aristophanes, *Birds* 876–77 (Phrygia, through the link with Phrygian Sabazios); Diogenes, fr., Athenaios 1.2 = Nauck p. 776. The assertion of Robertson 1996: 239–41 and passim, that the historically attested Mother of the gods was an "age-old" Greek divinity with little Anatolian connection is highly speculative; he relies heavily on a literal reading of mythical accounts recorded during Roman times or in late antiquity, and dismisses the preponderance of the ancient evidence connecting the deity with Anatolia as elements brought to Greece by private persons from the fourth century and later.

3. Epigraphical testimony, Guarducci 1970. Votive statuettes, F. Naumann 1983: 110–35. Literary citations collected by Schwenn 1922c: 2250 ff., and Burkert 1985: 177–79.

4. The clearest statement of orgiastic rites and mystery cult in connection with Meter is in the opening chorus of Euripides, *Bacchae* 76–86, 126–29; for a negative view of ecstatic rites, see Demosthenes, *On the Crown* 260. This negative point of view is echoed by several modern scholars as well; see Bömer 1963: 866–67; Burkert 1985: 179; Versnel 1990: 105–11.

lenic elements, a circumstance that gave her cult and her character a stamp that was neither totally Greek nor totally Phrygian.

Let us start by reviewing the written data for the earliest appearance of the Greek Mother. We recognize this goddess, first and foremost, by her name, Meter. This was derived from her cult title in Phrygia, Matar (Mother), a name that in two (and only two) extant Paleo-Phrygian texts is qualified by the adjective *kubileya,* a Phrygian word that probably meant "of the mountain."[5] In Greek literature, the goddess was usually called Kybele, a Greek name taken from this Phrygian epithet. In inscribed votives dedicated to her, the goddess is regularly addressed as Μήτηρ, Meter, her cult title in Greece. In cult hymns she could be addressed as Meter or as Meter Kybele, indicating that the Greeks equated the two names.[6] The title Meter can appear alone, but the goddess is usually addressed as Μήτηρ θεῶν, "Mother of the gods."[7] This is similar to, but not equivalent to the Phrygian name Matar, and in itself introduced a slightly different definition of a mother goddess, one that was to contribute to the goddess's distinctive identity in the Greek world.

Meter first comes to our attention, in a forceful and evocative way, through the fourteenth Homeric Hymn. The Hymn to the Mother of the gods comprises only six lines, but it forms what was to be a classic statement of the Mother Goddess in Greece, her attributes, her personality, and the impression she made on the Greek world:

> Μητέρα μοι πάντων τε θεῶν πάντων τ' ἀνθρώπων
> ὕμνει, Μοῦσα λίγεια, Διὸς θυγάτηρ μεγάλοιο,
> ᾗ κροτάλων τυπάνων τ' ἰαχὴ σύν τε βρόμος αὐλῶν
> εὔαδεν ἠδὲ λύκων κλαγγὴ χαροπῶν τε λεόντων
> οὔρεά τ' ἠχήεντα καὶ ὑλήεντες ἔναυλοι.
> Καὶ σὺ μὲν οὕτω χαῖρε θεαί θ' ἅμα πᾶσαι ἀοιδῇ.

Sing to me, clear-toned Muse, daughter of great Zeus, of the Mother of all gods and of all human beings; she takes pleasure in the resounding of castanets and tympana and the roar of flutes, the cry of wolves and bright-eyed lions, the echoing mountains and the wooded glens. And hail to you too, and all the goddesses who join in song.

Here the Mother is presented as the omnipotent goddess, progenitor of all divine and human life. She is accompanied by wild animals whose untamed nature is appropriate to her own open character. The goddess loves the outdoors and eschews urban areas. She surrounds herself with musical instruments that make loud raucous noises, castanets and tympana (tambourines), replicating the sounds of her animal

---

5. See the discussion in chapter 4 above.

6. Pindar fr. 80 (Snell); Aristophanes, *Birds* 875–77; Euripides, *Bacchae* 78. The evidence is discussed by Henrichs 1976: 253–54.

7. Note a fourth-century B.C. votive relief of Meter from the Athenian Agora, *CCCA* II, no. 3, one of the earliest of many such dedications; examples have been collected in *CCCA* II: 250.

companions. The hymn ends with an invocation to the Muses; thus it lacks the statement, found in other Homeric hymns, saluting the deity and promising to address her again, an ending that is generally interpreted to signify that the hymn formed a prelude to a longer poem. The ending of this hymn suggests that the poem was intended to be a complete unit in itself.

The date of the hymn is uncertain. This work, one of the corpus of hymns written in epic meter and style but composed after the Homeric poems, has traditionally been placed in the mid sixth century B.C., largely on the basis of its epic meter and its use of Homeric grammar forms and compound epithets—for example, μεγάλοιο, χαροπῶν. This date is somewhat problematic, however, for the Hymn to Meter contains only a few such epic forms; other details in the hymn, such as the different structure of the ending and the reference to tympana, which did not appear in the goddess's visual iconography until the late sixth century, suggest that the date may be somewhat later, perhaps the last quarter of the sixth century B.C. The epic language of the hymn would then be a product of self-conscious imitation.[8] The hymn certainly implies, though, that Meter had a firm place in Greek cult, for she was to be addressed in the same language used for other, more central Greek deities. She was a definite, if ancillary, member of the family of Greek gods, invoked through the Muses, as the other gods were.

Was this Meter the Anatolian goddess? One complication lies in the fact that the Greeks used the title Meter for more than one divinity. The Greeks knew that Mother Kybele had come to Greece from Anatolia, but they also addressed the divinity Rhea, the Mother of the original six Olympian gods, as a mother goddess.[9] The hymn, however, provides several strong allusions to the Phrygian goddess: her home in the mountains, her accompanying predators, her music. As we shall see, these points are all present in the Greek visual representations of Meter, drawn from the images of Matar's Anatolian homeland, suggesting that the goddess honored by this hymn was still close to her Phrygian forebear.

Certain evidence of Greek knowledge of the Phrygian goddess appears even earlier, in a graffito on a sherd of local fabric from Epizephyrian Lokri, in southern Italy, probably dating to the late seventh or early sixth century B.C.[10] Clearly visible on it is the goddess's Greek name Ϙυβάλας, Kybele, as written in the Doric dialect using the epichoric alphabet of Lokri,[11] indications that the word had already become a part of the Greek language.

---

8. Such archaistic language could persist until the Hellenistic period; cf. West 1970: 212–15, who argues for a third-century B.C. date for a Hymn to Meter from Epidauros, *IG* iv² 131, which uses imagery similar to Homeric Hymn 14.

9. The relationship of the Anatolian Mother Goddess to other Mother divinities in Greek society, including Rhea and Demeter, the archetypal divine mother, is explored more fully in chapter 6.

10. Guarducci 1970. The piece was found under the foundations of a wall dated by the presence of Middle Corinthian pottery to the first half of the sixth century B.C.

11. In Paleo-Phrygian texts, *kubileya* is written with a *k,* not a qoppa.

Apart from this sherd, however, recognition of the Mother Goddess is more difficult. In early literary texts, the Phrygian goddess's presence is signified by the occurrence of the name Κυβήβη, Kybebe, in the work of the early lyric poets Semonides of Amorgos and Hipponax of Ephesos, and the logographer Charon of Lampsakos. In each case, the name occurs in a brief fragment, quoted out of context by a later author or lexicographer. Hipponax records that the daughter of Zeus was addressed as Kybebe or Thracian Bendis.[12] Charon reported that Aphrodite was called Kybebe by the Phrygians and Lydians.[13] According to Semonides, the name given to the goddess's wandering priests, later known as *metragyrtai*, was Κυβήβος, Kybebos,[14] and it seems likely that the masculine form of the word derives from the feminine theonym Kybebe.

The Kybebe of these texts is surely the Hellenized form of Kubaba, the name of the Anatolian goddess who was worshipped in the Neo-Hittite states of the Early Iron Age and the deity whom Herodotos calls the local goddess of Sardis.[15] Thus her appearance in Greek poetry of the sixth century B.C. shows Greek knowledge of an Anatolian goddess. Whether this was the Mother Goddess of the Phrygians is less certain, for as we have seen, the Phrygian goddess of the mountains was a separate deity from the Neo-Hittite city goddess Kubaba.[16] It is quite possible, however, that ethnic distinctions between the religious practices of different Anatolian peoples had little meaning to the Greeks. The words Κυβήβη (Kybebe) and Κυβέλη (Kybele), while distinctive in their Anatolian languages, are only slightly different in Greek, and the Greeks may well have conflated them.[17] In addition, Kubaba's prominence at Sardis, a city with which the Greeks had much contact during the sixth century, may have caused the two divine names to merge and the two Anatolian deities to be absorbed into Greek cult practice as one unit. The confusion of names is especially plausible in the case of Hipponax of Ephesos (who also speaks of Kybele), for several Lydian words appear in his poetry.[18] The presence of the name Kybebe in these texts of East Greek authors may reflect the Lydian strain in the identity of the Greek Meter, a point that we shall also see attested archaeologically.

The use of the name Kybele, the derivative of the Mother's Phrygian epithet, is somewhat clearer. It first appears in a citation of Hipponax, in which the poet equates Κυβελίς (Kybelis) with Rhea, another indication that the Phrygian goddess had become the Greek Mother Goddess, subsuming any indigenous mother deity.

---

12. Hesychios, s.v. Κυβήβη, Masson 1962: fr. 127 and p. 168; West 1989–92: Hipponax fr. 127.

13. Charon of Lampsakos, *FGrHist* 262 F 5.

14. West 1989–92: Semonides fr. 36, quoting Kratinos. Versnel 1990: 109, has suggested that this is the earliest reference to a begging eunuch priest of Kybele, later called a *metragyrtos* or *Gallos*.

15. Kubaba as a Neo-Hittite deity, Laroche 1960, Hawkins 1981a, 1981b; Kubaba in Sardis, Herodotos 5.102. On the equation of Kubaba with Kybebe in Greek, see Brixhe 1979: 40–41.

16. Graf 1984: 119; Roller 1994b. See the discussion in chapter 3 above.

17. Brixhe 1979: 40–41.

18. Masson 1962: 31–32; Brixhe 1979: 41.

The goddess's name supposedly was derived from a Phrygian city where she was honored, called Kybella.[19] During early fifth century B.C., Pindar addressed the goddess as Δέσποινα Κυβέλη Μήτηρ, Mistress Kybele the Mother.[20] This is the earliest known equation of the name Kybele with the title Meter, demonstrating clearly that Kybele was the Greek Mother Goddess. By the latter half of the fifth century, the name Kybebe was no longer used, and the theonym Kybele is the principal name of the goddess, found in Aristophanes' *Birds*[21] and in an emotionally charged passage in Euripides' *Bacchae*.[22] In most subsequent literary texts from mainland Greece, Kybele is the Mother Goddess's name.

While it is uncertain why the Greeks turned the Phrygian epithet *kubileya* into a proper noun, it seems likely that the Greeks were aware of its meaning in the Phrygian language. The Greek Mother was also addressed as Μήτηρ ὀρεία, "Mother of the mountains,"[23] indicating that the Greeks, too, valued the Mother's close connection with mountains. The Phrygian epithet may have been chosen because it recalled the Mother's home. Creating a Greek name for the Phrygian Mother appears as a part of the process of syncretism, giving the goddess a name that alluded to her Phrygian origins, yet was specifically Greek.

Archaeological data supplement the slender written information and provide a more detailed way to trace the spread of the cult. The presence of the name Kybele in Italy indicates a wide spread of the goddess's cult to the Greek west, and since it is unlikely that the cult leapt directly from Phrygia across the Mediterranean to Italy, we should assume that at this early date, there were intermediate stations in the eastern parts of the Greek world where the goddess was worshipped. What those intermediate stations may have been is best indicated by finds in a number of Greek cities of small statuettes and votive reliefs depicting the goddess.[24] These votive objects bring their own difficulties of interpretation, for many are poorly preserved or lack information on provenience and context, making chronology a problem. Nonetheless, the early Greek votives show strong affinities with the images of Phrygian Matar and provide the best evidence for the geographical spread of the Meter cult. The earliest examples of such works are found, not surprisingly, in the Greek cities on the west coast of Anatolia, but several are known from mainland Greece as well.

19. Tzetzes, in Lycophron, *Alex.* 1170. Masson 1962: no. 156 and p. 177; West 1989–92: Hipponax fr. 156.

20. Pindar fr. 80 (Snell). Henrichs 1976: 253–54.

21. Aristophanes, *Birds* 877.

22. Euripides, *Bacchae* 78–79.

23. Euripides, *Hippolytos* 141–44, and note also *Bacchae* 76–79, the Great Mother worshipped in the mountains (these are discussed in greater detail in chapter 6). Adjectives mentioning specific mountains were to become common epithets of Meter in the fourth century B.C. and later, including a text from Chios in which the goddess is addressed as Μήτηρ Κυβελείη, Forrest 1963: 59–60 no. 11. Other topographical epithets used to address the goddess include Idaia, Sipylene, Dindymene, and other examples discussed in chapter 7 below. All are drawn from names of topographical features, usually mountains.

24. The earliest Greek votive reliefs of Meter have been treated as a group by F. Naumann 1983: 110–17 (standing goddess) and 117–34 (seated goddess).

We may begin with a number of small marble reliefs depicting the goddess standing in a frame that imitates the walls and gabled roof of a building. Several were found in Miletos, and others are likely to be from Miletos too, although their provenience is less secure (fig. 37).[25] These reliefs were almost certainly intended as votive offerings. Their identification specifically as Meter votives comes primarily from the standing pose of the figures and from the architectural frame, the naiskos, in which they are placed, both features consistently present in Phrygian depictions of the Mother Goddess.[26] One Milesian naiskos has a gable decorated with relief sculpture, strengthening the reference to an actual building.[27] Another, recently published example has painted designs on the gabled façade; these include a geometric band on either side of the niche, a central Ionic column in the pediment and a double-horned volute akroterion.[28] The details of the Ionic column capital and akroterion are taken from Greek, not Phrygian architecture, but the allusion to a Phrygian architectural façade with its geometric patterning seems too pronounced to be accidental. No other Greek deity was consistently represented in a naiskos. In later times, the naiskos type, often identified by inscription, was the standard votive offering to Meter, which suggests that these early naiskoi reliefs represent Meter also.

Apart from the Anatolian feature of the standing pose in the naiskos, the standing figures in the Miletos votives are fully Hellenized in costume, pose, and attributes. In each relief, the standing female figure wears the typical costume of an Ionic kore, the chiton, mantle, and veil. She normally has one hand at her side, and in some cases, she appears to hold her skirt to the side in a manner reminiscent of Archaic Greek korai.[29] Several of these female figures hold an object in one hand across the breast, which in some cases is depicted clearly enough to be identified as a pomegranate.[30] Two reliefs depicting a pair of standing female figures in a naiskos, both holding an object across the breast, may also indicate Hellenic influence, for these anticipate the examples of double naiskoi among Classical and Hellenistic Meter votives, but form a break from the Phrygian Matar, who always stands alone.[31] A fur-

25. F. Naumann 1983: nos. 37–43, gives seven examples of naiskoi with a standing female figure; of these, nos. 40–43, now in the Izmir Museum, apparently came from Miletos. To her list should be added three reliefs from Miletos now in Berlin (C. Blümel 1964: nos. 44 and 45), several recent finds at Miletos (von Graeve 1986a: pl. 9, nos. 1–4; 1986b: 43–47; 1986c: 21–25), and several unpublished examples in the Miletos museum and storerooms (Mary Jane Rein, personal communication). On Miletos as the most likely provenience for this group of reliefs, see Rein 1993.

26. Another correspondence, the pomegranate held by the figure within the naiskos, is reminiscent of the round object held by the goddess in the Phrygian relief from Boğazköy, Bittel 1963: pl. 1. This is a unique example of the attribute in Phrygia, a notable contrast to the situation in Greece where it appears to be the standard attribute in early representations of Meter.

27. F. Naumann 1983: no. 37.

28. Von Graeve 1986c: 22, fig. 1.

29. C. Blümel 1964: pl. 126; F. Naumann 1983: nos. 39, 41, 43; von Graeve 1986c: pl. 6,1. Two examples, F. Naumann 1983: no. 37 and no. 42, are shown with both hands by the side.

30. F. Naumann 1983: no. 39; von Graeve 1986c: 23.

31. C. Blümel 1964: no. 44; von Graeve 1986a: pl. 9, 3. Double Meter votive naiskoi are discussed by Price 1971: 53–54.

ther remove from a Phrygian antecedent is presented by one of the two double naiskoi: while it is otherwise identical with the reliefs designated as Meter votives, it bears a dedication to the Nymphs.[32] Meter appears together with the Nymphs in Late Classical and Hellenistic reliefs, and it is possible that the connection between Meter and the Greek Nymphs was made as early as the sixth century B.C.[33]

The date of these Milesian reliefs, suggested by parallels with Ionian korai, should probably be placed in the second quarter of the sixth century B.C. This raises the question of why these Meter votives first appeared in the Greek world during the first half of the sixth century. The Greeks certainly knew of the Phrygians well before this time. They had had commercial and diplomatic contacts with central Phrygia since at least the eighth century B.C.;[34] moreover, there are several references to Phrygians in early Greek poetry, particularly the *Iliad*.[35] Some have suggested that the Anatolian Mother was known earlier but had been absorbed into the cult of a more powerful Greek divinity. Finds at the sanctuary of Artemis at Ephesos, for example, suggest that more than one female divinity was worshipped there during the seventh century B.C., but the separate cults had been subsumed into the single cult of Artemis a century later. If one of these were the cult of Meter (as the excavator postulated), this might explain why an early cult of Meter left few traces in the archaeological material.[36]

The large corpus of Meter votives from Miletos suggests a more probable explanation. While the Greeks' knowledge of Meter could have come through contacts between the cities of central Phrygia and the Ionian coast, a closer and more contin-

32. Von Graeve 1986c: 25, pl. 6, 2.

33. I think this is more likely than von Graeve's interpretation that the piece depicts two Nymphs (von Graeve 1986c: 25), for Nymphs are not normally shown in a naiskos frame. For a later example of Meter with the Nymphs, note a relief from Paros, F. Naumann 1983: no. 427, pl. 29. Meter's relationship with the Nymphs is discussed in chapters 6 and 7. Note also a Hellenistic statuette of Meter dedicated to the Muses, Roller 1991: 134; this piece demonstrates that Meter votives could be dedicated to other divinities.

34. The evidence is discussed by DeVries 1980, Roller 1983: 299–301, and Muscarella 1989. Herodotos 1.14, records that Midas, the Phrygian ruler at Gordion during the late eighth century B.C., dedicated his throne at the sanctuary of Apollo at Delphi.

35. *Iliad* 2.862, 3.184–85 and 401, 16.718–19 (Hekabe's home on the Sangarios River), 18.291, 24.545; Homeric Hymn to Aphrodite 112, 137; Archilochos, West 1989–92: fr. 42; Alcman, Page 1962: fr. 126; Hipponax, West 1989–92: fr. 27; Stesichoros, Page 1962: fr. 212.

36. Bammer 1982: 81–84; 1984: 11 (an explanation also adopted by Rein 1993: 59–63). The so-called hawk priestesses, the ivory statuettes of women carrying a hawk in their hands or on their heads (Akurgal 1961: figs. 167–69; Muss 1983: 102–4; Bammer 1985: figs. 21, 22), have often been thought to support a connection between Artemis and Meter because of the frequency of the hawk as an attribute of the Phrygian Matar. I am not persuaded by these arguments. The hawk-bearing figures may simply allude to Artemis's persona as goddess of the hunt. Note that in Sardis, the site of another prominent Artemis sanctuary, the deities Artemis and Meter were clearly separate entities (see Hanfmann and Waldbaum 1969). Moreover, there is no evidence of the identity of the earliest deities worshipped at the Ephesian Artemision. It is quite possible that a native Anatolian cult underlies the Artemision; Strabo 14.1.21 reports that the shrine was founded on an earlier Carian site. Bammer's statement that this deity was Meter/Kybele is, however, unfounded speculation. Although there was a cult of Meter at Ephesos, discussed below and in chapter 7, it was not located in the area of the Artemision, but on the Panayir Dağ, several kilometers away.

uous point of contact was available through Greek colonies in the region of the Sea of Marmara and on the southern shore of the Black Sea. The city of Miletos led the way with its colonies at Kyzikos and Sinope, founded during the late seventh and sixth centuries B.C.[37] There was also a prominent Phokaian colony, Lampsakos, on the Sea of Marmara. In this area, on the northwestern border of Phrygian territory, the Greeks would have lived as close neighbors with Phrygian settlements. The material culture at the nearby Phrygian sites of Daskyleion and Doryleion clearly shows the impact of the Greeks on their Phrygian neighbors.[38] Phrygian religious practices could have had an equally strong impact on the Greeks, a point implied by Herodotos's lively anecdote about the Meter cult in Kyzikos.[39] Religious ties between colony and mother city, always one of the strongest bonds in a Greek community, could have led to the introduction of the Meter cult into Miletos and Phokaia, and Miletos's position as leader of the Ionian league would have facilitated the spread of the cult in Ionia.

Another point where Ionian Greek and Anatolian cult interests intersected was in Lydia, specifically through Ionian contacts with Sardis. The excavations at Sardis have yielded evidence of the cult of a female deity strongly resembling Meter. The material remains of cult practice include an altar and a few examples of naiskoi with a standing draped female figure in the architectural frame, similar to the Milesian reliefs of the goddess.[40] Of particular value is a three-dimensional model of an Ionic temple that depicts a goddess standing as if in the temple door (fig. 38).[41] The identity of this goddess is uncertain, and one would assume that the Lydians called her Kubaba, the native Anatolian goddess attested through Herodotos's testimony and by inscription.[42] The pose and costume of the Sardis goddess and her placement in the "temple" frame, however, present close formal similarities to the Ionian statuettes of Meter. The Sardis goddess stands in a perfectly frontal pose, flanked by upright wavy lines, perhaps indicating snakes. She wears a Greek chiton and mantle,

37. Graf 1985: 111–15; Rein 1993: 40–44; Rein 1996: 229–30.
38. For a discussion of Greek colonization in the region of the Sea of Marmara, see Graham 1971: 39–42. Graham's lucid discussion of Greek-Phrygian relations in this area is marred by his assumption that Phrygian influence in the region would have ceased after the pressures of the Kimmerians on Phrygia in the early seventh century B.C. In fact, Phrygia remained a strong cultural (if not political) force in the region well into the sixth century B.C., as material from the recent excavations at Daskyleion indicates (see Mellink 1993: 121). As an example of the melding of Greek and Phrygian religious symbolism, note a Phrygian grave stele from the Phrygian city of Dorylaion (modern Eskişehir) illustrating a winged female figure holding a lion cub upside-down (F. Naumann 1983: pl. 12a), a piece in Hellenic style but very close to Phrygian iconography.
39. Herodotos 4.76. This passage is discussed further in chapter 6 below.
40. On the altar, located in the Pactolus North section of Sardis, see Rein 1993: 64–67. On the naiskoi, see Hanfmann 1961: 48–49, fig. 31 (from Dede Mezari, a nearby site); 1964: 40–45, fig. 25, and 43–44, fig. 27.
41. Hanfmann 1964: fig. 25, described more fully in Hanfmann and Ramage 1978: no. 7, 43–51, figs. 20–50, and Rein 1993: 75–112, a special study devoted to this relief.
42. Herodotos 5.102; the inscription, *kuvav* incised on a pottery sherd, is discussed by Gusmani 1975: 28–30.

FIGURE 37. Meter naiskos
from Miletos. Early sixth century B.C.
Courtesy, Deutsches Archäologisches
Institut, Istanbul.

and holds her skirt to the side in her right hand, while in her left hand is an object
held across her chest. This object is much worn, but the folds of the drapery over the
left breast suggest that it was something small, perhaps a bird or a pomegranate,
on analogy with contemporary statuettes from Samos or Miletos.[43] Thus the Sardis
goddess is a direct Lydian counterpart to the early Greek images of the standing
goddess. Her name may have been Kubaba, but her iconographic form is that of the
Greek Meter.

43. The Miletos statuettes are cited above; for parallels with contemporary statuettes from Samos,
see Rein 1993: 103–4. Hanfmann and Ramage 1978: 45, assumed that the Sardis goddess held a lion across
her chest, and Hanfmann thought he could see a lion's paw, but Rein 1993: 78–79, states that she is unable to detect this.

The sculpted decoration on the other three sides of the Sardis temple model adds further information on cult rites. On the sides and back of the piece are engaged Ionic columns. In between them is relief sculpture, placed as if to imitate relief or painted designs that would have been found on an actual temple. Several of these panels depict activities that presumably formed part of the ritual activities included in the worship of the goddess, such as prayer, drinking, and dancing. Other panels illustrate scenes that seem to allude to the mythological ancestry of the Lydian royal house. On both sides of the temple model are lions, shown so that they seem to disappear behind the columns.[44] The lions have no part in the narrative scenes, but rather appear to have a symbolic function, serving as an emblem of the goddess's strength and power.

The Sardis piece seems to be transitional between the Phrygian and Ionian Greek depictions of the goddess. The figure of the goddess herself is Greek in style, although the snakes on either side of her may refer to Lydian myth.[45] The scenes on the back of the temple model also seem to treat Lydian myth, while the lions on the

44. Hanfmann and Ramage 1978: figs. 33–37, 39–41 (the scenes of worship); figs. 47–48 (scenes of myth); figs. 42–43 (lions); Rein 1993: 81–99, figs. 9–26
45. Rein 1993: 79–80.

side of the Sardis temple model were surely influenced by Paleo-Phrygian rock reliefs such as Arslankaya or Arslantaş, not only in the choice of the lion, but also in the formal symmetry of the placement. Thus the Sardis temple model, in combining both Greek and Anatolian features, illustrates how Greek style could be adapted to Anatolian iconography, and conversely how Anatolian themes could be treated by a sculptor with close affinities to Greek art.

The conspicuous placing of the lions on the Sardis piece is a point of particular interest. The lions on the Sardis temple monument may be more than a Lydian adaptation of a Phrygian religious motif, for the lion was also a powerful symbol of the Lydian royal family, used in coinage and in royal cult objects.[46] The prominence of the lion in cult objects dedicated to Kubaba, a goddess who protects cities, may have served a dual function: it advertised the goddess's power and also reinforced the power of the Lydian king by symbolizing the support he enjoyed from Kubaba/Meter. The lion of Lydian cult is noteworthy also for its impact on the Greeks. While the lion is not, apart from the Arslankaya façade, one of the common attributes of Phrygian Matar, it was to become a standard attribute of the Greek Meter, as discussed below. The lion's frequency in Lydian cult objects may have been one reason for its ready acceptance as a symbol of Greek Meter.

Greek images of Meter move one step further from their Anatolian counterparts during the mid sixth century B.C. with the appearance of a series of reliefs depicting a seated figure. First found in several Ionian Greek cities, including Smyrna, Erythrai, Klazomenai, Miletos, Ephesos, and Kyme,[47] the type spread to the Aegean islands of Samos, Chios, Thasos, and Amorgos,[48] and was carried by emigration to the western Mediterranean, to Sicily, southern Italy, and the Phokaian colony of Massalia (modern Marseilles).[49] These objects depict a female figure seated on a substantial throne, wearing a long gown and a low headdress with a veil. She is framed within a niche resembling an architectural façade, her naiskos, usually with a pointed

46. Note the conspicuous presence of the lion on early coinage from Lydia (Kraay 1976: 24, 29–31) and in Lydian sculpture (Ratté 1989: 380). Croesus dedicated a gold lion to the cult of Apollo at Delphi (Herodotos 1.50).

47. Möbius 1916: 166, n. 2, gives a list of the seated Meter votives (known at that time). For Meter reliefs in north Ionia, see Graf 1985: 318 (Erythrai), 388–89 (Klazomenai), 419–20 (Phokaia), and in general 108. Meter reliefs from Ionia are discussed as a group by F. Naumann 1983: 124–36, nos. 48–68. To her list should be added a work from Didyma, Tuchelt 1970: L 87.

48. F. Naumann 1983: nos. 56, 56a (Chios); nos. 61, 62 (Samos); nos. 113–17 (Thasos); no. 65 (Amorgos).

49. Seated Meter votives in Sicily and Italy, Sfameni Gasparro 1996: 54–55. Votives from Massalia, Froehner 1897: 11–18, nos 23–63 = F. Naumann 1983: nos. 69–108. Froehner's no. 40 is not an image of Meter; it is identified by him as Venus, but Vermaseren, *CCCA* V, no. 292, calls this a sixth-century B.C. image of Attis. The piece very likely does represent Attis, for the figure wears the typical pointed cap and short tunic of later Attis representations, but it is unlikely to be a work of the sixth century B.C. The form of the naiskos, with elaborate Ionic capitals on Corinthian pilasters, and the use of a drill on the piece suggest a Roman work. Froehner's description of the context of all these pieces merely states that they were found lying face down, used as the underpinning of an (undated) mosaic floor; this context would not rule out a later date.

gable. While the goddess can be shown with her hands resting on her knees,[50] often she has an object in her lap, which in a few examples is clear enough to be identified as a lion.[51] One group of six naiskos reliefs depicting the goddess holding her lion was found in graves near Kyme (fig. 39),[52] and other examples of the goddess with lion type are known from Smyrna, Samos, Thasos, and Massalia.[53] Thus these statuettes introduce the seated pose, costume, and lion attribute of the goddess that was to become her standard iconography in the Greek world until late antiquity.

Exactly why the goddess's visual form changed from the standing image found in Phrygia and Lydia to a seated image is uncertain. It is possible that familiarity with the Greek tradition of seated statues at Ionian sanctuaries such as Didyma may have made the seated pose more attractive. Indeed, several of the seated Meter votives, such as the pieces from Kyme, depict the seated goddess wearing a chiton with three vertical folds in between the legs, a detail also found on seated figures from Didem.[54] It may also be that, to a Greek, the pose of the deity enthroned projected a stronger expression of power and awe, an important element in the worship of Meter.[55] The large relief of a seated female figure carved into the rock façade on Mount Sipylos, near Kyme, may have furnished a model for such a figure of awe; although this is a work of the Hittite Empire period, it was identified by Hellenistic Greek inscriptions as Meter Sipylene, and the Greeks of the sixth century B.C. may have also have connected this figure with the goddess Meter.[56]

The date of the Greek seated figures of Meter is suggested through parallels with seated figures from Didyma, from the mid sixth century B.C. The only known historical context useful for chronology, that of the group of seated statuettes from the Phokaian colony of Massalia, supports this suggestion. The colony was founded about 600 B.C., and the mother city of Phokaia was abandoned in the middle of the sixth century B.C.[57] This indicates that the iconographic type had been formed by that time, since it was available to the Phokaians to transfer to their new settlement in the west.

The naiskoi from Ionian Greek cities suggest how the visual form of the Greek Mother Goddess developed, first as a standing image and then in the seated pose with the attribute of the lion. This image of the seated goddess with lions quickly

50. F. Naumann 1983: nos. 48–55. Salviat 1964: no. 92.
51. In one example, F. Naumann 1983: no. 66, the goddess holds a hare on her lap.
52. Reinach 1889. He describes five statuettes (three now lost) and one under life-size statue.
53. Smyrna, F. Naumann 1983: cat. no. 60; Samos, Freyer-Schauenburg 1974: no. 69; Thasos, Salviat 1964: 241, no. 2, fig. 3; Massalia, F. Naumann 1983: no. 90.
54. Compare two seated female statues from Didyma, Tuchelt 1970: K 45 (now in London), K 58, and a seated male, K 55, with one of the seated statuettes from Kyme, Tuchelt 1970: L 90. All have the same trait of vertical folds falling between the two legs.
55. Connor 1988: 186, makes a similar observation on the seated image of the Nymph.
56. For a discussion of this relief and its identification as Meter Sipylene, see chapter 7, p. 200 and n. 58 there.
57. Langlotz 1966: 16–17.

spread to other parts of the Greek world. It appears in the western Mediterranean
not only at Massalia but also in southern Italy at Velia.[58] In addition, the type appears in Aigina and in Athens, as indicated by a series of terracotta figurines from the
Acropolis in Athens that depict a seated female figure with a lion on her lap; these
date from the second half of the sixth century.[59]

The Peloponnesos has also furnished several examples. Two small statuettes de-

58. Ibid.: 32, fig. 38, a piece from Velia. For the Massaliote examples, see n. 49 above.
59. Statuette from Aigina, F. Naumann 1983: no. 112. Terracotta figurines from Athens, Franz Winter
1903: I, 43, n. 4; 50, n. 2a, b, c, 3; *CCCA* II no. 359. F. Naumann 1983: no. 111, pl. 19, 3, identified a statuette depicting a seated female figure from the Athenian Acropolis as a sixth-century B.C. Kybele votive,
but damage to the figure's lap has erased any trace of an object such as a lion, making this identification
tentative; cf. the comments of La Genière 1985: 696, n. 15.

picting a female figure seated on a throne flanked by lions are known from Sparta,[60] and a statuette found in Arkadia may also be an early cult image.[61] Another sanctuary to Meter was located in Akriai, in the southernmost part of the Peloponnesos, a site that Pausanias identified as an ancient shrine of the Mother of the gods.[62] Taken together, the presence of these statuettes of Meter suggests a well-established cult in several areas of the Peloponnesos by the end of the sixth century. The transmission of the cult to the Peloponnesos may well have been facilitated by contact with Lydian cult centers. Direct communication between Sardis and Sparta is attested by Herodotos, and religious and intellectual contacts between the two areas are underlined by the ancient tradition that the poet Alcman was born in Sardis but produced his poetry in Sparta.[63]

Thus far we have considered only Phrygian and Lydian models for Greek cult images of Meter. There were, however, other sources of influence within the Aegean world that probably had a significant effect in forming the visual image and character of the Greek Meter. One is a possible antecedent in Minoan and Mycenaean religious practice. The only suggestion of a Mother Goddess in Mycenaean cult is one citation on a Pylos tablet, which records a large quantity of oil dedicated to Mater Teija, the Divine Mother.[64] Since this title only occurs once, its precise meaning is unknown, but this figure is not the Mother of the gods, and thus seems unlikely to be the ancestress of the first-millennium Meter Kybele.[65] Minoan cult, however, offers a possible model in a frequently recurring scene in Minoan art, the figure of a standing female deity flanked by lions, found on seals and sealings.[66] This deity is often shown standing on mountaintops, suggesting that her power derives from control over the untamed mountain environment, as symbolized by her lion attendants.[67] The specific identity of the Bronze Age goddess is unknown, but the corre-

60. La Genière 1985: figs. 2, 5; 1993, figs. 1, 3.

61. La Genière 1985: 711–13, figs. 7–8; 1993, figs. 4–6. On the cult of Meter in Arkadia, see Pausanias 8.44.3.

62. Pausanias 3.22.4. La Genière 1986: 31, fig. 1.

63. Herodotos 1.69–70. On Alcman, see the *Suda*, s.v. Ἀλκμάν, and an epigram in the *Anthologia palatina* 7.709, a Hellenistic work but ascribed to Alcman; it refers to the poet's interest in the cult of Kybele. For a discussion of the material, see La Genière 1985: 699–700.

64. Pylos tablet PY 1202; for the text, see Palmer 1963: 241, Gérard-Rousseau 1968: 138, and Bennet and Olivier 1973: 154. The quantity of oil dedicated implies a figure of some importance, perhaps to be identified with Demeter (thus Gérard-Rousseau) or with a minor deity called Theia, otherwise unknown, apart from a brief mention by Hesiod, *Theogony* 135, 371. Palmer proposed that this title did not refer to a divinity, but to a human priestess. The statement of Robertson 1996: 240, that this was "one of the few major deities named in Linear B" is inaccurate; not only do other Greek major deities appear in Linear B tablets, but a single mention of Meter Theia does not prove that she was a major deity.

65. The arguments of Robertson 1996: 302–3, that the historically attested Mother of the gods was a Mycenaean pastoral deity are unpersuasive; neither the Phrygian Matar nor the Meter of Homeric Hymn 14 has any connection with pastoralism, but rather with predators and the untamed wilds of the mountains, the antithesis of pastoralism.

66. For examples, see Spartz 1962: 28–31, 99–101, nos. 1–6, 15. Mycenaean renderings of this scene are heavily dependent on Minoan precedents, so I consider the scene Minoan.

67. See Peatfield 1989, on the importance of peak sanctuaries in Minoan palatial religion and their survival in popular cult after the collapse of the palatial hierarchy.

spondences in iconography between this deity and the earliest representations of the Phrygian Mother Goddess in the Greek world are striking. One recognizable descendant of the Bronze Age goddess in first-millennium B.C. Greece may be the seated goddess depicted with lions above the lintel of the seventh-century B.C. temple at Prinias, on Crete.[68] There is no evidence that the Prinias figure was regarded as a mother goddess, but one wonders if survival of an Aegean predecessor, whose status was indicated through the symbolism of powerful animals, was one reason why the Phrygian Mother Goddess found ready acceptance in Greece. The similarities of iconography (both deities appear with lions) and sacred space (both are associated with mountains and with doorways) seem too close to be coincidental. As we shall see, in the fifth century B.C., there are frequent references to close links between Meter and Crete, and this link may well derive from memory of cult practice on Crete.[69]

Another visual image that may have influenced early Greek depictions of Meter is the motif of the Potnia Theron, or Mistress of Animals, a class of images found in the Orientalizing period (so called because of the preponderance of motifs from the Near East in Greek art). The motif consists of a standing female figure (the Potnia) flanked by a pair of wild animals; these are usually lions, but can also be birds, deer, or fantasy animals such as griffins.[70] The identity of the Potnia ("Powerful Lady" in Greek) is uncertain. She may simply be an abstract genius figure or she may be a goddess, in which case she could be identified with any one of several Greek goddesses, including Artemis and Hera as well as Meter. As a symbol of nature and power, she moves in the same sphere as the Phrygian Mother Goddess.[71] The type seems to have been introduced into Greece from the Near East during the second millennium B.C. and became common in Minoan and Mycenaean art. Near Eastern centers such as Assyria and Cyprus furnished additional source material during the Early Iron Age.[72] The motif was widely used as a decorative design in vase painting, small plaques, jewelry, and other minor arts.[73] The very ubiquity of the motif and its usage in contexts unconnected with cult may mean that it need not be directly con-

68. Vermaseren 1977: fig. 2; Boardman 1978: fig. 32.4 The connection between the seated image of Meter and the Prinias figures is discussed by Christou 1968: 47.

69. Note the comments of La Genière 1985: 715–16.

70. The phrase originally referred to Artemis (*Iliad* 21.470). For a discussion of the Potnia Theron in early Greek art, see Spartz 1962 and Christou 1968. On the Potnia Theron motif in Anatolian monuments, F. Naumann 1983: 101–10.

71. As F. Naumann 1983: 101–10 noticed, the Potnia Theron motif is found in Phrygia also, notably on a stele from Dorylaion depicting a winged genius figure (F. Naumann 1983: pl. 12, 1) and on an alabastron from Gordion (F. Naumann 1983: pl. 12, 2). Like the seated pose of the goddess, the Potnia Theron motif seems, however, to have come to Phrygia from Greece, and it was not a feature of Phrygian iconography developed from the representations of Matar.

72. Spartz 1962: 99–105, nos. 1–38.

73. A well-known example of the motif used as a decorative ornament on pottery is found on the handle on the François krater, *ABV* 76, 1; for the Potnia Theron on jewelry, see Christou 1968: 213, no. 19; 220, nos. 13–22; 225, nos. 10–12. Other examples have been collected by Christou 1968: 211–28.

nected with sacred images. Its presence does, however, establish Greek interest in the concept of a powerful goddess as tamer of animals.

As an example of the conflation of images in early Greek art, we may consider a large Boiotian relief pithos of the seventh century B.C., originally placed over a grave.[74] The relief scene on the pithos depicts a standing female deity wearing a long formal gown and a crown with leafy branches extending from it. She is shown as if embraced at the waist by two smaller female figures, and the group of three is flanked by two lions standing upright on their hind legs, with their mouths open, as if roaring. The chief female figure has been identified as Artemis or Hera, but may simply be an unnamed divinity of regenerative powers over both plants and animals, shielding her human devotees.[75] Her animal companions, the rampant lions, are very reminiscent of the lions that flank the Phrygian Mother Goddess in Arslankaya, in southwestern Phrygia, and the presentation of this figure, the female divinity who represents both power and protection for her worshippers, strongly echoes the role of the Phrygian Mother. Although probably not directly influenced by the Phrygian Mother Goddess, the figure on the pithos vividly illustrates Greek receptiveness to the image of a powerful goddess accompanied by lions.

In the late sixth century B.C., a new element appears in the iconography of Greek Meter votives, one that was to become an important symbol in the Hellenic cult of Meter. This is the tympanum, regularly depicted as if balanced on the left arm of Meter. While the Greek image of the seated goddess with the lion on her lap can be traced, however indirectly, to Anatolian representations, the attribute of the tympanum has no Anatolian precedent. Among the earliest examples are votive reliefs depicting the seated goddess holding a tympanum in her left arm from Thasos. In two such reliefs, the goddess appears seated with a tympanum on her left arm, a lion in her lap, and a shallow bowl in her outstretched right hand, in other words, with the three attributes that were to form the standard iconography of Meter during the fifth century B.C. and later.[76] Other examples of Meter with the tympanum may be found in a rock sanctuary near Phokaia, discussed below, and in Ephesos.[77] From

74. Christou 1968: 210, no. 2. Vermaseren 1977: fig. 1.
75. Identification as Artemis, discussed by Christou 1968: 16; as Hera, Vermaseren 1977: fig. 1. Christou 1968: 18–19, interprets the figure as a *kourotrophos*, a nurturing female divinity derived directly from a Near Eastern model.
76. Salviat 1964: no. 2, fig. 3; no. 5, fig. 7. Note also Salviat 1964: no. 4, fig. 6, and F. Naumann 1983: no. 113; both of these works also depict the seated goddess with lion, but no tympanum. In one example, the goddess apparently once held an object in her left arm, but its identity is no longer clear, Salviat 1964: no. 1, fig. 4; F. Naumann 1983: no. 114.
One other example of a goddess with lions, the goddess shown driving a lion chariot, has been attributed to the Archaic period; in this context the female divinity driving a lion chariot on the north frieze of the Siphnian Treasury at Delphi has often been identified as Kybele (see. F. Naumann 1983: no. 121, pl. 21, 2; *CCCA* II: no. 41). This deity is not Kybele, however; see E. Simon 1984: 7, and Brinkmann 1985: 101, who identifies the figure as Themis. Another pose, which was to be popular later, that of the goddess sitting on the back of a lion, did not enter the Greek iconographic repertory until the later fourth century B.C. (Pliny, *NH* 35.36.109; F. Naumann 1983: 233).
77. F. Naumann 1983: cat. no. 64; see the discussion of F. Naumann on p. 136.

this point on, the tympanum was to be one of the most common attributes of Meter, surviving until the late Roman era. It was routinely depicted on the left side of the goddess, held in the crook of her arm resting on the throne. The implication seems to be that the goddess will strike this instrument with her right hand, as her worshippers did.

The comparatively late date of the tympanum's appearance may seem surprising, given its prominence and ubiquity in later images of Meter; in fact, the Greeks themselves assumed that the tympanum had always been one of the goddess's chief symbols.[78] The origin of the tympanum did indeed lie in the ancient Near East, where it was used in cult rituals in Assyria, in the Neo-Hittite centers in southeastern Anatolia, and on Cyprus, although there is as yet no evidence for its use in Phrygia.[79] The Greeks were surely aware of the instrument's Oriental origin, and may have associated the tympanum with the Phrygian goddess because she too came to Greece from the Orient. The prominence of the instrument in Greece is especially interesting, however, because the presence of the tympanum implies the use of loud pulsing percussion in cult rituals; thus it appears to signal elements of emotional tension leading to open, unrestrained behavior among the goddess's followers. Such emotionalism and unrestrained behavior has always been thought to be typical of the Phrygian rites of Meter, directly transferred from her Anatolian background, but the presence of the tympanum only in Greek Meter votives, not in Phrygian ones, calls that assumption into question. The Greek Mother of the gods loved the sound of the tympanum and castanets, as the fourteenth Homeric Hymn assures us, but one wonders whether it was Meter's marginal status in the Greek world that made her cult an attractive forum for open emotional expression through raucous music. I shall return to this point again, but it is worth emphasizing that the only empirical evidence for the origin of such emotional expression in the Meter cult suggests that the concept was originally Greek, not Phrygian.

The early images of Meter were surely votive offerings, but their exact use, in public urban shrines, private domestic shrines, or in extra-urban sanctuaries, is uncertain. The statuettes from Kyme were found in graves, and some of the Milesian examples were from mixed debris with other votive offerings, but most of the other examples are casual finds without informative context.[80] Only occasionally is there evidence for the circumstances under which the goddess was worshipped. The sanc-

78. Note *Anth. pal.* 7.709, a Hellenistic epigram by Alexander of Aetolia (fl. ca. 280 B.C.), attributed to the seventh-century B.C. poet Alcman of Sparta, which mentions the clashing tympana of Kybele. Tympana are also mentioned in Homeric Hymn 14.

79. Aign 1963: 58–64, 158–62 (Cyprus), 173–77 (Karatepe, a Neo-Hittite site), 366 (Assyria). As an example of early Greek knowledge of the tympanum, note the depiction of the instrument on a Phoenician bronze bowl of ca. 700 B.C., found at Olympia (Aign 1963: 161, n. 1) and on a bronze bowl from Cyprus, found in Sparta (Canciani 1970: pl. VI, VII).

80. On the Kyme statuettes, see Reinach 1889. The recently discovered statuettes from Miletos came from a pit of mixed debris that included pottery and a fragment of a kouros (von Graeve 1986b: 43–47). Almost all other examples are without context or were recovered from later reuse.

tuary at Daskalopetra on Chios, dated to the late sixth or the fifth century B.C., furnishes one example. This monument, a natural rock formation shaped into a shrine, includes a carved niche with a female figure seated on a throne, with her feet resting on a footstool.[81] She may have held a lion on her lap, as was recorded by earlier travelers, although few traces of this remain now.[82] The niche in which the goddess sits is framed by pillars with bases carved in the form of lions' claws, while a low gable surmounts the opening.[83] Thus the niche imitates the façade of a building, a likeness further emphasized by reliefs of two striding lions on the two side walls of the "building." Along the east side of the monument, facing the goddess's image, and along the monument's north and south sides were low benches carved out of the natural rock. The "bench" on the east side may have been an altar for animal sacrifices and for placement of votive offerings.[84] Thus the Daskalopetra Monument may be the earliest extant cult image of Meter (as opposed to a votive offering) in the Greek world.

The Daskalopetra Monument is similar in several key points to the Phrygian monuments of the Mother Goddess. These include the placement of the goddess's image within a carved niche imitating an architectural structure, the lions on either side of the niche, and the setting of the monument, a natural rock formation outside an urban area. The location of this shrine near a spring also recalls the frequent association of Phrygian shrines with springs. Yet, while the overall plan of Daskalopetra is reminiscent of Phrygian shrines, the details of the low flat gable, lion-footed pillars,[85] and seated statue are of Hellenic origin. The monument has become an Ionic shrine to the Greek Meter.[86]

Another Ionic shrine in a rural setting is found near the city of Phokaia. Here a set of rock-cut stairs leads up to a cliff carved with close to a hundred votive niches.[87] Most of these were empty, but at least two of them retain traces of a female figure carved at the back of the niche, in one case standing and holding a tympanum, and in another case seated, without attributes. The poor state of preservation makes it uncertain how many other niches also contained a carved figure. The earliest phases of the sanctuary are probably to be dated to the late sixth or the fifth century B.C. Both the rock-cut statues and the niches appear to derive from the Phrygian tradition of cutting small schematic idols of the goddess onto rock outcrops.[88] During the fourth century B.C. and later, such rock-cut niches were to become a feature of

81. For discussions of this monument, see Rubensohn and Watzinger 1928; Boardman 1959: 193–96; Romano 1980: 344–49; F. Naumann 1983: 150–53; Graf 1985: 107–13.
82. Graf 1985: 107.
83. Boardman 1959: 193–96.
84. Romano 1980: 344–49.
85. According to Boardman 1959: 191–96, the use of lions' paws was a characteristic feature of Chian architecture.
86. Graf 1985: 109.
87. Langlotz 1969: 383–85; F. Naumann 1983: 153–55; Graf 1985: 419–20.
88. A close parallel is furnished by rock-cut niches at Findik, near Kütahya (Haspels 1971: 92).

Meter sanctuaries in other Ionian cities, including Ephesos, Erythrai, and possibly Samos,[89] but the Phokaian niches seem to have been among the earliest in the Greek world.

The placement of these cult objects and sanctuaries suggests that Meter was worshipped primarily at extra-urban shrines and in private cult. Evidence of Meter's presence in urban centers is much rarer. The figurines from the Athenian Acropolis indicate interest in the cult of Meter in the city of Athens during the sixth century B.C., but these too appear to be private votives, not part of a cult of the Athenian polis. Only in the early fifth century B.C. did Meter receive an official civic cult center in Athens, the Metroön in the Athenian Agora.[90]

In sum, Meter appears in the Greek world during the late seventh or the sixth century B.C. She was a vivid and forceful character, at home in the mountains with predators and clashing castanets and tympana. Scattered literary references and numerous statuettes depicting the goddess indicate that by the second half of the sixth century, her worship had become widespread throughout the Greek world, in Ionia, Athens, the Peloponnesos, southern Italy, Sicily, and southern France. Both the Greek name of the goddess, Kybele, and her cult title, Meter, were derived from her Phrygian counterpart, as were the earliest Greek representations of her. Taken together, the evidence gives the impression of a cult that gradually filtered into the Greek world through personal exchanges between Greeks and Anatolians, as the Greeks gained increasing knowledge of Anatolia through commercial, military, and settlement contacts. It became established earlier in the cities of Ionia and their colonies, both northern and western, which had more contact with the Phrygians and Lydians. Meter's acceptance may have been aided in part by the fact that visual images of her made use of a symbol system, the heraldically placed lions flanking the goddess, that was already known in Greece and used for other Greek deities and for indefinite figures such as the Potnia Theron.

During this early period of contact, however, the Hellenic Mother Goddess underwent certain changes in both name and appearance that mark her as a deity whose subsequent cult would be different from that of her Anatolian predecessor. One of the Phrygian Mother's epithets had become her principal Greek name, Kybele. The Hellenic Mother Goddess was shown wearing a Greek, not a Phrygian costume. The visual image of Meter changed significantly as the goddess turned into an imposing seated figure. The Greek Meter used only one of the Phrygian goddess's attributes, the lion, and she acquired a new attribute, the tympanum, which had no antecedent in Anatolia, yet was to become a crucial symbol of her character in the Greek world. This mixture of Phrygian names and cult symbols with symbols not of

89. Graf 1985: 420.

90. A sixth-century B.C. Metroön, identified by H. Thompson 1937: 135–40, 205–7 (for the proposed reconstruction, see H. Thompson 1972: pl. 4), probably never existed; see the discussion by Stephen G. Miller 1995: n. 5. The history of the Metroön in the Agora is discussed in chapter 6.

Phrygian origin undoubtedly facilitated the acceptance of the non-Greek goddess into Greek cult, yet created an identity and visual form that marked Meter as a distinct entity.

The actual evidence for the establishment of the cult of Meter, slender as it is, gives a glimpse of the progress of her reception in the Greek world during the sixth century B.C. The sporadic nature of the evidence, however, makes the character of the early Meter cult and the reasons for its attraction more difficult to assess. To determine the nature of the early cult of Meter in Greece, we shall have to move beyond a simple review of the evidence.

One significant difference between the Phrygian and Greek cults of the Mother is noteworthy: while the cult monuments of Phrygian Matar seem to represent both elite and popular religious expression of the Phrygian state, the Greek votives were rarely associated with the emerging Greek city-state, the polis. The sanctuaries of Meter in the Peloponnesos and at the rock monuments of Phokaia and Chios were located well away from urban settlements. The goddess appears to have attracted a wide following, but her shrines were not markers of territorial sovereignty around which the Greek polis coalesced.[91] Nor is there any evidence that Meter received the kind of wealthy offerings that the Artemision at Ephesos or the Heraion at Samos attracted; the naiskos statuettes were small, simple objects, and there is no evidence of a temple or other impressive shrine.

Meter's relationship to her Phrygian background poses other problems. Some scholars have assumed that Meter's assimilation into Greek cult involved a process of "domestication" designed to eliminate the "barbarous" features of Phrygian cult.[92] The surviving material, however, gives us no hint of any barbarous features— that is to say, features indicating wild or uncivilized activity—either in Phrygia or in Greece. Moreover, the early iconography of Meter does not seem to have marked her as a distinctly foreign deity or emphasized her non-Greek origins. That was a distinction in status that was to come later.[93]

Another difficulty in assessing the basis of Meter's appeal lies in the uncertainty concerning the meaning attached to the early goddess's title as a Mother Goddess. There is no intimation that she was the Mother and protector of the state, a status I have postulated for the Phrygian Matar. Homeric Hymn 14 addresses her as the Mother of everything, but this seems a little too vague to be meaningful. The concept of a divine mother was already represented in the Hellenic pantheon by well-established female deities such as Rhea, Hera, and Demeter; and as the progenitor

91. On rural sanctuaries and the Greek polis, see de Polignac 1994.
92. The assumption of "barbarism" (usually undefined) in Phrygian cult can be found, inter alia, in La Genière 1985: 716 and Versnel 1990: 107–8. As discussed in chapters 6, 7, and 8, many of the so-called barbarous features of the Meter cult, such as the cult of Attis, were of Greek origin, not Phrygian.
93. See the introductory discussion of Hall 1989, on the ideological division between Greek and barbarian, a division that hardened only after the Persian Wars in the early fifth century B.C.

of all life, Meter impinged on the territory of Aphrodite as well. The use of the Meter votives in private contexts and extra-urban sanctuaries may well reflect the desire of her adherents not to infringe on the gods of the Greek polis.

At the same time, the vagueness in the definition of Meter's divinity suggests the basis of her appeal. The fourteenth Homeric Hymn leads us into a world of wild animals and wild spaces, a world where Meter's preferred residence is apart from the artificial environment, both architectural and social, of human society. This most distinctively Phrygian characteristic of the goddess is resonant in both the archaeological and literary evidence for Meter in the Archaic period. It suggests that the Greeks found in the Meter cult a particular quality of unstructured contact with the divine, a quality that we shall see more forcefully in evidence during the fifth and fourth centuries B.C. Such unstructured contact may have resounded even more powerfully in Greece than it did in Phrygia, because of the private, low-key nature of the Meter cult.

It is interesting to compare the image evoked by the Homeric Hymn to Meter with the sentiments expressed by Homer in book 9 of the *Odyssey*.[94] As Odysseus and his crew arrive at the land of the Cyclopes, they note the natural beauties and abundance of the landscape, but compare these unfavorably with a Greek settlement. A Greek, Odysseus says, would have built a beautiful harbor and ships; he would have tilled the land and made something of the place, not left it in its wild state, as the Cyclopes did. But the Greek Mother of the gods, by avoiding the works of human beings and preferring the wild state of nature, announced a cult presence that was to contrast sharply with many of the Greek definitions of civilization.

Thus by the end of the sixth century, the Greek Meter had entered Greek cult as the deity of wild places and free expression of religious emotion. As the mother of all gods and all humanity, her powers were all-inclusive. Yet she was not a deity whose worship reinforced communal bonds or defined civic identity within a Greek community. These points were to be significant in the goddess's cult during the fifth century B.C. and later.

94. *Odyssey* 9.125–39.

6 · THE CLASSICAL PERIOD

The Anatolian Mother arrived in the Greek world during the late seventh and sixth centuries B.C. Votive offerings to her with a recognizably Hellenic iconography testify that her cult spread rapidly and was well established by the early fifth century. During the Classical period, the fifth and fourth centuries B.C., we see an even more vivid picture of Meter. Not only is there more evidence for the goddess's appearance, rites, and personality, but the evidence offers a richer cross-section of the Greeks' reactions to her, both positive and negative.

In this chapter we can therefore move beyond a chronological summary of the evidence for the Meter cult to a broader consideration of her place in Greek society. We find the goddess a conspicuous figure in Greek cult practice, worshipped at public sanctuaries and addressed with hundreds of private votives. Increasingly, she was assimilated with other Greek goddesses, including Rhea and Demeter, and her rites were linked with those of important Greek divinities such as Dionysos and Pan. Despite this, Meter still occupied a space apart from the Olympian gods, and her rites were often regarded as antithetical to the religious practice of a Greek community. This tension between the conflicting features of the Meter cult, which was absorbed into the mainstream of Greek cult practice yet was held at arm's length, is a key motif in the goddess's position in Classical Greece.

One factor influencing our view of Meter during the Classical period lies in the geographical centers of the Greek world where her cult is best attested. During the fifth and fourth centuries B.C., evidence for the Meter cult is drawn largely from cities on the Greek mainland, with the material from Athens playing an increasingly prominent role. The cities of Ionia, which had formed a crucial intermediary with Anatolia during the period of the goddess's absorption into Greek cult, offer much less information during these two centuries. This, however, is, doubtless a result of their conquest by the Persian Empire and consequent impoverishment, rather than a lack of interest in the cult of Meter, for, as we shall see in chapter 7, the goddess is abundantly represented in Ionia during the Hellenistic period. The resulting emphasis on the Greek mainland in itself imposes a certain slant on our view of the goddess, for the investigation will focus on Greek cities that were further removed from the goddess's Anatolian roots and that often regarded those roots as the mark of an inferior people. Within these cities, Meter came to represent, not the religion and culture of Phrygia, but the Greek concept of an Oriental barbarian deity. This distinction will become important as we review the evidence on Meter in Classical Greece.

RITES AND CULT PRACTICES

Let us look first at Meter's Greek identity and the rituals celebrated for her. The Hellenic concept of Meter is evident, first and foremost, through her titles. Her most frequent form of address was as Μήτηρ θεῶν, the Mother of the gods, a title that first appeared in Homeric Hymn 14 and was to become a standard part of her definition in the Greek world.[1] By the early fifth century, the Greek Mother had become the Μήτηρ Μεγάλη, the Great Mother; to Pindar, who also addresses her as [δέσπ]οιν[αν] Κυβέ[λαν] Ματ[έρα], Mistress Kybele, the Mother.[2] The goddess was the Great Mother to Aristophanes and Euripides as well.[3] In one of the few direct references to her Phrygian identity as a goddess of the mountains, the Greeks addressed her as Μήτηρ ὀρεία, the Mother of the mountains.[4] The association with mountains and wild spaces is more theoretical than actual in the fifth and fourth centuries, for no rural shrines to Meter on the Greek mainland during this period are known; Meter's identification with mountains was not a reference to one sacred place, but a general description of a deity of wild and unknown country.[5] Thus to the Greeks of the

1. Aristophanes, *Birds* 876; Hippocrates, *On the Sacred Disease* 4.22; Euripides, *Helen* 1302; Menander, *Theophoroumene* 27; Page 1962: frs. 764 (Melanippides) and 935, 4 ff. (a hymn from Epidauros; see West 1970: 212–13). The title is standard in votive offerings; note a fourth-century B.C. statuette found in the Athenian Agora, inscribed Κρίτων Μητρὶ θεῶν, (Thompson 1937: 204, fig. 124 = *CCCA* II no. 3 [here fig. 40]), and numerous other examples cited in *CCCA* II (see p. 250).
2. Meter Megale, Pindar, *Dithyramb* II, 9, and fr. 95 (Snell). Despoina Kybele, Pindar, fr. 80 (Snell); for the corrected reading of this fragment, see Henrichs 1972: 84–86. The titles of Meter are extensively discussed by Henrichs 1976; for a list of ancient citations, see pp. 253–54 n. 3. *Despoina*, meaning "Powerful Lady," is not a title unique to Meter but a general term of address used for several goddesses; it is the equivalent of the later *Kyria*, also applied to Meter (see Henrichs 1976: 272 n. 50).
3. Aristophanes, *Birds* 876; Euripides, *Bacchae* 78–79.
4. Sophocles, *Philoktetes* 391–94; Timotheos, Page 1962: no. 791, line 124; Euripides, *Hippolytos* 144, *Cretans* (Austin 1968: fr. 79, line 13), *Helen* 1301–2; Aristophanes, *Birds* 875.
5. Topographical epithets such as Idaia or Dindymene, drawn from a specific mountain sacred to the goddess, were to become common in the Hellenistic and Roman periods, but these rarely occur in Classical Greece. One exception is Euripides' *Orestes* 1453, where the Phrygian slave calls on "Meter Idaia," a form of address perhaps intended to emphasize the character's Phrygian background.

Classical period, the goddess was Kybele, a name regularly used in literary texts, although not in cult votives and inscriptions. She was the Mistress, the Great Mother, and the Mother of the gods. And she was the Mother of the mountains, although in the rather vague sense of a divinity outside the settled landscape, not the guardian of a specific place.

The clearest picture of Meter comes from the large number of votive statuettes and reliefs depicting her. The visual image of Meter, adopted directly from Phrygian representations of her, had become extensively Hellenized by the end of the sixth century B.C. and varied little from that point on. During the Classical period, Meter was normally shown seated on a throne. She wears a chiton, pinned on both shoulders, and a himation, or mantle, draped across her lap; the sculptors often detailed the contrast between the vertical folds of her chiton skirt and the horizontal catenary folds of the mantle over it. She often has a low crown, or polos,[6] and in some cases a veil extending down her back. She carries a tympanum in the crook of her left arm, which rests on the arm of the throne, while her right hand holds an open bowl, a phiale, the standard Greek vessel for pouring offerings to the gods.[7] In many cases, a lion lies curled up in her lap, or two lions in the crouching position appear on either side of throne. Not all images of the goddess have every one of these attributes; combinations of two of the three—for example, lion and phiale, phiale and tympanum, lion and tympanum—are common.

The depiction of Meter that was to be the single most influential representation of the goddess was a cult statue made in the latter part of the fifth century B.C. by Agorakritos of Paros, a pupil of Pheidias, for the Metroön, her temple in the Athenian Agora. This statue has not survived, but literary descriptions and small copies of it provide a fairly clear indication of its appearance.[8] The goddess was seated on a throne, and held a tympanum in her hand; two lions sat under (i.e., next to) her throne. Copies of Agorakritos's work, or variations of it, supplied the model for numerous small votives dedicated to Meter (figs. 40, 41). The literally hundreds of examples that survive show little deviation from this model during the ensuing centuries of her worship, lasting nearly a millennium. The sheer abundance and repetitive nature of these statuettes and reliefs create a sense of monotony, and this circum-

6. The so-called mural crown, the turreted crown that was a common feature of the goddess's iconography in Rome, appears in the Greek world only in the Hellenistic period; the earliest examples may be two terracotta figurines from Pergamon, discussed in chapter 7 (see Töpperwein 1976: nos. 190 and 199).

7. The Latin name of the vessel, *patera,* has gained wider currency in scholarly literature.

8. The work is mentioned by Pliny, *Natural History* 36.17; Pausanias 1.3.5; and Arrian, *Periplous* 9; see Wycherley 1957: testimonia nos. 402, 468, 489, and F. Naumann 1983: 159. The most detailed description is that of Arrian. This statue is variously attributed to Pheidias or his pupil Agorakritos, but it seems more likely that Agorakritos was the sculptor; see von Salis 1913, Despines 1971: 111–23, and F. Naumann 1983: 159–69.

FIGURE 40. Meter naiskos dedicated by Kriton, from the Athenian Agora. Fourth century B.C. Courtesy, American School of Classical Studies at Athens: Agora Excavations.

stance, added to the fact that many of these objects have no secure archaeological context, provenience, or date, limits their usefulness as a source of information on the Meter cult in Greece.[9]

Some useful observations can be made, however, about the source and meaning of the goddess's attributes. The open bowl that the goddess carries in her right hand is perhaps the least distinctive, for such a vessel can be held by several Greek divinities.[10] It symbolizes the liquid offerings made to the divinity by worshippers, and thus proclaims the figure's status as a divinity. A similar vessel is found in representations of Matar in Phrygia, where the Phrygian goddess, not surprisingly, carries a

9. For a list of some of the many hundreds of surviving examples, see F. Naumann 1983: nos. 123–421, statuettes derived from the Agorakritos model; and 422–45, representations of Meter other than the Agorakritos type. Vermaseren, *CCCA* II, lists several hundred examples from various sites in Greece, although his catalogue mixes Classical, Hellenistic, and Roman objects together indiscriminately, and his lists should be used with caution. In particular, *CCCA* II, nos. 683–84 and 695–720, from Cyprus, are not Archaic Greek works, but of late Roman date (cf. Lambrechts 1962: 45, and F. Naumann 1983: 239–40). The remark of Will 1960: 95–96, on the ironic contrast between the abundance of Meter depictions available and the lack of information afforded by them, is very appropriate.

10. On the type of sacrificing deity, see E. Simon 1953. As Simon, p. 7, notes, the type of sacrificing deity becomes especially prominent in the fifth century B.C.

FIGURE 41.   Meter naiskos with male and female attendants,
from the Athenian Agora. Fourth century B.C. Courtesy, American
School of Classical Studies at Athens: Agora Excavations.

Phrygian vessel.[11] The Greek use of a phiale may only be the replacement of a Phrygian vessel with a Greek one. This replacement, however, carried a critical difference in meaning. The Phrygian vessel held by the Phrygian Matar is a common pottery shape, one that would have been in daily usage by human beings, but the Greek phiale was almost always a ritual vessel used for pouring libations. Its presence in Greek Meter votives adds an element of ritual distance to the figure of the Greek goddess. The Greek phiale, moreover, was normally used to pour out libations, not to consume them—in other words, to make an offering, not to receive one.[12] The vessel alludes, not the goddess's character, but to actions that her followers will perform in her honor.

The lion, Meter's regular animal companion, seems the most direct reference to her Anatolian roots. In Phrygia, however, the lion was only one of her animal attributes, and not the most frequent one. The predatory bird, the Phrygian Mother Goddess's most ubiquitous symbol, drops out of the Greek iconography of Meter/Kybele altogether, and with it any implication of the directly helpful benefits from the hunting goddess symbolized by the Phrygian bird of prey. The lion of the Greek Meter votives symbolizes the goddess's strength and power, but also forms a more general allusion to the goddess's Oriental background, a steady reminder of her foreign origins.[13]

If the lion was a Greek adaptation, the tympanum was a Greek addition to the Meter icon. In Greek images, the goddess is always shown holding the tympanum in her left hand, as if preparing to strike it with her right hand. The instrument does not allude to the goddess's sphere of influence, but rather to rites to be performed in her honor, incorporating the emphatically percussive music played by her worshippers, which, as we shall see, formed a distinctive feature of the goddess's rites in Greece. Like the phiale, Meter's tympanum symbolizes the actions of her worshippers, not of the goddess herself.

Thus the Greek iconography of Meter/Kybele presented a goddess who had departed quite far from her Anatolian origins. Some of her Anatolian symbols had disappeared, while others, such as the lion and the phiale, were adapted from her Anatolian origins but carried a different meaning. And one key symbol, the tympanum, had acquired a prominence that it did not have in Anatolian tradition. The goddess had not really been transferred into a Greek deity: few Greek deities are associated with lions,[14] and none apart from Meter/Kybele holds a tympanum. She had, how-

11. Note the round bowl or a spouted jug held by the goddess in Paleo-Phrygian votive reliefs from Gordion, Ankara, and Ayaş, described in chapter 4.

12. E. Simon 1953: 7–8.

13. The lions are usually thought to be symbolic of the wild and unrestrained rituals of Meter's worshippers; note the comment of Versnel 1990: 109, "There were the silent lions of iconography and the roaring adepts in ritual to recall them." This point is explored in greater detail below.

14. Apollo was frequently associated with lions; note, e.g., the row of sculpted lions at the Apollo sanctuary on Delos and an ivory figure of Apollo with a lion from Delphi (Cahn 1950: fig. 1). Shapiro

ever, moved away from a Phrygian image into a Greek concept of what an Oriental deity looked like.

The most memorable picture of the Greek Meter comes, not from her titles or her votive images, but from the actual rituals celebrated by the Greeks for the goddess. These are known through literary texts covering the whole span of the fifth and fourth centuries, and the descriptions they offer of the rituals for Meter express the emotional content of her cult and hint at its appeal to her worshippers.

The rites of Meter were mystery rites, ceremonies that were not held openly for all to see and participate in, but celebrated privately, limited to those who had been initiated into the cult, the mystai.[15] The prohibition against revealing the actual practices of such mystery religions was taken quite seriously by the Greeks,[16] and so we have little idea about the actual sequence of the rites, although there is no reason to suspect that they included anything disreputable.[17] The rites evidently took place at night, and frequent references to the use of torches give a sense of visual drama.[18] The tools of mystery rites, the torches and vessels for purification, appear frequently in the hands of young female and male attendants depicted on Meter reliefs (figs. 41, 42).[19]

The visual drama of such nocturnal rites would have been enhanced by music, and indeed, it is the presence of this music in the rites of Meter that seems to have made the strongest impact on her worshippers and on their often unsympathetic contemporaries. The tympanum, the goddess's newly acquired attribute, figures promi-

1989: 59 (pl. 29c), discusses a black-figured amphora in the British Museum, London B 49; the scene on this vase has been interpreted as depicting Kybele in her naiskos (e.g., by Schefold 1937: 38–39; fig. 5; F. Naumann 1983: 117), but is more likely to represent Apollo.

15. Euripides, *Cretans* (Austin 1968: fr. 79, 10–13); *Bacchae* 78–79. The rites are described as ὄργια (Euripides, *Bacchae* 78) and τελετάς (*Bacchae* 73), the same terms used for mystery rites of other deities, especially Demeter and Dionysos. Another important source of information on the mysteries of Meter is a Hellenistic relief from Lebadeia, *CCCA* II: no. 432, discussed in chapter 7 below.

16. On the strict penalities meted out to those who violated the Mysteries, see Thucydides 6.28; Andokides, *On the Mysteries* 11. Livy 31.14.6–9 records an incident in 200 B.C. in which two young men of Akarnania unwittingly compromised the secrecy of the Eleusinian Mysteries and were put to death as a result.

17. Several modern scholars, e.g., Foucart 1873: 64–65; Bömer 1963: 870–74; and Versnel 1990: 109–10, have implied that the rites of Meter were somehow disgraceful and barbarous. Much of the evidence they cite, however, is drawn from Roman, not Greek literature. In particular, Foucart 1873: 71, n. 3, and Bömer 1963: 873, rely for their judgments on descriptions of the Roman Galli, yet fail to explain why descriptions of Roman activities should be taken as evidence for religious practice in Greek society several centuries earlier. Only rarely does the primary evidence from Classical Greece support such an unattractive picture of the cult of Meter.

18. Nocturnal rites: Pindar, *Pythian* 3.79. Torches: Pindar, *Dithyramb* II.12 (Snell); Euripides, *Cretans* (Austin 1968: Κρῆτες, fr. 79, 13–14); *Bacchae* 146–47.

19. Torch bearers, usually young women: *CCCA* II: nos. 45, 54, 82, 96, 124, 182, 186, 207, 248, 251, 330, 339, 340, 362, 382, (all from Athens), 267, 278, 279, 310, 311, 320 (from the Piraeus), 402 (from Euboia). Meter with a human attendant bearing a jug, *CCCA* II, nos. 45, 54, 186, 208, 248, (from Athens), 267, 278, 310, 311 (from the Piraeus), 386 (from Philiati), 483 (perhaps from Patrai), 519 (Corcyra), 529 (Thasos), 575, 576, 579 (Samos), 583 (Tenos), 668 (Kalymna); jug carried by Hermes, *CCCA* II, nos. 362 (from Athens), 508 (unknown).

FIGURE 42. Votive relief of Meter and two attendants, from the Piraeus. Mid fourth century B.C. Courtesy, Antikensammlung, Staatliche Museen zu Berlin, Preussischer Kulturbesitz.

nently in descriptions of her rituals,[20] as do the flute and the cymbals.[21] The flute can be ἀδυβόας, sweet-breathing,[22] but the percussive instruments clearly were used to create a sense of emotional tension. The use of terms like βρόμιος, roaring, and κτύπον, resounding, to describe the aural effects of these instruments evokes their loud, pulsing rhythm, a point often reinforced through the meter and rhythm of the poetry, most notably in the opening chorus of Euripides' *Bacchae*.[23] A passage from a fragmentary tragedy of the late-fifth-century B.C. poet Diogenes gives an especially lively account of the goddess's music:

τυμπάνοισι καὶ ῥόμβοισι καὶ χαλκοκτύπων
βόμβοις βρεμούσας ἀντίχερσι κυμβάλων
σοφὴν θεῶν ὑμνῳδὸν ἰατρόν θ' ἅμα

[the Phrygian women who] with their tympana and the whirling of the resounding brass and the clashing of cymbals in their hands roar out the wise and healing music of the gods.[24]

The music was often accompanied by dance, and the frenzied movements and gestures of the dance are vividly described.[25] A fragmentary passage by an unknown tragedian combines all these elements, the Phrygian flute, the cymbals, the tympanum, the encircling dance; all these, we are told, are pleasing to the Great Goddess.[26]

We get some sense of the total effect of music and dance from an Attic red-figured volute krater, now in Ferrara, from the Group of Polygnotos, of about 440 B.C.[27] The main scene on the krater illustrates two divinities, one female, one male, both seated within a naiskos framed by Doric columns (fig. 43). Each holds out a phiale in the right hand as if making an offering. The female deity is surely Kybele/Meter; this is indicated by her crown and by the crouching lion who is shown perched on her left arm, probably placed there to make its presence more visible than it would be on the goddess's lap. Her male companion, shown equal in size with Meter,

20. Homeric Hymn 14. Pindar, *Dithyramb* II.10 (Snell). Euripides, *Helen* 1347; *Palamedes* (Strabo 10.3.13 = fr. 586 Nauck); *Bacchae* 124–25. Diogenes (fr. 776 Nauck).
21. Flute music: Euripides, *Bacchae* 127–28; cymbal music: Homeric Hymn 14; Pindar, *Dithyramb* II.11 (Snell); Euripides, *Helen* 1308; Diogenes (fr. 776 Nauck). On loud music in the cult of Meter, see Strabo 10.3.15–17.
22. Euripides, *Bacchae* 127.
23. βρόμια, Euripides, *Helen* 1308, and κτύπον, Euripides, *Bacchae* 129. On the trancelike state induced by such rhythm, see Bremer 1984: 278–86.
24. Diogenes, Athenaios 1.2 = Nauck p. 776.
25. Euripides, *Bacchae* 130–34, and generally the first chorus, 64–169. On ritual dancing in the rites of Meter, see Plato, *Ion* 534a, 536c; Strabo 10.3.15. On the so-called Phrygian dance, see Lawler 1964: 114–15 and Hall 1989: 132–33, citing Aeschylus's *Phryges*.
26. Kannicht and Snell 1981: fr. 629.
27. *ARV*² 1052, 25; Matheson 1995: 278, assigned by her to the Curti Painter. The most comprehensive illustrations can be found in Aurigemma 1960: 48–51, pls. 19–30. For some preliminary remarks on the difficulty on interpreting this vase, see Bérard et al. 1989: 24–29.

FIGURE 43.
Attic red-figure krater
from Ferrara, Side A.
Early fifth century B.C.
Courtesy, Archaeological
Museum of Ferrara.

wears a long colorful robe and has a snake tied like a fillet in his hair. Apart from this he has no attributes, and so his identity remains uncertain. His placing, in a pose of balance and equality with Meter, would seem to imply that he is her consort, but we have no knowledge that Meter had a consort during this time. The god may not be one identifiable deity. He seems close to Dionysos: the snake fillet is reminiscent of Dionysos's menads, although it is not worn by the god himself, but the lack of the god's most characteristic attributes, the kantharos, ivy, and thyrsos, make his identification as Dionysos uncertain.[28] The emphasis of the work seems to lie in the rites

28. Menads in Dionysiac company often handle snakes; for examples, see *ARV²* 182, 6, amphora by the Kleophrades Painter, and *ARV²* 371, 14, cup by the Brygos Painter. The identity of this male god has been much discussed, and suggestions have included Iacchos, Dionysos, Sabazios, and Hades. For a summary of recent scholarly opinion, see F. Naumann 1983: 171–75. Naumann identifies the god as Sabazios, as does Matheson 1995: 278–79. The strongest arguments for Sabazios were made by E. Simon 1953: 83–85, drawing attention to the Phrygian origins of both deities and the marked similarity between the scenes of ritual on the vase and the activities in the rites as described by Demosthenes, *On the Crown*

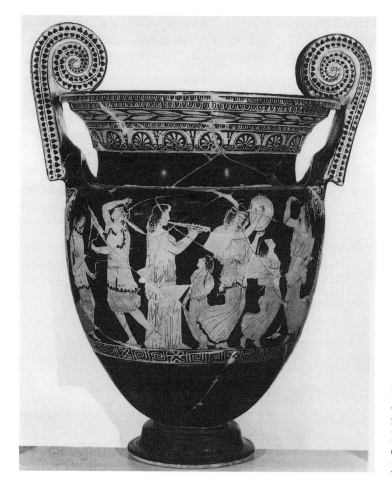

FIGURE 44.
Attic red-figure krater
from Ferrara, Side B.
Early fifth century B.C.
Courtesy, Archaeological
Museum of Ferrara.

directed to the divine pair, and since rites for Meter were often closely intertwined with those of Dionysos,[29] a figure who alludes to Dionysos may have been appropriate.

Of greater interest is the scene that fills the rest of the vase. This depicts the ritual performed by human devotees in honor of the two divinities (fig. 44). We see a row of figures winding around the vase, starting with a woman, who faces the goddess,

260. Yet the god seems too central a figure to represent a minor deity like Sabazios, and his visual iconography here bears little relationship to images of Sabazios from later Greek and Roman art (unlike Meter, whose pose, costume, and attributes remained fairly constant). Loucas 1992 interprets the god as Dionysos and the scene as a depiction of Orphic ritual honoring a local divinity at the Attic deme of Phlya; the unusual features of the scene would reflect local cult practices. I suggest that the scene was intended, not as an actual portrayal of cult ritual, but rather as an ironic commentary on Meter's rituals, in which case there may be no one identifiable male god.

29. Pindar, *Dithryamb* II.6–9 (Snell). The *locus classicus* is the opening chorus of Euripides' *Bacchae*, lines 64–168; cf. also Euripides, *Cretans* (Austin 1968: fr. 79, 11–12) and *Palamedes* (fr. 586 Nauck), and, in general, Strabo 10.3.14–15.

and ending with a male flute player, who stands at the left of the male god, with his back to the naiskos. The lead figure stands beside a low altar and carries on her head a basket containing the sacred objects of the mysteries; these are covered by a cloth, for they would have been too precious to display openly. The procession that stretches behind her consists of a woman playing the flute, followed by twelve dancing figures, another woman flutist who stands in the midst of the dancers, and the male flutist who brings up the rear. The dancers comprise a mixed group of seven adult women, one adult man, and four children, three girls and a boy. Some of the women are smaller than the others, which may indicate that they are adolescents. The children mimic the actions of the adults, and the last of them, a girl, seems to peek out from behind the long robe of the male flute player. The cross-section of ages and sexes may indicate that a family group is being depicted.

All of the dancers toss their heads back, kick their legs up, and open their mouths, using gestures and movements very reminiscent of the poses used by Dionysiac menads as they dance in the mysteries of Dionysos.[30] Several of the figures lift snakes into the air and dance with them, their open and free movements forming a counterpoise to the sedate poses of the flute players. Two of the women strike tympana, while the boy clacks the castanets. The intense, yet unrestrained expressions of the worshippers, all of whom are deeply engaged in their activities, contrast sharply with the rigid, detached demeanor of the two seated deities toward whom the procession is focused.

In this vase scene, we come as close as we are likely to come to the mystery rites of Meter. We cannot be sure how accurately the scene portrays these rites, but the activities of the individuals depicted on the vase echo to a striking degree the words of Demosthenes more than a hundred years later:

τοὺς καλοὺς θιάσους ἄγων διὰ τῶν ὁδῶν, τοὺς ἐστεφανωμένους τῷ μαράθῳ καὶ τῇ λεύκῃ, τοὺς ὄφεις τοὺς παρείας θλίβων καὶ ὑπὲρ τῆς κεφαλῆς αἰωρῶν, καὶ βοῶν εὐοῖ σαβοῖ, καὶ ἐπορχούμενος ὑῆς ἄττης ἄττης ὑῆς, ἔξαρχος καὶ προηγεμὼν καὶ κιττοφόρος καὶ λικνοφόρος καὶ τοιαῦθ' ὑπὸ τῶν γρᾳδίων προσαγορευόμενος.

And you [Aischines] used to lead your fine band through the streets crowned with fennel and white poplar, and you used to squeeze fat-cheeked snakes and lift them over your head and shout out *evoi saboi* and dance along to *hyes attes attes hyes;* you were the head, the leader, the ivy bearer, the liknos [covered basket] bearer, and you were saluted as such by the old women.[31]

---

30. See, e.g., an amphora by the Kleophrades Painter, *ARV*² 182, 6, and a cup by Makron, *ARV*² 462, 48; note the remarks of Keuls 1984: 289.

31. Demosthenes, *On the Crown* 260. Demosthenes did not record the name of the god for whom the rites he described were being celebrated. Most scholars have assumed that these must have been rites of Phrygian gods, noting the similarity of the words in the ritual cry σαβοῖ and ἄττης to the names of the Phrygian gods Sabazios and Attis (e.g., E. Simon 1953: 83–85; F. Naumann 1983: 172). The passage may

Since Demosthenes here uses his opponent's participation in the mystery rites as a form of political attack, he clearly expected his audience to disapprove of these activities. Did the vase painter (or his patron) disapprove of them too? The piece is a volute krater, made for a symposium, a drinking party for fashionable young men in Athens. This was exactly the kind of forum in which such outlandish activities might well have been the object of derision, and the clumsy way in which the children parody the actions of the adults does add a certain degree of irony to the scene. The intent of the scene on the krater may have been to present, not a literal illustration of Meter's mystery rites, but a somewhat sarcastic version of the way these rites were viewed by uncomprehending contemporaries.

Apart from this vase scene and comments such as Demosthenes', the details of such mystery rites are lost to the modern world. We must wait for Christian reporters to find any direct description of the ceremonies involved, and the information they give makes these ceremonies seem surprisingly flat: "I have eaten from the tympanum, I have drunk from the cymbal, I have carried the ritual vessel, I got under the veil," Meter's initiates would cry, according to Clement's mocking report in the second century C.E.[32] His cynicism may well have found its counterparts in fifth- and fourth-century B.C. Athens. One might expect that an unsympathetic observer would not respond warmly to the type of activities illustrated on the krater; indeed, to those outside the cult, the actions of the initiates must have seemed more than a little bizarre.

Yet both the krater and the literary descriptions communicate, even if unintentionally, the emotional content of the mysteries of Meter, for the individuals depicted are engaged in activities of deep personal intensity. The musical instruments, the flutes and tympana, the dance, and the generally heightened atmosphere of emotional expression confirm the impression of joyous abandonment described so vividly by Pindar and Euripides. This atmosphere goes far toward explaining the attraction of the Meter cult to her worshippers, for it responds to a need, felt by many individuals (not only in ancient Greece), to cut through the pomp and circumstances that normally surround the officially sanctioned religion of the state and seek direct contact with the divine.[33] As the comments of Christian authors make clear, Meter's ability to satisfy this need was to last until late antiquity.

---

be less a reference to Phrygian gods, however, than a scornful summary of the impression made on Greek society by charismatic ritual. Moreover, it is not at all certain whether Sabazios and Attis were indeed Phrygian gods; for analysis of the origin of the Attis cult, see Roller 1994a.

32. Clement, *Protrept.* 2.14. Clement's word for "veil," *pastos,* was normally used for a bridal bed curtain (see Lane 1988); was he referring to some form of mystic union between the worshipper and the deity? Cf. also Firmicius Maternus 18, who offers two other readings for the final lines, "I have learned the secrets of religion" (Latin text), or "I have become an initiate of Attis" (Greek text). This text clearly reflects later accretions to the rituals of Meter, for it is highly unlikely that Attis played any part in these rituals before the fourth century B.C.

33. On ecstatic religion in general, see Lewis 1989. Versnel 1990: 110, offers a good description of the appeal of such an experience: "the eternal tension between the 'routinization' of religion and the craving for the immediate experience of god."

This sense of total abandonment to an altered mental state induced by Meter is described in several sources, not always in connection with specific ritual activity. This altered state of consciousness could be frightening: even an unwilling person could become a μητρόληπτος, a person "seized by Meter."[34] When Phaedra acts strangely, her nurse wonders if the Μήτηρ ὀρεία, the Mountain Mother, has possessed her; being transported to the Mother's mountainous realm meant abandoning the restraints of civilized behavior.[35] The goddess's power could lead to frenzy, for the Mother of the gods was one of the deities believed responsible for the "Sacred Disease," epilepsy. "If a patient roars or suffers convulsions on the right side, [the healers] say the Mother of the gods is to blame," reports the author of the Hippocratic treatise.[36] Plutarch preserves a dramatic anecdote describing an incidence of (faked) possession by the Mother:

> All of a sudden he threw himself on the ground, in the midst of his discourse, and after having lain there some time without speaking, as if he had been in a trance, he lifted up his head, and turning it round, began to speak with a feeble trembling voice, which he raised by degrees; and when he saw the whole assembly struck dumb with horror, he threw off his mantle, tore his vest in pieces, and ran half-naked to one of the doors of the theater, crying out that he was driven by the Mothers.[37]

This individual was feigning ritual possession by the Mothers in order to escape a difficult political situation in Sicily, but this does not alter the fact that to his contemporaries, such behavior in the grip of ritual possession was highly credible.

Herodotos offers another vivid description of the rites of Meter in his account of the Skythian Anacharsis. On his way home from a grand world tour, Anacharsis stopped at Kyzikos and encountered the local citizens celebrating a splendid festival to the Mother of the gods. He was so impressed that he vowed that if he should return home safely to Skythia, he would sacrifice to the goddess according to Kyzikene custom. Upon his return, he went to a remote wooded area of Skythia and conducted the appropriate ritual, a nighttime ceremony during which he beat on the tympanum and decked himself out in sacred images. The Skythian king Saulios was informed of these goings-on, whereupon he shot and killed Anacharsis with an arrow.[38] While the accuracy of this story has been contested,[39] Herodotos's descrip-

34. Hermias, *In Platonis Phaedrum Scholia*, ed. P. Couvreur, p. 105a.
35. Euripides, *Hippolytos* 141–44. On the frightening image of mountains, see Osborne 1987: 189–92.
36. Hippocrates, *On the Sacred Disease* 4.
37. Plutarch, *Marcellus* 20. The translation is that of Bolton 1962: 137–38. In general, see Dodds 1951: 75–79, and the valuable discussion by Connor 1988: 155–66.
38. Herodotos 4.76.
39. Features such as the the vagueness of the locale (somewhere in Skythia) and the legendary nature of Anacharsis's voyage (one thinks of the wandering sage Solon) have led several scholars to doubt the validity of a historical Anacharsis. The arguments against the historicity of the episode are summarized by Kindstrand 1981: 20–23. See also Hartog 1988: 62–84 and passim, on Herodotos's use of the Skythians as a metaphor for a remote "Other."

tion of the rites of Meter, with its nocturnal festival, tympana, and images worn by the celebrants, is consistent with other descriptions of her rites in the Greek world.[40] Herodotos may not give us direct information about Skythian history, but he does offer a sense of the impact of the Meter cult, simultaneously appealing and frightening, on a non-initiate.

Yet not every episode of mental abandonment to the Mother Goddess brought unpleasant consequences. Often the heightened emotional awareness of such encounters brought highly desirable results. Plato reports that devotees of Meter could find an inner peace through such awareness in their dance,[41] and he was clearly interested in the altered states that such rituals could induce.[42] "I seem to hear [the Laws of Athens] talking to me as clearly as the Korybants [followers of Meter] hear the music of their flutes," Socrates tells Crito at the end of their conversation shortly before his death.[43] Here the Meter cult offers a metaphor for a divine conduit of spirituality, which aided Socrates in a difficult crisis. Possession by Meter could bring a heightened fluency and heightened awareness, perhaps even an awareness of inner wisdom and spiritual guidance. The fragment from Diogenes quoted above makes this explicit, for the roaring of Meter's cymbals brings σοφὴν ὑμνῳδὸν ἰατρόν θ', a wise and healing singing.[44]

The general sense of these passages is that Meter, like Dionysos, Pan, and the Nymphs, was one of a group of deities who could directly affect the psyche, the intimate core of personality. Contact with Meter could come suddenly to an unwilling or unaware individual, through disease or ritual possession, or one could deliberately seek out such contact for its benefits. Clearly, the rites of Meter, described by the poets and depicted on the Ferrara krater, were designed to induce this contact for individuals who, unlike Socrates and the epileptic, had not been directly favored by divine visitation. Thus to the participants, the rites of Meter were not frightening but liberating. Despite their supposedly wild nature, they were a form of religious expression shared by many Greeks, one that could also be associated with the cults of other Greek divinities, including such critical figures as Dionysos, Apollo, the Muses, and the Nymphs.[45]

Such ecstatic rites formed one aspect of the Greek cult of Meter. Yet it is likely that Meter was worshipped not only through mystery cult but also through expressions of individual reverence. Such personal devotion is depicted on several votive reliefs.

40. This is the earliest reference to the images of Meter worn by her priests. For examples of such images, see Reeder 1987: 440, a discussion of a bronze matrix (illustrated here, figs. 58–59) that may have furnished master forms for such images.

41. Plato, *Ion* 536c.

42. Plato, *Phaedrus* 265 B.

43. Plato, *Crito* 54d.

44. Diogenes (fr. 1, p. 776 Nauck), quoting Athenaios 14.636. Note a citation of Apollodoros, *Bibliotheke* 3.51, in which Dionysos, struck with madness by Hera, was cured by Kybele.

45. On the general question of divine possession, see Dodds 1951: 64–101, and Connor 1988.

FIGURE 45. Relief from Thasos with two votaries and the statue of a goddess seated in a niche. Early fifth century B.C. Courtesy, Collection of the J. Paul Getty Museum, Malibu, California.

One example, from Thasos, shows two women with doves as offerings, approaching the goddess in her niche (fig. 45). A fourth-century B.C. relief from the Piraeus (fig. 46) illustrates a man addressing the goddess (the dedication uses a plural verb, so originally there must have been at least two worshippers), and a second-century B.C. work now in Venice depicts a mother and her daughter in Meter's presence (fig. 60).[46] This type of individual devotion must explain the hundreds of small Meter statuettes and reliefs so frequently found near Meter shrines, in domestic contexts, and simply scattered throughout the Greek world (figs. 40, 41, 47).

Only rarely do objects from the fifth and fourth centuries offer a hint as to why someone wished to approach Meter, but in some cases we can sense the individual need that led to the petition. One such example is furnished by a mid-fourth-century stele from the Piraeus, offered to Meter, ὑπὲρ τῶν παιδίων, on behalf of the children.[47] Other votive statuettes from Athens and Kyme depict Meter on her throne

46. The Thasos relief, Salviat 1964: 239, a = CCCA II: no. 528; the relief from the Piraeus, Walter 1939: 54, fig. 22 = CCCA II: no. 270; and the one from Venice, Linfert 1966: fig. 2.
47. Piraeus stele, CCCA II: no. 308. In this volume, see fig. 48.

FIGURE 46. Votive relief with Kouretes and Nymphs, dedicated to Meter, from the Piraeus. Fourth century B.C. (After M. J. Vermaseren, *Corpus Cultus Cybelae Attidisque* II, no. 270, Études Préliminaires aux Religions Orientales dans l'Empire Romain 50/2 [Leiden, 1982]; after *Jahresheft des Österreichischen Archäologischen Instituts* 31 [1939]: 54, fig. 22.)

with lions, but holding a child, in the pose of a *kourotrophos*.[48] A particularly striking example from Argos, perhaps a cult statue, was placed in a sanctuary of Eileithyia, goddess of childbirth.[49] These objects imply that for some women, the goddess was worshipped literally as the protector of mothers. Others may have sought help for other ills. Such personal approaches to a mother goddess would likely have been very frequent, given the uncertain vicissitudes of life in the ancient world (no less than today), and this circumstance may account both for the great number of small Meter votives and for their anonymity, given the fact that the sorrows of humble people are rarely of great concern to those who record affairs of state.

48. Price 1978: 64–65. Note also fig. 60 in this volume, one of a pair of parallel votive reliefs, now in the Archaeological Museum, Venice; the other (Linfert 1966: fig. 1) was dedicated by a father and son to Herakles. Three votives from the Piraeus, *CCCA* II: nos. 273, 275, 276, address the goddess as "gracious midwife"; see chapter 7.
49. Charitonidis 1954: 414–15, 425, and fig. 1. Charitonidis assumes that the child on the goddess's lap must be Attis, but its poor state of preservation makes this uncertain.

FIGURE 47. Meter naiskos with two attendants, from the Piraeus. Courtesy, National Archaeological Museum, Athens.

In sum, Meter was a multifaceted deity who was worshipped in both open and closed rites, with group and individual activities. The ecstatic rituals of music and dance and the personal requests and thank offerings were two aspects of a similar experience, a way of seeking direct contact with the deity.

SANCTUARIES OF METER AND
THE STATUS OF METER IN THE GREEK POLIS

In addition to private rites for Meter, the goddess was also worshipped in public temples and shrines to her, or Metroa, in a number of Greek cities and sanctuaries. The presence of a Metroön implies a more official cult, with sacrifices and prayers open to many people. We shall want to explore this more public side to Meter too, to see how her mystery rites and her personal interactions with individuals compare with her public presence.

We have a number of descriptions concerning the establishment of the cult of Meter in various Greek communities. In 464 B.C., Themistokles established a cult in Magnesia to the Mother of the gods after she appeared to him in a dream and warned him about a planned assassination attempt; the cult was an offering of thanks for saving his life.[50] Also in the fifth century B.C., Pindar states proudly in his third Pythian Ode that he founded a shrine to the goddess Meter near his house, where she was worshipped with torchlit processions and all-night choruses.[51] The rituals celebrated at the poet's shrine correspond to the mystic cult of Meter, which suggests a private foundation, but the poet's language implies that the shrine was accessible to anyone who wished to worship Meter.[52]

At the end of the fifth century B.C., a Metroön was built in the sanctuary of Zeus at Olympia. The building has been identified through excavation, but its function and place in Olympian cult is still uncertain.[53] The interest in introducing the cult of Meter to Olympia seems to lie in the identification of Meter with Rhea. The existence of an altar built at the same time as the temple demonstrates that Meter/Rhea had a cult there, but we have little idea of how extensive a role she played in the sanctuary. Pausanias, who is our principal ancient source, provides little information on

50. Plutarch, *Themistokles* 30, discussed by Garland 1992: 78 and Borgeaud 1996: 29. There were similar cult foundations for Pan in Athens (Herodotos 6.105) and Boiotia (Plutarch, *Aristides* 11).

51. Pindar, *Pyth.* 3.77–79; Pausanias 9.25.3. A scholiast on the Pythian Ode, *Σ Pyth.* 3.137–139, offers additional detail, reporting that while in the Boiotian mountains, the poet saw a vision in which an image of Meter descended from the sky toward him. For a discussion of the passage, see Haldane 1968: 18–31. Slater 1971, doubts the validity of this foundation, preferring to place it in Sicily, but his argument ignores the evidence of Pindar, frs. 80, 95, and 96 (Snell). For a fuller refutation of Slater's ideas, see Henrichs 1976: 256, n. 10.

52. Ironically, the poet's shrine outlived him to become one of the few survivals of the glory of Thebes. During the sack of Thebes in 335 B.C., it was spared by Alexander (Pliny, *NH* 7.29.109; Arrian, *Anabasis* 1.9.10), and it was virtually the only building in Thebes still standing in the second century C.E. (Pausanias 9.25.3). The poet may have wished to honor Meter, but the sanctuary owed its fame to the goddess's disciple, Pindar himself.

53. Pausanias 5.20.9. For the date and location of the building, see Hitzl 1991: 8–14.

the building, apart from reporting that in his day the Metroön was used for the Roman imperial cult.

The cult of Meter in Athens presents a different situation. Meter had received private cult offerings from Athenians during the sixth century B.C., but the construction of a shrine to Meter in the Athenian Agora in the early fifth century B.C. is the earliest example of the goddess's presence in a Greek city center and a conspicuous testimony to the importance of Meter in that city's political and religious life. This first civic Metroön is the building on the west side of the Agora identified in earlier publications as the Old Bouleuterion (Council House). It was evidently planned as part of a building program in the Agora begun shortly after the reforms of Kleisthenes in 508 B.C.,[54] suggesting that Meter had already found a place in civic cult practice. The original Metroön should be restored as a rectangular building with two internal partitions creating three rooms, which faced east toward the open area of the Agora; an altar stood in front of it.[55] The foundations would later be reused for a Hellenistic Metroön, constructed around 150 B.C., a building whose identity is secure through the description of Pausanias and the discovery of roof tiles stamped "Sanctuary of the Mother of the gods."[56] It therefore seems almost certain that its early-fifth-century predecessor was also a Metroön.[57] This early Metroön was destroyed during the Persian invasion in 480 B.C., as was the rest of the Agora, but the ruined Metroön was repaired around 460 B.C. and was used as a depository for state archives from at least the late fifth century, if not earlier.[58] The placement of the building in the Agora indicates that the cult of Meter was an important one to the Athenians, a point reinforced by the creation of Agorakritos's cult statue of Meter during the latter part of the fifth century B.C. A statement by Demosthenes, that it was the practice of the Athenian *prytaneis* (presiding council members) to sacrifice to

54. Thompson 1937: 135–40, 205–7. A date of ca. 500 B.C. for the earliest building program in the Agora has recently been reemphasized in a thorough study by Leslie Shear (1993: 418–22).

55. For the excavation of the Metroön, see Thompson 1937: 205 ff., and Thompson and Wycherley 1972: 29–38. In this discussion of the building history of the Athenian Metroön, I am following the arguments of Stephen G. Miller. For the new proposed reconstruction, see S. G. Miller 1995: figs. 4–5. On the date preceding the Persian sack of Athens, see Shear 1993. Doubts about Thompson's reconstruction of the building history of the Athenian Metroön were also expressed by Francis 1990, although his argument is flawed by the presumption that a negative taint of Oriental rites colored Meter's Athenian cult from its inception; a similar flawed presumption underlies the arguments of Shear 1995.

56. Pausanias 1.3.5; Thompson and Wycherley 1972: 29–30 (the tile is illustrated in pl. 30c).

57. The suggestion of Boersma 1970: 31–333, that the earliest temple was dedicated to Zeus Eleutherios is not convincing. The building was a shrine to Meter from at least the late fifth century B.C. (Athenaios 9.407b–c = Wycherley 1957: no. 470), and it seems unlikely that Zeus would have been displaced from his home by Meter less than a hundred years after its dedication to him.

58. Thompson and Wycherley 1972: 35. For the epigraphical testimonia, see Wycherley 1957: 151–60, nos. 465–519. On the establishment of the Athenian state archive, see Boegehold 1972; see also Stroud 1974: 174, on the Metroön as the depository for counterfeit coins. The earliest attested use of the Metroön as the Athenian archive room in the late fifth century B.C. is described in an incident connected with Alcibiades (Athenaios 9.407b–c = Wycherley no. 470). The altar to Meter may have been located outside the Metroön; this is implied by Aischines, *Timarchos* 60–61, who describes how a certain Pittalakos came to the Agora and sat naked at the altar of Meter in the presence of a large crowd.

the Mother of the gods, along with sacrifices to Zeus, Athena, Apollo, and the other gods, supports this.[59] Taken as a whole, the evidence implies a close integration of Meter with the respected cults of the Athenian democracy.

While the importance of the Athenian Metroön is clear, it is much less clear why the cult of Meter should have occupied such a conspicuous place in Athenian civic life, and the ancient sources give no reason for this. A key factor may be Meter's Ionian background. Her cult had originally reached the Greek mainland from Ionian cities such as Miletos, and this may have had a special resonance in Athens, which identified itself as the mother city of the Ionians.[60] It is interesting to note that temples of Meter occupied conspicuous positions in other Ionian cities, including Smyrna and Kolophon, where the Metroön also served as an archive building. The evidence for these Ionian civic Metroa is from the fourth century B.C. and later, but they may well have existed earlier.[61] It is also possible that the populist character of the early Meter cult, evident through the large number of private votive offerings, made her a divinity with particular appeal to the Athenian democracy. Another reason may be Meter's close association with the important Athenian civic deity Demeter, also a mother goddess.

Given the prominence of the Athenian Metroön and its role in the Athenian democracy, it seems all the more surprising that several of the ancient sources recording its establishment describe extensive resistance to the foundation of the Athenian Metroön and the worship of Meter. This point of view can be traced to the fourth century B.C., as we learn from a scholiast on Aischines' oration against Ktesiphon. The passage records that the Athenians made a part of the Bouleuterion a sanctuary of Rhea on account of "that Phrygian man": μέρος τοῦ Βουλευτηρίου ἐποίησαν οἱ Ἀθηναῖοι τὸ Μητρῷον, ὅ ἐστιν ἱερὸν τῆς ῾Ρέας, διὰ τὴν αἰτίαν ἐκείνου τοῦ Φρυγός. The scholiast cites as his source a work entitled *Philippics;* while its authorship is uncertain, this was surely part of the anti-Macedonian literature from the second half of the fourth century B.C.[62] The earliest account of "that Phrygian man" and his role in the foundation of the Metroön appears only much later, in the *Orations* of the fourth-century C.E. Roman emperor Julian. The episode next appears in the works of Byzantine lexicographers, with the fullest account found in the works of Photios, writing in the ninth century C.E.[63] Photios's narrative agrees with the account of Julian, but offers more extensive detail:

59. Demosthenes, *Prooemia* 54.

60. Simms 1985: 85; Parker 1996: 159.

61. On Metroa in Kolophon and Smyrna, see chapter 7. On the Metroön as an archive center in Kolophon, see *CCCA* I: 599, 601–5.

62. Σ Aischines 3.187. Wycherley 1957: 151–52, ascribes the *Philippics* quoted here to Anaximenes or Theopompos. The identity of "that Phrygian man" is discussed below.

63. Julian 5.159a; *Suda,* s.v. μητραγύρτης; Photios, s.v. μητραγύρτης. The ancient testimonia on the Metroön have been collected by Wycherley 1957: 151–60.

μητραγύρτης. ἐλθών τις εἰς τὴν Ἀττικὴν ἐμύει τὰς γυναῖκας τῇ μητρὶ τῶν θεῶν,
ὡς ἐκεῖνοί φασιν. οἱ δὲ Ἀθηναῖοι ἀπέκτειναν αὐτὸν ἐμβάλλοντες εἰς βάραθρον ἐπὶ
κεφαλήν. λοιμοῦ δὲ γενομένου ἔλαβον χρησμὸν ἱλάσασθαι τὸν πεφονευμένον.
καὶ διὰ τοῦτο ᾠκοδόμησαν βουλευτήριον, ἐν ᾧ ἀνεῖλον τὸν μητραγύρτην. καὶ
περιφράττοντες αὐτὸν καθιέρωσαν τῇ μητρὶ τῶν θεῶν ἀναστήσαντες καὶ
ἀνδριάντα τοῦ μητραγύρτου. ἐχρῶντο δὲ τῷ μητρώῳ ἀρχείῳ καὶ νομοφυλακείῳ,
καταχώσαντες καὶ τὸ βάραθρον.

metragyrtes: a certain man came to Attica and initiated the women into the mysteries
of the Mother of the gods, as some say. The Athenians killed him by throwing him
into a pit on his head. When a plague occurred they received an oracle ordering them
to propitiate the murdered man. And because of this they built the Bouleuterion, [on
the spot] on which they killed the *metragyrtes*. Having made a fence around it, they
consecrated it to the Mother of the gods, and set up a statue of the *metragyrtes*. They
used the Metroön for an archive and repository of law, and they filled up the pit.

A scholiast on Aristophanes' *Ploutos* draws on the same tradition, but offers an alternative explanation for the priest's murder: τὸν Φρύγα τὸν τῆς Μητρὸς ἐνέβαλον ὡς
μεμηνότα ἐπειδὴ προέλεγεν ὅτι ἔρχεται ἡ Μήτηρ εἰς τὴν ἐπιζήτησιν τῆς Κόρης (They
[the Athenians] threw Meter's Phrygian [into the pit] because they considered him
mad, since he proclaimed that the Mother was coming on her quest for Kore).[64]

This story has a number of odd features, many of which have been extensively discussed in secondary literature without achieving any consensus.[65] Its historicity is a
particular problem. Some have assumed that the narrative is a literal account of the
execution of a *metragyrtes* and should be connected with the construction of the first
Metroön in the Agora in the early fifth century B.C.[66] Others have argued that the
plague mentioned in Photios's account must be the plague at the outset of the Peloponnesian War in 430 B.C.[67] Neither of these proposed dates corresponds with the
evidence. In the early fifth century B.C., Meter was an Ionian deity, already well
known through private votives, and so her public position in the city is not surprising. And a foundation during the late fifth century makes no sense; one cannot
"found" a cult that is already well established. Moreover, the whole atmosphere of
resistance to a new god or new cult seems inconsistent with the open system of polytheism, in which new deities were routinely accommodated without stress.[68] It

64. Σ Aristophanes, *Ploutos* 431 = *Suda*, s.v. βάραθρον.
65. Among the many treatments of this episode in modern literature, I have found the studies of Cosi
1980–81, Cerri 1983, and Versnel 1990: 105–11, especially helpful. See also Foucart 1873: 64–66; Nilsson
1967: 725–27; van Straten 1976a: 42–43; Vermaseren 1977: 32–35; Simms 1985: 69–70; Frappicini 1987; and
Parker 1996: 189–91. My discussion here also draws on my own treatment of the story, Roller 1996.
66. This was the opinion of the excavator of the Agora, Homer Thompson (Thompson 1937;
Thompson and Wycherley 1972). See also Nilsson 1967: I, 737, Vermaseren (*CCCA* II no. 1), and Versnel
1990: 107.
67. Foucart 1873: 64–66; Picard 1938 and 1954, Boersma 1970, Cosi 1980–81, Cerri 1983, Frappicini
1987.
68. Burkert 1985: 176–79. Note Plato's favorable comments on the new festival of the Thracian goddess Bendis in Athens (*Republic* 1.327a).

seems particularly inconsistent with the social atmosphere in Athens, where, we are told, the Athenians welcomed so many outside cults that they became a source of ridicule for the comic poets.[69]

Were it not for some details suggesting a core of historical actuality, we would be tempted to reject the account of the *metragyrtes*' death altogether.[70] The close relationship between Bouleuterion and Metroön is one. Another is the reference to the *barathron*, the pit into which the Mother's priest was thrown; this was in fact the method of capital punishment used in Athens during the fifth and fourth centuries, although it had long been abandoned by the time of the sources recording the incident.[71] On the other hand, the appearance of this story in such late sources makes one suspect that several aspects of it have been translated through numerous retellings and through the changing status of the Mother of the gods herself. The identity of "that Phrygian man," credited by the Aischines scholiast with the creation of the Metroön, is also perplexing, because this emphasizes Meter's foreign roots and stresses the anomaly of her home in the Agora of Athens.

We need first to consider who and what the *metragyrtai* were. The term was derived from two Greek words, $M\acute{\eta}\tau\eta\rho$, Mother, and $\dot{\alpha}\gamma\acute{\upsilon}\rho\tau\eta\varsigma$, a collector, taken from the verb $\dot{\alpha}\gamma\epsilon\acute{\iota}\rho\epsilon\iota\nu$, meaning to gather or collect; a *metragyrtes* was, then, "one who gathers for the Mother." The word denoted a priest of Meter who went around begging alms for the cult (and probably also for himself). The earliest citation of the word occurs in the fourth-century comic poet Antiphanes, where the *metragyrtes* is clearly an object of ridicule.[72] Aristotle defined the *metragyrtes* as $\ddot{\alpha}\tau\iota\mu\sigma\varsigma$, someone dishonorable, contrasting a *metragyrtes* with a *dadouchos*, a torch bearer, an honorable religious office.[73] Athenaios, describing Dionysios of Syracuse, commented that he spent his last days as a *metragyrtes*, a mark of how low the former Sicilian tyrant had sunk.[74] The general image is of someone disreputable, on the fringes of Greek society, with whom respectable people would not associate.[75] Putting a statue of a public disgrace like a *metragyrtes* into an important public shrine like the Athenian

<hr>

69. Strabo 10.3.18; Parker 1996: 158–59.

70. This is the conclusion of Wilamowitz 1879: 195 n. 4, Will 1960: 101, n. 2, and Bömer 1963: 10, n. 4.

71. Cerri 1983: 161–62.

72. A title of a comedy by Antiphanes, fr. 154 (Kock II 74), cf. also fr. 159, the *metragyrtes* as a magician. Other examples cited by Bömer 1963: 871, and Versnel 1990: 109. One should note, though, that Menander's *Priestess*, assumed by Webster 1960: 150, and Bömer 1963: 869–70, to be a condemnation of the Meter cult, may have nothing to do with Meter, for the deity whom the priestess (of the title) worships with *tympana* and *orgia* is masculine, not feminine.

73. Aristotle, *Rhetoric* 1405a.

74. Athenaios 12.541e. Similarly disparaging remarks were made about a *metragyrtes* of Ptolemy IV; see Plutarch, *Cleomenes* 36.

75. This is certainly the definition adopted by Foucart 1873: 160–61; Bömer 1963: 869–70; and Versnel 1990: 110, although much of the more extravagant evidence they cite about the *metragyrtes*' appearance and clothing is drawn from Roman, not Greek sources. Foucart and Bömer were particularly influenced by the vivid picture of the Galli, the priests of the Roman Magna Mater, found in Apuleius's *Golden Ass* 8.24–31, without explaining why a Roman work of the second century C.E. should be taken as evidence for Greek religious practice of the fifth and fourth centuries B.C.

Metroön does seem inconsistent, and it is not surprising that many scholars have been troubled by it. For this reason, the current weight of scholarly opinion is that the *metragyrtes* story records an active tradition of resistance within Athens to the cult of the Phrygian Mother Goddess.[76]

A different approach may help resolve the confusion. Discarding such a literal historical reading of this narrative enables us to see it as a well-known myth type, one with special resonance for Classical Athens. The outlines of the myth type are clear: an outsider comes into town, converts one group of the population, the women, to a new deity. As a result, the principal group in the community reacts violently and kills the outsider, whereupon the deity takes revenge by causing a plague (or some other form of retaliation). The community then recognizes the power of the deity by according it even greater honor. This is an ahistorical pattern characteristic of a resistance myth that has many parallels, including at least one anecdote connected with the cult of the Magna Mater in Rome.[77] The function of the myth is not to condemn the deity's priest but to praise the deity, and the concept of resistance in the myth forms a foil to the deity's power, demonstrating the deity's ability to overcome all challenges to its authority. Indeed, the story of the *metragyrtes* winning converts to a new god is one found in several religions, including Christianity. The tone of the narrative, implying resistance to conversion, is more reminiscent of St. Paul traveling through Asia Minor, winning converts among the women and being thrown into prison because of this,[78] than it is of the fluid nature of Greek paganism. Given the late date of our sources, one wonders whether their perspective may have been colored by contact with proselytizing Christianity. And the use of a plague to punish people who do not honor a deity's priest is a story pattern as old as Homer's *Iliad*.[79]

Yet the story has a well-known parallel with a work very close in time to Agorakritos's cult statue of Meter—namely, Euripides' *Bacchae*. In this play, too, a stranger comes into town and initiates the women into his mysteries. The dominant male voice (Pentheus) tries to stop him, even throws him into prison, and the reaction of the deity is violent. The new god punishes the community and forces it to accept him. The intermingling of ecstatic rituals for both Meter and Dionysos in the opening chorus of the *Bacchae* makes this parallel even more striking. In the *Bacchae*, the myth type is confused by the fact that the priest and the new deity are one and the

76. Thus Cosi 1980–81, and Cerri 1983, with earlier bibliography; note also Versnel 1990: 105–6, "the legend retains the memory of an actual event, the historicity of which has been convincingly demonstrated." Parker 1996: 190, is more skeptical.

77. On the *metragyrtes* in Rome, see Plutarch, *Marius* 17.9 and Diodoros 36.13, discussed by Versnel 1990: 105, n. 35. The *logos* of Anacharsis discussed above, Herodotos 4.76, exhibits the same pattern of introduction, resistance, and death of the deity's celebrant. Other parallels are cited by Burnett 1970: 26; note also the very modern parallel discussed by Oranje 1984: 1–3.

78. Cf. the incident described in Acts 16.

79. *Iliad* 1.8–52; another parallel may be found Herodotos 1.167, the description of a plague and an expiating cult founded to honor the Phokaians killed in a sea battle.

same; even so, both the plot and the message are remarkably similar to Photios's *metragyrtes* story. Few would make a serious argument that the *Bacchae* is recounting an actual historical event.[80] Rather, the desire is to confirm the high status of the deity and create public acceptance of the deity's ecstatic rituals.

The alternative account of the Aristophanes scholiast may aid in placing the *metragyrtes* story in an Athenian framework. According to this, the *metragyrtes* was killed because he proclaimed that the Mother was coming to look for Kore. This may conceal a more specific reference—namely, that the *metragyrtes* had profaned the Eleusinian Mysteries, an action punishable by death.[81] This statement gains credibility from the close identification of Meter with Demeter. A specific historical context is suggested by the charge of profaning the Eleusinian Mysteries leveled against Alcibiades in 415 B.C., a charge that gained greater public attention because of its connection with the Sicilian disaster.[82] This is not the only example of the act of profaning the Mysteries being severely punished, but it is one of the more notorious ones. Its timing corresponds to the prominence of Meter on the Athenian stage, where the cult of Meter figures in nine plays, produced within a span of some twenty-five years (ca. 430–405 B.C.).[83] A particularly noteworthy example is that of Euripides' *Helen,* produced in 412 B.C., for in this play the conflation of the Phrygian Mother with Demeter is especially close.[84]

At this point it is difficult to determine whether the legend of the *metragyrtes* is essentially a fiction, created to explain the prominence of the Metroön in Athens, or whether it was prompted by the actual execution of a *metragyrtes* on the charge of profaning the Eleusinian Mysteries, preserved by collective memory in the more familiar form of a resistance myth. The story, however, suggests as a historical context, not the cult's foundation, but rather a reaction to the cult of Meter in the late fifth or the early fourth century B.C., during which time a *metragyrtes* had become symbolic of the disgraceful Oriental barbarian.[85] The prominent position of a deity attended by disgusting barbarian priests would have needed an explanation of a sort that had not been necessary two generations earlier, and the *metragyrtes* tale served that function.

The foundation legend of the Athenian Metroön raises interesting issues beyond

---

80. This was the contention of Dodds 1960: xi, but as the discussion of Henrichs 1978 shows, this is most unlikely. Cf. also Parker 1996: 160, n. 27. On the antiquity of the god Dionysos in Greece, note the occurrence of his name in a Linear B text, Ventris and Chadwick 1959: 127, PY Xa06.

81. Versnel 1990: 109.

82. Thucydides 6.27–28; Plutarch, *Alcibiades* 18–22. Charges of profaning the Mysteries were also leveled against the fifth-century poet Diagoras of Melos (Σ Aristophanes, *Birds* 1073; Diodoros 13.6). For other examples of profaning mystery rites, see n. 16 above.

83. Euripides' *Cretans* (performed ca. 430 B.C.), *Hippolytos* (428 B.C.), and *Palamedes* (415 B.C.); Aristophanes' *Birds* (414 B.C.); Sophokles' *Philoktetes* (409 B.C.); Euripides' *Helen* (412 B.C.) and *Bacchae* (405 B.C.); a fragment of a play by Diogenes, produced near the end of the fifth century (Nauck p. 776) and a fragment of unknown authorship and date.

84. This chorus and Meter's relationship to Demeter are discussed further below.

85. Note that all the references to a *metragyrtes* in Greece are of the early fourth century B.C. and later.

the question of its historicity. The implication of the legend is that in bringing the cult of Meter, the Mother's Phrygian priest brought something new, dangerous, even frightening to Athens. At first glance the central location of the Metroön, its splendid cult statue, and the frequency of votive offerings in the vicinity do not seem to support this negative judgment. Yet the *metragyrtes* legend is one of several factors creating the impression that by the late fifth century, the cult of Meter had acquired a distinctively negative tone. The horrific conclusion of the *Bacchae* vividly illustrates a profound uneasiness with religious rites that included the open expression of emotion and ecstasism, rites to which Meter's tympana contributed their share. We read in Menander's *The Priestess*, a late-fourth-century play, that women are warned away from the seductive rites of the cymbals.[86] The prosecution of Ninos, a priestess of Sabazios (supposedly a Phrygian god), during the fourth century B.C. underscores the dangers that the Athenians perceived in Phrygian rites.[87]

These negative judgments reflect a wider set of negative Greek attitudes, not only toward Oriental cults, but toward Orientals in general and toward Phrygians in particular.[88] Many Greeks had long regarded Phrygians with disdain and considered them primarily as slaves,[89] but this personal attitude reached almost the status of public ideology during the second half of the fifth century B.C. The Phrygians, a historical people with whom the Greeks had had regular contact since at least the eighth century B.C., became confused with the mythical Trojans; Aeschylus, we are told, presented the two peoples as equivalents on the tragic stage.[90] Thus the Phrygians were actively identified with the hereditary enemies of the Greeks. During the fifth century, the Trojans came to be stereotyped as Oriental barbarians, a circumstance encouraged by parallels drawn between Trojans and Persians in Greek tragedy[91] and in Greek vase painting.[92] As a result, the Phrygians came to stand indirectly for Persians, who personified the Oriental menace to Greek, and especially Athenian, freedom.

86. Menander, Ἱέρεια, see Webster 1960: 149–50, and Bömer 1963: 869–70. Note also Menander's highly fragmentary *Theophoroumene*, in which a woman is possessed by the Mother of the gods.

87. Demosthenes 19.281, and Σ 87.19.431; Josephus, *Against Apion* 2.267; see Versnel 1990: 114–18.

88. See Roller 1983 on the negative judgment of Phrygians implicit in the Greek treatment of the myth of the Phrygian king Midas, and, in general, Hall 1989, on the growth of negative racial stereotypes in Athens during the fifth century B.C.

89. Archilochos 42 (West 1989–92), the Phrygians as drunkards; Hipponax 27 (West 1989–92), the barbarian Phrygians sold to Miletos to grind barley.

90. Σ *Iliad* 2.862; Strabo 12.8.7. The ancient citations are discussed by Hall 1988. Note the shift between *Iliad* 2.862 and the Homeric Hymn to Aphrodite, lines 111–16, where the Trojans and Phrygians are clearly represented as two separate peoples, and Euripides, *Iphigenia in Aulis*, passim, where the sacrifice of Iphigenia clears the way for Agamemnon to go to Phrygia (not Troy).

91. See Hall 1989: 102, for a discussion of Trojans in Greek tragedy. On the merging of Trojans and Persians in fifth-century B.C. imagery, see Bacon 1961: 101, and Hall 1989: 68–69.

92. The representations of the Trojan Paris offer the best example of this. Beginning in the middle of the fifth century B.C., Paris is represented in the Achaemenian costume of long-sleeved tunic, trousers, boots, and soft, pointed cap. One of the earliest examples may be a hydria by the Painter of the Carlsruhe Paris, *ARV*² 1315, 1, and a hydria of the Kadmos Painter, Berlin F 2633 (now lost), *ARV*² 1187, 32, discussed in Roller 1994a: 251–52.

Under these circumstances, the prominence of Meter, a deity with a Phrygian background, not just in the Athenian Agora, but next to the Bouleuterion, the institution that symbolized Athenian democracy and freedom, may have been seen at the least as a contradiction, and perhaps even as a source of embarrassment to Athens. Stigmatizing the so-called wilder aspects of the Mother's worship as a series of rites associated with undesirables and foreign priests may have been one way of resolving that embarrassment.[93] As we shall see, the process had repercussions well beyond Athens, for it created a judgmental review of the Meter cult that was to survive until late antiquity.

THE PLACE OF METER IN THE GREEK PANTHEON

It has long been recognized that the Greek Meter was a highly syncretistic deity, embodying not only an Anatolian predecessor but also traits of a Hellenic or pre-Hellenic Mother Goddess.[94] The Classical goddess was both $M\acute{\eta}\tau\eta\rho$, Meter, the Mother, a direct transfer from her Phrygian cult name Matar, and also $M\acute{\eta}\tau\eta\rho\ \theta\epsilon\hat{\omega}\nu$, the Mother of the gods—that is, of the Olympian pantheon. This dual identity caused the Anatolian Mother Goddess to become conflated in Greek literature and cult practice with other Greek mother deities, each of which would contribute to her personality and to her identity in the perception of both Greeks and Romans. As the Mother of the gods, she was identified with Gaia (Earth) and, more especially, with Rhea, wife of Kronos and mother of the six original Olympian gods. As Meter, the Mother Goddess, she became closely allied with the Greek deity who exemplified motherly devotion, Demeter. The fusion was never complete, and the constituent deities who formed elements of Meter during the Classical period were recognized and often addressed as separate entities. Yet the separate elements of Meter's personality were no longer distinct either, and the assimilation of Meter with other figures such as Gaia, Rhea, and Demeter only underscores how widely the syncretism had progressed and how much the character of the Anatolian Mother had come to influence her Hellenic counterparts.[95]

One aspect of Meter's identity was as Mother Earth. Earth, $\Gamma\hat{\eta}$ or $\Gamma a\hat{\imath}a$ in Greek, the Mother of all life, was already a potent figure in Hesiod's *Theogony*.[96] Not only did she symbolize the agricultural fertility of the land, but she was also, in Hesiod's

93. Hall 1989: 149, has a particularly good discussion of this development. See also Versnel 1990: 110–18.

94. Will 1960: 96–97, who summarizes the opinions of earlier scholars. See also Parker 1996: 189.

95. Will 1960: 110–11, attributes the title of Great Mother goddess to the Phrygian deity, and the title of Mother of the gods to a Greek Meter. As we shall see, however, this is much too compartmentalized: the iconography of the Phrygian Mother was used for Rhea, Mother of the gods, and the Phrygian deity's imagery also influenced the Greek mother goddess Demeter.

96. Hesiod, *Theogony* 116–56.

poem, literally the progenitor of all beings, divine and human. The sixth-century B.C. Homeric Hymn to Γῆ Μήτηρ Πάντων, Earth Mother of all, stresses agricultural bounty of the goddess, while addressing her as θεῶν Μήτηρ, Mother of the gods.[97] The Athenian Solon addressed her as "Black Earth, the Great Mother of the Olympian deities," using cult titles later applied to Meter Kybele and to Rhea, Mother of the Olympians.[98] In the fourth century B.C., this identification of Meter with Gaia is made explicit in the Derveni Papyrus, which gives a broad definition of Meter as equivalent to all Mother deities in Greek cult practice: Γῆ δὲ καὶ Μήτηρ καὶ Ῥέα καὶ Ἥρη ἡ αὐτή (Earth and Meter and Rhea and Hera are the same thing).[99] The concept of Mother Earth, however, seems to have been a fairly abstract one to the Greeks. Mother Earth was only rarely represented in Greek art, and is usually shown as a mature woman rising up from the ground.[100] She was not the goddess with tympanum and lions.

More concrete is the figure of Rhea, the wife of the Titan Kronos, who also figures prominently in Hesiod's *Theogony*. Hesiod's account of the birth of Rhea's six divine children became one of the classic stories of Greek mythology: Kronos swallowed each of his children at birth until Rhea, angered by her husband's behavior, gave him a stone to swallow while she spirited away the youngest, the baby Zeus, to the island of Crete.[101] Later versions of the story report that the infant Zeus was cared for on Crete by a group of young men known as Kouretes, a term derived from the Greek word *kouros,* or youth.[102] The Kouretes clashed their shields together to drown out the baby's cries so that his father would not learn of his existence.

Several aspects of this story were to have a lasting influence on the identity of Meter Kybele. In the mid sixth century B.C., the Greek poet Hipponax equated Kybele, the Anatolian Mother, with Rhea, the Mother of the gods.[103] By the fifth century B.C., this syncretism had developed to the point where the cult figure Meter could be addressed as either Kybele or Rhea. In tragedy, both Kybele and Rhea used

97. Homeric Hymn 30. For the dating, see Janko 1982: 156. The hymn follows the Hesiodic genealogy, addressing Mother Earth as the wife of Ouranos.

98. Solon (Bergk) fr. 36.

99. Derveni Papyrus, col. XVIII, line 7, published in *Zeitschrift für Papyrologie und Epigraphik* 47 (1982), suppl. For commentary on the passage, see Kannicht 1969: 330 and West 1983: 93.

100. Mother Earth is shown rising up from the ground in in vase scenes depicting the birth of Erichthonios and the Gigantomachy; for examples, see Carpenter 1991: 73–75.

101. Hesiod, *Theogony* 453–91.

102. Zeus's upbringing on Crete is described by Euripides, *Bacchae* 120–25; Apollodoros 1.1.6–7; Diodoros 4.79–80, 5.64–65; and Pausanias 5.7.6. Alternative traditions connected the event with other sites in Greece as well: in Arkadia (Pausanias 8.36.2) and in Messenia (Pausanias 4.33.1). The location of the incident in Crete seems to have been the most widely reported tradition, and the claims of other areas may result from different sites in Greece desiring to be associated with the prestige of the birthplace of the premier Olympian god.

103. Hipponax, West 1989–92: I, fr. 156, discussed in chapter 5 above.

the tympanum and were at home in the mountain environment.[104] In the *Bacchae,* Euripides clearly ascribes these elements of raucous music and ecstatic dance to the goddess's Phrygian origins, although in another work, the *Cretans,* he connects such rituals with Mount Ida and Crete.[105] The fifth-century poet Telestes equated the Mother of the gods with Rhea,[106] and Rhea and Meter, like Gaia, are said in the fourth-century Derveni Papyrus to be one and the same. The Aischines scholiast discussed above refers to the Athenian sanctuary of Rhea (i.e., the Athenian Metroön) and her Phrygian priest,[107] indicating that Rhea and the Phrygian Mother were perceived as the same goddess.

There seem to have been several reasons for the syncretism of these two figures. Rhea was a divine mother, as was the Phrygian Mother Goddess, and so identifying the outsider with the local Mother of the gods was a means of assimilating the foreign deity into the Greek pantheon. The connection served to define the Phrygian goddess more sharply; she had always been Meter, the Mother, but there was little hint as to what she was the mother of, and the identification with Rhea made her specifically the Mother of the gods. This assimilation may also have been aided by a similarity in names leading to a false etymology: the Greeks were evidently aware that the Greek name Kybele was derived from the Phrygian epithet meaning "mountain," and so the Phrygian goddess, Matar Kubileya, or Mother of the mountains, became Μήτηρ ὀρεία, Mother of the mountains, in the Greek language.[108] The Greek word ὀρεία, *oreia,* is close in sound (although unrelated in meaning) to Rhea, further facilitating the equation between the two. A third factor may be that, apart from the story of the birth of Zeus, Rhea was a fairly colorless individual in the Greek pantheon with no strong local cult or identifiable activity under her control. She does not appear in Greek art until the fourth century B.C., when her visual iconography and attributes were clearly copied from those of Phrygian Kybele.[109] The Phrygian Mother Goddess could therefore adopt Rhea's name and her position in the Greek pantheon without dislodging an established visual tradition or strong local cult following. The assimilation was furthered by a similarity of toponyms con-

104. Cf. Sophokles, *Philoktetes* 391–92, where the Mountain Mother, i.e., Kybele, is called the Mother of Zeus; and Euripides, *Bacchae* 58–59, 78–79, 126–29, in which Meter is addressed both as Kybele the Great Mother and Mother Rhea of the Phrygian flutes.

105. Euripides, *Bacchae* 58–59. See also Diogenes (fr. 1, p. 776 Nauck; see n. 158 below). Euripides, *Cretans* (Austin 1968: fr. 79).

106. Telestes, Page 1962: fr. 764 (= fr. 809): Μητέρα θεῶν . . . Τελέσ[της ἐν Διὸ]ς γονα<ῖ>ς τὸ [αὐτὸ κ]αὶ ʽΡέαν.

107. Σ Aischines 3.187, on *Ktesiphon.* Arrian's description of the cult statue in the Athenian Metroön calls this a statue of Rhea (Arrian, *Periplous* 9).

108. Timotheos, *Persians,* in Page 1962: fr. 791, line 124; Euripides, *Hippolytos* 144; cf. also Sophokles, *Philoktetes* 391.

109. A good example in E. Simon 1966: 76–78, pl. 18, 19.2, a fourth-century Attic pelike illustrating an episode from the Homeric Hymn to Demeter. Rhea is present, shown holding the tympanum of Meter Kybele, despite the fact that the Phrygian goddess does not appear in the hymn.

nected with the cult of Meter: the Zeus/Rhea cult was located on Mount Ida in Crete, while the Phrygian Mother was at home on Mount Ida in northwestern Anatolia.[110]

There was, however, another consequence of the assimilation between Rhea and the Phrygian Mother, more meaningful and lasting than mere accommodation to the foreign deity—namely, the use of this assimilation to explain the elements of wild music and ecstatic behavior in the cult of Meter. The cause seems to lie in the connection of Zeus and Rhea with Crete. Just as the baby Zeus had been cared for on Crete by the Kouretes, who sang and danced and clashed their shields, so the followers of Rhea/Meter would also sing and dance and make raucous noises during their rites, in imitation of the Kouretic attendants of her son Zeus. This mythological aition was used by several Classical authors to rationalize the elements of wild music, unrestrained behavior, and open expression of emotional tension that, as we have seen, often characterized the cult of Meter in the Greek world.[111]

The Kouretic attendants themselves shared in the confusion between the Cretan and Phrygian origins of Meter, for they were often conflated with another band of youths, the Korybantes, also followers of Meter noted for their trancelike music and dance, who were said to be of Phrygian origin.[112] Euripides uses both terms for the attendants of Rhea/Kybele,[113] implying that this ecstatic element could be associated with either group. Diodoros straddles the issue by saying that the mysteries of Meter came from Mount Ida in Phrygia, but were brought by the Idaian Daktyls to Crete.[114] Strabo attempted to systematize a rather odd assortment of mythic followers of Rhea/Meter, brought together not because of common origin but because of the common use of rites involving music and dance.[115] This array of demi-gods confuses rather than clarifies any efforts to sort out the distinctions between Meter

110. Strabo 10.3.12 on Mount Ida in Phrygia; 10.3.20 on Mount Ida in the Troad and on Crete.

111. Euripides, *Bacchae* 120–29; Strabo 10.3.11. Meter's worship connected with that of Zeus: Pindar, *Dithyramb* II (Snell); Euripides, *Cretans* (Austin 1968: fr. 79, 10–13).

112. Korybantic dancing: Plato, *Crito* 54d, *Ion* 536c; Korybantes as armed bands, Aristophanes, *Lysistrate* 558; Korybantes from Phrygia, Aristophanes, *Wasps* 8. See Linforth 1946, an interesting discussion of Korybantic rites, and Graf 1985: 319–34, evidence on the cult of the Korybantes in Erythrai.

113. Euripides, *Bacchae* 120–25.

114. Diodoros 5.65; he names the fourth-century historian Ephoros as his source. The picture is further complicated by the presence of other groups of minor divinities, many of whom were connected with Meter. Their numbers expanded to include not only the Kouretes and Korybantes but also the Daktyls and the Telchines, who were known as wizards and magicians associated with metalworking. (On the Idaean Daktyls as attendants of Meter, note Sophokles, *Kophoi Satyroi*, fr. 337 Nauck; Diodoros 5.64, quoting Ephoros. See also Hemberg 1952 and Burkert 1983b.) These various groups had in common the fact that they consisted only of male figures, in contrast to most group divinities in Greek cult, such as the Muses, the Nymphs, or the Graces, who are normally female, and that they often brought special skills, such as metalworking or the ability to contact the deity through mystery rites.

115. The ancient sources that mention these two groups have been collected by Schwenn 1922a, s.v. "Korybanten": 1441–46; 1922b, s.v. "Kureten": 2205–6. The principal source is Strabo 10.3.10–24, a long discussion of the different types of male demi-gods; here the Korybantes are described as Phrygian (Strabo 10.3.12). Strabo states that his source was Demetrios of Skepsis, fl. ca. 180 B.C. Note also the discussion of Jeanmaire 1939: 593–616, who plausibly suggests that the Hellenistic mythographer Apollodoros may also have been one of Strabo's sources.

Kybele and Rhea in Classical Greece. Indeed, the overlapping identities of the various groups attendant on Kybele and Rhea demonstrate that the two mother deities were so closely conflated that such separation may not be possible.

One consistent thread linking all of these figures, goddesses and demi-gods, is their association with ecstatic ritual. This is clear from a fourth-century B.C. votive relief from the Piraeus mentioned earlier, depicting a man approaching the Mother of the gods (fig. 46).[116] Above his head is a cloudlike object supporting three Nymphs and three armed youths, the Kouretes. The presence of figures floating on a cloud indicates that the individual making the dedication had received contact with the divinity through a dream, and the Kouretes, along with the Nymphs, were the source of the dream contact, communicating the message from the goddess to her human followers.[117] Rhea's demi-gods offered another model through which their human followers could enter a similar dreamlike state and contact the divinity on their own. Evidently by the fifth century B.C. (if not earlier), the story of Rhea and the birth of Zeus described another form of ecstatic religion. Rhea and the Asiatic Kybele may originally have been two separate figures, but they eventually became two manifestations of the same religious phenomenon.

The fusion of the Asiatic Kybele and the Cretan Rhea has another interesting ramification, suggested by archaeological evidence indicating that the ecstatic rites of Meter may well originally have been at home on Crete. The tympanum first appears in Greek art in the eighth century B.C. on Crete, illustrated on a bronze disc, a votive offering found in a cave sanctuary of Zeus on Mount Ida; the votive offerings in the cave also included several bronze shields.[118] In antiquity, the birth of Zeus was assigned to a variety of caves on Crete, and finds of bronze shields and bronze discs, perhaps cymbals, at several Cretan sites suggest ecstatic worship there.[119] Such objects, dating to the eighth and seventh centuries B.C., indicate that the elements of ecstatic religion were part of the cult of the Hellenic Rhea well before she became conflated with Kybele. As Rhea and Phrygian Matar, both deities personified as mothers, became assimilated, the religious fervor expressed through raucous music and dance passed from the Greek cult of Rhea into the composite cult image of

---

116. The Kouretes also appear in two other Meter votives, a relief from Lebadeia (Walter 1939: 59, fig. 23, = *CCCA* II 432) and a bronze matrix in New York (Reeder 1987: fig. 3, top). These two works, to be discussed in more detail in chapter 7, establish the suitability of the Kouretes' presence in the cult of Meter.

117. Note also a relief from the Athenian Acropolis, Acropolis Museum 2455, F. Naumann 1983: no. 426, *CCCA* II: no. 190. The relief, of which only the lower left-hand corner survives, depicts two armed youths approaching Meter, who is seated at the left. Here the youths, probably the Kouretes, are presented in the normal pose of worshippers approaching the deity, thus taking on the role of suppliants and adorants, not attendants. For a discussion of divine contact through dreaming, see van Straten 1976b.

118. For the disc, see Kunze 1931: no. 74, pl. 49; Barnett 1960: pl. IVa. Canciani 1970: 55, is correct in criticizing Kunze's assumption that the disc itself was a tympanum, but the repoussé work on it depicts two winged genius figures, each holding two tympana.

119. R. W. Hutchinson, in Bosquanet 1939: 62–65; Kunze 1931: 6–35; Canciani 1970: 20–52.

Phrygian Kybele, as she adopted Rhea's position as *Μήτηρ θεῶν*. The syncretism may perhaps have taken place in the latter half of the sixth century B.C., the time when Meter acquired a tympanum, symbol of her ecstatic rites.

There is yet another aspect to the cult of Meter that may derive from Crete, one that adds an interesting dimension to the Greek definition of a Mother Goddess. I have noted that Meter was valued not only for her link with ecstasy, but also for her kindly, helpful qualities. Diodoros records an interesting discussion of the cult of the Mothers (plural) at Engyion in Sicily. This town, supposedly settled from Crete, had an important shrine to the Mothers, honoring the goddesses who saved Zeus on Crete from his father, Kronos. These goddesses and their helpers, the Kouretes, were honored also for their useful skills, which they taught to human beings; such skills included metallurgy, the domestication of animals, the technique of hunting, and also political and social harmony. The teaching was carried out through mystery rites.[120] This tradition may well reflect an indigenous Meter cult among the Sicilians that was absorbed into the Greek mythological framework after the area was settled by Greeks. Diodoros's report confirms that Meter could be associated with helpful and kindly actions. And the Kouretes assisted in these helpful activities by acting as intercessors in the rites through which one contacted Meter.

The identification of the Phrygian Mother with Rhea, Mother of the gods, and the fusion of the cult symbols and rites of these two goddesses furnish one example of syncretism. A very different situation resulted from the conflation of the Phrygian Mother with the Greek Demeter. In this instance it was not a case of blending two cults together, but rather of adapting the symbols and rituals of one deity to another, while keeping their cult identities separate.[121] As we shall see, this transference of symbols could pass both ways.

Meter had been associated with Demeter since at least the late sixth century B.C., as demonstrated by a votive statuette of Demeter from a sixth-century sanctuary in the Sicilian city of Gela, depicting the goddess seated on a throne with a lion in her lap, the standard iconography of Meter.[122] This use of shared symbols increased during the fifth and fourth centuries. Pindar addresses Demeter as the goddess with resounding cymbals, using the imagery of Meter, and the fifth-century B.C. poet Melanippides states explicitly that the two goddesses were regarded as identical: *Μελανιπ[πί]δης δὲ Δήμητρ[α καὶ] Μητέρα Θεῶν φ[η]σιν μίαν ὑπάρχ[ειν]* (Melanippides says that Demeter and the Mother of the gods are one).[123] The Derveni Papyrus

---

120. Diodoros 4.79–80, 5.64–65. Diodoros quotes Ephoros for the second passage.
121. For a general discussion of the relationship of Meter and Demeter, see Graf 1974: 155, n. 24, van Straten 1976a, and Versnel 1990: 108, although, unlike Versnel, I see the process as one of bilateral assimilation rather than the deliberate acculturation of a foreigner.
122. Van Straten 1976a: 42–43, fig. 1.
123. Pindar, *Isthmian* 7.3–4; Melanippides, Page 1962: fr. 764.

makes the same claim, stating that Demeter received her name Γῆ Μήτηρ because she was a fusion of both goddesses.[124]

The syncretism seems to have been particularly strong in Athens and Attica. Vessels similar to those used in the rites of Demeter were found near the Metroön in the Athenian Agora, suggesting some conflation of cult.[125] Such conflation is further implied by an Attic black-figured olpe of the late sixth century B.C., which depicts Demeter and Kore holding a stalk of wheat while accompanied by a lion.[126] An altar dedicated to the two goddesses of Eleusis, placed next to the Athenian Metroön, offers further evidence.[127] Influence could also flow in the opposite direction, for statuettes of Meter enthroned were found in the sanctuary of Eleusis.[128] The association was formalized through an important shrine, the Metroön in Agrai; this sanctuary, near the Ilissos River in Athens, was the site of the Lesser Mysteries, the first stage of initiation ceremonies for the Eleusinian Mysteries.[129] The syncretism of cult was reflected in literature, as the two deities are intertwined in the third chorus of Euripides' *Helen*, in which the Mountain Mother of the gods, named ὀρεία Μήτηρ θεῶν, wanders across the world with her κρόταλα βρόμια, her resounding castanets, and her σατίνας, her Phrygian chariot drawn by lions, looking for her daughter.[130] The classic story of Demeter's search for Persephone has been outfitted with pseudo-Phrygian trappings.

Many scholars have denied that this intermingling of the symbols of Demeter and Meter was a natural coherence of functions, preferring to see it as a self-conscious effort on the part of the Greeks, particularly in Athens, to "domesticate" and channel the wilder aspects of the Phrygian goddess's rites into publicly acceptable (and controllable) cult practices.[131] Yet this line of argument ignores the likelihood that the so-called wilder aspects of the Meter cult were well entrenched in Greek practice and perhaps even originated there. Moreover, this dual aspect of religious expression in public and personal rites was a long-standing part of Greek religious tradi-

124. Derveni Papyrus, col. XVIII, line 8, published in *Zeitschrift für Papyrologie und Epigraphik* 47 (1982), suppl. For commentary on the passage, see Kannicht 1969: 330.

125. H. Thompson 1937: 205–8; Nilsson 1967: 726.

126. Metzger 1965: 22, no. 43.

127. Arrian, *Anabasis* 3.16.8.

128. Graillot 1912: 504–5, 507. Graf 1974: 155, n. 24.

129. Möbius 1935–36: 243–53; Kannicht 1969: 327–60; E. Simon 1983: 26–27. For the possible location of the temple, see Travlos 1971: 112–13, 289–91. On the close relationship of Meter and Demeter, see Simms 1985: 66–67.

130. Euripides, *Helen* 1301–65. The word σατίνας was evidently Phrygian for "chariot"; it is used by Sappho (Lobel and Page 1955: fr. 44, 13) and Anakreon (Page 1962: fr. 388) and appears in the Homeric Hymn to Aphrodite, 13. For discussions of this chorus, see Sfameni Gasparro 1978; Kannicht 1969: II, 327–59; Cerri 1983; Roller 1996: 310–13.

131. Cf. Möbius 1935–36: 245, quoting Wilamowitz: "the Meter worshipped in Attica was the Mother worshipped everywhere, with no taint of the scandalous Phrygian creature." Similar sentiments are expressed by Mylonas 1961: 290–91 and Versnel 1990: 107–8, who maintains that Kybele was identified with Demeter in order to control the Phrygian deity.

tion, particularly evident in the worship of Demeter. In assimilating Eleusinian symbolism and cult practice with that of Meter, the Greeks were not Hellenizing the acceptable aspects of a distasteful foreign cult, but rather were recognizing that both goddesses spoke to both public and personal needs, which by nature involve variable forms of expression.

The ready transference of cult symbols and images between the Hellenic Mother goddesses and the Phrygian Mother in itself undercuts any assumption of barbarisms and inferiority in the cult of Meter, at least in the early stages of Meter's presence in the Greek world. The frequent and widespread mingling of the Phrygian Mother with Rhea and Demeter implies a voluntary syncretism between the foreign and the Hellenic Mothers, and bringing Meter into the circle of the most respected Greek gods was one aspect of this syncretism. This action in itself reinforces Meter's central position in Greek cult. No other foreign god was equated with a Greek deity or brought into the heart of the Greek pantheon to the extent that the Phrygian Mother was,[132] nor did any other foreign deity alter the cultic identity of indigenous Greek deities as the Phrygian Mother did.

In addition to the direct conflation of Meter with the Greek mother deities Rhea and Demeter, the cult of Meter was closely allied with that of several other Greek deities, including Hermes, Dionysos, and Pan. The first two need be discussed only briefly. Meter's links with Hermes are apparent through his presence on several Meter votive reliefs, where he stands next to the seated goddess. The connection between the two seems to arise, not from a shared mythic tradition, but from Hermes' function as the divine herald. In this capacity, Hermes becomes the god who conducts mortals in the mysteries of Meter and so is represented as her attendant.[133]

The connection with Dionysos, described by many authors, and realized most vividly by Euripides,[134] does not derive from any common bond of myth, but from the similar rituals and similar forms of ecstatic spiritual expression used to approach both deities. Meter was appropriately linked with Dionysos, the older and more respected deity, whose affinity with ecstatic ritual is well known. Like Meter, Dionysos was a deity at home both in the city and in wild, unsettled places. His worship too cut across the bounds of public and private religious expression.

Pan's connection with Meter is more direct. It is made explicit by Pindar, who

132. Other non-Greek deities were integrated into Greek tradition to an extent. The Syrian god Adonis, whose early death was lamented by Greek women, was drawn into the mythic cycle of Aphrodite and Persephone, and the Thracian goddess Bendis was frequently portrayed in Greek art as a Thracian Artemis and received an important festival in the Piraeus (Plato, *Republic* 1.327a), although Bendis did not appear in any Greek mythic cycle. On this question, see Simms 1985.

133. For examples, see *CCCA* II, nos. 362 (from Athens), 508 (unknown provenience). See also Reeder 1987: 431–32. Additional votive reliefs from Ephesos depicting Meter and Hermes jointly are discussed in chapter 7 below.

134. Pindar, *Dithr.* II.6–9 (Snell). Euripides, *Palamedes* (fr. 586 Nauck), and *Bacchae,* lines 1–169 and passim. Plato, *Phaedrus* 244a, and Hermias, *Σ* ad loc., pp. 104–105A (ed. P. Couvreur). Strabo 10.3.13. For a general discussion of the ancient evidence, see Kannicht 1969: II, 331–32.

calls him the comrade of the Great Mother and states that the two are worshipped side by side in Pindar's own shrine.[135] Elsewhere, Pindar calls Pan the κύνα, or dog, of Meter, no doubt alluding to the god's status as her faithful companion.[136] As the Greek god of the mountains and the woodlands, Pan was a logical associate of the Mother of the mountains.[137] He appears in this role in several votive reliefs of Meter, usually with his typical attributes, the syrinx, his shepherd's pipes, and the pedum, or shepherd's crook, which were appropriate for his pastoral life.[138] Pan had a natural affinity with Meter for another reason, since he was a deity, not only of the pastoral countryside, but also of the countryside of wild, uncontrolled nature.[139] Such lack of control is exemplified by the ecstatic state found in the rites of both Meter and Pan: one could become a Πανόληπτος, a person seized by Pan, just as one might be seized by Meter or by the Korybantes, and with equally disturbing results.[140] His ability to inspire "panic" emphasizes the irrational quality of this type of divine contact.[141] As a model for human relations with the divine, both Pan and Meter symbolized a somewhat frightening image. Pan, however, was consistently a respected, if minor, Greek deity; his position as a native Greek divinity kept him free of negative associations such as those of Meter's Phrygian background.

METER AND ATTIS

One deity with whom Meter was to be intimately associated was Attis, prominent in later myth and cult as the castrated lover of Mother Kybele. Yet Attis has formed no part in the discussion of Meter's Greek cult up to this point. The reason for this is simple: before the mid fourth century B.C., there is no evidence for the presence of Attis in the cult of Meter. Given Attis's colorful role in later Greek and Latin literature, this may seem surprising, yet the vivid descriptions of the Meter cult by the fifth-century poets and tragedians make no mention of him. Even Demosthenes, in attacking Aischines for his participation in ecstatic religious rites, never alludes to the eunuch god; given the virulence of Demosthenes' language, one imagines that he would have used Attis's deviant sexuality as grounds for further attacks if the tradition of Attis's castration had been known. Some scholars have assumed that the cult of Attis must have existed before the fourth century and cite as proof an incident described by Plutarch, an episode of self-castration in the Athenian Agora before the

---

135. Pindar, fr. 95–100 (Snell), and *Pythian* 3.78. On Pindar and Pan, see Haldane 1968.
136. Pindar, fr. 96 (Snell). Henrichs 1976: 256.
137. On the association of Pan and the Mother, see Brommer 1949–50: 12, and Borgeaud 1988a: 55, 147–48.
138. *CCCA* II, nos. 66, 180, 182, 339 (from Athens), 279 (from the Piraeus), no. 432 (from Lebadeia). See Borgeaud 1988a: 52–53.
139. Osborne 1987: 189–92.
140. Hermias, *In Platonis Phaedrum Scholia*, p. 105a (ed. P. Couvreur).
141. Like Meter, Pan was one of the deities suspected of influencing Phaedra's unusual behavior (Euripides, *Hippolytos* 142).

Sicilian expedition in 415 B.C.[142] This interpretation, however, ignores the fact that Plutarch's narrative makes no mention of either Meter or Attis; his context suggests, not a religious cult practice but rather the unusual action of one psychologically disturbed individual, the impact of which was enhanced by the subsequent Sicilian disaster.[143] It also seems unlikely that the absence of Attis before the fourth century B.C. resulted from the Greeks' rejection of his cult because they found the god too "barbaric" and "repulsive."[144] This assumption is undercut by the great frequency and spread of Attis figurines among these same Greeks in the second half of the fourth century and later. The figure of Attis is an intriguing example of the ways in which the Phrygian cult of the Mother Goddess was transformed to respond to the different social and political realities of Greek cult practice. As we shall see, the Attis of Greek cult and Greek myth was largely a Greek creation.

Before inquiring into the source of Attis in Greek art and Greek cult, one crucial point should be emphasized: unlike Meter, whose ancestry can be traced to the Phrygian goddess Matar, there is no indication of a god equivalent to Attis in Phrygian art or cult practice. In Phrygia, the name Attis functioned as the title of a priest of Meter until at least the first century C.E.[145] It was a priestly title in Greece also, at Rhamnous and at Samothrace,[146] suggesting that the Greeks' interest in the figure of Attis came through knowledge of this Phrygian usage. Yet in Greek (and later in Roman) society, the title Attis normally refers, not to a priest, but to a deity, albeit a minor deity, in the sphere of Meter Kybele. Thus in including the god Attis in the cult of Meter, the Greeks were making a significant addition to it rather than following a Phrygian precedent.

Attis's Greek character and form are already apparent in the earliest representation of him, a votive stele from the Piraeus dated to the mid fourth century B.C. (fig. 48).[147] The piece consists of an inscribed shaft with a sculpted relief above de-

142. Plutarch, *Nikias* 13.2. The suggestion was first made by Foucart 1873: 64–65, and followed by Burkert 1985: 177–79, Garland 1987: 130–31, and Versnel 1990: 107.

143. Burkert 1979a: 105 and 1985: 159, stresses that the use of a stone for self-castration in Plutarch's report must mean that the incident was connected with the cult of the Mother Goddess, noting the use of a stone in Roman narratives that do quite clearly relate to Attis, e.g., Catullus 63.3, Ovid, *Fasti* 4.237. This, however, ignores the fact that in numerous descriptions of the Attis cult, a different instrument was used, either a metal weapon (Lucretius 2.621; Martial 2.45; Lucian, *Dea Syria* 51) or a pottery sherd (Pliny, *NH* 35.165; Juvenal 6.514).

144. Kern 1935: II, 232; Ferguson 1944: 110–11; Versnel 1990: 107–8. Their comments reflect an attitude common in modern scholarship, that the legend of Attis must have been a traditional Phrygian tale, because no Greek would have countenanced such actions. For a further discussion of this problem, see chapter 1.

145. Polybios 21.37.4–7. Epigraphical evidence discussed by Welles 1934: nos. 55–61 and Virgilio 1981. The question of Attis's identity is considered in greater detail in chapters 7, 8, and 11.

146. At Rhamnous, Roussel 1930: 5–8 = *CCCA* II: no. 245. On Samothrace, Hippolytus, *De refutat. omn. haeres.* 5.8.9; 5.9.1–11.

147. Berlin, Staatliche Museen, inv. no. 1612, Kekulé von Stradonitz 1922: 198. The piece itself has long been known; it was discovered in the Piraeus in illicit excavation during the nineteenth century and was acquired by the Pergamon Museum in the early years of this century. The work is illustrated and discussed by Vermaseren 1966: pl. 11; *CCCA* II: no. 308: and F. Naumann 1983: pl. 40, 1, no. 552; the latter

FIGURE 48. Votive relief of Angdistis and Attis from the Piraeus. Mid fourth century B.C. Courtesy, Antikensammlung, Staatliche Museen zu Berlin, Preussischer Kulturbesitz.

picting two figures, a male seated at the left and a standing female at the right. On the shaft below the relief an inscription, written in clear, non-stoichedon lettering, reads: Ἀνγδίστει καὶ Ἄττιδι Τιμοθέα ὑπὲρ τῶν παιδίων κατὰ πρόσταγμα (Timothea [dedicated this] to Angdistis and Attis on behalf of the children according to command).[148] Therefore we can securely identify the two figures as Attis at the left, and Angdistis at the right.

The stele depicts Attis in profile, seated on a rock and facing right. He wears a dis-

---

two works give previous bibliography. The inscription is published as *IG* ii² 4671. The stele has been mentioned earlier in connection with Meter's function as a *kourotrophos*. My own views on this stele and on the origin of a god Attis in Greek cult have been argued at length in Roller 1994a, and so I give only a summary of the argument here.

148. Vermaseren, in *CCCA* II: 93, reads the text as ὑπὲρ τῶν παιδῶν, but the stone is clearly inscribed παιδίων.

tinctive costume, a long-sleeved, belted tunic, trousers, and soft boots with pointed toes. On his head is a close-fitting cap with a pointed tip extending forward; flaps hanging from the back of the cap fall over his shoulders. His left hand, resting on his left knee, holds a syrinx, while he extends his right hand forward in order to receive a small trefoil jug from Angdistis. A long curved stick, his crook, leans against the rock on which he sits. The female divinity opposite him, the Phrygian Mother Goddess, is addressed here neither as Meter nor as Kybele but as Angdistis, a name she bore in Phrygia and one that we shall meet with frequently in Hellenistic cult material.[149] She stands and faces Attis, wearing a peplos and low headdress with a veil extending down her back almost to her feet. In her right hand, she holds the small jug that she extends to Attis, while in her left hand, she holds a round flat disk, her tympanum, against her left leg.

Attis can be recognized not only from his name but also from his costume and attributes, both of which were routinely used in later representations to identify Attis as an Oriental shepherd and companion of Meter.[150] We should note, though, that neither costume nor attributes were original to Attis. The costume is a modification of Achaemenian Persian dress, widely used in Greek art to depict not only Persians but also Oriental figures of myth such as Amazons and Trojans.[151] In particular, this costume appears regularly in depictions of the Trojan Paris, during the mid fifth century B.C. and later.[152] The association of the costume with Paris and the conflation of Trojans and Phrygians on the Attic stage may well have encouraged the suitability of this dress for a Phrygian figure. Attis's later identification as a Phrygian shepherd may well stem from this connection with the Trojan shepherd Paris.[153] The attributes of Attis, his shepherd's crook and pipes, may also have been influenced by the woodland deity Pan, Meter's frequent companion.

On this stele, however, Attis is not the youthful shepherd of myth, but a god, the divine companion of Meter/Angdistis. His divinity is made clear not only from the fact that the stele is dedicated to him, but also from Angdistis's gesture of handing him her vessel, the instrument by which she received votive offerings. The gesture surely indicates that it was suitable for Attis to receive votive offerings too. We may compare a similar gesture made by the Greek divinity Themis toward the Thracian goddess Bendis, illustrated on an Attic red-figured skyphos of the later fifth century

---

149. Angdistis was apparently the personal name of the goddess in Anatolia, as opposed to her cult title of Matar; see Strabo 10.3.12, 12.5.3. See also a series of inscriptions on votive altars from the Phrygian site of Midas City, dedicated to Angdistis the Mother Goddess or Angdistis the Mother of the gods, discussed by Haspels 1971: 195–200, 295–301, esp. nos. 6, 8, 13; and in general, Gusmani 1959. Further examples of cult objects dedicated to Angdistis are discussed in chapter 7.

150. The typical Attis representation is abundantly illlustrated in Vermaseren and de Boer 1986.

151. For examples, see Roller 1994a: 250–51.

152. Note the two vases cited in n. 92 above.

153. On Attis as a Phrygian shepherd, see Theokritos 20.40.

B.C.; this action indicates that it is proper, *themis,* to worship Bendis.[154] The parallel gesture of Angdistis on this stele suggests that Attis was now an established part of Greek cult.

The appearance of a new god in Greek cult may seem unusual, but it was not unknown. The clue to the origin of Attis as a divinity may lie in the passage from Demosthenes' speech *On the Crown* 260, where *attes* is a ritual cry shouted by followers of mystic rites. The god Attis may be a divine personification of that cry, here embodied as an Oriental shepherd. A good parallel is furnished by the god Iacchos, a follower of Demeter in the Eleusinian Mysteries; his origins too lie in the mystic cry *iache,* and the deity is a personification of that cry. The close integration of the cults of Meter and Demeter, especially in Attica, makes this parallel all the more likely.

Thus Attis entered Greek art and Greek cult, probably during the early fourth century B.C., as the companion and attendant of Meter. Within a century, depictions of Attis in sculpted reliefs and terra-cotta figurines had become quite common and were widely disseminated throughout the Greek world, with examples known from Athens, Sicily, Amphipolis, Olynthos, and Delos, among other places.[155] The fact that depictions of him became so widespread so quickly indicates that Attis rapidly became an essential element in the cult of Meter. The Greeks explained this circumstance with an elaborate mythical tradition that made Attis Meter's lover. This is explored more fully in chapter 8, but its meaning can be briefly summarized here. Although it contains some aspects of Phrygian cult practice—namely, the connection of the Phrygian Mother Goddess with the rulers of the Phrygian state, and the fact that the goddess was attended by eunuch priests in Phrygia—the myth is of a specifically Greek type, that of the powerful goddess who destroys her lover, as in the tale of Aphrodite and Adonis.

Here we are concerned not so much with myth as with cult practice, in particular, the place of Attis in the cult of Meter. The function of the god Attis in Greek cult is suggested by representations of him, particularly the terra-cotta figurines. Many of these show him dancing, leaping, or playing an instrument, in other words, performing the same actions that the human devotees of Meter performed during their

---

154. Tübingen F 2, unattributed but mentioned in *ARV*² 1023, 147. For a discussion of Themis and Bendis on this vase, see E. Simon 1953: 25–26.

155. For a general summary of Attis depictions, see Vermaseren and de Boer 1986: 22–44. For late-fourth-century B.C. depictions of Attis in Athens, see Thompson 1951: 53 and pl. 26b; in Sicily, at Akrai, Sfameni Gasparro 1973: 269–70; in Amphipolis, Mollard-Besques 1972: nos. D 251, 252; and *Olynthus* XIV: 21–33 and pl. 42. For other examples from Amphipolis, Olynthos, and other sites in northern Greece, see *Olynthus* XIV: 119–21. By the third century B.C. and later, the type was extremely widespread; in addition to the sites listed above, examples of Attis figurines are known from Delos (*Délos* XXIII: nos. 364–69), from numerous sites in Asia Minor (Franz Winter 1903: 372, nos. 4, 5, 7, 10; Mollard-Besques 1972: D 649, D 865, D 1410, D 2291–2301, E 19, E 235–41), and from Italy (Winter 1903: 372, nos. 1–3; 373, nos. 2–5).

rites. In these objects, Attis stands as a substitute for the human worshipper, and so in offering a figurine of Attis, the human devotee was offering a part of him/herself. Other figures depict Attis in a more sedate pose, as on the fourth-century Piraeus stele. Here I think we should understand Attis in the role of an intercessor. The human worshipper of Meter was making a request of the goddess or thanking her for the fulfillment of a request (on behalf of the children, as in this case), and Attis has become the divine figure who reinforces the request or thank offering. In no case is there an intimation of anything disreputable in these Attis votives, nor is there any allusion to deviant sexual practices. The "Phrygian flasher" type, the Attis figurine with exposed genitalia, first appears in Rome in the second century B.C., and its meaning should be interpreted with reference to the cult of the Roman Magna Mater.

Attis cannot be used to explain the negative connotations that the cult of Meter acquired in Classical Greece. Indeed, the standard image of Attis in later Greek and Roman literature and art is more likely to be a result of those negative connotations, for the mythical image of Attis was surely influenced by the prevailing Greek stereotype of the Phrygian as effeminate Oriental barbarian. Away from the world of racial stereotypes and mythical images, Attis was the divine companion and attendant of Meter. People turned to his cult for the same reasons as they turned to the cult of Meter—namely, to obtain personal petitions and to enjoy personal contact with the divine.

METER'S PLACE IN GREEK SOCIETY

The question of the social status of Meter in the Greek world is inevitably linked to the question of who the goddess's worshippers were. Here the evidence fails us almost totally, for the majority of Meter votives are anonymous. The frequency, ubiquity, and varied quality of the fifth- and fourth-century Meter votives suggests, though, that the goddess's followers were a diverse group.[156] The unspoken assumption behind the foundation legend of the Athenian Metroön and negative connotation of the *metragyrtes* is that the Meter cult appealed to lower-class types and undesirables,[157] but this may not have been the case. The sympathetic treatment by important poets such as Pindar and Euripides of the religious experience offered by Meter speaks strongly for the broad attraction of the goddess to citizens and noncitizens, male and female.

There is, however, some evidence to suggest that the goddess had an especial

---

156. One point in support of this is the evidence from the Hellenistic cult of Meter in the Piraeus, discussed in chapter 7, where it is clear that Meter's adherents included people of both genders and varying social status.

157. This point of view has been taken for granted by several modern commentators, e.g., Bömer 1963: 871–74, "primarily a slave religion"; and Versnel 1990: 107–8, who takes for granted the need to "domesticate" the unpleasant associations of her foreign origin and nature.

appeal to women. Our evidence is somewhat equivocal on this point, and several of the connections of the Meter cult with women may reflect literary or social convention rather than reality. For example, women make up the tragic choruses that worship Meter with hymns, in the *Helen*, the *Bacchae*, and in the chorus of Phrygian women described in a fragmentary play of Diogenes:

καίτοι κλύω μὲν Ἀσιάδος μιτρηφόρους
Κυβέλας γυναῖκας, παῖδας ὀλβίων Φρυγῶν

I hear the women with their mitred heads, followers of Asiatic Kybele, daughters of the blessed Phrygians.[158]

This need not be an accurate reflection of cult practice, since women, especially foreign women, were often featured in tragic choruses to give an emotional, exotic flavor to the action.[159] Similarly, Demosthenes' attack on Aischines' mother for her adherence to ecstatic rites implies that nocturnal processions, loud noises, and snake handling are typical behavior of women; such actions are a product of women's unstable emotional state, which men (like the Athenian jury he is addressing) should reject.[160] And women were always regarded as particularly vulnerable to possession by a deity, particularly when this caused their behavior to become irrational or threatening.[161]

More telling of actual practice is the scene on the Ferrara krater, interpreted as a depiction of a set of rites, especially dances, connected with Meter. Here the majority of the participants in these rites are indeed women; in fact, there is only one adult male shown among the group. And we should note that one of the most damning charges laid against the *metragyrtes* in the foundation legend of the Athenian Metroön is that he had come to initiate the women of Athens into the mysteries of Meter. One can read this challenge to traditional authority as part of the mythic pattern of the story, but it may also be that the tradition preserved some truth, that women did find the cult of a mother goddess more appealing.[162] We have already noted that Meter functioned as a *kourotrophos*, a deity with special regard for mothers and young children. Women's sympathy for the Meter cult is also supported by a scattering of gravestones depicting a woman holding a tympanum. These may well

---

158. Diogenes, in Athenaios 1.2 (fr. 1, p. 776 Nauck). The Theban Semele is speaking.

159. E.g., the chorus of Persian women in Aeschylus's *Persae*, the Egyptians in the *Suppliants*, the Carian women in the *Libation Bearers*, the barbarian women in Euripides' *Phoinissai*, and many other examples; see Hall 1989: 115–16, 130–32.

160. Demosthenes, *On the Crown* 259–60. This too is a point of view supported by modern commentators; note the remarks of Foucart 1873: 60: "Cults of foreign deities made substantial progress, especially among women."

161. Padel 1983.

162. For a general discussion of women and ecstatic religion, see Lewis 1989: esp. 26–27.

have belonged to women who had served as priestesses of Meter, and their families were eager to publish that fact as a mark of distinction.[163]

At the same time, it would be wrong to claim that the cult of Meter appealed only to women. The earliest inscribed Meter votive from the Athenian Agora was dedicated by Kriton, a masculine name. The presence of a male worshipper in the Meter votive relief illustrating the Kouretes demonstrates clearly that men honored Meter as women did. While she may have functioned as the kindly Mother to women, the goddess's sphere of influence cut across gender and class lines. Our inability to define the goddess's worshippers more closely may in itself reflect how widespread her appeal was and how deeply it was rooted in Greek society.

SUMMARY: NOTHING TO DO WITH PHRYGIA?

During the fifth and fourth centuries B.C., the Greek Meter was an established figure in Greek cult. Her Phrygian origins, already greatly modified by the Greeks during the Archaic period, receded further into the background as her name, cult titles, and visual image developed away from her Phrygian predecessor into a specifically Greek definition of a Mother Goddess. A principal component of this definition was Meter's identification in myth and cult with the Greek goddesses Rhea and Demeter, particularly Rhea. Meter became the Mother of the gods, both in the indefinite sense as the progenitor of life and in the specific sense as the mother of the Olympian deities, honored with the Olympian pantheon even if she was not part of it.

The evidence from Classical Greece paints a lively portrait of a goddess who, despite her foreign origins, was very much at home in Greek society, worshipped by poets, politicians, and common people. Meter was an established deity in city life, particularly in Athens, where her roots as an Ionian goddess gave her a central role in the political life of the community, as guardian of the archives of the Athenian democracy. On a more personal level, people worshipped her through a type of rite designed to induce an altered mental state, whereby the participant could come into direct contact with the divine. This was a recognized aspect of Greek religious experience, associated with many deities including Apollo, Dionysos, and the Nymphs. To an extent, this was a legacy of Meter's Phrygian origins, for her identity as the Mother of the mountains made her the deity of the wild and untamed landscape. Yet the Phrygian Mother's affinity with mountains, caves, and springs is more muted in Greece during the Classical period. Her terrain was less the physical landscape of the countryside, as it had been earlier, and more the mental landscape of unrestrained behavior.

Perhaps because of this, the rites of Meter and the open expression of the altered

---

163. Two examples from the Piraeus, Möbius 1968: 39, pl. 24a; Clairmont 1970: 98, pl. 13a. Another very similar fourth-century B.C. gravestone of a priestess of Meter, of unknown provenience, is now in the Ashmolean Museum, see *Archaeological Reports* 1960–61: 59.

emotional state that these rites induced seemed somewhat threatening, as if they were encouraging people to throw off the bonds formed by membership in their Greek community. As a result, the rites of Meter evoked a mixed reaction, frequently bordering on disapproval. This seems to have become more pronounced during the latter part of the fifth century B.C., when Meter's Phrygian connections were revived and used to classify her as a barbarian goddess. She was still the Mother of the gods, but she was also the symbol of an Asiatic people regarded largely as a source of slaves and increasingly identified with the Trojans and Persians, the great enemies of Greek freedom.

The irony of this increasing "Orientalizing" of Meter is that the Oriental qualities ascribed to her had little foundation in her Phrygian background. The most visible symbols of her ecstatic rites, her tympana, cymbals, and castanets, were assigned a Phrygian origin, but this, as we have seen, is inaccurate. Instead, the putative Asiatic origin of Meter's rites was less real than it was a product of fifth-century political image-making, a way of assigning the open emotionalism expressed during her rites to a non-Greek people and thereby lessening its value.

Thus the Meter of Classical Greece, while a revered cult figure, increasingly reflected the changes in Greek society. She had entered Greece as a deity of the countryside, but by the end of the fifth century her cult on the Greek mainland was largely urban. In the early fifth century she was a fully Hellenized deity, equated with Rhea and worshipped with Demeter, but by the fourth century she was the goddess whose rites were suspect and whose priests were stigmatized as "those Phrygians!" Yet by this time, Meter had become a fully formed member of the Greek religious community; her rites could be derided, but not ignored. This process of development in the Classical Greek world gave a lasting stamp to Meter's personality and cult rituals, which was to survive and influence subsequent definitions of the Mother Goddess in the Hellenistic and Roman worlds.

7 · THE HELLENISTIC PERIOD

The centuries between the death of Alexander in 323 B.C. and the beginning of the Roman Empire under Augustus in 31 B.C. form a time when the cultural development of the Greek world was both uneven and diffuse. This circumstance will inevitably affect an attempt to follow the development of the cult of Meter, the Greek Mother Goddess. In the earliest phase of Meter's worship in the Greek world, we can trace the progress of her cult as it moved from central Anatolia to the Greek coastal cities and the islands, the Greek mainland, and the western Mediterranean. The cult of Meter in Classical Greece demonstrates how the rituals and activities of the goddess and her followers had an increasing impact on Greek literature, art, and social attitudes, most evident in Athens. In contrast, the ensuing Hellenistic age offers no single guiding thread with which to follow the cult of Meter. In part this is because the cult itself covered a much broader geographical area, comparable to the contemporary spread of Hellenism. Moreover, the issues raised by the status of Meter during this time are much more varied. We shall see the impact of the Greek Meter on the older Anatolian cult centers of Phrygian Matar, the Meter cult in established Greek cities, and Meter's presence in new city foundations. Yet despite the centrifugal quality of the material, the cult of Meter during the Hellenistic period continues to instruct us, both about Greek religious practice and about Greek society as a whole. Not only is there more material available for study, but the more extensive documentation enables us to hear a greater variety of voices reacting to the goddess, voices that tell us that the Mother Goddess had lost none of her power.

Evidence for the Meter cult in the Hellenistic Greek world comes from a variety of sources. The numerous shrines and sacred places of Meter illustrate the extent of her worship. Several epigraphical documents that preserve cult regulations and other information provide a clearer picture of cult rituals and practices. There is, however, no Hellenistic counterpart to the literary texts from the fifth and fourth centuries B.C. that offer such vivid descriptions of the goddess and the emotional reactions of her followers; in the few surviving Hellenistic texts in which Meter does appear, she is often a figure of lighthearted fun, and the power that her worshippers found in her cult takes second place to an artificial literary image.

The geographical spread of the Meter cult in the Hellenistic Greek world is extensive.[1] While the campaigns of Alexander had no immediate impact on the cult of Meter, the political realignments that took place after his death affected the diffusion of the goddess's cult and the range of cities and cult centers where she was worshipped. The Greek cities in western Asia Minor, where the cult of the Phrygian Mother Goddess had long been prominent, regained their freedom and their prosperity, and they once again furnish abundant evidence of the cult of Meter. One newly founded Hellenistic city, Pergamon, became an important center for the goddess's cult. In addition, the spread of Hellenism that followed Alexander's conquest of the Persian Empire had a marked impact on the cities and cult centers of the non-Greek Anatolian peoples. The older Anatolian languages and cultural forms disappeared, as centers such as Gordion, Ankara, Pessinous, and Sardis became increasingly Hellenized. The effect of the spread of Hellenism on the cult of the Phrygian Matar was not simply a replacement of Anatolian forms with Greek ones but a blending of the two that created a new formulation of Meter. One of the most significant results of this blending occurred during the third century B.C., when the cult of Meter was imported from Asia to the city of Rome. While this event is fully explored in chapter 9, it is important to remember that the transfer took place in the Hellenistic milieu, which experienced the resurgence of older cult forms and the spread of new shrines and sanctuaries.

During this same period, however, there is much less evidence of the Meter cult in mainland Greece. Of the mainland Greek sites discussed earlier, only Athens continued to have a prominent shrine of Meter, the Metroön in the Agora, rebuilt in the second century B.C. Yet there is other evidence of the continuing impact of Meter on private cult, both in the frequency of individual offerings to the goddess and in the existence of private cult organizations. One interesting example of the latter is furnished by the inscriptions of the *orgeones,* the governing body of the Meter cult, in Athens's port, the Piraeus. Here a rich body of epigraphical and archaeological data offers valuable insight into a flourishing cult of Meter in this community.

---

1. In addition to the Meter votives from Anatolia and the Greek world, cult objects have been found in Sidon (*CCCA* I: no. 895), Neapolis in Palestine (*CCCA* I: no. 896), Panticapaeum in the Ukraine (n. 43 below), Egypt (ibid.), and Bactria (*CCCA* I: no. 900).

METER IN PHRYGIA AND LYDIA

The Mother's older cult centers in Phrygia and Lydia form a good starting point. The Phrygian goddess Matar was still very much at home at several of her earlier shrines, but like many aspects of Anatolian life, her cult there was affected by the increasing influence of Hellenism, starting in the late fourth century B.C. Rather than simply absorbing Greek forms wholesale, however, the worship of Matar in Anatolia evolved into a hybrid that retained some aspects of the Phrygian Mother Goddess but took on features of Greek Meter as well.

The Hellenization of Matar's cult in Phrygia is evident in her nomenclature. She was now addressed exclusively in Greek, usually by her title as Mother, Meter, coupled with a topographical adjective. We learn of Meter Dindymene, an epithet alluding to a sacred mountain; this could be one of several, including a mountain near Aizanoi and one near Pessinous, as well as others near the Greek cities of the coast. The goddess was also worshipped at Aizanoi as Meter Steuene; in this case, the goddess was named for a cave sacred to her.[2] Meter Zizimmene was honored in southeastern Phrygia, at Sizma, near modern Kayseri.[3]

In addition to the application of Greek names, there was some real blending of Phrygian and Hellenic cult practices. The older Phrygian center of Gordion furnishes a good example. Gordion had long since lost its prominence as the capital of an independent Phrygian polity, but it retained a regional importance as a market town. Numerous Hellenistic images indicate the continuing cult of the Phrygian Mother, but for the first time, all these images, both imported and locally made objects, were based on Hellenic models. Among the imported objects are a marble statuette of the enthroned goddess with phiale and lions (fig. 49) and several terracotta figurines depicting the goddess seated either on her throne or on the back of a lion (fig. 50). Examples of local pieces include an alabaster statuette of the seated goddess with her lion and several terracotta images, of which the most impressive is a large, handmade figure of the enthroned goddess with phiale and tympanum (fig. 51).[4] Another object suggesting Hellenic influence on the cult of Meter at Gordion is a statuette of a young woman bearing a torch, probably also a Greek import; this work recalls the nighttime festivals of the goddess described in Classical Greek literature and depicted on Greek Meter votives.[5] The strongest iconographic influence on the Gordion Meter cult seems to come from Pergamon: several of the imported

---

2. Pausanias 10.32.3. Robert 1937: 301; R. Naumann 1967.
3. Ramsay 1906: 246; Mitchell 1982: no. 361, on Meter Zizimene.
4. Marble statuette, Roller 1991: pl. IIIc; terracotta statuettes, Romano 1995: 22–28, nos. 54–64; alabaster statuette, Romano 1995: pl. 41. For further discussion of this material, see Roller 1991.
5. For the piece, see Roller 1991: pl. IVa. Nocturnal festivals of Meter are discussed in Roller 1991: 140–41 and chapter 6 above.

FIGURE 49. Marble statuette of Meter
from Gordion. Late third–early second century B.C.
Courtesy, Gordion Excavation Project.

FIGURE 50. Terracotta statuette of Meter seated on a lion's back, from Gordion. Late third–early second century B.C. Courtesy, Gordion Excavation Project.

FIGURE 51. Terracotta statuette of Meter enthroned, from Gordion. Late third–early second century B.C. Courtesy, Gordion Excavation Project.

pieces were made in Pergamon, and some of the locally made objects, including the large handmade terracotta work, imitate a Pergamene model. All of these objects were found in household contexts, several of them in what are clearly household shrines.[6]

Yet it is doubtful whether the adoption of Hellenic imagery effected a change in cult practice. As in the earlier Phrygian period, small household shrines remained common, but there is as yet no evidence of a temple to the goddess. Meter's consort Attis remains an uncertain and inconspicuous figure in Gordion.[7] And at least one older Phrygian feature was retained, the connection of the goddess with funerary rites.[8] Taken as a whole, the Gordion material shows the eagerness of the local people to adopt and imitate Greek iconographic forms, but it also demonstrates the long life and essential conservatism of the cult of the Phrygian Mother in her ancestral home. Another Phrygian sanctuary, Midas City, suggests a similar pattern.[9] Here the presence of a small Hellenistic shrine on the high point of the older Phrygian settlement (now deserted) demonstrates the enduring connection of the Mother's cult with the high places of Phrygia.

The changing political landscape of central Anatolia brought an important new Meter shrine, Pessinous, to the fore. This Phrygian site, renowned in Roman history and legend as the oldest and most venerable sanctuary of Meter, has produced surprisingly little material related to the cult of the Phrygian Mother.[10] The site was occupied from at least the fifth century B.C., and a small stepped altar in the countryside nearby, similar to many other open-air shrines in Phrygia, indicates interest in the cult of Matar.[11] There is, however, little sign that Pessinous was a large or important Phrygian settlement, and neither is there much evidence before the Hellenistic period to suggest that this was the site of a major religious center.[12] The site

6. Provenience of the Gordion figurines, Romano 1995: 23–25; on household shrines, Romano 1995: 24.

7. Romano 1995: 41–42, tentatively identifies a terracotta statuette (no. 97) as Attis, although the figure's poor state of preservation makes this uncertain, and other interpretations, such as an Amazon, are also possible.

8. Note a miniature votive altar with relief doors on it, imitating a common type of Phrygian funerary monument; this was found in the same votive deposit as the marble statuette of Meter, Roller 1991: 141 and pl. IVb.

9. Haspels 1971: 154–55.

10. No written source before the second century B.C. mentions Pessinous, although Ammianus Marcellinus 22.9.7, in his description of the fourth-century C.E. emperor Julian's interest in the Meter cult, notes that the fourth-century B.C. Greek historian Theopompos records the founding of Meter's sanctuary at Pessinous by the Phrygian king Midas. Cicero, *De harus. res.* 13.28, states emphatically that Pessinous had been revered by the (Achaemenian) Persians, (Seleucid) Syrians, and all the kings who ruled in Europe and Asia. These comments may reflect the generally high status of Phrygian Matar in Anatolia rather than the historical prominence of this one shrine; see Virgilio 1981: 57–59. See also Diodoros 35.33.2; Strabo 12.5.3; Livy 29.10.5, 29.11.7; Valerius Maximus 8.5.3; Pausanias 7.17.9–12; Arnobius 5.5–7. For a general discussion of these sources, see Gruen 1990: 16, nn. 51, 52. The role of Pessinous in legends pertaining to the Meter cult is treated further in chapter 8.

11. On the earliest occupation of Pessinous, see Devreker and Waelkens 1984: 13–15, and Waelkens 1986: 37–39. For the altar, see Devreker and Vermeulen 1991: figs. 9, 10, and chapter 4 n. 87 above.

12. For evidence of the pre-Hellenistic settlement at Pessinous (still extremely scanty), see Devreker and Waelkens 1984, 13–14, and Waelkens 1986: 38–39. The site is still under investigation, and so any com-

would seem an unlikely candidate for a Phrygian sanctuary; it lies in a deep valley that is regularly subject to alternate bouts of extreme desiccation and flooding,[13] a situation quite unlike that of the mountain shrines that were the principal haunt of Matar. Ancient sources are quite insistent, however, on both the antiquity and the prominence of the Pessinuntine sanctuary, and the inhospitable nature of the site and its location away from natural resources and lines of communication may even support this point (for why else would anyone go there?).[14] Pessinous may well have taken on a greater significance during the Hellenistic period, when the importance of earlier cult centers such as Midas City and Gordion was substantially diminished.

Clear evidence for the cult of Meter at Pessinous emerges when the sanctuary attracted the attention of the Attalid kings of Pergamon, who built a temple and colonnades of white marble there. At that time, Pessinous was temple-state ruled by priestly dynasts.[15] Strabo, our main source for this event, unfortunately does not say which Attalid king first developed an interest in Pessinous, and so his information does not enable us to determine whether the Attalid dynasty had any direct contact with the site during the year 205/204 B.C., when the Romans reportedly removed the cult image of Meter from Pessinous and took it back to Rome.[16] Pergamene interest in the site is well attested for the mid second century B.C., however, through the correspondence between the Pergamene rulers Eumenes II and Attalos II and the dynasts of Pessinous.[17] Seven letters are known, dating from the period between 163 and 156 B.C., although they were inscribed on stone only in the first century B.C., probably on the walls of the Attalid temple.[18] This correspondence offers insight into the place of the Pessinuntine sanctuary in the world of Hellenistic power politics.

The letters record communications from Eumenes and Attalos to the priestly dynasts, all of whom took the title of Attis, perhaps a survival of the era when the name was used by Phrygian kings.[19] Attis continued to be a priestly title even when the

---

ments must be considered tentative; for a summary of the earlier excavations conducted by Pieter Lambrechts, see Devreker and Waelkens 1984.

13. Waelkens 1971: 349–50.

14. The literary sources on the status of Pessinous are discussed by Devreker, in Devreker and Waelkens 1984: 14–28, and chapter 9 below. On the inhospitable location of Pessinous, note the comments of Waelkens 1971: 349–52, and Devreker and Vermeulen 1991: 116.

15. Strabo 12.5.3. Waelkens 1986: 68–69.

16. This event is discussed at greater length in chapter 9. I find the comments of Gruen 1990: 16–19, persuasive; he argues that the Pergamene kings exercised no control over the region around Pessinous in the late third century B.C., and that the Romans were more likely to have taken the goddess directly from Pergamon itself or from the sanctuary of Meter on Mount Ida near Troy, legendary home of Aeneas, ancestor of Rome.

17. This correspondence has been extensively discussed by Welles 1934: nos. 55–61, and Virgilio 1981.

18. The blocks were reused in the Armenian cemetery at the nearby town of Sivrihisar, where the documents were seen and copied (the blocks have since disappeared). See Welles 1934: 241; Virgilio 1981: 13–20, and pls. 1–7.

19. See the discussion on the name Attis in chapters 4 and 8. Polybios 21.37.4–7 records that the names of the two chief priests at Pessinous were Attis and Battakes.

office was not held by a Phrygian; this is clear from the fact that one priest Attis had a brother named Aiorix, a Celtic name, indicating that by the second century B.C., the sanctuary was under the control of the Galatians.[20] The desire of the Pessinuntine dynasts to maintain the goodwill of the Pergamene rulers is clearly evident from the letters, as is the willingness of the Pergamenes to use Pessinous to further their own aims; in one instance, the Pergamenes clearly put the interests of Rome ahead of the needs of Pessinous.[21] We receive the distinct impression that Pergamon was the dominant partner in this relationship.

The cult of Meter figures surprisingly little in these letters. This should not be unexpected; while Pergamene interest in Meter is certainly well documented (as we shall see below), Pergamene interest in Pessinous resulted less from the site's status as a sanctuary of Meter than from its position as an independent state in Galatian territory, which the Pergamenes wished to control.[22] In the one letter that does refer specifically to the goddess, Eumenes expresses the wish that the goddess do a better job of caring for her priests when someone insulted them,[23] perhaps implying that it was up to the goddess (not Pergamon) to look out for Pessinuntine interests. In general, the letters establish Pergamon's interest in the site and in the cult but seem to suggest a time when the political influence of the Pessinuntine sanctuary was waning. As a result, Pessinous's heyday was brief; Strabo (a contemporary of Augustus) tells us that in his time, the dynasts had very little power and the city was much less prosperous, although the Meter cult was still important.[24] This is undoubtedly why the later priests of Pessinous published their predecessors' correspondence with Pergamon over a hundred years after the letters were written; they were seeking to bolster their claim to hegemony over the sanctuary and region.[25] The letters constituted the final display of Phrygian power in political and religious affairs.

Away from the world of power politics, we get a radically different view of the Phrygian Mother and her followers from a document of a private community under the protection of the goddess. The text, found in Lydian Philadelphia, dates from the late second or the first century B.C.[26] It regulates a household cult established by a certain Dionysios, who was led to found this group because of a vision he had re-

---

20. Virgilio 1981: 25–26, letter 1. For Galatians in Anatolia, see Allen 1983: 136–44; Mitchell 1993: I, 48–49 and passim. For Galatian influence on Phrygian culture, see Roller 1987b: 106, 129 no. 56; Frederick Winter 1988: 64–68; and DeVries 1990: 402–5.

21. On Pessinuntine support for Pergamon, letter 5 (Virgilio 1981): Attis sacrifices for the safety of the brother of Attalos II. On Pergamon's manipulation of Pessinous, letter 1 (Virgilio): Pessinous to capture the Pessongi by stealth, to benefit Pergamene interests. On Rome's interests outweighing those of Pessinous, letter 7 (Virgilio).

22. Virgilio 1981: 59–62.

23. Welles 1934: 242–43, letter 56; Virgilio 1981: 25, letter 2.

24. Strabo 12.5.3.

25. Welles 1934: 247; Virgilio 1981: 35–36.

26. The definitive edition of the text is Weinreich 1919. For bibliography, see Sokolowski 1955: no. 20, and more recently, the study of Barton and Horseley 1981. A portion of the text appears in *CCCA* I: no. 489.

ceived in a dream. This in itself is not unusual, for many such private cult foundations were established during the Hellenistic period.[27] The purpose of this foundation was not to honor one individual in perpetuity, however, but to establish a community of worshippers who would agree to abide by a strict code of personal behavior. According to the terms of the foundation, altars were to be set up for Zeus, Hestia, and the Θεοὶ Σωτῆρες, the Savior Deities, whose number included Eudaimonia (favorable spirit), Ploutos (wealth), Arete (virtue), Hygeia (health), Agathe Tyche (good fortune), Agathos Daimon (good spirit), Mneme (memory), the Charites (the Graces), and Nike (victory). The community would meet in the οἶκος, or house, of Dionysios. It would welcome men and women, free and slave, on equal terms. The text strictly prohibits the use of magic spells, love potions, abortifacients, and contraceptives, and enjoins a strict code of sexual behavior on its adherents, both male and female; adultery and fornication are strictly forbidden among freeborn cult members, and sexual relations between freeborn men and married female slaves are also prohibited (although the text does not appear to forbid prostitution). The whole community was to be under the protection of Angdistis, the Phrygian Mother Goddess, here addressed not by her title of Matar but by her personal name, which people used for her in Phrygia.[28]

This text has many interesting features, not the least of which is the close association between the Phrygian Mother Angdistis and correct moral behavior. This is a feature of the Phrygian cult that is attested more frequently in the first centuries C.E.[29] The text also offers one of the earliest explicit references to the goddess as a savior deity, another aspect that appears in later texts and cult dedications. The Savior Deities may well be a traditional feature in this cult, as a reference to ritual and cathartic prescriptions indicates; these are to be carried out κατά τε τὰ πάτρια καὶ ὡς νῦν, both according to ancestral tradition and as it is prescribed now (i.e., in this document). This raises the interesting question of what was being changed. Was it the addition of a new deity or of the behavioral code? Most commentators have suggested the former, assuming that the Greek deities were being incorporated into the cult of the Anatolian deity Angdistis.[30] This may well be the case: the city of Philadelphia was a recent Greek foundation and so the worship of Greek divinities is fully to be expected. The cult of Angdistis, the Phrygian Mother, was well known in Lydia also, as is demonstrated by the goddess's presence in a cult regulatory decree of the fourth century B.C. from Sardis.[31] Thus the Philadelphia text becomes an ex

27. Note a private foundation to honor Meter in Halikarnassos, Sokolowski 1955: no. 72, discussed below, and the wide variety of private Hellenistic cult foundations described by Laum 1914. On divine commands transmitted through dreams, see van Straten 1976b: 16.

28. Strabo 12.5.3. On the name Angdistis, see Gusmani 1959.

29. Note the increasing importance of the gods Hosios and Dikaios (Holy and Just), Mitchell 1982: see the discussion on p. 16 and nos. 44, 45, 242. See also chapter 11 below on sexual chastity in the Meter cult in the second century C.E.

30. Weinreich 1919: 31; Barton and Horsely 1981: 13.

31. Robert 1975.

cellent example of Hellenistic syncretism, blending the cult of a local divinity with Greek divinities and Greek personifications.

One may wonder, however, if the behavioral code was also novel, particularly for a Greek community. The concept of a closed group whose members are treated equally without regard to gender or legal status is highly unusual for this time.[32] As a divinity who reached her worshippers through direct personal inspiration, Meter/Angdistis already had a strong positive ethical influence. This document indicates that the goddess's influence extended not only to individuals but also to a larger group. The group's members were asked to renew their vows at regular intervals, monthly or yearly, and to assist in identifying members who did not abide by the community's moral code. One receives the impression that the adherents of this community took their obligations seriously, and that the Mother's ancestral prominence contributed to their sense of commitment.

Evidence for the cult of Meter in Lydia during the Hellenistic period is also found in Sardis, the old Lydian capital. Meter's ancestral presence is recalled by a dedication to the Lydian Mother of the gods, Μητρὶ Θεῶν Λυδ[ίαι], found near Sardis.[33] A relief of the early fourth century attests the goddess's continuing presence in the city; this illustrates Meter holding her lion while standing to the right of the figure of Artemis, who stands and holds a roe deer (fig. 52).[34] Two small human worshippers stand at the far right. The whole group is framed within a naiskos replicating the form of a Greek temple. Artemis is slightly taller than Meter, a circumstance indicating that hers is the more important cult. While this is not surprising, since Artemis was honored with the major temple in Sardis, the relief indicates that Meter retained an important status. Meter also received an important sanctuary, and the walls of the temple in this sanctuary were used to record and display public documents and correspondence with the Seleucid kings.[35] A few private votives from Sardis depict Meter in a conventional pose, seated on a throne with her tympanum, phiale, and lions.[36]

Another source of evidence for the continuing strength of the Mother's cult in Hellenistic Anatolia is a number of private votives dedicated to Angdistis. Although

32. The concept of a closed group formed to worship Meter was not unique to this community, however, for we shall see another example (without the moral restrictions on behavior) in the Piraeus.

33. From a site near Sardis, Robert 1982: 360–61.

34. Hanfmann and Waldbaum 1969; Hanfmann and Ramage 1978: 58–60, no. 20; Hanfmann 1983: 223, fig. 1.

35. Hanfmann 1983 et al.: 130; Gauthier 1989: 47–58. One document that specifically mentions the Metroön, a decree honoring the queen Laodike of 213 B.C., was to be inscribed on the pilaster (parastade) of the temple within the Metroön, implying that the Metroön was a sanctuary precinct with more than one building. A figure with a turreted crown that appears on Hellenistic coins of the city may be Meter, or perhaps Tyche (Hanfmann 1983 et al.: 130; Gauthier 1989: 55).

36. Hanfmann and Ramage 1978: 60–61, no. 25, and 169–70, no. 259 = CCCA I: no. 463. Hanfmann and Ramage suggest that a fragmentary relief of the late second or early first century B.C. depicting a female figure with a high, tubelike crown, no. 159, may represent Meter, but this is uncertain. Meter votives from the Roman era are discussed in chapter II.

FIGURE 52.
Votive relief of Artemis and
Meter from Sardis. Fourth
century B.C. Courtesy, The
Archaeological Exploration
of Sardis.

absent in Paleo-Phrygian texts, Angdistis became an increasingly frequent name for
the Mother Goddess in the Hellenistic period. In addition to shrines in Sardis and
Philadelphia noted above, there was also an important cult of Angdistis at Dokimeion in Phrygia, where she appears on coins minted by the city.[37] Numerous votives, generally small inscribed altars, were dedicated to her at Midas City,[38] and
inscribed votive statuettes are known from Bithynia and Pisidia.[39] All of these dedications address the goddess solely as Angdistis. There are in addition several votives

37. Robert 1980: 237, figs. 10–14.
38. Haspels 1971: 295–302, nos. 1–5, 7, 9–12, 14–17.
39. Bithynia, Schwertheim 1978: 798, no. I A8 (Kandira); *MAMA* VIII: 70 no. 396, Robert 1980: 239,
CCCA I: no. 767 (Viranköy). Pisidia, a small votive altar found in the village of Arvaliköy, south of Burdur, Robert 1980: 239 = *CCCA* I: no. 768.

from Midas City and Eumeneia dedicated Ἀνγδίστει Μητρὶ θεᾷ, to Angdistis the Mother Goddess, and Ἀνγδίστει Μητρὶ θεῶν, to Angdistis Mother of the gods,[40] as well as a text, now in Venice, whose provenience is unknown.[41] This indicates clearly that Angdistis was the name of the Phrygian Mother, a point explicitly stated by Strabo and Hesychios.[42]

An abundance of offerings from other parts of the Hellenistic world indicates that the name was not merely a local one. Outside of Anatolia, inscriptions and votive statuettes to Angdistis are known from Attica, Lesbos, Paros, Egypt, and Pantica-paeum on the northern shore of the Black Sea.[43] In these inscriptions, too, Angdis-tis was equated with Meter. The equation is further confirmed by the placement of a dedication to Angdistis on a typical Meter votive, a statuette of the seated goddess with lions and tympanum; this can be seen on pieces from Ephesos, Bithynia, and the one now in Venice.[44] These demonstrate the continuing importance of the Mother Goddess, both in Phrygia and well beyond her Anatolian homeland.

In sum, Meter continued to be a powerful force in the religious life of the non-Greek Anatolian peoples during the Hellenistic period, and her cult flourished in many older Anatolian centers. Most of Meter's shrines were now simple affairs, and her votive objects were small and unprepossessing, reflecting the economic and po-litical decline of the region. Only the sanctuaries at Pessinous and Sardis seem to have had conspicuous temples, and these owed their prominence to the support of Hellenistic dynasts. Yet interest in the Mother Goddess clearly remained strong in personal cult, reflecting the strength of her position in the lives of the Anatolian peoples.

THE GREEK METER IN WESTERN ANATOLIA

During the Hellenistic period, Meter was once again a real presence in the Greek cities of western Anatolia. The Greek Meter in Asia was still addressed by her tradi-tional titles of Μήτηρ Μεγάλη, the Great Mother,[45] and Μήτηρ θεῶν, the Mother of the gods, and the title Μήτηρ ὀρεία, the Mountain Mother, leaves no doubt about her identification as a mountain goddess.[46] In addition, the goddess was often ad-dressed with topographical epithets referring to a particular mountain sacred to her,

40. Midas City, Haspels 1971: 295–302, nos. 6, 8, 13. Eumeneia, *CIG* III 3886.
41. *CIG* IV 6837; *CCCA* I: no. 888.
42. Strabo 10.3.12. Hesychios, s.v. Ἀγδιστις.
43. Attica, a stele from the Piraeus, *IG* ii² 4671 = *CCCA* II, no. 308, here fig. 48, and a text of cult reg-ulations from Rhamnous, Roussel 1930: 5–8. Lesbos, *IG* xii, no. 118; Robert 1980: 238–39. Paros, *SEG* 13: 108, no. 445; *CCCA* II, no. 647. Egypt, *OGIS* no. 28. Panticipaeum, *CCCA* VI: no. 561; Robert 1980: 238.
44. From Ephesos, Keil 1915: 75, item L. The Bithynian pieces and the statuette in Venice are cited in nn. 39 and 41 above. There are a few objects dedicated both to Angdistis and to Meter, naming them as separate entities. *CIG* 3993, from Iconium; and at Sizma near Iconium, Robert 1980: 239.
45. In Erythrai, Sokolowski 1955: no. 25, line 96, no. 26, line 98; Engelmann and Merkelbach 1973: no. 207, Graf 1985: 162, 317. In Ephesos, Graf 1985: 317.
46. In Chalkedon, Sokolowski 1955: no. 4, line 12; in Ephesos, Keil 1926: 256–61, figs. 50, 51.

a circumstance noticeable in virtually every district of western Anatolia. The goddess in Ionia was particularly rich in epithets. In the town of Magnesia on the Sipylos, Meter became Meter Sipylene or Meter Plastene.[47] In Erythrai, she was Meter Kybeleie, an epithet that drew on the Paleo-Phrygian *kubileya* to refer to a specific mountain on the peninsula of Erythrai.[48] The goddess was Meter Antaia in Kolophon,[49] and in Smyrna, she was addressed both as Meter Sipylene and with the local epithet Meter Smyrnaike.[50] The Gallesion mountain south of Smyrna was the site of the shrine of Meter Gallesia.[51]

In other parts of western Anatolia, the picture is similar. In northwestern Anatolia, on the Aspordenon Mountain near Pergamon, the goddess was worshipped as Meter Aspordene.[52] In the Troad, she was Meter Idaia, the goddess of Mount Ida,[53] and in Kyzikos, Meter Dindymene, the goddess of Mount Dindymon, near the Sea of Marmara.[54] In Caria, near the city of Sparza, the goddess was addressed as Meter Sparzene.[55] In addition to epithets referring to specific sacred places, the Greeks in western Anatolia, in Ephesos, Erythrai, and Troy, remembered Meter's origins in the title Μήτηρ Φρυγία, the Phrygian Mother. Her antiquity was honored in Ephesos and Kyzikos as Μήτηρ Πατρωίη, the ancestral Mother.[56]

These epithets are particularly appropriate to the cult of Meter in Asia Minor, for they do more than reinforce the connection of Meter with specific places. They demonstrate that the Greeks were still very conscious of her origins, her geographical origin in Phrygia and her cultic origin in the mountains. But even more than the connection with specific locations, such epithets effectively emphasize the continuing connection between the goddess and the landscape, especially the mountains and hollows where she was most at home. Many of the Greek shrines of the goddess in Anatolia were located in remote mountainous areas, well away from urban centers, reinforcing the association of the goddess with the natural environment. This

47. Meter Sipylene: Homolle 1894, *CCCA* I: nos. 543, 544, 545, 546, 549, 550, 551, 555, 564, 571, 575, 576, 580, 582, 583, 584. These were all found in Smyrna. For Meter Plastene, see *CCCA* I: nos. 452, 453; cf. Pausanias 5.13.7. Both epithets refer to the same site, a shrine at the base of a mountain near Magnesia where a large relief of a seated figure carved into the side of the mountain (probably a Hittite relief—see Spanos 1983) was identified as a seated image of Meter; see nn. 58, 59 below.

48. Strabo 14.1.33; Graf 1985: 318.

49. *CCCA* I: nos. 599, 604.

50. Petzl 1990: no. 743, 11 = *CCCA* I: no. 547.

51. Meriç 1982: 28–30, cf. Strabo 14.1.27.

52. Strabo 13.2.6. The site, to be discussed below, was excavated in 1909; see Conze and Schazmann 1911. The topographical designation was also used to distinguish this aspect of Meter from the goddess worshipped in the city of Pergamon, where she was addressed as Μήτηρ Βασίλεια, cf. Ohlemutz 1940: 181 (discussed in chapter 11 below).

53. Strabo 10.3.12.

54. On Mount Dindymon near Kyzikos, Apollonios Rhodios 1.1092–1152. On other locations of Mount Dindymon, see Jessen 1903, and Santoro 1973: 73–74.

55. Robert 1937: 334 n. 3.

56. In Ephesos, Keil 1926: 256–61, *CCCA* I: nos. 624, 625; Graf 1985: 317; in Erythrai, Engelmann and Merkelbach 1973: no. 218; in the Troad, Strabo 10.3.12; in Kyzikos, Schwertheim 1978: 820, no. II A15. In general, see Robert 1982.

aspect of her identity had been a key feature of the goddess Matar in Phrygia, and Homeric Hymn 14 stresses its importance in the definition of the Greek Meter. Nonetheless, it is interesting to see how enduring this phenomenon was during the Hellenistic era (as it would be in Roman Anatolia as well). This tenacity emphasizes the essential conservatism of the region and shows that the power of Anatolian landscape was still a vital force in shaping the goddess's cult.

Several examples of Meter's mountain shrines are known. One is the shrine of Meter Sipylene, the Mother of Mount Sipylos, also known as Meter Plastene.[57] Pausanias reports that the image of Meter Sipylene was the most ancient of all the images of the Mother of the gods,[58] describing a seated figure carved out of the natural rock of the north slope of the mountain, not far from the modern town of Manisa. The sculpture, which can still be seen, depicts a seated figure in a long robe, although it is a Hittite image, not Phrygian.[59] Yet epigraphical citations and Meter votives from the site indicate that Pausanias's identification was already fixed in the Hellenistic period. To Greek eyes, a seated figure on the mountain had to be Meter.

Ephesos furnishes another example of a mountain sanctuary of Meter.[60] Located at the base of the Panayir Dağ, the sanctuary consists of niches carved into the side of the mountain, some of them empty and some them still containing images of the goddess carved from the live rock. On the rock plateau in front are additional cuttings and a large projection carved into the form of an altar. Several of the niches bear inscriptions, which variously address the goddess as Μήτηρ Ὀρείη, Μήτηρ Πατρωίη, and Μήτηρ Φρυγίη, indicating that to the Ephesians, she was the Mountain Mother, the ancestral goddess, and the Phrygian. Meter did not dislodge the cult of Artemis at Ephesos, and she never received a major temple, valuable votive offerings, or the type of public notice that made Ephesian Artemis so prominent. Yet the Meter cult continued to be an important part of Ephesian life.

The Ephesian sanctuary has also produced a series of small votive reliefs depicting the goddess standing, accompanied by one or two lions, which crouch on their haunches by her side.[61] In several examples, a young male stands at her right, and in a few cases, she has both a young man at her right and an older man on her left (fig. 53). An inscription to Zeus Patroös on a nearby rock altar identifies the older god as Zeus,[62] while other inscriptions record dedications both to Hermes and to

57. For the shrine, see Wolters 1887: 271–74. The inscriptions are published by Ihnken 1978: nos. 36–38.

58. Pausanias 3.22.4; 5.13.7. Pausanias's reference to Phrygian Pelops in the latter passage indicates that he had the Phrygian Mother Goddess in mind.

59. A Hittite hieroglyph to the upper right of the figure identifies it as a work of the Late Bronze Age; for a second Hittite Empire inscription next to this figure, see Güterbock and Alexander 1983. Spanos 1983 identifies the figure as male, but the relief is so worn that its gender is uncertain.

60. On the cult of Meter in Ephesos, see Keil 1915, Keil 1926: 256–61, Knibbe 1978: 490–91, and F. Naumann 1983: 214–16.

61. The reliefs have been collected and analyzed by Keil 1915; see also F. Naumann 1983: 218–23.

62. Keil 1926: fig. 50.

FIGURE 53. Votive relief of Meter with older and younger god
from Ephesos. Third–second century B.C. Archaeological Museum of
Izmir. (After F. Naumann, *Die Ikonographie der Kybele in der phrygischen
und der griechischen Kunst* [Tübingen, 1983], pl. 34, fig. 2.)

Apollo Patroös, making the identity of the young god less certain.[63] The figure's flat
hat and boots indicate, however, that he is Hermes, a regular companion of Meter
in the Greek world since the fifth century B.C. Similar reliefs are known from other
proveniences as well, including votive reliefs carved into niches in the hillsides at
Samos, a piece from the sanctuary of Meter Plastene near Mount Sipylos, and others with no secure provenience.[64]

The reliefs depicting Meter with male divinities are of an iconographic type new

63. Ibid.; *CCCA* I: no. 618 (Apollo). On the inscriptions, see Keil 1926: 259–61; F. Naumann 1983: 216.
64. Examples of the triad relief from Samos, Horn 1972: nos. 174 a–d. On the shrines of Meter in
Samos, in use from the late fourth century B.C. until the early first century C.E., see F. Naumann 1983: 217.
Mount Sipylos, Wolters 1887: 271–74. Unknown provenience, Keil 1915: 69–74, reliefs F–M.

to the Hellenistic period and provide further evidence of syncretism between Greek and Anatolian cult practice. In the Greek world, Hermes was the god who conducted initiates into the mysteries. He had a very specific connection with Meter, that of expiation,[65] and his presence here may reinforce the ethical function of Anatolian Meter, evident in the text from Lydian Philadelphia discussed earlier. The presence of Zeus is less expected, since this god had previously had no formal connection with the Greek Meter. During the first centuries B.C. and C.E., however, Zeus was to become a prominent part of the Meter cult in Pergamon and Aizanoi, a circumstance that resulted from the assimilation of Meter to Rhea and the legend of the birth of Zeus; thus Anatolian Meter was increasingly honored as the mother of Zeus. The votive reliefs from Ephesos and other Ionian sites suggest that such syncretism was well established by the early Hellenistic period.

Another mountain shrine lies on the Gallesian Mountain south of Smyrna, near the ancient city of Metropolis, which surely derived its name from this sanctuary.[66] The Meter sanctuary, located in a cave at the foot of the mountain, was in use from the fourth century B.C. until late antiquity. Cult activity is attested by numerous animal bones, the debris of sacrificial victims, and several statuettes and votive reliefs of the goddess, in both terracotta and stone.[67] The terracotta images depict the standard type of seated Meter votive, while the stone votives follow the Ephesian model of the standing goddess accompanied by an older and a younger male figure. The frequency of the type at these sites suggests that representation of Meter with two male gods was characteristic of this region.

In addition to her rural shrines, Meter functioned as a civic deity as well. The Mother Goddess of Smyrna, often addressed as Meter Sipylene, is attested through many inscriptions and through a large number of Meter votive statuettes.[68] Her temple, the Metroön, located on the plain in the main part of the city, was reputed to have been one of the most beautiful in Smyrna.[69] There was a prominent Metroön in Kolophon also, located in the city center, and a fourth-century B.C. text mentions

65. Hermes conducts initiates into the Lesser Mysteries in Athens, mysteries that supposedly originated in the expiation of Herakles; see the valuable discussion of Reeder 1987: 431–32. The Hermes figure has often been identified as Kadmilos, a minor divinity who could function as an attendant (Conze 1880, 1881, 1888, 1891), but this seems very unlikely; Kadmilos was a serving deity of the Great Gods at Samothrace (Cole 1984: 3), but there is no evidence to suggest that he had any connection with Meter. Keil 1915: 76, identified the group as a divine triad of father, mother, and child, but that concept seems more appropriate to Christianity than to Greek paganism.

66. For the ancient name, see Strabo 14.1.1, and a fourth-century B.C. inscription, Sokolowski 1955: no. 29. The site has been surveyed by Recep Meriç; see esp. Meriç 1982: 28–30 on the sanctuary. Note that the name Metropolis was used for several sites in Asia connected with the Mother goddess cult, including Metropolis in Phrygia (Haspels 1971: 210), and in Lydia (Steph. Byz., s.v. Μητρόπολις).

67. Meriç 1982: nos. TK 6–12 (terracotta figurines), and ST 14–15, stone statuettes.

68. On the inscriptions, see *CCCA* I: no. 547 = Petzl 1990: no. 743, 11, Meter Smyrnaike, and n. 47 above, Meter Sipylene, clearly the main identity of Meter in Smyrna. For the statuettes, see *CCCA* I: nos. 553, 556, 558–60, 577 (Meter standing), 554, 557, 561, 563, 565–66, 569–70, 572–73, 579 (Meter seated).

69. On the temple, see Strabo 14.1.37; Pliny, *NH* 14.6.54; Aristeides, *Or.* 15 (Dindorf, p. 375), who comments on its beauty, although he may have been partial to his home town. Nothing of the building survives today.

Meter, here worshipped as Meter Antaia, as one of the five principal deities of the city.[70] The decrees of the Boule, the democratic council of Kolophon, were to be written up on a stone stele, with a copy placed in the Metroön.[71] This is an instructive parallel to Athenian practice and one that reflects the importance of Meter in the political life of the Ionian Greeks. Another civic Metroön was found in Erythrai, attested by an inscription of the first half of the third century B.C. recording the sale of priesthoods.[72] The priesthood of Μήτηρ Μεγάλη cost 480 drachmas, making it one of the more expensive offices, exceeded in value by only seven of the fifty-four offices that changed hands. The purchaser, a certain Molion, son of Dionysios, is also known as an official in charge of the city mint;[73] his prosperity and position of authority mark him as an important person in Erythrai, and his willingness to commit resources to the cult of Meter speaks highly for the status of the cult in this community. Meter also appears in a second-century B.C. civic calendar of religious festivals in Erythrai and in one private dedication.[74] The continuing importance of Meter on Chios is also demonstrated by inscriptions, including one to Μήτηρ Κυβελείη, referring back to her Phrygian nomenclature.[75] One particularly interesting text records that a certain Kallisthenes undertook the ceremony of the στρωτή and the καθέδρα, the "spreading" and the "throne," for Meter.[76] Both of these are rituals that suggest an interesting fusion of Anatolian and Greek cult practices, which we shall meet with again in connection with Meter and Attis in the Piraeus.

The shrine of Meter in Priene suggests a different pattern.[77] It was a small, unprepossessing affair, an open-air sanctuary located in the residential quarter near the west city gate. Terracotta figurines and marble statuettes of the seated goddess with her lion provide the identification of the sanctuary, and charred animal bones and offering vessels confirm its ritual usage. Other statuettes, reliefs, figurines, and one rather crude statue depicting the goddess were found in various locations throughout the city.[78] The modesty of the shrine, combined with the lack of any reference to Meter in inscriptions or coins from Priene, suggests that the goddess played little or no role in the formal cults of the polis. Yet the frequent occurrence of Meter votives

70. *CCCA* I: no. 599.

71. *CCCA* I: 601, 602, 605.

72. Engelmann and Merkelbach 1973: no. 201; the priesthood of Meter is mentioned on side A, line 50 (= Sokolowski 1955: no. 25, line 96).

73. Graf 1985: 317.

74. The sacred calendar, Engelmann and Merkelbach 1973: no. 207, line 98 (= Sokolowski 1955: no. 26 line 98). The section that mentions Meter is too badly damaged to ascertain anything but the name. The private dedication appears on a small altar of the late second or first century B.C., offered to Μήτηρ Φρυγία, Engelmann and Merkelbach 1973: no. 218.

75. Forrest 1963: 59–60 no. 11 (Chios). Hekataios says Kybeleia was the name of a city on the Erythraian peninsula (*FGrHist* 1 F 230; cf. Strabo 14.1.33), which may mean that there was a Μήτηρ Κηβελείη near Erythrai (this was the opinion of Engelmann and Merkelbach 1973: 365–66).

76. Forrest 1963: nos. 9, 10; no. 9 mentions the στρωτή.

77. On Meter in Priene, see Wiegand and Schrader 1904: 171–72 and Schede 1964: 101.

78. For other representations of Meter at Priene, see Wiegand and Schrader 1904: 373–74 and F. Naumann 1983: 261–62.

illustrates that the lack of official patronage did not prevent the cult of Meter from playing a significant role in the personal lives of private citizens. Further north, both Meter and Attis are abundantly attested in the rich group of late Hellenistic figurines from Myrina; most of these were found in graves and demonstrate the continuing influence of Meter in private cult.[79]

A third-century B.C. text from Halikarnassos also documents Meter's role in personal cult.[80] A certain Poseidonios was ordered by the oracle of Apollo at Telmessos to found a family cult, with provisions for sacrifices to the Ἀγαθὴ Τύχη (Good Fortune) of Poseidonios's parents and the Ἀγαθὸς Δαίμων (Good Spirit) of himself and his wife. Other deities to be honored by this foundation were Zeus Patroös, Apollo Telmessos, the Moirai, and the Mother of the gods. Something of a pecking order emerges in the provisions for the sacrificial victims: Zeus, Apollo, and the Moirai were all to receive a ram, while Meter was to get only a goat. The text confirms Meter's regular presence in personal cult and her subordination to the other deities of the Greek pantheon.

Meter also enjoyed a special prominence in northwestern Anatolia. She received cult honors in Chalkedon,[81] as well as in Kyzikos, where she was worshipped with a variety of topographical epithets, not only as Meter Dindymene, but also with other topographic epithets.[82] The foundation of the cult of Meter Dindymene was ascribed to Jason and the Argonauts at the start of their voyage across the Black Sea, an event featured by Apollonios of Rhodes in the *Argonautika*.[83] The importance of Meter Dindymene may be inferred from the value of the cult statue, supposedly taken by the Kyzikenes from their neighbors in Prokonnesos; Pausanias reports that the statue was of gold, while the goddess's face was made from hippopotamus ivory.[84] There is also a rich series of inscribed votive reliefs from Kyzikos illustrating scenes of sacrifice to the goddess.[85] A typical example depicts the seated goddess at her altar, while a procession of worshippers approaches with hands raised in adoration and an attendant leads two sheep forward for sacrifice (fig. 54).[86] The text below, primarily a list of names of officials with their titles, imputes a certain degree of prestige to the individuals involved in the cult.

79. Burr 1934: nos. 63–64; Burr dated these to the first century B.C. Other examples are illustrated in *CCCA* I: 498–510.

80. Sokolowski 1955: no. 72. Strictly speaking, Halikarnassos was a Carian, not an Ionian city, but by the third century B.C. the city was so thoroughly Hellenized that it seems best to discuss this inscription here.

81. Sokolowski 1955: no. 4.

82. Hasluck 1910: 214–22, dedications to Μήτηρ Πλακιανή, Κοτυιανή, Τολυπιανή, Ανδιρηνή, and Λοβρινή.

83. Apollonios, *Argonautika* 1.1092–1152.

84. Pausanias 8.46.4.

85. The cult of Meter in Kyzikos has been the subject of a special study by Schwertheim 1978: 809–26. nos. IIA and B.

86. A dedication to Meter Tolypiane, illustrated by Schwertheim 1978: 817, no. IIA 11; F. Naumann 1983: no. 581, pl. 44, 1 = *CCCA* I: no. 289.

FIGURE 54. Votive relief of Meter
with worshippers from Kyzikos. Second century B.C.
Courtesy, National Museum, Copenhagen, Department
of Near Eastern and Classical Antiquities.

The cult of Μήτηρ Ἰδαία, the Idaean Mother, in the newly established city of Ilion is of special interest, for this was revered as the site of Homer's Troy. Cult activity on the southwest side of the mound of Bronze Age Troy during the sixth century B.C. is attested by the presence two temples, although the identity of the deities worshipped there is unknown.[87] In addition, two open-air sanctuaries, an upper and a lower level, have been identified from the Hellenistic period, each containing an altar.[88] The lower sanctuary has yielded numerous terracotta figurines and marble statuettes of Meter, two figurines of Attis, and several figurines of draped women. Worth noting is a figurine of Attis as an infant, a rare type in Anatolia, although the piece came from a mixed context and so is not definitely Hellenistic.[89] The sanctuary to the goddess on Mount Ida, well known during the Roman era, also appears to have been active during the Hellenistic period, and terracotta figurines found in several sections of the Trojan settlement attest to the goddess's presence in private cult.[90] The prominence of Meter at Troy was to receive even greater attention in the year 205/4 B.C., when the Romans brought the goddess to Rome to be the Mater Deum Magna Idaea, the Great Idaean Mother of Rome. As a result, the city of Ilion received a number of special privileges: it was formally recognized by the Roman Senate as the mother city of the Romans in 188 B.C. and was granted additional territory and immunity from taxation.[91] From the perspective of a Hellenistic Greek city, however, the cult of Meter in Troy was little different from that in other contemporary Greek cities—namely, a cult practiced on the goddess's sacred mountain, within her urban sanctuary, and throughout the households of the city.

Among the Greek cities in Asia, we see Meter most vividly in the new foundation of Pergamon, where she had a conspicuous presence both in the city and in two open-air shrines in the mountains nearby.[92] The ruling Attalid dynasty took a strong interest in the goddess, as indicated by their support for her sanctuary at Pessinous, and a series of inscriptions, a fine life-size statue, and several statuettes and terracotta figurines from Pergamon demonstrate that this interest was widespread.

87. Rose 1995: 85–88; 1997: 76–86.

88. The sanctuary area at Troy, first noted and briefly described by C. W. Blegen (Blegen et al. 1958: 259–73, 303–7), is currently being investigated by a team from the University of Cincinnati; for reports on the Hellenistic levels, see Rose 1993b: 98–104, 1994: 76–86, 1995: 85–94; 1997: 86–92. Since the site is still under investigation, this description should be considered tentative. I am grateful to C. Brian Rose for sharing information on his work in progress with me.

89. D. B. Thompson 1963: 77–84, nos. 16–51; Stella G. Miller 1991: 39–43; CCCA I: nos. 329–30 (statuettes). The figure of the baby Attis (Miller 1991: 42–43 and fig. 2) came from a context ranging from the third century B.C. to the fourth century C.E.

90. Dion. Hal. 1.61. D. B. Thompson 1963: 79 discusses two terracotta plaques perhaps depicting the cult monument at this sanctuary on Mount Ida. On figurines from domestic shrines, see ibid.: 80.

91. Livy 38.39.8–11; Strabo 13.1.27. See the discussion in Rose 1994.

92. The cult of Meter in Pergamon has been carefully discussed by Ohlemutz 1940: 174–91. On the two extramural shrines, see Conze and Schazmann 1911 (Mamurt Kale) and Nohlen and Radt 1978 (Kapikaya).

Let us look first at the evidence for the cult of Meter within the city of Pergamon. The goddess worshipped at Pergamon was Μήτηρ Μεγάλη, the Great Mother, a cult title that, although widely used, was not distinctive to this city. As Meter Megale, the goddess had a city sanctuary called the Megalesion, located near the city wall, as we learn from a citation of the Roman author Varro.[93] This may well be a survival, otherwise rarely attested in Hellenistic Greek cities, of the older Phrygian function of Matar as the protector of gates and boundaries. A potential candidate for this sanctuary at Pergamon is the series of foundations located near the main gate leading to the upper city, where a life-size statue, possibly the most impressive sculptural representation of Meter surviving from the ancient world, was discovered (fig. 55).[94] The statue, dated to the second century B.C., is derived from the Agorakritan model. The goddess is shown seated on a large, elaborate throne with a footstool. She wears a chiton, belted under her breasts, and a mantle draped over her lap, its horizontal folds contrasting with the vertical folds of the chiton. Her left arm rests on the arm of the throne, and its upper surface has been hollowed out to insert a round object, surely the tympanum, which was probably made separately. The work lacks the head and right arm, and so it is uncertain whether the goddess held an offering vessel in her right hand, although contemporary terracotta figurines suggest that this is likely. A marble lion, surviving only in fragments, may have been placed by the goddess as her companion.[95] Apart from the high quality of the workmanship of the statue, the most noteworthy thing about it is its conservatism, for it closely follows the Classical schema of Meter representations. The piece may very well have been a cult statue, and its prestige may well have confirmed this schema, for we find the Pergamene model widely distributed in other Anatolian cult centers, in places as diverse as Troy and Gordion.[96]

Numerous stone statuettes and terracotta figurines depicting Meter were also found throughout the city.[97] Two of the Pergamene figurines depict the goddess wearing a high crown in the form of a tower, the earliest examples of the so-called mural crown that was to be so popular in Roman representations of the Mother Goddess (fig. 56).[98] This too may be an allusion to Meter's function as the protector of Pergamene gates and walls. These statuettes and figurines appear to have been used in household shrines, a situation similar to that noted in Troy and Priene.

93. Varro, *De ling. lat.* 6.15; cf. Ohlemutz 1940: 183–85.
94. Now in the State Museum in Berlin; see Franz Winter 1907: no. 45, pl. 12; F. Naumann 1983: no. 554 (with previous bibliography), pl. 41; *CCCA* I: no. 349.
95. For the lion, see Winter 1907: no. 165.
96. Roller 1991: 137–38.
97. The statuettes, Franz Winter 1907: nos. 239 (standing figure), 240–43 (seated figures); the figurines, Töpperwein 1976: 49–53, nos. 188–202. All but one of the more than sixty Meter figurines from Pergamon show her seated.
98. Töpperwein 1976: nos. 190 and 199.

FIGURE 55.   Marble statue of Meter
from Pergamon. Second century B.C. Courtesy,
Antikensammlung, Staatliche Museen zu Berlin,
Preussischer Kulturbesitz.

FIGURE 56.
Terracotta statuette of
Meter from Pergamon.
Third–second century B.C.
Courtesy, Deutsches
Archäologisches Institut,
Istanbul.

Meter also appears on the Great Altar of Pergamon, where she is seated on a lion. While reflecting Pergamene interest in the goddess, the figure on the altar alludes to the Rhea of Greek mythology, not to the Mother of Anatolian cult.[99]

Equally important to the Pergamene cult of Meter, if not more so, were the extramural sanctuaries of the goddess located in the mountains near Pergamon. The major one, known as Mamurt Kale, lies about thirty kilometers southwest of the city. Strabo called this the most important Pergamene sanctuary of Meter, who here was worshipped as Meter Aspordene.[100] Despite its proximity to the city of Pergamon (one can see the city from this sanctuary), the place is difficult of access, located on a mountaintop in desolate country. Yet the site was honored by the Pergamene

99. E. Simon 1975: 32, pl. 27. The iconography of the Mother of the gods seated on the back of a lion was probably introduced into the Greek world in the late fourth century; according to Pliny 35.36.109, this scene was painted by Nikomachos, son and pupil of Aristeides.

100. Strabo 13.2.6. The sanctuary was excavated by the German Archaeological Institute in 1909; see Conze and Schazmann 1911 and a good summary in Ohlemutz 1940: 174–81. The terracottas from the site were published by Töpperwein in Nohlen and Radt 1978: 77–87.

kings from the inception of the city. The first ruler of Pergamon, Philetairos, created a sacred enclosure there with an altar and temple, which bore on its architrave the inscription Φιλέταιρος Ἀττάλου Μητρὶ θεῶν, Philetairos son of Attalos [dedicated this] to the Mother of the gods. This inscription was damaged at some point, but was repaired using the same text. Along the center back wall of the temple was found a large stone basis, evidently for a cult statue. The basis appears to be older than the temple, suggesting that the Pergamene kings did not found the sanctuary but developed an already existing shrine. We may assume that during the period when the Attalid dynasty was establishing itself in the new city, the rulers would have taken care to support the established local cults in the region. The continuing interest of the Attalids in the goddess's mountain sanctuary is demonstrated, not only by the repair of the temple inscription, but also by the discovery of two other inscriptions connecting the Attalid family with the site, one a gift from a cousin of Philetairos, who dedicated a statue of his wife to Meter, and the other a dedication to Attalos I Soter by the priestess Metreis.[101]

Evidence for a more popular use of this mountain sanctuary is furnished by the large number of terracotta figurines found there.[102] Several are freestanding pieces depicting Meter seated, with her regular attributes of lion, tympanum, and phiale. Others are relief plaques in which the goddess is shown within a naiskos, usually an Ionic temple, recalling the archaic images of Meter seated within her naiskos. Two examples depict Meter in the famous Pergamon Altar pose, riding on a lion's back. Other figurines depict standing figures, often veiled women, holding up a tympanum; these may represent cult worshippers performing the music used in the goddess's rituals. A number of handmade animal figurines may allude to gifts of animals for sacrifice, and one figurine shows the goddess enthroned with a small child on her lap,[103] an interesting type, which should be added to the limited but nonetheless persistent evidence that Meter played the role of *kourotrophos*—that is, a goddess who nourished mothers and small children.[104]

In addition to these predictable Hellenistic types, several of the figurines from Mamurt Kale show close affinities to statuettes of Meter made in the sixth and fifth centuries B.C., supporting the observation of the excavators that the Attalid cult structures were built on the site of an earlier sanctuary. The figurines include seated images of Meter with no lion, whose closest parallels are with the late Archaic figurines from

101. Conze and Schazmann 1911: 7, 38; Ohlemutz 1940: 178.
102. For the terracottas, see Conze and Schazmann 1911: pls. 11–13; Töpperwein, in Nohlen and Radt 1978: 77–90.
103. Töpperwein, in Nohlen and Radt 1978: pl. 36, no. MK 16. See also Conze and Schazmann 1911: pl. 12, no.4, interpreted by Ohlemutz 1940: 178, as the goddess in the role of *kourotrophos*. This piece has since been lost.
104. It is also possible that Meter may be shown in her mythic role as the Mother of Zeus, a mythological tradition attested in Pergamon in the second century C.E., but that may be older. See chapter 11 below.

Kyme.[105] In the Hellenistic period, worshippers surely would have come from Pergamon, and remnants of stoas were found near the sanctuary; these may have been used to house pilgrims.[106] The continuing use of the sanctuary is attested by Hellenistic terracottas and coins,[107] but these cease after the first century B.C., suggesting that the sanctuary may have been abandoned during the Roman era.

Another extra-urban Meter sanctuary, known as Kapikaya, lies about five kilometers northwest of Pergamon.[108] Its identification as a Meter sanctuary is secure through the finds of several terracottas depicting the goddess seated on her throne with her lion, and one vessel inscribed *Μητρ[ὶ] Θεῶν*. A much simpler shrine than Mamurt Kale, Kapikaya consists of a small grotto with a natural spring and a rock terrace in front. A stepped altar and several niches were carved into the rock, and steps and niches are found in the grotto as well. The arrangement is very reminiscent of the stepped niches and rock altars found at Phrygian shrines such as Kalehisar, and it is also similar to the carved niches found in the rock cliffs at Phokaia and Ephesos. The site was evidently used as a Meter sanctuary from the early third through first centuries B.C., but during the first century C.E., it was transformed into a Mithraeum, at which point evidence for its use in the cult of Meter ceases.

The ample data pertaining to the cult of Meter in Pergamon and the surrounding region enable us to draw a clearer picture of the goddess, her rituals, and her status within the community. Meter was clearly an important deity—her patronage by the ruling dynasty and the high quality of her cult statue attest to that. At the same time, she was not one of the most important deities of the city, on par with Athena and Zeus. She apparently did not have a conspicuous temple, and her cult shrines did not serve as a focus for important construction programs within Pergamon. The pattern of the Meter cult in Pergamon replicates that noted in several other Hellenistic Greek cities—namely, that the goddess was worshipped primarily in open-air shrines, household cult, and extramural mountain sanctuaries. Meter in Pergamon retained many characteristics of the older Phrygian Matar, including her conspicuous position near the city gate, her prominence in mountain shrines, and her appeal to people of both high and low social status. The visual image of the goddess in Pergamon was, however, thoroughly Hellenized, derived from representations developed in Greece. This blend of Hellenic and Anatolian forms was to be important,

---

105. The goddess is shown wearing a skirt with folds depicted as three vertical ridges between the legs, cf. Töpperwein, in Nohlen and Radt 1978: pl. 36, nos. MK 14, 16. Töpperwein, ibid.: 86, states that close parallels exist in style and clay composition between the Mamurt Kale figurines and figurines from Larissa, but the current excavator of Pergamon, Wolfgang Radt (cited in Romano 1995: 23), believes that the figurines are of Pergamene manufacture.

106. Ohlemutz 1940: 177.

107. Ibid.: 180; Töpperwein, in Nohlen and Radt 1978: 86.

108. The site, first noted by Conze and Schazmann, was investigated primarily as a salvage excavation by the German excavators of Pergamon, Klaus Nohlen and Wolfgang Radt, in a six-week period during the fall of 1972; see Nohlen and Radt 1978.

since the Pergamene image of Meter was to have a substantial impact on the Mother Goddess who appeared in Rome.

One aspect of the Meter cult in the Greek cities of western Asia has so far been mentioned only briefly—namely, Attis, that most problematical of figures, who was at home neither in Phrygia nor fully in Greece. The god Attis was a development of mainland Greek cult, first appearing in Athens and Attica in the fourth century B.C. and spreading from there to Greek cities on the Aegean islands and in northern Greece. Thus his presence in the Greek cities of Anatolia would have been somewhat intrusive, for he was not part of the original Meter cult, but a borrowing from the Greek cities on the mainland. For that reason, it is not surprising that Attis only rarely appears in the finds from the Hellenistic cult of Meter in western Asia Minor. In addition to the terracotta Attises of uncertain date from Troy, a single Attis figurine is known from the city of Pergamon.[109] A single arm, clothed in the long-sleeved garment characteristic of Attis depictions, was found among the terracotta figurines at Mamurt Kale, and a vessel inscribed with the name Ἄττιν was found at the same site.[110] Neither of the Mamurt Kale pieces, however, is an absolutely certain indicator of an Attis cult; the arm could come from a figure such as an Amazon, traditionally dressed in Oriental costume, and Attis was a common personal name in Anatolia, so the name on the bowl could be that of a human being, not a god.[111] The scarcity of Attis figurines at Pergamon contrasts sharply with the abundance of Meter/Kybele representations, of which more than sixty survive.[112]

Attis was most definitely at home in the urban cult of Meter at Pergamon, however, represented there by an over-life-size marble statue of the god, now in Berlin (fig. 57).[113] The Pergamene Attis lacks attributes, but can nonetheless be identified as Attis by the characteristic costume of an Oriental shepherd. While found in an uncertain context, the piece is similar in style and workmanship to the large marble statue of Meter discussed earlier, and it is quite plausible that the two were made as a pair and were exhibited together in the same shrine.[114] Both the size and high quality of the piece indicate that Attis formed an important part of the Meter cult. Attis may have been a more essential part of Meter's cult in the city, because the urban cult of Meter was more thoroughly Hellenized. His absence from extra-urban mountain shrines suggests that the mountain shrines remained closer to the older Anatolian cult forms.

109. Attis at Pergamon, Töpperwein 1976: no. 390, pl. 55. Another example may be a terracotta arm clothed in the long-sleeved garment normally worn by Attis, Töpperwein 1976: no. 391, pl. 55.

110. Conze and Schazmann 1911: pl. 12, no. 4 (the figurine arm, now lost); pl. 13, no. 4 (the inscribed vessel).

111. We should recall that Attis, in a variety of spellings, was one of the most common personal names in Anatolia; see Zgusta 1964: 105–9, nos. 119–1 through 119–19.

112. Töpperwein 1976: 49.

113. Franz Winter 1907: no. 116, pl. 27; F. Naumann 1983: 249–50; CCCA I: no. 359.

114. F. Naumann 1983: 249.

FIGURE 57. Marble
statue of Attis from Pergamon.
Second century B.C. Courtesy,
Antikensammlung, Staatliche
Museen zu Berlin, Preussischer
Kulturbesitz.

FIGURE 58.   Bronze matrix illustrating votive reliefs, provenience unknown. Side A. Third–second century B.C. Courtesy, Metropolitan Museum of Art, New York: Rogers Fund, 1920.

An interesting piece of evidence attesting to the worship of Attis in Ionia has been found in Ephesos, under the Augustan Basilica. A terracotta figurine, dated from its context to the first century B.C., illustrates a youth lying on his back. On his head is the peaked cap frequently found on figurines of Attis, while his body is tightly wrapped in cloth strips except for the male genitalia, which are left conspicuously unbound.[115] The excavator suggested that the piece must represent Attis after his death through self-castration. The parallels cited in support of this are, however, of the second century C.E. or later, and illustrate a different scene, a youthful Attis falling under a pine tree, clutching his genitals.[116] The Ephesos piece shows an immature youth, quite clearly uncastrated, and the wrappings could easily be the swad-

115. Karwiese 1968–71: figs. 1, 2.
116. Ibid.: fig. 3, a rock relief from Hamamli, in Lydia, of the second or third century C.E. (discussed in chapter 11 below), and fig. 8, a coin from Kyzikos of the late second century C.E.

dling of an infant. The piece may allude to the tradition that Attis was the son of
Meter/Kybele, making this a type of Attis previously unattested in Anatolia. The
piece furnishes another example of the influence of Hellenic myth on Meter's Anatolian cult.

Apart from the formal shrines of Meter, there are numerous Meter statuettes and
relief naiskoi from Hellenistic Asia Minor without any clear provenience. While we
cannot learn much about individual sanctuaries from these pieces, their abundance
attests again to the goddess's popularity. In some cases, the very lack of provenience
may have some meaning, for Meter was frequently worshipped in private household
shrines, and many of the representations of her may never have been intended for a
sanctuary.

Some votive images of Meter were meant to travel away from their place of origin. A bronze matrix, now in New York, offers one model of how this was done
(figs. 58, 59). Of unknown provenience, the matrix can be assigned by stylistic analy-

sis to Anatolia, probably Ionia.[117] The piece is crowded with inverted relief scenes, both large and small, which would have been used to make smaller plaques in metal and terracotta to serve as votive offerings by individual worshippers. All of the scenes are connected with Meter. The major scene, occupying most of one side of the matrix, depicts the goddess enthroned in a naiskos, flanked by Hermes and a torch-bearing maiden; above the naiskos are two groups of three armed youths, surely the Kouretes. Other smaller scenes on the matrix show the goddess sitting, standing, or riding in a chariot drawn by lions; scenes of individual worshippers, including a Hermes and a torch-bearing female attendant, are also present. The matrix offered the potential for making a variety of images to suit different tastes and pocketbooks. Such images could have circulated widely in personal and cultic use. A plaster relief in Cairo and a gilded bronze relief found in Mesembria may illustrate the types of objects made from such a matrix.[118] Small plaques made from such a matrix may even have been worn as personal adornment, such as the plaques worn by the Skythian Anacharsis, as described by Herodotos,[119] or by Meter's priests in Rome (fig. 70).[120]

METER IN GREECE

In contrast to the Greek cities in Asia Minor, where the Meter cult was an active part of both urban and rural life, Meter was a more muted presence on the Greek mainland and the Aegean islands during the Hellenistic period. Yet, while there are few formal shrines of the goddess, Meter continued to exercise a significant influence in private cult, in circumstances ranging from childbirth to the grave.

The most impressive evidence of the strength and breadth of the Hellenistic cult of Meter continues to be the large number of votive offerings dedicated to her. The standard image of the goddess, enthroned with her attributes of lion, tympanum, and phiale, was a popular subject, in stone and terracotta, in both freestanding figures and reliefs illustrating the goddess within her naiskos. These are found not only in older Greek cities but also in communities that first become prominent at the end of the fourth century and later, such as Olynthos, Amphipolis, and Delos.[121]

---

117. Reeder 1987: figs. 1–4, illustrate the matrix. On its probable Asiatic origin, see Reeder 1987: 433–36.

118. The Cairo plaster relief, Reeder 1987: 428, fig. 5. The Mesembria plaque, Babritsa 1973: fig. 93a; Reeder 1987: 430, fig. 6.

119. Herodotos 4.76.

120. Described by Polybios 21.6.7; 21.7.5. Livy, 38.18.9, refers to the *insignia* of the Galli who met Manlius Volso on his approach to Pessinous (see chapter 9).

121. The standard collection of Meter votives in the Greek world remains that of Vermaseren, *CCCA* II, with additional material in *CCCA* VI (Macedonia). The material is arranged topographically rather than chronologically, and Hellenistic votives are thus scattered randomly among material of both earlier and later periods within the entry for each individual site. F. Naumann 1983: 239–82, devotes a section of her analysis of Greek "Kybele" images to Hellenistic material, although, perhaps tellingly, almost all of her examples are taken from Anatolia. The Hellenistic images of Meter from the Greek mainland seem to

Several of the naiskoi reliefs depict two images of the goddess seated side by side; the doubling could have indicated two different aspects of the goddess or it may have been intended to reinforce her power.[122] There are several dedicatory inscriptions on Meter votives using a phrase such as κατὰ πρόσταγμα or κατ' ἐπιταγήν, according to command, an expression used most frequently in votives that record a very personal involvement of the dedicator with the deity.[123] This language confirms that Meter's capacity to speak to her devotees directly continued during the Hellenistic period. In addition to depictions of the goddess herself, her companion Attis, a development of fourth-century Greek art and cult, is represented with increasing frequency, attesting to his increasing prominence.[124]

The reservations expressed earlier about the limited usefulness of such small votive objects, however, are applicable to the Hellenistic material as well. Most of the votives have little individuality and offer no new insight into cult practices. Rarely were they found in a context that offers much information on their chronology or function. They attest to the continuing strength of the goddess in private cult, but to understand the reasons for her strength, we have to turn to examples of specific communities where Meter was prominent. Fortunately, there are several of those, offering a broader picture of Hellenistic Meter.

Meter's temple in Athens, the Metroön, furnishes one of the few instances in which the goddess was honored by a public cult. In the middle of the second century B.C., a new structure was built on the site of the older Athenian Metroön, adjacent to the Bouleuterion, consisting of four parallel, non-connecting rooms, joined at front by a colonnaded porch; the second room to the south served the cult of Meter.[125] The new building provided separate structures for the cultic and record-keeping functions of the Metroön. The discovery of numerous statuettes and fig-

---

have been a rather conservative group; rarely were new features introduced into the goddess's visual iconography. The exceptional examples are discussed below.

122. Double images of Meter from mainland Greece, Price 1971: 55–56; *CCCA* II: nos. 90, 183, 193, 239, 241, 328, 341, 386 (from Attica), 454 (from Isthmia), 509 (location unknown). On the meaning of double representations in Greek art, see Price 1971, esp. 52–54.

123. For a discussion of this phrase, see van Straten 1976b. It occurs on the Piraeus votive to Angdistis and Attis; a similar phrase, *kat' epitagen*, is found on another dedication to Meter from the Piraeus, *IG* ii² 4038. Van Straten 1976b: 1–38, suggests that this phrase might mean that the dedicator received the command in a dream. He cites several votives dedicated to Meter, in which the text specifically mentions that the dedicator received instructions through a dream (ibid., 21–27): from Thasos (no. 4.32), Epidauros (no. 4.22), Kyzikos (no. 1.9), and the Phrygian sites of Uşak (no. 8.7), Ayazviran (no. 9.5), and Himmetli (no. 12.39). The phrase also appears in *SIG*³ 1153, a dedication to Meter from Athens, and *SIG*³ 1127, 1129, 1131, 1138, private dedications from Delos. Note also the fourth-century B.C. votive cited in chapter 6, Walter 1939: fig. 22.

124. For a general summary of Attis depictions, see Vermaseren and de Boer 1986. For late fourth-century B.C. depictions of Attis in Athens, see H. Thompson 1951: pl. 26b; in Sicily, at Akrai, Sfameni Gasparro 1973: 269–70; in Amphipolis, Mollard-Besques 1972: D 251, 252; in Olynthos, *Olynthos* XIV: nos. 21–33 and pl. 42. By the third century B.C. and later, the type was extremely widespread; in addition to the sites listed above, examples of Attis figurines are known from Delos (Laumonier 1956: nos. 364–69) and Italy (Franz Winter 1903: 372, nos. 1–3; 373, nos. 2–5).

125. Pausanias 1.3.5; H. Thompson 1937: 192–93; Thompson and Wycherley 1972: 36–38, fig. 10.

urines nearby testifies to the Athenians' continuing interest in the Meter cult.[126] We hear for the first time of an Athenian festival, the Galaxia, held to honor the Mother of the gods; this took its name from a porridge of milk and barley consumed during the festival.[127] Sacrifice to Meter was also one of the standard religious obligations of the ephebes.[128] Clearly the long-standing association of the Meter cult with the Athenian democracy still had force in the Hellenistic period, although given the limited power of the Athenian Boule, one suspects that these rites involved more show than substance. The construction of the Hellenistic Metroön was contemporary with the building of the Stoa of Attalos, a Pergamene donation from Attalos II.[129] The strong interest of the Pergamene kings in the Meter cult may well have contributed support to the continuing prominence of Meter in Athens.

In addition to the formal public temple of Meter in the Athenian Agora, the goddess also had an active cult in the port city of Athens, the Piraeus. There her cult was managed by a private organization for the benefit of its adherents. The cult officials recorded many of their activities on stone, and, when added to numerous private dedications, votive offerings, and funerary stelai from individual devotees of Meter, their documents give us one of the clearest pictures of Meter's status and appeal. The range of evidence on the Piraeus cult extends from the fourth century B.C. to the fourth century C.E., but much of it is concentrated in the Hellenistic period, offering an interesting view of Meter's community during this time.

The actual site of the Piraeus Metroön remains uncertain. A small Metroön in the Moschaton district, consisting of a cella and pronaos, has been excavated, together with its cult statue,[130] but this may have been the shrine of an independent community. The majority of the inscriptions and votives from the Piraeus were found in uncontrolled excavations near the Akte peninsula, and it seems likely that the central place of the goddess's worship lay near here, in a site yet to be uncovered.[131]

The decrees relating to the administration of the cult provide much information on the organization of the cult and the people who were involved with it.[132] Nine of these are decrees of a standard type, praising someone for services performed for the cult; an additional decree, inscribed on the same stone as one of the honorific de-

---

126. For Meter statuettes from the Agora, see Thompson and Wycherley 1972: pl. 31; *CCCA* II: nos. 3, 38–179.

127. Theophrastus, *Characters* 21; Bekker, *Anecdota* 1.229.25; Hesychios, s.v. Γαλάξια.

128. *IG* ii² 1006.23; 1009.7; 1011.13; 1028.40; 1029.24; 1030.35.

129. H. Thompson 1937: 192.

130. For the excavation of the temple, see Papachristodoulou 1973; for the statue, see Despines 1971. Temple and statue are noted briefly in *CCCA* II: nos. 306–7. The statue from the Metroön in Moschaton uses a schema similar to that of the small Meter votive reliefs and statuettes, except for the lack of the tympanum and the fact that the lion was made separately and placed at the goddess's right side.

131. Garland 1987: 146. A large number of sculptures, inscriptions, and other objects related to the cult of the Mother were excavated in the Piraeus in 1855, in an area between Mounychia and the Zea harbor, simply referred to as "the Mills"; see Michon 1915–18 for a discussion of the circumstances of their finding.

132. These have been collected and analyzed by Ferguson 1944; see esp. pp. 107–15.

crees, deals with financial and organizational arrangements. Despite the formulaic nature of the texts, we learn a fair amount about the cult, including its organization, the rites celebrated in it, and the people who were involved.

Of particular interest is the identity of those involved in the cult. In many of the decrees, the individuals named, either the proposer or the honorand, are Athenian citizens. Twelve different individuals, approximately one-third of the total, are identified as Athenian citizens by their demotics;[133] most are not from the Piraeus. Names of Greek metics (free noncitizens) from Troizen, Herakleia, and Poros are also recorded.[134] The remaining individuals have Greek names, but no identification of origin; these may be citizens or metics. The individual priestesses mentioned all have Greek names, including the two known from funerary epitaphs. In one, the priestess's husband is also named; he too has a Greek name, although no citizenship is given.[135] Thus most of the devotees of Meter appear to have been Athenian citizens, or Greeks from other cities. Of the names connected with the cult in administrative texts, votive dedications, and funerary offerings from the Piraeus, only one is clearly a non-Greek name, the Anatolian Manes, which appears on a small naiskos relief of the enthroned goddess (fig. 47).[136] This name appears as part of a joint offering with Mika, presumably his wife, who had a Greek woman's name, although her precise origin is unknown. The cult's membership as a whole reflects the varied population of the Piraeus, but it does not suggest a cult that appealed primarily to non-Greeks.

This is an important point, because evaluation of the Meter cult in the Piraeus has been colored to a large extent by an assumption that Meter was a foreign deity and that her cult appealed primarily to foreigners and noncitizens. According to this view, the cult's governing body would have reflected this by organizing itself first as a thiasos, a religious association for noncitizens, and then later as a group of orgeones, the citizens who controlled religious associations formed primarily to administer the cults of heroes and foreign deities. Such a development would parallel the evolution of the first foreign cult to be formally established in the Piraeus, that of Bendis, whose members were organized as thiasotai for noncitizens, and orgeones for citizens.[137]

Yet the organizational documents of the Piraeus Meter cult do not reveal any separation between citizens and noncitizens. The earliest surviving administrative text, *IG* ii[2] 1316, from 246/5 B.C., grants honors to Agathon and his wife Zeuxion, a priestess of the cult, for financial contributions; here the cult leaders are called orgeones in

---

133. The corpus of inscriptions connected with the cult, including administrative decrees, votive offerings, and funerary texts, yields a count of thirty-seven names, excluding the archons' names.

134. Metics from Troizen and Herakleia, *IG* ii[2] 1273; from Poros, *IG* ii[2] 1328 I, 1328 II, and 1327.

135. Möbius 1968: 39, pl. 24a.

136. *IG* ii[2] 4609 = *CCCA* II: no. 267.

137. Ferguson 1944: 108–9.

the text, although they are named thiasotai in the heading. This could be an error of the stonecutter,[138] but it is also possible that either there was no clear difference between the two bodies, or that there were two groups, one of metics and the other of citizens, who worked closely together and may have seen the legal distinction between them as less compelling than their common bond in the cult. The honorees are both Athenian citizens. The next text in the revised chronological sequence is *IG* ii² 1273, which contains two honorary decrees, both proposed by metics and both honoring metics, one from Troizen and one from Herakleia.[139] Here the governing individuals are quite clearly named thiasotai.[140]

In the remaining administrative decrees, from 220/19 to 70 B.C., the issuing body is consistently the orgeones of the cult. Each decree in the series, apart from the first two mentioned above, uses the same prescript. This suggests that some formal reorganization of the cult took place in the late third century B.C. From this point on, the orgeones were in control. Another point of consistency found in the later decrees is the individual officiating at the cult. In the first two decrees, a married couple and a man, respectively, serve as priests, but in the succeeding decrees, the sacred official is always a woman; this too suggests some reorganization in the cult.

The varied status of the cults' members seems especially clear in one of the decrees of the orgeones, *IG* ii² 1327. Here the proposer, a metic from Poros, is also named as one of the *epimeletai* (managers). Another epimeletes is an Athenian citizen from the deme of Cholarge, while the third is merely named Ergasion, with no patronymic or civic affiliation. This, plus the name itself, "Worker," suggests that Ergasion may have been a freedman. This implies that metics, both freeborn foreigners and freedmen, had been absorbed into the orgeones and were treated on equal footing with Greek citizens in the context of the cult's administration.

One aspect of the Piraeus cult of Meter that emerges from the administrative decrees is a strong sense of a close-knit community among the cult's members. This appears in several references to financial issues. Individuals are praised for contributions to the cult from their own private funds, although this was a fairly common practice, indeed, expected of the wealthy. One decree, *IG* ii² 1328 I, however, spells out specifically that the financial burdens of the cult had become greater than could be met from the cult's funds and implies that in the past such a shortfall would have been met by the priestess; this situation was evidently no longer feasible and there-

138. Thus Ferguson 1944: 138–39. If so, this may be because the inscription is, in fact, the product of two different hands, one in the heading and one in the text. I have not examined the stone personally and photographs do not permit certainty on this point.

139. The honorand of the second decree is the proposer of the first decree, suggesting some collusion among the members of the *thiasos*.

140. *IG* ii² 1273, originally dated to 284/3 B.C., was supposedly the earliest decree pertaining to the cult of Meter. In this decree, the administrators of the cult are the thiasotai. A recently revised reading of the archon's name in this text as Euxe[i]nos indicates, however, that the inscription should be dated to 222/1 B.C.; see Oikonomides 1978; Habicht 1980.

fore other arrangements had to be made. Another, *IG* ii² 1329, honors a certain Chaireas for sharing benefits, φιλάνθρωπα, perhaps monetary payments, with the people and for lending money to the cult without interest while the treasurer was out of town. The Piraeus decrees also allude to other aspects of sharing among the members. A kitchen is mentioned in one decree, *IG* ii² 1301, implying communal dining, and provisions for a common eating club and burial fund are found in another text, *IG* ii² 1327.

Another indication of a close-knit community comes from the selection of priestesses. Several funerary monuments depict a seated woman holding a tympanum, which indicates that the woman (or her family) considered the position of priestess prestigious enough to be commemorated after death. One of these is a dedication by a husband, suggesting that he sympathized with his wife's views. This relief shows the seated woman holding a temple key and being greeted by a young girl, who holds a tympanum in her right hand; the epigram indicates that the girl is a granddaughter who will continue the family tradition of service to the goddess.[141] Another text, *IG* ii² 1328 II, of 175/4 B.C., states specifically that religious offices could remain in one family. Here one individual, Metrodora, daughter of the priestess Euaxis, is named *zakoros* (temple attendant) for life; one wonders if she had been named "gift of Meter" to show the family's pride in the priestly office. One decree, *IG* ii² 1328 I, guarantees the priestesses their annual vote of thanks, and some of the priestesses who are praised will also be honored with a painting of themselves set up in the goddess's precinct; this honor was extended to generous financial benefactors as well.[142]

Several administrative texts also provide evidence on cult ritual. Some of these are fairly standard practices, found in many cults. The priestess was to conduct sacrifices on entering office, the εἰσιτήρια (*IG* ii² 1315), but how many other sacrifices took place is not known; a reference in the same text to other sacrifices held "on the appointed days" indicates that there would have been several sacrifices and festivities in the course of a year.

Two particular rituals, the *strosis,* or spreading, and the *agermos,* or collection, seem especially appropriate to the cult of Meter. The action of the "spreading" is described in one decree concerning the priestess's financial obligations, *IG* ii² 1328 I, where she is required to "spread out the two thrones as beautifully as possible and put the silver decoration on the female libation bearers and the other women around the goddess during the collection" (lines 9–11: [σ]τ[ρω]ννύειν/ θρόνους δύο [ὡς] καλλίστους, περιτιθέναι δὲ ταῖς φιαληφόροις καὶ τ[α]ῖ[ς πε]/ρὶ τὴν θεὸν οὔσαις ἐν τῷ ἀγερ-

141. Möbius 1968: 39, pl. 24a. Clairmont 1970: 98, pl. 13a = *IG* ii² 6288 (the monument described in the text). Another very similar fourth-century B.C. gravestone of a priestess of Meter, of unknown provenience, is now in the Ashmolean Museum, Oxford (*Archaeological Reports* 1960–61: 59).

142. Priestesses honored: *IG* ii² 1314 and 1334; financial benefactors: *IG* ii² 1327 and 1329.

μ[ῶ]ι κόσμον ἀργυροῦν). The "spreading" is also mentioned as an important duty in other texts, *IG* ii² 1315 and 1329 (I discuss its meaning further in connection with the cult of Attis).

IG ii² 1329 also mentions the *agermos*. This has been widely assumed to refer to a collection of offerings for the goddess by the *metragyrtai,* the mendicant priests of Meter.[143] Although almost always a term of scorn in literature, the word *metragyrtes* never appears in any epigraphical document dealing with the cult of Meter, and there is no indication that the *agermos* consisted of begging priests passing the hat. In *IG* ii² 1329, Chaireas is praised for joining in the liturgy for the *agermos* and the *strosis,* suggesting that the *agermos* was another instance of community sharing.[144]

In addition to information in these administrative texts, further evidence on the rites of Meter can be gleaned from the votive offerings dedicated to her. The Piraeus has yielded a rich assortment of Meter votive statuettes and naiskoi, as well as several inscribed bases and small altars.[145] Most of the statuettes and naiskoi follow the standard iconography of Meter representations, showing the seated goddess with her lion, tympanum, and phiale. Almost all are uninscribed and many are of uncertain provenience, and so the information they can offer is limited. Nonetheless, their abundance in this one community offers further proof of the goddess's popularity there.

A few reliefs use different schemata. An especially fine example is a relief now in Berlin, a work of the early fourth century B.C., which illustrates the seated goddess being approached by two figures, a young man holding a large trefoil jug and a torch-bearing maiden (fig. 42). These attendant figures, present in many other Meter reliefs, both Classical and Hellenistic, allude to mystery rites in the worship of Meter.[146] Meter's capacity to induce personal inspiration is also demonstrated by two other reliefs from the Piraeus discussed in chapter 6, a relief dedicated to Meter by two (or more) individuals, prompted by the Kouretes and the Nymphs (fig. 46),[147] and the votive relief dedicated to Angdistis and Attis (fig. 48). Other evidence citing Meter's individual support includes three texts, two on a statue base (*IG* ii² 4714, 4759) and one on a small altar (*IG* ii² 4760), dedicating the object "to the Mother of

---

143. On the role of the *metragyrtai* in the Greek cult of Meter, see chapter 6 above.

144. The term *agermos* appears in cult regulations from several Greek cities—the cult of Demeter on Kos, *SIG*³ 1006; of Artemis at Halikarnassos, *SIG*³ 1015; of Zeus Sosipolis at Magnesia, *SIG*³ 589; of Apollo at the Ptoan sanctuary in Boiotia, *SIG*³ 635; other examples given by Burkert 1985: 101. In each case, the *agermos* represents funds for a sacrifice collected from public contributions of the citizens.

145. Twenty-three naiskos reliefs, twenty-two statuettes, six votive altars and bases, and one second-century C.E. bust of a priestess are listed in *CCCA* II: nos. 267–322 (nos. 309 and 314 are probably grotto reliefs of Hekate, however, not of Meter). Apparently there were also several terracotta statuettes of the goddess, noted by Graillot 1912: 506–7; but these have disappeared. The extant glyptic representations of Meter from the Piraeus are discussed as a group by Petrocheilos 1992.

146. Note the discussion in chapter 6 above.

147. Walter 1939: 54, fig. 22 = *CCCA* II, no. 270.

the gods, the gracious midwife."[148] Another (*IG* ii² 4038) preserves an offering by a mother on behalf of her daughter. In one epigram from the tombstone of a priestess (*IG* ii² 6288), the goddess is addressed as Μήτηρ Παντότεκνος, the Mother who begets all. All of these objects stress the close ties people felt with Meter and the beneficial personal contact they perceived themselves as receiving from her.

The Piraeus relief illustrating Attis and Angdistis is especially interesting because the Piraeus is one of the few Greek sites to furnish evidence on the cult rituals of Attis. In addition to this relief, one inscription, *IG* ii² 1315, mentions a set of rites for Attis, the Attideia; the text praises the priestess for "spreading the couch at both Attideia." From this we learn that there were two festivals of Attis, and that the ceremony of the *strosis*, the "spreading" mentioned in two other texts noted above, was connected with Attis in some way. Let us look more closely at the Piraeus evidence to examine Attis and his status in Greek cult.

We have already seen that in Anatolia, Attis was not the name of a god but a priestly title, a survival of the time when Phrygia was an independent kingdom and Attis had been a frequent name in the Phrygian royal family. In addition, we should note that the cult of the Anatolian Mother was apparently connected with funerary ritual, very probably the funerary rites of Phrygian rulers. Within the framework of Greek myth, of course, Attis was the lover of Kybele, who died young, and the literary treatments of the myth of Kybele and Attis consistently mention the death of Attis and the rites of mourning for him that formed a part of his festival.[149] The myth may be reflecting an actual practice, a Phrygian ritual honoring a dead king named Attis, and this ritual survived in Greek myth and Greek cult through the rites of the Attideia, especially the *strosis*, the act of spreading the couch at the Attideia (as described in *IG* ii² 1315). Myth and cult jointly suggest that the *strosis* entailed spreading a funerary couch, on which an image of Attis was laid as if for ritual mourning. A clear parallel to such a ritual is supplied by the Adonia described by Theokritos, in which the image of the dead Adonis was laid out every year on a lavishly appointed couch.[150] In another example of *strosis*, *IG* ii² 1328 I, the priestess is ordered to spread two thrones, which implies that an image of Attis would have been seated on a throne parallel to that of Meter. Perhaps these were the two Attideia, the ritual marriage and the ritual mourning for the god; each would have involved the spreading

148. Note also an amphora with a dedication to the *kourotrophos*, found in Mounychia, the same district as the presumed location of the principal Metroön of the Piraeus (Price 1978: 120). This maternal facet of the goddess's character is found in other parts of the Greek world too, as in a relief now in Venice (fig. 60), discussed by Linfert 1966: 497–501, Havelock 1981: no. 171, and F. Naumann 1983: 242–46. The piece, a dedication by a mother and daughter, forms a contrasting pair with a parallel votive relief dedicated by the father and son to Herakles (Linfert 1966: 500).

149. Diod. Sic. 3.59; see in general, Hepding 1903: 130–34. This concept is developed further in chapter 8 below.

150. Theokritos 15.85–86.

of a couch, one connubial and one funereal. The Piraeus was not the only Greek community to celebrate such rites, for a Hellenistic text from Chios also mentions a throne and the *strote,* or spreading,[151] suggesting that Attideia were held here too.

Yet another text, *IG* ii² 1327, prescribes sacrifices for τοῖς θεοῖς, the gods (unnamed); the stele bearing this inscription was to be set up in the Metroön. This may furnish an additional example of Meter worshipped in conjunction with Attis. A more puzzling reference is found in *IG* ii² 1329, in which Chaireas is praised for his piety to τὰς θεὰς, the goddesses. The identity of these goddesses is uncertain, but a likely female partner for Meter is Demeter, the deity most often associated with her in earlier Greek literature and cult.[152]

I have described the evidence on the cult of Meter in the Piraeus at length, not because it was atypical (in fact, many aspects of the Piraeus cult were quite typical of Greek practice in other cities), but because the varied nature of the Piraeus's evidence offers a special insight into the organization, rituals, and emotional content of the Greek cult of Meter. This deity was outside the circle of the Olympic pantheon, and so a separate structure, the orgeones, had to be created to administer her cult, but her iconography and that of her companion Attis were part of the Greek artistic and religious tradition. The cult was well integrated into the Piraeus community, attracting adherents from among citizens, Greek metics, and non-Greeks alike. Its great popularity must have derived in part from the close community of worshippers that grew up around it and from its ability to speak directly to its worshippers and to respond to the most basic elements of human existence: food, birth, and death. The antipathy toward Meter expressed in the literature of Classical Athens is in no way supported by evidence for the cult of Meter. Nor is there any intimation that Meter in the Piraeus was a foreign divinity. The strength of the cult may have derived from the fact that it flourished outside of the traditional polis structure of Greek civic cult and from its ready acceptance of foreigners and freedmen along with citizens. The Meter cult illustrates one aspect of the transition to the more private and personal cults of the Hellenistic period, which may have claimed more loyalty than the older cults of the state.

The mysteries of Meter continued to be celebrated in other Greek cities as well. A second-century B.C. inscription from Troizen records the establishment of a house

---

151. Forrest 1963: no. 9.

152. In addition to the material cited in chapter 6 above, see Reeder 1987: 436, who discusses the conflation of the visual images of Meter and Demeter during the Hellenistic period. One of the texts prescribing the religious duties of the Athenian ephebes, *IG* ii² 1009.7, directs the young men to offer a phiale to Demeter, Kore, and Meter, thus reinforcing the pairing of Meter and Demeter in Attica. Ferguson 1944: 138 assumed that the phrase τοὺς θεοὺς referred to Meter and Attis, while the reference to τὰς θεὰς indicated joint worship of Meter and Attis after his emasculation. Garland 1987: 129 suggests that τοὺς θεοὺς were the Mother of the gods and Attis, while the phrase τὰς θεὰς indicates Meter and another foreign goddess, perhaps Nana. Neither of these suggestions is compelling, since both rely on the assumption that Meter was a foreign deity.

F I G U R E 6 0.   Relief of Meter and Attis,
provenience unknown. Late second century B.C.
Courtesy, Archaeological Museum, Venice.

for the initiates of the Great Mother, to be used also for the protection of the city.[153]
In another instance, a most interesting votive relief from Lebadeia provides yet another insight into Meter's role in personal cult (fig. 61).[154] The piece, probably to be
dated to the early Hellenistic period, illustrates what appears to be a scene of initiation into the cult of Meter. In the relief, Meter, shown in profile, sits at the left with
her phiale and lion. Approaching her are eleven standing figures; all are equal in
height, but each one has a distinctive attribute. At the left is a young woman holding a key, probably Persephone with the key (literally and symbolically) to the mysteries of Meter. With her left hand, she leads forward a standing figure, whose costume, veil, and long robe mark the individual as an initiate of the cult. To the right
of the initiate can be recognized Dionysos with his thyrsos, Pan with his pipes, and

153. *IG* iv.757 B.
154. Walter 1939: 59–80, fig. 23; F. Naumann 1983: 191–193, no. 422, pl. 28, 1; *CCCA* II: no. 432.

FIGURE 61. Votive relief illustrating Meter
and hero cult, from Lebadeia. Fourth–third century B.C.
Courtesy, National Archaeological Museum, Athens.

a woman holding two torches, who may be Hekate or an anonymous torch-bearing
attendant. Beyond this figure is a mature, bearded male god holding a horn of
plenty and flanked by two snakes; this may be the local god Trophonios, who had a
famous oracular shrine near Lebadeia,[155] or Zeus Meilichios. To the right of the
bearded god stand three armed youths, the three Kouretes, and behind two youths
with pointed caps, the Dioskouroi.

In front of the Dioskouroi are four much smaller figures, a woman and three children, whose size indicates that they are human, not divine. They stand before a low
table on which are placed pyramidal cakes of the sort regularly used in funerary
meals as offerings to the dead.[156] Thus we see that the work is a funerary relief
offered by the wife and children to the deceased, presumably the father of the family, who is the veiled initiate being presented to Meter. Despite his mortal origins, he
stands equal in stature and apparently on equal footing with the gods, indicating
that this is a relief of the heroized dead.

All of the deities in this relief have some chthonic symbolism, appropriate in a
scene with powerful funerary connotations, and all have some connection with
Meter. Persephone, Dionysos, and Pan had long been her companions, as had the
Kouretes. A torch-bearing woman is a frequent attendant on Meter reliefs; if she is
Hekate, there would be a common association with Meter in mystery cult.[157] One
interpretation of the work proposes that the relief illustrates a scene of the dead

155. Pausanias 9.39.
156. Thönges-Stringaris 1965: 19, 56–63.
157. For Meter's connection with Persephone (and Demeter), Dionysos, Pan, and the Kouretes, see
chapter 6 above. On Meter and Hekate, see Roller 1991: 141–42.

man's initiation into the mysteries of Trophonios,[158] but the initiation ceremonies are directed, not to Trophonios, but to Meter. The relief vividly illustrates Meter's prominence in funerary cult and implies that initiation into her mysteries offers the deceased passage to a better life in the next world.

The same sentiment may underlie a series of reliefs in which Meter is depicted attending a funerary banquet.[159] One example of this type is a relief from Kos, a small stele of the late fourth century B.C.[160] The relief depicts a couple, the man reclining, the woman seated, at a banquet table presided over by Meter, present with her usual attributes of lion, tympanum, and phiale. Below this group a man stands with upraised right hand; beside him is a large snake, which reinforces the chthonic character of the scene. Meter's position at the banquet also helps demonstrate the goddess's special affinity for the heroized dead.

Other reliefs depicting Meter may also refer to mystery rites, although without the funerary connotation. A complex relief carved onto a natural rock outcrop on the island of Paros depicts Meter seated in the company of several divinities including Pan and the Nymphs, who are being approached by a group of human worshippers, now barely identifiable.[161] The Thracian goddess Bendis appears to the left of the Nymphs, and beyond Bendis sits Meter. An inscription records that the relief was dedicated by a Thracian, Adamas the Odrysian, to the Nymphs. The poor condition of the relief precludes certain identification of many of the figures on it, but drawings by earlier travelers to the island indicate that a torch-bearing young woman was depicted on the relief near Meter, an allusion to mystery rites in which Meter would participate.[162] Another interesting series of open-air reliefs depicting Meter, Attis, and their attendants were carved onto cliffs near Akrai, in Sicily. These reliefs, dating from the fourth through second centuries B.C., are in poor condition, but the scenes on them offer testimony to the widespread connection of the goddess with a mountain environment and to the power of mystic rites for Meter in Sicily during the Hellenistic period.[163]

METER IN HELLENISTIC LITERATURE AND SOCIETY

Apart from the profundities of cult ritual and mystic imagery, a radically different world appears in several literary texts of the Hellenistic period. Here the treatment

158. Walter 1939, whose careful discussion of the work is still of great value; on his suggestion concerning Trophonios, see esp. pp. 60–65.

159. These have been studied as a group by Mitropoulou 1996, although the identification of some examples in her corpus is tentative.

160. Mitropoulou 1977: 137–38, no. 29; F. Naumann 1983: no. 423; Mitropolou 1996: 138–39, K5.

161. F. Naumann 1983: no. 427 (with earlier bibliography), pl. 28, 2 and pl. 29.

162. For a careful discussion of this relief and the drawings of it by earlier travelers, see Bodnar 1973.

163. For discussion of the Akrai reliefs, see Sfameni Gasparro 1973: 267–76, and 1996; F. Naumann 1983: 202–8, nos. 428–39.

of Meter (usually called Kybele or Rhea) and her attendants exemplifies the intellectual gap between educated men and ordinary people. The goddess herself is less a figure of awe, and more one designed to introduce a note of exoticism or eccentricity into a narrative. A rather amusing example can be found in the Epidaurian Hymn to the Mother of the gods, dated to the third century B.C.[164] After beginning with an invocation to the Pleiades, the hymn conflates Meter with Demeter, portraying the Mother of the gods wandering across the earth, as if searching for her daughter.[165] Father Zeus calls her back to heaven, lest she meet up with bright-eyed lions and gray wolves (as in Homeric Hymn 14.4). The goddess refuses to do so, and indeed, why should she? Lions and wolves are her natural companions.[166] Instead, she continues to wander.

Clearly, at the time this text was written, Meter's association with the mountains and with wild animals was not expressive or threatening, as it had been in the *Bacchae,* but merely idiosyncratic. At one point (line 7), she even shakes her wild hair, an action often ascribed to her human followers but not to the goddess herself. In taking on the eccentric qualities of her human attendants, Meter has ceased to be a figure of dignity, and the poem, while drawing on earlier, more emotionally dramatic treatments of her personality and doings, presents her as a subject for parody, not a figure of respect. A similar example is found in Theokritos's twentieth idyll. The poet tells us that just as Rhea weeps for her country boy (Attis), so the country bumpkin of this poem should expect favors from his true love.[167] The poet has reduced the emotional expression of Meter's rituals to the aspect of a figure of fun, on par with the nymphs and shepherds of pastoral poetry.

Meter evidently figured in the work of Kallimachos, although the texts are so fragmentary that their context must remain uncertain. Kallimachos comments on the exotic behavior of Meter's followers in his third *Iambos,* where the poet refers to one who "tosses Phrygian hair to Kybebe [*sic*] and cries out to Adonis."[168] In the fourth *Iambos,* the laurel tree swears "by the Mistress [$\Delta\acute{\epsilon}\sigma\pi o\iota\nu a$] to whom cymbals resound."[169] Here the association of Meter Kybele with uncontrolled emotional behavior is automatic. The poet may well be expressing the disdain felt by many educated Greeks for the unusual behavior and open expression of emotion that the cult of Meter was supposed to induce.

This disdainful humor extends to Meter's attendants, as a new character enters the

---

164. Hymn to Meter from Epidauros, *IG* iv² 131. Here I follow West 1970: 212–15, who dates the text to the third century B.C. on metrical grounds. This date fits well with the lighthearted treatment of the goddess and the implied parody of Euripides' *Helen* 1301–68.

165. Cf. the conflation between Meter and Demeter in the third choral ode from Euripides' *Helen.* This conflation is reinforced by the subsequent lines ("Father Zeus calls you"), a clear reference to *Hom. Hymn Dem.* 460–61.

166. As West (citing Latte) pointed out (West 1970: 214).

167. Theokritos 20.40.

168. Kallimachos, *Iambos* 3.35 (Pfeiffer fr. 193).

169. Ibid. 4.105 (Pfeiffer fr. 194).

literary horizon. For the first time we meet a figure who was to bulk large in later Greek and Roman literature and cult practice, Meter's eunuch priest, the Gallos. This individual appears in a theme popular with Hellenistic epigrammatists, the encounter of the Gallos with a lion. Five examples survive, dating from the late third and early second century B.C., *Anth. pal.* 6.217–20 and 237, and a sixth, *Anth. pal.* 6.234, also concerns a Gallos.[170] Each recounts a similar story: the eunuch priest of Meter either takes shelter in a cave (*Anth. pal.* 6.217, 219, 220) or wanders in the deserted countryside (*Anth. pal.* 6.218, 237). Here he is attacked by a lion, but is able to frighten away the animal by beating on his tympanum and waving his wild mop of hair. As a mark of his gratitude to the goddess for saving him, he makes a dedication to the goddess (called both Kybele and Rhea), offering his robes and hair, (6.217, 237), his tambourine (6.220), or an image of the beast that attacked him (6.218).[171]

These epigrams mark the earliest appearance of the word "Gallos" to denote a priest of Meter.[172] They also provide the earliest clear evidence that these priests were eunuchs. Given the notoriety that these priests were to receive in later Greek and Roman literature, their late appearance in the cult of Meter is surprising. One reason for this may be that the word "Gallos" itself was new, created by the Greeks during the Hellenistic period to describe these priests. Its source is uncertain, but it is likely that the term was a shortened form of the word "Galatos," or Galatian, referring to a Celtic group that entered Anatolia in the early third century B.C.[173] The Galatians settled in the older Phrygian heartland of central Anatolia, where they became such a dominant presence that the region came to be called Galatia. We have already seen that Galatian priests were active at Meter's Pessinuntine shrine. Under these circumstances it would not be surprising if "Galati" or "Galli" became generic terms for the priests of Meter.

These priests were not always regarded with amused contempt, for we learn from Polybios and Livy that they could be influential figures within their communities. Two incidents are particularly telling: during the Roman siege of Sestos, in western Asia Minor, in 190 B.C., the Galli approached the Roman army and persuaded it to spare the city (Polybios 21.6; Livy 37.9.9), and in 189 B.C., when the Roman army was maneuvering near Pessinous, the Galli met the army and predicted victory, thus

---

170. The texts of *Anth. pal.* 6.217–20 are taken from Gow and Page 1965, that of 237 from Gow and Page 1968. For a discussion of these poems, see Gow 1960. Note also *Anth. pal.* 6.234, a dedication by a Gallos, although lacking reference to a lion.

171. Gow and Page 1965: II, 24–25, suggest that this is a painting of the episode, and propose that all four epigrams were derived from a common source, an inscription on a painting depicting the event.

172. Kallimachos's *Aitia*, fr. 789 (Pfeiffer 1949), includes the word Γάλλος, the Gallos, here meaning a river in Phrygia; see also Pliny, *NH* 31.5.9, fr. 411 Pfeiffer. Pfeiffer fr. 791, the word Γάλλος as the title of an unknown work by Kallimachos.

173. Lane 1996. Both ancient and modern sources connect the term with the river Gallos, which flows through Pessinous. Kallimachos, in Pliny, *NH* 31.5.9; Alexander Polyhistor, *FGrHist* 273 F 74; Ovid *Fasti* 4.361–66; see also Cumont 1910: 674–76 and Waelkens 1971: 364–67. Lane 1996: 131, proposes inverting this argument, suggesting that the river Gallos took its name from the Galatian people who settled in that region.

encouraging the Romans' military efforts (Polybios 21.37.4–7; Livy 38.18.9–10). In both situations, the Galli were met with respect, although Livy does comment on their strange appearance and fanatical songs. It is noteworthy, though, that in contexts where the Galli were engaged in serious diplomatic activity, their appearance and sexual status are not used to degrade them.

In these epigrams, however, we see an individual whose appearance, actions, and sexual status mark him as a deviant. To an extent, this is not surprising; the Gallos was a descendant of the *metragyrtes* of fourth-century sources, as is clear in one epigram where the word *metragyrtes* is substituted for *Gallos*,[174] and the *metragyrtes* of earlier Greek literature was clearly a figure of disdain. Yet the appearance of the *metragyrtes* is rarely a source of comment, and his sexuality is never mentioned. In contrast, the sexual status of the Galli in the epigrams is clearly a point of emphasis. They were castrated (νεήτομος, 6.234) and effeminate (ἡμιγύναικα, 6.217). Moreover, they had distinctly feminine appearance and personalities: they had long loose hair (6.217, 219, 220, 234), sometimes perfumed (6.234), and they wore women's clothing (6.219). In the course of their rituals, they shrieked (6.219, 234), waved their hair wildly (6.218, 219, 220), and banged on various noisy instruments (6.217, 218, 220, 237). This same image occurs in a passage preserved by Hephaestion, ascribed by him to "one of the more recent [i.e., Hellenistic] poets"; here it is the feminine form "Gallai" that refers to the wandering priests of Meter, with their erratic behavior and use of raucous music:

Γάλλαι μητρὸς ὀρείης φιλόθυρσοι δρομάδες
αἷς ἔντεα παταγεῖται καὶ χάλκεα κρόταλα

The roaming thyrsus-loving Gallai of the Mountain Mother clash their instruments and bronze castanets.[175]

This passage too suggests that individuals with such outré appearance and habits had become almost a cliché of un-Hellenic appearance and manners.

Was the picture of the Galli drawn by the Greek poets accurate? Several of the activities described in the epigrams were not new to the Meter cult; the participants in the rituals illustrated on the Ferrara krater (figs. 43, 44) also toss their hair about while striking tambourines and castanets. The implication here, however, is that such behavior is indicative of deviant sexuality and effeminacy. The Galli's activities

174. In *Anth. pal.* 6.218 the priest is called a Μητρὸς ἀγύρτης, but in the other four epigrams the word *Gallos* is used.

175. Hephaestion p. 39, van Ophuijsen 1987: 109–10. Pfeiffer 1949: fr. 761, cautiously attributes this passage to Kallimachos, one of his "Fragmenta Incerti Auctoris." The couplet is in galliambic meter, so named because it was used in hymns to the Mother of the gods (the same meter is used by Catullus in his poem 63). Hephaestion records that Kallimachos wrote in galliambics, and on that basis Wilamowitz 1879: 198 ascribes this fragment to Kallimachos, but Hephaestion's text does not support that assumption.

in honor of their goddess served as a form of caricature at best and of degradation at worst.

We have no information suggesting that castration and effeminacy were typical of the Meter cult. The Galli never appear in any cult regulation or decree, and their activities seem to have been limited to Asia Minor (no Galli are attested in the Piraeus material, for example.) The Hellenistic epigrams appear to exaggerate the characteristics of the Galli to create an artificial literary image, that of a despised group of castrati (the feminine form Γάλλαι anticipates Catullus 63) and foreigners whose eccentric appearance and behavior put them beyond the pale of respectable society.

These references to Meter and her priests in Hellenistic literature, although brief and fragmentary, exhibit several trends. We see no personal accounts of religious rituals observed or emotional involvement experienced, as was the case in the descriptions of Pindar and Euripides. Instead, Meter has become a figure of lighthearted mockery, and her legendary background, her priests, and her rituals are flippantly dismissed. It is interesting to compare Pindar, who, as an adherent of the goddess, describes the Meter cult from the inside, with Kallimachos, who describes the trappings of the Meter cult from the outside. Whereas Pindar proudly announces that he worships the goddess with nocturnal choruses in his own home (*Pythian* 3.77–79), Kallimachos treats Meter's rites as bizarre, behavior with which he felt no sympathy.

In the opinion of learned men, Meter had become a symbol of uncivilized—that is, non-Hellenic—behavior. The appearance of the word "Gallos" to refer to a priest of Meter reinforces this attitude. Since the term never appears in any text describing religious activity, its use in literature may be another way of downgrading the adherents of Meter's rites by describing the goddess's priests as Galatian foreigners, members of an ethnic group that the Greeks found troublesome at best and destructive barbarians at worst.

This negative attitude toward the Meter cult finds echoes in other sources. An explicit example is found in a third- or second-century B.C. Pythagorean text, a treatise on the modesty of women.[176] In giving examples of proper female behavior, the text states that women are to be permitted to leave the house to participate in the cults of the polis, but enjoins them against taking part in orgies and rites of Meter (ὀργιασμῶν δὲ καὶ ματρῳασμῶν), for these lead to drunkenness and ecstasy of the soul, behavior unbecoming to the mistress of the household. A late-second- or first-century B.C. cult regulation from Eresos, on Lesbos, reflects a similar attitude.[177] The text gives a list of prohibited activities within an unidentified sacred temenos: access to the area is denied to women who have recently given birth, Galli, and

---

176. Phintys, *On the Modesty of Women*, p. 593, ed. Thesleff 1965: 151–54.
177. Schwyzer 1923: no. 633.

women who γαλλάζειν—that is, hold Gallic rites to Meter. Such statements may well reflect a common public attitude toward Meter and her followers—namely, that participating in Meter's rites was something that decent people did not do. They suggest that the cynicism of the poets was closer to the dominant public opinion of the Meter cult.[178]

SUMMARY: METER AND HELLENISTIC SOCIETY

The evidence on Meter in Hellenistic society vividly illustrates the intensity, ubiquity, and tenacity of the Mother Goddess cult. Within this general pattern, though, there are several trends. We see distinct regional responses to the Meter cult; Meter has become less a civic deity and more a deity of private cult; and there is a widening gap between the actions of ordinary people and the reactions of intellectuals and literati. The one overriding aspect of the Meter cult is its prominence in so many Hellenistic cities and its ability to touch the lives of people so forcefully.

By the end of the Hellenistic period, the cult of the Phrygian goddess had moved far from Anatolia, and it is informative to trace the differing regional patterns in her cult. In Phrygia, many of the features of the Phrygian Matar remained strong. She was still the preeminent divinity, attracting support in older Phrygian centers. No important monuments comparable to the impressive carved Phrygian façades were created during this time, but this was a result of the decline of Phrygia as political power and the absence of a wealthy elite able to sponsor such monuments, not a lack of interest in Meter. Only in Pessinous was the Meter cult important enough to exercise some political clout, and this was due to patronage from outside Phrygia, from the Attalid dynasty. In Lydia, Meter continued to be one important deity among many, and the status of her cult, especially in Sardis, reflects both her subordinate status to other deities and, again, the importance of Greek patronage, in this case from the Seleucid dynasty.

In the Greek cities of Asia Minor, Meter shared her position with the traditional Olympian pantheon. While rarely the most important deity, Meter was a visible presence in the cities of this region, as is clear from her urban shrines both in older cities such as Kolophon and Smyrna and in the new city of Pergamon. She also continued to be a deity of the landscape, worshipped in the mountains, hollow valleys, and caves where she had always been most at home. In some areas, the need to communicate with the Mountain Mother in her outdoor home was clearly powerful and

---

178. In the same vein, a third-century B.C. letter talks of a festival for the women in which music will be provided by Phrygian flutes and a musician called Zenobios the Effeminate, with his tympanum, cymbals, and castanets; see Grenfell and Hunt 1906: *Hibeh Papyri* I.54.

led to the establishment or revival of extramural sanctuaries at sites such as Metropolis, Mamurt Kale, and Kapikaya. In another trend, Meter became an increasingly strong presence in private cult, commemorated in household shrines and graves.

In Greece itself, Meter's connection with the outdoor environment had never been strong, and apart from Athens, she had never been a significant force in political cult. In this region, however, Meter had long been valued as a source of personal inspiration, a trend that continued, since Meter increasingly became a deity of personal cult. Her visual image and the rites celebrated for her illustrate that people considered her a fully Hellenized deity, but her cult did not occupy a prominent place in public life. Instead, she was the deity invoked to preside over birth and death, and was supported by private organizations whose membership cut across social and legal status. Her cult is a vivid demonstration of the changing social fabric of religion in the Hellenistic Greek cities, as the older cults of the polis, which had reinforced the bonds of class and citizenship, gave way to the religious expressions of individuals.

This is the message that comes through most clearly in religious communities such as those in Philadelphia and the Piraeus—namely, that Meter's power in private cult derived from her ability to respond to her worshippers' most personal needs. The material from these groups does much to explain the appeal of the goddess and also to indicate why we see so many votive offerings to her, yet hear so little of her in the formal cults of the polis. The cult's wide diffusion and continuing ability to draw followers from a broad cross-section of people show clearly that the goddess's power derived, not from a provincial Anatolian culture, but from a very forceful concept of her personal interaction with people's daily lives.

The reaction to this personal cult, however, was also forceful. Underlying some of the ancient material (and much of the modern discussion of it) is the implication that Meter's adherents were people on the margins of Greek society. To an extent, this may be true, for apart from a few areas (Pergamon is one example), Meter seems not to have been a deity who commanded the attention of the ruling elite and the intellectual class. Indeed, the almost cynical treatment she received in Hellenistic literature implies that many educated Greeks considered her cult an object of scorn, and the social makeup of the community of Meter in the Piraeus, whose membership included women and noncitizens, may indicate why this was so. The text from Eresos even implies that some of Meter's functions, her association with birth and death, may have brought a form of ritual pollution on her adherents. The Hellenistic literary tradition strengthens this marginalization by implying that the cult was under the control of effeminate, desexed barbarians, often eccentrics of unusual appearance and behavior. The extensive finds of votive offerings to the goddess and the cult regulations of Philadelphia and the Piraeus tell us that most of Meter's adherents were not eccentrics and social deviants; indeed, some may even have maintained a stricter behavioral code than the general public. This negative reaction, however, reinforces a point made several times in this chapter, that the cult of Meter was in many cases outside the mainstream cults of the Hellenistic Greek city. This antithesis between the negative public image of the Meter cult and the private reality of the positive experience that individuals found in it may be the most salient characteristic of Meter in the Hellenistic era.

3 · FROM CULT TO MYTH

8 · THE MYTH OF CYBELE AND ATTIS

The Mother's shrines, cult images, votive offerings, hymns, and dedicatory texts form the actual remains of cult practice. They illustrate how people in the ancient Mediterranean world worshipped a mother goddess, and offer some insight as to why they did so. A rather different view appears in the major narrative cycle concerned with the goddess. This is the myth of Cybele, the Mother of the gods, and her youthful lover Attis.[1] The story, recounted over several centuries and by many authors, describes the essential elements of the life of Cybele: the circumstances of her birth, her recognition as a goddess, her relationship with the young shepherd Attis, and the castration and death of Attis. The narrative brings the goddess out of the world of abstract religious imagery and invests her with a dramatic reality as vivid as that of any Homeric deity.

Yet the myth was more than a dramatic story. It acquired the status of a *hieros logos,* a sacred tale whose function was to introduce the Phrygian divinities Cybele and Attis to the Greek and Roman world. Learned men of Greece and Rome invoked the myth to explain the variety of cult practices connected with the Great Mother of the gods and to offer a rationale for some of the cult's unusual features, notably the castration of the goddess's priests. An analysis of this myth is therefore an important part of any attempt to understand the nature of the Mother Goddess. We shall need

---

1. I use the word "myth" here in the sense of a traditional tale told with reference to the gods or religious ritual. When discussing the myth, I call the goddess Cybele, since this is the name that many literary sources use when describing her role in the traditional tale. This will help keep Cybele, the figure of myth, distinct from the figure of cult who was addressed as Matar, Meter, Magna Mater, or the Mother of the gods.

to consider the origin of the myth, its relation to cult ritual, and the nature of its transmission through written sources. An analysis of the myth will also demonstrate the long life and staying power of the goddess, for the many peoples who worshipped the Mother Goddess both absorbed and in turn helped shape the myth.

A key feature of the myth of Cybele and Attis is its connection with Anatolia. The story reputedly originated there, and, as the worship of the Phrygian Mother Goddess spread to the west, the myth of Cybele and Attis was used to connect the rites held for Meter/Magna Mater outside of Phrygia with her Anatolian homeland. For this reason, the story of Cybele and Attis should be distinguished from other myths and legends about the Mother Goddess. We have already seen several examples of Greek myths that became enmeshed with the Phrygian Mother Goddess: her association with Demeter and Kore, her conflation with Rhea, and her assimilation with the story of the birth of Zeus on Crete. Another powerful example is found in Rome, where the Magna Mater became attached to the legend of Aeneas on Mount Ida and the founding of Rome. This chapter focuses on a different story, one that both Greeks and Romans called Phrygian. The ethnic identity of the myth, however, raises several problems. Knowledge of it comes to us entirely through Greek and Latin texts, and the syncretisms that shaped the Mother Goddess's cult in Greek and Roman society have clearly left their mark on these texts. As we shall see, authentic Phrygian material does underlie the myth, but the narrative as it is preserved for us bears the imprint not only of Phrygia but of the cultures that preceded the Phrygians in Anatolia as well. It also reflects the perspectives of the Greeks and Romans, who presented the myth in a way that suited their own religious and political needs and their view of the Phrygians.

Thus this myth is central to the cult of the Mother in Phrygia, Greece, and Rome. Yet the written accounts of it will lead us primarily to Greek and, especially, Roman perspectives. For this reason, I have placed the discussion of it between the presentation of cult material from Greece and that from Rome. While analyzing the narratives about Cybele and Attis, we should remember that we are hearing the voices of Greek and Latin authors talk about Phrygia, rather than the voices of the Phrygians talking about their own myth and cult. We shall need to sort out these disparate voices in order to find the Phrygian elements in this tale of the Phrygian Mother Goddess.

THE MYTH AND ITS SOURCES

I have used the phrase "the myth of Cybele and Attis," but as is so often the case in ancient myths and legends, there is no single narrative describing the life of these two figures. Instead, the story of Cybele and her consort exists in a number of versions, each with a slightly different slant to it. This analysis will thus begin with a summary of the basic plot.[2] In most accounts of the myth, the story falls into two parts: (1) the origin and background of Cybele, and (2) her love affair with Attis and its unfortunate aftermath. The first part, dealing with the origin of the goddess, appears less frequently in the surviving sources, although it is known in two quite different versions, that of Diodoros,[3] and that of Pausanias and Arnobius.[4] The second part, the relationship of Cybele and Attis, appears in virtually all references to the myth. These accounts fall into three general story patterns: (1) a version preserved by Pausanias, who credits it to Hermesianax (I shall call this Pausanias A);[5] (2) the account of Diodoros; and (3) the account attributed to the priesthood in Pessinous and preserved at length by Ovid,[6] Pausanias (Pausanias's second version of the story, here called Pausanias B),[7] and Arnobius.[8]

The first element in the story is the background of the goddess before she met Attis. Diodoros's account is in the form of a story pattern occurring widely in Greek myth and folklore, telling of a child who is exposed at birth, miraculously survives, and is later recognized by its parents under unusual circumstances. In this case the child was a daughter of Maion, king of Lydia, and his wife Dindymene. Exposed at birth by her father on Mount Cybelon, she was fed by wild animals and received the name Cybele from the place where she was exposed. She was widely known for her kindness to young animals and children and thus acquired the names "Great Mother" and "Mother of the mountains." Having reached adulthood, she fell in love with a Phrygian youth, Attis, and became pregnant by him, at the point when she was reunited with her parents. (The subsequent events in Diodoros's narrative recounting the fate of Cybele and Attis are given below.)

A more complex tale on the goddess's origins is that of Arnobius and Pausanias B. Neither author uses the name Cybele at all; instead, both introduce the Magna Mater as the oldest of the gods. In Arnobius's version, Jupiter attempts to rape the

2. The ancient sources for the myth of Cybele and Attis have been collected in several modern works, of which the most complete are Rapp 1890–94, Drexler 1894–97, and Hepding 1903: 5–97. Hepding focuses primarily on the legend of Attis, and brings in Cybele only when her story relates to that of Attis. Vermaseren 1966 and id. 1977: 88–95 also emphasize the legend of Attis, but in both of these discussions, Vermaseren focuses on creating an internally coherent and attractive version of the story. In doing so, he smooths over many inconsistencies in detail and unevenness in the accuracy of the various written sources, thus depriving his studies of much critical value.

3. Diodoros preserves two versions of the myth of Cybele. The first, Diodoros 3.57, which may be called a Greek version, links the origin of the Mother Goddess with the Greek myth of Ouranos and Ge. In the second version, 3.58–59, the emphasis is on Phrygia and the Phrygian figures of Cybele, Attis, Marsyas, and Midas.

4. Pausanias 7.17.10–11; Arnobius, *Ad. nat.* 5.5–7.

5. Pausanias 7.17.9, the so-called "Lydian" version. A narrative fairly similar to Pausanias's is given by Servius, *Comm. ad Aen.* 9.115.

6. Ovid, *Fasti* 4.221–44.

7. Pausanias 7.17.10–12, the so-called Phrygian version. The reasons why Pausanias preserved two such differing versions of the myth are discussed below.

8. For a summary of the different versions of the myth and the principal sources of each version, see the end of this chapter.

Magna Mater as she lies sleeping on Mount Agdos in Phrygia. Frustrated in the attempt, the god pours out his semen on the mountain, which becomes pregnant and gives birth to a wild and uncontrollable creature named Agdestis (*sic*), with the genitals and libido of both sexes. Pausanias preserves a tale similar to this, stating that Zeus, while asleep, poured out his sperm on the earth, which in time brought forth the androgynous Agdistis.[9] Agdistis's dual sexuality and the violent lust resulting from it form a threat to gods, who react by chopping off the male genitalia. As these fall to the ground, they produce an almond tree; whereupon the daughter of Sangarios (a major river in Phrygia) picks the fruit of the tree and immediately becomes pregnant, giving birth to the beautiful child Attis. In each case, Arnobius and Pausanias use this episode to lead into the passion that Agdistis conceives for the young Attis, strongly implying that Agdistis is playing the role given to Cybele in other versions of the myth. Arnobius does mention the Magna Mater as the rival of Agdistis for the love of the young Attis, but Agdistis is clearly the center of Arnobius's story. For both authors, the purpose of this part of the myth seems to be to introduce Agdistis into the narrative and to lay the groundwork for the connection between sexuality and violence.

The second and more widely known aspect of the myth of Cybele and Attis describes the relationship between the two, namely, their love affair and its tragic consequences, ending in Attis's death, usually through self-castration. This is clearly the focal point of the myth. It was the section of the traditional tale that attracted the most attention in Mediterranean antiquity, in part because of the sensational nature of the material and in part because it provided the rationale for the self-castration of the Mother's priests, an act otherwise inexplicable to the Greeks and Romans. I shall summarize the three versions of the story of Attis noted above.

The version offered by Pausanias A is the only one that lacks any reference to a personal attachment between the goddess and Attis.[10] Here Attis is a human being who achieves his divine status through his devotion to the goddess, and his divinity is explained, not through a love affair, but through his support of the goddess's cult. In this account, Attis was born in Phrygia of human parents, normal except for the fact that he was unable to beget children. As an adult, he moved to Lydia and established the rites of the Mother there. These rites attracted an enormous following, more so than the cult of Zeus, with the result that Zeus was jealous and sent a boar to kill Attis. In view of the manner of his death, the Galatian residents of Pessinous refused to eat pork.[11]

9. I use the spelling Agdistis for this bisexual creature, since this is the form most frequently attested in the literary sources that record the myth. Several variant spellings of the name occur in Anatolia; see the examples cited in n. 26 below.

10. Pausanias 7.17.9.

11. A more grisly variant on this narrative can be found in Servius's Commentary on *Aeneid* 9.115. In Servius's story, too, Attis becomes conspicuous for his devotion to the Magna Mater, but in this account Attis's undoing is his physical beauty, which attracts the attention of the king of his (unnamed) city. To

The other accounts of the Attis myth focus on the personal relationship between Cybele and Attis. Diodoros preserves a rather simple tale in which the human Cybele, cast out by her parents, falls in love with the handsome young shepherd Attis. She becomes pregnant by him but then is recognized by her parents and taken in again. When they learn of her pregnancy, they cause Attis to be killed, whereupon Cybele goes mad with grief and wanders through the countryside. Eventually, after a famine, she is recognized as a goddess and Attis is worshipped with her. Because his body had long since disappeared, an image of him served as the focal point of his cult.

The third version is surely the most memorable one, the story of the passionate affair between the two principals that ends with the castration and death of Attis. In addition to the narratives of Pausanias and Arnobius mentioned above, this myth is recounted in detail by Ovid and appears in the work of several other authors, including Theokritos, Seneca, Lucian, and many authors of late antiquity, both pagan and Christian.[12] The large number and long chronological span of the extant accounts of this tale suggest that this was the version that circulated most widely. The internal details of the various authors are somewhat inconsistent, but the general outline of the plot follows a standard program. The goddess, variously called Magna Mater (Ovid, Arnobius), Agdistis (Pausanias B, Arnobius), or simply the turret-crowned goddess (Ovid), conceives a grand passion for the handsome young Attis. In every version, it is clear that the affair was an unhappy one, whether because Attis himself was unfaithful (Ovid) or because Attis was drawn away into an arranged marriage with the daughter of the king of Pessinous (Pausanias B and Arnobius, who names the Pessinuntine king Midas). As a result of this intervention by an outside party, Attis castrates himself (Ovid, Pausanias B, Arnobius) and dies of his wounds, proclaiming as he does so that his death is deserved because of his unfaithfulness to the goddess. The goddess mourns his death profoundly, and because of her sincere unhappiness, Zeus grants her requests that Attis's body remain uncorrupted (Pausanias B, Arnobius) and that his self-castration be followed by his priests (Ovid).

---

escape the advances of this king, Attis flees from the city to the forest, but the king pursues him and rapes him. Attis retaliates by castrating the king, who then castrates Attis in turn. Attis is found by the attendants of the Mother's temple lying under a pine tree, dying of his wounds. They try unsuccessfully to save him, and after his death, they institute an annual period of mourning in his honor, during which the goddess's attendants, here called *archigalli,* castrate themselves in memory of Attis.

12. Pagan authors: Theokritos 20.40; Seneca, *Agamemnon* 686–90; Lucian, *On Sacrifices* 7, *Dialogue of the Gods* 12; Julian, *Oration* 5; and Sallustius, *De natura deorum* 4. Christian authors in addition to Arnobius: Clement, *Protrep.* 2.13–14; Tertullian, *Ad nat.* 1.10.45; Firmicus Maternus, *De err. prof. relig.* 3 and 8, 1–3; Prudentius, *Ad Symmachum* 1.187, 2.51–52, 2.521–23, and *Peristephanon* 10.154–60, 10.196–200, 10.1006–90; Hippolytus, *Refutat. omnium haeres.* 5.7.138, 5.7.140, 5.8.162, 5.8.168–70; Socrates, *Hist. eccl.* 3.23; Eusebius, *Praeparatio ev.* 2.3.18; Augustine, *Civ. Dei* 6.7.71–74. The complete texts of the ancient sources, both Greek and Latin, are given by Hepding 1903: 5–77. This summary of the myth is taken from the three principal sources, Ovid, Pausanias, and Arnobius; the other ancient references add little to their information.

I give more detailed consideration below to a number of points raised in this composite summary. Yet even this cursory account brings up some obvious artificialities, use of aetiology, and repetition of folktale motifs drawn from other Greek legends. The different versions of the myth are confusing and contradictory—sometimes, it appears, intentionally so. In earlier discussions of the myth, the standard way of addressing these artificialities and contradictions was to allocate the varying versions of the myth to three different points of geographical origin. The first, expounded by Pausanias (Pausanias A), has been called the "Lydian" version, in which Attis is a human priest of Cybele who introduces her cult into Lydia. The second, the "Phrygian" version, whose origin was attributed to Pessinous, describes the love affair of Cybele and Attis and the subsequent castration of Attis; this is the version of Ovid, Pausanias B, and Arnobius, and has been considered by previous scholars to be the oldest and most genuine tradition. The third account is the "euhemeristic" version, or rationalization of the myth, presumably of Greek origin, as known from Diodoros.

This tripartite theory, first promulgated in detail by Hepding in 1909, has won many converts.[13] Yet it has several flaws. It attributes the most distasteful behavior, particularly the sexually deviant behavior, to the Phrygians, and dismisses, with little discussion, Diodoros's alternative version of the tale as an impossible fiction. This circumstance in itself lays the theory open to suspicions of Orientalist prejudice of the sort discussed in chapter 1. Such an approach also assumes that the Classical authors are reproducing Phrygian, especially Pessinuntine, cult practice accurately, without offering any discussion of the Phrygian evidence for such cult practices. Moreover, despite the fact that the sources that record the myth stretch over a period of several centuries and purport to record ritual of greater antiquity still, this approach assumes that the myth was a static, unchanging entity, and that as a result written sources of the third and fourth centuries C.E. must accurately record rituals and traditions formed many centuries earlier.

A more fruitful way to understand the myth is to analyze the various stages of the narrative and demonstrate their relationship, if any, to their Phrygian origins. A comparative analysis that concentrates only on the surviving literary sources and fails to take into account the inconsistencies between the Anatolian background of the myth and the Greek and Latin treatments of it will inevitably be limited in the insight it can offer.[14] Once the Phrygian core of the myth has been identified, it will be easier to suggest what the original structure and purpose of the story may have

13. Hepding 1903: 121–22; see also Vermaseren 1977: 90–92; Borgeaud 1988b: 88–91. For earlier discussions of the source of the myth, see Baumeister 1860; Cumont 1896: 2249–50. The approach of Walter Burkert (1972: 80–82; 1979a: 104–5), who maintains that the myth of Cybele and Attis represents a collective cultural memory of Paleolithic hunting rituals, is of little value; see the discussion in chapter 1 above.

14. Extensive comparative analyses have been offered by previous scholars, of which the most complete are Hepding 1903: 121–22; Vermaseren 1977: 88–95; Borgeaud 1988b and 1996: 56–88.

been. We shall also be able to see what the non-Phrygian elements in the story are and then determine how they became attached to the core story and why.

Critical to such an analysis is a consideration of the problems inherent in the written sources that preserve the myth. The first is the question of chronology. Brief allusions to the myth appear in literature of the second century B.C.,[15] but the earliest continuous narrative that survives, that of Diodoros, dates to the first century B.C. The fullest records of the myth are later still, namely, those supplied by Ovid, writing in the early first century C.E., Pausanias in the second century, Arnobius in the late third century, and Julian in the fourth century C.E.[16] Several of these later authors claim to draw on written sources of an earlier period; Pausanias states that his source is Hermesianax, a writer of the early third century B.C., and Arnobius claims to draw on the work of an earlier writer named Timotheos. Since these earlier sources are no longer extant, the accuracy with which writers such as Pausanias and Arnobius reproduce material much earlier than their own time period is difficult to determine, and this chronological gap will have to be taken into account. Thus in reading the myth, we cannot be sure whether we are reading a tradition formed in the third century B.C., an account of the third century C.E., or some pastiche of material formed over a period of many centuries.

The late date of our extant sources poses another problem. As the abundant archaeological evidence makes clear, the cult of the Mother Goddess was prominent in Phrygia from the early first millennium B.C. It was practiced in the Greek world from the sixth century B.C., and it arrived in Rome in the late third century B.C. During the many centuries of its existence, the cult changed considerably, and although the surviving written sources claim to explain rituals and beliefs of a much earlier time, it is clear that they reflect cult practices and attitudes of their own times as well. The most conspicuous example of this is the figure of Attis himself. The cult of Attis first appears in the Greek world in the mid fourth century B.C.,[17] and there is no evidence in Phrygia to suggest that a god named Attis was worshipped there before the Roman period. Yet the myth implies that Attis had been an essential part of the cult of the Mother Goddess in Phrygia from its earliest stages. Attis's relationship with the goddess, the key component of the myth, thus constitutes a contradiction, undercutting the modern assumption that the myth is a close record of Phrygian ritual. Earlier scholars have noted the lack of evidence concerning Attis in the Classical world before the fourth century B.C., but they explained this by assuming that a Phrygian god named Attis must have existed, but had been deliberately suppressed

15. Theokritos 20.40. Several of the epigrams in the *Anthologia palatina* describing the encounter of the Gallos and the lion may derive from the second century B.C., i.e., *Anth. pal.* 6.217, 218, 219, 220, and 237; see also Gow 1960.

16. Julian, *Orations* 5.165.

17. On the origin of the cult of Attis, see Roller 1994 and chapter 6 above. Lambrechts 1962: 62, argues that Attis was purely a phenomenon of the western Roman Empire; this is not correct, but his statement that there was no god Attis in Phrygia is accurate.

from the cult of the Greek Meter; he was supposedly too "barbaric" for Greek sensibilities.[18] The differences between Phrygian cult and the Greek and Roman records of the myth of Cybele and Attis cannot, however, be explained away as distaste for a barbarian ritual that the more enlightened culture of Hellenism rejected.

In addition to problems of chronology, there are problems of ideology. Many vivid details of the love affair of Cybele and Attis come from the writings of the Christian apologists of the third and fourth centuries C.E.,[19] several of whom use the myth as ammunition in their attacks on pagan religious practices. In particular, Arnobius, who has left the most extensive account of the myth, clearly has an ideological agenda, for his version of the Cybele and Attis story is framed within a narrative that deliberately dwells on the most unattractive aspects of pagan myth and cult. Since the identity of the Timotheos he quotes is uncertain,[20] his claim to give an accurate account of earlier material should be regarded with skepticism. He may have taken the basic outline of the narrative from an earlier source—the similarity of his tale to that of Pausanias B suggests this—but the tone of Arnobius's account lies in Christian polemic, and much of the lurid detail he records may also.

These inconsistencies of chronology, ideology, and content suggest that the myth of Cybele and Attis is not merely a Greek and Roman record of a Phrygian tradition. To understand the origins of the myth and the reasons for its association with Phrygian cult ritual, we shall have to dig a little deeper.

Let us begin by looking at the principal actors in the myth. All of the participants in the story are known in Phrygia, where they appear in a variety of contexts, religious, mythical, and historical, and we can compare their place in Phrygian society with their role in the story. The goddess herself, the subject of this study, needs no further introduction other than to note again that her Phrygian name was Matar, or "Mother," the equivalent of Meter in Greek or Mater in Latin. Cybele was not her name in Phrygia, but an epithet derived from the Phrygian word for "mountain."[21] The other figures in the myth, Attis, Agdistis, Midas, have independent personalities in Phrygian history and cult and need a more careful review.

Attis, the other central figure in the myth, has already been introduced in chapters 4 and 6. He was certainly at home in Phrygia, but not as a god. Attis is, in fact, the

18. Kern 1935: II, 232; Ferguson 1944: 107–15, esp. 110; Versnel 1990: 108. Such negative stereotypes of the Phrygians had a long history in the Greek world; note the comments of Hall 1989: 103, 124–25, on the Greek stereotype of Phrygians as effeminate cowards, and the discussion in chapter 1.

19. For sources, see n. 12 above.

20. Weinreich, "Timotheos," in *RE* 26 (1937), 1342; Nilsson 1961: 641; and Borgeaud 1988b assume that Arnobius's source was a Eumolpid priest active in Egypt in the early third century B.C.; yet R. Laqueur, "Timotheos," also in *RE* 26 (1937), 1338, states that this Timotheos is otherwise unknown. The fact that Timotheos was one of the commonest Greek names precludes certainty as to the identity of Arnobius's source.

21. As noted in chapter 4, it is uncertain whether the epithet Kybele, or *kubileya* in Paleo-Phrygian texts, was the general Phrygian word for mountain or the name of one specific mountain. Diodoros's connection of the goddess's name with Mount Kybelon suggests that he associated her with this one particular place.

most frequently attested personal name in Phrygia, found in numerous texts, ranging from large, impressive inscriptions like that on the Midas Monument to graffiti
scratched on common household pottery.[22] These graffiti, surely notations of own-
ership, demonstrate that among the Phrygians, the name Attis was an ordinary one,
with no special religious or social significance. This fact should be kept in mind
when evaluating occurrences of the name Attis in Greek texts where the context is
unconnected with the myth of Cybele. Often the name Attis may be nothing more
than a Greek author's choice of a typical ethnic name to give an Anatolian "flavor-
ing" to a particular episode being recounted, much as an Englishman might use the
name Paddy in a story about an Irishman.[23] This is the most likely interpretation of
the tale Herodotos recounts about Atys, son of Croesus, and his death during a boar
hunt.[24] Several scholars have explained this episode as a sanitized version of the
myth of Cybele and Attis, but a more plausible explanation lies at hand: Herodotos
may have named the young man Atys simply because, to a Greek, especially one who
was a native of Anatolia, as Herodotos was, this was the prototypical Anatolian
name.[25] When the name Attis does occur in a religious context in Phrygia, it refers
to a prominent member of the Phrygian ruling class, perhaps the king himself, who
would have been the principal individual responsible for venerating his kingdom's
chief divinity. We have already seen how the priestly function of the king was commemorated by using the royal name Attis as the title of the Mother Goddess's chief
priest in Pessinous.

Another figure who appears prominently in the Cybele and Attis narrative is
Agdistis. In the account of Pausanias B, this hermaphroditic figure plays the role of
the alter ego of Cybele; and for Arnobius, Agdistis was the rival of the Magna Mater
for the affections of Attis. Agdistis, too, we have met before, for she is well documented, in Phrygia and in other areas of the Mediterranean, as a female divinity, regularly equated with the Mother Goddess in title and iconography. Her name is most
commonly given as Angdistis.[26] The name may have been derived from a toponym,

22. Note the examples cited in chapter 4, n. 42, and Roller 1987b: nos. 48, 51.
23. See Boardman 1970: 21 for a similar suggestion on the use of the Lydian name Manes. Note the
occurrence of the name in a fragment of the fourth-century B.C. comic poet Theopompos (fr. 27 [Kock]).
The fragment appears in the *Suda,* s.v. "Attis," where the commentary connects it with the Mother of the
gods, but a more likely explanation is that the original text refers to a man and his Phrygian slave.
24. Herodotos 1.33–44.
25. The assumption that this must be the Attis of the Cybele myth was first proposed by Baumeister
1860, who saw in Herodotos's narrative the same tale as the "Lydian" version of Pausanias 7.17.9.
Baumeister notes that both the Atys of Herodotos and the Attes of Pausanias were killed by a boar,
recalling also Pausanias's comment that the Galatian residents of Pessinous do not eat pork. In this conclusion he was followed by Hepding 1903: 5; Vermaseren 1977: 88–90; Burkert 1979a: 104; and Borgeaud
1988b: 88 and 1996: 57. Herodotos's account, however, is cast in the form of a folktale (note its similarity
to the myth of Adonis, the young lover of Aphrodite, also killed by a boar), and it seems more likely that
both Herodotos and Pausanias were drawing on folktale motifs than that Herodotos was describing cult
ritual. It is also possible that Herodotos calls Croesus's son Atys because this was in fact his name, continuing the name of his grandfather Alyattes.
26. In Anatolia Agdistis's name is found in several variant spellings. Votive texts from Midas City
refer to Angdissi, Andissi, Agdissi, and Andxi (all datives), and the additional spellings Angdessi and

perhaps that of the mountain Agdos, as Arnobius reports, and thus Angdistis may have referred to the Mountain Mother as she was worshipped in one specific place, as opposed to the other topographic epithets used for the goddess. A substantial concentration of votives to Angdistis in the vicinity of Dokimeion and Midas City suggests that the mountain Agdos may have been located in this region. Nowhere in Anatolia is there any hint of Angdistis's dual sexuality, or of any negative or cruel features such as those Arnobius describes. In fact, the contrary is true, for Angdistis is frequently invoked together with deities regarded as healing or savior deities.[27]

The other figure who appears in some accounts is Midas. In Diodoros's version, Midas was a king of Phrygia who was especially devoted to the cult of Cybele. In Arnobius's account, Midas was the king of Pessinous whose daughter was betrothed to Attis; it was this betrothal that precipitated the crisis resulting in Attis's self-castration. Midas, too, is well known apart from this myth. He was a ruler of Phrygia in the late eighth and early seventh centuries B.C., and his life and activities are independently attested in Assyrian and Greek historical records.[28] His reign evidently coincided with the greatest extent of the Phrygian kingdom; and as a result Midas left a powerful impression on his contemporaries and followers, although the seat of his kingdom was Gordion, not Pessinous.[29] The appearance of his name on the important cult relief at Midas City implies strongly that Midas figured in the goddess's cult, perhaps in a role analogous to that of Attis—namely, as a ruler linked to the goddess by his priestly duties. There are a scattering of Classical references to a connection between Midas and the Mother Goddess; Greek sources credit him with the establishment of the goddess's rites, and he is also called the son of Cybele.[30] These references may recall the historical Midas, although it is also likely that when later authors wanted to name a specific Phrygian king, they simply used the best-known Phrygian royal name without any clear idea of who this was.

The principal figures in the myth of Cybele and Attis are thus in fact a mixed group, consisting of genuine deities, such as the Mother Goddess and Agdistis, and human beings, such as Midas and Attis. With this in mind, let us return to the myth. We shall want to examine its Anatolian background and the ways in which the Anatolian elements are presented in Greek and Latin texts.

Andixeos occur at other Anatolian sites. On votives from the Piraeus, Paros, and Egypt the name appears as Angdistis, but variants with a tau are less common in Anatolia. The differing spellings may well represent regional variations. For discussion of the name's orthography, see Gusmani 1959: 203–6 and Robert 1980: 239. On the basis of the nomenclature used on the coinage from Dokimeion, Robert argues that the standard spelling of the name in Anatolia was Angdissis.

27. Note the Philadelphia text discussed in chapter 7, Weinreich 1919 = Barton and Horseley 1981, where Angdistis is one of the *theoi soteres;* also *CIG* III 3993 = *CCCA* I: no. 777, Angdistis paired with "the helpful Mother," and *MAMA* VI 394, Angdistis paired with Asklepios.

28. For the source material relating to a historical Midas, see Roller 1983: 299–302 and Muscarella 1989. Midas may have been a dynastic name used by several kings, but all the historical references in both Assyrian and Greek texts relate only to this one individual of the late eighth century B.C.

29. See Roller 1984 for a discussion of Midas and the foundation legend of Gordion.

30. For the references, see Roller 1983: 309.

ANALYSIS OF THE MYTH: FROM PHRYGIA TO THE WEST

Let us begin by looking at the myth as a whole. All versions of the myth combine elements of three quite different types. The first is a traditional tale of the creation of the gods through successive generations. This tale had its roots in the Anatolian Bronze Age, but it continued to enjoy an active life in the Classical world. The second is a record of the cult rituals of Phrygia, several of which are present in the myth, although in a highly altered form. The third element is the distorted lens through which Greeks and Romans observed Phrygian customs, distorted in part through the use of the myth to explain the rituals of the goddess in the West, particularly those of the Magna Mater in Rome, which were not always identical with the rituals of Phrygia. The Graeco-Roman view of the goddess and her rituals is also strongly colored by a heritage of regarding the Phrygians as inferior Asiatic barbarians and Phrygian religious practice as typical of such low-life types.[31]

All of these elements, the generation myth, the Mother's Phrygian rituals, and the reaction of the West to these rituals, contain a great deal of tension, since each includes sexually explicit material whose presentation may well be colored by the personal reactions of an individual author. This is particularly true of the focus on castration, which tends to acquire a prurient fascination of its own, thereby obscuring the explanatory function of the myth and its relationship to a Phrygian background. I suspect that it is this personal tension and the varying motives of different authors for relating the story that contributes to such radically differing versions of it. Before we consider the reasons for such individual variation, let us examine each of the three elements posited above and then consider how they might have been combined in the form known through the surviving written sources.

The first element, the myth of the creation of the gods through successive generations, was an old one in the ancient Near East. We meet it in the background story of Cybele related by Pausanias B and Arnobius, who use it to describe the rape of the earth and the birth of the monstrous Agdistis. According to Arnobius, Zeus tried to rape the Mother as she was sleeping; his seed fell on the rock Agdos and produced Agdestis (*sic*) instead. In Pausanias's B version, Zeus simply pours out his semen onto the earth (no rape being involved), and Adgistis is born. Both of these versions conflate the Mother Goddess with Mother Earth and tell of the union of the male sky god with female earth.[32]

While this is a myth of long standing in the ancient Mediterranean world, best known through the *Theogony* of Hesiod,[33] the myth of divine succession is far older

---

31. See Hall 1989: 154 on Greek attitudes; Beard 1994 on Roman attitudes.
32. Schibli 1990: 61–62.
33. Hesiod, *Theogony* 132–38.

than Hesiod. Its roots lie in Bronze Age Anatolian, specifically Hittite, tradition, where we find elements of the story of Cybele and Attis paralleled by two myths, the myth of Kumarbi and the Song of Ullikummi.[34] There are several points of correspondence with the myth of Cybele. In the myth of Kumarbi, Anu, the Hittite god, is deposed from his position as principal god by Kumarbi, who castrates him by biting off his genitals. Kumarbi swallows the genitals and becomes impregnated with five powerful deities.[35] In a parallel move, the gods attempt to depose Agdistis from power by ripping off (surely as violent as biting off) the male genitals; nobody swallows them, but the genitals are thrown on the ground, resulting in the pregnancy of Sangarios's daughter. This last detail may be present in the Kumarbi myth also, as Kumarbi spits out the genitals of Anu onto the earth, which then conceives.[36] In both cases the locus of the deity's power is his male organs, and the intent is to remove this power by removing those organs. In each case, though, the threatening god's power is not eliminated but merely transferred to the next generation.

The Song of Ullikummi also contains at least one element that appears in the Phrygian tradition. In this poem, Kumarbi wishes to overthrow the Storm God, one of the deities whose birth resulted from Kumarbi's swallowing Anu's genitals. To achieve this, Kumarbi begets a monster, the Storm Monster Ullikummi, by spilling his semen on a rock, which then becomes pregnant with Ullikummi,[37] an episode paralleling that of the birth of Agdistis as related by Arnobius. The intent of Kumarbi's action is to produce a creature who will have both the strength and the hardness of a rock, but the result is to create a being that is difficult to control, as Agdistis is too.

These unusual birth and castration patterns are not limited to Hittite epic tradition. In Greek literature, the castration of Ouranos described in Hesiod's *Theogony* immediately springs to mind.[38] Although Ouranos is masculine, not bisexual, the castration is carried out for the same reasons as the attack on Agdistis—namely, to make him passive and eliminate the threat of violence. In another parallel action, Ouranos's severed genitals drip blood onto the earth, which immediately becomes pregnant with the Erinyes, Giants, and Nymphs. The actual male genitalia, thrown into the sea, create Aphrodite, goddess of beauty,[39] in a manner reminiscent of the beautiful Attis being born of the severed male genitalia of Agdistis.

In addition to the *Theogony,* there are other Greek parallels to the Agdistis story. A

34. For the text of the Song of Ullikummi, see Güterbock 1952. An English translation of both myths by Albrecht Goetze appears in Pritchard 1969: 120–28. For a discussion of their impact on Greek literature, see Walcot 1966: 1–26; for their relationship to Phrygian myth: Meslin 1978: 767; Burkert 1979b; Borgeaud 1988b: 92.

35. Albrecht Goetze, in Pritchard 1969: 120–21; Walcot 1966: 2–5.

36. Goetze, in Pritchard 1969: 120.

37. Güterbock 1952: 14–15; Goetze, in Pritchard 1969: 121.

38. Hesiod, *Theogony* 176–82. This connection was also made in antiquity by Dionysius of Halikarnassos 2.19, who also links the castration of Ouranos and the more extreme rites of the Magna Mater.

39. Hesiod, *Theogony* 183–200.

striking one, with an impeccable Greek pedigree, is the attempted rape of Athena by Hephaistos. Like Zeus, Hephaistos is frustrated in his attempt and pours his semen on the rock of the Acropolis, resulting in the birth of the monstrous Erichthonios.[40] In another version, the sixth-century B.C. historian Pherekydes recorded a theogony in which Zas (Zeus) and Chthonie/Ge (Earth), two of the three original divine beings, marry and produce a monstrous offspring, which then forms a threat to the power of Zeus and Earth.[41] There is also an amusing parallel to the Agdistis episode in the tale recounted by Aristophanes in Plato's *Symposium,* where the original beings on earth were double creatures, many of them androgynous.[42] In this case, too, the double sexuality of the creatures constitutes a threat to the gods, and so they have to be separated to make them more docile. While the tone is different, the result is the same—namely, the separation of a hermaphroditic being into constituent male and female parts as a form of control.

Other parallels are known from much later sources. The Christian apologist Clement of Alexandria, writing in the second century C.E., preserves a bizarre account of the Eleusinian Mysteries, in which Zeus tries to rape Demeter; when she rejects his advances, he cuts off the testicles of a ram and flings them into her lap.[43] This is reminiscent of the attempted rape of the Magna Mater (closely identified with Demeter) and the castration of Agdistis. The second-century C.E. mythographer Philo of Byblos wrote a *Theogony* in which Ouranos is castrated by his son and his severed genitals mingle with the water of the springs and rivers, just as the severed genitals of Agdistis mingle with (i.e., impregnate) the Sangarios River's daughter.[44] A variant on this appears in the fifth-century C.E. writer Nonnos, who describes how Zeus pursued Aphrodite and tried to rape her, unsuccessfully, whereupon his semen dropped to the ground, giving birth to a race of centaurs.[45]

No one of these episodes repeats exactly the story of Agdistis and the birth of Attis. This material does, however, demonstrate that many of the more bizarre elements of the Cybele/Attis story, such as the rape of Earth, the castration of a powerful male deity, and the passage through the fruit of this castration to a new generation of gods and heroes, were known in both Anatolian and Greek tradition.[46] The elements of violence and sexuality within the Phrygian myth that seemed most disturbing to ancient (and modern) scholars were probably not original to the Phry-

40. Euripides, *Ion* 267–70. The meaning of the Athena-Hephaistos episode is quite different from that of the Phrygian story, for the result is a desirable one—namely, to make the Athenian nobility (supposedly descended from Erichthonios) god-born without compromising the virginity of Athena.
41. Kirk and Raven 1963: s.v. "Pherekydes," frs. 51–54; Schibli 1990: 50–69, 78–103.
42. Plato, *Symposium* 189e–190d.
43. Clement, *Protreptikos* 2.13.
44. Philo of Byblos, *FGrHist* 790 F 2.
45. Nonnos 5.611–15, 14.193–202, 32.71–72. See Walcot 1966: 21.
46. One specific detail mentioned only by Arnobius, that the rock Agdos was the same rock as was thrown by Deucalion and Pyrrha to create humanity, widens the story by placing the creation of human beings within this framework of successive generations.

gians; rather, they belong to a wider pattern of creation myths. The Phrygians were exposed to this mythical tradition both as the heirs of the Hittites in central Anatolia and through their contacts with Anatolian Greeks. Since A(n)gdistis is merely the Phrygian name for the Mother Goddess, the story of her creation and subjugation through castration may originally have been a Phrygian variant of this wider story pattern, designed to place the Phrygian Mother within the myth of generations focused on Mother Earth.

Yet, while many elements of the birth of Cybele appear in the traditions of other Mediterranean peoples, the story of Cybele and Attis is unique. An explanation for the relationship of the two may lie in Phrygian cult practice. Therefore it will be valuable to review what features of Phrygian cult monuments and religious practice can be related to the narrative details of the myth.

One such feature is the Phrygian Mother's identity as the Mother of the mountains. Diodoros, while stating that the goddess had human parents, gives the name of her mother as Dindymene, thereby alluding to Meter Dindymene, one of Meter's most common epithets. Diodoros also recognized, perhaps only unconsciously, that the goddess's name Cybele was derived from a term connected with the Phrygian word for mountain, *kubelon*. Arnobius's account also connects the goddess with the mountains, for his description recalls the Mother's association with wild and remote landscape, her natural haunt: "in Phrygiae finibus inauditae per omnia vastitatis petra est quaedam, cui nomen est Agdus" (at the boundaries of Phrygia is a certain rock of unheard-of desolation throughout, named Agdus) (Arnobius 5.5). Ovid, too, places the goddess in the mountains, although his main interest was in the Trojan mountains and their connection with the legendary past of Rome:

> Dindymon et Cybelen et amoenam fontibus Iden
> semper et Iliacas Mater amavit opes.

> The Mother always loved Dindymon and Cybele and Ida, pleasant with fountains, and the wealth of Troy.

> (Ovid, *Fasti* 4.249–50)

Despite the variant details, the Mother's mountain home, a key point in the myth, is derived from Phrygian cult.

Another Phrygian feature that survives in Graeco-Roman narratives is the fate of Attis. Here the connection with Phrygian religious practice is not so obvious, and so we need to review the archaeological evidence from Phrygia.

Underlying the account of Attis's death and burial is the similarity of Phrygian cultic and funerary monuments. Phrygian cult architecture, particularly the rock-cut cult façades of the goddess that form such a striking feature of the Phrygian highlands, resembles several of the most conspicuous Phrygian grave monuments; many of the funerary monuments were also cut into the live rock, and in several cases, they use similar iconographic features, such as the representation of predators.[47] This circumstance, noted by many travelers in Anatolia, originally led to difficulties in determining which of the Phrygian rock monuments were for divine use and which for human use. This blurring of functions may well have been intentional, as if the iconography of strength and power that the predators represent was suitable for both cultic and funerary monuments.[48] A similar correlation can be noted in central Phrygia, in the district around Ankara and Gordion. In this region, there are no cliffs available for rock-cut tombs, but the freestanding stone reliefs of the goddess, clearly religious monuments, can also have funerary connections, as is demonstrated by the reliefs from Ankara, found in proximity with groups of burial tumuli.[49]

How does this relate to the myth of Cybele and Attis? I have drawn attention to the close relationship between Phrygian religious and funerary symbolism because of the one feature in the myth that appears in every version of the story—namely, the profound mourning for the death of Attis. This appears consistently in accounts such as those of Diodoros and Arnobius, which otherwise vary significantly, and is present in both of Pausanias's versions, as well as in almost every minor reference to the goddess. It is given as the rationale for many of the cult's unusual practices, such as the use of wild music and the frenzied behavior of the cult's followers. Let us recall how frequently this point is emphasized in Greek and Roman literature:

And you, Rhea, weep for the cowherd.
> (Theokritos 20.40)

And Cybele became maddened because of her grief for the youth [Attis] and wandered around the countryside.
> (Diodoros 3.57.6–7)

The crowd beats its breast for the turreted Mother, as she mourns Phrygian Attis.
> (Seneca, *Agamemnon* 688–90)

And you, foolish boy, have persuaded Rhea to long for the Phrygian youth . . . and now she is wandering up and down Ida mourning for Attis.
> (Lucian, *Dialogues of the Gods* 20,
> Aphrodite speaking to Eros)

47. Haspels 1971: 98–99, on the confusion of sepulchral and religious monuments; 112–38, on the iconography of sepulchral monuments.

48. The reasons for this remain obscure to us, and I am not prepared to speculate on the meaning of Phrygian funerary iconography in the absence of written texts.

49. Buluç 1988. In most cases the precise relationship between the reliefs and the tumuli was not recorded when they were initially excavated. Elizabeth Simpson (1996: 198–201) has proposed that some of the objects found in the Gordion tumuli MM and P also have reference to the cult of the Mother Goddess; in particular, she sees the horned rosette design on the inlaid serving stands from these tumuli (originally called screens, Young et al. 1981: Tum P 151, MM 378, 379) as a symbol of the goddess.

The Phrygian Rhea is honored at Pessinous by the Phrygian mourning for Attis.

(Arrian, *Tactica* 33.4)

In the annual rites honoring the earth, there is drawn a cortege of the youth's funeral.

(Firmicus Maternus, *De err. prof. rel.* 3)

The youth must be wept through the many sacred rites of the Mother.

(Prudentius, *Peristephanon* 10.200)

The tone can be solemn or humorous, respectful or critical, but the mourning rite is always the central core of the narrative.

This may be the clue to a major enigma in the myth, namely, the role of the god Attis. If, as I have postulated above, the Phrygian rulers maintained a close relationship with the Mother's cult as part of their official obligations, the funeral of one of these rulers would have been an occasion for official mourning, being seen as the loss of the goddess's most important earthly devotee, perhaps even of her earthly consort.[50] After the disappearance of kingship in Phrygia, the cult responsibilities of a royal, human Attis would have been taken over in part by the human priest, as we know from the documents of Hellenistic Pessinous. The mourning may have referred to the funeral of a high priest Attis, or it may have evolved into an annual ritual for an abstract figure of a king named Attis, perhaps a ritual analogous to a Greek hero cult, all the more important to the Phrygian people because it was a survival from Phrygia's period of glory.

This hypothesis finds support in virtually all of the written sources on the myth. In the accounts of Diodoros, Pausanias A, and Servius, Attis is a human being, and Pausanias A makes Attis exactly what the epigraphic evidence from Pessinous proves he was—namely, a human male and the Mother Goddess's principal devotee. The other sources make Attis's devotion to Cybele personal, not ritual, and Diodoros records that because Attis was no longer present, an image had to be created to substitute for him. For Pausanias B and Arnobius, the image was the body of Attis himself, which would never decay, and his death occasioned annual mourning. Can we not see in this an aetiological explanation of Phrygian ritual? Such annual mourning would have reaffirmed the goddess's power and her close contact with her people through her love for their ruler. It would also have maintained the Phrygians' sense of themselves as a distinct people, despite their loss of political independence.

The roots of the other memorable feature of the myth—namely, Attis's castration of himself and, in consequence, the self-castration of the goddess's priests—also lie in Phrygian religious ritual, although the actual practice was quite different from

50. We have no idea whether the ritual of a sacred marriage played a part in Phrygian tradition, but such a ritual is attested in Hittite religious practice (see T. Özgüç 1988) and could well have survived into the first millennium B.C.

that imputed in the myth. Recall the silver Phrygian statuette of a mature but unbearded male (fig. 36) found together with a statuette of the Mother Goddess in a Phrygian tomb.[51] The piece probably represents a priest of the Mother Goddess, and the lack of a beard may well signify that the individual was a eunuch. Ritual castration in Anatolia was not limited to the cult of the Phrygian Mother either; Strabo reports that the priests of Ephesian Artemis, the Megabyzoi, were originally eunuchs, and that this was considered a position of great honor.[52] No direct evidence providing a rationale for the practice of ritual castration survives from Anatolia, but there are indirect connections that suggest how this custom came about and what it meant to the Phrygians.

Several scholars have noted that the Phrygians showed a marked preference for deities that personified positive moral and ethical values.[53] The Phrygian Mother fit well into this preference, for she was frequently worshipped in connection with the so-called Savior Deities.[54] This is particularly striking in the Hellenistic and Roman eras, where the presence of several texts from Phrygia, written in the Greek language, enables us to gain some sense of why her worshippers were attracted to her. The important second-century B.C. text from Anatolian Philadelphia discussed in chapter 7 is particularly informative in this context.[55] The text, which records the establishment of a closed community to worship Angdistis, the Phrygian Mother Goddess, spells out several cult regulations requiring a high degree of morally uplifting behavior from those who worshipped the goddess. This extended to sexual fidelity, since fornication and adultery were expressly forbidden.

In this context, it may be that the goddess's principal devotees, namely, her priests, were expected to make a permanent commitment to sexual chastity through castration. The context of the Philadelphia inscription implies that this would have been seen as an affirmative action, publicly declaring a man's fidelity to the goddess and his determination to maintain the vows of chastity necessary for total commitment to her cult. A hint of this may survive in Ovid, who states that total chastity is part of Attis's devotion and fidelity to the goddess, "Semper fac puer esse velis" ("Act so that you may always wish to be a boy," i.e., sexually inexperienced) (*Fasti* 4.226); this was the commitment that Attis promised the Mother. Such castration may be repugnant to us, but it was likewise advocated by many Christians of the second through fourth centuries C.E., and for the same reason—namely, to remove oneself permanently from the temptations of the flesh so as to be able to devote oneself to

51. Özgen 1988: 38, no. 41. For a more detailed discussion of the statuette, see chapter 4.
52. Strabo 14.1.23. Smith 1996 examines the evidence for the eunuch *megabyzoi* and casts doubt on their existence, but the citation of Strabo seems to indicate that such eunuch priests did exist, although they may have been few.
53. See Mitchell 1982: 6–7; Roller 1988a: 47–48; Lane Fox 1986: 405–6, on the straightlaced character of the Phrygians.
54. Note the material cited above, n. 27, on the connection of Angdistis with Savior Deities.
55. Weinreich 1919: 4–8; Barton and Horseley 1981. Note esp. lines 25–29.

one's religious vows.[56] The application of this attitude to Phrygian cult can only be inferred, not proven, but I think it goes far toward explaining what the practice meant in Phrygia, and why it would not have been condemned among the Phrygians as it was among the Greeks and Romans.[57]

This also addresses a key issue that has rarely been noted in other discussions of the myth—namely, the inconsistent congruence between castration and death in the story of Cybele and Attis. It is, after all, the emphasis on the annual mourning for Attis that is really the key to the myth, and it is here that the source of the ritual lies, in the creation of an image and the perpetual honor accorded it (as stated by Diodoros, Pausanias A and B, Arnobius, and others). As a guiding theme of the myth, the motif of castration makes no sense. It is absent from several versions of the story altogether, indicating that the castration episode was not essential to the myth. Even when it is present, it lacks a coherent connection to the story. Nowhere is it explained why self-castration killed Attis. It clearly did not kill most of his priests, who were supposedly following the god's example.[58] Viewed in this light, the scene of the castration of Attis seems like a late addendum to the myth, one that was designed to combine two basic features of Phrygian cult practice, the annual mourning for an Attis and the self-castration (for whatever reasons) of Phrygian priests of the Mother.

In addition to the background of Phrygian ritual, a third factor, the perspective through which the Greeks and Romans recorded Phrygian customs and ritual, is also crucial in explaining the formation of the myth. While the source of the myth did indeed lie within Phrygian cult practice and tradition, the form in which it was translated to the West distorted both the meaning and the intent of Phrygian cult.

There are several reasons for this. One has been alluded to earlier—namely, the conflation of the Cybele/Attis myth with other similar myths and with folktale patterns. Each version of the story furnishes examples. We have already noted one, the

56. Cf. the strong case that Origen makes for castration (Origen, *On Matt. 19.12, 15.1–5*). Origen took his own teachings seriously and was castrated voluntarily. Note also the *Sentences of Sextus,* ed. Chadwick 1959: 13, 71a, 273, in which the devout man is urged, "Cast away any part of the body which leads you into intemperance," "Conquer the body in every way," and "Men ought to cut off some parts of their members for the health of the rest." Cf. also the evidence collected by Brown 1988: 168–70.

57. A similar idea was proposed by Nock 1925: 28. It has been criticized by Rousselle 1988: 126 n. 84, on the grounds that abscission of the testicles need not interfere with a man's capacity to have sexual relations, and there is certainly plenty of evidence from Rome to suggest that the Galli did enjoy sexual relations (see chapter 10). The evidence from Phrygia suggests strongly, however, that there (if not elsewhere in the Roman Empire) chastity was an important value.

58. Cf. Lucretius 2.618–23, in which the priests of the Magna Mater in Rome march through the streets in procession, brandishing the weapons with which they have just castrated themselves. This point is noted by Rousselle 1988: 122–23, who analyzes the evidence for the means of castration in Mediterranean antiquity and provides a sober discussion of its actual effect, in many cases little more than that of a modern vasectomy. Rousselle undercuts her arguments, however, by assuming that the Mother's priests would have chosen a simple and private method, such as tying up the testicles to cause permanent damage to the vas deferens; while this was practiced by some men, the ancient evidence suggests that the Mother's priests chose the more dramatic way of cutting off their testicles to create a public show of the finality of the act.

exposure of the infant Cybele and her miraculous survival, mentioned by Diodoros. This same story pattern recurs in the version reported by Arnobius; here it is Nana, the daughter of Sangarios, whose child Attis is exposed and miraculously survives through his nourishment by a goat. Diodoros's picture of Cybele wandering the countryside, maddened with grief, is another story type; this recalls the wandering of Demeter looking for her daughter, a parallel that gains force when we recall that Euripides uses exactly this blending of images in the third chorus of his tragedy *Helen*.[59]

A different story type occurs in a specific incident mentioned by Arnobius in his account of Agdistis. Arnobius reported that the emasculation of Agdistis was achieved through the actions of Dionysos, who poured wine into the fountain where Agdistis normally drank, making him/her drunk. This parallels exactly a crucial detail in one of the Greek legends connected with the Phrygian king Midas, who was said to have used just this method to capture the satyr in order to question him and thus acquire wisdom.[60] Arnobius (or his source) was evidently familiar with the tradition that made Midas into a figure of Greek myth, indicating that in recounting the story of Agdistis, he was drawing on a Hellenic source rather than on Phrygian tradition.

In addition to mythic parallels with these specific incidents, the Cybele and Attis myth as a whole is an example of a Greek myth type, the separation of a powerful goddess from her beloved, often a human being. Similar tales include the stories of Eos and Tithonos and Selene and Endymion, but the closest example is probably the story of Aphrodite and Adonis. This is a compelling parallel, not only because of the similar details of the handsome lover dying young from the attack of a wild boar, but also because elements in the characters of both Aphrodite and Persephone, rivals for the love of Adonis, are strongly identified with Cybele, Aphrodite through her capacity to inspire irrational sexual acts and Persephone through her association with Demeter, also a Mother Goddess.[61] In general, such use of folktale motifs often makes it difficult to determine when the Greek and Latin sources are relating a traditional tale about Cybele and when they are summarizing such traditional tales in general.

Another reason for the distortion of Phrygian cult ritual is the desire of later authors to use the myth to explain cult rituals of the Mother outside of Phrygia. The very fact that the Mother's cult was so widespread throughout the Mediterranean world made her myth unlike other Greek myths that claimed to elucidate ritual.

---

59. Euripides, *Helen* 1301–65.

60. This episode was widely recorded in Greek literary and pictorial sources; for an analysis of the evidence, see Roller 1983: 303–6 and M. Miller 1988.

61. On the Adonis myth type, see Ribichini 1981: 24–26 and passim, with earlier bibliography. A summary of the Adonis myth and its treatment in both ancient sources and modern scholarship is given by Tuzet 1987: 11–94; on the syncretism with the Attis story, see 31–32.

Most aetiological myths were closely linked to a specific site, such as the story of Demeter and Kore and the Eleusinian Mysteries. Yet the myth of Cybele and Attis was not connected solely with one place or one cultural group, but reflected the differing experiences and motivations of the diverse peoples who worshipped the Mother Goddess. It is not surprising that such a variety of cultures and customs would lead to a variety of narrative accounts.

The myth's function as an explanation of ritual appears most noticeably in its connection with the cult festival of the Magna Mater in Rome. Ovid's narrative in the *Fasti* is quite explicit in this regard. To him, each aspect of the Roman Megalesia, including the music played and the food served there, could be understood through references to the myth of Cybele in Rome. The same situation is found in other accounts: Servius asks why the pine tree is sacred to the goddess; Pausanias asks why the Galatians do not eat pork, and the differing versions of the myth provide the answer. And the basic question, why the priests of the Magna Mater castrate themselves, is posed by virtually every author. We can see that the myth's rationale for castration is exactly the reverse of cult practice: the Mother's priests did not castrate themselves in imitation of Attis; rather, the tradition of eunuch priests was an old one in Anatolia, and the myth was developed to explain this tradition by imputing the action to a god, Attis. Yet the need to explain the features of a prominent Roman cult whose origins lay outside of Rome must have been a powerful incentive to continue retelling the myth.

A third reason for the variations in the mythical accounts lies in the varying Western attitudes toward the Phrygians. This again is most prominent in Rome, where, on the one hand, the Phrygians were equated with the Trojans, the respected ancestors of the Romans, yet, on the other hand, contemporary Phrygians were largely regarded as slaves and Oriental barbarians. We can see this dichotomy in the diametrically opposing motivations imputed to Attis's actions in the separate versions of the myth: on the one hand (Diodoros, Pausanias A) Attis is punished for his devotion to the Mother, and on the other (Ovid, Pausanias B, Arnobius) for his lack of devotion. Yet both situations are used to explain Attis's death. The effect is to present Attis in a positive light in one case, and in a negative light in the other. Such radically different accounts indicate that there was no general consensus among Greek and Roman writers about the point of the myth. Some saw it as a sensible explanation of a cult derived from Phrygia, while others saw it as an example of the depths to which Oriental (and, in the opinion of some Christian authors, pagan) behavior could sink.

Yet, judging from the frequency with which it is cited, the negative image was more powerful and widespread. Beneath this negative image surely lies the low opinion that the Greeks and Romans held of their Oriental neighbors, evident in a wide range of material, from the unattractive depiction of Phrygians in Greek tragedy through the metaphor of the Phrygian as effeminate weakling in Virgil's *Aeneid*.[62] This negative attitude has found a powerful modern echo in the assessments of nineteenth- and twentieth-century scholars, who have assumed, almost unanimously, that the violent stories of Pausanias B and Arnobius must represent the older, more accurate version, simply because their emphasis on violence and sexuality gives a more unattractive picture of the Mother Goddess.[63]

The chronology of the myth's sources provides additional insight into the Greek and Roman perspective on the story. After the cult of Attis appeared during the fourth century B.C., Attis quickly became a prominent figure among the Greeks, and his cult spread throughout the Greek world and then to Rome. A myth would be needed to explain a cult figure who went from nonexistence to prominence in the space of less than a century. It is probably not accidental that the oldest version of the myth, Pausanias's source Hermesianax (fl. ca. 300 B.C.), appears shortly after the first monuments relating to Attis. Indeed, it seems highly likely that some version of the myth of Cybele and Attis was first developed in the Greek world during the early Hellenistic period. The evolution of the cult of the god Attis took the myth even further away from the Phrygian rites and traditions that lay behind it. Pausanias virtually acknowledges this in introducing his two versions of the Attis story. The first, which appears to be much closer to Phrygian practices, he credits to a specific third-century B.C. author, but the second, more fantastic story, he attributes to contemporary—that is, second-century C.E.—popular opinion. Placing the myth's theater of action in Pessinous is another example of this. It reflects the position of Pessinous as a major Phrygian shrine during the second century B.C. and later, the time period of the extant accounts of the myth, and ignores the fact that Pessinous had not been a particularly prominent cult center before that time. A further indication of Hellenistic origin is the fact that Pausanias's first version of the story (Pausanias A) uses the myth to explain the food preferences of the Galatians in Pessinous. This would have made sense only after the Galatian invasion of Asia Minor in the third century B.C.[64]

The differing versions of the myth among Classical authors may also be ascribed to their different purposes in relating the story. Ovid's goal was to explain the Magna Mater's public festival in Rome and the practice of ritual castration that took place there; this custom seemed bizarre and meaningless to the Romans, who looked upon the Magna Mater as a national deity and a fertility goddess. Pausanias, a native

62. See Hall 1989: 153–54, on the use of Kybele by the Greeks to indicate strange and wild behavior, and Wiseman 1984: 119–20, on the negative symbolism of Phrygians in the *Aeneid*.

63. As an example of this, note that Pausanias mentions Pessinous in both his version A and version B, but only the second, more violent one has traditionally been called Pessinuntine, or Phrygian, in modern scholarly literature (Hepding 1903: 98–111).

64. On the status of Pessinous before its enlargement by the Attalid kings, see Devreker and Waelkens 1984: 13–14, Gruen 1990: 19, and Devreker and Vermeulen 1991: 109.

of Anatolia, knew more about actual Anatolian cult practice and understood that there were regional differences in the Mother's cult. Arnobius was intent on proving the superiority of Christianity and so preserved the most violent and unattractive version of the myth. He had a personal stake in emphasizing the elements of incest, rape, and deviant sexuality in a cult that was to him the epitome of pagan disgrace. His stress on the abnormal sexual practices described in the myth should be read in the context of the general criticisms leveled by contemporary Christian authors against pagan sexual practices.[65] The virulence with which he writes suggests, moreover, that the force of the goddess's appeal was very powerful and could not be ignored.[66]

With these factors in mind, we can return to the issues raised at the beginning of this chapter. Phrygian history, cult practice, and ritual all played a part in shaping the myth of Cybele and Attis, for the basic core of the myth reflects the close association between the Phrygian goddess and the Phrygian state. The venerable legend of the birth of the gods and the passage of power through successive divine generations also contributed to the formation of the myth, as did a number of the traditional story patterns of Greek myth, including the separation of a powerful goddess from her beloved and the exposure at birth of a miraculous child who will survive to affect its parents' lives. The myth evolved as the Mother's cult in the Classical world evolved, reflecting both the spread of the cult and its changing position in different regions of the Mediterranean world. Greek and Roman misunderstandings of older Phrygian rites, particularly the rites of mourning for a dead priest-king and the eunuch status of the Mother's priests, appear to have been critical in the formation of the written versions of the myth as we know them. Equally influential were the (usually negative) perceptions of the Phrygians held by many Greeks and Romans. By combining these elements, the Greek and Latin narratives give us a sense of the power behind the myth of Cybele and Attis and open a window onto Phrygian cult practices, a world whose roots were much earlier than the Classical narratives that describe them and that would survive to influence Christian practice and belief in turn.

65. Note the continuing strong attack on the goddess and her cult, Arnobius, *Ad. nat.* 5.8–17. The role of the Mother Goddess cult in the third- and fourth-century C.E. debate between pagan and Christian falls outside of the time limits I have set for myself in this study, but it is a critical issue and deserves more attention that it has received thus far. For some good introductory remarks, see Rousselle 1988: 120–28.

66. His passion is echoed in numerous early Christian references to the cult of Attis, which clearly characterize this as one of the most popular, if distressing, alternatives to Christianity. The sources are given in n. 12 above.

PRINCIPAL SOURCES FOR
THE MYTH OF CYBELE AND ATTIS

The Origin of Cybele

A. Cybele is born, is exposed, survives, and is reconciled with her parents—Diodoros 3.58 (1st c. B.C.)

B. Agdistis, a bisexual monster who doubles as Cybele, is born of a rock. S/he is castrated, and the castration results in the birth of Attis—Pausanias 7.17.10–11 = Pausanias B (2d c. C.E.); Arnobius, *Adversus nationes* 5.5–7 (3d c. C.E.)

The Relationship of Cybele and Attis

A. Attis is a human priest and follower of Cybele who is killed because of his devotion to the goddess—Pausanias 7.17.9 = Pausanias A (2d c. C.E.); Servius, *Comm. ad Aen.* 9.115 (4th c. C.E.)

B. Attis and Cybele fall in love; Cybele becomes pregnant, and Attis is killed; Cybele wanders maddened through the countryside and is later recognized as a goddess—Diodoros 3.58–59 (1st c. B.C.)

C. Cybele takes Attis as a lover; he is unfaithful to her, and she drives him mad; he castrates himself and dies, and she mourns his death—Ovid, *Fasti* 4.221–44 (1st c. C.E.); Pausanias 7.17.10–12 = Pausanias B (2d c. C.E.); Arnobius 5.5–7 (3d c. C.E.); and many others (see n. 12).

4 · THE ROMAN MAGNA MATER

9 · THE ARRIVAL OF
THE MAGNA MATER
IN ROME

The prominence of the cult of the Magna Mater in Rome is unquestioned. Numerous literary sources, lengthy and brief, mention the cult, describing the origins, history, and rituals of the Roman Great Mother Goddess. A wealth of archaeological testimonia, including shrines of the goddess in Rome and numerous pictorial representations of her, provides further evidence. In contrast to efforts to examine the cult of the goddess in Anatolia and Greece, where there are many critical gaps in our knowledge, the abundance of material connected with the cult of the Mother Goddess in Rome seems overwhelming and the full discussion of it in modern scholarship intimidating. Often, however, earlier works discussing the identity and status of the Magna Mater have focused on the arrival and development of her cult primarily as a reflection of the Roman political atmosphere. As a result, cult practices and the place of the cult in Rome have received less attention. An effort to see the Roman goddess in the broader context of ancient Mediterranean society may provide a clearer picture of why this divinity maintained such a strong hold on the city of Rome and the Roman people. We will want to know what was uniquely Roman about these people's response to the Mother Goddess.

In Anatolia and Greece, the evidence for the worship of the goddess Matar/Meter comes into view slowly. From a modern perspective, one gradually becomes aware of a cult that had evidently been gathering strength and adherents over a period of time before its impact on the wider social fabric made it more visible. In Rome, by contrast, there is a clear starting point: the importation of the Magna Mater into Rome in 204 B.C. The impact of the cult of the Mother Goddess in Rome was real, vivid, and public from the very beginning. This cult was actively sought and openly encouraged by many segments of Roman society. One pertinent question here is why the Roman situation was so different. Why was the Magna Mater a central feature of Roman religious life, when her position in the Greek world was often so marginal? Did the Romans require different things from the Magna Mater, which enabled her cult to fit into Roman life? What was her role in the religious and social structure of the community?

An analysis of the circumstances surrounding the arrival of the cult in Rome is the first step in answering these questions. The advent of the Magna Mater in Rome made an enormous and lasting impression on its contemporaries, judging from the frequency with which it is cited and discussed by later authors, both Latin and Greek. The sources are all much later than the event; the earliest accounts are from the first century B.C., from Cicero and Diodoros, and the most complete testimonia are from the Augustan period, especially the descriptions of Livy and Ovid. There are numerous other references to the cult's arrival by Strabo, Varro, Pliny, and Seneca, to name but a few of the many ancient commentators on the event.[1] All agree on placing the Mother's arrival in Rome in 204 B.C., but they differ on several key points, including the motive for the cult's introduction and the place from which the Magna Mater came to Rome. In several cases, the reasons for their disagreements may provide interesting insights into the cult's status in Rome. But before examining these testimonia in detail, let us look at the generally accepted aspects of the narrative concerning the Mother's arrival in Rome.

In the year 205 B.C., a wave of religiosity, fueled in part by frequent showers of stones from the sky, led the Romans to consult the Sibylline Books. This religious anxiety was exacerbated by the stresses of the Second Punic War, and several ancient authors connect this action directly with Hannibal's presence in Italy,[2] although as we shall see, this connection may have been made well after the event. Livy records that the Sibyl's response was to state that a foreign enemy would be expelled from Italy if the Magna Mater were brought to Rome.[3] The place where the Romans were ordered to seek the goddess varied, but the majority of the ancient sources name Pessinous, the Phrygian sanctuary of the Mother in central Anatolia.[4] Contrasting traditions do exist, however; Varro states that the goddess was brought from a shrine called the Megalesion in the city of Pergamon,[5] while Ovid locates the Mother's

---

1. For a full review of the ancient sources on the event, see Schmidt 1909: 1 n. 1. The advent of the Magna Mater in Rome has been the subject of numerous modern studies, of which the works of Schmidt 1909, Lambrechts 1951, Köves 1963, Thomas 1984: 1502–8, and Gruen 1990 are especially helpful.
2. Cicero, *De harus. res.* 13.27; Silius Italicus 17.1–47; Appian, *Hannibal* 7.9.56; Arnobius, *Ad. nat.* 7.49; Ammianus Marcellinus 22.9.5–7; Anon., *De viris illus.* 46; Julian 5.159c.
3. Livy 29.10.4–6.
4. Cicero, *De harus. res.* 13.28; Livy 29.10.6; Diodoros 34.33.1–3; Strabo 12.5.3; Cassius Dio 17.61; Appian, *Hannibal* 7.9.56; Herodian 1.11.1–2; Valerius Maximus 8.15.3; Ammianus Marcellinus 22.9.5–7; Arnobius, *Ad. nat.* 7.49; Anon., *De viris illus.* 46.
5. Varro, *De ling. lat.* 6.15.

home on Mount Ida near the ancient city of Troy,[6] which was under Pergamene control at that time. Livy seems to combine the two traditions in reporting that the Romans sought the help of the Pergamene king Attalos I in obtaining the goddess from Pessinous. Precisely what the Romans obtained is described in several sources: it was a small, dark sacred stone, not formed into any iconographic image, that had fallen to the shrine of Pessinous from the sky.[7]

The Sibylline Books were also quite specific about how the goddess was to be received into Rome. The Romans were to name the best man in the city, the *vir optimus,* to receive her. The choice of *vir optimus* was Publius Cornelius Scipio Nasica, son of the Scipio who had been killed in Spain in 211 B.C. and cousin of Scipio Africanus. He was a young man at the time and had not yet started a political career.[8] In addition to her masculine host, the Mother was to be received by the women of Rome, either by a group of Roman matrons who were to escort her into the city,[9] or, in the majority of the ancient testimonia, by the best woman in the city. According to most sources, this was Claudia Quinta, either a matron or a Vestal Virgin, a member of another prominent family.[10]

The Mother's arrival apparently occasioned great excitement. Livy reports that when Marcus Valerius Falto, the ambassador to Pergamon who was to negotiate the goddess's transfer, announced in the Senate that the ship bringing the Magna Mater to Rome had arrived in Ostia, the people, led by Scipio Nasica, rushed to the port of Ostia to greet her. From this point on, the tradition diverges. In Livy's version, Scipio Nasica went on board the ship and accepted the black stone, which he then turned over to the matrons of Rome, and these women passed the goddess (i.e., the stone) on to Rome and to the Temple of Victory on the Palatine. Ovid preserves a more sensational story, however, which appears in many later accounts of the event. According to Ovid, the intent was to bring the ship with the image of the Magna Mater directly to Rome. However, as it was being towed up the Tiber River, it became stuck in the sand and could not be dislodged. At this point, Claudia Quinta

6. Ovid, *Fasti* 4.263–64.

7. Appian, *Hannibal* 7.9.56; Herodian 1.11.1; Ammianus Marcellinus 22.9.5–7. Arnobius, *Ad. nat.* 7.49, describes the stone in some detail, stating that it was was small enough to be held in one hand; it formed the face of the Magna Mater's cult statue in her Palatine temple.

8. On the choice of Scipio Nasica as *vir optimus,* see Cicero, *Brutus* 20.79; Livy 29.14.5–14; Pliny, *NH* 7.120.34–35; Silius Italicus 17.1–47; Cassius Dio 17.61; Ammianus Marcellinus 22.9.5–7; Velleius Paterculus 2.3.1; Augustine, *Civ. Dei* 2.5. Livy describes him as *adulescens nondum quaestorius.*

9. Livy 29.14.12.

10. For Claudia Quinta as the best woman, see Cicero, *Pro Caelio* 14.34; Propertius 4.11.51; Livy 29.14.5–14; Ovid, *Fasti* 4.305–48; Pliny, *NH* 7.120.35; Suetonius, *Tiberius* 2.3; Silius Italicus 17.33–47; Appian, *Hannibal* 7.9.56; Herodian 1.11.4–5; Statius, *Silvae* 1.2.245–46; Anon., *De vir. illus.* 46; Augustine, *Civ. Dei* 10.16. In Diodoros's account, 34.33.2–3, the name of the Roman matron who received the goddess is Valeria. In most sources, Claudia is called a matron, although in some instances she is identified as a Vestal Virgin (Statius; Herodian; Anon., *De vir. illus.*). Livy is quite explicit, however, that the goddess was to be received by the matrons of Rome, and it seems most likely that Claudia was a married woman. See also Bömer 1964: 148.

stepped forward and the famous miracle took place. Claudia had been accused of improper behavior and appealed to the Mother to redeem her reputation and reveal her to be chaste. She then unfastened her belt and looped it around the tow rope of the ship. Pulling lightly on it, she was able to dislodge the ship from the sandbar and tow it into Rome, thus proving that hers was the *casta manus,* the chaste hand that the Sibyl had foretold.[11] In Ovid's version, too, the Romans received the Mother joyfully and installed the sacred stone on the Palatine in the Temple of Victory. Then followed a splendid celebration, with banquets and games, to honor the arrival of the goddess.[12] A temple for the Magna Mater on the Palatine was begun, which was completed and dedicated in 191 B.C. by Marcus Junius Brutus, during the consulship of Scipio Nasica.[13]

These are the basic facts of the tradition. A review of the ancient testimonia, however, immediately raises several problems. There are significant inconsistencies, both within the work of certain authors and among the various sources. Moreover, there are undercurrents of contemporary events, strongly implied but not stated openly. In particular, the motives offered by Cicero, Livy, et al. for the Romans' importation of the cult are not entirely satisfactory. Why did the Romans want to bring the Magna Mater to Rome? Why did they adopt the cult of the Phrygian goddess so enthusiastically?

For the ancient commentators on the event, the answer lay readily at hand. Many of their testimonia connect the Magna Mater's arrival with the Romans' war against Carthage and Hannibal's subsequent invasion of Italy, a series of campaigns lasting from 218 to 203 B.C. Several authors, including Cicero, Livy, and Appian,[14] vividly describe the sense of popular hysteria engendered by the fear of Hannibal's presence in Italy, and clearly record the sense of relief inspired by the goddess's arrival. Some modern commentators have interpreted these remarks to imply that the Magna Mater arrived when Rome was at a low ebb, and that the goddess's arrival turned the tide against the African invader.[15] In fact, this is not the case. In 204, Hannibal had been openly unsuccessful in his Italian campaign for some time, and he was on the verge of withdrawing from Italy to Africa (presumably without pressure from the Magna Mater). To a modern observer, the arrival of the Magna Mater had little to do with the Carthaginian Wars.[16] The reasons for it must be sought elsewhere.

I shall return below to a discussion of what those reasons might have been. It

11. Ovid, *Fasti* 4.260. According to Cicero, *De harus. resp.* 13.27, Claudia was *castissima matronarum.* See also Silius Italicus 17.33–47; Statius, *Silvae* 1.2.245–46.

12. Livy 29.14.14; Cicero, *De senec.* 13.45 (citing Cato).

13. Livy 36.36.3–5.

14. Cicero, *De harus. res.* 13.27; Livy 29.10.4–6; Silius Italicus 17.1–5; Appian, *Hannibal* 7.9.56; Arnobius, *Ad. nat.* 7.49; Ammianus Marcellinus 22.9.5; Anon., *De viris illus.* 46.

15. This was the opinion of Graillot 1912: 30–32 and Cumont 1929: 43–44.

16. As was noted by Schmidt 1909: 21–23; Lambrechts 1951: 46–47; Thomas 1984: 1503; Gruen 1990: 6–7.

should be noted first, however, that such a conclusion, while probably correct, must still take into account the weight of ancient tradition associating the two events. By the first century B.C., the time of our earliest sources on the goddess's arrival, the event had been incorporated into the Roman historical tradition on the Punic Wars. According to Cicero, the Magna Mater brought relief to weary Rome.[17] Livy credits her with having given a renewed sense of vigor and purpose to the war effort.[18] The myth of her effectiveness as a savior of Rome was evidently a very powerful one and subsumed other, more probable explanations of her advent. And this association expanded with each successive retelling, to the point where, by the third century C.E., the Magna Mater was held to have been directly responsible for driving Hannibal out of Italy.[19] Her reputation as the divinity who could drive a foreign foe from Italian soil was reinforced by giving her the Temple of Victory as her first Roman home. This picture of the Magna Mater as a positive force, an asset to Rome, clashes with the many ambivalent associations attached to the goddess after her cult had become established in Rome. Conspicuous among these are the comments of Dionysios of Halikarnassos, who emphasizes the "un-Roman" nature of the cult, and poem 63 of Catullus, with its vivid and rather horrifying description of self-castration by the goddess's devotees.[20] The sources that describe the goddess's transfer, including those contemporary with Dionysios and Catullus, are, however, in agreement: the Romans wanted the Magna Mater to come; they actively sought her presence and regarded her arrival as a significant turning point in their history.

Moreover, the role of the Magna Mater's two prominent recipients, Scipio Nasica and Claudia Quinta, took on distinctly patriotic overtones, and their reputation as saviors of Rome became proverbial. This is particularly noticeable in the case of Nasica. Despite the fact that he never did have a particularly distinguished public career, his name became legendary and was frequently cited by later authors as a symbol of Republican virtue.[21] Claudia too became symbolic as the embodiment of feminine virtue. The legend surrounding her actions became increasingly elaborate as the story was retold by later authors. For example, according to Cicero and Livy, Claudia was a married woman,[22] but Silius Italicus and Statius make her a Vestal

17. Cicero, *De harus. resp.* 13.27: "defessa Italia Punico bello atque ab Hannibale vexata, sacra ista nostri maiores ascita ex Phrygia Romae collocarunt" (when Italy was exhausted by the Punic War and hard pressed by Hannibal, our ancestors settled in Rome those sacred rites that they had acquired from Phrygia). Bömer 1964: 138–41 suggests that the Magna Mater became a respected Roman deity only during the Augustan era, but Cicero's comments indicate that the deity enjoyed a high status before the Principate of Augustus.

18. Livy 29.10.7–8.

19. Arnobius, *Ad. nat.* 7.49; Anon., *De viris illus.* 46. According to Julian, 5.159c, the Magna Mater was Rome's ally in the war against Carthage.

20. Dionysios of Halikarnassos 2.19.4–5. Catullus 63. Both of these passages are discussed in further detail in chapter 10.

21. Cicero, *De harus. res.* 13.27, *De finibus* 5.64; Valerius Maximus 7.5.2, 8.15.3; Pliny, *NH* 7.120.34; Silius Italicus 17.5–17; Cassius Dio 17.61; Juvenal 3.137; Augustine, *Civ. Dei* 2.5.

22. Cicero, *De harus. res.* 13.27. Livy 29.14.12.

Virgin,[23] a version followed in subsequent retellings of the story. This seems to be a transformation of the original tale about a chaste woman into an assumption that she must represent the ultimate symbol of official chastity.[24] The increasingly exaggerated nature of these legends makes it difficult to determine the actual events of 204 B.C. They do, however, indicate the enduring strength of the tradition and its close involvement with a critical moment in Roman history.

If the danger from Hannibal's troops did not provide sufficient motivation for the event, then an alternative explanation is needed. Several contributing factors have been advanced by other scholars. One frequently repeated idea, originally proposed by Cumont, is that the Romans merely followed the guidelines of the Sibylline Books without reflecting on the implications of the Sibyl's command; that is, they did not know what they were getting.[25] Other issues, such as Rome's perception of its own past, the status of foreign gods in Rome, and internal and external Roman politics, have also received extensive attention. Rather than speculate on the relative weight of these issues at this point, it seems more fruitful to review the evidence for cult practice in Rome of the late third and second centuries B.C. Clearly any explanation of why the cult of the Magna Mater was adopted and how it fitted into Roman society will depend on exactly what it was that the Romans received.

What type of cult the Romans received depends in part on the shrine from which the goddess came. In the majority of the sources, this was Pessinous.[26] In the third century B.C., however, Pessinous lay in territory controlled by the Galatians.[27] According to Livy, the Roman legation relied on the help of the Pergamene king Attalos I, who conducted them to Pessinous and negotiated the transfer of the goddess. Yet it is most unlikely that Attalos's authority extended into the interior of Phrygia at that time.[28] The Romans' ability to reach Pessinous and negotiate with the high priests there in 204 B.C. is therefore quite improbable. Pessinous has a strong claim to be the principal shrine of the goddess in Asia Minor during the first century B.C. and later, the period contemporary with the earliest ancient sources describing the cult's transfer to Rome, and so it is not surprising that Cicero, Diodoros, Livy, Strabo, and other commentators named Pessinous as the original home of the Roman Magna Mater.[29] Yet in a later passage, Livy himself clearly implies that the Romans had not been in contact with Pessinous. Both Livy and the summary of

---

23. Silius Italicus 17.33–47. Statius, *Silvae* 1.2.245.

24. For a discussion of the position of Claudia Quinta under the early Empire, see chapter 10, pp. 313–14, below.

25. Cumont 1929: 48. See also Thomas 1984: 1504; Wiseman 1984: 117–19. The principal ancient support for this argument is Dionysios of Halikarnassos 2.19.4–5.

26. For the ancient sources connecting the Roman goddess with Pessinous, see n. 4 above. These are followed by many modern commentators on the Magna Mater's arrival; see (among others) Warde Fowler 1911: 330; Magie 1950: 25; Bayet 1957: 124.

27. Virgilio 1981: 45, 73–75. See the discussion in chapter 6.

28. Allen 1983: 143; Gruen 1990: 16.

29. Schmidt 1909: 23–26; Gruen 1990: 16–17.

Polybios state that in 189 B.C., a Roman army under Manlius Volso was advancing into the interior of Galatia. When they reached the Sangarios River, the Pessinuntine priests Attis and Battakes, wearing their religious insignia, met the army and foretold victory over the Galatians.[30] The context of Livy's description clearly implies that the Romans had not been to Pessinous before and had previously had no direct contact with Meter's shrine there.

Livy's conflicting testimony on Pessinous is not the only inconsistency in the ancient sources to cast doubt on the accuracy of the tradition concerning this site. Other commentators give a sense of how the legend surrounding Pessinous was embroidered in successive retellings. The image of the Mother in Pessinous was said to be so ancient that it was not made by human hands, but had fallen from the sky. This later gave rise to a suggested etymology for the site, that the name Pessinous derived from the circumstance of the image's falling (ἀπὸ τοῦ πεσεῖν; *pesein* meaning "to fall").[31] Livy's account of how the Romans were persuaded to look for guidance in the Sibylline Books by the occurrence of a shower of stones was elaborated to the point where Appian, writing in the second century C.E., proclaimed that from this very shower of stones came the image of the Magna Mater, falling on Pessinous.[32] Taken together with Livy's remarks on Manlius Volso's campaign, this suggests that the later prominence of Pessinous artificially forced this site into the limelight.

The status of Pessinous in 204 B.C. should also be considered. This site, often claimed to be the oldest and most significant Phrygian shrine of the Mother Goddess, is in fact a cult place of no great antiquity, and there is little to suggest that it was a major shrine before the Hellenistic period.[33] During the second century B.C., it attracted the patronage of the Pergamene rulers,[34] but it is doubtful how widespread the reputation of the sanctuary was before that time. It appears to have been a cult center of purely local importance, and only the Attalids' support increased its prestige beyond the territory of Phrygia. The connection of the Magna Mater's arrival with Pergamon and the Pergamene kings may have caused the Roman legend about the goddess's origins to be sited in a Phrygian shrine where Pergamon had a strong presence.

The minority tradition reported that the goddess came to Rome from a site in northwestern Anatolia. Varro named Pergamon,[35] and Ovid, followed by Herodian, states that Mount Ida, near Troy, was her home.[36] Because they are less frequently cited than Pessinous as the seat of the goddess's cult, these two sites have received less credence as a possible source for the Romans' borrowing. Yet Pergamon,

30. Livy 38.18.9–10; Polybios 21.37.4–7; Gruen 1990: 17.
31. Appian, *Hannibal* 7.9.56; Herodian 1.11.1; Ammianus Marcellinus 22.9.5–7.
32. Appian, *Hannibal* 7.9.56.
33. Virgilio 1981: 64, Devreker and Waelkens 1984: 14 and the discussion in chapter 7 above.
34. Strabo, 12.5.3.
35. Varro, *De ling. lat.* 6.15.
36. Ovid, *Fasti* 4.264; Herodian 1.11.

or the Pergamene region of Ida, under Pergamene control in the late third century,[37] is the stronger candidate than Pessinous for the event, on both political and cultic grounds. In 205 B.C., the Romans had no formal relations with the Attalid monarchy, but according to Livy, they were directed by the oracle of Apollo at Delphi to seek help from Attalos I.[38] Thus divine guidance led the Romans to northwestern Asia Minor, an area where the cult of Meter, the Greek Magna Mater, was already strongly established. Pergamon itself was an important center of Meter's worship, both in the urban sanctuary of the Megalesion and in the rural shrines of the mountains near Pergamon. And the city of Troy and the rural area of Mount Ida also contained shrines of Meter. If the Romans did indeed seek the help of Attalos to find the Mother, they need have looked no further than Attalos's own home territory.

Moreover, the divine guidance of Apollo would have reinforced the Romans' awareness of northwestern Asia Minor, an awareness sharpened by their growing interest in the purported Trojan heritage of Rome. The territory around Mount Ida, near Troy, was important to the Romans because this was the birthplace of their legendary ancestor Aeneas.[39] Ida was also the place to which Aeneas and his followers retreated after the fall of Troy, before starting on their voyage to Italy. And the Mater Magna Idaea, the goddess of Mount Ida, guided this undertaking. This is a prominent theme in Augustan literature and later: it is found in the account of Ovid,[40] and throughout the *Aeneid* of Virgil;[41] Herodian also emphasizes this, stating that the Romans acquired the Magna Mater from the Phrygians by citing kinship ties and descent from Aeneas.[42] Yet these sources connecting Mount Ida with Rome's legendary past are not merely ex post facto revisions of the legend. The conjunction of Aeneas, Troy, and Rome was one of long standing, already well known in the late third century B.C.[43] Indeed, another prophecy concerning military activity in the Punic Wars had addressed the Romans as descendants of the Trojans.[44] It

37. Magie 1950: 6.
38. Livy 29.11.5–6.
39. Homer, *Iliad* 2.820–21; Hesiod, *Theogony* 1008–10.
40. Ovid, *Fasti* 4.179–372; cf. esp. *Fasti* 4.272: "In Phrygios Roma refertur avos" (Rome is returned to her Phrygian [i.e., Trojan] forefathers).
41. Virgil, *Aeneid*: 2.693–97; 2.788; 3.111–14; 6.784–89; 7.138–40; 9.77–122; 10.156–58; 10.219–35; 10.252–55. See Wiseman 1984 and the discussion in chapter 10.
42. Herodian 1.11.3; on this passage, see Gruen 1990: 16.
43. The legends surrounding Aeneas and the origins of Rome are extensively treated by Perret 1942, Galinsky 1969, Poucet 1985, and Gruen 1992: 6–51. The earliest author to connect Aeneas, Mount Ida, and Rome may have been Hellanikos, writing in the fifth century B.C., who makes Mount Ida the starting point for Aeneas's voyage; see Perret 1942: 13. Perret suggests that the campaigns of Pyrrhos in Italy during the early third century B.C. may have been the chief factor in drawing attention to the legend of Aeneas and its connection with Italy (note Pausanias 1.12.1), but it is likely that the legend had already taken shape in the late fourth century; see Dumézil 1970: 487; Gruen 1990: 10–19; and Gruen 1992: 28. Bömer 1964: 138–46, supported by Thomas 1984: 1505, suggests that the connection of the Magna Mater with Pergamon and Mount Ida was an artificial creation of Augustan propaganda, but others, including Lambrechts 1951, Galinsky 1969: 176–77, Gérard 1980, and Gruen 1990: 20 and 1992: 47, have demonstrated that the Aeneas connection was a factor in Roman political consciousness well before that time.
44. Livy 25.12.5: "amnem, Troiugena, fuge Cannam" (flee the Canna River, Trojan race).

would not be surprising if the Trojan connection formed part of the Romans' interest in the Magna Mater cult.

The contact with Pergamon is relevant here also, for this was a key factor in directing the Romans to the Idaean shrine. Both Livy and Ovid convey a sense of randomness about the Romans' quest for the Mother, which Attalos may have exploited in giving them the sacred stone.[45] The sacred stone itself, described by Livy, makes no sense, since the images of both Phrygian Matar and Greek Meter were fully iconic, not pieces of unformed stone. But if the Romans did not have a clear idea of what they were seeking, their search may well have ended in or near Pergamon with the discovery that the local Mother Goddess was also the divinity of their own heroic ancestor; she was the Mater Magna Idaea, the Great Mother of Mount Ida, even to Livy, who stresses the Pessinuntine origin of her cult.[46] By establishing ties with this Magna Mater, the Romans were able to import the cult, not as a foreign deity in the city, but as their own ancestral protector who was coming home to her own people.

Thus the Romans' lack of access to Pessinous makes this site a dubious source of the goddess's cult. On the other hand, a growing interest in Pergamene territory and its connections with the Romans' own legendary past make Pergamon, either the city or the Pergamene shrine on Mount Ida, a much likelier source of the Roman Magna Mater. This point will be significant for an evaluation of the cult in Republican Rome, for the cult practices of the Mother in the Phrygian heartland and in the Greek world were not identical. If the Romans took the cult from a Greek city such as Pergamon, one would expect to find evidence of a cult that was much Hellenized, with little reference to its Phrygian roots. The evidence from Rome suggests that this was indeed the case.

In recent years, the slender evidence to be gleaned from Roman historical sources on the Magna Mater and her cult in the late third century B.C. has been supplemented by data obtained from extensive archaeological activity on the Palatine in the area of the temple of the Magna Mater.[47] This has greatly enlarged our knowledge of the temple of the Magna Mater and its relationship to other structures in the area, and has also provided additional information on Roman cult practices.

The site of the principal shrine of the Magna Mater in Rome has long been

---

45. Livy 29.11.7: "sacrumque iis lapidem quam matrem deum esse incolae dicebant tradidit ac deportare Romam iussit" (he handed over to them the sacred stone that the inhabitants claimed was the Mother of the gods and ordered them to take it to Rome). Is there a note of sarcasm in *dicebant* (the inhabitants *claimed* this was the goddess)? In a similar vein, cf. Ovid, *Fasti* 4.261–62: "patres . . . errant / quaeve parens absit, quove petenda loco" (our ancestors were uncertain who this parent was or in what place she was to be sought).

46. Livy 29.10.5–6; Ovid, *Fasti* 4.249; Praenestine calendar, *CIL* I, 1 p. 235.

47. The first systematic investigation of the area was the excavation conducted by Romanelli; see Romanelli 1963 and 1964. The more recent work of Patrizio Pensabene has been published in a series of preliminary reports, Pensabene 1978–1985a and 1988. Pensabene 1982 and 1985b provide general summaries of work in progress, and Pensabene 1988 summarizes the architectural history of the site.

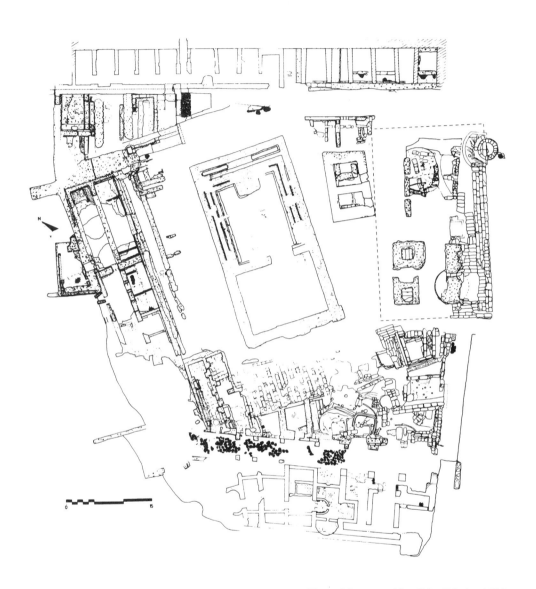

FIGURE 62. Plan of the west side of the Palatine hill in Rome, showing the location of the Magna Mater temple. Late second–first century B.C. (After P. Pensabene, *Archeologia Laziale* 9 [1988]: fig. 1.)

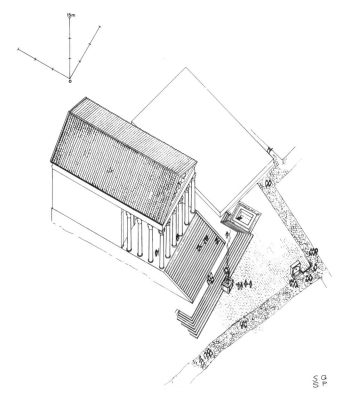

FIGURE 63. Restored elevation of the Magna Mater temple on the Palatine, Rome. Late second–first century B.C. (After P. Pensabene, *Archeologia Laziale* 9 [1988]: fig. 6.)

known.[48] It was located on the southwest side of the Palatine, near the early Republican Scalae Caci, the temple of Victory, and another structure, which has been identified, perhaps incorrectly, as the Auguratorium (fig. 62).[49] Other ancient and important shrines lay nearby: the hut of Romulus on the top of the Palatine hill and the Lupercal at the base of the Scalae Caci.[50] The position of the Mother's shrine, in a prominent place in the heart of Rome and in close proximity to other venerable Republican monuments, is in itself a statement about the high esteem in which the Romans held this cult.[51]

48. For a description of previous archaeological research on the temple, see Nash 1961: 30; Romanelli 1963: 202; Pensabene 1982: 70–72; 1985b: 179. Because the site of the temple is still under investigation, this summary should be considered preliminary and subject to modification.

49. For the identification as the Auguratorium, see Platner and Ashby 1929: 61. Pensabene 1981 discusses the earlier history of this building, in which terracottas representing Juno Sospita were found, although the deity to whom the temple was dedicated remains unknown. Pensabene 1988: 57, proposes a tentative identification as the temple of Victoria Virgo, founded by Cato in 193 B.C.

50. For the location of these shrines, see Platner and Ashby 1929 and Nash 1961: 163–69; see also Wiseman 1984: 126 on the topography of the house of Augustus, which was later built nearby.

51. Coarelli 1982: 37.

The plan of the earliest sanctuary is fairly clear. The original temple built to honor the Magna Mater was of a standard Roman type consisting of cella and pronaos. Built on a high podium, it had six columns across the front, probably in the Corinthian order.[52] The platform of the cult statue survives, together with evidence of a narrow opening at one side, which may have given access to a stairway leading to a series of subterranean rooms, whose function is uncertain.[53] This was the temple begun shortly after the Mother's arrival in 204, and dedicated in 191 B.C.[54] The temple itself seems to have been part of a larger building program, which developed the southwest side of the Palatine from an area of small houses into an area of public monuments.[55] In III B.C., the superstructure of this temple was severely damaged by fire, but in constructing the second temple, the builders were able to make use of the existing podium and foundations, and so the second temple followed the plan of the earlier structure (fig. 63).

An important feature of the Magna Mater temple was the treatment of the area in front of the temple. In front of the earliest temple (of 191 B.C.) was a staircase extending down from the temple podium to a large paved piazza; this led to a street at the foot of the Palatine, probably in place before the temple construction. At the foot of this staircase on the edge of the piazza was a large fountain with a basin, which may have been an integral part of the cult's rites.[56]

The steps, open square, and waterworks all played important parts in cult ritual. The steps, forming a structure like the cavea of a theater, were evidently designed to provide an area in which people could stand and watch the Ludi Megalenses. These games, mentioned in several ancient sources as an essential feature of the cult from its inception, consisted of dramatic performances and contests held in the piazza at the foot of the temple steps.[57] The provision for water in the cult, also a key element in both Republican temples, may reflect the need to wash the image of the goddess. In the Imperial era, this ritual was carried out in the Almo River,[58] but in earlier times the *lavatio* could well have been performed at a place closer to the other cult rites held in the temple.

In addition to clarifying the early history of the cult structures, investigations of the area have revealed large deposits of terracotta figurines, which provide impor-

52. For a plan of the area, see Pensabene 1988: 58, fig. 5, and 59, fig. 6. Little of the superstructure of the first temple has survived, but the second temple, rebuilt on the same spot, was definitely built in the Corinthian order, making it probable that the first temple was also.

53. Pensabene 1988: 58–59, suggests that these rooms were used by the goddess's clergy to celebrate the Hilaria, the rites of Attis.

54. The erroneous dating sequence proposed by Romanelli 1963: 202–14 and Romanelli 1964 was corrected by Coarelli 1977: 10–13.

55. Pensabene 1981.

56. For an attempted reconstruction of the area, see Pensabene 1980 and 1985b: 183–84.

57. Dionysios Hal. 2.19.2–5; Livy 36.36.3–5; Cicero, *De harus. res.* 11.22, 12.24; Valerius Maximus 2.4.3. For the reconstruction of this area, see Pensabene 1985b: 183 and id. 1988. For its use as a theater, see Hanson 1959: 13–16.

58. Ovid, *Fasti* 4.339–40; Valerius Flaccus, *Argonautica* 8.239–42. Coarelli 1982: 46.

FIGURE 64. Head from terracotta figurine of Magna Mater, from votive deposit near Magna Mater temple on Palatine, Rome. Second century B.C. Courtesy, Soprintendenza Archeologica di Roma.

FIGURE 65. Terracotta figurine of Attis, from votive deposit near Magna Mater temple on the Palatine, Rome. Second century B.C. Courtesy, Soprintendenza Archeologica di Roma.

tant evidence on cult practice. The figurines were buried under the foundations of the second temple, in other words before the construction of this temple; thus they date to the period between 191 and 111 B.C.[59] There are various figurine types. Some, such as figures of unidentified men and women, are fairly common and show no obvious connection with the Magna Mater. The majority of the figurines, however, do have some direct reference to the cult of the Magna Mater. These include eleven representations of the goddess herself, three heads of Dionysos, and ninety-four images of Attis (figs. 64, 65). There are, in addition, a dozen or more terracottas de-

59. The first group of terracotta votives was uncovered in the excavations conducted on the Palatine by Romanelli, between 1949 and 1952, and was mistakenly dated by him to the period of the second temple, after 111 B.C. (Romanelli 1963: 262; 1964: 620). This dating was corrected by Pensabene (see Pensabene 1982: 86; Wiseman 1984: 118 n. 9). Another group of terracotta figurines pertinent to the cult was uncovered in earlier excavations by G. Boni on the Palatine, near but not within the temple of the Magna Mater. It contains a similar mix of types, including several examples of Attis and of the glans penis. These are illustrated by Vermaseren *CCCA* III, 1977: 10–11, nos. 12–13.

FIGURE 66. Terracotta glans penis, from votive deposit near Magna Mater temple on the Palatine, Rome. Second century B.C. Courtesy, Soprintendenza Archeologica di Roma.

picting the glans penis (fig. 66). There are several figures of dancing women and models of theater masks. Other types include a figurine depicting the upper part of a human torso with multiple breasts, two pairs of lovers embracing, and several cistae of fruit. Terracotta images of evergreen cones (pine cones?) (fig. 67) and of lions are also present, as well as a variety of other animal figurines, horses, pigs, goats, rams, dogs, and cocks.[60]

Several of the figurine groups will repay closer inspection. The images of the goddess tend to follow her standard Hellenistic iconography, depicting a seated draped female accompanied by a lion, either at her side or on her lap. This type, of Greek origin, had by the second century B.C. become widely dispersed throughout virtually every Mediterranean center and so offers little definite information on provenience. One valuable detail, however, lies in representations of the goddess that depict her wearing a headdress like a mural crown (fig. 64).[61] This type, while not common in the Hellenistic Greek world, is found at Pergamon, where it appears to symbolize the status of the goddess as a protector of the city. One unusual figurine depicts the goddess standing, with her right hand holding an object across her chest; she wears a high polos rather than a crown, a feature reminiscent of sixth-century B.C. representations of the goddess from Ionia.[62] The presence of both Magna

60. The figurine group is described by Romanelli 1963: 262–90; 1964: 621; and Pensabene 1982: 85–88. For illustrations of the figurines found in Romanelli's earlier excavations, see Romanelli 1963: figs. 32–63; 1964: pls. 36–37. The complete corpus is published by Vermaseren in *CCCA* III: nos. 13–199. Pensabene 1982: pls. 5–8 illustrate the pieces found in his more recent excavations.

61. Pensabene 1982: 86; pl. 7, nos. 2, 3, 4. *CCCA* III: no. 149.

62. For the Roman piece, see Pensabene 1982: pl. 7, 1. F. Naumann 1983: pl. 13, illustrates comparable Archaic Greek examples. There are several terracottas depicting Kybele from third- and second-century B.C. contexts in Troy that show her wearing a high polos, similar to this piece from the Palatine. In all the Trojan works, however, the goddess is shown seated on a throne holding a tympanum, features not present in the Roman piece. For the terracottas from Troy, see D. B. Thompson 1963: pls. 7–15.

FIGURE 67. Terracotta evergreen cone, from votive deposit near Magna Mater temple on the Palatine, Rome. Second century B.C. Courtesy, Soprintendenza Archeologica di Roma.

Mater types in a second-century B.C. Roman context may be another indication that the Roman goddess's origin lay on the west coast of Asia Minor.

Of greater interest are the representations of Attis. He can appear in a variety of poses: standing, seated, on a rock or on horseback, or moving, either dancing or simply walking forward. He is often shown with one or both of his two characteristic attributes, the syrinx and the shepherd's crook. Most of the figurines show him wearing the specific costume that had become a standard feature in the iconography of Attis, a pointed cap, long-sleeved tunic, and baggy trousers. Several figurines show Attis with his clothing pulled back to reveal his abdomen and genitalia (fig. 65).

By the second century B.C., Attis was a well-known figure in the cult of the Mother Goddess in the Greek world, and his iconography, including his characteristic costume and attributes, created under Greek stylistic influence, was widely disseminated.[63] Nevertheless, this is an unusually large concentration of Attis figurines at a shrine of the Mother. On the Palatine, the Attis figures outnumber images of the Magna Mater by almost ten to one. They demonstrate that Attis was an essential part of the Mother's cult from its inception in Rome, far more prominent there than in the eastern Mediterranean region. Clearly, the Magna Mater's eunuch consort came with her to her new home in Rome.

The votive terracottas add further information on cult rites and attitudes that characterized the cult. Among the animal types, the presence of lions surely alludes to the goddess's favorite animal companion, while the other animals may represent sacrificial victims. The masks and dancing figures presumably symbolize the Ludi Megalenses. There are also many objects with sexual imagery. The phalli and breasts allude to human sexual generation and nurturing, while other images, such as those

63. For examples, see Vermaseren and DeBoer 1986.

of baskets of fruit and lovers embracing, suggest reproduction and fertility. Further-more, several of the Attis figurines from the Palatine draw attention to his sexual or-gans. This circumstance is found only infrequently in Attis figurines from the Greek world, and indeed the type may appear here in this Roman context for the first time.[64]

Taken together, the physical evidence of architecture and votive figurines is infor-mative in several ways. The material confirms the hypothesis drawn from textual evi-dence, that Pergamon was the source from which the Romans received the Magna Mater. The Palatine figurines find their closest parallels in terracottas from Perga-mon, not only in the use of the mural crown, but also in the depiction of the god-dess's throne. These details also appear in fictile material from Troy, Smyrna, and other cities on the west coast of Anatolia,[65] strongly suggesting that, together with the unformed stone, the Romans imported the iconographic models of western Asia Minor, particularly Pergamon. A Pergamene origin is further suggested by the epi-thet Megalesian, for according to Varro, the name was derived from the Pergamene shrine Megalesion.[66] This name clearly comes from the Greek adjective *megale,* or great, a standard epithet for the goddess in the Greek and Roman world, although unattested in Phrygia.

A more telling point for the goddess's origin is the presence of Attis. The promi-nence of Attis in the Palatine material recalls his presence in Greek ritual, particularly that described in third- and second-century B.C. cult regulations from the Piraeus.[67] The worship of Attis was a feature of the Pergamene cult also, as is shown by the finds of a life-size marble statue and terracotta figurines depicting Attis there.[68] A deity named Attis is not attested either epigraphically or iconographically at any Phrygian site, however, until well after the Roman conquest of Asia Minor,[69] and his cult in Rome is thus unlikely to derive from a Phrygian shrine. Therefore Attis too links the Roman cult closely to Pergamene, or Greek, rather than Pessinuntine Phrygian practice.

In addition to the question of the cult's origin, the Palatine material demonstrates

---

64. For examples of Attis with exposed genitals, see Vermaseren and De Boer 1986: nos. 37–53, 57–61, 64, 80, 85–88, 101, 104, 115, 125–31, 135–38, 149, 195, 211–13, 224, 235–36, 257, 262, 271–73, 282, 287–96, 298, 424, 439. Most of these have no secure provenience or date, although a few were found in Tarsos (Ver-maseren and De Boer 1986: nos. 212, 235, 250, 272, 273); these may date to the late second or first century B.C. None of the Attis figurines with exposed genitalia from the Greek world can be definitely shown to be earlier than the Palatine group.

65. Pensabene 1982: 89. For parallels, see Conze and Schazmann 1911: pls. 11, 12, figs. 1–10, and Töp-perwein 1976: 49–53, pls. 30–33.

66. Varro, *De ling. lat.* 6.15. Ohlemutz 1940: 183–85. See the discussion of Pergamene cult in chapter 7 above.

67. The Attideia, a festival of Attis, is mentioned in a *lex sacra* from the Piraeus, *IG* ii² 1315, line 10 = *CCCA* II: no. 262; note the discussion in chapter 7 above.

68. Franz Winter 1907: no. 116, pl. 27 (the statue; see fig. 57); Conze and Schazmann 1911: pl. 12, 3, and Töpperwein 1976: nos. 390–91 (the figurines). On Attis in Pergamon, Ohlemutz 1940: 179.

69. F. Naumann 1983: 99; see the discussion in chapter 7.

that the specifically Roman rituals held to honor the goddess were in place from the cult's inception. The games, the Ludi Megalenses, were one of these. While the name of the festival may be Greek, there is no evidence from any Greek city of performances celebrated in honor of the Mother. Yet the games clearly were an important part of the Roman cult, and the original temple complex was designed to accommodate them. First held in 194 B.C., with Plautus's play *Pseudolus* as part of the inaugural performance,[70] they became an annual festival of theatrical entertainments. The aspect of purification, the washing of the goddess's statue, was also a key Roman ritual from the start, and provisions were made in the first Magna Mater sanctuary for that as well. The central place of these Roman rituals, unattested in the Greek cult of Meter, confirms the Romans' desire to make the Magna Mater a Roman deity and place her in the heart of the city's religious life.

The early cult material also confirms the Magna Mater's central role in Roman history and ideology. One symbol from the Palatine terracottas, the evergreen cones, suggests Rome's connection with Mount Ida and the intertwining of the Magna Mater with the legend of Aeneas. Although later mythological tradition recalled that one evergreen, the pine, became a special symbol of Attis because he had castrated himself under it,[71] this seems an artificial aetiology, designed to explain the presence of this symbol in Roman cult. The pine (or any other evergreen tree) is nowhere attested as a Phrygian cult symbol, nor are pine cones found among the images connected with the goddess or Attis in the Greek world. A comment by Ovid in the *Fasti,* however, is very enlightening in this context.[72] The poet states that the ship built to carry the Magna Mater to Rome was constructed from the very same sacred pines of Mount Ida that Aeneas used when building the ships with which he escaped from Troy. According to Ovid, the pine thus became a sacred symbol of the Mother, Aeneas's protector. A similar point is emphasized by Virgil in the *Aeneid,* where Aeneas's ships are saved from attack because they were constructed from the Mother's sacred pines.[73] The votive pine cones at the Magna Mater's shrine in the early second century B.C. indicate that the cult of the Magna Mater was already linked with Rome's legendary origins.[74]

---

70. On the first Megalesian Games, see Livy 34.54.3. On the play, *Pseudolus, didascalion,* see Beare 1950: 47–48. Ovid, *Fasti* 4.326, suggests that the story of Claudia Quinta formed part of the Ludi, although it is difficult to be certain whether this quasi-historical pageant was included in the second-century B.C. rites of the goddess.

71. On Attis's castration under a pine tree, see Arnobius, *Ad. nat.* 5.7.

72. Ovid, *Fasti* 4.273–77; cf. with 4.251–54.

73. *Aeneid* 9.85–89.

74. Graillot 1912: 37 and Wiseman 1985: 201 and 1995: 56 have proposed another connection with Rome's legendary origins, namely, the identification of the Magna Mater with Rhea Silvia, mother of the twins Romulus and Remus, through the Greek Meter's conflation with Rhea, wife of Kronos. This would make the Magna Mater both the Mother of the gods and the Mother of Rome. The connection between the two Rheas was certainly made in the first century B.C. and later (Lucretius 2.633–38; Ovid, *Fasti* 4.195–210), but it is uncertain whether this tradition was active in the third century B.C., at the time of the Magna Mater's arrival.

The Romans gave the Magna Mater an individual stamp in other ways. One novel characteristic of the Roman cult is the attention paid to themes of sexuality and fertility. The large number of Attis figurines and their rather exhibitionist poses stress this, as do the many objects from the Palatine votive deposit illustrating human sexual organs, breasts, loving couples, and baskets of fruit, signifying baskets of plenty. This emphasis on sexuality and fecundity was not only human but also agricultural. Pliny comments that the year after the Magna Mater arrived in Rome, the crops were especially bountiful.[75] Ovid, too, in his account of the legend of Claudia, stresses the barrenness of the earth before the Mother's arrival, presumably to be improved by her presence.[76] This forms a contrast with both Phrygian Matar and Greek Meter, for whom fertility was rarely an issue, and whose association with wild and unstructured mountain landscape was directly at odds with agriculture and the settled countryside. It is a point worth stressing, in view of the many distasteful associations found in Latin literature concerning the presence of Attis and the elements of deviant sexual behavior among his priests. In the early cult of the Magna Mater in Rome, Attis and the overtones of sexuality that went with him were attractive features, to be encouraged through offerings and gifts.

The discussion thus far has stressed the uniqueness of the Magna Mater cult and its particular place in Roman history. There are, however, many features of the Magna Mater and her worship that were quite characteristic of Roman religious practice, and a discussion of those features will show that the Magna Mater's arrival was not an anomaly.

One is the relationship of the Magna Mater to other foreign gods in Rome. The Magna Mater was only one of several foreign deities that the Romans imported in the Republican era to help address a severe internal crisis.[77] In the early third century B.C., the Romans solicited an important Greek god, Asklepios (Aesculapius), for assistance in eliminating a serious plague.[78] In the *Metamorphoses,* Ovid gives a vivid account of the healing god's arrival in Rome,[79] and many aspects of the narrative, such as the description of the crowd that thronged the port to greet the sacred snake and the ship's miraculous gliding up the river, are oddly reminiscent of the legends surrounding Claudia Quinta and the Magna Mater. The transfer of Venus Erycina from Sicily to Rome in 215 B.C. brought another foreign divinity to the city, one with a mix of Greek and non-Greek traits.[80] This goddess, who arrived in the wake of the

75. Pliny, *NH* 18.4.16.
76. Ovid, *Fasti* 4.299.
77. On foreign cults in Rome, see Latte 1960: 213–63; Bloch 1966: 143–48. Lambrechts 1951: 44–45, citing the Roman reaction to the god Dionysos, felt that the warm welcome afforded the cult of Cybele was out of keeping with the Romans' normally hostile response to foreign divinities, but, as noted by Warde Fowler 1911: 223–47, Bayet 1957: 120–27, and Gruen 1990: 7–9, several foreign deities were welcomed to Rome.
78. Livy 10.47.6–7; Valerius Maximus 1.8.2; *De vir. ill.* 22. See Schmidt 1909 and Latte 1960: 225–27.
79. Ovid, *Metamorphoses* 15.626–744.
80. Livy 22.9.9–10. For a discussion of the event, see Gruen 1990: 8–9.

Roman military defeat at Trasimene, also brought the promise of future success to Rome and, like the Magna Mater, was received into the city by the first man in the state.[81]

In addition to these foreign cults that became resident in the city, the Romans also used foreign deities to advance their own interests. In 222 B.C., the Romans dedicated an important votive offering, a golden bowl, to Apollo at Delphi in thanks for victory over the Gauls.[82] More significant, they also sought the aid of Pythian Apollo in the war against Hannibal.[83] And Apollo was also the deity who directed the Romans to seek the aid of the Pergamene king Attalos in order to bring the Magna Mater to Rome.[84] In this broader context, the arrival of the Magna Mater appears to follow an established pattern of using foreign divinities, both fully Greek and mixed Greek/non-Greek, to satisfy Rome's needs.

We should note also that the Magna Mater may not have been an altogether unfamiliar deity. Although her cult did not reach the city of Rome until the end of the third century B.C., the goddess was known in Etruria well before this date, as is demonstrated by a black-figured Pontic vase of the mid sixth century B.C., now in Munich. The piece illustrates an enthroned Cybele framed within a naiskos, the classic Greek iconography, yet the goddess is shown wearing the typical Etruscan cap, the *tutulus,* indicating that the vase illustrated the Etruscan concept of the goddess.[85] The goddess was honored in other parts of Italy as well. She was depicted in a series of reliefs carved onto a hillside at Akrai, in Sicily, probably of the early third century B.C., and was worshipped in several cities in southern Italy.[86] Since the Romans had active contacts with all of these areas before 204 B.C., this suggests that upon her arrival in the city, the goddess came not as a stranger but as a deity whose presence was already well established in Italy and thus somewhat familiar in Rome.

The connection between the Magna Mater's arrival and Republican politics should also be considered.[87] It is surely no accident that the names of those involved in the cult's transfer were among the most distinguished of the Roman Republic. The *vir optimus* who welcomed the goddess, Publius Cornelius Scipio Nasica, represented one of the most politically prominent families in Rome of that generation. Nasica's personal role as host, *hospes,* of the goddess, is stressed by several sources.[88] Yet Na-

81. Livy 22.10.10. This was Q. Fabius Maximus, the man chosen as the individual with the greatest *imperium* in the state.

82. Plutarch, *Marcellus* 8.6.

83. Livy 28.45.12, 29.10.6.

84. Livy 29.11.6.

85. E. Simon 1978–80: 29–30, figs. 1–2. E. Simon 1990: 151, fig. 191, also identifies a figure on a late-fourth-century B.C. bronze cist from Praeneste as Attis. The identification is not certain, since it is also possible that the figure is Adonis.

86. *CCCA* IV: nos. 152–64. Sfameni Gasparro 1973: 267–76; 1996.

87. This feature of the Magna Mater's arrival has been extensively discussed in modern scholarly literature and so can be more briefly summarized here. For fuller treatments of this issue, see Köves 1963, Bömer 1964, Scullard 1973, Gérard 1980, Thomas 1984: 1505–8, Gruen 1990: 21–27.

88. Livy 29.11; Juvenal 3.137; Valerius Maximus 8.15.3; Anon., *De vir. illus.* 46.

sica himself clearly comes across as a compromise candidate. The choice of a young man with no personal influence on Roman politics evidently gave a distinguished public honor to a weak member of that family, one whose potential to reap benefits from his prestigious honor would be limited.[89]

The choice of the best woman is also instructive. The legend recounting the miracle of Claudia Quinta leaves us with the impression that her position as *castissima femina* was a spontaneous reaction to the situation, that she simply stepped out of the crowd so that the goddess might demonstrate her power and Claudia's chastity. Yet this seems too contrived to be the case. As a member of yet another leading family, her role in the cult's introduction gave the Claudii a position of special honor. In hindsight, it seems that the attention paid to Claudia was deliberately designed to place this family in the limelight as well.[90] And Claudia's prominence was more enduring than that of Scipio Nasica. Not only did her part in the goddess's arrival become increasingly exaggerated with each retelling, but the legend extended to her statue, placed in the temple of the Mater; this was said to have warded off the flames from the goddess's first temple when it burned in 111 B.C.[91] Moreover, a number of votive reliefs and coin portraits depicting the miracle suggest that Claudia herself became the object of cult. Ovid's statement that the story of Claudia Quinta was put on stage implies that her role in the goddess's arrival became part of the popular legend about the Magna Mater.[92] All of these circumstances attest to the increasing fame and prestige that the Magna Mater cult brought to the Claudian gens for several centuries.[93]

In addition, a large delegation was sent to Pergamon to negotiate the goddess's removal to Rome, led by five individuals, M. Valerius Laevinus, M. Valerius Falto, S. Sulpicius Galba, M. Caecilius Metellus, and Cn. Tremellius Flaccus, each of whom had already held public office.[94] The composition of the delegation may well have been designed to cover a broad range of political factions, all participating in the honor of receiving the Magna Mater.[95] The descriptions in sources some two

---

89. Köves 1963: 325; Thomas 1984: 1505; Gruen 1990: 26. Köves undercuts his argument by suggesting that Nasica was chosen specifically because of his youth, since he was intended to personify the god Attis (Köves 1963: 330).

90. Köves 1963: 339–47; Gérard 1980: 156–58. Köves, followed by Wiseman 1979: 97–98, convincingly suggests that Livy and Ovid were following two annalistic sources, one that stressed Nasica's role (Livy) and one giving great prominence to Claudia (Ovid) and barely mentioning Nasica.

91. Valerius Maximus 1.8.11; Tacitus, *Ann.* 4.64.

92. *Fasti* 4.326: "mira sed et scaena testificata" (a wonder, yet it is attested on the stage).

93. Bömer 1964: 146–51. Gérard 1980 argues that the connection of Claudia with the legend of the Magna Mater received greater prominence during the late Republic and early Empire because of contemporary political events, the career of Publius Clodius Pulcher (as known from Cicero, *Pro Caelio*), and the prestige of the Julio-Claudian family (note the comment of Suetonius, *Tiberius* 2.3). See also Wiseman 1979: 94–99. For the development of the legend of the Magna Mater's arrival during the Augustan Principate and the cult of the *Navisalvia*, see Gerard 1980: 169–75 and chapter 10 below. The suggestion of Bremer 1979: 9–11 that Claudia represented an outsider and that her part in the legend was symbolic of the rites of passage is unconvincing.

94. Livy 29.11.3.

95. Thomas 1984: 1505–7; Gruen 1990: 25.

hundred years after the event have the effect of glossing over any internal differences, but from our modern perspective, we can see that a considerable amount of personal and familial rivalry for the honor of welcoming the Magna Mater to Rome may well lie behind the legend of the goddess's arrival.[96] Adding further distinction to the goddess's transfer was the presence of five large warships that supported the delegation. Clearly, the whole event was orchestrated to make an impressive public appearance, and our sources leave the impression that many illustrious families and individuals wanted to play a part in that public appearance.

The desire of important political families and groups to maintain a strong and publicly visible presence in the Magna Mater cult is further confirmed by the practice of a Roman ritual formed to celebrate the goddess. An entry in the Praenestine sacred calendar under April 4, the day of the Megalesian festival of the Mater Magna, records that it was the custom for the nobility to hold lavish banquets, *mutitationes cenarum,* on that day, for this was the anniversary of her arrival in Rome.[97] This text, written in the first decade C.E., is supplemented by a reference in Aulus Gellius, where it is stated that the patricians were accustomed to exchange hospitality, *mutitare soliti sunt,* at the Megalesian festival, while the plebeians did so at the festival of Ceres.[98] The prominent role of the Roman aristocracy in the Magna Mater's rites was surely a further source of prestige for the cult.

The Magna Mater cult may well have played a role in another broad political issue, the increasing influence of Hellenism on Roman society. Despite its originally Phrygian roots, the cult that came to Rome was the cult of Meter, a self-consciously Hellenized cult. Installing this Greek goddess on the Palatine near the ancestral home of Romulus and other important Republican shrines made a clear statement that Greek religious practices were to be included in Roman ritual.[99] These Hellenic associations were to be a continuing feature. Cicero stressed that even though the Magna Mater was a respected Roman deity, her foreign origins were always remembered: she had been settled in Rome from a faraway land, and her games were the only ones not called by a Latin name.[100] Her hymns were always sung in Greek, never Latin.[101] The subsequent tensions between the so-called foreign, un-Roman ways of the goddess and her prominence in Roman cult, as emphasized by Dionysios of Halikarnassos, may reflect similar tensions surrounding the debate over her arrival.

---

96. Livy 29.14.5–8. In general, see Scullard 1973: 56–89.

97. *CIL* I, 1, p. 235. Cf. Cicero, *De senec.* 13.45.

98. Aulus Gellius 2.24.2.

99. Bailey 1932: 123–28; Scullard 1973: 76; Gruen 1990: 10; Gruen 1992: 47.

100. Cicero, *De harus. res.* 12.24: "ludos eos . . . ex ultimis terris arcessita in hac urbe consederit; qui uni ludi ne verbo quidem appellantur Latino" (those games settled in this city from faraway lands, these games alone are not called by a Latin name).

101. Servius, Commentary on Virgil, *Georgics* 2.394: "hymni vero matris deum ubique propriam, id est graecam, linguam requirunt" (The hymns of the Mother of the gods everywhere require their own language, that is, Greek). See the comments of Sfameni Gasparro 1985: 5.

Thus the Magna Mater cult comprised both unique characteristics and features that reappear in several religious and political issues of the third and second centuries B.C. With these factors in mind, we should return to the questions posed at the beginning of this chapter—namely, why the Romans wanted to bring the Magna Mater to Rome, and what exactly it was that they brought. As one of several foreign deities who found a home in Rome, the Magna Mater came to Rome as a positive force, one that quickly took a central place in Roman religious practice. She came at the specific behest of the Sibyl, who directed the Romans to look to Asia in order to find the goddess. In Asia, the Romans found their Mother in Pergamon; this is clear from the fact that her cult in Republican Rome had significant affinities with Pergamene Greek practice but shows only limited knowledge of traditional cult practice in the interior of Phrygia. Yet if, as Livy reports, the Romans had no allies in Asia, we would like to know why the Romans directed their attention to Pergamon at this juncture.[102] Perhaps just as the fame of Aesculapius as a healer had spread to Rome, so the Mother's reputation as a protector of cities, a key part of her identification in Pergamon, was also known. The goddess gained further prestige in Roman eyes because one of her home shrines in Asia was the home of Aeneas, legendary ancestor of the Roman people.[103] For all these reasons, she would have been the deity ideally placed to support the Romans' sense of destiny in the late third century and their quest for victory. Her presence brought assurance that the safety of the state was under divine protection.

Moreover, the evidence concerning the goddess's arrival suggests that the Roman cult quickly took on a distinctive character, one that separated it from its Anatolian or Greek origins. While many aspects of Roman cult practice can be traced to Pergamon, the Romans used only those parts of the Pergamene cult that were expedient for their own purposes. In Rome, the cult was exclusively urban, with no interest in the goddess's sacred settings in remote locations, particularly on sacred mountains. The one such setting that the Romans did make use of was Mount Ida, but this, as we have seen, was important to them because of its association with Rome's legendary past. The Mother's association with personal cult and with direct divine inspiration, so prevalent in the Greek world, seems to have found no echo in Roman practice. Instead, the Magna Mater was emphatically a state deity and a symbol of fecundity, aspects of her identity that seem to have been stressed much more in Rome than in Anatolia. The Romans also used the figure of Attis and enlarged his role in the cult beyond what he enjoyed in the Greek world.

The evidence also suggests that distinctively Roman imagery and rituals were established for the Magna Mater at the time of her first appearance in Rome. She

---

102. Livy 29.10.4–29.11.1 implies that the oracle from Delphi, while not naming a specific place, served to reinforce the Sibyl's naming of Asia.

103. Lambrechts 1951: 47; Gruen 1990: 11–19.

received a fine temple in one of the most prominent locations in the city. Her arrival was supported by two of the most distinguished families in Rome. Provisions were made for her *lavatio* and scenic games. As the terracotta votives demonstrate, the music, the orgiastic rituals (dancing, flute music, playing the tympanum), and the cult of Attis were all found in Republican Rome. Taken together, these features indicate that the point of view espoused by some modern scholars, principally Cumont, that the Romans were poorly informed about the nature of the cult before it arrived in Rome, is not correct. The Romans wanted the Magna Mater to come, adopted her cult enthusiastically, and installed it in a place of honor in the heart of the city. Their desire both to import the Mother Goddess and to establish her as a Roman deity was powerful enough to overrule any difficulties they may have had with her origins and her rites.

Thus several strands of Roman political, social, and religious tradition formed the backdrop to the advent of the Magna Mater. With the aid of the Sibylline Books, the Romans found a deity who would not only drive out the foreign foe but also protect the city and lead it on to greater victory in the future. Throughout, we sense a feeling of confidence, a desire to celebrate Rome's origins and take a more active role in a wider political theater. The pattern of prominent worship and support in the early Magna Mater cult would continue and even intensify in succeeding centuries.

10 · THE REPUBLIC
AND EARLY EMPIRE

The Magna Mater came to Rome with great fanfare and public ceremony. After her dramatic arrival, however, the goddess seems to have settled down in her home on the Palatine and become a regular part of Roman religious life. This chapter explores the Magna Mater's place in that life, her temple and images, her public festivals, and the public and private reaction to her cult. Since there is a rich body of information on the Magna Mater cult in the city of Rome, the investigation focuses on this, following the role of the goddess from her arrival until the early Principate, the first half of the first century C.E. We shall want to consider how the goddess fit into the religious and social life of the city, and we shall need to examine what aspects of Roman life and society shaped the Mother's cult. Of special concern will be the Mother's *Romanitas,* the qualities that set her Roman cult apart from her cult in Anatolia and Greece and gave a distinctly Roman stamp to her character.

THE MAGNA MATER CULT
DURING THE REPUBLIC

I shall start with a consideration of the evidence for the Magna Mater cult between ca. 200 and 60 B.C. After the wealth of information about her arrival, our written sources provide many fewer details about the goddess's cult in Rome during the first century and a half of her residence in the city. While some have interpreted this gap as a mark of hostility to the cult that developed as people became more familiar with its priests and rituals,[1] the scant information probably reflects the opposite, that

---

1. The strongest statement espousing this point of view is Bömer 1964; see also Galinsky 1969: 185–87. The assumption is that once the Romans learned of the Magna Mater's ecstatic rituals and eunuch

nothing unusual occurred, and that the cult practices established upon the goddess's arrival were maintained. A few scattered anecdotes suggest that the cult of the Magna Mater continued to have an effect on Roman politics. There is also an increasingly clear picture of the rites that were celebrated for the goddess in Rome.

The strongest indication of the Magna Mater's continuing presence in Roman religious life is the goddess's sanctuary on the Palatine, where her temple continued to be a major center of Roman cult. After the fire of III B.C. destroyed the first temple, it was soon rebuilt. The second building replicated the plan of the earlier structure, a prostyle, hexastyle building with a single cella.[2] New were the addition of an internal colonnade and benches running along the length of the interior walls and across the back on either side of the cult statue.[3] In addition, the general area of the sanctuary was enlarged and made more grandiose with the addition of a larger piazza at the foot of the steps in front of the temple. As in the earlier temple, there were settling basins for water. The whole level of the piazza was raised and supported by an extensive substructure consisting of a series of barrel vaults that contained a row of *tabernae* (shops), reached by a covered street.[4] These vaults would have supported the open square used for the theatrical performances, the *ludi scaenici,* at a higher level (figs. 62, 63).[5] The elaboration of the Magna Mater complex fits into the general trend toward monumentalization of important sanctuaries, observable at other Republican sanctuaries of the same period, such as those at Praeneste and Tibur.[6]

The rites that were celebrated at the Magna Mater's festival in the spring became an increasingly important part of Roman life. Scattered anecdotes offer a picture of the events that took place and also something of the lively atmosphere that accompanied them. The festival of the Megalesia, started in 194 B.C., now lasted a week, from the fourth to the tenth of April. The plays, the ludi scaenici, evidently occupied the greater part of this time. In addition to Plautus's *Pseudolus,* written for the inaugural festival, we have four plays of Terence produced at this festival, the *Andria,* the *Hecyra,* the *Heautontimoroumenos,* and the *Eunuchus,* from the period 166–161 B.C.[7] They were performed on the open plaza at the base of the temple's steps.[8] Cicero's comment on the setting of the plays, "ante templum in ipso Matris Magnae

---

priests, they were so repelled that they neglected the cult. The argument, however, relies extensively on the silence of imperfectly preserved historical records, and ignores the fact that the sources recording the goddess's arrival in Rome are all much later than the event they describe. The full ramifications of the Magna Mater cult may not have been known in the late third century B.C., but they were certainly known to Cicero, Livy, and Ovid, and these authors offer no indication that the Romans were to regret their decision to bring the Mother to Rome.

2. Coarelli 1977: 13; Pensabene 1985b: 182–83; 1988: 59–60.
3. Pensabene 1985b: 182–83.
4. Pensabene 1988: 60–62.
5. Pensabene 1985b: 185–86; 1988: 54–61.
6. Pensabene 1988: 60. Boëthius 1978: 157–78.
7. Beare 1950: 94; Gruen 1992: 186.
8. Hanson 1959: 13–16, 25.

conspectu" (in front of the temple, actually in the sight of the Great Mother),[9] emphasizes the intimate connection between the goddess and the theater. The festive ambiance of these comedies was increased by the addition of carnival entertainments. An episode described by Terence illustrates this: in 165 B.C., during the first production of the *Hecyra,* the play had to compete with the more enticing charms of a rope dancer who set up his act nearby; the second showing was disrupted by a promise of gladiatorial games that distracted the audience and, according to the playwright, ruined the performance.[10] By the first century B.C., chariot races had been added to the ludi scaenici. Held in the Circus Maximus, at the foot of the Palatine, also in sight of the Magna Mater,[11] the races were preceded by an elaborate procession, in which the statues of the gods were carried.[12] The games, originally under the care of the curule aedile, provided an opportunity for lavish public display, important to the ambitious young politician, as Julius Caesar discovered.[13] After 23 B.C., the games were held by the praetor.[14]

The practice among the aristocracy of holding festive banquets, the *mutitationes,* on April 4 continued as well. Such banquets evidently became occasions for extravagant display, so much so that in 161 B.C., sumptuary legislation had to be introduced to control them. Thereafter, the senatorial class was limited to an expense of 120 *asses* on the dinner and the hosts were forbidden to display more than 120 pounds of silverware or to serve foreign wine.[15] This custom of reciprocal entertainments was still active during the early Empire.[16]

While rites such as these were not unique to the Megalesia, such lengthy and elaborate celebrations were generally limited to the major civic cults.[17] Even more than the presence of prominent political families, the physical facilities and the rituals of the Magna Mater illustrate the important role of her cult in Roman public life.

The cult's connections with civic life are also reinforced by the appearance of the Magna Mater on a number of Republican coin issues. The earliest known example is a denarius of 102 B.C., on which a bust of the Magna Mater wearing the turreted crown is paired with an image of Victory on the reverse, advertising the Mother's

9. Cicero, *De harus. resp.* 12.24.

10. Terence, *Hecyra,* prologue. Beare 1950: 173 and Scullard 1981: 97–101 take these anecdotes from the play's prologues at face value. Gruen 1992: 210–18 suggests that these performances of the *Hecyra* in fact never took place, and that the description of confused and competing performances instead refers to the games held by L. Anicius Gallus in 166 B.C. to celebrate his triumph over the Illyrians.

11. Ovid, *Fasti* 4.389–92.

12. Ovid, *Amores* 3.2.43–57.

13. Livy 34.54.3; Cicero, *De harus. res.* 13.27. Boyancé 1954: 340–42 cites numismatic evidence. Julius Caesar celebrated the Megalesian games with especial splendor (Cassius Dio 37.8.1).

14. Cassius Dio 54.2.3.

15. Scullard 1981: 97–101.

16. Ovid, *Fasti* 4.353–57.

17. There were five official festivals with games during the Republic, honoring Jupiter, Apollo, Hercules, and Liber and Ceres, in addition to the Magna Mater; the most magnificent were probably the Ludi Romani, held for Jupiter Optimus Maximus (Dionysios of Halikarnassos 7.72; Scullard 1981: 40).

long-standing connection with Victory.[18] Other Republican coins of the first century B.C. also depict the goddess with the turreted crown, sometimes only her head (fig. 68), sometimes the goddess in her chariot drawn by lions (fig. 69). Several of these no doubt served to advertise the aedile, the official responsible for the Megalesian Games,[19] but at least one other example, an aureus of 43 B.C. depicting the Magna Mater in her lion chariot, may be an allusion to victory, in this case the expected victory of Octavian.[20]

During the period between the Magna Mater's arrival and the mid first century B.C., a few anecdotes indicate the goddess's impact on the political scene. One example is known from Livy's *History,* the encounter of Manlius Volso's army with the Mother's priests, the Galli, at Pessinous in 189 B.C.[21] The chief priests, Attis and Battakes, met the Roman army and predicted victory in the forthcoming battle with the Galatians, support that was warmly welcomed by the Roman general.[22] The continuing interest of Pessinous in Rome is further attested by an incident in 102 B.C., when one of the Mother's priests, another Battakes, came to Rome and petitioned to address the Senate.[23] According to Diodoros, his motive was to complain of impieties that had profaned the temple of the goddess, while Plutarch records that he came to predict that the Romans were to gain victory and power in war. Diodoros and Plutarch agree that the Senate supported the priest, and even voted a

18. Crawford 1974: 326–27, no. 322. This issue, contemporary with the visit to Rome by the priest Battakes (Diodoros 36.13; Plutarch, *Marius* 17.5) (see below), may refer specifically to the campaign against the Cimbri. For an overview of the Magna Mater on Republican coinage, see Turcan 1983: 5–23.

19. Examples are illustrated by Crawford 1974: 356, 1a, denarius, head with turreted crown; 385, 4, denarius, goddess in lion chariot; 409, 2, denarius, goddess with turreted crown and forepart of lion; 431, 1, denarius, goddess with turreted crown. The first, third, and fourth of these were issued by the curule aedile, the official in charge of the games. Summers 1996: 344.

20. Crawford 1974: 500–501, no. 491.

21. Polybios 21.37.4–7; Livy 38.18.9–10; chapter 7 above. Polybios names the priests; Livy refers to them simply as Galli.

22. The Romans had encountered the Galli the previous year at Sestos, when the priests had interceded, successfuly, on behalf of their people to end the Romans' siege (Livy 37.9.9; Polybius 21.6).

23. Diodoros 36.13; Plutarch, *Marius* 17.5–6.

temple for the Magna Mater. Diodoros gives a vivid picture of the priest's colorful attire and headdress, like a crown, with regal connotations unwelcome to the Romans. The plebeian tribune Aulus Pompeius opposed allowing the Phrygian priest to speak, but when this same tribune died suddenly of a fever shortly thereafter, the circumstance was seen as an omen of the goddess's power. The people became even more convinced of the Mother's strength and escorted the departing priest from Rome with public acclamation.

The latter incident is one of the few episodes during this period in which we receive any insight into popular reaction to the Mother's cult in Rome. On the surface, it has many of the characteristics of a resistance myth, such as the one told about the *metragyrtes* and the Meter cult in Athens, in which opposition to the goddess's priest was met with a fresh demonstration of her power.[24] Yet we should assume a core of reality to the story, for the event was one of a series of incidents that were later seen to foretell the Romans' victory in their campaigns against the barbarians north of the Alps.[25] In many ways, the episode is reminiscent of the circumstances that had brought the Mother to Rome a century earlier, for at that time, too, her cult had contributed to victory against a foreign foe, a point acknowledged by its original housing in the temple of Victory. The story does, however, sound the first note of ambivalence in Roman reaction to the Magna Mater, implying that the goddess's message was welcome in Rome, but her foreign priest was not.[26]

The circumstances surrounding the rebuilding of the temple of the Magna Mater on the Palatine after its destruction in III B.C. provide further insight into the cult's status. The name of the temple's rebuilder is given by Ovid as Metellus,[27] and it has been plausibly argued that this was C. Metellus Caprarius, who would have built the temple with funds from military spoils and dedicated it in 101 B.C.[28] Here again the cult of the Magna Mater furnished an opportunity for a politically prominent family to gain attention through a pious act, a temple restoration that brought favorable publicity.[29]

24. Versnel 1990: 105 n. 35.
25. The beneficiary of the priest's visit seems to have been Marius, who claimed that the victory promised by the Mother was his victory over the Teutones and made special sacrifices to her in consequence. Plutarch, *Marius* 31.1. See Broughton 1953–54: 210–11.
26. Some have interpreted the incident to mean that the cult was a focus for class conflict, since the Senate was willing to listen to the Pessinuntine priest, while the tribune of the plebs opposed it. Bömer 1964: 136, argues that the Senate must have favored the priest; in contrast, Coarelli 1982: 41, 66, claims that it was the plebs that most strongly supported the Magna Mater. The issue may be moot since, as Thomas 1984: 1511, has noted, the tribune could well have been manipulated by opposing senatorial factions.
27. Ovid, *Fasti* 4.347–48.
28. Morgan 1973: 238–39.
29. Ibid.: 241–45, expanding on Broughton 1953–54: 211, has argued that internal political struggles very likely played a part in Metellus's action as well, since the family of the Metelli was opposed to that of Marius, the individual favored by the Pessinuntine priest's visit to Rome the year before. Yet Plutarch, *Marius* 17.5, does not say that the priest favored Marius, merely that the priest predicted victory for the Romans. To read Metellus's action as an example of manipulative politics seems to be overstating the evidence.

Two other historical anecdotes from the late second and early first centuries B.C. present a rather different picture. Both concern the first unequivocal evidence for self-castration in honor of the Magna Mater and the Roman reaction to it. In 101 B.C., a slave of a certain Servilius Caepio castrated himself in the service of the Mater Idaea; as a result he was exiled from Rome and forbidden ever to return.[30] In itself, this need not indicate total condemnation of the cult, for exile was a comparatively mild punishment for a slave.[31] The second anecdote is more telling: in 77 B.C., a slave named Genucius received an inheritance from a freedman named Naevius Anius. Genucius, a priest of the Magna Mater, was a eunuch and was ultimately denied his inheritance on the grounds that he was neither man nor woman. Moreover, Genucius was not even allowed to plead his own case, lest the court be polluted by his obscene presence and corrupt voice.[32] Valerius Maximus, who describes the incident, reinforces his account with a strong tone of moral condemnation, the first we note, of the eunuch Galli in Rome.[33] Roman approval of the goddess did not extend to her eunuch priests.

The incidents described above create a variable picture. The Romans evidently admired certain aspects of the Magna Mater and advanced her rites as one of the strong religious cults concerned with the safety of the state. At the same time, support for the goddess was by no means unanimous. And the goddess's eunuch priests were becoming an increasingly visible presence in Rome, making the Magna Mater cult even more problematic. Already we can see the Romans' two-edged reaction to the Mother Goddess, a deity both embraced as a key part of Roman religious life and held at arm's length.[34] This two-edged reaction would become even more prominent in the succeeding century.

THE LATE REPUBLIC AND EARLY EMPIRE: LITERARY FIGURES

The varied character of the Magna Mater's cult comes into sharper focus in the mid first century B.C., when our information about the goddess increases substantially, because of the greater number of sources and the richness of detail that they provide. From this point on, we get a much fuller picture of the goddess and her place in Roman society. We can now penetrate the surface, as it were, and sense some of the

30. Obsequens 44a. This incident may have taken place at the dedication of the second temple of the Magna Mater on the Palatine (Morgan 1973: 233–34).
31. Morgan 1973: 234; Thomas 1984: 1510. Bömer 1964: 136 sees the slave's permanent exile as a mark of severe criticism of the cult by the Roman state.
32. Valerius Maximus 7.7.6.
33. Wiseman 1985: 204; Beard 1994: 177.
34. This ambivalent quality is well described by Beard 1994. However, I take exception to her attribution of the more distasteful aspects of the Magna Mater cult, particularly the eunuch priests, to its foreign origins. The two sides of the Magna Mater were not "the Roman and the foreign"; both sides were equally Roman. Therein lies the paradox and the fascination of the cult.

emotional reaction to the goddess—both the hold that she had on her followers and the antipathy that her cult aroused among its detractors.

The comments of Dionysios of Halikarnassos provide a good starting point, since his work is the most explicit statement of the ambivalent response to the Magna Mater.[35] In describing the customs of Roman religion, Dionysios wrote:

> And one thing I have marveled at the most, namely, that although many thousands of races have come into the city, who need to honor their native gods according to the customs of their homelands, the city has not emulated any of the foreign customs publicly, a thing that has happened in many cities; even if the rites were brought in according to oracles, such as the rites of the Idaean goddess, she honors them according to her own traditions, rejecting all fabulous sophistry. The praetors hold annual sacrifices and games for the goddess according to the laws of Rome, but a Phrygian man and a Phrygian woman act as priests for her. They carry her through the city, begging alms in her name according to their custom, wearing pectoral images and playing the Mother's hymns on the flute for their followers and beating the tympana. But according to law and the Senate's decree, no native Roman may go about through the city decked out in a brightly colored robe and playing the flute while begging alms, or celebrate the goddess's orgies in the Phrygian manner. So careful is the city about religious customs other than its own; so ominously does it regard all unseemly nonsense.

This passage, which the reference to the praetors places after 23 B.C.,[36] brings into focus the contrasting nature of the Magna Mater cult. Dionysios clearly saw a real distinction between the customary Roman rites of the Mother, the sacrifices and the games, and the foreign rites, with their loud music, public begging, and foreign priests in strange outfits. For him, this constituted a value judgment on the cult's origins: what was good about the goddess came from old Roman tradition, while the bad side of her rites could be ascribed to foreigners, specifically to Phrygians.[37]

Dionysios was certainly correct in locating the origin of several of the Magna Mater's rites outside of Rome. His comments on Phrygians in their fancy robes remind one of the beautiful garments with intricately woven patterns that were (and are) a long-standing tradition on the Anatolian plateau,[38] although one can see how a Phrygian in a elaborately embroidered robe might have clashed noticeably with the plain, largely monochromatic Roman tunic and toga.[39] The use of pectoral images is well attested in Asia Minor also, through literary references and surviving

---

35. Dionysios of Halikarnassos 2.19.3–5.
36. Cf. Cassius Dio 54.2.3. See also Wiseman 1984: 117.
37. In this he has been followed by almost every modern scholar writing on the Magna Mater, from Graillot 1912 and Cumont 1929 to Thomas 1984, Wiseman 1984, and Beard 1994: 176.
38. Boehmer 1973. See also Simpson 1988 on the Phrygian fondness for complex patterns.
39. Zanker 1988: 162–65, on Augustus's efforts to stress the white toga as the proper dress for Romans.

FIGURE 70. Statue of a
Gallus, from Rome. Second
century C.E. Courtesy, Capitoline
Museum, Rome.

FIGURE 71. Bronze group illustrating the Magna
Mater seated in her chariot, pulled by lions. Second
century C.E. Courtesy, Metropolitan Museum of Art,
New York: Gift of Henry G. Marquand, 1897.

examples of the master forms used to create such images (figs. 58, 59).[40] The effect of
these images is well illustrated by sculptural representations of individuals wearing
them, particularly a striking image of an *archigallus* (high priest) in Rome (fig. 70).[41]

The other supposedly Phrygian features are more likely to be of Greek origin. We
have no evidence in Anatolia either for processions in which the image of the goddess was carried aloft or for ritual collections, although both of these formed a part
of the goddess's Greek cult.[42] Greek was also the established language of her cult,
both within and outside of her homeland, even in Rome.[43] While there is evidence

40. The Galli wearing images in Pessinous, Polybios 21.37.4–7; Livy 38.18.9–10. For the bronze matrix, see Reeder 1987: 423–40.
41. Gow 1960: 90, fig. 1, and pl. 8, 1; *CCCA* III: nos. 249, 250.
42. Both features are attested in the Piraeus: processions, *IG* ii² 1328 I; ritual collections, *IG* ii² 1328 I,
1329.
43. Servius, Commentary on Virgil, *Georgics* 2.394.

for music in the Mother's Phrygian cult,[44] the tympanum was a Greek attribute of the goddess, never found in Anatolia until after the Phrygian visual types had disappeared.

Thus we can see that Dionysios's observations about the dual origins of the Magna Mater rites have some factual basis. His comments about the dual character of the cult, however, appear to be less an inquiry into its roots and more a reaction to a difference of manners: the calm, controlled part of the Magna Mater's ritual was a product of Roman culture, but the noisy and colorful aspects Dionysios clearly viewed as vulgar and unseemly (his own word), and therefore un-Roman. Yet was it merely a matter of assuming that when rites were conducted in a decorous manner, one was acting like a Roman? By this time, all of the cult's strands, Phrygian, Greek, and Roman, had become thoroughly enmeshed with one another to create a uniquely Roman progression of ceremonies. The Magna Mater could be a deity of the old Roman state; she could be the miraculous prophet of a new world order; and, as a goddess of fertility, she could represent people's most intimate sexual desires. Both the controlled state channels and the loud ecstatic clamor were essential to her character and her place in Roman life.

The Magna Mater never lost her identity as a deity of the state. Brought to Rome to ensure victory and reinforce Rome's ties with its legendary past, she was an honored part of Roman public life. This is richly emphasized by Cicero in his conflicts with Publius Clodius Pulcher. The archetype of the unscrupulous politician, Clodius used the Magna Mater to advance his own career on several occasions: he incited the Galatian Brogitarus to sack the Mother's shrine at Pessinous and disrupt her rites,[45] and he created a public disturbance in Rome by breaking up the games of the Megalesian festival with gangs of slaves recruited for this purpose.[46] Moreover, we are told, only free men could attend these games. Clodius thus not only polluted the games, but introduced the lowest class element, slaves, into the goddess's rites, heretofore the privilege of Roman citizens.

To Cicero, the fact that even the venerable Megalesian Games had been desecrated showed how low public morality had sunk. The goddess and the games had been *casti, sollemnes, religiosi* (chaste, traditional, religious), until defiled by Clodius.[47] His sister Clodia, notorious for her loose morals, also came in for attack, for she compared badly with her ancestress Claudia Quinta, the miraculously demonstrated *castissima femina* of the Mother's arrival. The modern reader may wonder how seriously to take these allegations; Terence's depiction of the varied entertainments at

---

44. Note the sixth-century B.C. image of the goddess accompanied by flute and lyre from Boğazköy, Bittel 1963: 7–21, pl. 1–8 (here fig. 10). This was reproduced in terracotta in the first century C.E., see *CCCA* I: 200, pl. 37.

45. Cicero, *De harus. resp.* 13.28.

46. Ibid. 11.22–23.

47. Ibid. 12.24.

the Ludi Megalenses suggests an atmosphere that was far from *castum* and *religio-sum*. Yet the image evoked by Cicero of a dignified public festival is clearly compelling. It speaks strongly for the continuing functioning of the Magna Mater as an official deity of the city of Rome.

Cicero's words lead us to the rites celebrated for the Magna Mater at her state festival. We can glimpse both the form and the emotional content of this festival in the animated account of it by Lucretius. For Lucretius, writing in the mid first century B.C., the Magna Mater symbolized the world order. The goddess played a prominent role in Lucretius's own definition of the heavenly cosmos, since she was equated with Earth.[48] She is the *magna deum mater materque ferarum et nostri genetrix* (2.598–99), the Mother of the gods, the Mother of wild beasts, and our creator. She becomes a metaphor for Lucretius's vision of the gods as beings independent of humanity, suspended in air:

> aëris in spatio magnam pendere docentes
> tellurem neque posse in terra sistere terram

> [T]hey teach that the great earth hangs in the middle of the air, and earth cannot rest on earth.

> *(De rerum natura 2.602–3)*

Just as Mother Earth cannot rest on earth, so the Magna Mater does not rest on earth, but is carried aloft.[49]

Lucretius incorporates this metaphor into a description of the principal Roman ritual of the goddess, a formal parade through the city streets during which a statue of the deity in her lion chariot (see fig. 71 for an idea of what this looked like) was carried aloft by the Galli, the Mother's eunuch priests:[50]

> quo nunc insigni per magnas praedita terras
> horrifice fertur divinae matris imago.

> Adorned with this insignia the image of the divine mother is borne fearfully across great lands.

> (2.608–9)

The poet presents a lively picture of the combination of awe, fear, and excitement that the procession evoked:

> tympana tenta tonant palmis et cymbala circum
> concava raucisonoque minantur cornua cantu,

48. Lucretius 2.598–660.
49. Bailey 1947: 898–909.
50. Summers 1996 clearly shows that Lucretius was drawing an actual Roman event.

et Phrygio stimulat numero cava tibia mentis.

The taut drums thunder under the palms, the hollow cymbals resound, the horns threaten with raucous song, and the hollow pipes stimulate the mind with their Phrygian mode.

(2.618–20)

The impact of this emotionally arousing spectacle is increased by the appearance of the armed bands that accompany the goddess's image:

hic armata manus, Curetas nomine Grai
quos memorant, Phrygias inter si forte catervas
ludunt in numerumque exultant sanguine laeti,
terrificas capitum quatientes numine cristas

Here an armed band, which the Greeks name Curetes, disport themselves randomly among the Phrygian troops, and leap up among their group, joyful in blood, shaking the frightful crests by the nodding of their heads.

(2.629–32)

Lucretius is particularly interesting here because of the way in which he combines his rather terrifying vision of the Mother's rites with the positive values of Roman society. The goddess's lions, the wild beasts that draw her chariot, come to symbolize the fact that wild offspring can be softened by the nurturing actions of their parents (2.604–5). The castrated Galli are a reminder that those who are ungrateful to their parents (both to the Great Mother and to human parents) do not deserve children of their own (2.614–17); thus the Mother's cult encourages family bonds and filial devotion. By playing on the Latin words *Phrygias* (Phrygian) and *fruges* (fruits, i.e., grain), the poet uses the goddess's Phrygian background to emphasize her role as bringer of fruits—that is, fertility—to mankind (2.610–13).[51] Even Lucretius's frightening image of the armed bands who attend the Mother, the Curetes (the Greek Kouretes), serves a didactic purpose, for the Curetes used their arms to protect the baby Jupiter from his father Saturn; this enables the poet to finish with an exhortation that these same martial virtues may be passed on to the youth of today:

propterea Magnam armati Matrem comitantur,
aut quia significant divam praedicere ut armis
ac virtute velint patriam defendere terram,
praesidioque parent decorique parentibus esse.

---

51. This undoubtedly refers to Herodotos's statement that the Phrygians were the oldest race and the originators of bread (Herodotos 2.2).

Therefore armed bands accompany the Great Mother, because they signify that the goddess commands that they may want to defend their fatherland by arms and courage, and prepare to be both protection and pride to their parents.

(2.640–43)

Lucretius has integrated a frank acknowledgment of the problematic features of the cult, including the public presence of the Galli and the violence and sexuality that they represent, into an endorsement of the traditional Roman virtues of filial piety, honor to the gods, and willingness to defend the fatherland. The fervor of the Magna Mater's rites, while frightening, serves the special purpose of emphasizing the high worth of the values that the goddess represents.

The position of the Magna Mater as beneficial state deity was enlarged and elaborated still more during the Augustan era. Ovid played a major role in this process by bringing together several aspects of the goddess, her Roman rituals, the myth of her Phrygian lover Attis, and the legend of her arrival, into his book of Roman festivals, the *Fasti* (4.179–372). Ovid's description of the Megalesian festival, like Lucretius's, evokes the disquieting emotions of the spectacle:

ibunt semimares et inania tympana tundent,
aeraque tinnitus aere repulsa dabunt;
ipsa sedens molli comitum cervice feretur
urbis per medias exululata vias.

The half-men will come and thump their empty drums, and bronze clashed on bronze will give its ringing note; she herself [the goddess] is borne on the soft neck of her comrades, with howls, through the middle of the streets.

The poet confesses himself frightened by the spectacle (*Fasti* 4.189–90). Yet he integrates the most disturbing aspect of the Magna Mater cult, the legend of Attis and its rationale for the castration of the Galli, into the most traditionally Roman part of her story, the miracle of Claudia Quinta. Ovid stresses that the annual performance of this legend, enacted as a pageant on the public stage, proves its accuracy (*Fasti* 4.326).

Above all, the *Aeneid* of Virgil places the Great Mother of Ida, the Magna Mater Idaea, in the forefront of the gods responsible for the greatness of Rome. As the nurturer of Aeneas, she is the divinity who protects the hero and, by implication, the city of Rome, which his descendants will found.

The Magna Mater is a significant presence throughout the *Aeneid*.[52] During the sack of Troy, her light on Mount Ida is the first sign of a more hopeful future for the

52. On the Magna Mater in the *Aeneid*, see R. G. Austin 1977: 241–42, Arrigoni 1984, and Wiseman 1984, who collects all the references to the Magna Mater cult in the poem and correctly points out a significant dichotomy between the favorable image of the goddess and the unfavorable image projected

beleaguered Trojans (*Aeneid* 2.693–97). It is she who decrees that Aeneas's wife Creusa should remain behind in Troy, freed by death from Greek slavery ("sed me magna deum genetrix his detinet oris": the great Mother of the Gods detains me on these shores [*Aeneid* 2.788]). A side visit to Crete emphasizes the Cretan elements of the Mother, alluding strongly to her background in Greek cult (*Aeneid* 3.111–14). And when the Trojans arrive in Italy, the Magna Mater takes on an even more active role as the protector of Aeneas. She averts the fire of his Rutulian enemies in Italy from his ships (*Aeneid* 9.77–83, 9.107–22). Her symbols provide the insignia for Aeneas's ships:

> Aeneia puppis
> prima tenet, rostro Phrygios subjuncta leones;
> imminet Ida super, profugis gratissima Teucris.

> Aeneas's ship holds the fore, with Phrygian lions at the prow, while Ida rides above, most pleasing to the fleeing Trojans.

> > (*Aeneid* 10.156–58)

She figures frequently in his prayers (*Aeneid* 7.139; 10.251–55), and her own wishes can persuade even great Jupiter to act on Aeneas's behalf (*Aeneid* 9.82–106). And, perhaps most significant, it is the Magna Mater who epitomizes the great and glorious future Rome was to have, as revealed to Aeneas by Anchises in the Underworld. Just as the Great Mother is blest in her godlike descendants, so Rome will be blest:

> qualis Berecyntia mater
> invehitur curru Phrygias turrita per urbes,
> laeta deum partu, centum complexa nepotes,
> omnis caelicolas, omnis supera alta tenentis.

> Just like the Berecynthian Mother in her turreted crown who is carried through Phrygian cities, happy in the birth of the gods, embracing a hundred descendants, all heavenly dwellers, all holding the lofty skies.[53]

> > (*Aeneid* 6.784–87)

To Virgil, the procession of the Magna Mater's image, the principal rite at her annual festival, was the evocation of Rome's present grandeur.

In Virgil's poetry, the Magna Mater has gone beyond her long-standing role as protector of the state. As a deity whose original home was on Ida, she is the natural

---

by the Galli. I think, however, that Wiseman has missed the mark in querying the favorable image of the Magna Mater as the issue to be explained. The key role of the goddess in the safety of the state was a long-standing feature of her cult by Virgil's time, as was the goddess's connection with Mount Ida. It is the equation of Aeneas's followers with the Galli, the band of *semiviri*, that seems out of character and requires explanation.

53. For a full discussion of these passages, see Wiseman 1984: 120–22.

support of Rome's great hero, who was born on Ida.[54] In saying this, Virgil drew in part on the well-established interest in the Magna Mater cult, deriving from the third century B.C., when the oracles of the Sibyl and Apollo first directed Roman attention to Asia and thereby reinforced Rome's parallel interest in its Trojan origins. In the Augustan ideology, however, the paths of both goddess and hero were more closely aligned: both were originally at home in Asia, where they received modest recognition, but both had to come to Italy in order to realize their potential and fulfill their part in making Rome a great city.[55] Thus it is highly appropriate that the Magna Mater should have a key role in enabling Aeneas to achieve his destiny.[56] She was an essential link between Rome's heroic past and its future greatness.

Yet the goddess of the state celebrated by the poets had an alien side, which was equally compelling. The Magna Mater was not only the representative of the noble past and the glorious future of Rome, but also a seducer and destroyer of men. As a goddess surrounded by effeminate *castrati,* she came to represent the male's uncertainty and ambivalence about, even fear of, his own sexuality.

This sexual image was most frequently expressed, not by the Magna Mater herself, but by the Galli. Although derisively described as *semiviri* or *semimares* (half-men), the latter appear to have become an increasingly conspicuous presence in late Republican and Imperial Rome. We know little about them, however, and have no reliable information about their origins, background, or family connections. We know that Galli could not be Roman citizens, but that left many candidates for the role of Gallus, including many who had been born in Rome and were thus thoroughly acquainted with Roman customs, even though their ancestors had come to Rome from abroad.

The undisguised contempt of the Romans for the Galli comes across loud and clear. The Galli not only castrated themselves but emphasized their artificial femininity through feminine dress and manners, so their high-pitched voices, long wild hair, and garish costume made them instantly recognizable.[57] Moreover, the implicit degradation of such female appearance reinforced popular assumptions about their licentious behavior. Their castrated status made it impossible for them to reproduce, but this did not appear to inhibit their sexual appetites or keep them from erotic liaisons with both men and women. Numerous anecdotes and references portray the Galli as the purveyors of offbeat sexual activities, clearly exciting to respectable

---

54. Homer, *Iliad* 2.820–21; Hesiod, *Theogony* 1008–10.

55. This is quite specifically spelled out by Ovid, *Fasti* 4.250–54.

56. I am not convinced by the arguments of Bömer 1963, Austin 1977: 241, and Wiseman 1984, who attribute the prominent role of the Magna Mater in the *Aeneid* as Augustan rehabilitation of a foreign cult. Given the goddess's long-standing (nearly two hundred years) status as the protector of Rome, it would be more surprising if she did not play a role in supporting Aeneas.

57. Half-men: Ovid, *Fasti* 4.183 (*semimares*); Varro, *Saturae Menippeae,* Cèbe fr. 24 (Nonius fr. 140); Juvenal 6.513. Voice: Valerius Maximus 7.7.6. Unkempt hair: Thyillos, *Anth. pal.* 7.223; Augustine, *Civ. Dei* 7.26. Odd dress: Varro, *Saturae Menippeae,* Cèbe frs. 19–22 (Nonius frs. 135–38); Diodoros 36.13; Dion. Hal. 2.19. For a detailed discussion of Roman reaction to the eunuch priest, see Roller 1997.

people.[58] From Philodemus, we hear of the Gallus Trygonion, the "Little Dove," active in the priestly house of the Galli on the Palatine.[59] Thyillos (a contemporary of Cicero) writes of Aristion, who once tossed her hair to Cybele, but is now dead from the excesses of heavy drinking and all-night festivals of love.[60] To Horace (quoting Philodemus), the Galli were suitable liaisons for a coy married woman; a real man would prefer a straightforward prostitute.[61] Indeed, women were considered especially susceptible to the charms of the Galli, whose sterility may have made them a favored choice among women for extramarital relationships.[62] We receive the impression that the ambiguous sexual status of the Galli was precisely the thing that made them covertly attractive.

This degrading image lies behind several passages in the *Aeneid* alluding to the Galli.[63] When Aeneas and his companions first arrive in Carthage, the Carthaginian Iarbas disparagingly describes him as "ille Paris cum semiviro comitatu" (that Paris with his half-male band, *Aeneid* 4.215). This point is repeated later by Turnus, in Italy, on the eve of battle:

> da sternere corpus
> loricamque manu valida lacerare revolsam
> semiviri Phrygis et foedare in pulvere crinis
> vibratos calido ferro murraque madentis.

> Grant that I may strike down his body and tear open with my strong hand the breastplate of this Phrygian eunuch, and befoul his hair, curled with a hot iron and wetted with myrrh, in the dust.

(*Aeneid* 12.97–100)

Aeneas and his followers, the founders of Rome, have become effeminate men who, like the Galli, frizz their hair and drench themselves with perfume. Similarly, in another battle scene, Numanus taunts the Trojan warriors as desexed Orientals prone to orgiastic ritual, outsiders who cannot stand up to the deeds of real (Latin) men:

58. E.g., Martial 3.81: the Gallus as cunnilingus who makes up with his mouth what he lacks in his genitals; "It's your head that should have been castrated," the poet says. This attitude appears in the passage from Varro's *Eumenides* discussed below.

59. Philodemus, Epigram 26, in Gow and Page 1968: 366–67. For the Palatine clubhouse of the Galli in Rome, see Wiseman 1982: 475–76.

60. *Anth. pal.* 7.223. Cf. also Juvenal 8.176, the Gallus as a heavy drinker.

61. Horace, *Satires* 1.2.119–22.

62. Juvenal 2.111–16, and esp. 6.521–26, on the influence the Galli held over Roman matrons; cf. Richard 1966. Note also the fragment of a second-century A.D. novel on papyrus, published by Parsons 1974: no. 3010 and Reardon 1989: 816–18, in which a certain Iolaos wishes to take instruction in the mysteries of the Magna Mater in order to pose as a Gallus and thereby obtain access to a desired female companion. Galen, *On the Use of the Parts of the Human Body* 14.647 (Kühn 4: 190) 190, comments on the eunuch's capacity for sexual pleasure. In a different context, Basil of Ancyra, *De virginitate,* writing in the fourth century C.E., warns Christian virgins to avoid eunuchs, because their castrated state is no guarantee of chastity. Rousselle 1988: 158 collects evidence for Roman knowledge of postpubertal castration and its effect on sexual and reproductive capacity. Note also the comments of Brown 1988: 169–70.

63. Wiseman 1984: 119–20.

O vere Phrygiae, neque enim Phryges, ite per alta
Dindyma, ubi adsuetis biforem dat tibia cantum;
tympana vos buxusque vocant Berecyntia matris
Idaeae: sinite arma viris et cedite ferro.

O truly Phrygian women—for you are not Phrygian men—go to the heights of
Dindyma, where the flute gives a two-pronged song to your accustomed ears. The
drums and the Berecynthian boxwood of the Idaean Mother call you: leave fighting
to the men and yield to the sword.

(*Aeneid* 9.617–20).[64]

Here even the epithet Berecyntia Mater, which elsewhere evokes the most positive
picture of Rome's future (*Aeneid* 6.784), is used to symbolize weakness and effeminacy.

This characterization of Aeneas as a despised and effeminate Gallus seems totally
inconsistent with the powerful portrait of the Magna Mater discussed above, which
permeates the whole *Aeneid*. The key to understanding both the inconsistency and
the force of this negative sexual stereotyping may lie in a speech given by Juno at the
end of the poem. Yielding to Jupiter's plan that the Trojans prevail, Juno imposes
one last condition, that the conquered Italians not change their voices or their clothing: "ne . . . vocem mutare viros aut vertere vestem" (*Aeneid* 12.825); even though
the Trojans have won, good sturdy Italian speech and manners will prevail. In other
words, Italian men will never adopt the speech and costume of effeminate Orientals
such as the Galli. In likening Aeneas and the Trojans to this contemptuous image,
Virgil may have been attempting to come to terms with contemporary opinion of
the Magna Mater cult held by many Romans, that it represented a threatening combination of domination and debauchery, of "madness and high camp."[65] Virgil was
also alluding to the equation of "Trojan" with "Phrygian," current in literary vocabulary since the fifth century B.C.[66] In so doing, the poet could acknowledge the unattractive side of the Magna Mater cult, but excuse it as a product of her Eastern,
barbarian origins. As the poet states, Troy will fall, to be succeeded by Roman stock,
powerful in Italian virtue: "Romana potens Itala virtute propago" (*Aeneid* 12.827).

This reinforces an earlier point: just as the Magna Mater fulfilled her destiny by
coming to Rome, so Aeneas will put away the trappings of his Phrygian (i.e., Trojan) background and become Latin. He will rid himself of the effeminacy of the Oriental in order to fulfill his destiny as the ancestor of Rome. Here Virgil is echoing
the sentiments of Dionysios of Halikarnassos (2.19.3–5). According to both Dionysios and Virgil, a good Roman could be devoted to the Great Idaean Mother of the

64. A similar idea is expressed by Ovid, *Metamorphoses* 3.534–37.
65. Peter Wiseman's wonderful phrase (Wiseman 1984: 119).
66. The equation of Trojan with Phrygian was first made by Aeschylus; see Hall 1988 and the discussion of this issue in chapter 6 above.

Roman state, yet abstain from the alien character of the Galli. Far from being critical of the Magna Mater, the metaphorical equation of Aeneas with a Gallus serves to reinforce both the power of the goddess and the superiority of Rome.[67]

A more complex portrait of the dark side of the Magna Mater, one that adds a more serious note to the sexual aspect of her character, is that of Catullus, in his poem 63. His picture of the goddess, savage and domineering, is thoroughly compelling and has been one of the most influential on subsequent conceptions of her. It is neither titillating in its hints of unusual sexual behavior nor judgmental in its attribution of the effeminate stereotype to inferior foreigners. Instead, it evokes the confused psychological state of an individual who is both attracted to and repelled by the power of a sexually dominant woman.

The poem explores the reactions of Attis, a young devotee of the Magna Mater, who castrates himself abruptly while in a trance induced by the wild music and orgiastic excitement of her rituals. In his new state as a *notha mulier,* a bastard woman (63.27), his initial reaction is one of exultation.[68] He leads the goddess's band of followers on into a kind of frenzy, ended only by the cleansing quiet of sleep. The coming of the light, however, wakens him from this trance and makes him aware of what he has done. He gazes out to sea, lamenting his action bitterly: he has cut himself off from everything of value, from country, family, friends, and the important social contacts that define his world. The goddess's reaction is to draw Attis into her world, loosening her constant companion, her lion, from her chariot and sending it to drive Attis into the dark forests where he will spend the rest of his life as her slave. The poem then shifts voice to close with the poet's first-person prayer that the goddess may divert such madness away from him:

> Dea magna, dea Cybebe, dea domina Dindymi,
> procul a mea tuus sit furor omnis, era, domo:
> alios age incitatos, alios age rabidos.

> Great goddess, goddess Cybele, goddess and mistress of Dindymus, may all your insanity, Lady, be far from my home. Drive others to frenzy, drive others mad.

(63.91–93)

67. In proposing this explanation of Virgil's two-sided attitude toward the Magna Mater cult, I am, to an extent, following the arguments of Wiseman 1984; but, as I stated in n. 52, I think his emphasis on the unattractive features of the Magna Mater cult is overdone. Augustus did not have to "rehabilitate" the goddess, for she had never ceased to be an important part of Roman religious practice. It is the prominence of the Galli and the cult of Attis that evokes surprise in the modern reader, and the reason for this may lie in the fact that both the Attis cult and the Galli were becoming much more of a public presence in first-century B.C. and C.E. Rome than they had been two centuries earlier.

68. After Attis's castration (lines 4–7), the poet consistently uses the feminine forms of pronouns and adjectives to describe Attis. I have chosen to retain the masculine pronoun in this discussion, however, since it seems to me that Catullus is not creating the character of a woman, but rather that of a man who is uncertain of his own gender identity.

This poem has been much discussed, which is hardly surprising, given the emotional intensity and the complexity of the images in it.[69] While it is not my goal to locate it in the context of Catullus's entire oeuvre, a task that is beyond the scope of a work focused on the Magna Mater cult, it is important to ask why the poet has chosen this religious cult as his subject and what he wishes to say about it. One line of analysis regards the poem as a strong condemnation of the contemporary (i.e., first-century B.C.) cult of Cybele and Attis, warning of the cult's destructive effects on Roman society; according to this view, the poet is reflecting sentiments similar to those of Dionysios of Halikarnassos, expressing the desire to separate the so-called Phrygian elements of the cult from the proper Roman elements.[70] Yet this seems too didactic an approach to Catullus, who is more concerned with private emotions than with public morals. Moreover, Catullus's vision of the strong sexual element in the cult of Cybele and Attis was completely at home in Rome, and had been so for well over a hundred years. It is hard to see how the goddess would have been more dangerous now than she had been at the time of her cult's foundation in Rome. The same criticism can be applied to those who see the poem as a product of Catullus's time in Bithynia, and assume that the scene he describes had little to do with the Roman experience of the Magna Mater.[71] Indeed, poem 63 presents the antithesis of the Mother's Anatolian cult; the wild mountain scenery and the passionate all-night rituals, so moving to the goddess's Anatolian and Greek followers, bring only grief to this Attis.

This poem should not be seen as an expression of a public agenda, but rather as a metaphor for the sexual feelings and emotional state of the poet.[72] The effectiveness of the metaphor is reinforced by the use of the galliambic meter, the same meter used for hymns sung by the Galli to the Magna Mater.[73] There may also be an allusion, in lines 76–90, to the confrontation of the Gallus with the lion, a popular theme in Hellenistic poetry.[74] Yet the encounter of this Attis with the goddess is less ritual than personal. He is caught up swiftly in her spell (he travels *vectus celeri rate,*

69. Recent summaries of the bibliography and criticism on this poem can be found in Small 1983, Holoka 1985, and Ferguson 1988. I have found the studies of Elder 1947, Putnam 1961 and 1974, Wiseman 1985: 198–206, and Takács 1996 especially helpful.

70. This point of view has been argued most persuasively by Wiseman 1985: 198–206, who suggests that the poem was a hymn to be sung at the Megalesia, the goddess's principal Roman festival. The prayer at the end would be meant to distance the poet and his audience at the festival from the wilder, "unRoman" aspects of the cult. See also Ferguson 1988: 20–21.

71. Small 1983: 71–72, 118, with earlier bibliography; Ferguson 1988: 34.

72. Note the comment of Elder 1947: 395, the poem is "a dramatization of a mental state . . . a sympathetic delineation of a mind undergoing a psychological experience of a most powerful sort." Cf. also Putnam 1961: 166, "Catullus speaks through characters, but very much for himself. . . . We seek to discover Catullus' mind at work even in his longer poems"; Takács 1996: 382, "an integral part of Catullus' many-faceted love poetry."

73. Hephaestion 12.3, and the comments of van Ophuijsen 1987: 109–10; Terentianus 2889–91; Martial 2.86.4–5. The Hephaestion passage is discussed in chapter 7 above. See Mulroy 1976; Wiseman 1985: 200.

74. Gow and Page 1968: 30; *Anth. pal.* 6.217–20, 234, 237, discussed in chapter 7 above.

on a swift ship, *citato pede,* with swift foot) and castrates himself for no reason other than the confused state of his mind. Sleep and darkness shroud the immediate impact of his action, but the return of light reveals to him that he has sacrificed himself (since his genitals symbolize his own individuality) to a goddess who cares nothing for him. He has permanently lost the bonds of citizenship, family, and friends, "patria, bonis, amicis, genitoribus abero" (63.59), and the social contacts of the gymnasium, forum, and palestra that define the masculine place in society: "abero foro, palaestra, stadio et gumnasiis" (63.60). Not only his gender but also his civic identity ("ubinam aut quibus locis te positam, patria, reor?" [63.55]) and his freedom ("semper omne vitae spatium famula fuit" [63.90]) are gone. Because of excessive sexual passion for a cruel mistress, he has allowed himself to adopt the powerless status of a real slave in Rome.[75]

It is hard to be certain how personal Catullus intended his work to be. The Attis of the poem is surely the poet himself, who has chosen to present himself in this mythological role. Yet the mythological Attis we meet here is not the god who was worshipped along with Cybele on the Palatine, but rather a human being who acts out the part of the human companion and doomed lover of the goddess: "ego nunc deum ministra et Cybeles famula" (I am now a handmaid of the gods and a slave of Cybele) (63.68). The poet, as Attis, has become both the principal celebrant of the goddess and her principal victim. The love/hate relationship of the poet with Lesbia, which forms such a major theme in his work, is certainly pertinent here, as Cybele becomes, like Lesbia, the powerful mistress who seduces, maddens, and destroys.[76] If one accepts the identity of Lesbia as Clodia, sister of P. Clodius Pulcher, Catullus's metaphor of the poet as Attis gains special force, for Clodius was the man who used the cult of the Magna Mater for his own personal advantage, disrupting the Megalesian Games in 56 B.C., close in time to the composition of Catullus's poem.[77] Catullus could write such a pointed allusion to his powerful mistress who draws innocent young men into her circle, then gelds and enslaves them, knowing that his attack was effective on both personal and political levels.

Yet one suspects that the poet wanted to do more with this metaphor than communicate his own experiences with misdirected romantic passion. The poem also enables the poet, as Attis, to explore the nature of his own masculine identity. He can speak in a feminine voice, mirroring the state of a woman who was seduced and abandoned and whose life was completely altered as a result. We see this through several striking parallels between Attis and Ariadne, whose fate as the abandoned

75. Cybele becomes the *domina,* both the mistress of Catullus's mind and the slave mistress of his body; cf. Wiseman 1985: 181.
76. Cf. Putnam 1974: 80; and the comment of Wiseman 1985: 175, "It is often thought that the choice and treatment of Catullus' mythological themes were influenced by his own experience in love."
77. Cicero, *De harus. res.* 22–29. On the dates of Catullus, see Wiseman 1985: 206. On Clodius's actions and their relationship to his political career, see Gallini 1962 and Michels 1966, whose comments on Lucretius are valuable here as well.

lover of Theseus is explored in poem 64: both travel swiftly across the sea in the hope of finding new love; both find passion at night but awake to desertion in the morning; both have confused the superficiality of external attraction with the reality of internal values.[78] Yet in poem 63 the poet remains acutely conscious of his own masculinity; he now has new insight into the powerless status of a woman, and he does not want to be a woman. Thus the shifting of Attis's social role, from goddess's lover to goddess's slave, mirrors the shifting of gender roles by Catullus's Attis, as the change of pronouns from masculine to feminine within the poem emphasizes. If accepting his mistress means rejecting his own sexuality (the followers of Cybele castrate themselves "Veneris nimio odio," because of excessive hatred of Venus, i.e., of erotic love), then this is no option for him.

We must assume that the poet's use of the Magna Mater's imagery in communicating a love/hate relationship with the masculine sexual identity was effective precisely because the images he evoked were familiar to his audience. The tone of half-fascination, half-horror that the poet brings to the figure of Attis mirrors a similar emotional intensity experienced during the course of the Mother's Roman rites (as Lucretius 2.618–23 brings out forcefully). The poet may be directing our attention to the externally attractive features of those rites, for the voyage to a new place, the wild music, the trancelike state of her followers, seem at first to offer the capacity to transform oneself into a new and potentially better person. But this proves illusory; Cybele does indeed have the power to transform who one is, but for the worse, not for better. Catullus emphasizes this further by inverting the message of the story of the Gallus and the lion. In the Hellenistic version, the Gallus, by performing the goddess's ritual dance and music, saves himself from the lion, but in Catullus's version the lion, the wild beast, is triumphant, conspiring with the goddess to drag the innocent Attis under.

Interestingly, Catullus uses the Cybele imagery to discuss several of the same themes as his contemporary Lucretius. Lucretius stresses the contrast between the destructive emotion of the goddess's rites and the productive love between parent and child (Lucretius 2.614–17), a theme that recurs in Catullus's work, since he contrasts the passion of erotic love with the pure love of a father.[79] Moreover, for both poets, the destructive violence of the goddess draws men away from their privileges and duties as citizens of the state (Lucretius 2.641–43; cf. Catullus 63.50, 55–59). Yet while Lucretius could use these themes to warn and advise, Catullus concentrates on the aftermath of self-indulgence, leaving the reader with the sense of the hopeless inevitability of men's inability to cope with the consequences of passionate excess. The prayer at the end seems more a desperate plea than a hopeful appeal to the goddess for a better future.

78. This is well explored by Putnam 1961: 168–71.
79. Catullus, poems 64.212–50 and 72; see Putnam 1961: 167, 187.

A lighter look at the sexual side of the Magna Mater cult appears in the *Eumenides* of M. Terentius Varro, one of his Menippean satires, composed around 70–60 B.C. While the surviving text is highly fragmentary, the sections relevant to the Magna Mater have been reconstructed to present a fairly coherent account.[80] According to the premise of the work, the unnamed protagonist attempts, ultimately unsuccessfully, to find meaning in the world through adherence to mystery cults in first-century B.C. Rome.[81] The protagonist describes his encounter with the Magna Mater cult in the first person: while going home, he hears the sound of cymbals and is attracted to activities inside. He puts on women's clothing (and thus presumably escapes notice because he is dressed like one of the Galli), and enters the temple. He observes the crowd of Galli chanting to the goddess, while the aedile places the crown brought from the theater on the head of the goddess (this indicates that the incident took place during the Megalesian festival).[82] He is impressed by the delicacy and beauty of the Galli and by the charm of their feminine costumes—they look like Naiads, he tells us—and especially by the high priest, whose purple robe and golden crown gleam with light. The bewitching music and song add to the intoxicating atmosphere, and the narrator is attracted by assurances of good sense and chastity by the cult's priests. Then, suddenly, he curses the insanity he finds in the cult, as the Galli try to pull him down from the altar, where he has perhaps taken refuge to avoid forcible castration (the text is unclear at this point). The story breaks off abruptly as the narrator moves on to a new episode in his search for meaning, to the cult of Serapis.

While the reconstruction of the narrative is tentative, the separate fragments offer several notable insights into the status of the Magna Mater cult in Rome. The two-edged reaction to the cult is clear: on the one hand, the ambiguous costume and un-Roman appearance of the Galli are stressed, yet the goddess clearly enjoys the official approval of the state, as witnessed by the presence of the aedile at these rites. The element of sexual ambiguity is also prominent: the narrator escapes detection by dressing as a woman but is attracted (as a man might be) to the enticing feminine qualities of the priests. He adopts a woman's appearance for the sake of cult practice, yet is repelled by the idea of being a woman. Unlike Catullus's Attis, Varro's narra-

---

80. This discussion of Varro's work follows the text of Cèbe 1977: Varro, *Eumenides* frs. 16–27 (Nonius, frs. 132–43). The commentary of Wiseman 1985: 269–72 is also of great value.

81. Cèbe 1977: 563 locates the action of the satire in Athens, citing the prominence of the Metroön in the Athenian Agora, and the lack of an official cult of Attis in Rome. Other scholars who have analyzed these fragments (e.g., Graillot 1912: 103; Wiseman 1985: 269) have, however, assumed that the scene must be laid in Rome. The temple of the Magna Mater in Rome was certainly as prominent as that in Athens, and the cult of Attis and the practice of ritual castration is more frequently attested in Rome. Moreover, if the scene is not set in Rome, it becomes difficult to account for the presence of the theatrical games mentioned in fr. 134.

82. I follow Wiseman 1985: 271, in reading *e scena coronam adlatam* rather than the reading of Cèbe 1977: 531, *messem hornam adlatam*. I also follow Graillot and Wiseman in reading *aedilis*, rather than Cèbe's reading of *aedituus*.

tor sees the consequences of losing his own gendered identity before any disastrous action occurs, but he, too, discovers that the outward attractiveness of the Cybele cult masks a destructive loss of self. And this poem, too, closes with a plea that the deceptive madness of the goddess be kept at bay: "apage in dierectum a domo nostra istam insanitatem" (to hell with it! drive that insanity away from our home! [Cèbe, fr. 142]).

The text also hints at another source of the cult's attraction, its dual political and social status. The Magna Mater lies within the group of officially recognized state cults, yet outside the bounds of decent behavior, thereby offering the chance of an illicit, and potentially titillating, experience. The male participant in the cult could toy with transvestitism, bisexuality, and emotional release, all within one of Rome's most hallowed shrines. Thus the appeal of the cult appears to lie in the narrator's need to come to terms with both sides of his nature, the lawful and the lascivious. Small wonder that men kept returning to mistress Cybele!

THE LATE REPUBLIC AND EARLY EMPIRE: MONUMENTS AND RITUALS

These literary sources of the first centuries B.C. and C.E. give such a richly varied picture of the Magna Mater that one would expect equally rich insight from the Roman cult monuments of the same period dedicated to her. The information derived from pictorial and archaeological evidence for the goddess and her cult is, however, much more limited. Most Roman representations of the Magna Mater follow the standard Greek iconography, depicting her as a mature woman, seated on a throne, with a tympanum on her left arm and a lion by her side. Specifically Roman iconography can be found in a few monuments, the best-known perhaps being the third temple of the Magna Mater on the Palatine. Augustus himself took personal credit for the temple's reconstruction, rebuilding it in an even more elaborate form after the second temple burned in 3 C.E.[83] The temple now had a marble façade and sculptural decoration, preserved today through a relief on the Ara Pietatis (figs. 72, 73).[84] The temple's pedimental sculpture depicts a throne in the center with a turreted crown resting on it, two reclining male figures leaning on a tympanum on either side, presumably Attis represented twice, and two lions tamely drinking out of bowls. This is a representation of the *sellisternium,* a Roman ritual at which images of the gods were set on chairs in front of a banquet table, as if the deity were actually present at the banquet.[85] The Magna Mater was to be represented at the banquet by her turreted crown, while her companion Attis reclines beside her. Even her animal com-

83. *Res gestae divi Augusti* 3.19; Ovid, *Fasti* 4.348.
84. *CCCA* III: no. 2, pls. 9–12.
85. Taylor 1956; Hanson 1959: 15; Weinstock 1957: 147–48.

panions, her lions, join in the festivities by lapping up their dinner from bowls. All the elements of the traditional cult are there, the crown symbolizing the goddess as the protector of the city, the prominence of Attis and his accepted place as her companion, the tympanum, symbol of the goddess's rites, and the lions, the wild beasts who have been tamed and are, so to speak, eating out of her hand, at her table.

Specifically Roman associations can also be found in the more traditional representations of the Magna Mater, such as that on a marble base from Sorrento.[86] Originally designed to support three statues, one of which was surely a representation of Augustus, the base bears sculpted reliefs on all four sides depicting Roman deities. The Magna Mater appears on one lateral face, shown in her standard Hellenistic iconography of a figure seated on a throne, wearing a turreted crown, veil, and tunic, with a lion crouching at her right. She is attended by a dancing Corybantic figure at

86. Guarducci 1971: 94–112.

F I G U R E 7 3.   Detail from the Ara Pietatis relief illustrating the
pedimental sculpture on the Augustan temple of the Magna Mater. Mid
first century C.E. Courtesy, German Archaeological Institute, Rome.

the left, and at the far left by a standing veiled woman, probably Juno Sospita.[87]
Juno Sospita was depicted in the terracottas found in the earliest Palatine temple of
the Magna Mater,[88] and the coupling of the two on this clearly Augustan monument
is another indication of how Augustan iconography preserved and enhanced the old
Roman order of the gods, in this case two deities who had been linked since the late
third century B.C.

The Magna Mater on the Sorrento base seems to allude to the goddess's Palatine
cult, perhaps specifically to the Augustan rebuilding of her temple in 3 C.E., and, in
conjunction with the goddess's prominence in the *Aeneid*, offers a further example
to connect her cult with the emperor. The Palatine temple was adjacent to the house

87. Ibid.: 111–12.
88. Pensabene 1981 postulates that there may have been an earlier temple to Juno Sospita on the Palatine, superseded by the first temple to the Magna Mater. In support of this, note Ovid, *Fasti* 2.55–56, the
Phrygian Mother and Juno Sospita as former neighbors on the Palatine.

MATRIDEVMETNAVISALVIAE
SALVIAEVOTO SVSCEPTO
CLAVDIA   SYNTHYCHE
    D   D

FIGURE 74. Relief of Claudia Quinta and the *Navisalvia,* from Rome. Second century C.E. Courtesy, Capitoline Museum, Rome.

FIGURE 75. Marble
statue of the Magna Mater
from the Palatine, Rome. Late
first century C.E. Courtesy,
Fototeca Unione at the
American Academy at Rome.

of Augustus and Livia, and this physical proximity of the emperor to one of Rome's major shrines surely reinforced his interest in the cult.[89] An even more striking piece of evidence of the emperor's personal association with the goddess is offered by a portrait statue in the J. Paul Getty Museum.[90] The work depicts a seated Magna Mater, a fairly standard pose, but with a portrait head of the empress Livia. The body is that of a mature woman wearing a turreted crown, holding a tympanum (now missing), and accompanied by a lion at her right. She holds two additional attributes, a rudder and a cornucopia. But the head of the piece has been given the facial features of Livia, and the work, although clearly a posthumous portrait,[91] demonstrates a close connection between the goddess and the Imperial family.

Another votive of interest, a marble relief in the Capitoline Museum, illustrates the figure of Claudia Quinta (fig. 74). There seems no reason to doubt that this Roman matron, representative of a prominent Republican family, played a part in the events of the goddess's arrival in 204 B.C. Claudia's reputation clearly underwent an enlargement and elaboration and acquired specifically political overtones during the early Principate, however, as her high status, reinforced by a personal sign from

89. Wiseman 1984: 126.
90. Bieber 1968: pls. 1–4.
91. Livia was deified by Claudius in 43 C.E., and the piece has been variously dated to the Claudian (Vermaseren, *CCCA* III: 84–85, no. 311) or Antonine (Bieber 1968: 16–17) periods.

the Magna Mater herself, undoubtedly enhanced the prestige of the Claudian gens and thereby the Imperial family. The legend of the chaste woman was treated by the Augustan poets Ovid and Propertius.[92] As an exemplar of Republican virtue, Claudia became a standard-bearer of old-fashioned morality, a prominent part of Augustan propaganda.[93] The Capitoline relief emphasizes this point. Claudia, shown at the right, wears the costume of a Vestal Virgin, indicating that the depiction on the relief has been influenced by the increasingly fabulous character of the story. In her right hand, she holds a rope attached to a ship, on which a seated figure is placed, undoubtedly the statue of the Magna Mater. An inscription underneath the relief identifies the object as a votive to the Mother of the gods and the ship of salvation, the *Navisalvia*.[94] Other inscriptions dedicated to the goddess and the ship indicate that the sacred ship itself seems to have become a focus of the Magna Mater cult, at a shrine probably to be localized at a site along the Tiber where the Mother's ship first docked in Rome.[95]

The Magna Mater's arrival in Rome was honored with another shrine, a tholos of the goddess along the Via Sacra leading to the Colosseum. The location of this building, described in detail by Martial,[96] may be identified with a set of semicircular foundations near the southwest corner of the Basilica of Maxentius.[97] The building has been plausibly identified as the location of the house of Publius Cornelius Scipio, not Nasica, the famous receiver of the Mother upon her arrival in Rome, but his son, P. Cornelius Scipio Corculum, consul in 162 B.C. The shrine described by Martial may have been in place from the mid second century B.C., but the interest in glorifying this aspect of the cult's reception seems to have gained greater significance in the first century C.E. as the role of Scipio Nasica was glorified more greatly.[98]

During the late Republic and early Empire, however, the majority of the visual images of the goddess remain surprisingly static, following the visual form of the goddess imported from Pergamon. A good example of this is the over-life-size marble statue of the goddess found in the nineteenth century in the Palatine temple (fig. 75).[99] The piece depicts a seated woman wearing a tunic, belted under her breasts, and a mantle over her shoulders, which is drawn up across her lap. Probably

92. Ovid, *Fasti* 4.305–48; Propertius 4.11.51–52.
93. Bömer 1964: 146–51; Wiseman 1979: 94–99; Gérard 1980: 174–75.
94. *CCCA* III: no. 218. The sculpted votive altar in the Capitoline Museum probably dates to the first or second centuries C.E. (see Schmidt 1909: 2, Helbig 1912: I, no. 798, Bömer 1964: pl. 33, fig. 1). For a discussion of the monument, see Bömer 1957–58: II, 235; Bömer 1964: 146–51; Coarelli 1982: 42–43.
95. Note another votive altar with an almost identical inscription, but no relief, *CCCA* III: no. 219; an inscription with a similar votive dedication, *CIL* VI 494, the offering of a certain Telephus, *magister* of the college of the cult; and a medallion of Diva Faustina illustrating Claudia pulling on the ship's rope, Bömer 1964, pl. 33, figs. 4, 5. For the location of this shrine, see Coarelli 1982: 42–46.
96. Martial 1.70.
97. Coarelli 1982: 35.
98. Note the lavish praise for Nasica by Valerius Maximus 8.15.3, and Juvenal 3.137–38.
99. *CCCA* III: no. 3, pls. 13–15.

a work of Augustan classicism, it was surely drawn from a Pergamene prototype.[100] The great majority of the surviving Roman votive reliefs and figures follow this schema, with variations often found in Greek works, such as the lion in the goddess's lap rather than at her side, or the presence of the tympanum.[101] This was, as we have seen, the most frequent form of the goddess in the second-century B.C. votives from the Palatine, and it was surely the one used for the cult statue placed in the Palatine temple.[102]

Another well-attested image, although appearing less frequently in surviving monuments, is that of the goddess seated on a lion's back. This was displayed in the spina of the Circus Maximus, where the goddess's games were held. The original statue was probably set up during the reconstruction of the Circus Maximus after the fire of 31 B.C.,[103] but it was copied many times, in freestanding pieces, in relief sculpture, and in other media.[104] This, too, was a Greek iconographic image, one prominent in Pergamon, as shown by its presence on the Pergamon Altar[105] and in terracotta figurines from Pergamon and other Anatolian sites.[106]

By the first century C.E., the Magna Mater was thus a divinity with a central place in Roman life. And the place of honor created for her cult in the first two centuries of its existence in Rome continued under the early Empire. Augustus brought the cult more closely under imperial control by putting priests chosen from his *liberti,* his freedmen, in charge of it,[107] a departure from earlier practice, when attendance at the Magna Mater's festivities was limited to freeborn Roman citizens.[108] The emperor Claudius reportedly supported the cult and took pride in the pious recognition of his chaste ancestress Claudia. During his reign, Attis was officially admitted to the Roman pantheon, and Roman citizens were permitted to participate in his priesthood;[109] a priestly body, the *quindecemviri,* took over formal administration of

---

100. For a close parallel, see the second-century B.C. life-size statue of the goddess from Pergamon, Franz Winter 1907: pl. 7 (here fig. 55). Note the high belting of the tunic, the catenary folds of the goddess's tunic across her knees, the way in which her right knee is thrust forward and slightly out, and even the sandals she wears, all found in the Pergamene work.

101. See the discussion in Bieber 1968: 3–5, figs. 9–10, coin pls. I, II. Other examples are illustrated in *CCCA* III: nos. 247, 248, 256, 268, 280.

102. Note the seated statue of the Magna Mater on the Haterii relief, perhaps representing the image in her Palatine temple, *CCCA* III: no. 200.

103. Platner and Ashby 1929: 119; Coarelli 1982: 41–42.

104. Freestanding sculpture, *CCCA* III: nos. 306, 470; relief sculpture, *CCCA* III: nos. 237, 241a, 252, 286; lamps, *CCCA* III: nos. 330, 439, 440; mosaics, note the representation from Piazza Armerina, Gentili 1959: pl. IX.

105. E. Simon 1975: 30–34, pl. 27. The type may have been invented by the Greek painter Nikomachos, son and pupil of Aristeides in the late fourth century B.C. (Pliny, *NH* 35.36.109).

106. The type appears in terracottas from the Pergamene sanctuary at Mamurt Kale, Conze and Schazmann 1911: pl. XII, no. 3. Note also a Pergamene piece found in Gordion (here fig. 50) and a marble votive relief from Didyma, F. Naumann 1983: pl. 47, fig. 1. Both of these works date from the second century B.C.

107. *CIL* 6.496.

108. Cicero, *De harus. res.* 13.27.

109. Johannes Lydus, *De mensibus* 4.59.

his cult. Attis received his own festival, the Hilaria, celebrated on March 15–27, although its rites are only known through descriptions in much later sources.[110] While the Magna Mater disappeared from the repertory of gods on Roman coins in the early Imperial period, she reappeared during the reign of Hadrian, a time marked by a self-conscious revival of older cults.[111] As a part of Roman history and Roman society, the Magna Mater was never ignored, but as was true of many cults, her future fluctuated with the reigning emperor and his choice of favored gods.

THE MATER DEUM MAGNA IDAEA: ANALYSIS AND CONCLUSIONS

The prominence of the Magna Mater in literature, art, and practice speaks of a cult that lay at the very center of the Roman religious experience. Her temple was located in the heart of the city, near its most venerable shrines. Her rites followed the standard Roman program of procession, sacrifice, and games. Her visual image, while derived from a Greek prototype, stressed her Roman character, particularly the turreted crown, an attribute alluding to her role as protector of cities. Her presence at the *sellisternium,* depicted on her temple on the Palatine, further underscores her full integration into Roman religious practice. Her frequent appearance in the major texts of Roman literature demonstrates that her presence was not an empty shell, but one that had an impact on people's views of their history, their values, and themselves.

The goddess's prominence can be directly tied to her association with the safety of the state. This theme is conspicuous in the Magna Mater's first appearance in Rome in the third century B.C., and it continued to be a factor in her Roman character throughout the early Imperial period. It is stressed by Lucretius, with his emphasis on martial valor; by Ovid, with his vivid narrative of Claudia, the *castissima femina;* and by Virgil, with his portrait of the close relationship between the Magna Mater and Aeneas. We can see a growing rationalization in the mythical tradition surrounding the Magna Mater, as the unattractive foreign features, particularly the legend of Attis and the allusions to the Galli, were criticized more sharply, while the Roman elements, especially the story of Claudia Quinta, became increasingly glorified and fantastic. Yet the close intertwining of the goddess and the Roman state was consistent, vivid, and real. The Magna Mater was a deity of patriotism.[112] She was the Mother of the state, and literally the mother of the state's most important deity, Jupiter.[113] The theatrical works produced at her Palatine temple reinforced the pub-

---

110. Fasce 1978 gives a thorough description of the rites connected with Attis.
111. Bömer 1964: 145.
112. In stating this, I am following the line of argument laid out by Lambrechts 1951 and Boyancé 1954.
113. *Aeneid* 9.82–84.

lic perception of her importance to the state and the intertwining of her legend with Roman history. The political careers of virtually every politically important family, from the Scipiones through Augustus, touched on the cult of the Magna Mater.

This last circumstance becomes even more striking when one compares the status of the Roman Magna Mater to that of the goddess Meter in Greece. No major Greek political figure ever aligned himself closely with Meter. Even in Athens, where the temple of Meter, the Metroön, occupied a central position in the Agora, men like Perikles, Lykourgos, and Demetrios of Phaleron never paid much attention to Meter, certainly not in any official capacity. In Rome, however, the situation was reversed: a whole range of public figures advertised their association with the Magna Mater.

Because the Magna Mater became such a basic part of Roman life, the ambivalence that colors much of the Roman reaction to her seems paradoxical and needs to be addressed. I suggest that the paradox results in large part from the Mother's position as an official Roman deity. Because of this, the Romans required different things from the Magna Mater cult than was the case in Anatolia or Greece. In Anatolia, the Mother's roots seem to have lain deep within popular Anatolian tradition. Although the elite of the Phrygian polity supported her cult as a means of advancing their own status, the Mother outlived the Phrygian state and maintained a strong hold on the Anatolian populace. In the Greek world, the Mother was essentially a deity of private cult. Despite her position as the keeper of laws in several Ionian Greek cities, including Athens, she was not a deity who defined and guarded the polis. In Rome, however, the Magna Mater's alliance with the health and safety of the state was a major condition of her arrival and continued to be prominent throughout the Augustan Principate. As a result, many of the aspects of the Mother's worship that remained private in Anatolia and Greece, such as the use of ecstatic rites and eunuch priests, became public rituals in Rome, and therefore were subjected to a kind of public scrutiny that changed their character.

We can see this clearly in the Romans' puzzled reaction to the goddess's ecstatic rites. In the Greek world, the outward manifestations of ecstasism, particularly the loud, pulsing music and dance, were designed to introduce an interior state of openness to communication with the deity. This was evidently a very personal act, one designed for a participant, not a spectator; furthermore, our information suggests that such activities were normally part of a mystery rite and were rarely carried out in public. In contrast, the Mother's Roman cult offers no private inspiration by individual devotees; in fact, there is no indication that the Magna Mater was one of the deities to whom ordinary people turned for private consolation. The outward forms of ecstatic ritual were entirely public, carried out by her priests in the context of the goddess's public festival, where the place of the Roman public was merely that of an observer at what must have seemed like a baffling performance. Since there was no participation by the population at large, it is hardly surprising that the original meaning of the goddess's ecstatic ritual became perverted into a bizarre public spectacle.

The place of the eunuch priests in the Roman Magna Mater cult is equally problematic. Despite the attribution of this priesthood to an Eastern origin, the custom of self-castration is attested far more frequently and vividly in Rome than in any other part of the ancient Mediterranean world. The reason for this must lie in the same factors noted above, that the Romans had different requirements of the cult and practiced it in a public forum.

One uniquely Roman feature of the Mother Goddess cult is the strong emphasis on fertility. Neither the Anatolian nor the Greek Mother was a fertility deity, but for the Romans, this was an essential part of the Magna Mater's character. It encompassed both human sexuality, as witnessed by the presence of votive terracottas depicting male and female reproductive organs, and agriculture, for the Magna Mater brought rich crops and new life to barren fields, as Lucretius, Ovid, and Pliny emphasize. The results in the first case could be a happy outcome for parents, leading to children who brought promise of the future (Lucretius), or an unhappy outcome to those who denied sexuality, such as Catullus's Attis. The strong element of sexuality was surely a major source of the goddess's appeal to a society where fertility was frequently emphasized and the abundant production of children in marriage was practically a national duty.

The Magna Mater's identity as a symbol of fertility was clearly at odds with her attendance by eunuch priests. Yet the castration of the Magna Mater's priests was an essential aspect of the cult. It seems probable that the eunuch priests of the Mother came with her from Anatolia to Rome in 204 B.C. and thus were part of the goddess's Roman cult from the beginning; the frequency of Attis figurines near the early Magna Mater temple certainly suggests this. Thus the eunuch priesthood was so deeply embedded in the cult's identity that public condemnation of it had little effect.[114]

Here again the Roman shift from private to public cult may have caused a real shift in meaning. In Anatolia, the evidence for ritual castration is sparse and equivocal; the practice was apparently limited to an elite class within the priesthood and may have originated in a form of ritual chastity.[115] There is no evidence at all from the Greek world for ritual castration until the Hellenistic period, when the Galli

114. We should remember that bizarre, even offensive practices were found in other Roman cults besides that of the Magna Mater, including cults whose Italian ancestry was unquestioned. At the Lupercal, for example, naked men ran through the streets whipping women as a means of encouraging their fertility. Here many of the elements of the Mother's cult, sexuality, violence, and fertility, were combined in one of the oldest Roman religious shrines. Wiseman 1984: 126; Zanker 1988: 129.

115. A series of inscriptions of the first century C.E. from Pessinous, describing the office of priest held by a father and son, indicates that castration was not a requirement for the priesthood in the goddess's important Anatolian shrine; see Devreker and Waelkens 1984: 221, nos. 17, 18, and the discussion in chapter 11. On ritual chastity, see chapter 8.

appear in a few places in Asia Minor. In contrast, the evidence suggests that eunuch priests were a common sight in Rome. The prominence of these priests in Roman society may have resulted from the secure position given to eunuchs by the Magna Mater cult. Such a protected status could have caused their number to multiply, as the priesthood proved a magnet for transsexuals, transvestites, and others who found themselves on the margins of society. Our sources strongly imply that in Rome there was a substantial subculture of such individuals whose desire to be outside the confines of standard sexual roles and family obligations led to their decision to choose this asexual path. While individuals like this have existed in almost every society, Rome was unusual in offering such people a formal public outlet in a respected religious cult. This may well have caused their numbers to grow to the point where they became quite a conspicuous part of the social scene. They may also have been feared for their power; the anecdote about the priest Battakes' visit to Rome in 102 B.C. (see pp. 290–91 above) served as a vivid reminder of what would happen to those who publicly opposed the Galli.

The strong Roman contempt for the Galli should be seen in this context. It seems unlikely that the Galli's castrated condition per se was distressing to the Romans; eunuchs, after all, were regularly used as slaves and must have been familiar to most people.[116] Rather, the disturbing issue lay in the fact that this particular group of eunuchs enjoyed a sacred status in an important state cult, affording the Galli a position of inviolability and social standing denied to slaves. Their status was quite inconsistent with Roman concepts of hierarchy, where males were expected to be dominant over females and freeborn Roman citizens over slaves and foreigners.[117] The sanctity of these effeminate foreigners brought this power inversion into the open in an inescapable way and made the eunuch priests doubly offensive, even as their presence had to be tolerated.[118]

Thus we can see that the public and patriotic character of the Magna Mater made her a Roman deity of a very composite nature. Some of the original characteristics of the Phrygian Matar Kubileya were present, some aspects of the goddess reached Rome through the filter of Greek practice, and some parts of her character and rituals were either reshaped into Roman practices or created anew to make her Roman. And the power of this Roman image of the Mother Goddess and her cult was enormous. The pastiche of elements that originally made up her identity was forgotten as the cult extended beyond the city of Rome and was widely disseminated throughout the Empire. Her companion Attis, whose connection with Phrygia was always the loosest element in the identity of the Roman Mother, became an increasingly

116. Hug 1918: 451; Hopkins 1978: 192. Terence's play *The Eunuch* certainly seems to take their presence for granted.
117. Wiseman 1985: 10–14.
118. There are many valuable insights into the status of sacred eunuchs in the selection of papers published by Herdt 1994. See also the Appendix to this chapter.

important figure in his own right. From this point on, the cult of the Magna Mater and her consort Attis lost the limited connection it had with its Anatolian ancestry, and the Roman redefinition of the Mother's cult eventually extended even to the goddess's original Anatolian homeland. Chapter 11 seeks to discover to what extent the Roman concept of the Mother Goddess influenced her identity and worship in the older cult centers in Anatolia.

APPENDIX

Much valuable insight into the status of the Magna Mater cult in Rome and the public's reaction to it can be gained through a comparison of the cult of the Roman goddess with the cult of another mother goddess, whose worship continues in twentieth-century India. There are a number of striking parallels between the Indian deity, known simply as Mata (Mother), and the Roman goddess: both are mother goddesses, both inspire simultaneous adoration and fear among the populace, and, perhaps most telling, both are attended by priests who castrate themselves voluntarily in the goddess's service. The cult of this Indian mother goddess and the role of her castrated attendants have been the subject of a study by Serena Nanda entitled *Neither Man nor Woman,* and I shall draw on her work to help shed light on the cult of the Magna Mater in Rome.[119] I am particularly interested in the identity of the Indian goddess and in the activities and status of her priests, as well as in the general public reaction to them.

The characters of the two maternal divinities are similar, but not identical. Unlike the Magna Mater, the Hindu mother goddess Mata is not a goddess of the state; rather, her sphere of influence lies on a personal level and is concentrated on human fertility. The major ceremonies in her honor take place on the occasion of marriages and at the birth of children, especially sons. Her power as a fertility goddess is administered on the human level by castrated priests called *hijras,* whose most important ritual activity is to sing and dance and perform blessing ceremonies at weddings and at the naming feasts of sons. Thus the Hindu mother goddess's cult practice is informed by the dichotomy between the celebration of fertility and attendants who personify the impossibility of fertility.

The personality of Mata can be highly variable. Nanda describes her position in the Hindu belief system as that of a deity "having both a beneficent and a destructive aspect,"[120] although, as she correctly notes, this is a definition that fits other mother goddesses, and indeed, a great many divinities in other cultures. In the case of the Indian mother goddess, however, the accent seems to be on the destructive. This takes many forms, including a variety of "images of the Mother Goddess en-

119. Nanda 1990.
120. Ibid.: 33.

gaging in aggressive acts—devouring, beheading, and castrating."[121] The goddess's image as a powerful aggressor is particularly prominent in her role as castrator of her mortal consort. There is an elaborate mythic tradition describing the Mother as a castrating queen, which forms a rationale for the eunuch status of her priests. According to this myth, Mata was married to a handsome young prince, but the marriage was never consummated. When the goddess confronted her prince with his impotence, he confessed that he was incapable of sexual activity; he was "neither man nor woman." The goddess was so angry at this that she castrated him, and he took the form of a woman. Because of this, the hijras say, "The goddess is always with us and we live in her power."[122]

While this story is not an absolute corollary to the myth of Cybele and Attis, some interesting parallels can be noted. In both tales, the powerful goddess marries a handsome young human lover, yet the marriage is not successful. The reasons for this vary: in the Hindu tradition, it is impotence, whereas in the Graeco-Roman tradition infidelity causes the rupture. Yet the outcome is similar. The crisis results in the youth's castration, either by the goddess (Hindu) or by himself, under pressure from the goddess (Graeco-Roman). In both cultures, the mythic aetiology of ritual castration seems highly artificial, very much an ex post facto explanation designed to rationalize the existence of a eunuch priesthood understood by neither culture but felt by both to be essential.

It is the character and activities of the hijras, the eunuch priests of the Hindu Mata, which provide the greatest point of comparison with the Roman Magna Mater and her Galli. In India, as in Rome, the imperative for the castrated state of the hijras, while widely accepted, is not understood on any logical level. The emphasis on castration in the cult of Mata is all the more surprising, given the Hindu mother goddess's concern with human reproduction. Yet the hijras' emasculated condition is considered a necessary part of their religious status, and the rituals they perform at weddings and at the birth of children are intended to ensure the goddess's beneficence to her followers. Nanda describes several instances in which families did not want hijras at these important family ceremonies, yet felt that they had to tolerate them because of the goddess's power and the unfortunate consequences of ignoring it.[123]

This uneasy toleration results from the hijras' two-edged ability both to help followers of the goddess and to harm those who do not respect her. They can use this power with devastating results, as the following story illustrates:

A group of hijras came to the house of a wealthy man whose daughter-in-law had recently given birth to her first son. The hijras offered to bless the newborn, but the

121. Ibid.
122. Ibid.: 25–26.
123. Ibid.: 4–9.

father-in-law was insulted at the prospect of having no-good eunuchs in the house and threw them out. As they were leaving, the lead hijra retorted with the following curse: "Just as you have kicked us down, so your grandson's bier will go down the same way." The next day the small boy fell sick and soon died. When the father-in-law met later with the lead hijra, he wept and cried: "I sent you away with kicks and blows. Now my daughter-in-law's lap is empty. I had a gift from heaven and now God has taken that gift away."[124]

Nanda was assured by the hijra priest who reported this story that the episode was genuine. Yet in its present form, the narrative is highly reminiscent of the resistance myths told about the arrival of the Phrygian Mother in Greece and Rome. It is particularly close to the story of the eunuch priest Battakes who addressed the Roman Senate on behalf of the Magna Mater in 102 B.C. and the tribune who opposed him, "kicked him down," so to speak, resulting in the tribune's speedy death.[125] In Hindu society, too, insulting a priest of the mother goddess results in a clear demonstration of her authority and enhancement of her status. Such anecdotes give us a greater insight into why the Mother's eunuch priests might be privately despised but publicly tolerated, even praised.

Clearly, the castrated state of the hijras lies at the core of the uneasy reaction to them. In particular, the voluntary choice of emasculation as an adult places the hijra outside the norms of society, on both ritual and personal levels. Officially, it gives the hijra a sacred status. The religious ideology of the hijras defines them as people who live asexual lives, who have supposedly chosen to renounce sexual activity in order to devote themselves to asceticism.[126] They claim to earn their living as servants of Mata by performing at her festivals and by religious mendicancy.

The private reality is quite different. Most men are attracted to the hijra community not because of religious piety, but because they are impotent. Able to play neither a male nor a female role in reproduction, they choose the life of the sacred castrato, because this gives them a status and a community group in which to live. Many are clearly transsexuals, having "a woman's mind in a man's body."[127] Hijras were all born men, but they identify strongly with the female role in society: they dress as women, wear their hair as women do, wear women's jewelry and makeup, take women's names, and always use the feminine pronoun when referring to themselves or to other members of their community. Most hijras come from the lower middle class or working class in Indian society; very few come from the lowest social caste. They claim to be ascetics in order to secure greater prestige for their ritual activities of participation at weddings and births. Yet it is clear that most hijras do not

124. Ibid.: 8–9.
125. Diodoros 36.13; Plutarch, *Marius* 17.
126. Nanda 1990: 29–32.
127. Nanda 1990: xiv, quoting Karl Ulrich's 1864 work *Inclusa: Anima muliebris corpore virili inclusa*.

renounce sexual activity. Many, perhaps the majority, are prostitutes.[128] Others link up in a long-term relationship with men whom they regard as husbands and seek respectability in a semblance of family life.[129] They are well aware that engaging in prostitution and other sexual activities undercuts their claim to special ritual status as ascetics, but prostitution offers a source of income that few can do without. It is the contradiction between their ritual pose of purity and chastity and the private reality of regular engagement in illicit sexual activities that makes the hijras a particularly despised group in India. This is so despite the fact that, as noted above, their public role in fertility rituals makes many Indians feel unable to ignore them without risk.

The parallels between the hijras and the Roman Galli are numerous and enlightening. It is here, in exploring the psychology and the activities of the hijras, that Nanda's work is particularly valuable to the student of Mediterranean antiquity. She was able to talk to several of these individuals in depth and probe their attitudes toward their asexual identity and their reasons for choosing this path, something we clearly cannot do with the Roman Galli. Before exploring the parallels between the two groups, though, we should stress the substantial inequity in such a comparison, for in discussing the Roman Galli, we are discussing the Romans' descriptions of them, not the opinions of the Galli about themselves. We inevitably evaluate the Galli based on the opinions of people who not only looked down on them but may have been repeating information based on stereotypes and hearsay, rather than facts gained from personal contact with them.

One obvious parallel lies in the physical appearance of the two groups. The Romans, too, saw the Galli as women, and used the feminine pronoun to describe them.[130] Comments were made on their feminine appearance and dress, which could elicit approval and even sexual excitement from men.[131] The outlandish behavior of the hijras and their noisy activities are another point of comparison, for as was also the case with the Galli, such activities are designed to attract attention to the eunuch priesthood. One Indian newspaper has described the hijras as "eunuchs wearing garish makeup, gaudy saris, bangles and bells,"[132] a description reminiscent of Dionysios of Halikarnassos's observation that the Galli went "through the city in gaudy robes, begging, and escorted by flute players."[133]

Another parallel lies in their method of earning a living. Like the hijras, the Galli were known for performances at religious festivals, although they did not (as far as we know) perform at private family gatherings, but at the public festival of their

128. Nanda states that all the hijras she met either were or had been prostitutes.
129. Nanda 1990: 122–25.
130. Catullus 63; Hephaestion p. 39, van Ophuijsen 1987: 109–10.
131. Note the description of the Galli by Varro, Cèbe 1977: Varro, *Eumenides* frs. 16–27 (Nonius, frs. 132–43).
132. Nanda 1990: 38, quoting an Associated Press report from Bhopal in 1984.
133. Dionysios of Halikarnassos 2.19.5.

deity, the Magna Mater. Lucretius's vivid description of the public performance of the Galli at that festival is memorable: drums thunder, cymbals clash, horns resound, and flutes agitate the mind,[134] all of which find echoes in the raucous and noisy performances of the hijras.[135] Another common source of income is religious mendicancy. The Galli engaged in public begging at religious festivals on behalf of their goddess and, of course, themselves, an activity that apparently made them particularly despised in both Greece and Rome, but one that was nonetheless tolerated because of its ritual associations.[136] Begging is a regular activity of the Indian hijras too, one that they undertake because it reinforces the image of religious asceticism, although in practice most hijras prefer not to beg, since it is hard work, nets little money, and subjects them to public scorn.[137]

The chief point of contact between the two groups is, clearly, their emasculated sexual condition and the liminal status in society that results from this. The sexual parallel between the two groups is not exact, for the hijras undergo total castration, while the Galli, as far as we can tell, removed the testicles only. In both groups this condition was undertaken voluntarily, a circumstance that puts the individuals who select this path outside the bounds of normal behavior, both physically and psychologically. The act of castration does not, however, make these eunuch priests asexual beings, and as with the Galli, prostitution and other sexual activities contribute to the marginal status of the hijras. In India, hijra prostitutes service male customers only, but in Rome, the Galli seem to have been attractive to both men and women.[138] In both cases, the act of castration makes the group's members more sexually available, and those who wish to earn money from prostitution can benefit from this.[139]

Nanda's conversations with the hijras offer some insight into the choice of self-castration. In Hindu cult, the followers of Mata undergo castration self-consciously and deliberately, after a long period of apprenticeship in the cult.[140] This warns against the common interpretation that the self-castration of the Roman Galli was an act of ritual madness. The comment of Walter Burkert is typical of the opinion of many classicists: "It is clear that the act [of self-castration] was performed in a state

134. Lucretius 2.618–20.
135. Nanda 1990: 1–3.
136. Cicero, *De legibus* 2.22; Dionysios of Halikarnassos 2.19.5. On begging in the cult of the Mother Goddess in Greece and Rome, see Aristotle, *Rhetoric* 1405a; Athenaios 12.541e; Plutarch, *Cleomenes* 36; Lucretius 2.626.
137. Nanda 1990: 50–51.
138. Attractiveness to men, Varro (n. 131 above); to women, Philodemus, Epigram 26, in Gow and Page 1968: 366–67; Horace, *Satires* 1.2.119–22.
139. Nanda 1990: 52–54, indicates that the hijra is considered a more attractive source of sexual favors than a female prostitute. We have no idea whether a comparable situation obtained among the Galli in Rome, but certainly the comments of Horace (n. 138) and Martial 3.81 indicate that this might have been so.
140. Nanda 1990: 26–29.

of mind when the man could not give reasons for what he did."[141] Yet this attitude seems to be more a reflection of the modern repugnance toward castration than of any ancient description. Our ancient sources on the Galli give no indication that these individuals were mad; rather, they seem to have flaunted their castrated status and enjoyed the special position that it brought them,[142] a situation that also obtains for the hijras.

The chief social result of voluntary castration, however, is to set the castrato outside the cultural norms of his society. This makes such an individual vulnerable to abuse, as numerous anecdotes, ancient and modern, relate. On the other hand, the ambiguous sexual status of the eunuch priest is also a source of power, because service to a powerful goddess makes most people reluctant to provoke her eunuch priest in a public confrontation. Thus the sacred eunuch can engage in outrageous behavior with impunity, trading on a disreputable image to dress, talk, and act in what many consider a shameful way. The opportunity for such extreme appearance and behavior may even attract members to the group.

I am reluctant to press the parallels between these two groups of castrated priests too closely, for the status and activities of the Roman Galli are known to us only imperfectly and only through hostile sources, and it is always a daunting task to speak for the silent dead. Yet the comparison with the hijras of India is instructive in several ways. It shows the fear that the sacred eunuchs could arouse in people because of their perceived power, and the need to tolerate them, however reluctantly, because of this power. It also gives us an insight into why a man would choose such a life. The parallels with Hindu cult suggest that by enveloping transsexual behavior in religious garb, the status of eunuch priesthood offered an aura of respectability to a man whose natural sexual inclinations would in any case have put him outside the norms of conventional social behavior. And, perhaps most important, by illustrating how a mother goddess can enjoy high status while her priests inspire disgust, the modern Hindu mother goddess and her eunuch priests provide a living example of the coexistence of both attractive and unattractive elements in the same cult. Religious practice, ancient and modern, resists easy categorization.

141. Burkert 1979a: 105. Cf. also Wiseman 1984: 119.
142. E.g., Lucretius 2.631; Juvenal 6.511–16.

11 · THE ROMAN GODDESS IN ASIA MINOR

The Magna Mater became an integral part of the Roman state and the Roman religious experience. One of the most striking phenomena of the goddess's worship was its tendency to follow the spread of the Roman state throughout the Mediterranean world. As the Romans gained control of Spain, Gaul, Britain, the Rhine and Danube valleys, and North Africa, the cult of the Magna Mater became part of life in the western provinces as well. In these areas, the Magna Mater cult was strongly influenced by the Roman model, and the impact of the goddess's Phrygian origins was much less pronounced. Yet the high degree of popularity that the Magna Mater enjoyed testifies abundantly to the attractiveness of her cult and its ability to transcend regional and cultural boundaries.

It is not the purpose of this study to follow the Magna Mater to all corners of the Roman Empire, a task beyond the scope of a single volume, and one that has been addressed in part by Maarten Vermaseren's catalogues, the *Corpus Cultus Cybelae Attidisque,* volumes 4 through 7.[1] Instead, I wish to continue to explore the Anatolian definition of the Mother Goddess, and the tensions between the Eastern and Western aspects of her cult, and so I shall return now to the Roman East. In several of the Roman provinces of Asia Minor, the cult of the goddess continued to enjoy great popularity. Here, however, the Romanized Magna Mater coincided with the well-established persona of the Hellenistic Meter, who was herself a fusion of the older Anatolian Mother Goddess with Greek cult. The blending of the various strands of the Mother's cult offers an interesting perspective on the wider problem of the extent of Romanization (and Hellenization) in the eastern half of the Empire.

---

1. Graillot 1912: 412–533 remains the best general synthesis on the spread of the Meter cult, although much new material has become available for study since its publication.

In focusing on the cult of the Mother Goddess in Asia Minor during the first two centuries of Roman rule, this chapter thus returns this survey of the Mother's cult to the goddess's Anatolian homeland.

As in the Hellenistic period, the Mother Goddess of Roman Asia spoke in multiple voices. She was still very much at home in the older Phrygian centers of her cult; in fact, the cult of Meter in one of those centers, Pessinous, is better documented during this time than it had been in previous centuries. In addition, the Mother Goddess was still a strong presence in several important Greek cities of western Asia, as she had been during the Hellenistic period. Indeed, dividing this discussion of Meter in Asia into two separate sections, one on Hellenistic and one on Roman material, introduces an artificial break into the material that did not exist in practice. There are, however, some noticeable changes in the cult of Meter in Asia that can be traced to Roman influence. The figure of Attis, a key element in the goddess's Roman persona, became a stronger presence in Asia. More generally, the influence of Meter herself weakened, as the Meter cult lost ground to the civic cults of the established Greek gods and to the Roman Imperial cult.

This discussion will concentrate on the areas where the Meter cult was a strong presence in Roman Asia. While evidence of the worship of Meter can be found in virtually every area of Roman Asia Minor, the Meter cult is best attested in western and central Anatolia. It formed a distinctive feature of the religious practices of western and northwestern Asia Minor, in Ionia, Aeolis, Mysia, and Bithynia. Meter also had a strong presence in Caria, Lydia, Phrygia, and the older Phrygian heartland, now the province of Galatia.

A wide range of epithets were used to address the goddess. She was still addressed by the general term of $M\acute{\eta}\tau\eta\rho$ $\acute{o}\rho\epsilon\acute{\iota}a$,[2] the Mountain Mother, but more frequently her worshippers tried to pin the goddess down to a specific community in order to stress her connection with their particular locale. As a result, the goddess's topographical epithets in Anatolia, always numerous, mushroomed during the first two centuries C.E., to the point where every little town and village claimed its own individual form of Meter. We hear of a wide variety of epithets from Phrygia, Meter Salsaloudene[3] and Meter Tazene,[4] Meter Pontanene and Meter Malene, the last two from towns near Midas City.[5] A Meter Kiklea appeared in a small town near Aizanoi.[6] One noteworthy epithet is found on a second-century C.E. votive altar from a rural site north of Midas City, dedicated to Meter Kybele.[7] This recalls the Phrygian epi-

---

2. In Lycia, Latte 1920: 104, no. 11, a text from Oinoanda; cf. Robert 1937: 403. In Caria, Reinach 1908, a text from Apollonia (see n. 43 below). See also Σ Apollonios Rhodios 2.722.
3. *IGRRP* IV.755, near modern Kabalar, in Phrygia.
4. *IGRRP* IV.1371.
5. Haspels 1971: 199–200.
6. *IGRRP* IV.604.
7. Drew-Bear 1978: no. 9 = *MAMA* V: no. 213.

thet *kubileya* and reminds us again that in Anatolia, "Kybele" was only an epithet, not the goddess's name.

In other examples, "Meter" appears with a proper name in the genitive, recording the name of an individual who made donations to the cult, for example, Μήτηρ Καλλίππου[8] and Μήτηρ Ἀδράστου.[9] Meter can also appear with a descriptive epithet, such as Μήτηρ ἀπὸ σπηλείου, the Mother of the cave,[10] Μήτηρ ἐπήκοος, the Mother who listens,[11] or Μήτηρ τετραπροσώπος, the Mother of four faces—that is, the Mother who sees all.[12] The greater proliferation of such Meter epithets surely reflects the greater proliferation of the cult itself. It may also result from the greater spread of literacy in the first two centuries C.E., which enabled more people in remote areas to record their dedications to the goddess.

The range of the Meter cult is also evident from the abundant evidence of small votive statuettes, altars, and inscribed plaques dedicated to her. The standard Meter votive continued to be a small statuette or relief depicting the goddess seated on her throne, holding her phiale and tympanum, and accompanied by lions. By the first century C.E., the type was so prevalent that its broad dispersion in Anatolia calls for little comment. While virtually every museum in Turkey has one or more of these statuettes, a lack of firm information on their provenience and date undercuts their potential to offer new information on the Meter cult, apart from attesting to its general popularity and wide distribution.

Small altars and stelai dedicated to Meter form another class of material that becomes abundant during the first two centuries C.E. The majority of these record only that individuals honored Meter in fulfillment of a vow, εὐχή. Occasionally there is an indication of what the person wanted from Meter; the most common reasons are the health and safety of the individual, or his family or friends.[13] One individual sought Meter's help for the return of a sum of gold stolen from its owner; the goddess is directed to punish the thieves "in accordance with her power so that she will not become an object of derision."[14] We also learn of individuals who made dedications to Meter in expiation for a sin.[15]

---

8. Ibid.: no. 10. The practice of using a genitive as a Meter epithet was apparently fairly common (see Haspels 1971: 196).

9. Sheppard 1981: 24–25, no. 5. This is from the Lydian city of Attouda (modern Hisarköy), where Adrastos was the name of a wealthy citizen in the community.

10. Robert 1955.

11. An inscription from Sivrihisar, perhaps originally from Pessinous, Graillot 1912: 354 n. 6.

12. *MAMA* V: no. 101.

13. Some examples (by no means an inclusive list): "for the safety of the *demos* and the children" (Körte 1897: 31, no. 6, from Pessinous); "on behalf of all men and animals" (*MAMA* V: no. 101, from north Galatia); "on behalf of the children" (Schwertheim 1978: 794–95, no. I A3 from Hadrianoi, in Bithynia); "for the neighborhood" (Corsten 1991: 74–75, no. 50, from Prusa, in Bithynia). See n. 35 below and fig. 76 for an interesting example from Kyzikos of Meter petitioned to save a friend from pirates (Schwertheim 1978: 810–12, no. II A3).

14. Dunant 1978; Versnel 1991: 74, a text on a bronze plaque from Asia Minor, provenience unknown, dated from 100 B.C. to 200 C.E.

15. *IGRRP* IV.1371.

Numismatic material is another abundant source of evidence attesting to the frequency and influence of the Meter cult. Roman coins illustrating the goddess appear on individual coin issues from virtually every major city in western and central Asia Minor. The evidence, gathered by Graillot in his monumental study of the Mother Goddess in the Roman Empire, dates mostly from the late first, second, and third centuries C.E.[16] In a few places, such as Aizanoi (discussed below), the coin evidence reflects a specific change in cult practice. The more common pattern, however, is that found in cities such as Phokaia, where the image of Meter on the city's coinage is joined with that of Tyche, the city's tutelary deity.[17] Often the image of Meter on civic coinage is shown with the turreted crown of the Roman city deity, suggesting that here, too, the goddess was envisioned as the deity who supported and protected the city.[18] Meter's presence on the coin issues of the cities of Roman Asia Minor may not reflect an important civic cult of the goddess, for her shrines were rarely among a city's most prominent religious sanctuaries. It seems more likely that the goddess's identity as a protective deity was analogous to her situation in Rome, where the Magna Mater was primarily an urban deity associated with the safety of the city of Rome.

In contrast, many of the actual cult shrines of Meter are located in more remote rural areas, indicating that the goddess's worship was most prominent in districts where the mountainous terrain led to a natural interest in the cult of the Mountain Mother. Thus we can see two quite separate tendencies in the cult of the Mother Goddess during the first two centuries C.E.: her function as a protective deity of cities and her function as the guardian of the countryside. These tendencies reflect the broader pattern of social development in Roman Asia, a contrast between the highly Hellenized urban centers and the life of the countryside, where local traditions remained stronger.

I shall discuss the cult of Meter in western and northwestern Anatolia first. Many cities with a Hellenistic cult of Meter have produced evidence of a Meter cult in the Roman Imperial era as well, attested through shrines and individual dedications. In Smyrna, the goddess continues to figure prominently in the epigraphical material of the first two centuries C.E., where Meter was frequently the divinity used as a witness for contracts and oaths.[19] The temple of Meter, described by Aelius Aristeides as the most beautiful building in Smyrna, presumably continued to add luster to the city, although nothing survives of it.[20] The prestige of the Meter cult is further sug-

---

16. Graillot 1912: 346–411. Graillot gives extensive sources for his examples, and so his data will not be repeated here. Graillot relied almost exclusively on numismatic evidence for his picture of Meter in Roman Asia Minor, in large part because little other evidence was available to him.

17. Graf 1985: 388.

18. In Erythrai, Graf 1985: 388. Cf. Graillot 1912: 360–61, who cites numerous examples from Phrygia, Lydia, and Caria.

19. Petzl 1990: no. 641, worshipped as Μήτηρ Σιπυληνή; 744, Μήτηρ Θεῶν; 743, Μήτηρ Σμυρναϊκή.

20. Strabo 14.1.37; Pliny, NH 14.6.54; Aelius Aristeides, Smyrnaean Orations 15, p. 232 (Dindorf).

gested by a second-century C.E. inscription honoring one of its priestesses, Ulpia Marcella, a member of a wealthy and distinguished family in Thyateira, who was chosen priestess of the Smyrnaean Meter for life, indicating that families of important social position wished to be publicly associated with Meter.[21]

In Ephesos, the cult of Meter continued to flourish alongside that of Artemis, and a series of reliefs depicting Meter with a young and an elderly god shows that the Hellenistic shrine of Meter on the Panayir Dağ was still an active cult center.[22] Two statues of Attis of the later first and second centuries C.E. indicate that Meter's divine companion had become part of her cult in Asia.[23]

There is no evidence of new foundations of Meter in Ionia during this time, however, and at least one Meter sanctuary, that in Magnesia on the Meander, founded by Themistokles, had been abandoned by the first century C.E.[24] We receive the impression that the interest in the Meter cult in Ionia continued more through the force of tradition than because of any active presence of the goddess in the life of the region. Further south, near Iasos, an inscription records the construction of a "house"—that is, shrine—for Meter, paid for by subscription of the local people; perhaps tellingly, the first two names on the subscription list are Attes, a Phrygian name, and Tibeios, a Paphlagonian name.[25] The cult of Meter in this region may have been supported by immigrants from interior regions where the goddess's presence was stronger.

In northwestern Asia Minor, the Meter cult is better documented. At Ilion, or Troy, the discovery of several terracotta figurines of the goddess indicates that she was worshipped in the city, although it is unclear whether she received her own sanctuary or was worshipped only in household shrines, as was the case in many cities of Asia Minor during the Hellenistic period.[26] Meter was also worshipped on the summit of Mount Ida, where, according to ancient tradition, her sanctuary had been founded by Idaios, son of Dardanos, the eponymous hero of Troy.[27] According to Plutarch, Meter was worshipped on Ida jointly with Zeus.[28]

The cult of Meter flourished in Pergamon also. The strong interest in the goddess during the Hellenistic era, exhibited by the Attalid kings and by private citizens, continued during the first two centuries of the Roman era, and Meter's status at Pergamon was enhanced to the point where her cult became interwoven with the

21. Graillot 1912: 368; *IGRRP* IV.1254 (= 1423).
22. Keil 1915: 74–75, fig. 47, showing an *archigallus* wearing a plaque depicting Meter with an older and a younger god; cf. also Keil 1926: 256–61.
23. *CCCA* I: nos. 636, 638.
24. Strabo 14.1.40.
25. For the inscription, see W. Blümel 1985: no. 229. The text is discussed by Robert 1982: 361.
26. S. G. Miller 1991; Rose 1993a: 341; 1993b: 98–105; 1995: 81–94; 1997: 74–92. Thus far it has not been possible to connect a substantial sanctuary located on the southwestern slope of the Bronze Age Acropolis with a deity (or pair of deities, since the sanctuary was divided into two separate areas), although the presence of Meter figurines suggests that her worship may have played a role in the area's use.
27. Dionysius of Halikarnassos 1.61.4.
28. Plutarch, *De fluv.* 13.4.

mythic prehistory of the city. This is attested by the oracle of Apollo at Klaros, whom the Pergamenes consulted during the second century C.E., probably during the reign of Marcus Aurelius, for help during a plague. To rid their city of the disease, the citizens of Pergamon were told to organize four choirs to honor the gods Zeus, Dionysos, Athena, and Asklepios; as the divinity who gave birth to Zeus, Meter was to be honored too, for Zeus's birthplace was located on the highest point of the Pergamene acropolis.[29] Although first mentioned in this context, the tale was surely not new then, and it may even have been developed at the time of the founding of the city. The story reflects a fusion of the Greek Meter, here assimilated to Rhea, mother of Zeus, and the cult of the Anatolian Mother of the mountains, located on the heights of the Pergamene mountain. It is an interesting example of how Meter, never one of the most influential deities in the city, could still have an impact on the cults of more major deities, particularly that of Zeus.[30]

On an individual level, Pergamene interest in the Meter cult is attested to by a number of private votives. Several dedications address the goddess as Meter Basileia, the Royal Mother; this may refer to the Attalid patronage of Meter, or to ties between the goddess and the cult of Zeus. Other texts honor individual women who served as priestesses of Meter. In one votive dedication, the dedicator identifies himself as a *mystes,* an initiate into the rites of Meter, thus indicating that the goddess was honored with mystery rites in Pergamon, as she was in cities on the Greek mainland.[31]

A rich group of monuments connected with Meter has been found in the districts of Mysia and Bithynia.[32] Both areas had important cults of Meter, and Mysia in particular supported a prominent cult of the goddess in the city of Kyzikos and its surrounding communities, supposedly dating from the heroic voyage of Jason and the Argonauts. A series of votive reliefs and texts dating from the first century B.C. and the first two centuries C.E. record individual offerings from inhabitants of the Kyzikene region.[33] One of these reliefs, dedicated to the ancestral Mother, Μητρὶ Πατρώιᾳ, shows the interest in identifying the cult of Meter with the city's past.[34] We meet a eunuch priest of the Meter cult on an inscribed relief from Kyzikos, dating from the year 46 B.C., dedicated by one Soterides (fig. 76), who petitions Meter

<hr/>

29. The legend is recorded in an inscription that preserves the oracular text, *CIG* 3538 = Fränkel 1890–95: 239 no. 324, lines 17–19. See also Ohlemutz 1940: 181.

30. Arrian, *Bithyniaka, FGrHist* 156 F 22, implies a further connection between Meter and Zeus: "The Bithynians go up to the heights of the mountains and call Zeus *Pappas,* and they call Attis by the same name." See also the cult of Meter Steuene, discussed below.

31. The texts, all of the early Roman period, are given in Fränkel 1890–95: nos. 481–83, honorific inscriptions from the acropolis; no. 484, an honorific inscription found, divided, in the theater and in the precinct of the Athena temple (these four = *CCCA* I: nos. 352–55); the votive inscription, Fränkel 1890–95: no. 334 = *CCCA* I: no. 351.

32. The monuments connected with the cult of Meter in Mysia and Bithynia have been the subject of a special study by E. Schwertheim (see Schwertheim 1978).

33. These have been collected by Schwertheim 1978: 809–27, nos. IIA (inscriptions) and B (reliefs).

34. Schwertheim 1978: 820, no. II A15.

FIGURE 76. Votive relief of Meter dedicated by Soterides, from Kyzikos. First century B.C. Courtesy, Musée du Louvre, Paris.

to help his friend Markos, who had fought with Pompey's fleet and been captured by pirates in a sea battle.[35] Soterides identifies himself in the text as a Gallos, a status reinforced by his feminine dress. This may be the earliest known use of the word "Gallos" in Anatolia in a votive text, and one of the very few instances where the eunuch priesthood of Meter is attested in Asia Minor. The presence of a Gallos may reflect the more visible status of the Galli in the Roman world, rather than Anatolian tradition. The cult of Attis was known in Kyzikos as well, attested by Attis's depiction on the city's coinage.[36]

35. *IGRRP* IV.135 = Schwertheim 1978: 810–12, no. II A3. For a discussion of the relief, see van Straten 1993: 255–56, fig. 17.
36. Karwiese 1968–71: 60–61.

The cult of Meter continued to be a significant presence in Kyzikos during the first two centuries C.E. We hear of Sosigenes, priest of Meter, who also kept the Imperial cult and paid for its games. The same honor was accorded to another unknown individual; these texts are both Hadrianic.[37] Since the principal prerequisite for these offices was a generous income, we may assume that in most cases serving as priest of Meter was a civic honor that carried a certain amount of prestige for well-to-do individuals. The continuing importance of the Kyzikene Meter cult is also made evident by an anecdote from late antiquity, recounting that Constantine admired its cult statue so much that he had it brought to Constantinople.[38]

The picture in Bithynia is a little different. Greek city foundations had come later to this mountainous area southeast of the Sea of Marmara, and so it is not surprising that most Meter votives from Bithynia come from rural sites. The younger Pliny describes a temple of Meter in Nikomedia, evidently a prominent landmark in the city; he describes it as *vetustissima* (very ancient), and this may well have been the case, since he notes that this temple was substantially lower than other major buildings in the city.[39] Apart from this, however, urban shrines of Meter are rare. The city of Kios, a Milesian colony, has produced no monuments of the Meter cult, and the city of Apameia has yielded only Hellenistic material. Meter appears on Roman Imperial coins at Klaudiu Polis, but no Meter votives have been found there.[40] In contrast, several small votives and altars have been found at various rural sites. Most of these are dedicated, not to Meter, but to the goddess Angdistis, Θεᾷ Ἀνγδίστει, or simply to Θεᾷ, the goddess, often qualified with a topographical adjective such as would be used with the name Meter.[41] A continuing series of small altars and stelai record that individuals honored Meter in fulfillment of a vow, εὐχή, suggesting that she was still the divinity called on to address personal needs, a point reinforced by several texts that speak of contact with the goddess in a dream.[42] One has the impression that in urban centers in northwestern Anatolia, interest in the cult of Meter was fairly limited, while the cult in the countryside seems to have been a much more active, ongoing part of people's lives.

We see this continuing connection of the goddess with the countryside in Caria also. An inscription from the city of Apollonia Salbake, near Aphrodisias, records the erection of a house for the Parthenoi, the Maidens, who attended the cult of Meter.[43]

37. *IGRRP* IV.117.
38. Zosimos 2.31.2.
39. Pliny the Younger, *Epistles* 10.49–50.
40. Becker Bertau 1986: 21, 29–30.
41. Note the material collected by Schwertheim 1978: 792–803, nos. I A1–14. Nos. 1, 2, 7, and 12 are inscribed with the word Μητρί; nos. 8 and 9 are dedicated to Angdistis; no. 10 mentions a metroac thiasos.
42. Schwertheim 1978: 792–99, nos. I A1, 2, 5, 9.
43. Originally published by Reinach 1908. For a further discussion of the text, see Robert 1937: 106–8, and 1954: 41–42.

The responsibility for the house's construction and maintenance is carefully spelled out: a body of men was to build the structure, roof it, decorate it in stucco, and paint it. The group is a rare one in ancient literature: they are the ὀροφυλακήσαντες, the guardians of the mountains, a type of local police force assigned to patrol this rugged mountainous area of Caria. The παραφύλαξ, the police chief, his company of the mounted patrol, and their slave attendants all joined in a subscription to support the building. The goddess honored is the Μήτηρ θεῶν ὀρεία ἐπήκοος θεά, the Mountain Mother of the gods, the goddess who listens. The text is a forceful statement of the strength of the Mountain Mother and her hold on the people of the countryside, to the point where even the local police force needed to respect and propitiate her.

The building to which the police contributed is interesting too; it is a Parthenon, a house of the virgins, here not for a virgin goddess, as in Athens, but rather for the virgin priestesses of the cult. The use of virgin priestesses to attend to a religious cult is fairly rare; other examples include virgin attendants on the cult of Meter in Kyzikos, and cults of Artemis in Magnesia and of Demeter in Hermione.[44] All are female divinities, and both Artemis and Demeter were deities of special concern to women, suggesting that the use of a Parthenon for Meter's attendants may be another instance of women's interest in the Mother Goddess. The Virgins' House also reinforces the evidence from Hellenistic Anatolia alluding to the concern for sexual chastity in the Meter cult.

The inland areas of Lydia, Phrygia, and Galatia present a somewhat different situation. Lydia had been an important center of the Mother Goddess's worship since the Archaic period, and the Lydians continued to be conscious of their special affinity with Meter. Numismatic evidence indicates that Meter was honored in virtually every major city in Lydia.[45] Two inscriptions from the first centuries B.C. and C.E., dedicated to Μητρὶ Λυδ[ίαι], the Lydian Mother, were found near Lake Gyges, near Sardis.[46] Votive images of Meter dating from the first centuries C.E. were also found at Sardis.[47] These follow the standard form of Meter votive, depicting the goddess seated on a throne with her lion and tympanum; while they are not very individualized, these votives do tell us that the cult of Meter was an ongoing part of the city's religious life.

During the Roman era, we find the first reference to the god Attis in Lydian cult practice. His cult presence at Sardis is attested through sculptural representations and inscriptions of the second century C.E. and later.[48] There is also an interesting

---

44. Reinach 1908. The cults noted range in date from the second century B.C. (Kyzikos) to the third century C.E. (Hermione in the Argolid).

45. Graillot 1912: 372.

46. Robert 1982.

47. Hanfmann and Ramage 1978: no. 256 (second or third century C.E.); no. 164 (third century C.E.).

48. Hanfmann 1983: 231.

series of Lydian reliefs from the Lydian site of Hamamli, depicting Attis shown as if lying under a pine tree. Dated to the late second or third century C.E., these reliefs illustrate a particular episode in the myth of Cybele and Attis, the death of Attis from self-castration.[49] This scene, closely following the literary version of the tale given by Ovid and others, is one of the few visual records of the myth, and may well reflect the imprint of Roman mythic tradition in Anatolia. The comparatively late date of these reliefs supports the suggestion made in chapter 8, that the myth as it survives in Graeco-Roman literary sources is not a traditional Anatolian tale of great antiquity. Taken together, the evidence for the cult of Attis in Lydia offers an interesting demonstration of the prestige of the Graeco-Roman definition of the Mother Goddess, outweighing the older Lydian cult forms.

In Phrygia, the Mother Goddess remained a strong presence in local religious practice during the Roman era. The mountainous area of central Phrygia, the site of the earlier Phrygian highland shrines, was now much less populated; people no longer needed to retreat to the hilltop settlements, the old Phrygian *kales,* for security, and so these were largely deserted. A sanctuary at one of these older Phrygian centers, the acropolis of Midas City, enjoyed a brief revival in the second and third centuries C.E. Its sacred usage is attested by a series of small inscribed round altars and plaques. These are dedicated to Angdistis, in several cases also called the Mother of the gods or the Mother Goddess.[50] The objects are all simple offerings, dedicated by private individuals in fulfillment of a vow. Votive offerings to Meter have also been found on other mountain summits in the region, including the Türkmen Baba, the high mountain overlooking Midas City.[51] Here, too, we see the Mother of the mountains honored in her ancestral home.

A Meter shrine of a very different type is found at the important sanctuary of Aizanoi, near Kotyaion (modern Kütahya). This site, in a fertile river valley, was settled in the early third century B.C.[52] While political control of the area passed back and forth between Pergamon and Bithynia, the settlement itself prospered and became an important center of commerce in the region. Aizanoi's success was due in part to its location near a major sanctuary of Zeus, which brought in considerable wealth to the region. This sanctuary was regularly under the patronage of either the Attalid kings of Pergamon or the Bithynian kings of Prusa, and the desire to control the sanctuary of Zeus seems to have been a major reason for the political contention over Aizanoi.[53] In the second century C.E., the sanctuary received its first temple, a pseudo-dipteral structure in the Ionic order, built near the city between 126 and 157

49. Karwiese 1968–71: figs. 2–3. Karwiese discusses several other representations of the prostrate Attis; most come from the western half of the Empire, and all are of the second century C.E. or later.
50. Haspels 1971: 188–89.
51. Ibid.: 199–200.
52. Strabo 12.8.12. For the history of Aizanoi, see R. Naumann 1979: 8–11, and Levick et al. 1988: xxxiv.
53. Levick et al. 1988: xxxiv.

(fig. 77).[54] The impressive remains of this temple, which still dominate the landscape today, indicate clearly that the site had more than local importance.[55]

The cult of Meter played a critical role in the Zeus sanctuary at Aizanoi. Local tradition recorded that Zeus's birth took place in the nearby Steunos cave, and Meter, long since identified with Rhea, was acknowledged as Zeus's mother.[56] Pausanias, our principal source for this tradition, states that the original settlers in Aizanoi came from Azania, in Arkadia.[57] While the aetiology connecting the Phrygian city with an eponymous Greek ancestor is fairly transparent, Pausanias is surely recording a common type of syncretism, through which Greek settlers in the area identified their Mother Goddess Rhea with the local Phrygian Mother Goddess. As a result, the Meter cult at Aizanoi was localized in the Steunos cave, and the goddess was worshipped there as Meter Steuene.

This cave, located some three kilometers from the temple at Aizanoi, has been carefully investigated.[58] The cult statue of the goddess that, according to Pausanias, stood in front of it is long since gone,[59] but finds of votive offerings confirm the cave's sacred function and indicate that it was in use as a sanctuary from the first century B.C. until the mid second century C.E.[60] The votives included pottery and terracotta figurines, among them several representations of the goddess with her lion and tympanum, and also figurines that depict the goddess holding an infant.

Other features of the cave sanctuary offer an interesting mix of traditional Phrygian and Hellenic cult fixtures, demonstrating that the Hellenic settlers were accommodating themselves to existing religious usage. At the entrance to the cave are several arched niches carved into the rock; these are now empty, but they were probably intended to contain votive offerings, such as small statuettes and reliefs. The form of these niches is very similar to that of the niches found at the Greek cities of Phokaia and Ephesos, but the practice of cutting votive niches into the live rock was an old one in Phrygia, found, among other places, at the nearby Phrygian settlements at Midas City and Findik.[61] Above the mouth of the cave is a steplike structure, carved into the natural rock, probably a stepped altar of the kind found at virtually every Phrygian shrine of Matar.[62] Its location, on the high point of the ridge above the cave, is characteristic of such Phrygian stepped altars. These would have

54. For the publication of the temple of Zeus, with earlier bibliography, see Weber 1969 and R. Naumann 1979.

55. Levick et al. 1988: xxxiv.

56. Pausanias 10.32.3.

57. Pausanias 8.4.3.

58. R. Naumann 1967 gives an account of the discovery and investigation of the cave sanctuary.

59. Pausanias 10.32.3.

60. R. Naumann 1967: 237–45.

61. Haspels 1971: fig. 32 (Midas City), figs. 227–29, 232 (Findik).

62. R. Naumann 1967: 228–31, discusses possible interpretations of the structure, and suggests that the structure may be a throne. Parallels for stepped altars can be found at Midas City (see Haspels 1971: figs. 25–31) and Findik (ibid.: figs. 230–31).

FIGURE 77. Temple of Zeus and Meter, Aizanoi. Second century C.E. Photograph by author.

been the places where offerings to the goddess were made, in her mountaintop home. As the finds from the Angdistis sanctuary at Midas City indicate, these stepped altars continued in use during the Hellenistic and Roman eras.

Equally interesting are two round structures on the ridge above the cave. These consist of blocks of drafted masonry lining circular shafts, one somewhat larger than the other, providing openings from the upper ridge into the cave ceiling. The excavator of the site, Rudolf Naumann, identified the larger of these shafts as a structure designed for a taurobolium, a bull sacrifice, and the smaller one as for a criobolium, the sacrifice of a ram,[63] but this seems very unlikely. Naumann assumed that these shafts would have been used in a form of the taurobolium as described by the Christian apologist Prudentius, during which a bull was placed on a wooden platform set above a subterranean pit and then stabbed slowly to death, so that the animal's blood ran down onto a person standing below.[64] Yet there is no evidence to indicate that this type of taurobolium was ever practiced in Anatolia, and no evidence that the stabbing sacrifice of a bull took place at all before the fourth century C.E., by

63. R. Naumann 1967: 239–41, followed by Levick et al. 1988: xxxiii. The diameters of the two shafts are 3.95 and 3.6 meters.

64. Prudentius, *Peristephanon* 10.1006–50, dating from the fourth century C.E.; see Vermaseren 1977: 101–7, for a dramatic account of the ritual.

FIGURE 78. Temple of Zeus and Meter.
Underground shrine to Meter, Aizanoi. Second
century C.E. Photograph by John Wagoner.

which time the cave of Meter Steuene had been abandoned.[65] The shafts above the
Aizanoi cave do, however, recall similar shafts found in Phrygian sanctuaries, often
located behind or near rock-cut niches in which cult statues of the deity were placed;
these occur widely at Phrygian highland sanctuaries, at the nearby sites of Midas
City, Findik, Deliklitaş, and at several sites in the Köhnüş Valley.[66] The shafts at the
older Phrygian sites were probably used as deposits for votive offerings to the goddess. It seems likely that the Aizanoi shafts, with their carefully laid out circular tun-
nels, served a similar function, particularly since they lie directly above the cave containing the main sanctuary of the goddess.

65. The ritual described by Prudentius was celebrated only in the Roman West, and was not practiced
before the fourth century C.E. The form of taurobolium sacrifice attested in epigraphical records from
Anatolia was a very different affair, more analogous to a bull-running contest. For a full discussion of the
ancient evidence on the taurobolium, see Rutter 1968 and Duthoy 1969; both works review the primary
data and note that the texts from Asia Minor that mention the taurobolium have no connection with the
cult of Meter.
66. Haspels 1971: 77, 82, 86.

The cave shrine of Meter Steuene ceased to be used at a comparatively early date, not because of lack of interest, but because the Meter sanctuary was removed in the second century C.E. to the temple of Zeus. Here the joint worship of these two divinities united the cult of the most important male deity with that of the powerful local female deity.[67] This temple contained two cellas. The main one, on ground level, was the sanctuary of Zeus; following the traditional plan of a Greek temple, it faced east and was entered through the pronaos. The second cella, the new sanctuary of Meter Steuene, consisted of a vaulted underground room, accessible by means of a flight of stairs from the opisthodomos of the Zeus sanctuary (fig. 78).[68] The underground chamber was surely intended to reproduce the atmosphere of the older Steunos cave shrine, a feat admirably accomplished by the fine masonry-vaulted room, whose excellent state of preservation enables us to experience the original cavelike space with light coming from small windows set in the foundation walls underneath the Zeus temple. The integration of the two cults is further demonstrated by an inscribed votive plaque dedicated to both Zeus and Meter: Διὶ καὶ Μητρὶ Θεῶν Στευηνῇ Ἀρτεμίδωρος Διονυσίου Αἰζανείτης ἱερεὺς κτίστης ἐκ τῶν ἰδίων (Artemidoros son of Dionysios of Aizanoi, priest and founder, [dedicated this] to Zeus and Meter Steuene, Mother of the gods, from his private funds).[69]

The combined cult of Meter Steuene and Zeus is further illustrated on a series of Aizanetan coins dating from the second and third centuries C.E., depicting Meter enthroned, holding the infant Zeus in her arms.[70] Often the Kouretes are shown as well, clashing their shields as they drown out the cries of the newborn god. Such images appear not only on the coins of Aizanoi, but also on those of other Phrygian cities, including Akmonia, Apameia, Laodicea, and Tralles. In some cases, the local river god, personifying the river Penkalas, is also shown holding an infant on his arm.[71] The intent seems to have been to combine the by now classic story of the birth of Zeus (traditionally located on Crete) with the Anatolian cult of Meter, fusing the cults of Hellenized and pre-Greek religious practice in Asia Minor.[72] We see this fusion fully realized in the architecture, epigraphy, and numismatics of the second century C.E., but the assimilation may well have started several centuries earlier. This is suggested by the earlier terracotta votives from the Steunos cave depict-

67. R. Naumann 1979: 65–67; Levick et al. 1988: xxxiv.

68. This follows a pattern found in other Anatolian temples containing double cults, in which the principal deity, a male, was worshipped in the main cella, and the secondary deity, a female, was worshipped in the opisthodomos. The closest parallels are furnished by the temple of Rome and Augustus in Ankara and the temple of Zeus Sosipolis and Tyche in Magnesia on the Meander. See Krencker and Schede 1936: 43, and Humann 1904: 152, 165; see also Akurgal 1978: 284–85 (Ankara), 180–83 (Magnesia), and Levick et al. 1988: xxxiv.

69. An inscription found in Gediz, Buresch 1898: 159 = Levick et al. 1988: xxxiii.

70. Robert 1981: 353–59, fig. 18.

71. Ibid.: 355–58.

72. The emperor Julian, writing in the fourth century C.E., expressed the same sentiment: "She is the one who bore and nourished the great Zeus" (Julian, *Oration* 5.166a).

ing Meter holding a young child; they may well represent the Mother of Zeus holding her divine son.

More than any other sanctuary of Meter during the first two centuries C.E., Aizanoi shows us the strength and long life of the cult of the Anatolian Mother, and its ability to accommodate itself to the changing political and religious realities of the Greek and Roman presence. It may even have caused the tradition of worshipping Meter in a cave to gain strength during the first two centuries C.E., a point suggested by the frequency of other dedications to Meter that identify her as the goddess of the cave.[73]

A different pattern of the Romanization of the Mother Goddess cult can be observed at Pessinous. In Roman Pessinous, Meter remained an independent deity, not formally allied with the cult of another deity. Despite the Roman claim that this was the oldest and most important Phrygian shrine of Meter, there is little evidence from Pessinous to suggest that the Meter sanctuary there was unusually illustrious, and the site appears to have owed its prominence largely to Pergamene support during the Hellenistic period and to the Pergamenes' need to deal with the local Galatian tribes, which controlled the area. The Romans inherited this history of troubled relations with the Galatians, finally organizing the region as the province of Galatia in 25 B.C.[74] During the first two centuries C.E., the city continued to serve as an important commercial center, although Strabo reports that in his time (the late first century B.C.), the city's prosperity was much reduced.[75]

To date archaeological investigations at Pessinous have failed to uncover the Meter sanctuary.[76] The most prestigious sanctuary known is that of the Imperial cult, prominently represented at the site with a large temple-theater complex.[77] Most of our information about the cult of Meter is provided by epigraphical data, including a group of inscriptions alluding to cult ritual. We learn about the existence of the Attabokaoi, a group responsible for conducting the mysteries of the goddess.[78] The group is otherwise unknown, although the use of the name Attas in their title probably refers to an association with the Pessinuntine priesthood and not to a divinity named Attis.

There is also a series of honorific inscriptions praising various individuals for their

---

73. Robert 1955: 110–13, publication of an altar from Roman Phrygia (exact provenience unknown) dedicated Μητρὶ ἀπὸ σπηλέου, the Mother from the cave; Petzl and Pleket 1979: 294–95, dedication to Meter carved on the rock at the mouth of a cave near Akçaalan, in Lydia. For other examples, see Robert 1955.

74. On the earlier history of Pessinous, see Devreker and Waelkens 1984: 13–18; Waelkens 1986: 38–39. For Roman campaigns against the Galatians in 189 B.C., see Livy 38.18.9–10; on Clodius's attempt to undermine Rome's Galatian ally Deiotarus in 58 B.C., see Cicero, *De harus. res.* 13.28.

75. Strabo 12.5.3; Mitchell 1993: II, 20–22.

76. Waelkens 1986: 37–39; Devreker and Vermeulen 1991: 109–10.

77. Waelkens 1986: 57 and passim. This temple, begun in the reign of Augustus and completed under Tiberius, is the building erroneously identified as the temple of Cybele in many plans and guidebooks.

78. Körte 1897: 38, no. 23, lines 20–22 = Devreker and Waelkens 1984: 221, no. 17; Körte 1900: 437–39, no. 63, line 7 = Devreker and Waelkens 1984: 221, no. 18.

involvement with the cult. One first-century C.E. inscription by an individual refer-ring to himself as Attis the priest, Ἄττις ἱερεὺς, indicates that the name Attis re-mained a priestly title.[79] Another pair of texts from the second century C.E. suggest that at this time, the priesthood of Pessinous was a form of public honor and pri-marily a perquisite of wealthy families. We hear of Tiberios Klaudios Heras, active in the religious life of the community, who was *archiereus*, chief priest, of Meter nine times, along with six terms of service as priest of the Imperial cult and one as high priest of the *koinon*, the community. His Romanized Galatian name suggests that he was part of the local Galatian hierarchy who had become Roman citizens, and as chief priest of Meter, he held the title of Attis, an honor that he shared with his son, Tiberios Klaudios Deiotaros, who also bore a distinguished Galatian name.[80] This clearly indicates that not all the Pessinuntine priests of Meter were eunuchs dedi-cated to life service of the goddess. The formulae used to praise these two men are fairly standard and do not imply that being an Attis, a chief priest of Meter, was an extraordinary step for a local citizen. In fact, we receive the opposite impression, that serving as priest of Meter was one of many public honors sought by prominent members of the community of Pessinous, and neither the only one nor necessarily the most distinguished one.[81] T. Klaudios Heras was also priest of Meter at nearby Midaeion, the site of another Meter sanctuary, known only through the presence of the goddess on the city's coins.[82]

At another Phrygian site, Dokimeion, near modern Afyon, the goddess is also richly attested on the city's coinage and on small altars that served as votive dedica-tions; here she was known by her local name of Angdistis.[83] Dokimeion was famous for its marble quarries, particularly for white marble enlivened with streaks of red. Roman legend recorded that this was caused by the blood of Attis washing through the stones,[84] a further indication that the Graeco-Roman mythic cycle of the death of Attis had influenced local Anatolian tradition.

In sum, the cult of Meter continued to thrive in Anatolia during the first centuries C.E. Virtually every community had its shrine of Meter, where the goddess was wor-shipped under her local epithet as the protector of individuals and their families and

79. Körte 1897: 38, no. 22; Devreker and Waelkens 1984: 24.
80. Körte 1897: 38, no. 23 = Devreker and Waelkens 1984: 221, no. 17; Körte 1900: 437–439, no. 63 = Devreker and Waelkens 1984: 221, no. 18. See also Devreker in Devreker and Waelkens 1984: 19–20.
81. On Attis as a priestly title in Pessinous, see chapter 8 above. Carcopino 1942: 158–67, argues that the existence of this father-son pair serving as Meter's priests in Pessinous reflects the more civilized tone introduced into the metroac cult during the reign of Claudius, implying that the Pessinuntine cult had rejected the practice of eunuchism under the civilizing influence of Rome. A more likely explanation, however, is that during the first two centuries C.E., the cult of Meter was one of the regular civic cults in the city (and perhaps less prestigious than the Imperial cult). For a private citizen to serve as a priest of Meter was a way of advertising one's status in society; it did not imply a condemnation, or even a comment on eunuchism, and indeed the evidence for eunuch priests at Pessinous during this period is very slim.
82. Körte 1897: 38–39.
83. Robert 1980: 236–40.
84. Statius, *Silvae* 1.5.37–38; 2.2.87–89. See Robert 1980: 235–36.

friends. The goddess was present in the urban centers of the region, but she was still most at home in her mountain and rural shrines. Her cult was rarely the most important in a given region; where a sanctuary of Meter was unusually prominent, it was often because of its association with a prestigious patron in the past (Aizanoi, Pessinous) or with another prestigious cult, such as that of Zeus (Pergamon, Aizanoi). The simple mountain shrines at Midas City and in Bithynia are probably typical of Meter shrines that lacked such patronage: unpretentious places where the local people came to pray for help in their troubles or to absolve themselves of their sins.

EPILOGUE

The Phrygian Mother Goddess did not fade away after the second century C.E. Quite the contrary; the cult of the Mother spread throughout the length and breadth of the world touched by ancient Mediterranean civilization, from Britain to Afghanistan. Nor did the goddess fade away from the Mediterranean heartland, for we find the Roman Magna Mater playing a vivid role in the political and religious life of the Empire in late antiquity. The strength of the Mother's cult in late antiquity, the revival of mysticism, and the growing prominence of Attis as an independent deity are all topics that will reward further examination.

It therefore seems inappropriate to offer a comprehensive discussion summarizing the meaning of the Mother Goddess in ancient Mediterranean life, since my narrative breaks off very much in the middle of the goddess's story. Rather, my goal has been to describe how the Mother developed from her provincial origins to a deity with a wide following throughout the Mediterranean world. A key part of this effort is a definition of what made the Phrygian Mother Goddess individual. The Phrygian Mother first appears to us as a product of the Anatolian landscape, and the qualities that made her distinctive, the power and awe communicated by a mountain environment and the ability to transcend boundaries between unstructured space and a highly structured human community, reflect part of the universal human experience. Not all of these qualities were transferred with the goddess to the Greek and Roman worlds, but her cult clearly had a form of staying power that enabled it to move beyond any strictly local manifestation.

Under certain circumstances, the Mother's power was used for specific regional and political purposes: she was part of the power structure of the Phrygian state and she contributed to the Romans' sense of self-definition as the people destined for victory. But her appeal went beyond any narrow political or ethnic definition and spoke to the human needs of many peoples of the ancient Mediterranean world. We receive only indirect hints about what those needs were; there is no ancient equivalent of a diary or confessional text enabling us to probe into the mind of an initiate into the Mother's mysteries. We can, however, see clearly that the response to the Mother's power was very real. Thus, even without carrying the chronological narrative forward to the end of Mediterranean antiquity, I hope to have shown how this deity, the product of a regionally limited culture and a populace that was rarely a major player in the power politics of ancient Mediterranean life, produced such a strong response in people and places that were not her own.

A study of the Mother Goddess's cult is also useful in offering another tool to examine the social world of Mediterranean antiquity. The varying reactions to the Mother among different Mediterranean groups, the peoples of ancient Anatolia, the Greeks, and the Romans, help illuminate many of the significant changes in Mediterranean society and also mark the constancies that shaped the lives of many of the people who lived there. Moreover, the cult of the Mother enables us to hear the voices of humble people as well as great, and rural communities as well as major urban centers. In communicating the changes and constancies found in the worship of the Mother Goddess, these voices remind us forcefully that religious practice was one of the most significant forces shaping people's lives.

BIBLIOGRAPHY

Aign, B. 1963. *Die Geschichte der Musikinstrumente des ägäischen Raumes bis um 700 vor Christus.* Frankfurt a/M.

Åkerström, Å. 1966. *Die architektonischen Terrakotten Kleinasiens.* Lund, Sweden.

Akurgal, E. 1949. *Späthethitische Bildkunst.* Ankara.

———. 1955. *Phrygische Kunst.* Ankara.

———. 1961. *Die Kunst Anatoliens von Homer bis Alexander.* Berlin.

———. 1962. *The Art of the Hittites.* New York.

———. 1978. *Ancient Civilizations and Ruins of Turkey, from Prehistoric Times until the End of the Roman Empire.* Translated by John Whybrow and Mollie Emre. Istanbul.

Albright, W. F. 1929. "The Anatolian Goddess Kubaba." *Archiv für Orientforschung* 5: 229–31.

Allen, R. E. 1983. *The Attalid Kingdom.* Oxford.

Arrigoni, G. 1984. "Cibele." In *Enciclopedia Virgiliana,* ed. U. Cozzoli, 2: 770–74. Rome.

Aurigemma, S. 1960. *Scavi di Spina.* Rome.

Austin, C. 1968. *Nova Fragmenta Euripidea in Papyris Reperta.* Berlin.

Austin, R. G. 1977. *P. Vergili Maronis Aeneidos Liber Sextus. Commentary.* Oxford.

Babritsa, A. 1973. "Ἀνασκαφὴ Μεσημβρίας Θράκης." *Praktika:* 70–82.

Bachofen, Johann Jakob. 1861. *Das Mutterrecht: Eine Untersuchung über die Gynaikokratie der alten Welt nach ihrer religiösen und rechtlichen Natur.* Stuttgart.

———. 1967. *Myth, Religion, and Mother Right: Selected Writings of J. J. Bachofen.* Translated from the German by Ralph Manheim. With a preface by George Boas and an introduction by Joseph Campbell. Princeton, N.J.

Bacon, H. 1961. *Barbarians in Greek Tragedy.* New Haven, Conn.

Bailey, C. 1932. *Phases in the Religion of Ancient Rome.* Berkeley and Los Angeles.

———. 1947. *Titi Lucreti Cari, De Rerum Natura, Libri Sex. Prolegomenon, Critical Apparatus, Translation, and Commentary.* Oxford.

Bammer, A. 1982. "Forschungen im Artemision von Ephesos vom 1976 bis 1981." *Anatolian Studies* 32: 61–87.

———. 1984. *Das Heiligtum der Artemis von Ephesos.* Graz.

———. 1985. "Neue weibliche Statuetten aus dem Artemision von Ephesos." *Jahresheft des österreichischen archäologischen Instituts* 56: 39–58.

Barnett, R. D. 1960. "Some Contacts between Greek and Oriental Religions." In *Éléments orientaux dans la religion grecque ancienne,* 143–53. Travaux du Centre d'Études supériores specialisé d'histoire des religions, Strasbourg. Paris.

Barton, S. C., and G. H. R. Horseley. 1981. "A Hellenistic Cult Group and New Testament Churches." *Jahrbuch für Antike und Christentum* 24: 7–41.

Baumeister, A. 1860. *Commentationen de Atye et Adrasto conscriptam.* Leipzig.

Bayet, J. 1957. *Histoire politique et psychologique de la religion romaine.* Paris.

Beard, M. 1994. "The Roman and the Foreign: The Cult of the 'Great Mother' in Imperial Rome." In *Shamanism, History, and the State,* ed. N. Thomas and C. Humphrey: 164–90. Ann Arbor, Mich.

Beare, W. 1950. *The Roman Stage.* London.

Becker Bertau, F. 1986. *Die Inschriften von Klaudiu Polis.* Bonn.

Bennet, E. L., and J.-P. Olivier. 1973. *The Pylos Tablets Transcribed.* Rome.

Beran, T. 1963. "Eine Kultstätte phrygischer Zeit in Boğazköy." *Mitteilungen der deutschen Orient-Gesellschaft* 94: 35–52.

——. 1967. *Die hethitische Glyptik von Boğazköy* I. Wissenschaftliche Veröffentlichung der deutschen Orient-Gesellschaft 76. Berlin.

Bérard, C., C. Bron, J.-L. Durand, F. Frontisi-Ducroux, F. Lissarague, A. Schnapp, and J.-P. Vernant. 1989. *A City of Images: Iconography and Society in Ancient Greece.* Translated by D. Lyons. Princeton, N.J. Originally published as *Une cité des images.* Lausanne, 1987.

Bergk, T. 1883. *Anthologia Lyrica.* Leipzig.

Bieber, M. 1968. *The Statue of Cybele in the J. Paul Getty Museum.* J. Paul Getty Museum Publication No. 3. Malibu, Calif.

Bittel, Kurt. 1963. "Phrygisches Kultbild aus Boğazköy." *Antike Plastik* 2: 7–21.

——. 1976a. *Die Hethiter.* Munich.

——. 1976b. *Beitrag zur Kenntnis hethitischer Bildkunst.* Sitzungsberichte der Heidelberger Akademie der Wissenschaften, phil.-hist. Klasse. Heidelberg.

——. 1981. "Kubaba. B. Ikonographie." In *Reallexikon der Assyriologie* 6: 261–64. Berlin.

Blegen, C. W., C. G. Boulter, J. L. Caskey, and M. Rawson. 1958. *Troy* [excavations conducted by the University of Cincinnati, 1932–38], vol. 4: *Settlements VIIa, VIIb, and VIII.* Princeton, N.J.

Bloch, R. 1966. *The Origins of Rome.* New York.

Blümel, C. 1964. *Die archaisch griechischen Skulpturen der staatlichen Museen zu Berlin.* Berlin.

Blümel, W. 1985. *Die Inschriften von Iasos.* Bonn.

Boardman, J. 1959. "Chian and Early Ionic Architecture." *Antiquaries Journal* 39: 170–218.

——. 1970. "Pyramidal Stamp Seals in the Persian Empire." *Iran* 8: 19–44.

——. 1978. *Greek Sculpture: The Archaic Period.* Oxford.

Bodnar, E. W. 1973. "A Quarry Relief on the Island of Paros." *Archaeology* 26: 270–77.

Boegehold, A. L. 1972. "The Establishment of a Central Archive at Athens." *American Journal of Archaeology* 76: 23–30.

Boehmer, R. M. 1972. *Die Kleinfunde von Boğazköy: Aus den Grabungskampagnen 1931–1939 und 1952–1969.* Wissenschaftliche Veröffentlichung der Deutschen Orient-Gesellschaft, Boğazköy-Hattusas 7. Berlin.

——. 1973. "Phrygische Prunkgewänder des achten Jahrhunderts." *Archäologischer Anzeiger* 2: 149–72.

Boersma, J. S. 1970. *Athenian Building Policy from 561/0 to 405/4 B.C.* Groningen.

Boëthius, A. 1978. *Etruscan and Early Roman Architecture.* Harmondsworth, Eng.

Bolton, J. D. P. 1962. *Aristeas of Proconnesus.* Oxford.

Bömer, F. 1957–58. *P. Ovidius Naso: Die Fasten.* Translation and Commentary. Heidelberg.

———. 1963. *Untersuchungen über die Religion der Sklaven in Griechenland und Rom.* Vol. 4. Mainz.

———. 1964. "Kybele in Rom: Die Geschichte ihres Kults als politisches Phänomen." *Römische Mitteilungen* 71: 130–54.

Borgeaud, P. 1988a. *The Cult of Pan in Ancient Greece.* Translated by K. Atlass and J. Redfield. Chicago. Originally published as *Recherches sur le dieu Pan.* Rome, 1979.

———. 1988b. "L'écriture d'Attis: Le récit dans l'histoire." In *Métamorphoses du myth en Grèce antique,* ed. C. Calame: 87–104. Geneva.

———. 1996. *La Mère des dieux: De Cybèle à la Vierge Marie.* Paris.

Bosanquet, R. C. 1939. "Dicte and the Temples of Dictaean Zeus." *Annual of the British School at Athens* 40: 60–77.

Boyancé, P. 1954. "Cybèle aux Mégalésies." *Latomus* 13: 337–42.

Bremer, J. 1979. "The Legend of Cybele's Arrival in Rome." *Studies in Hellenistic Religions,* ed. M. J. Vermaseren: 9–22. Leiden.

———. 1984. "Greek Maenadism Reconsidered." *Zeitschrift für Papyrologie und Epigraphik* 55: 267–86.

Brinkmann, V. 1985. "Namenbeischriften an Friesen des Siphnierschatzhauses." *Bulletin de Correspondance Hellénique* 109: 77–130.

Brixhe, C. 1979. "Le nom de Cybèle." *Die Sprache* 25: 40–45.

———. 1982. "Palatalisations en grec et en phrygien." *Bulletin de la société linguistique de Paris* 77: 209–49.

Brixhe, C., and T. Drew-Bear. 1982. "Trois nouvelles inscriptions paléo-phrygiennes." *Kadmos* 21: 64–87.

Brixhe, C., and M. Lejeune. 1984. *Corpus des inscriptions paléo-phrygiennes.* Paris.

Brommer, F. 1949–50. *Pan im 5. und 4. Jahrhundert v. Chr.* Marburger Jahrbuch für Kunstwissenschaft 15. Marburg.

Broughton, T. R. S. 1953–54. "Notes on Roman Magistrates: Marius and the Magna Mater." *Historia* 2: 209–13.

Brown, P. 1988. *The Body and Society: Men, Women, and Sexual Renunciation in Early Christianity.* New York.

Buluç, S. 1988. "The Architectural Use of the Animal and Kybele Reliefs Found in Ankara and Its Vicinity." *Source* 7: 16–23.

Buresch, K. 1898. *Aus Lydien: Epigraphische-geographische Reisefrüchte.* Leipzig.

Burkert, W. 1979a. *Structure and History in Greek Mythology and Ritual.* Berkeley and Los Angeles.

———. 1979b. "Von Ullikummi zum Kaukasus: Die Felsgeburt des Unholds." *Würzburger Jahrbücher für die Altertumswissenschaft* 5: 253–61.

———. 1983a. *Homo Necans.* Translated by Peter Bing. Berkeley and Los Angeles. Original German edition, Berlin, 1972.

———. 1983b. "Tradition in Greek Religion." In *The Greek Renaissance of the Eighth Century B.C.: Tradition and Innovation,* ed. R. Hägg: 85–89. Stockholm.

———. 1985. *Greek Religion.* Translated by J. Raffan. Cambridge, Mass. Originally published as *Griechische Religion der archaischen und klassischen Epoche.* Stuttgart, 1977.

Burnett, A. P. 1970. "Pentheus and Dionysus: Host and Guest." *Classical Philology* 65: 15–29.

Burney, C. 1957. "Urartian Fortresses and Towns in the Van Region." *Anatolian Studies* 7: 37–53.

Burr, D. 1934. *Terracottas from Myrina in the Museum of Fine Arts, Boston*. Vienna.

Cahn, H. 1950. "Die Löwen des Apollon." *Museum Helveticum* 7: 185–99.

Canciani, F. 1970. *Bronzi orientali e orientalizzanti a Creta nell'VIII e VII secoli A.C.* Rome.

Carcopino, J. 1942. "La réforme romaine du culte de Cybèle et d'Attis." In *Aspects mystiques de la Rome païenne*: 149–71. Paris.

Carpenter, T. H. 1991. *Art and Myth in Ancient Greece*. New York.

Cèbe, J.-P., ed. 1977. *Varron: Satires ménippées*. Translated and edited, with commentary. Vol. 9. Collection de l'École française de Rome. Rome.

Cerri, G. 1983. "La madre degli dei nell'*Elena* di Euripide: Tragedia e rituale." *Quaderni di storia* 18: 155–95.

Chadwick, H. 1959. *The Sentences of Sextus: A Contribution to the History of Early Christian Ethics*. Cambridge.

Charitonidis, S. 1954. "Recherches dans le quartier est d'Argos." *Bulletin de Correspondance Hellénique* 78: 410–26.

Christou, C. 1968. *Potnia Theron: Eine Untersuchung über Ursprung, Erscheinungsformen und Wandlungen der Gestalt einer Gottheit*. Thessaloníki.

Çilingiroğlu, A., and D. H. French, eds. 1994. *Anatolian Iron Ages 3: The Proceedings of the Third Anatolian Iron Ages Colloquium Held at Van, Turkey, 6–12 August 1990 (= Anadolu Demir Çağlari 3: III Anadolu Demir Çağlari Sempozyumu Bildirileri Van, 6–12 Ağustos 1990)*. British Institute of Archaeology at Ankara monograph 16. London.

Clairmont, C. W. 1970. *Gravestone and Epigram: Greek Memorials from the Archaic and Classical Period*. Mainz.

Coarelli, F. 1977. "Public Building in Rome between the Second Punic War and Sulla." *Papers of the British School at Rome* 45: 1–23.

———. 1982. "I monumenti dei culti orientali in Roma." In *La soteriologia dei culti orientali nell'Impero Romano*, ed. U. Bianchi and M. J. Vermaseren: 33–67. Leiden.

Cole, Susan Guettel. 1984. *Theoi Megaloi: The Cult of the Great Gods at Samothrace*. Leiden.

Connor, W. R. 1988. "Seized by the Nymphs: Nympholepsy and Symbolic Expression in Classical Greece." *Classical Antiquity* 7: 155–89.

Conze, A. 1880. "Hermes-Kadmilos." *Archäologische Zeitung* 38: 1–10.

———. 1881. "Zur Jahrgang XXXVIII." *Archäologische Zeitung* 39: 59.

———. 1888. "Hermes-Kadmilos." *Athenische Mitteilungen* 13: 202–6.

———. 1891. "Hermes-Kadmilos." *Athenische Mitteilungen* 16: 191–93.

Conze, A., and P. Schazmann. 1911. *Mamurt Kaleh: Ein Tempel der Göttermutter unweit Pergamon*. Jahrbuch des deutschen archäologischen Instituts, suppl. 9. Berlin.

Cook, B. F. 1966. "The Goddess Cybele: A Bronze in New York." *Archaeology* 19: 251–57.

Corsten, T. 1991. *Die Inschriften von Prusa ad Olympum*. Bonn.

Cosi, D. M. 1980–81. "L'ingresso di Cibele ad Atene e a Roma." *Atti del centro ricerche e documentazione sull'antichità classica* 11: 81–91.

Cox, C. W. M., and A. Cameron. 1937. *MAMA*, vol. 5. Manchester.

Crawford, N. 1974. *Roman Republican Coinage*. Cambridge.

Crossland, R. A. 1982. "Linguistic Problems of the Balkan Area in Late Prehistoric and Early Classical Periods." In *Cambridge Ancient History*, 2d ed., ed. J. Boardman, I. E. S. Edwards, N. G. L. Hammond, and E. Sollberger, 3.1: 834–849. Cambridge.

Cumont, F. 1896. "Attis." In *RE* 2, pt. 2: 2247–52.

———. 1906. "L'Asie mineure." In *Les religions orientales dans le paganisme romaine: Conférences faites au collège de France en 1905*: 43–68. Paris. 4th ed., 1929, reprinted 1963.

———. 1910. "Gallos." In *RE* 7, pt. 1: 674–82.

Deighton, H. 1982. *The "Weather-God" in Hittite Anatolia: An Examination of the Archaeological and Textual Sources.* British Archaeological Reports, International Series, 143. Oxford.

Delcourt, M. 1961. *Hermaphrodite: Myths and Rites of the Bisexual Figure in Classical Antiquity.* Translated from the French by J. Nicholson. London. Original ed., Paris, 1956.

Despines, G. I. 1971. Συμβολὴ στὴ μελετὴ τοῦ ἐργοῦ τοῦ Ἀγορακρίτου. Athens.

Devreker, J., and F. Vermeulen. 1991. "Phrygians in the Neighbourhood of Pessinous (Turkey)." In *Liber Amicorum Jacques A. E. Nenquin Studia Archaeologica*: 109–17. Brugge.

Devreker, J., and M. Waelkens. 1984. *Les fouilles de la Rijksuniversiteit te Gent a Pessinonte, 1967–1973.* Vol. 1. Brugge.

DeVries, K. 1980. "Greeks and Phrygians in the Early Iron Age." In *From Athens to Gordion: The Papers of a Memorial Symposium for Rodney S. Young.* University Museum Papers, University of Pennsylvania, 1: 33–49. Philadelphia.

———. 1988. "Gordion and Phrygia in the Sixth Century B.C." *Source* 7: 51–59.

———. 1990. "The Gordion Excavation Seasons of 1969–1973 and Subsequent Research." *American Journal of Archaeology* 94: 371–406.

———. 1998. "The Assyrian Destruction of Gordion?" *American Journal of Archaeology* 102: 397.

Dodds, E. R. 1951. *The Greeks and the Irrational.* Berkeley and Los Angeles.

———, ed. 1960. *Euripides' Bacchae.* Oxford.

Drew-Bear, T. 1978. *Nouvelles inscriptions de Phrygie.* Zutphen, Netherlands.

Drexler, W. 1894–97. "Meter." In *Lexikon der griechischen und römischen Mythologie,* ed. W. H. Roscher, 2, pt. 2: 2848–2931. Leipzig.

Dumézil, G. 1970. *Archaic Roman Religion.* Translated by P. Knapp. Chicago.

Dunant, C. 1978. "Sus aux voleurs! Une tablette en bronze à inscription grecque du Musée de Genève." *Museum Helveticum* 35: 241–44.

Dupont-Sommer, A., and L. Robert. 1964. *La Déesse de Hiérapolis-Castabala (Cilicie).* Paris.

Duthoy, R. 1969. *The Taurobolium: Its Evolution and Terminology.* Leiden.

Ehrenburg, M. 1989. *Women in Prehistory.* London.

Elder, J. P. 1947. "Catullus' 'Attis.'" *American Journal of Philology* 68: 394–403.

Engelmann, H., and R. Merkelbach. 1973. *Die Inschriften von Erythrai und Klazomenai.* Vol. 2. Bonn.

Fasce, S. 1978. *Attis e il culto metroaco a Roma.* Genoa.

Ferguson, J. 1988. *Catullus.* Greece & Rome: New Surveys in the Classics 20. Oxford.

Ferguson, W. S. 1944. "The Attic Orgeones." *Harvard Theological Review* 37: 62–144.

Fleischer, R. 1973. *Artemis von Ephesos und verwandte Kultstatuen aus Anatolien und Syrien.* Leiden.

Forrest, W. G. 1963. "Inscriptions of SE Chios I." *Annual of the British School at Athens* 58: 53–67.

Foucart, P. 1873. *Des associations religieuses chez les grecs.* Paris.

Francis, E. D. 1990. "The Mother, the Demos, and the Demosion." In *Image and Idea in Fifth-Century Greece: Art and Literature after the Persian Wars,* ed. Michael Vickers: 112–20. London and New York.

Fränkel, M. 1890–95. *Die Inschriften von Pergamon.* Vols. 1–2. Königliche Museen zu Berlin, Altertümer von Pergamon 8. Berlin.

Frankfort, H. 1958. "The Archetype in Analytical Psychology and the History of Religion." *Journal of the Warburg and Courtauld Institutes* 21: 166–78.

Frappicini, N. 1987. "L'arrivo di Cibele in Attica." *Parola del passato* 42: 12–26.

Frazer, J. G. 1906. *Attis, Adonis, and Osiris.* Studies in the History of Oriental Religion. London.

Freyer-Schauenburg, B. 1974. *Bildwerke der archaischen Zeit und des strengen Stils.* Samos 11. Bonn.

Friedrich, J. 1932. *Kleinasiatische Sprachdenkmäler.* Berlin.

———. 1941. "Phrygia." In *RE* 20, pt. 1: 781–891.

Froehner, W. 1897. *Catalogue des antiquités grecques et romaines du Musée de Marseilles.* Paris.

Gabriel, A. 1952. *La Cité de Midas: Topographie, Le site et les fouilles.* Vol. 2 of *Phrygie: Exploration archéologique.* Paris.

———. 1965. *La Cité de Midas: Architecture.* Vol. 4 of *Phrygie: Exploration archéologique.* Paris.

Galinsky, G. K. 1969. *Aeneas, Sicily, and Rome.* Princeton, N.J.

Gallini, C. 1962. "Politica religiosa di Clodio." *Studi e materiali di storia delle religioni* 33: 257–72.

Garland, R. 1987. *The Piraeus from the Fifth to the First Century B.C.* London.

———. 1992. *Introducing New Gods: The Politics of Athenian Religion.* Ithaca, N.Y.

Gauthier, P. 1989. *Nouvelles inscriptions de Sardes.* Vol. 2. Geneva.

Gentili, G. V. 1959. *La Villa Erculia di Piazza Armerina.* Rome.

Gérard, J. 1980. "Légende et politique autour de la Mère des Dieux." *Revue des Études Latines* 58: 153–75.

Gérard-Rousseau, M. 1968. *Les mentions religieuses dans les tablettes mycéniennes.* Rome.

Gimbutas, M. 1982. *The Goddesses and Gods of Old Europe.* Berkeley and Los Angeles.

———. 1989. *The Language of the Goddess.* San Francisco.

Glendinning, M. 1996a. "Phrygian Architectural Terracottas at Gordion." Ph.D. diss., University of North Carolina, Chapel Hill.

———. 1996b. "A Mid-Sixth-Century Tile Roof System at Gordion." *Hesperia* 65: 99–119.

Gow, A. S. F. 1960. "The Gallus and the Lion." *Journal of Hellenic Studies* 80: 88–93.

Gow, A. S. F., and D. L. Page. 1965. *The Greek Anthology: Hellenistic Epigrams.* 2 vols. Cambridge.

———, eds. 1968. *The Greek Anthology: The Garland of Philip and Some Contemporary Epigrams.* Cambridge.

Graeve, V. von. 1986a. "Über verschiedene Richtungen der milesischen Skulptur in archaischer Zeit." In *Istanbuler Mitteilungen,* suppl. 31, *Milet, 1899–1980: Ergebnisse, Probleme und Perspektiven einer Ausgrabung,* ed. W. Müller-Wiener: 81–94. Tübingen.

———. 1986b. "Milet 1985." *Istanbuler Mitteilungen* 36: 43–47.

———. 1986c. "Neue archaische Skulpturenfunde aus Milet." In *Archaische und klassische griechische Plastik,* ed. H. Kyrieleis, 21–29. Mainz.

Graf, F. 1974. *Eleusis und die orphische Dichtung Athens in vorhellenistischer Zeit.* Berlin.

———. 1984. "The Arrival of Cybele in the Greek East." In *Proceedings of the VIIth Congress of the International Federation of the Societies of Classical Studies,* ed. J. Harmatta, 1: 117–20. Budapest.

———. 1985. *Nordionische Kulte: Religionsgeschichtliche und epigraphische Untersuchungen zu den Kulten von Chios, Erythrai, Klazomenai und Phokaia.* Bibliotheca Helvetica Romana, 21. Vevey.

Graham, A. J. 1971. "Patterns in Early Greek Colonization." *Journal of Hellenic Studies* 91: 35–47.

Graillot, H. 1912. *Le culte de Cybèle, mère des dieux, à Rome et dans l'empire romaine.* Paris.

Graves, R. 1948. *The White Goddess: A Historical Grammar of Poetic Myth.* New York.

Grenfell, B. P., and A. S. Hunt. 1906. *Hibeh Papyri.* Vol. 1. London and Oxford.

Gruen, E. S. 1990. "The Advent of the Magna Mater." In id., *Studies in Greek Culture and Roman Policy*: 5–33. Leiden and New York.

———. 1992. *Culture and National Identity in Republican Rome.* Ithaca, N.Y.

Guarducci, M. 1970. "Cibele in un'epigrafe arcaica di Locri Epizefirî." *Klio* 52: 133–38.

———. 1971. "Enea e Vesta." *Römische Mitteilungen* 78: 73–118.

Gusmani, R. 1959. "Agdistis." *Parola del passato* 66: 202–11.

———. 1971. "Le religioni dell'Asia Minore nel primo millennio A.C." *Storia delle religioni* (Turin): 295–341.

———. 1975. *Neue epichorische Schriftzeugnisse aus Sardis.* Vol. 3 of *Archaeological Exploration of Sardis.* Cambridge.

Güterbock, H. 1940. *Siegel aus Boğazköy, I: Die Königssiegel der Grabungen bis 1938.* Archiv für Orientforschung, suppl. 5. Berlin.

———. 1942. *Siegel aus Boğazköy, II: Die Königssiegel von 1939 und die übrigen Hieroglyphensiegel.* Archiv für Orientforschung, suppl. 7. Berlin.

———. 1946. *Ankara Bedesteninde bulunan Eti Müzesi Büyük Salonunun Kilavuzu.* Istanbul.

———. 1952. *The Song of Ullikummi: Revised Text of the Hittite Version of a Hurrian Myth.* New Haven, Conn.

———. 1954. "Carchemish." *Journal of Near Eastern Studies* 13: 102–14.

———. 1974. "Kleine Beiträge zum Verständis der Ankara-Reliefs." *Bagdader Mitteilungen* 7: 97–99.

Güterbock, H., and R. L. Alexander. 1983. "The Second Inscription on Mount Sipylos." *Anatolian Studies* 33: 29–33.

Habicht, C. 1980. "Bemerkungen zum P. Haun. 6." *Zeitschrift für Papyrologie und Epigraphik* 39: 1–5.

Haldane, J. A. 1968. "Pindar and Pan: Frs. 95–100 Snell." *Phoenix* 22: 18–31.

Hall, E. 1988. "When Did the Trojans Turn into Phrygians?" *Zeitschrift für Papyrologie und Epigraphik* 73: 15–18.

———. 1989. *Inventing the Barbarian: Greek Self-Definition Through Tragedy.* Oxford.

Hamilton, N. 1996. "Figurines, Clay Balls, Small Finds and Burials." In Hodder 1996: 215–63.

Hanfmann, G. M. A. 1961. "The Third Campaign at Sardis (1960)." *Bulletin of the American Schools of Oriental Research* 162: 8–49.

———. 1964. "The Sixth Campaign at Sardis (1963)." *Bulletin of the American Schools of Oriental Research* 174: 3–58.

———. 1983. "On the Gods of Lydian Sardis." In *Beiträge zur Altertumskunde Kleinasiens*, 219–31. Mainz.

Hanfmann, G. M. A., W. E. Mierse, C. Foss, et al. 1983. *Sardis from Prehistoric to Roman Times: Results of the Archaeological Exploration of Sardis, 1958–1975.* Cambridge, Mass.

Hanfmann, G. M. A., and N. H. Ramage. 1978. *Sculpture from Sardis: The Finds through 1975.* Cambridge, Mass.

Hanfmann, G. M. A., and J. C. Waldbaum. 1969. "Kybebe and Artemis: Two Anatolian Goddesses at Sardis." *Archaeology* 22: 264–69.

Hansen, E. V. 1971. *The Attalids of Pergamon.* Ithaca, N.Y.

Hanson, J. A. 1959. *Roman Theater Temples.* Princeton, N.J.

Hartog, F. 1988. *The Mirror of Herodotos: The Representation of the Other in the Writing of History.* Translated by Janet Lloyd. Berkeley and Los Angeles. Original French edition, 1980.

Hasluck, F. W. 1910. *Cyzicus.* Cambridge.

Haspels, C. H. E. 1951. *La Cité de Midas: Céramique et trouvailles diverses.* Vol. 3 of *Phrygie: Exploration archéologique.* Paris.

———. 1971. *The Highlands of Phrygia.* Princeton, N.J.

Havelock, C. 1981. *Hellenistic Art.* New York.

Hawkes, J. 1968. *Dawn of the Gods.* New York.

Hawkins, J. D. 1972. "Building Inscriptions of Carchemish." *Anatolian Studies* 22: 87–114.

———. 1981a. "Kubaba. A. Philologisch." *Reallexikon der Assyriologie* 6: 257–61.

———. 1981b. "Kubaba at Karkamis and Elsewhere." *Anatolian Studies* 31: 147–76.

———. 1982. "The Neo-Hittite States in Syria and Anatolia." *Cambridge Ancient History,* 2d ed., ed. J. Boardman, I. E. S. Edwards, N. G. L. Hammond, and E. Sollberger, 3.1: 372–441. Cambridge.

Helbig, W. 1912. *Führer durch die öffentlichen Sammlungen klassischer Altertümer in Rom.* 2 vols. Leipzig.

Hemberg, B. 1952. "Die Idaiischen Daktylen." *Eranos* 50: 41–59.

Henrichs, A. 1972. "Towards a New Edition of Philodemus' *On Piety.*" *Greek, Roman, and Byzantine Studies* 13: 67–98.

———. 1976. "Despoina Kybele: Ein Beitrag zur religiösen Namenkunde." *Harvard Studies in Classical Philology* 80: 253–86.

———. 1978. "Greek Menadism from Olympias to Messalina." *Harvard Studies in Classical Philology* 82: 121–60.

Hepding, H. 1903. *Attis: Seine Mythen und sein Kult.* Giessen.

Herdt, G., ed. 1994. *Third Sex, Third Gender: Beyond Sexual Dimorphism in Culture and History.* New York.

Hitzl, K. 1991. *Die Kaiserzeitliche Statuenausstattung des Metroons.* Olympische Forschungen 19. Berlin and New York.

Hodder, I., ed. 1996. *On the Surface: Çatalhöyük, 1993–95.* British Institute of Archaeology at Ankara Monograph 22. Cambridge.

Holoka, J. P. 1985. *Gaius Valerius Catullus: A Systematic Bibliography.* New York and Los Angeles.

Hopkins, K. 1978. *Conquerors and Slaves.* Sociological Studies in Roman History, 1. Cambridge.

Horn, R. 1972. *Hellenistische Bildwerke auf Samos.* Samos 12. Bonn.

Hug, [A?]. 1918. "Eunuchen." In *RE,* suppl. 3: 449–55.

Humann, C. 1904. *Magnesia am Mäander.* Berlin.

Huxley, G. L. 1959. "Titles of Midas." *Greek, Roman, and Byzantine Studies* 2: 85–99.

Ihnken, T. 1978. *Die Inschriften von Magnesia am Sipylos.* Bonn.

Işik, C. 1986. "Neue Beobachtungen zur Darstellung von Kultszenen auf urartäischen Rollstempelsiegeln." *Jahrbuch des deutschen archäologischen Instituts* 101: 1–22.

Işik, F. 1987. "Zur Entstehung phrygischer Felsdenkmäler." *Anatolian Studies* 37: 163–78.

———. 1989. "Die Entstehung der frühen Kybelebilder Phrygiens und ihre Einwirkung auf die ionische Plastik." *Jahresheft des österreichischen archäologischen Instituts* 57, suppl. 7: 40–107.

Jacoby, F. 1926–1958. *Fragmente der griechischen Historiker.* Berlin.

James, E. O. 1959. *The Cult of the Mother-Goddess: An Archaeological and Documentary Study.* New York.

Janko, R. 1982. *Homer, Hesiod and the Hymns.* Cambridge.

Jeanmaire, H. 1939. *Couroi et Couretes: Essai sur l'education spartiate et sur les rites d'adolescence dans l'antiquité hellénique.* Lille. Reprint, New York 1975.

Jessen, [?]. 1903. "Dindymene." In *RE* 5, pt. 1: 651–52.

Jung, C. G. 1969. "Psychological Aspects of the Mother Archetype" [1938]. In *Four Archetypes: Mother, Rebirth, Spirit, Trickster,* trans. from the German by R. F. C. Hull. Princeton, N.J.

Junge, P. J. 1940. "Hazarapatis." *Klio* 33: 13–38.

Kabbani, R. 1986. *Europe's Myths of Orient.* Bloomington, Ind.

Kannicht, R. 1969. *Euripides' Helena. Text und Kommentar.* Heidelberg.

Kannicht, R., and B. Snell. 1981. *Tragicorum Graecorum Fragmenta.* Vol. 2. Göttingen.

Karwiese, S. 1968–71. "Der tote Attis." *Jahresheft des österreichischen archäologischen Instituts* 49: 50–62.

Keil J. 1915. "Denkmäler des Meter Kultes." *Jahresheft des österreichischen archäologischen Instituts* 18: 66–78.

———. 1926. "Vorläufiger Bericht über die Ausgrabungen in Ephesos." *Jahresheft des österreichischen archäologischen Instituts* 23: 247–99.

Kekulé von Stradonitz, R. 1922. *Die griechische Skulptur.* Berlin and Leipzig.

Kern, O. 1926–38. *Die Religion der Griechen.* Vols. 1–3. Berlin.

Keuls, E. C. 1984. "Male-Female Interaction in Fifth-Century Dionysiac Ritual as Shown in Attic Vase Painting." *Zeitschrift für Papyrologie und Epigraphik* 55: 287–97.

Kindstrand, J. F. 1981. *Anacharsis: The Legend and the Apophthegmata.* Uppsala.

Kirk, G. S., and J. E. Raven. 1963. *The Presocratic Philosophers.* Cambridge.

Knibbe, G. 1978. "Die 'anderen' ephesischen Götter." In *Studien zur Religion und Kultur Kleinasiens: Festschrift für Friedrich Karl Dörner,* ed. S. Şahin, E. Schwertheim, and J. Wagner: 489–503. Leiden.

Kohler, E. 1995. *Gordion Excavations Final Reports* II: *The Lesser Phrygian Tumuli.* Part 1. *The Inhumations. Gordion Excavations 1950–1973.* University of Pennsylvania, University Museum Monograph 88. Philadelphia.

Körte, A. 1897. "Kleinasiatische Studien II." *Athenische Mitteilungen* 22: 1–51.

———. 1898. "Kleinasiatische Studien III." *Athenische Mitteilungen* 23: 80–153.

———. 1900. "Kleinasiatische Studien VI." *Athenische Mitteilungen* 25: 398–444.

Körte, A., and G. Körte. 1904. *Gordion: Ergebnisse der Ausgrabung im Jahre 1900.* Jahrbuch des kaiserlichen deutschen archäologischen Instituts, suppl. 5. Berlin.

Köves, T. 1963. "Zur Empfang der Magna Mater in Rom." *Historia* 12: 321–47.

Kraay, C. 1976. *Archaic and Classical Greek Coins.* Berkeley and Los Angeles.

Krencker, D., and M. Schede. 1936. *Der Tempel in Ankara.* Berlin and Leipzig.

Kunze, E. 1931. *Altkretische Bronzereliefs.* Stuttgart.

La Genière, J. de. 1985. "De la Phrygie à Locres Épizéphyrienne: Les chemins de Cybèle." *Mélanges de l'École française de Rome. Antiquité* 97: 693–717.

———. 1986. "Le culte de la mère des dieux dans le Péloponnèse." *Comptes rendus de l'Académie des Inscriptions et Belles-Lettres:* 29–46.

———. 1993. "Statuaire archaïque de la Mère des dieux en Arcadie et en Laconie." In *Sculpture from Arcadia and Laconia,* ed. O. Palagia and W. Coulson: 153–58. Oxford.

Lambrechts, P. 1951. "Cybèle, divinité étrangère ou nationale?" *Bulletin de la Société royale belge d'Anthropologie et de Préhistoire* 62: 44–60.

———. 1952. "Les fêtes 'phrygiennes' de Cybèle et d'Attis." *Bulletin de l'Institute historique belge de Rome* 27: 141–70.

———. 1962. *Attis: Van Herdersknaap tot God.* Brussels.

Lane, E. 1988. "Παστός." *Glotta* 66: 100–123.

———. 1996. "The Name of Cybele's Priests the 'Galloi.'" *CARC:* 117–33.

Lane Fox, R. 1986. *Pagans and Christians.* New York. Reprint, San Francisco, 1995.

Langlotz, E. 1966. *Die kulturelle und künstlerische Hellenisierung der Küsten des Mittelmeers durch die Stadt Phokaia.* Arbeitsgemeinschaft für Forschung des Landes Nordrhein-Westfalen 130. Cologne and Opladen, Leverkusen, Germany.

———. 1969. "Beobachtungen in Phokaia." *Archäologischer Anzeiger* 84: 377–85.

Laroche, E. 1960. "Koubaba, déesse anatolienne, et le problème des origines de Cybèle." In *Éléments orientaux dans la religion grecque ancienne,* 113–28. Travaux du Centre d'Études supériores specialisé d'histoire des religions, Strasbourg. Paris.

Latte, K. 1920. *Heiliges Recht: Untersuchungen zur Geschichte der sakralen Rechtsformen in Griechenland.* Tübingen. Reprint, Darmstadt, 1964.

———. 1960. *Römische Religionsgeschichte.* Handbuch der Altertumswissenschaft 5.4. Munich.

Laum, B. 1914. *Stiftungen in der griechischen und römischen Antike.* Leipzig.

Laumonier, A. 1956. *Exploration archéologique de Délos,* vol. 23: *Les figurines terre-cuites.* Paris.

Lawler, L. B. 1964. *The Dance in Ancient Greece.* London.

Lejeune, M. 1969a. "Discussions sur l'alphabet phrygien." *Studi micenei ed egeo-anatolici* 10: 19–47.

———. 1969b. "Notes paléo-phrygiennes." *Revue des Études anciennes* 71: 287–300.

———. 1970. "Les inscriptions de Gordion et l'alphabet phrygien." *Kadmos* 9: 51–74.

———. 1979. "Regards sur les sonores i.-e. en vieux phrygien." In *Florilegium Anatolicum: Mélanges offerts à Emmanuel Laroche:* 219–24. Paris.

Levick, B., S. Mitchell, J. Potter, and M. Waelkens. 1988. *Monuments from the Aezanitis. MAMA,* vol. 9. Gloucester.

Lewis, I. M. 1989. *Ecstatic Religion: A Study of Shamanism and Spirit Possession.* 2d ed. London.

Linfert, A. 1966. "Zur zwei Reliefs." *Archäologischer Anzeiger:* 497–501.

Linforth, I. M. 1946. *The Corybantic Rites in Plato.* University of California Publications in Classical Philology 13, no. 5: 121–62.

Lobel, E., and D. Page, eds. 1955. *Poetarum Lesbiorum Fragmenta.* Oxford.

Loon, M. N. van. 1966. *Urartian Art.* Istanbul.

———. 1991. *Anatolia in the Earlier First Millennium B.C.* Iconography of Religions 15.13. Leiden.

Loucas, I. 1992. "Meaning and Place of the Cult Scene on the Ferrara Krater T 128." In *The Iconography of Greek Cult in the Archaic and Classical Periods,* ed. R. Hägg: 73–83. Athens and Liége.

Luckenbill, D. D. 1926–27. *Ancient Records of Assyria and Babylonia.* Chicago.

Macqueen, J. G. 1986. *The Hittites and Their Contemporaries in Asia Minor.* London.

Magie, D. 1950. *Roman Rule in Asia Minor.* Princeton, N.J.

Mallett, M. 1992–93. "An Updated View of the Çatal Hüyük Controversy." *Oriental Rug Review* 12 (Dec./Jan.): 32–43.

Mallowan, M. E. L. 1972. "Carchemish." *Anatolian Studies* 22: 63–86.

Masson, O. 1962. *Les fragments du poète Hipponax.* Paris.

Matheson, S. B. 1995. *Polygnotos and Vase Painting in Classical Athens.* Madison, Wis.

Mellaart, J. 1962. "Excavations at Çatal Hüyük." *Anatolian Studies* 12: 41–66.

———. 1963a. "Excavations at Çatal Hüyük 1962, Second Preliminary Report." *Anatolian Studies* 13: 43–104.

———. 1963b. "Deities and Shrines of Neolithic Anatolia." *Archaeology* 16: 29–38.

———. 1964. "Excavations at Çatal Hüyük 1963, Third Preliminary Report." *Anatolian Studies* 14: 39–121.

———. 1965. "Çatal Hüyük West." *Anatolian Studies* 15: 135–56.

———. 1966. "Excavations at Çatal Hüyük, 1965, Fourth Preliminary Report." *Anatolian Studies* 16: 165–192.

———. 1967. *Çatal Hüyük: A Neolithic Town in Anatolia.* London.

———. 1970. *Excavations at Hacilar.* Edinburgh.

———. 1975. *The Neolithic of the Near East.* London.

Mellaart, J., U. Hirsch, and B. Balpinar. 1989. *The Goddess from Anatolia.* Milan.

Mellink, M. J. 1963–64. "A Votive Bird from Anatolia." *Expedition* 6: 28–32.

———. 1965. "Mita, Mushki, and Phrygians." *Anadolu Araştirmalari* 2: 317–25.

———. 1979. "Midas in Tyana." In *Florilegium Anatolicum: Mélanges offerts à Emmanuel Laroche:* 249–57. Paris.

———. 1981. "Temples and High Places in Phrygia." *Temples and High Places in Biblical Times:* 96–104. Jerusalem.

———. 1983. "Comments on a Cult Relief of Kybele from Gordion." *Beiträge zur Altertumskunde Kleinasiens:* 349–60. Mainz.

———. 1991. "Archaeology in Anatolia." *American Journal of Archaeology* 95: 123–53.

———. 1993a. "Archaeology in Anatolia." *American Journal of Archaeology* 97: 105–33.

———. 1993b. "Phrygian Traits at Boğazköy and Questions of Phrygian Writing." *Istanbuler Mitteilungen* 43: 293–98.

Meriç, R. 1982. *Metropolis in Ionien. Ergebnisse einer Survey-Unternehmung in den Jahren 1972–75.* Königstein.

Meslin, M. 1978. "Agdistis ou l'androgynie malséante." In *Hommages à Maarten J. Vermaseren,* ed. M. B. de Boer and T. A. Eldridge, 2: 765–76. Leiden.

Metzger, H. 1965. *Recherches sur l'imagerie athénienne.* Paris.

Michels, A. K. 1966. "Lucretius, Clodius, and the Magna Mater." In *Mélanges d'archéologie, d'épigraphie, et d'histoire offerts à Jérôme Carcopino*: 675–79. Paris.

Michon, E. 1915–18. "Buste de Mélitiné." *Monuments antiques de France* 75: 91–129.

Miller, M. 1988. "Midas as Great King in Attic Vase Painting." *Antike Kunst* 31: 79–89.

Miller, Stella G. 1991. "Terracotta Figurines: New Finds at Ilion, 1988–1989." *Studia Troica* 1: 39–68.

Miller, Stephen G. 1995. "Old Bouleuterion and Old Metroon in the Classical Agora of Athens." In *Studies in the Ancient Greek Polis,* Historia Einzelschriften 95: 133–56. Stuttgart.

Mitchell, S. 1982. *Regional Epigraphic Catalogues of Asia Minor,* vol. 2: *The Inscriptions of North Galatia.* British Archaeological Reports, International Series 135. Oxford.

———. 1993. *Anatolia: Land, Men, and Gods in Asia Minor.* Oxford.

Mitropoulou, E. 1977. *Deities and Heroes in the Form of Snakes.* Athens.

———. 1996. "The Goddess Cybele in Funerary Banquets and with an Equestrian Hero." *CARC:* 135–65.

Möbius, H. 1916. "Form und Bedeutung der sitzenden Gestalt." *Athenische Mitteilungen* 41: 119–219.

———. 1935–36. "Das Metroon in Agrai und sein Fries." *Athenische Mitteilungen* 60–61: 234–68.

———. 1968. *Die Ornamente der griechischen Grabstelen.* Munich.

Mollard-Besques, S. 1972. *Catalogue raisonné des figurines et reliefs en terre-cuite grecs, étrusques, et romains,* vol. 3: *Époques hellénistique et romaine, Grèce et Asie Mineure.* Paris.

Morgan, M. G. 1973. "Villa Publica and Magna Mater." *Klio* 55: 231–45.

Mulroy, D. 1976. "Hephaestion and Catullus 63." *Phoenix* 30: 61–72.

Muscarella, O. W. 1974. *Ancient Art: The Norbert Schimmel Collection.* Mainz.

———. 1989. "King Midas of Phrygia and the Greeks." In *Anatolia and the Near East: Studies in Honor of Tahsin Özgüç,* ed. K. Emre, F. Hrouda, M. Mellink, and N. Özgüç: 333–42. Ankara.

———. 1995. "The Iron Age Background to the Formation of the Phrygian State." *Bulletin of the American School of Oriental Research* 299–300: 91–101.

Muss, U. 1983. "Studien zur Bauplastik des archaischen Artemisions von Ephesos." Ph. D. diss., Bonn.

Mylonas, G. E. 1961. *Eleusis and the Eleusinian Mysteries.* Princeton, N.J.

Nanda, S. 1990. *Neither Man nor Woman: The Hijras of India.* Belmont, Calif.

Nash, E. 1961. *Pictorial Dictionary of Ancient Rome.* 2d ed. Tübingen.

Nauck, A. 1877. *Tragicorum Graecorum Fragmenta,* ed. B. Snell. Hildesheim. Reprint, 1964.

Naumann, F. 1983. *Die Ikonographie der Kybele in der phrygischen und der griechischen Kunst.* Istanbuler Mitteilungen, suppl. 28. Tübingen.

Naumann, R. 1967. "Das Heiligtum der Meter Steuene bei Aezani." *Istanbuler Mitteilungen* 17: 218–47.

——. 1979. *Der Zeustempel zu Aizanoi.* Berlin.

Neumann, E. 1963. *The Great Mother: Analysis of an Archetype.* Princeton, N.J.

Neumann, G. 1959. "Die Begleiter der phrygischen Muttergöttin von Boğazköy." *Nachrichten der Akademie der Wissenschaften in Göttingen:* 101–5.

Neve, P. 1970. "Bericht über die Ausgrabungen der deutschen Boğazköy-Expedition im Jahre 1969." *Türk Arkeoloji Dergisi* 18: 151–59.

Nilsson, M. P. 1961. *Geschichte der griechischen Religion.* Vol. 2. 2d ed. Munich.

——. 1967. *Geschichte der griechischen Religion.* Vol. 1. 3d ed. Munich.

Nock, A. D. 1925. "Eunuchs in Ancient Religion." *Archiv für Religionswissenschaft* 23: 25–33.

Nohlen, K., and W. Radt. 1978. *Kapikaya, ein Felsheiligtum bei Pergamon.* Altertümer von Pergamon 12. Berlin.

Ohlemutz, E. 1940. *Die Kulte und Heiligtümer der Götter in Pergamon.* Würzburg. Reprint, Darmstadt 1968.

Oikonomides, A. 1978. "P. Haun. 6 and Euxenos the Athenian Eponymous of 222/1 B.C." *Zeitschrift für Papyrologie und Epigraphik* 32: 85–86.

Ophuijsen, J. M. van. 1987. *Hephaestion on Metre.* Mnemosyne suppl. 100. Leiden.

Oranje, H. 1984. *Euripides' Bacchae: The Play and Its Audience.* Leiden.

Orthmann, W. 1971. *Untersuchungen zur späthethitischen Kunst.* Bonn.

Osborne, R. 1987. *Classical Landscape with Figures: The Ancient Greek City and Its Countryside.* London.

Özgen, E., and I. Özgen. 1988. *Antalya Museum Catalogue.* Ankara.

Özgüç, N. 1965. *The Anatolian Group of Cylinder Seal Impressions from Kültepe.* Ankara.

Özgüç, T. 1969. *Altintepe II: Tombs, Storehouses, and Ivories.* Ankara.

——. 1971. *Kültepe and Its Vicinity in the Iron Age.* Ankara.

——. 1988. *Inandiktepe: An Important Cult Center in the Old Hittite Period.* Ankara.

Padel, R. 1983. "Women: Model for Possession by Greek Daemons." In *Images of Women in Antiquity,* ed. A. Cameron and A. Kuhrt: 3–19. Detroit.

Page, D. L., ed. 1962. *Poetae Melici Graeci.* Oxford.

——, ed. 1974. *Supplementum Lyricis Graecis.* Oxford.

Palmer, L. R. 1963. *The Interpretation of Mycenaean Texts.* Oxford.

Papachristodoulou, I. 1973. "Ἄγαλμα καὶ ναὸς Κυβέλης ἐν Μοσχάτῳ." *Archaiologike Ephemeris:* 189–217.

Parker, Robert. 1996. *Athenian Religion: A History.* Oxford.

Parsons, P. J. 1974. *Oxyrhynchus Papyri.* Vol. 42. London.

Patai, R. 1967. *The Hebrew Goddess.* New York.

Peatfield, A. 1994. "After the 'Big Bang'—What? or, Minoan Symbols and Shrines beyond Palatial Collapse." In *Placing the Gods: Sanctuaries and Sacred Space in Ancient Greece,* ed. S. Alcock and R. Osborne: 19–36. Oxford.

Pembroke, S. 1965. "Last of the Matriarchs: A Study of the Inscriptions of Lycia." *Journal of the Economic and Social History of the Orient* 8: 217–47.

——. 1967. "Women in Charge: The Function of Alternatives in Early Greek Tradition and the Ancient Idea of Matriarchy." *Journal of the Warburg and Courtland Institutes* 30: 1–35.

Pensabene, P. 1978. "Roma—Saggi di scavo sul tempio della Magna Mater del Palatino." *Archeologia Laziale* 1: 67–71.

——. 1979. "'Auguratorium' e tempio della Magna Mater." *Archeologia Laziale* 2: 67–74.

——. 1980. "La zona sud-occidentale del Palatino." *Archeologia Laziale* 3: 65–81.

——. 1981. "Nuove acquisizioni nella zona sud-occidentale del Palatino." *Archeologia Laziale* 4: 101–18.

——. 1982. "Nuovi indagini nell'area del tempio di Cibele sul Palatino." *La soteriologia dei culti orientali nell'Impero Romano,* ed. U. Bianchi and M. J. Vermaseren: 68–98. Leiden.

——. 1983. "Quinta campagna di scavo nell'area sud-ovest del Palatino." *Archeologia Laziale* 5: 65–75.

——. 1984. "Sesta e settima campagne di scavo nell'area sud-ovest del Palatino." *Archeologia Laziale* 6: 149–58.

——. 1985a. "Ottava campagna di scavo nell'area sud-ovest del Palatino." *Archeologia Laziale* 7: 149–55.

——. 1985b. "Area sud-occidentale del Palatino." In *Roma, Archeologia nel Centro,* ed. A. M. Bietti Sestieri et al.: 179–212. Rome.

——. 1988. "Scavi nell'area del Tempio della Vittoria e del Santuario della Magna Mater sul Palatino." *Archeologia Laziale* 9: 54–67.

Perret, J. 1942. *Les origines de la légende troyenne de Rome.* Paris.

Petrocheilos, I. 1992. "Ἀναθηματικὰ γλυπτὰ τῆς Κυβέλης ἀπὸ τὸν Πειραιά." *Archaiologike Ephemeris:* 21–65.

Petzl, G. 1990. *Inschriften von Smyrna.* Bonn.

Petzl, G., and H. Pleket. 1979. "Inschriften aus Lydien." *Zeitschrift für Papyrologie und Epigraphik* 34: 281–95.

Pfeiffer, R. 1949. *Callimachus.* Oxford.

Picard, C. 1938. "Le complexe Métrôon-Bouleutérion-Prytanikon, à l'Agora d'Athènes." *Revue Archéologique* 12: 97–101.

——. 1954. "Les métrôa grecs, temples et locaux d'archives." In *Urbanisme et Architecture: Études écrites et publiées en l'honneur de Pierre Lavedan:* 287–92. Paris.

Platner, S. B., and T. Ashby. 1929. *A Topographical Dictionary of Ancient Rome.* Rome. Reprint, 1965.

Polignac, F. de. 1994. "Mediation, Competition, and Sovereignty: The Evolution of Rural Sanctuaries in Geometric Greece." In *Placing the Gods: Sanctuaries and Sacred Space in Ancient Greece,* ed. S. Alcock and R. Osborne: 3–18. Oxford.

Poucet, J. 1985. *Les origines de Rome.* Brussels.

Prayon, F. 1987. *Phrygische Plastik.* Tübingen.

Price, T. H. 1971. "Double and Multiple Representations in Greek Art and Religious Thought." *Journal of Hellenic Studies* 91: 48–69.

——. 1978. *Kourotrophos.* Leiden.

Pritchard, J. B., ed. 1969. *Ancient Near Eastern Texts Relating to the Old Testment.* 3d ed. Princeton, N.J.

Putnam, M. C. J. 1961. "The Art of Catullus 64." *Harvard Studies in Classical Philology* 65: 165–205.

——. 1974. "Catullus 11: Ironies of Integrity." *Ramus* 3: 70–86.

Ramsay, W. M. 1888. "A Study of Phrygian Art." *Journal of Hellenic Studies* 9: 350–82.

——. 1895. *Cities and Bishoprics of Phrygia.* Oxford.

——. 1899. *A Historical Commentary on St. Paul's Epistle to the Galatians.* London.

——. 1906. "Preliminary Report on Exploration in Phrygia and Lycaonia." *Studies in the History and Art of the Eastern Provinces of the Roman Empire,* ed. W. M. Ramsay: 232–78. Aberdeen.

Rapp, W. 1890–94. "Kybele." In *Lexikon der griechischen und römischen Mythologie,* ed. W. H. Roscher: 1638–72. Leipzig.

Ratté, C. 1989. "Five Lydian Felines." *American Journal of Archaeology* 93: 379–93.

Reade, J. E. 1972. "The Neo-Assyrian Court and Army: Evidence from the Sculptures." *Iraq* 34: 87–112.

Reardon, B. P. 1989. *Collected Ancient Greek Novels*. Berkeley and Los Angeles.

Reeder, E. D. 1987. "The Mother of the Gods and a Hellenistic Bronze Matrix." *American Journal of Archaeology* 91: 423–40.

Rein, M. J. 1993. "The Cult and Iconography of Lydian Kybele." Ph.D. diss., Harvard University.

———. 1996. "Phrygian *Matar:* Emergence of an Iconographic Type." *CARC:* 223–237.

Reinach, S. 1889. "Statues archaïques de Cybèle." *Bulletin de Correspondance Hellénique* 13: 543–60.

———. 1908. "Παρθενών." *Bulletin de Correspondance Hellénique* 32: 499–513.

Renaud, E. B. 1929. "Prehistoric Female Figurines from America and the Old World." *Scientific Monthly* 28: 507–12.

Ribichini, S. 1981. *Adonis: Aspetti orientali di un mito greco*. Rome.

Rice, P. C. 1981. "Prehistoric Venuses: Symbols of Motherhood or Womanhood?" *Journal of Anthropological Research* 37: 402–12.

Richard, L. 1966. "Juvénal et les galles de Cybèle." *Revue de l'histoire des religions* 169: 51–67.

Ridgway, B. S. 1977. *The Archaic Style in Greek Sculpture*. Princeton, N.J.

Robert, L. 1937. *Études Anatoliennes: Recherches sur les inscriptions grecques de l'Asie Mineure*. Paris. Reprint, Amsterdam 1970.

———. 1954. *La Carie*, vol. 2: *Le plateau de Tabai et ses environs*. Paris.

———. 1955. "Autel au Musée de Smyrne." *Hellenica* 10: 110–13.

———. 1963. *Les noms indigènes dans l'Asie-Mineure gréco-romaine*. Paris.

———. 1975. "Une nouvelle inscription grecque de Sardes." *Comptes rendus de l'Académie des Inscriptions et Belles-Lettres:* 306–30.

———. 1980. "Stace, les carrières et les monnaies de Dokimeion, Attis et Agdistis." In id. *À Travers l'Asie Mineure: Poètes, prosateurs, monnaies grecques, voyageurs et géographie*, 221–56. Paris.

———. 1981. "Fleuves et cultes d'Aizanoi." *Bulletin de Correspondance Hellénique* 105: 331–60.

———. 1982. "La Mère des Dieux Lydienne." *Bulletin de Correspondance Hellénique* 106: 359–61.

Robertson, N. 1996. "The Ancient Mother of the Gods: A Missing Chapter in the History of Greek Religion." *CARC:* 239–304.

Roller, L. E. 1983. "The Legend of Midas." *Classical Antiquity* 2: 299–313.

———. 1984. "Midas and the Gordian Knot." *Classical Antiquity* 3: 256–71.

———. 1987a. *Gordion Special Studies*, vol. 1: *Nonverbal Graffiti, Dipinti, and Stamps*. University of Pennsylvania, University Museum Monograph 63. Philadelphia.

———. 1987b. "Hellenistic Epigraphic Texts from Gordion." *Anatolian Studies* 37: 103–33.

———. 1988. "Phrygian Myth and Cult." *Source* 7: 43–50.

———. 1989. "The Art of Writing at Gordion." *Expedition* 31: 54–61.

———. 1991. "The Great Mother at Gordion: The Hellenization of an Anatolian Cult." *Journal of Hellenic Studies* III: 128–43.

———. 1994a. "Attis on Greek Votive Monuments: Greek God or Phrygian?" *Hesperia* 63: 245–62.

———. 1994b. "The Phrygian Character of Kybele: The Formation of an Iconography and Cult Ethos in the Iron Age." In Çilingiroğlu and French 1994: 189–98.

———. 1996. "Reflections on the Mother of the Gods in Attic Tragedy." *CARC:* 305–321.

———. 1997. "The Ideology of the Eunuch Priest." *Gender and History* 9: 542–59.

Romanelli, P. 1963. "Lo scavo al tempio della Magna Mater sul Palatino." *Monumenti Antichi* 46: 201–330.

———. 1964. "Magna Mater e Attis sul Palatino." In *Hommages à Jean Bayet,* ed. Marcel Renard and R. Schilling: 619–26. Brussels.

Romano, I. B. 1980. "Early Greek Cult Images." Ph.D. diss., University of Pennsylvania. University Microfilms, Ann Arbor, Mich.

———. 1995. *Gordion Special Studies,* vol. 2: *The Terracotta Figurines and Related Vessels.* University of Pennsylvania, University Museum Monograph 86. Philadelphia.

Rose, C. B. 1993a. "Greek and Roman Excavations at Troy, 1991–92." *American Journal of Archaeology* 97: 341.

———. 1993b. "The 1992 Post–Bronze Age Excavations at Troia." *Studia Troica* 3: 97–116.

———. 1994. "The 1993 Post–Bronze Age Excavations at Troia." *Studia Troica* 4: 75–104.

———. 1995. "The 1994 Post–Bronze Age Excavations at Troia." *Studia Troica* 5: 81–105.

———. 1997. "The 1996 Post-Bronze Age Excavations at Troia." *Studia Troica* 7: 73–110.

Roussel, P. 1930. "Un sanctuaire d'Agdistis à Rhamnonte." *Revue des Études Anciennes* 32: 5–8.

Rousselle, A. 1988. *Porneia: On Desire and the Body in Antiquity.* Translated from the French by F. Pheasant. Oxford. Original ed., *Porneia: De la maîtrise du corps à la privation sensorielle, IIᵉ–IVᵉ siècles de l'ère chrétienne.* Paris, 1983.

Rubensohn, O., and C. Watzinger. 1928. "Die Daskalopetra auf Chios." *Athenische Mitteilungen* 53: 109–16.

Ruge, W. 1903. "Dindymon." In *RE* 5, pt. 1: 652–653.

———. 1941. "Phrygia." In *RE* 20, pt. 1: 761–868.

Rutter, J. B. 1968. "The Three Phases of the Taurobolium." *Phoenix* 22: 226–29.

Said, E. 1979. *Orientalism.* New York.

Salis, A. von. 1913. "Die Göttermutter des Agorakritos." *Jahrbuch des deutschen archäologischen Instituts* 28: 1–26.

Salviat, F. 1964. "Stèles et naïskoi de Cybèle à Thasos." *Bulletin de Correspondance Hellénique* 88: 239–51.

Salvini, M. 1994. "The Historical Background of the Urartian Monument of Meher Kapisi." In Çilingiroğlu and French 1994: 205–10.

Sams, G. K. 1971. "The Phrygian Painted Pottery of Early Iron Age Gordion and Its Anatolian Setting." Ph.D. diss., University of Pennsylvania. University Microfilms, Ann Arbor, Mich.

———. 1989. "Sculpted Orthostates at Gordion." In *Anatolia and the Near East: Studies in Honor of Tahsin Özgüç,* ed. K. Emre, F. Hrouda, M. Mellink, and N. Özgüç: 447–54. Ankara.

———. 1994. "Aspects of Early Phrygian Architecture at Gordion." In Çilingiroğlu and French 1994: 211–20.

Sams, G. K., and M. Voigt. 1990. "Work at Gordion in 1989." *Kazi Sonuçlari Toplantisi* 12: 455–70. Ankara.

Sanders, G. M. 1972. "Gallos." In *Reallexikon für Antike und Christentum* 8: 984–1034.

Santoro, M. 1973. *Epitheta Deorum in Asia Graeca Cultorum ex Auctoribus Graecis et Latinis.* Milan.

Schede, M. 1934. *Die Ruinen von Priene: Kurze Beschreibung.* Archäologisches Institut des deutschen Reiches, Abteilung Istanbul, Istanbuler Forschungen. 2d ed., 1964. Berlin.

Schefold, K. 1937. "Statuen auf Vasenbildern." *Jahrbuch des deutschen archäologischen Instituts* 52: 30–75.

Schibli, H. S. 1990. *Pherekydes of Syros.* Oxford.

Schmidt, E. 1909. *Kultübertragungen.* Giessen.

Schwenn, F. 1922a. "Korybanten." In *RE* 11, pt. 2: 1441–46.

———. 1922b. "Kureten." In *RE* 11, pt. 2: 2202–9.

———. 1922c. "Kybele." In *RE* 11, pt. 2: 2250–98.

Schwertheim, E. 1978. "Denkmäler zur Meterverehrung in Bithynien und Mysien." In *Studien zur Religion und Kultur Kleinasiens: Festschrift für Friedrich Karl Dörner*, ed. S. Şahin, E. Schwertheim, and J. Wagner: 791–837. Leiden.

Schwyzer, E. 1923. *Dialectorum Graecarum exempla epigraphica potiora*. Leipzig. Reprint, Darmstadt, 1960.

Scullard, H. H. 1973. *Roman Politics*. 2d ed. Oxford.

——. 1981. *Festivals and Ceremonies of the Roman Republic*. London.

Sfameni Gasparro, G. 1973. *I culti orientali in Sicilia*. Leiden.

——. 1978. "Connotazioni metroache di Demetra nel Coro dell' 'Elena' (vv. 1301–1365)." *Hommages à Maarten J. Vermaseren*, ed. M. B. de Boer and T. A. Eldridge, 3: 1148–87. Leiden.

——. 1985. *Soteriology and Mystic Aspects in the Cult of Cybele and Attis*. Leiden.

——. 1996. "Per la storia del culto di Cibele in occidente: Il santuario rupestre di Akrai." *CARC:* 51–86.

Shapiro, H. A. 1989. *Art and Cult under the Tyrants in Athens*. Mainz.

Shear, T. L. 1993. "The Persian Destruction of Athens." *Hesperia* 62: 383–482.

——. 1995. "Bouleuterion, Metroon, and the Archives at Athens." *Studies in the Ancient Greek Polis*, Historia Einzelschriften 95: 157–190. Stuttgart.

Sheppard, A. R. R. 1981. "R.E.C.A.M. Notes and Studies No. 7: Inscriptions from Uşak, Denizli, and Hisarköy." *Anatolian Studies* 31: 19–27.

Showerman, G. 1901. *The Great Mother of the Gods*. Madison, Wis. Reprinted, Chicago, 1969.

Simms, R. R. 1985. "Foreign Religious Cults in Athens in the Fifth and Fourth Centuries B.C." Ph.D. diss., University of Virginia.

Simon, C. 1986. "The Archaic Votive Offerings and Cults of Ionia." Ph.D. diss., University of California, Berkeley.

Simon, E. 1953. *Opfernde Götter*. Berlin.

——. 1966. "Neue Deutung zweier eleusinischer Denkmäler des vierten Jahrhunderts v. Chr." *Antike Kunst* 9: 72–92.

——. 1975. *Pergamon und Hesiod*. Mainz.

——. 1978–80 [1987]. "Kybele in Etrurien." *Anadolu* 21: 29–36.

——. 1983. *Festivals of Attica: An Archaeological Commentary*. Madison, Wis.

——. 1984. "Ikonographie und Epigraphik." *Zeitschrift für Papyrologie und Epigraphik* 57: 1–21.

——. 1987. "Griechische Muttergottheiten." *Bonner Jahrbücher des rheinischen Landesmuseums,* suppl. 44: 157–69.

——. 1990. *Die Götter der Römer*. Munich.

Simpson, E. 1988. "The Phrygian Artistic Intellect." *Source* 7: 24–42.

——. 1996. "Phrygian Furniture from Gordion." In *The Furniture of Western Asia: Ancient and Traditional,* ed. G. Herrmann, 187–209. Mainz.

Slater, W. J. 1971. "Pindar's House." *Greek, Roman, and Byzantine Studies* 12: 141–52.

Small, S. G. P. 1983. *Catullus: A Reader's Guide to the Poems*. Lanham, Md., and London.

Smith, J. O. 1996. "The High Priests of the Temple of Artemis at Ephesus." *CARC:* 323–35.

Snell, B. 1955. *Pindari Carmina cum Fragmentis*. Leipzig.

Sokolowski, F. 1955. *Lois sacrées de l'Asie Mineure*. Paris.

Spanos, P. 1983. "Eine Bemerkungen zum sogenannten Niobe-Monument bei Manisa (Magnesia ad Sipylum)." *Beiträge zur Altertumskunde Kleinasiens:* 477–83. Mainz.

Spartz, E. 1962. *Das Wappenbild des Herrn und der Herrin der Tiere in der minoisch-mykenischen und frühgriechischen Kunst*. Munich.

Stone, M. 1976. *When God Was a Woman*. New York.

Straten, F. T. van. 1976a. "Assimilatie van vreemde goden: Archeologisch bronnenmateriaal." *Lampas* 9: 42–50.

———. 1976b. "Daikrates' Dream: A Votive Relief from Kos and Some Other *kat' onar* Dedications." *Bulletin antieke Beschaving* 51: 1–38.

———. 1993. "Images of Gods and Men in a Changing Society: Self-identity in Hellenistic Religion." In *Images and Ideologies: Self-definition in the Hellenistic World,* ed. A. Bulloch, E. S. Gruen, A. A. Long, and A. Stewart: 248–64. Berkeley and Los Angeles.

Stroud, R. S. 1974. "An Athenian Law on Silver Coinage." *Hesperia* 43: 157–88.

Summers, K. 1996. "Lucretius' Roman Cybele." *CARC:* 337–365.

Takács, S. A. 1996. "Magna Deum Mater Idaea, Cybele, and Catullus' *Attis.*" *CARC:* 367–86.

Talalay, L. E. 1987. "Clay Figurines from Neolithic Greece: An Argument by Analogy." *American Journal of Archaeology* 91: 161–69.

———. 1991. "Body Imagery of the Ancient Aegean." *Archaeology* 4⁺: 46–49.

———. 1993. *Deities, Dolls, and Devices: Neolithic Figurines from Franchthi Cave, Greece.* Excavations at Franchthi Cave, Greece, fasc. 9. Bloomington, Ind.

———. 1994. "A Feminist Boomerang: The Great Goddess of Prehistory." *Gender and History* 6: 165–83.

Taylor, L. R. 1956. "Sellisternium and Theoxenia." In *Atti dell'VIII congresso internazionale di storia delle religioni:* 349–50. Florence.

Temizer, R. 1959. "Un bas-relief de Cybèle découvert à Ankara." *Anatolia* 4: 179–87.

Thesleff, H. 1965. *The Pythagorean Texts of the Hellenistic Period.* Åbo, Finland.

Thomas, G. 1984. "Magna Mater and Attis." *Aufstieg und Niedergang der römischen Welt* II.17.3: 1500–1555. Berlin and New York.

Thompson, D. B. 1963. *Troy: The Terracotta Figurines of the Hellenistic Period.* Supplementary Monograph 3. University of Cincinnati Excavations in the Troad, 1932–38. Princeton, N.J.

Thompson, H. 1937. "Buildings on the West Side of the Agora." *Hesperia* 6: 1–226.

———. 1951. "Excavations in the Athenian Agora: 1950." *Hesperia* 20: 45–60.

Thompson, H. A., and R. E. Wycherley. 1972. *The Athenian Agora,* vol. 14: *The Agora of Athens: The History, Shape and Uses of an Ancient City Center.* Princeton, N.J.

Thönges-Stringaris, R. N. 1965. "Das griechische Totenmahl." *Athenische Mitteilungen* 80: 1–99.

Todd, I. 1976. *Çatal Hüyük in Perspective.* Menlo Park, Calif.

Töpperwein, E. 1976. *Terrakotten von Pergamon.* Deutsches Archäologisches Institut, Pergamenische Forschungen 3. Berlin.

Toutain, J. F. 1911. *Les cultes païens dans l'empire romaine,* vol. 1, pt. 2: *Les provinces latines, les cultes orientaux.* Bibliothèque de l'École des hautes études, Sciences religieuses. Paris.

Travlos, J. 1971. *Pictorial Dictionary of Ancient Athens.* Tübingen.

Tuchelt, K. 1970. *Die archaischen Skulpturen von Didyma.* Berlin.

Turcan, R. 1983. *Numismatique Romaine du Culte Métroaque.* Leiden.

Tuzet, H. 1987. *Mort et résurrection d'Adonis.* Paris.

Ucko, P. J. 1962. "The Interpretation of Prehistoric Anthropomorphic Figurines." *Journal of the Royal Anthropological Institute* 92: 38–54.

———. 1968. *Anthropomorphic Figurines.* London.

Ussishkin, D. 1975. "Hollows, 'Cup-Marks,' and Hittite Stone Monuments." *Anatolian Studies* 25: 85–103.

Ventris, M., and J. Chadwick. 1959. *Documents in Mycenaean Greek.* Cambridge.

Vermaseren, M. J. 1966. *The Legend of Attis in Greek and Roman Art.* Leiden.

———. 1977. *Cybele and Attis.* London.

————. 1977–89. *Corpus Cultus Cybelae Attidisque.* 7 vols. Études préliminaires aux religions orientales dans l'Empire romain. Leiden.

Vermaseren, M. J., and M. de Boer. 1986. "Attis." In *Lexicon Iconographicum Mythologiae Classicae,* 3: 22–44. Basel.

Vermeule, E. 1964. *Greece in the Bronze Age.* Chicago.

Versnel, H. S. 1990. *Ter Unus. Isis, Dionysos, Hermes: Three Studies in Henotheism.* Vol. 1 of *Inconsistencies in Greek Religion.* Leiden.

————. 1991. "Beyond Cursing: The Appeal to Justice in Judicial Prayers." In *Magika Hiera: Ancient Greek Magic and Religion,* ed. C. A. Faraone and D. Obbink: 60–106. Oxford.

Virgilio, B. 1981. *Il 'tempio stato' di Pessinunte fra Pergamo e Roma nel II–I Secolo A.C.* Pisa.

Voigt, M. 1983. *Hajji Firuz Tepe, Iran: The Neolithic Settlement.* University of Pennsylvania, University Museum Monograph 50. Philadelphia.

————. 1994. "Excavations at Gordion 1988–89: The Yassıhöyük Stratigraphic Sequence." In Çilingiroğlu and French 1994: 265–93.

Waelkens, M. 1971. "Pessinonte et le Gallos." *Byzantion* 41: 349–71.

————. 1986. "The Imperial Sanctuary at Pessinus." *Epigraphica Anatolica:* 37–72.

Walcot, P. 1966. *Hesiod and the Near East.* Cardiff.

Walter, O. 1939. "Κουρητικὴ Τριάς." *Jahresheft des österreichischen archäologischen Instituts* 31: 53–80.

Warde Fowler, W. 1911. *The Religions of the Roman Empire.* Reprint, New York 1971.

Weber, H. 1969. "Der Zeus-Tempel von Aizanoi." *Athenische Mitteilungen* 84: 182–201.

Webster, T. B. L. 1960. *Studies in Menander.* Victoria University of Manchester Publications, Classical Series 7. 2d ed. Manchester.

Wehr, D. S. 1985. "Religious and Social Dimensions of Jung's Concept of the Archetype: A Feminist Perspective." In *Feminist Archetypal Theory: Interdisciplinary Re-Visions of Jungian Thought,* ed. E. Lauter and C. S. Rupprecht: 23–45. Knoxville.

Weinreich, O. 1919. "Stiftung und Kultsatzungen eines Privatheiligtums in Philadelphia in Lydien." *Sitzungsberichte der Heidelberger Akademie der Wissenschaften* 16: 1–68.

Weinstock, S. 1957. "The Image of the Chair of Germanicus." *Journal of Roman Studies* 47: 144–54.

Welles, C. B. 1934. *Royal Correspondence in the Hellenistic Period: A Study in Greek Epigraphy.* New Haven.

West, M. L. 1970. "Melica." *Classical Quarterly* 20: 205–15.

————. 1983. *The Orphic Poems.* Oxford.

————. 1989–92. *Iambi et elegi Graeci ante Alexandrum cantati.* 2 vols. 2d ed. Oxford.

Wiegand, T., and H. Schrader. 1904. *Priene: Ergebnisse der Ausgrabungen und Untersuchungen in den Jahren 1895–1898.* Berlin.

Wilamowitz-Moellendorff, U. von. 1879. "Die Galliamben des Kallimachos und Catullus." *Hermes* 14: 194–201.

Will, E. 1960. "Aspects du culte et de la légende de la grande mère dans le monde grec." In *Éléments orientaux dans la religion grecque ancienne,* 95–111. Travaux du Centre d'Études supériores specialisé d'histoire des religions, Strasbourg. Paris.

Winter, Franz. 1903. *Die Typen der figürlichen Terrakotten.* Vol. 3 (in 2 vols.) of *Die antiken Terrakotten,* ed. Reinhard Kekulé von Stradonitz. Berlin.

————. 1907. *Die Skulpturen mit Ausnahme der Altarreliefs.* Königliche Museen zu Berlin, Altertümer von Pergamon 7. Berlin.

Winter, Frederick. 1988. "Phrygian Gordion in the Hellenistic Period." *Source* 7: 60–71.

Wiseman, T. P. 1979. *Clio's Cosmetics: Three Studies in Greco-Roman Literature.* Leicester.

——. 1982. "Philodemus 26.3 G-P." *Classical Quarterly* 32: 475–76.

——. 1984. "Cybele, Virgil and Augustus." In *Poetry and Politics in the Age of Augustus*, ed. T. Woodman and D. West: 117–28. Cambridge.

——. 1985. *Catullus and His World.* Cambridge.

——. 1995. *Remus: A Roman Myth.* Cambridge.

Wolters, P. 1887. "Miscellen." *Athenische Mitteilungen* 12: 271–74.

Wycherley, R. E. 1957. *The Athenian Agora,* vol. 3: *Literary and Epigraphical Testimonia.* Princeton, N.J.

Young, R. S. 1951. "Gordion—1950." University of Pennsylvania, *University Museum Bulletin* 16, no. 1 : 2–19.

——. 1953. "Progress at Gordion, 1951–1952." University of Pennsylvania, *University Museum Bulletin* 17, no. 4: 2–39.

——. 1956. "The Campaign of 1955 at Gordion." *American Journal of Archaeology* 60: 249–66.

——. 1963. "Gordion on the Royal Road." *Proceedings of the American Philosophical Society* 107, no. 4: 348–64.

——. 1964. "The 1963 Campaign at Gordion." *American Journal of Archaeology* 68: 279–92.

——. 1966. "The Gordion Campaign of 1965." *American Journal of Archaeology* 70: 267–78.

——. 1969. "Doodling at Gordion." *Archaeology* 22: 270–75.

Young, R. S., K. DeVries, J. F. McClellan, E. L. Kohler, M. J. Mellink, and G. K. Sams. 1981. *Gordion Excavations Final Reports,* vol. 1: *Three Great Early Tumuli.* Philadelphia.

Zanker, P. 1988. *The Power of Images in the Age of Augustus.* Ann Arbor, Mich.

Zgusta, L. 1964. *Kleinasiatische Personennamen.* Československá akademie ved. Monografie Orientálního ústavu 19. Prague.

——. 1982. "Weiteres zum Namen der Kybele." *Die Sprache* 28: 171–72.

Zoroğlu, L. 1994. "The Iron Age of Cilicia Tracheia and the Relationship between East and West." In Çilingiroğlu and French 1994: 301–9.

Acropolis, in Athens, 133, 139, 173n; in Midas City, 336; in Pergamon, 332

Adonis, 176n, 223, 228, 255

Aelius Aristeides, 330

Aeneas, 2, 7, 238, 270, 279, 299–301, 302–4, 316

Aeolis, 328

Aeschylus, 168, 183n

Aesculapius, 280, 284

Agathe Tyche, 195

Agathos Daimon, 195

Agdistis, 240, 241, 244, 245–46, 247, 248, 249, 255, 259. *See also* Angdistis

Agermos, 221–22

Agora, in Athens, 139, 145, *146–47,* 162, 164, 165, 169, 175, 177, 184, 218, 308n, 317

Agorakritos of Paros, 145, 146n, 162

Agrai, 175

Agricultural imagery: and Magna Mater, 280, 318; and Meter, 169–70; prehistoric, 31, 36, 37

Aigina, 133

Aischines, 162n, 163, 165, 171, 177, 183

Aizanoi, 189, 330, 336–37, *338–39,* 340–41, 343

Akalan, 101

Akrai, 281

Akriai, 134

Alcibiades, 162n, 167

Alcman of Sparta, 134, 137n

Alexander the Great, 64, 102n, 108, 120, 161n, 187, 188

Alexander Polyhistor, 68

Altars: and Magna Mater, 314n; and Matar, 52, 65, 71, 79, *80, 82,* 96, *98,* 102, 109, 111; and Meter, 138, 195, 200, 203n, 204, 206, 209, 210, 211, 222, 329, 334, 336, 342

Alyar, 54

Amazons, 180, 192n, 212

Ammianus Marcellinus, 192n

Amorgos, 131

Amphipolis, 181, 216

Anakreon, 175n

Anatolia: climate of, 20, 21; Greek influence in, 64, 102n, 108, 139, 188, 189, 250; Hittites in, 3, 41–44, 62, 78, 79, 81, 250; matriarchy in, 11–13, 18; Neo-Hittites in, 3, 41–42, 44–48, 49, 52–53, 67, 71–72, 74, 82–83, 101, 109, 110, 124, 137; Orientalist views of, 20, 21; Urartians in, 3, 52, 53–54, 109, 113

Anatolia, Mother Goddess cult in: Bachofen on, 11, 12; Greek influence on, 143–44, *150,* 169, 198–204, 215; and Jungian psychology, 16, 18; and matriarchy, 12–13, 18; prehistoric predecessor of, 15, 16, 36, 41; and ritual, 15, 21; Roman influence on, 327, 328, 336; and sexuality, 16; and social development, 10–13, 18–19; transmission of, 19, 143. *See also* Ionia; Lydia; Phrygia

Ancuzköy, 47

Angdistis, 179–81, *179,* 195–98, 217n, 222, 223, 245–46, 250, 253, 336, 338, 342. *See also* Agdistis

Animal-human composite imagery: and Matar, 49; and Neo-Hittite art, 49

Animal imagery: and Magna Mater, 276, 277; and Matar, 74, 75, 104, 109; and Meter, 122, 135, 141, 148, 210, 228; and Potnia Theron, 135; and prehistoric artefacts, 29, 30–32, 35, 36, 37, 38; and prehistoric mother goddess, 38, 39. *See also* Lion imagery; Predator imagery; Raptor imagery; Snake imagery

Ankara, 42, 43, 48, 49, *57, 58*, 72, 73, 75, 79, 82, 83, 102, 188, 251

Antaia, 199, 203

Antiphanes, 165n

Anu, 248

Aphrodite, 141, 168n, 175n, 176n, 248, 249, 255

Apollo, 105, 148–49n, 157, 163, 184, 204, 222n, 270, 281, 289n, 301, 332

Apollodoros, 170n, 172n

Apollonios Rhodios, 110n, 204

Appian, 266

Apuleius, 165n

Ara Pietatis, 309, *310–11*

Archetypes, Jungian, 16–18

Architecture: Greek, 126; Neo-Hittite, 52; Neolithic, 28–29, 34; Phrygian, 52, 54, 61, 72–74, 84–86, 100–102, 109, 112–13, 250; Roman, 274, 288; Urartian, 54, 61, 109, 113

Arete, 195

Areyastis Monument, 89, *94*, 100, 101

Ariadne, 306

Aristeides, 209n

Aristocracy, 23, 24; and Magna Mater, 283, 289; and Matar, 111–12

Aristophanes, 125, 144, 164, 167, 172n

Aristotle, 165

Arkadia, 134, 170n, 337

Arnobius, 239–40, 241, 243, 244, 246, 247, 248, 250, 251, 254, 255, 256, 257, 258, 259

Arslankaya, 49, 54, 85, 86, *87–88*, 90, 101, 102, 104, 110, 131, 136

Arslantaş, 102, 103, 131

Artemis, 47, 105, 127, 135, 136, 176n, 196, *197*, 200, 222n, 253, 331, 335

Artemision, at Ephesos, 104, 140

Asklepios, 280, 332

Aspordene, 199, 209

Assyria, 135, 137, 246

Ates, 69, 70, 96, 111

Athena, 163, 211, 249, 332

Athenaios, 165

Athens: Acropolis in, 133, 139, 173n; Agora in, 139, 145, *146–47*, 162, 164, 165, 169, 175, 177, 184, 218, 308n, 317; Attis depicted in, 181; Bouleuterion in, 162, 163, 164, 165, 169, 217; democracy in, 163, 169, 184, 218; dramatic arts in, 119, 167; herms in, 21n; Meter cult in, 24, 119, 133, 139, 143, 158, 162–69, 171, 175, 182, 183, 184, 187, 188, 217–18, 219, 291, 317; Metroön in, 119, 139, 145, 162–67, 171, 175, 182, 183, 188, 217, 218, 308n, 317; and Orientalist scholarship, 24

Attalid dynasty, 193, 206, 210, 232, 269, 331, 336

Attalos I (Pergamene king), 265, 270, 281

Attica, 175, 198

Attis: on the Ara Pietatis, 309, *310–11;* castration of, 5, 6, 16, 17, 21, 113–14, 177, 214, 237, 240, 241, 252–54, 256, 259, 304, 306, 321, 336; Christian commentary on, 241, 244, 256, 258; and coins, 333; and costumes, 131n, 180, 212, 214, 277; and Cybele, 4n, 5, 16, 22, 237–59, 305–7, 321, 336; and dance, 181; and figurines, 178, 181–82, 204, 206, 212, 214, 275, *275*, 277, 278, 280, 318; and funerary rites, 252; and Greek cult, 113, 155n, 177–82, 192, 212, 215, 217, 223–24, 227, 228, 244, 257, 278; Greek origin of, 178, 181; and inscriptions, 178–79, 212, 335; and Ionian cult, 214–15; and Jungian psychology, 16, 17; and Lydian cult, 335–36; and Magna Mater, 113, 241, 245, 275, 277, 278, 280, 284, 285, 299, 304–7, 318, 319–20; and Meter, 113, 155n, 177–82, 192, 212, 215, 217, 223–24, 227, 228, 244, 331, 342n; and monuments, 257; and music, 181; and mystery, 181; and mythic narrative, 4n, 5, 237–59, 306, 321; and nomenclature, 70; Orientalist views of, 20, 21; and Pan, 180; and Pergamene cult, 212; and Phrygian cult, 114, 154–55n, 178, 181, 182, 192, 193–94, 237, 243–47, 250–54, 319, 342; and reliefs, 178–79, *179*, 181, 214n, 222, 223, *225*, 227, 336; and ritual, 181, 223, 252, 278, 316; and Roman cult, 21, 22, 113–14, 257, 275, 277, 278, 280, 284, 285, 299, 304–7, 315–16, 318, 319–20; and sacred tree, 279; and sexuality, 177, 182, 277, 278, 280, 304–7; as shepherd, 180, 181, 212, 237, 241, 277; and shrines, 212; and statues, 212, *213*, 278, 331; and statuettes, 192n; and votives, 178–80, *179*, 182, 222

Auguratorium, in Rome, 273

Augustus (Roman emperor), 4, 187, 309, 313, 315

Aulus Gellius, 283

Ayaş, 72–73, 74

Baba, 69, 70, 111

Bachofen, Johann Jakob, 10–12, 13, 14, 18, 19–20

Bactria, 188n

Bahçelievler, *57*, 72–73, 74, 82, 104, 111

Bakşeyiş Monument, 90, *97*, 98, 101, 102

Basil of Ancyra, 302n

Battakes, 23

Baumeister, A., 245n

Bayandir, 104

Bendis, 176n, 180–81, 219, 227

Beydeğirmen, 80

Birecik, 47

Bithynia, 64, 96, 197, 198, 305, 328, 332n, 334, 336, 343

Blegen, C. W., 206n

Boğazköy, 42, 43, 44, 48n, *59*, 72, 74, 77, 79, 81, 83, 102, 109–11, 112–14

Boiotia, 222n

Bömer, F., 121n, 149n, 182n, 270n, 291n, 301n

Bouleuterion, in Athens, 162, 163, 164, 165, 169, 217

Bremer, J., 282n

Bronze Age, 3, 41–45, 109, 134–35, 200n, 206, 247, 248, 331n

Bükyük Kapikaya, 54, 86, *89*, 100, 101

Burkert, Walter, 17, 18, 121n, 178n, 324–25

Büyükkale, 74

Calendar: and Magna Mater, 283; and Meter, 203

Carcopino, J., 342n

Caria, 199, 328, 334–35

Carthage, 302

Castration: and Agdistis, 240, 248, 249, 255, 259; and Attis, 5, 16, 17, 21, 113–14, 214, 237, 240, 241, 252–53, 256, 259, 304, 306, 320, 336; and Christianity, 253; and Greek literature, 248–49; and Hittite tradition, 248; and Jungian psychology, 16–17; and Magna Mater cult, 17–18, 98n, 113–14, 237, 240, 254n, 256, 257, 267, 292, 298, 299, 301, 304, 306, 307, 308, 318, 319, 320, 324–25; and Mata (Hindu mother goddess), 320–21; and Matar cult, 19, 98n, 113–14; and Meter cult, 113–14, 181, 230, 231, 237, 240, 250, 252–54; and myth of Cybele and Attis, 5, 237, 240, 241, 247, 252–54, 256, 259, 321, 336; Orientalist views of, 19, 20, 21, 22; and Ouranos, 248

Çatalhöyük, 3, 27–34

Cato, 273n

Catullus, 1, 5, 9, 267, 304–7, 318

Celaenae, 67, 68

Ceres, 283, 289n

Chalcolithic period, 34

Chalkedon, 204

Charites, 195

Charon of Lampsakos, 124

Childbirth: and Meter, 159, 233; and prehistoric imagery, 29, 30, 31, 35, 37. *See also* Pregnancy

Chios, 68, 69n, 125n, 131, 138, 140, 203, 224

Christianity: and castration, 253; and Greek mystery rites, 155; and maternal identity, 9; mother goddess cult subsumed by, 345; and myth of Cybele and Attis, 4n, 241, 244, 256, 258; and prehistoric mother goddess, 13; and resistance to conversion, 166

Chronology: and Matar, 64, 71, 81–83, 99–103, 108, 243; and Meter, 119, 123, 132; and myth of Cybele and Attis, 243–44

Cicero, 192n, 264, 266, 267, 268, 283n, 288, 296–97

Cilicia, 45, 80–81

Circus Maximus, in Rome, 289, 315

City-state, and Meter, 4, 121, 140, 233

Class. *See* Social class

Claudia Quinta, 265–66, 267–68, 280, 282, 296, 299, *312*, 313–14, 315, 316

Claudiopolis, 80

Claudius (Roman emperor), 313n, 315

Clement of Alexandria, 155, 249

Coins, 289–90, *290*, 316, 330, 333, 334, 335, 340, 342

Consciousness, development of, 10–11, 16–18

Constantinople, 334

Costumes: and Attis, 131n, 180, 212, 214, 277; and Kubaba (Neo-Hittite goddess), 47, 48, 72n, 128, 129; and Magna Mater, 210, 276, 310, 314, 315n; and Matar, 47–48, 71–72, 85, 104, 105–8; and Meter, 126, 128–29, 131–32, 139, 145, 180, 207; and Phrygian priesthood, 105

Creation myths, 247–50

Crete, 15, 135, 170, 171, 172, 173–74, 238, 300

Cumont, Franz, 13, 20, 21, 23, 268, 285

Curetes, 298

Cybele: and Attis, 4n, 5, 16, 22, 237–59, 305–7, 321, 336; and castration, 98n; and costumes, 281; and Jungian psychology, 16; and matriarchy, 13; and mythic narrative, 4n, 5, 237–59, 306, 321; and naiskoi, 281; and nomenclature, 2, 63, 67, 68, 250; prehistoric predecessor of, 27; and priesthood, 98n; universalization of, 18

Cyprus, 135, 137

Daktyls, 172n

Dance: and Attis, 181; and Kubaba (Anatolian goddess), 130; and Magna Mater, 285; and Meter, 151, 154, 161, 171, 172, 173, 183; and prehistoric imagery, 31

Daskalopetra, 138

Daskyleion, 128

Death: and Matar, 113; and Meter, 233; and prehistoric imagery, 29, 31

Deliklitaş, 85n, 98, 339

Delos, 148n, 181, 216, 217n

Delphi, 136n, 148n, 270, 281

Demeter, 19, 119, 134n, 140, 143, 149n, 163, 167, 169, 171n, 174–76, 181, 184, 185, 222n, 224, 228, 238, 249, 255, 256, 335

Demetrios of Skepsis, 172n

Democracy, 163, 169, 184, 203

Demosthenes, 121n, 152n, 154–55, 162, 177, 181, 183

Derveni Papyrus, 170–71

Diadem, 132

Diagoras of Melos, 167n

Didyma, 132

Dikaios, 195n

Dindymene, 66–67, 125n, 144n, 189, 199, 204, 239, 250

Diodoros, 170n, 172, 174, 239, 241, 242, 243, 246, 250, 251, 252, 254, 255, 256, 259, 264, 265n, 268, 290–91

Diogenes, 151, 157, 167n, 183

Dionysios of Halikarnasos, 22, 248n, 267, 283, 293, 296, 303, 305, 323

Dionysios of Syracuse, 165

Dionysos, 143, 149n, 152–54, 157, 166, 176, 184, 225, 226, 255, 275, 332

Dioskouroi, 226

Dokimeion, 197, 246, 342

Dömrek, 79, *80*, 81, 102, 111

Doryleion, 128, 135n

Drinking vessels: and Matar, 73, 109; and Meter, 145, 146, 148, 151–55, *152–53*

Earth, worship of, 10–11, 20. *See also* Mother Earth

Economic relations, and prehistoric imagery, 31, 34

Ecstasy: and Magna Mater, 287n, 296, 317–18; and Meter, 4, 20, 121, 155–57, 161, 166–67, 168, 171, 172, 173, 176, 177, 185, 231

Egypt, 15, 188n, 198, 216

Eileithyia, 159

Eleusinian Mysteries, 167, 175, 176, 181, 249, 256

Elmali, 104, 114

Emotional expression, and Meter, 137, 141, 149, 151, 155–57, 168, 172, 183, 185, 228

Endymion, 255

Eos, 255

Ephesos, 104, 127, 131, 136, 140, 198, 199, 200, *201*, 202, 211, 214, 253, 331, 337

Ephoros, 172n

Epidaurian Hymn, 228

Epilepsy, 156

Erichthonios, 249

Erinyes, 248

Erythrai, 131, 199, 203

Etlik, 49, *58*, 72, 73, 74, 82, 109, 110, 111

Etruria, 281

Eudaimonia, 195

Eumeneia, 198

Euripides, 5, 9, 121n, 125, 144, 149n, 151, 156, 166–67, 168, 170n, 171, 172, 175, 182, 183n, 228n

Façades: and Phrygian cult imagery, 71, 84–86, 89–90, 96–104, 112–13, 232, 250; and Phrygian cult inscriptions, 65–66, 68, 69–70; and Phrygian tombs, 61; and Urartian tombs, 61

Faharad Çeşme, 78, 80, 111

Father god: Bachofen on, 10–11; Graves on, 13; mother goddess superseded by, 10–11, 13

Feminism, 13–14

Ferguson, W. S., 24, 224n

Fertility: and gender of divinity, 15; and Magna Mater, 23, 257, 278, 280, 284, 296, 298, 318; and Mata (Hindu mother goddess), 320; and Matar, 110, 114, 280; and Meter, 114, 169, 280; and prehistoric figurines, 14–15, 16, 31, 36; and prehistoric imagery, 30–31, 32, 36, 37; and prehistoric mother goddess, 13, 14, 15, 16; and prehistoric society, 15. *See also* Childbirth; Pregnancy

Figurines: and Attis, 178, 181–82, 204, 206, 212, 214, 277, 278, 280, 318; and Magna Mater, 275–76, *275*, 277–78; and Matar, *106*; and Meter, 133, 139, 189, 203, 204, 206, 207, 210, 217–18, 331, 337; and Phrygian priest, 105, *107*; prehistoric, 14–16, 27, 29, 30, 31, 32, *32–33*, 34, 35–38, 41

Findik, 98, *99*, 337, 339

Firmicius Maternus, 155n

Foucart, P., 149n, 183n

Francis, E. D., 162n

Froehner, W., 131n

Funerary art: and Matar, 52, 74, 79, 102–4, 113; and Meter, 183, 189, 192, 204, 218, 221, 226, 250, 251

Funerary rites, 223, 226–27, 252, 258

Gaia, 169, 170, 171

Galatians, 229, 240, 245n, 256, 257, 268–69, 290, 296, 328, 341–42

Galaxia festival, 218

Galen, 302n

Gallesia, 199

Galli, 216n, 229–32, 254n, 290, 292, *294*, 297–99, 301–4, 305, 308, 316, 318–19, 323–25, 333

Gela, 174

Gender: and cult membership, 23, 183–84; and fertility deity, 15; and prehistoric society, 38; and scholarly preconceptions, 9, 10, 18

Geometric ornament: Greek, 126; Phrygian, 73, 85, 86, 89–90, 100–102, 126

Gérard, J., 282n

Giants, 248

Gimbutas, Marija, 16

Glans penis, terracotta image of, 276, *276*

Gordion, 42, 43, 48, *56*, 72–79, *76*, *77–78*, 81–83, 100–104, 105, 110–14, 135n, 188, 189, *190–91*, 192, 193, 207, 246, 251, 315n

Graces, 172n, 195

Graeve, V. von, 127n

Graham, A. J., 128n

Graillot, Henri, 13, 20, 21, 23, 330

Graves, Robert, 13

Great Mother, 16, 18

Greece: and Alexandrian conquests, 64, 102n, 108, 120; city-state in, 121; and influence in Phrygia, 64, 102n, 105–8, 128, 189, 192–98; and Persian Wars, 120

Greece, Mother Goddess cult in: and administrative documents, 218–24; and agricultural imagery, 169–70; and altars, 138, 222; and animal imagery, 122, 141, 228; and Apollo, 157; and Artemis, 127; Asiatic origin of, 9, 19, 20, 119, 121–22, 123–25, 144, 149, 168, 184–85; assimilation of, 19, 119, 143, 169–77; and Attis, 21, 113–14, 177–82, 217, 223–24, 237, 238, 240, 244, 257, 278; barbarity of, 140, 149n, 167, 168, 178, 185, 231, 233, 244; and castration, 113–14, 230, 231, 237, 240; Christian commentary on, 155; and chronology, 119, 123, 132; and costumes, 126, 131–32, 139, 145, 180; and Daktyls, 172n; and dance, 151, 154, 161, 171, 172, 173, 183; and Demeter, 19, 119, 140, 143, 163, 167, 169, 174–76, 181, 184, 185, 224, 228; and democracy, 163, 169, 184, 218; and Dionysos, 143, 152–54, 157, 166, 176, 225, 226; and drinking vessels, 145, 146, 148, 151–55, 152–53; and ecstasy, 4, 20, 121, 155–57, 161, 166–67, 168, 171, 172, 173, 174, 176, 177, 185, 231; and Eleusinian Mysteries, 167, 175, 176; and emotional expression, 137, 141, 149, 151, 155–57, 168, 172, 183, 185, 228; and fertility, 169, 280; and figurines, 133, 139, 217–18; and funerary art, 183, 218, 221, 226; and funerary rites, 223, 226–27; and Gaia, 169, 170, 171; and Galaxia festival, 218; and Galli, 229–32; and Graces, 172n; and Hekate, 226; and Hera, 140, 170; and Hermes, 176; and Homeric Hymns, 122–23, 137, 140, 141, 144, 170, 228; importation of, 19, 63, 119, 125; and initiation, 149, 225–27; and inscriptions, 120, 121, 126, 184, 188, 217, 224, 227; and Kouretes, 170, 172, 173, 174, 184, 222, 226; and Kubaba (Anatolian goddess), 124, 128–29; and lion imagery, 109, 131–34, 136, 138, 139, 145, 148, 151, 170, 216, 218n, 222, 225, 227; Lydian influence on, 124, 128–32, 134; marginality of, 119, 137, 143, 233; and maternal identity of deity, 38, 140; membership of, 182–84, 219–20, 224, 232, 233; and metragyrtai, 124, 164–68, 182, 183, 222, 230, 291; and Metroa, 119, 139, 145, 161, 162–67, 171, 175, 182, 183, 188, 217, 218, 223n, 224; and Minoan religion, 134–35; and monuments, 138, 221; and Mother Earth, 169–70; and mountains, 69, 125, 125n, 144–45, 156, 171–72, 177, 227, 228, 232, 280, 305; and Muses, 123, 127n, 172n; and music, 110, 122, 137, 139, 148, 149–51, 154, 155, 157, 161, 171, 172, 173, 185, 230, 232n; and mystery, 149, 154, 161, 172, 174, 176, 183, 222, 224, 225, 226–27; and myth of Cybele and Attis, 237, 238, 240; and naiskoi, 126–27, 128, 129, 131–32, 133, 140, 146–47, 151, 160, 216–17, 219, 222; and nature symbolism, 135, 141; and niches, 138; and nomenclature, 45, 46–47, 63, 66–69, 122, 123, 124–25, 139, 144–45, 169, 171, 189; and Nymphs, 127, 157, 159, 172n, 173, 222, 227; and orgeones, 188, 219–20; and orgies, 20, 121, 231; Orientalist views of, 20, 24; and Pan, 143, 157, 176–77, 180, 225, 226, 227; and Persephone, 175, 225, 226; and phiale, 145, 216, 222, 225, 227; Phrygian cult influenced by, 187, 188, 189, 192–98; Phrygian influence on, 4, 120–28, 130–31, 134–41, 144, 145, 148, 169, 171, 172, 173, 175, 176, 177, 184–85; and political relations, 184, 218, 233, 317; and Potnia Theron, 120, 135, 139; and power imagery, 38, 39, 148; and predator imagery, 139, 228; prehistoric predecessor of, 15, 16, 30; and priesthood, 113–14, 164–68, 185, 218, 221–22, 229–32, 237, 240; and private sphere, 4, 120, 139, 141, 143, 163, 164, 176, 188, 196, 206, 216, 217, 232, 233, 234, 317; and public sphere, 4, 120, 143, 161, 164, 176, 234; and relations with city-state, 4, 121, 140, 233; and reliefs, 119, 120, 121, 126–27, 131–32, 136, 145, 149, 150, 157–59, 158–59, 173n, 176, 177, 216, 218n, 219, 221, 222, 225, 225, 226, 226, 227; and Rhea, 19, 119, 120, 124, 140, 143, 161, 169, 170–74, 176, 184, 185, 228, 229, 279n; and ritual, 121, 137, 143, 148, 149–51, 154–57, 161, 169, 173, 174, 176, 177, 183, 184–85, 187, 188, 221–27, 228, 230–32; Roman cult influenced by, 283, 284, 295–96, 316; and sacred tree, 21; and sacrifice, 98n, 138, 163, 218, 221; and sanctuaries, 132, 134, 136, 137–39, 140, 141, 143, 161, 162, 171, 188, 233; and sexuality, 20; and shrines, 119, 137–38, 140, 158, 161, 162, 188, 216, 218, 233; and snake imagery, 152, 154, 226, 227; and social class, 182, 184, 233; and social relations, 185, 233; and springs, 138; and statuettes, 120, 121, 127n, 132, 133, 137, 139, 140, 145, 158, 175, 217, 218n, 222; and Telchines, 172n; and temples, 119, 161, 218; and thiasotai, 219–20; transmission of, 132–33, 134, 139, 187–88; and tympana, 110, 122, 123, 136–37, 138, 139, 145, 148, 149, 151, 155, 168, 170, 173, 174, 180, 183, 185, 216, 218n, 221, 222, 227, 296; universalization of, 18; and votives, 119, 120, 121, 125–27, 131n, 132, 133n, 136, 137, 138, 139, 141, 143, 145, 148, 157–59, 158–59, 164, 168, 173, 176, 177, 184, 188n, 189, 216, 217, 218, 219, 222, 225, 226, 233

Gusmani, Roberto, 13

Hacilar, 34–38
Hades, 152n

Hadrian, 316, 334

Halikarnassos, 204, 222n

Hannibal, 264, 266–67, 268, 281

Haspels, Emilie, 64n, 99n, 102n

Hekataios, 203n

Hekate, 47, 226

Hellanikos, 270n

Hepding, H., 239n, 242

Hephaestion, 230

Hephaistos, 249

Hera, 135, 136, 140, 170

Heraion at Samos, 140

Herakles, 159n, 202n

Hercules, 289n

Hermes, 176, 200–202, 216

Hermesianax, 239, 243, 257

Herms, 21n

Herodian, 269

Herodotos, 11, 13, 46, 69, 124, 128, 134, 156–57, 166n, 216, 245

Hesiod, 10, 134n, 169, 170, 247–48

Hestia, 195

Hesychios, 67, 68, 198

Hetaerism, 10, 12

Hijras, 320, 321–23

Hindu mother goddess, 320–22, 324–25

Hippocrates, 156

Hipponax of Ephesos, 124, 170

Hittites, 3, 41–44, 62, 78, 79, 81, 132, 200, 248, 249

Homer, 6, 122–23, 127, 137, 140, 141, 144, 168n, 170, 171n, 175n, 206, 228

Horace, 302

Hosios, 195n

Hunter-gatherer society, 17

Hunting imagery: and Hittite religion, 43, 62; and Matar, 48, 53, 78, 109; and Meter, 148; pre-historic, 29, 30–31

Hyacinth Monument, 89, 90, *93, 101*

Hygeia, 195

Iacchos, 152n, 181

Idaean Mother, 2, 206, 270, 271, 292, 299–301

Idaia, 67, 125n, 144n, 199

Ilion, 206

Initiation, and Meter cult, 149, 225–27

Inscriptions: and Angdistis, 198; and Attis, 178–79, 212, 335; and Matar, 65–66, 68–70, 96, 111; and Meter, 120, 126, 180n, 184, 188, 200, 203, 206, 210, 211, 217, 224, 227, 329, 331, 332, 334, 335, 341–42; and Midas (Phrygian king), 100, 111

Ionia, 105, 126–28, 131, 132, 138–39, 143–44, 163, 164, 184, 199, 202–3, 214, 216, 276, 317, 328, 331

Iron Age, 3, 19, 41–48, 49, 52–54, 79, 83, 124, 135

James, E. O., 16

Jeanmaire, H., 172n

Judaeo-Christian culture, 9

Julian, 163, 243

Julius Caesar, 289

Jung, Carl, 16–18

Juno, 273n, 303, 311

Jupiter, 239–40, 289n, 298, 300, 303, 316

Kadmilos, 202n

Kalehisar, 79, 81, *81–82, 102, 109, 111, 211*

Kallimachos, 228, 230n, 231

Kapikaya, 211, 233

Karatepe, 110

Karkamiš, 45, 47, 48, 49, *50–51,* 52, 72n

Kastabala, 45, 47

Keil, J., 202n

Kern, Otto, 21

Klazomenai, 131

Kleisthenes, 162

Kolophon, 119, 163, 199, 202–3, 232

Konya, 105, 108

Korai, 126–27

Kore, 164, 175, 224n, 238, 256

Korybantes, 157, 172, 177

Kos, 222n, 227

Kouretes, 170, 172, 173, 174, 184, 216, 222, 226, 340

Kraters, 151–55, *152, 153.* See also Drinking vessels

Kriton, *146*

Kronos, 169, 170, 174, 279n

Kubaba, 44–47, 48, 49, 52–53, *59,* 67, 72n, 124, 128, 129, *130,* 131

Küçük Kapikaya, 86

Kumarbi, 248

Kumca Boğaz Kapikaya, 86, *90*

Kybebe, 45, 46, 67, 69, 124, 125, 228

Kybele: Asiatic origin of, 119, 123–25; and Attis, 177–78, 215, 223; and costumes, 276n; and lion imagery, 151; and Mother Earth, 170; and mountains, 69, 125; and music, 110; and naiskoi, 149n; and nomenclature, 2, 45, 46–47, 63, 66–69, 123, 124–25, 139, 144–45, 171, 328; and Rhea, 6, 124, 170–74; and sacrifice, 98n; and tympana, 110, 148, 171n

Kyme, 119, 131, 132, 137, 158, 211

Kyzikos, 128, 156, 199, 204, 214n, 332–34

Lampsakos, 128

Laroche, Emmanuel, 45n, 46n

Lebadeia, 226

Lesbos, 198, 231

Leto, 105

Liber, 289n

Lion imagery: and Apollo, 148–49n; and Demeter, 174, 175; and Kore, 175; and Kubaba (Anatolian goddess), 49, 130, 131; and Magna Mater, 276, 277, *295*, 298, 309–10, 315; and Matar, 41, 49, 80, 85–86, 102–4, 108, 109–10, 131; and Meter, 109, 131–34, 136, 138, 139, 145, 148, 151, 170, 196, 200, 203, 207, 209, 210, 211, 216, 218n, 222, 225, 227, 329, 335, 337; and Minoan religion, 134–35; and prehistoric artifacts, 30, 31, 36, 37, 41; and prehistoric mother goddess, 39

Livia (Roman empress), 313

Livy, 149n, 229–30, 264, 265, 266, 267, 268–71, 284, 288n, 290

Lokri, 123

Loucas, I., 153n

Lucian, 241

Lucretius, 254n, 297–99, 307, 316, 318, 324

Ludi Megalenses, 274, 277, 279, 297

Ludi Romani, 289n

Lupercal, in Rome, 273, 318n

Lycia, 11–12, 13, 64, 105

Lydia, 46, 64, 70, 102, 124, 128–32, 134, 139, 189, 194–96, 202, 214n, 232, 239–40, 242, 328, 335–36

Magna Mater: and Aeneas, 2, 7, 238, 270, 279, 299–301, 302–4, 316; and agricultural imagery, 280, 318; and altars, 314n; and animal imagery, 276, 277; and Apollo, 270; and aristocracy, 283, 289; Asiatic origin of, 19; and Attis, 113, 241, 245, 275, 277, 278, 280, 284, 285, 299, 304–7, 318, 319–20; and castration, 18, 19, 254n, 256, 257, 267, 292, 298, 299, 301, 304, 306, 307, 308, 318, 319, 320, 324–25; and coins, 289–90, *290*; and costumes, 276, 310, 314, 315n; and Curetes, 298; and dance, 285; and Delphic oracle, 270; and Demeter, 249; and Dionysos, 275; and ecstasy, 287n, 296, 317–18; and fertility, 257, 278, 280, 284, 296, 298, 318; and figurines, 275–76, *275*, 277–78; and founding of Rome, 238, 270, 279; and Galli, 216n, 229–32, 254n, 290, 292, *294*, 297–99, 301–4, 305, 308, 316, 318–19, 323–25; Greek influence on, 283, 284, 295–96, 316; and Idaean Mother, 2, 206, 299–301; importation of, 4, 19, 22, 63, 263, 264–71, 279, 281–83, 314; and Jupiter, 239–40, 300, 316; and lion imagery, 276, 277, *295*, 298, 309–10, 315; maternal identity of, 38; and Megalesian festival, 283, 288–89, 290, 296, 299, 305n, 306; and monuments, 309, 311, 315; and music, 19, 285, 293, 304, 307, 308, 317, 324; and myth of Cyb-ele and Attis, 239–40, 241, 244, 245, 256, 305–7; and orgies, 285, 302, 304; Orientalist views of, 21, 22, 23, 24; Pergamene influence on, 264–65, 268, 269–71, 276, 278, 281, 282, 284, 314–15; Pessinuntine influence on, 264–65, 268–71, 290; Phrygian influence on, 293, 295–96, 303, 305, 319; and political relations, 263, 281–83, 288, 290–91, 317, 345; prehistoric predecessor of, 27; and priesthood, 4, 254n, 256, 287–88n, 290–91, 292, 297–99, 301–4, 308, 315, 317, 318, 319, 323–25; and public sphere, 287, 289, 296, 297, 304n, 317, 318, 319; and Punic Wars, 264, 266–67; and relations with state, 7, 284, 296, 297, 299, 308, 309, 316–17, 327; and reliefs, 309–10, *310–11*, 313, 315; and Rhea, 279n; and ritual, 19, 247, 256, 274, 279, 283, 284, 285, 287n, 288–89, 292, 293, 296–99, 304, 307, 308, 309, 316, 317–18; and sacred calendar, 283; and sacred ship, 314; and sacred tree, 256, 279; and sacrifice, 277, 293; and sanctuaries, 274, 288, 316; and sexuality, 277–78, 280, 296, 299, 301–2, 304–9, 318, 319; and shrines, 271, 273, 279, 314; and Sibylline oracle, 20, 264–65, 266, 268, 269, 284, 285, 301; and social class, 23–24, 291, 296; and statues, 274, *313*, 314–15; and temples, 264–65, 266, 267, 271, *272–73*, 273–75, 279, 282, 285, 288–89, 291, 309, 314, 316; and theatrical performances, 288–89, 316–17; transmission of, 327; and tympana, 309, 310, 313, 315; and votives, *276–77*, 277–78, 279, 280, 313–15, 318; and washing of images, 274, 279. *See also* Rome, Mother Goddess cult in

Magnesia, 161, 199, 222n, 331, 335, 340n

Mahrada, 47

Malatya, 47, 48, 72n

Maltaş Monument, 89, *95*, 98, 102, 110

Mamurt Kale, 209–11, 212, 233, 315n

Manlius Volso, 269, 290

Marcus Aurelius, 332

Marriage rites, 223–24

Martial, 302n, 314

Massalia, 131, 132, 133

Mata, 320–22, 324–25

Matar: and altars, 52, 65, 71, 79, *80, 82*, 83, 96, *98*, 102, 109, 111, 192, 337; and animal imagery, 74, 75, 104, 109; and aristocracy, 111–12; and castration, 19, 98n, 113–14; and chronology, 64, 71, 81–83, 99–102, 108, 243; and costumes, 47–48, 71–72, 85, 104, 105–8; and drinking vessels, 73, 109, 148; and fertility, 110, 114, 280; and figurines, *106*; and funerary art, 52, 74, 79, 102–4, 113; and Hellenization, 72n, 105, 123, 125, 126, 169, 173, 177, 189; and hunting imagery, 48, 53, 78, 109; and inscriptions, 65–66, 68–70, 86, 96,

Matar (continued)

III; and lion imagery, 41, 49, 80, 85–86, 102–4, 108, 109–10, 131; and monuments, 54, 61, 65–66, 69, 71, 82–83, 84–86, 89–90, *91–97*, 96–104, 105, 110, 140, 232; and mountains, 43, 44, 46, 54, 61, 66–67, 68, 98, 108, 113, 115, 193, 200, 280; and music, 73, 110; and nature symbolism, 43, 44, 54, 61, 62, 113, 114; and niches, 54, 71, 79, 84–86, 89, 96, 105, 108; and nomenclature, 2, 12, 45, 46–47, 66–70, 108, 113, 114, 189, 244; and political relations, 114; and pomegranates, 73, 110, 114; and predator imagery, 48, 53, 109, 114, 115; and priesthood, 98n, 105, 111–12, 114; and raptor imagery, 48, 53, 73, 75, 79, 83, 104, 108, 109, 110, 112, 127n, 148; and reliefs, 47–48, 52–53, *56–60*, 72–75, *76*, 79–82, 84–86, *88*, 96, 102–4; and ritual, 19, 41, 42, 79, 114; and sanctuaries, 79–80; and shrines, 79, 81, *81*, 83, 111, 193; and social class, 112; and springs, 43–44; and statues, 72, 86, 96; and statuettes, 104, 105, *106*, 114; and temples, 79, 112; and votives, 44, 71, 78–79, 102, 112

Maternal identity, 5–6, 9, 10; and Magna Mater, 38; and Matar, 105, 114; and Meter, 38, 210

Matriarchy: and Anatolian Mother Goddess, 12–13, 18; Bachofen on, 10–12, 13, 14; and historical scholarship, 10–13; and Jungian psychology, 16; and Matar, 20; and prehistoric mother goddess, 10–11, 14, 16; superseded by patriarchy, 11–13

Matriliny, 11–12

Megabyzoi, 253

Megalesian festival, in Rome, 283, 288–89, 290, 296, 299, 305n, 306

Megalesion, in Pergamon, 207, 264, 270, 278

Meher Kapisi, 54

Melanippides, 174

Mellaart, James, 30, 34

Mellink, M. J., 64n, 83

Men: in Meter cult, 183, 184; in Neolithic society, 38

Menads, 152, 154

Menander, 165n, 168

Merchants, 23

Meriç, Recep, 202n

Mesembria, 216

Messenia, 170n

Metellus, 291

Meter: and administrative documents, 218–24; and agricultural imagery, 169–70; and altars, 138, 200, 203n, 204, 206, 209, 210, 211, 222, 329, 334, 336, 342; and Angdistis, 198; and animal imagery, 122, 141, 210, 228; and Apollo, 157, 184, 201; and Artemis, 127, 196, 200; Asiatic origin of, 121–22, 123–24, 144, 149, 168, 184–85;

assimilation of, 19, 119, 143, 169–77; Athenian cult of, 24, 119, 133, 139, 143, 158, 162–69, 171, 175, 182, 183, 184, 187, 188, 217–18, 219, 291, 317; and Attis, 113, 155n, 177–82, 192, 212, 215, 217, 223–24, 227, 228, 244, 331, 342n; and Bendis, 227; Christian commentary on, 155; and chronology, 119, 123, 132; and coins, 330, 334, 335, 340, 342; and costumes, 126, 131–32, 139, 145, 207; and Daktyls, 172n; and dance, 151, 154, 161, 171, 172, 173, 183; and Demeter, 119, 143, 163, 167, 169, 174–76, 181, 184, 224, 228; and democracy, 163, 169, 184, 218; and Dionysos, 143, 152–54, 157, 166, 176, 184, 225, 226; and drinking vessels, 145, 146, 148, 151–55, *152–53;* and ecstasy, 4, 121, 155–57, 161, 166–67, 168, 171, 172, 173, 174, 176, 177, 185, 231; and Eleusinian Mysteries, 167, 175, 176; and emotional expression, 137, 149, 151, 155–57, 168, 172, 183, 185, 228; and fertility, 15, 169, 280; and figurines, 133, 139, 203, 204, 206, 207, 210, 217–18, 331, 337; and funerary art, 183, 204, 218, 221, 226; and funerary rites, 223, 226–27; and Gaia, 169, 170, 171; and Galaxia festival, 218; and Galli, 229–32; and Graces, 172n; and Hekate, 226; and Hera, 140, 170; and Hermes, 176, 200–202, 216; and Homeric Hymns, 122–23, 137, 140, 141, 144, 170, 228; and Idaean Mother, 206; and initiation ceremony, 149, 225–27; and inscriptions, 120, 121, 126, 184, 188, 200, 203, 206, 210, 211, 217, 224, 227, 329, 331, 332, 334, 335, 341–42; and Kouretes, 170, 172, 173, 174, 184, 216, 222, 226, 340; and Kubaba (Anatolian goddess), 124, 128–29; and lion imagery, 109, 131–34, 136, 138, 139, 145, 148, 151, 170, 189, 196, 198, 200, 203, 207, 209, 210, 211, 216, 218n, 222, 225, 227, 329, 335, 337; Lydian cult of, 194–96, 328, 335–36; and Lydian influence in Greece, 124, 128–32, 134; marginality of, 137, 143, 233; maternal identity of, 38, 140, 210; and *metragyrtai,* 124, 164–68, 182, 183, 222, 230, 291; and Metroa, 119, 139, 145, 161, 162–67, 171, 175, 182, 183, 188, 196n, 202–3, 217, 218, 223n, 224, 317; and Minoan religion, 134–35; and monuments, 138, 221, 332; and Mother Earth, 169–70; and mountains, 125n, 156, 171–72, 177, 198–200, 206, 209, 210, 211, 227, 228, 232, 270, 280, 330, 335, 336, 343; and Muses, 123, 127n, 172n; and music, 122, 137, 139, 148, 149–51, 154, 155, 157, 161, 171, 172, 173, 185, 210, 230, 232n; and mystery, 149, 154–55, 161, 172, 174, 176, 183, 202, 222, 224, 225, 226–27, 332; and naiskoi, 126–27, 128, *129,* 131–32, *133,* 140, *146–47,* 151, *160,* 196, 210, 215, 216, 217, 219, 222; and nature symbolism, 135, 141; and niches, 138, 200, 211, 337; and nomenclature, 68, 69n, 122, 123, 125, 139, 144, 169, 171, 189, 198–99, 328–29; and Nymphs, 127, 157, *159*, 172n, 173, 184, 222, 227; and *orgeones*, 188, 219–20; and orgies, 121, 231; Orientalist views of, 24; and Pan, 143, 157, 176–77, 180, 225, 226, 227; Pergamene cult of, 202, 206–7, 209–11, 218, 270, 331–32; and Persephone, 175, 225, 226; and phiale, 145, 189, 196, 210, 216, 222, 225, 227, 329; Phrygian cult of, 187, 188, 189, 192–98, 232, 328, 336–42; and Phrygian influence in Greece, 4, 120–28, 130–31, 134–41, 144, 145, 148, 169, 171, 172, 173, 175, 176, 177, 184–85; Piraeus cult of, 218–24; and political relations, 184, 193–94, 203, 218, 233, 317, 336; and Potnia Theron, 120, 135, 139; and predator imagery, 139, 148, 228, 251; and priesthood, 113–14, 164–68, 185, 203, 219, 221–22, 229–32, 332–34, 335, 342; and private sphere, 4, 120, 139, 141, 143, 163, 164, 176, 188, 196, 206, 216, 217, 232, 233, 234, 317; and public sphere, 4, 120, 143, 161, 164, 176, 234; and relations with city-state, 4, 121, 140, 233; and reliefs, 119, 120, 121, 126–27, 131–32, 136, 149, *150, 157–59, 158–59,* 173n, 176, 177, 196, 200–201, *201,* 202, 203, *205,* 210, *214–15,* 215–16, 218n, 219, 221, 222, 225, *225,* 226, *226,* 227, 329, 331, 332, *333,* 337; and Rhea, 6, 119, 120, 143, 161, 169, 170–74, 176, 184, 202, 209, 228, 229, 279n, 332, 337; and ritual, 121, 137, 143, 148, 149–51, 154–57, 161, 169, 173, 174, 176, 177, 183, 184–85, 187, 188, 203, 210, 211, 221–27, 228, 230–32, 338; and Roman influence, 327–28; and sacred calendar, 203; and sacrifice, 138, 163, 202, 203, 204, 210, 218, 221, 338; and sanctuaries, 132, 134, 136, 137–39, 140, 141, 143, 161, 162, 171, 188, 192, 196, 198, 200, 202, 203, 206, 207, 209–11, 215, 233, 270, 331, 336–41, 342; and sexuality, 20, 195, 253, 335; and shrines, 137–38, 140, 158, 161, 162, 188, 192, 198, 200, 202, 207, 210, 211, 215, 216, 218, 233, 269, 270, 330, 331, 334, 336, 342–43; and snake imagery, 152, 154, 226, 227; and social class, 182, 184, 211, 233; and springs, 138, 162–63, 211; and statues, 203, 204, 206, 207, *208,* 211, 212, 334, 337; and statuettes, 120, 121, 127n, 132, 133–34, 137, 139, 140, 158, 175, 189, *190–91,* 198, 202, 203, 206, 207, *209,* 210, 215, 217, 218n, 222, 329, 337; and syncretism, 19, 119, 143, 169–77, 202, 337; and Telchines, 172n; and temples, 119, 161, 192, 196, 198, 210, 211, 218, 330, 334, 336–37, *338–39,* 340; and thiasotai, 219–20; and tympana, 122, 123, 136–37, 138, 139, 145, 148, 149, 151, 155, 168, 170, 173, 174, 183, 185, 189, 196, 198, 207, 210, 216, 218n, 221, 222, 227, 329, 335, 337; and virgins, 334–35; and votives, 119, 120, 121, 125–27,

131n, 132, 133n, 136, 137, 138, 139, 141, 143, 145, *148,* 157–59, *158–59,* 164, 168, 173, 176, 177, 184, 188n, 189, 198, 200–201, *201,* 202, 203–4, *205, 214–15,* 215–16, 217, 218, 219, 222, 225, *226,* 233, 329, 332, *333,* 334, 335, 337; and Zeus, 200, 202, 210n, 226, 228, 331, 332, 337–41, 343

Metragyrtai, 124, 164–68, 182, 183, 222, 230, 291

Metroa, 119, 139, 145, 161, 162–67, 171, 175, 182, 183, 188, 196n, 202–3, 217, 218, 223n, 224, 308n, 317

Metropolis, 202, 233

Midaeion, 342

Midas (Phrygian king), 69–70, 83, 99n, 100, 111, 192n; and myth of Cybele and Attis, 241, 244, 246, 255

Midas City, 66, 69, 84, 86, 89–90, *91–93,* 96, *98,* 99, 102, 110–13, 180n, 192, 193, 197–98, 246, 336, 337–38, 343

Midas Monument, 61, 69, 70, 86, 89–90, *91,* 99–102, 245

Miletos, 119, 126, 128, 129, 131, 137n, 163

Miller, Stephen G., 162n

Minoan religion, 134–35

Mirrors, and Kubaba (Neo-Hittite goddess), 48, 49

Mistress of Animals, 135

Mithraeum, at Kapikaya, 211

Mneme, 195

Monotheism, 38

Monuments: and Attis, 257; and Magna Mater, 309, 311, 315; and Matar, 54, 61, 65–66, 69, 71, 82–83, 84–86, 89–90, *91–97,* 96–104, *105,* 110; and Meter, 138, 140, 221, 232, 250–51, 332; and Phrygian geometric ornament, 100–102; and Urartian religion, 54, 61

Mother Earth, 7, 10, 169–70, 247, 297

Mother goddess: and animal imagery, 38, 39; and Asiatic origin of, 9, 19–24; Bachofen on, 10–12, 18; and development of consciousness, 10–11, 16–18; and feminism, 13–14; and fertility, 13, 14, 15, 16; and gender, 9, 10; and hunter-gatherer society, 17; and Jungian psychology, 16–18; maternal identity of, 9, 10, 38; and matriarchy, 10–14, 16; and Orientalism, 20–24; and prehistoric evidence, 14–16, 27, 30, 34, 36, 38–39, 41; and race, 9, 19; scholarly preconceptions about, 9–10, 20–24; and social class, 9, 23; and social development, 10–13, 17, 18; superseded by father god, 10–11, 13; universality of belief in, 16, 18, 27, 38. *See also* Angdistis; Cybele; Kybele; Magna Mater; Mata; Matar; Meter

Mountains: and Hittite religion, 42–43; and Matar, 43, 44, 54, 61, 66–67, 68, 98, 113, 115, 193, 200, 280; and Meter, 69, 125, 125n, 135, 144–45, 156, 171–72, 177, 184, 189, 198–200,

Mountains *(continued)*
  206, 209, 210, 211, 227, 228, 232, 250, 270, 280,
    305, 330, 335, 336, 343; and Minoan religion,
    134–35; and myth of Cybele and Attis, 239–40,
    244; and Urartian religion, 54, 61
Muses, 122, 123, 127n, 172n
Music: and Attis, 181; and Magna Mater, 19, 110,
    256, 285, 293, 304, 307, 308, 317, 324; and Matar,
    73, 110; and Meter, 110, 122, 137, 139, 148,
    149–51, 154, 155, 157, 161, 171, 172, 173, 185, 210,
    230, 232n; and myth of Cybele and Attis, 251
Mycenaean religion, 134, 135
Myrina, 204
Mysia, 328, 332
Mystery rites: and Attis, 181; and Eleusinian Mys-
    teries, 167, 175, 176, 181, 249, 256; and Magna
    Mater, 23, 308, 317; and Meter, 149, 154–55, 161,
    172, 174, 176, 183, 202, 222, 224, 225, 226–27, 332

Naiskoi, 126–27, 128, *129,* 131–32, *133,* 140, *146–47,*
    151, *160,* 196, 210, 215, 216, 217, 219, 222, 281
Nanda, Serena, 320–24
Nature symbolism: and Hittite religion, 43–44;
    and Matar, 43, 44, 54, 61, 62, 113, 114; and
    Meter, 135, 141; and Urartian religion, 54, 61
Naumann, F., 133n, 152n, 216n
Naumann, R., 338
Neapolis, 188n
Neo-Hittites, 3, 41–42, 44–48, 49, 52–53, 67,
    71–72, 74, 82–83, 101, 109, 110, 124, 137
Neolithic period, 3, 14–16, 27–39, 41
Neumann, Erich, 16–18
Niches: and Matar, 54, 71, 79, 84–86, 89, 96, 105,
    108; and Meter, 138, 200, 211, 337; and Urartian
    religion, 54
Nike, 195
Nikomachos, 209n, 315n
Nomenclature: and Agdistis, 245–46n; and
    Angdistis, 245–46; and Attis, 70; and Magna
    Mater, 63; and Matar, 2, 12, 45, 46–47, 66–70,
    108, 114, 189, 244; and Meter, 45, 46–47, 63,
    66–69, 69n, 122, 123, 124–25, 144–45, 169, 171,
    198–99
Nonnos, 249
Nymphs, 127, 157, *159,* 172n, 173, 184, 222, 227, 248

Olympia, 119, 161
Olynthos, 181, 216
Oracles, 20, 204, 264–65, 268, 270, 301, 332
Orgeones, 188, 219–20
Orgies: and Magna Mater, 23, 285, 302, 304; and
    Meter, 20, 121, 231
Orientalism, 3, 20–24, 242
Origen, 254n

Ornamental art. *See* Geometric ornament
Orphic ritual, 153n
Ouranos, 248
Ovid, 67, 68, 239, 241, 242, 243, 250, 253, 256, 257,
    259, 264, 265, 266, 269, 270, 271, 279, 280, 282,
    288n, 291, 299, 314, 316, 318, 336

Paintings, prehistoric, 29, 30, 31, 32, 34, 37, 41
Palatine, in Rome, 4, 265, 266, 271, *272–73,*
    273–74, 277, 278, 279, 280, 287, 288–89, 291,
    302, 309, 311, 314–15, 316
Paleolithic period, 14, 16
Palmer, L. R., 134n
Pan, 143, 157, 176–77, 180, 225, 226, 227
Panayir Dağ, 200, 331
Panticapaeum, 188n, 198
Paphlagonia, 80
Paris, 168n, 180
Paros, 198, 227
Patriarchy, Bachofen on, 11, 12
Patriliny, 12
Paul, Saint, 166
Pausanias, 134, 161, 162, 170n, 200, 204, 239, 240,
    241, 242, 243, 244, 245n, 247, 251, 252, 254, 256,
    257, 259, 337
Peloponnesian War, 164
Pensabene, Patrizio, 271n, 273n, 275n, 311n
Pergamon, 188, 189, 192, 193, 202, 206–7, 209–12,
    218, 232, 264–65, 268, 269–71, 276, 281, 282,
    284, 314–15, 331–32, 336, 341, 343
Persephone, 175, 176n, 225, 226, 255
Persia, 180, 185; and Persian Empire, 144, 188; and
    Persian Wars, 120, 144, 162
Pessinous, 66–67, 79, 111, 188, 189, 192–94, 198,
    206, 229, 232, 239, 240, 241, 242, 245n, 246, 252,
    257, 264–65, 268–71, 290, 296, 328, 341–42, 343
Pheidias, 145
Pherekydes, 249
Phiale, 145, 146, 148, 189, 196, 210, 216, 222, 225,
    227, 329
Philadelphia, 194–95, 197, 202, 233, 253
Philodemus, 302
Philo of Byblos, 249
Phokaia, 128, 131, 132, 136, 138–39, 140, 166n, 211,
    330, 337
Photios, 163–64, 167
Phrygia: Achaemenian control of, 102; funerary
    rites in, 223; Galatians in, 229; Greek influence
    in, 64, 102n, 105–8, 128, 139, 189, 192–98; lan-
    guage of, 3, 65, 100; Lydian control of, 102;
    Neo-Hittite influence in, 83, 100; reign of
    Midas in, 69–70, 83, 100, 111, 246
Phrygia, Mother Goddess cult in: and altars, 52,
    65, 71, 79, *80, 82,* 96, *98,* 102, 109, 111, 180n, 192,

197, 336, 337–38, 342; and animal imagery, 74, 75, 104, 109, 135, 148; and aristocracy, 111–12; and Attis, 114, 154–55n, 178, 181, 182, 192, 193–94, 237, 238, 242–47, 250–58, 319, 342; barbarity of, 19–24, 140, 144, 176, 182, 247, 256; and castration, 19, 98n, 113–14, 181, 250, 252–54; and chronology, 64, 71, 81–83, 99–103, 108, 243; and costumes, 47–48, 71–72, 85, 104, 105–8; and creation myths, 250; and death, 113; and drinking vessels, 73, 109, 148; and façades, 65–66, 68, 69–70, 71, 84–86, 89–90, 96–104, 112–13, 232; and fertility, 110, 114, 280; and figurines, *106*, 189, 337; and funerary art, 52, 74, 79, 102–4, 113, 192, 250, 251; and funerary rites, 252, 258; Greek cult influenced by, 4, 120–28, 130–31, 134–41, 144, 145, 148, 169, 171, 172, 173, 175, 176, 177, 184–85; Greek influence on, 105–8, 120, 121–22, 123–28, 130–31, 135, 189, 192–98, 250, 336–39; and Hittite religion, 42, 43, 44; and hunting imagery, 48, 53, 78, 109, 148; and inscriptions, 65–66, 68–70, 96, 111, 180n; and Kubaba (Neo-Hittite goddess), 45, 46, 47, 48, 49, 52–53, 67; and lion imagery, 41, 49, 80, 85–86, 102–4, 108, 109–10, 136, 145, 189, 198; and maternal identity of deity, 105, 114; and matriarchy, 20; and monuments, 54, 61, 65–66, 69, 71, 82–83, 84–86, 89–90, *91–97*, 96–104, 105, 110, 140, 232, 250–51; and morality, 195–96; and mountains, 43, 44, 54, 61, 66–67, 68, 98, 113, 115, 135, 171–72, 189, 193, 200, 250, 280, 305, 336, 338, 343, 345; and music, 73, 110; and myth of Cybele and Attis, 237, 238, 242–47, 250–58; and nature symbolism, 43, 44, 54, 61, 62, 113, 114; and Neo-Hittite religion, 45, 46, 47, 48, 49, 52–53, 67, 82–83, 109, 110; and niches, 54, 71, 79, 84–86, 89, 96, 105, 108, 337; and nomenclature, 12, 45, 46–47, 66–70, 108, 114, 180, 244; Orientalist views of, 19–23, 242; patronage of, 111, 232; and phiale, 189; and political relations, 114, 193–94, 232, 336; and pomegranates, 73, 110, 114; and pottery, 73, 148; and power imagery, 109, 110, 114, 115, 251; and predator imagery, 48, 53, 109, 114, 115, 148, 251; prehistoric predecessor of, 39, 41; and priesthood, 105, 111–12, 181, 194, 252–54, 258; and raptor imagery, 48, 53, 73, 75, 79, 83, 104, 108, 109, 110, 112, 127n, 148; and relations with state, 111, 140, 181, 258, 317; and reliefs, 47–48, 52–53, *56–57*, 72–75, *76*, 79–82, 84–86, *88*, 96, 102–4, 192n, 337; and ritual, 19, 41, 42, 79, 114, 247, 252, 254, 258, 338; Roman cult influenced by, 293, 295–96, 303, 305, 319; Roman influence on, 33–43, 320; and sacrifice, 338; and sanctuaries, 79–80, 192, 193, 198, 264, 336–41; and shrines,

79, 81, *81*, 83, 111, 192, 193, 197, 198, 257, 268, 269, 336, 342–43; and social class, 112, 140; and sphinxes, 85; and springs, 43–44, 138; and statues, 72, 86, 96, 337; and statuettes, 104, 105, *106*, 114, 189, *190–91*, 198, 253, 337; and syncretism, 195–96; and temples, 79, 112, 192, 198, 336–37, *338*; transmission of, 19, 63, 80–81, 119, 125, 345; and tympana, 189, 198; and votives, 44, 71, 78–79, 102, 112, 180n, 192n, 198, 337; and winged sun, 49, 74

Pindar, 5, 125, 144, 161, 172n, 174, 176–77, 182, 231

Piraeus, the, 158, *159–60*, 178, *179*, 188, 203, 217n, 218–24, 233, 278

Pisidia, 197

Plastene, 199, 200, 201

Plato, 157, 172n, 249

Plautus, 279, 288

Pleiades, 228

Pliny, 209n, 264, 280, 318, 334

Ploutos, 195

Plutarch, 21n, 23n, 156, 161, 177–78, 290, 291n, 331

Polis. *See* City-state

Political relations: and Magna Mater, 263, 281–83, 288, 290–91, 317, 345; and Matar, 114; and Meter, 184, 193–94, 203, 218, 232–33, 317, 336

Polybios, 229, 269

Pomegranates: and Kubaba (Neo-Hittite goddess), 48; and Matar, 73, 110, 114

Potnia Theron, 120, 135, 139

Pottery: and Kubaba (Neo-Hittite goddess), 46; and Matar, 73; and Meter, 337; and Phrygian designs, 73; and Phrygian inscriptions, 65; and Potnia Theron, 135n

Power imagery: and Magna Mater, 38, 39; and Matar, 109, 110, 114, 115; and Meter, 38, 39, 148, 251; and prehistoric artifacts, 37; and prehistoric mother goddess, 39

Praeneste, 288

Predator imagery: and Matar, 48, 53, 109, 114, 115; and Meter, 139, 148, 228, 251; and prehistoric artifacts, 36; and prehistoric mother goddess, 39. *See also* Raptor imagery

Pregnancy, and prehistoric imagery, 35, 37

Priene, 203

Priesthood: and Artemis, 253; and Magna Mater, 4, 98n, 113–14, 165n, 216, 237, 240, 254n, 256, 287–88n, 290–91, 292, 297–99, 301–4, 308, 315, 317, 318, 319, 323–25; and Mata (Hindu mother goddess), 320, 321–23; and Matar, 98n, 105, 111–12, 114; and Meter, 113–14, 164–68, 181, 185, 194, 203, 219, 221–22, 229–32, 237, 240, 252–54, 258, 332–34, 335, 342; and myth of Cybele and Attis, 237, 240, 241

Prinias, 135

Private sphere: and Magna Mater, 287; and Meter, 4, 120, 139, 141, 143, 163, 164, 176, 188, 196, 206, 216, 217, 232, 233, 234, 317

Propertius, 314

Prudentius, 338

Psychology, Jungian, 16–18

Public sphere: and Magna Mater, 287, 289, 296, 297, 304n, 317, 318, 319; and Meter, 4, 120, 143, 161, 164, 176, 234

Punic Wars, 264, 266–67, 270

Pylos, 134

Pyrrhic Wars, 270n

Ramsay, William, 12, 18

Rape, in mythic narrative, 239, 247, 249, 258

Raptor imagery: and Artemis, 127n; and Hittite religion, 43; and Matar, 48, 53, 73, 75, 79, 83, 104, 108, 109, 110, 112, 127n, 148; and prehistoric mother goddess, 39

Reliefs: and Angdistis, 222, 223; and Artemis, 196, 197; and Attis, 178–79, 179, 181, 214n, 222, 223, 225, 227, 336; and Hittite religion, 43; and Kubaba (Neo-Hittite goddess), 47, 48, 49, 52–53, 59; and Magna Mater, 309–10, 310–11, 313, 315; and Matar, 47, 48, 52–53, 56–57, 72–75, 79–82, 84–86, 88, 96, 102–4; and Meter, 119, 120, 121, 126–27, 131–32, 136, 145, 148, 149, 157–59, 158–59, 173n, 176, 177, 192n, 196, 197, 200–201, 201, 202, 203, 205, 210, 214–15, 215–16, 218n, 219, 221, 222, 225, 225, 226, 226, 227, 329, 331, 332, 333, 337; prehistoric, 29, 30, 31, 37; and Urartian religion, 59, 109

Rhamnous, 178

Rhea, 6, 19, 119, 123, 124, 140, 143, 161, 169, 170–74, 176, 184, 185, 202, 209, 228, 229, 238, 251–52, 279n, 332, 337

Ritual: and Attis, 181, 223, 252, 278, 316; Dionysiac, 154; and Kubaba (Anatolian goddess), 130; and Magna Mater, 16–17, 19, 247, 256, 274, 279, 283, 284, 285, 287n, 288–89, 292, 293, 296–99, 304, 307, 308, 309, 316, 317–18; and Mata (Hindu mother goddess), 320, 321; and Matar, 19, 41, 42, 79, 114; and Meter, 121, 137, 143, 148, 149–51, 154–57, 161, 169, 173, 174, 176, 177, 183, 184–85, 187, 188, 203, 210, 211, 221–27, 228, 230–32, 247, 252, 254, 258, 338; and myth of Cybele and Attis, 238, 252, 254, 255–56, 258; and Neolithic symbolism, 29, 30, 31, 38; Orphic, 153n; and Phrygian male gods, 154–55n. See also Castration; Ecstasy; Funerary rites; Marriage rites; Mystery rites; Sacrifice

Robertson, N., 121n, 134n

Romanelli, P., 275n

Rome: Auguratorium in, 273; Circus Maximus in, 289, 315; festivals in, 274, 277, 279, 283, 288–89, 296–97, 299, 305n, 306; foreign deities in, 280–81, 284; founding of, 238, 270, 279; Lupercal in, 273, 318n; Palatine in, 4, 265, 266, 271, 272–73, 273–74, 277, 278, 279, 280, 287, 288–89, 291, 302, 309, 311, 314–15, 316; Senate in, 206, 290, 291n

Rome, Mother Goddess cult in: and Aeneas, 2, 7, 238, 270, 279, 299–301, 302–4, 316; and agricultural imagery, 280, 318; and altars, 314n; and animal imagery, 276, 277; and aristocracy, 283, 289; Asiatic origin of, 9, 19–20, 21, 22, 23, 277; and Attis, 21, 22, 113–14, 237, 238, 240, 256, 257, 275, 277, 278, 280, 284, 285, 299, 304–7, 318, 319–20; Bachofen on, 19–20; barbarity of, 22–23, 24; and castration, 17–18, 98n, 113–14, 237, 240, 254n, 256, 257, 267, 292, 298, 299, 301, 304, 306, 307, 308, 318, 319, 320, 324–25; and coins, 289–90, 290, 316; and costumes, 276, 308, 310, 314, 315n; and Curetes, 298; and dance, 285; and Delphic oracle, 270; and Dionysos, 275; and ecstasy, 287n, 296, 317–18; and fertility, 23, 257, 278, 280, 284, 296, 298, 318; and figurines, 275–76, 275, 277–78; and founding of Rome, 238, 270, 279; and Galli, 216n, 229–32, 254n, 290, 292, 294, 297–99, 301–4, 305, 308, 316, 318–19, 323–25; Greek influence on, 283, 284, 295–96, 316; and Idaean Mother, 2, 206, 299–301; importation of, 19, 22, 63, 263, 264–71, 279, 281–83, 314; and lion imagery, 276, 277, 295, 298, 309–10, 315; and maternal identity, 38; and Megalesian festival, 283, 288–89, 290, 296, 299, 305n, 306; membership of, 23; and monuments, 309, 311, 315; and music, 19, 110, 256, 285, 293, 304, 307, 308, 317, 324; and mystery, 23, 308, 317; and myth of Cybele and Attis, 237, 238, 240, 256, 305–7; and nomenclature, 63; and orgies, 23, 285, 302, 304; Orientalist views of, 21, 22–23, 24; patronage of, 22; Pergamene influence on, 264–65, 268, 269–71, 276, 278, 281, 282, 284, 314–15; Pessinuntine cult influenced by, 341; Pessinuntine influence on, 264–65, 268–71, 290; Phrygian influence on, 293, 295–96, 303, 305, 319; and political relations, 263, 281–83, 288, 290–91, 317; and power imagery, 38, 39; prehistoric predecessor of, 16, 27, 30; and priesthood, 4, 98n, 113–14, 165n, 216, 237, 240, 253n, 256, 287–88n, 290–91, 292, 297–99, 301–4, 308, 315, 317, 318, 319, 323–25; and public sphere, 287, 289, 296, 297, 304n, 317, 318, 319; and Punic Wars, 264,

266–67; and relations with state, 7, 284, 296, 297, 299, 308, 309, 316–17, 327; and reliefs, 309–10, *310–11*, 313, 315; and Rhea, 279n; and ritual, 16–17, 19, 247, 256, 274, 279, 283, 284, 285, 287n, 288–89, 292, 293, 296–99, 304, 307, 308, 309, 316, 317–18; and sacred calendar, 283; and sacred ship, 314; and sacred tree, 21, 256, 279; and sacrifice, 277, 293, 316; and sanctuaries, 274, 288; and sexuality, 277–78, 280, 296, 299, 301–2, 304–9, 318, 319; and shrines, 271, 273, 279, 314; and Sibylline oracle, 20, 264–65, 266, 268, 269, 284, 285, 301; and social class, 23, 24, 291, 296; and statues, 274, *313*, 314–15; and temples, 264, 266, 267, 271, *272–73*, 273–75, 279, 282, 285, 288–89, 291, 309, 314, 316; and theatrical performances, 288–89, 316–17; transmission of, 327; and tympana, 309, 310, 313, 315; universalization of, 18; and votives, *276–77*, 277–78, 279, 280, 313–15, 318; and washing of images, 274, 279

Romulus and Remus, legend of, 279n

Rousselle, A., 254n

Sabazios, 152–55n, 168

Sacrifice, 17, 18, 96; and Magna Mater, 277, 293, 316; and Meter, 98n, 138, 163, 202, 203, 204, 210, 218, 221, 338

Salmanköy, 48, *60*, 74–75

Samos, 129, 131, 132, 140, 201

Samothrace, 178, 202n

Sanctuaries: and Hittite religion, 43–44; and Magna Mater, 274, 288; and Matar, 79–80; and Meter, 132, 134, 136, 137–39, 140, 141, 143, 161, 162, 171, 188, 192, 193, 198, 200, 202, 203, 206, 207, 209–11, 215, 233, 264, 270, 331, 336–41, 342; and Zeus, 336–41

Sappho, 175n

Sardis, 45–46, 64, 101, 124, 127n, 128–31, 134, 188, 195, 196–97, 198, 232, 335

Saturn, 298

Savior Deities, 195, 253

Scipio Corculum, 314

Scipio Nasica, 265, 266, 267, 281–82, 314

Selene, 255

Seleucid dynasty, 232

Semonides of Amorgos, 124

Seneca, 241, 264

Servius, 240–41n, 252, 256, 259, 283n

Sexuality: and Anatolian Mother Goddess, 16; and Angdistis, 246; and Attis, 177, 182, 277, 278, 280, 304–7; and Galli, 230, 254n, 301–2, 324; and hijras, 322–25; and Magna Mater, 277–78, 280, 296, 299, 301–2, 304–9, 318, 319; and Meter, 20, 195, 253, 335; and myth of Cyb-

ele and Attis, 240, 246, 247, 257, 258, 305; and Plato's *Symposium,* 249; and prehistoric figurines, 14, 15

Shear, T. L., 162n

Ship, sacred, *312*, 314

Showerman, Grant, 13

Shrines: and Attis, 212; and Hittite religion, 43; and Magna Mater, 271, 273, 279, 314; and Matar, 79, 81, *81*, 83, 111; and Meter, 119, 137–38, 140, 158, 161, 162, 188, 192, 193, 197, 198, 200, 202, 207, 210, 211, 215, 216, 218, 233, 257, 268, 269, 270, 330, 331, 334, 336, 342–43

Sibylline oracle, 20, 264–65, 266, 268, 269, 284, 285, 301

Sicily, 139, 174, 181, 227, 280, 281

Sidon, 188n

Simon, E., 152n

Simope, 128

Simpson, Elizabeth, 251n

Sipylene, 67, 125n, 132, 199, 200, 202

Sizma, 189

Skythia, 156–57

Slater, W. J., 161n

Slaves, 23, 168, 182n, 195, 256, 292, 296, 306, 319

Smyrna, 119, 131, 132, 163, 199, 202, 232, 278, 330–31

Smyrnaike, 199

Snake imagery: and Asklepios, 280; and Meter, 152, 154, 226, 227

Social class, 3, 9, 23, 24; and Magna Mater, 291, 296; and Matar, 112; and Meter, 140, 182, 184, 211, 233

Social development, 10–13, 17, 18–19, 330

Social relations: and Meter, 185, 233; and prehistoric imagery, 31, 32, 34, 38

Solon, 170

Sophokles, 167n, 171n, 172n

Sorrento, 310–11

Sparta, 134

Sparzene, 199

Sphinxes: Greek, 101; Neo-Hittite, 101; Phrygian, 85, 101

Springs: and Hittite religion, 43–44; and Matar, 43–44; and Meter, 138, 184, 211

State: and Magna Mater cult, 7, 284, 296, 297, 299, 308, 309, 316–17, 327; and Matar cult, 111, 140; and Meter cult, 140, 181, 258, 317. *See also* City-state

Statues: and Attis, 212, *213*, 278, 331; and Kubaba (Neo-Hittite goddess), 52; and Magna Mater, 274, *313,* 314–15; and Matar, 72, 86, 96; and Meter, 203, 204, 206, 207, *208*, 211, 212, 334, 337

Statuettes: and Attis, 192n; and Demeter, 174; and Matar, 104, 105, *106*, 114; and Meter, 120,

121, 127n, 132, 133–34, 137, 139, 140, 145, 158, 175, 189, *190–91*, 198, 202, 203, 206, 207, *209*, 210, 215, 217, 218n, 222, 253, 329, 337; and Phrygian priest, 105, *107*, 114, 253; prehistoric, 37
Stelai: Greek, 178–81, 218, 224; Phrygian, 61, 78, 79, 80, 109, 135n; Urartian, 61
Stephanus of Byzantium, 68
Strabo, 66–67, 172n, 193, 194, 198, 209, 253, 264, 268, 341
Strosis, 221, 223–24
Sun Goddess of Arinna, 42
Sun, winged, 49, 74
Syncretism: and Angdistis, 195–96; and Meter, 19, 119, 143, 169–77, 202, 337

Takmaköy, 105
Taş Kapisi, 54
Telchines, 172n
Telestes, 171
Telmessos, 204
Temples: and Hittite religion, 42, 43, 44, 78, 79, 81; and Kubaba (Anatolian goddess), 52, 130–31; and Magna Mater, 265, 266, 267, 279, 282, 285, 288–89, 291, 309, 314, 316; and Matar, 79, 112; and Meter, 119, 161, 192, 196, 198, 210, 211, 218, 330, 334, 336–37, *338–39*, 340
Terence, 288–89
Thasos, 131, 132, 158
Thebes, 161n
Theia, 134
Themis, 136n, 180
Theokritos, 223, 228, 241
Theopompos, 192n
Thiasotai, 219–20
Thomas, Garth, 22–23, 24
Thompson, H., 162n
Tibur, 288
Timotheos, 243, 244
Tithonos, 255
Tombs: Phrygian, 61, 102–4; Urartian, 61
Tree, sacred, 20, 21, 256, 279
Troizen, 224
Trophonios, 227
Troy, 168, 180, 185, 199, 206, 207, 212, 250, 256, 265, 269, 270–71, 276n, 278, 299–301, 302–3, 331
Tudhaliyas, funerary complex of, 43
Tušpa, 53, 54
Tyana, 64
Tyche, 330, 340n

Tympana: and Magna Mater, 309, 310, 313, 315; and Meter, 110, 122, 123, 136–37, 138, 139, 145, 148, 149, 151, 155, 168, 170, 173, 174, 180, 183, 185, 189, 198, 216, 218n, 221, 222, 227, 296, 329, 335, 337

Ullikummi, 248
Unfinished Monument, at Midas City, 89, 90, *92*, 101
Universality, of belief in mother goddess, 16, 18, 27, 38
Urartians, 3, 52–54, 109, 113

Valerius Maximus, 292
Varro, 207, 264, 269, 278, 308–9
Velia, 133
Venus, 131n, 280, 307
Vermaseren, Maarten, 16, 18, 131n, 146n, 216n, 239n, 327
Versnel, H. S., 21, 121n, 148n, 155n, 175n, 182n
Vestal Virgins, 265, 267–68, 314
Victoria Virgo, 273n
Virgil, 5, 7, 9, 22, 257, 270, 279, 299–301, 302–3, 304n, 311, 316
Votives: and Angdistis, 196–97, 222, 246; and Apollo, 281; and Attis, 178–80, *179*, 182, 222; and Claudia Quinta, 282; and Demeter, 174; and Magna Mater, *276–77*, 277–78, 279, 280, 313–15, 318; and Matar, 44, 71, 78–79, 102, 112; and Meter, 119, 120, 121, 125–27, 131n, 132, 133n, 136, 137, 138, 139, 141, 143, 145, 157–59, *158–59*, 164, 168, 173, 176, 177, 180n, 184, 188n, 189, 192n, 198, 200–201, *201*, 202, 203–4, *205*, *214–15*, 215–16, 217, 218, 219, 222, 225, *226*, 233, 329, 332, *333*, 334, 335, 337

Weather god: Hittite, 43; Neo-Hittite, 48
White Goddess, 13
Wilamowitz-Moellendorff, U. von, 175n
Will, E., 146n, 169n
Wiseman, T. P., 300n, 301n, 303n, 304n, 305n
Women: in Magna Mater cult, 23; in Meter cult, 183–84; in Neolithic society, 32, 34, 37–38

Yazilikaya, 43
Yeşilaliç, 54, *55*

Zeus, 70n, 161, 162n, 163, 170, 171, 172, 173, 174, 195, 200, 202, 204, 210n, 211, 222n, 226, 228, 238, 240, 247, 249, 331, 332, 336–37, 343
Zincirli, 47
Zonguldak, 105, 108

D